The
Sacred Paths
of the
East

The Sacred Paths of the East

THEODORE M. LUDWIG
Valparaiso University

Macmillan Publishing Company
New York

Maxwell Macmillan Canada
Toronto

Editor: Maggie Barbieri
Production Supervisor: Bert Yaeger
Production Manager: Su Levine
Text Designer: Jill Bonar
Cover Designer: Tom Mack

This book was set in Electra by Carlisle Communications, Ltd., and was printed and bound by R.R. Donnelley & Sons Company. The cover was printed by New England Book Components.

Macmillan Publishing Company
866 Third Avenue
New York, New York 10022

Macmillan Publishing Company is part of the
Maxwell Communication Group of Companies.

Maxwell Macmillan Canada, Inc.
1200 Eglinton Avenue East, Suite 200
Don Mills, Ontario M3C 3N1

Library of Congress Cataloging-in-Publication Data

Ludwig, Theodore M.
    The sacred paths of the East / Theodore M. Ludwig.
        p.   cm.
    Includes bibliographical references and index.
    ISBN 0-02-372163-4 (paper)
    1. Religions. 2. India—Religion. 3. China—
Religion. 4. Japan–
  –Religion.   I. Title.
BL80.2.L83   1993
291'.095—dc20   92-31725
                                                         CIP

Printing: 1   2   3   4   5   6   7   Year: 3   4   5   6   7   8   9

To Kathy, Kevin, Jim, Greg, and Keith

Preface

This book stems from a larger study of the whole range of the world's religious traditions, *The Sacred Paths: Understanding the Religions of the World* (Macmillan, 1989). The material on the religions of the East has been extensively revised for this volume for those who want to concentrate on this group of religions—a group that includes the religious experience of nearly half the people in the world today.

This volume takes up the religions of the East in two main "family" groupings. One group is made up of the religions arising from India, including Hinduism, Buddhism, Jainism, and Sikhism. The other group includes the religious traditions of China and Japan, especially Confucianism, Taoism, Shinto, and Mahayana Buddhism. These groupings represent religions that have grown up together historically and culturally, with considerable mutual influence and sharing.

Ideally, to understand the religions of the East, one should live in those lands, learn their languages, participate in their cultures, make friends with the people, and learn their literature and traditions. Until we can do that, however, a first step in understanding these religions, as any religious tradition or culture, is to get a sense of what they mean for the people who practice them and live by them. It is important, of course, to study the historical development of each religious tradition—its origin, its development, and its expansion into different sects or subgroups. Each religion is a living and growing organism that cannot be understood apart from its historical and cultural development. But more is needed to *really* understand each religion. It is essential to become conversant with the self-understanding of the people, as expressed in their sacred stories, their general worldview, their basic ideas about life, and their ritual and ethical practices. Only by somehow putting oneself in the place of those people can one begin to understand what it means to live by that religion, to view the world in terms expressed by that religion, and to make sense out of life by means of rituals, ideas, and living community of that religion.

In order to reach as complete an understanding as possible of each of the religious traditions of the East, this book combines discussion of historical development with a thematic approach based on general questions of human existence that are of central concern in all religions. As explained in the Introduction in Chapter 1, these are questions about identity, ultimate reality, human nature, and the right way to live. These are questions with which the reader can identify from personal experience, and they can thus open windows toward understanding the meaning and guidance that people find in their religion. Against the background provided by these thematic questions, the book presents the master story (or stories) of each religion, its ideas and teachings, and its ritual and ethical practices.

Each religious tradition is a highly complex living organism, with various movements, sects, or groupings at different points in its history. In keeping with this book's purpose, the general mainstream of each tradition is presented, with some of the major alternatives given where appropriate. This work is a basic introduction for students who are beginning their exploration of the religions of the East; it does not attempt to be a complete catalog of each religious tradition. For more thorough descriptions of the various movements that make up each religious system, the student can consult the works on each religion listed in the bibliography.

Again, since the purpose of this book is to help students become conversant with basic religious issues and with the major religions of the East, discussion of the more technical topics has been minimized; for example, the history of the academic study of religion, the various scholarly approaches to studying the religions, and the philosophical schools that evolved in connection with each religion. Further, simplified spellings rather than scholarly transcriptions of terms from the different languages have been used. All these aspects of religion are important, of course, and advanced students are encouraged to consult the *En-cyclopedia of Religion* and other works listed in the Bibliography.

To assist students in attaining familiarity with these religions, a number of study features have been included here. Maps are given to help visualize the geographical location of each tradition and time lines listing important events within the development of each religion are presented. A list of key terms and definitions at the end of discussions will facilitate review of the main aspects of each religion. Discussion questions at the end of each chapter are intended to encourage reflection about the meanings people find in their religion. And the Bibliography lists selected works that will be helpful as students probe deeper, including both general works and specialized studies that provide more depth in certain areas.

Many have helped along the way toward the completion of this volume. Thanks are due especially to Maggie Barbieri of Macmillan Publishing Company, who facilitated the process of publishing this study. And I here want to express my appreciation to the following scholars who have read the revised manuscript and made valuable suggestions: Sandra Lubarsky of Northern Arizona University, Bruce M. Sullivan, also of Northern Arizona University, and Charles White of The American University. Their critical suggestions have been most helpful in sharpening the focus of this work.

Brief Contents

Contents

The
Sacred Paths
of the
East

CHAPTER 1

Introduction: Basic Dimensions of Religion

In this book, we embark on a journey of understanding of some of the religions of the East, with their ideas and teachings, their rituals and art, and their societies and ways of life. Most importantly, we want to understand what these religions mean to the people who practice them and live by them.

As we study, we also will attempt to understand some fundamentals of religion as a significant human activity, across cultural lines. In the Introduction we will reflect on some important dimensions of religion to guide us as we study the diverse and fascinating religious traditions of the East.

RELIGIONS OF THE EAST

In attempting to gather the vast religious traditions of the world into several simple groupings, we find that they are sometimes divided very broadly into religions of the West and religions of the East. Those of the West include Judaism, Christianity, and Islam, the major world religions that have had a strong impact on the history and culture of the West. Religions of the East include Hinduism, Buddhism, Jainism, Sikhism, Confucianism, Daoism, and Shinto. A third grouping can be added, religions of the tribal, nonliterate peoples in many parts of the world such as traditional Africans, Native Americans, and Melanesians.

Our concern here is with that grouping called religions of the East. What we are calling the "East" is actually a vast panorama of peoples, cultures, and languages, from Calcutta to Tokyo, from Jakarta to Beijing. This group of peoples encompasses most of Asia, except for the western and northern reaches that shade over into Islamic states and Russia. And the "East" encompasses at least one-half of the world's population.

Obviously, we cannot look at all the numerous peoples and religions of Asia. We focus on two central groups or families: those religions arising in India, and those found in East Asia (especially China and Japan).

The group of religions arising in India share a common historical development in the first millennium B.C.E. and a set of common perspectives on the world and the path to follow. These religions include the traditions known as Hinduism, Buddhism, and Jainism. Sikhism developed much later, in the seventeenth and eighteenth centuries of the Common Era, but it still shares many of the same perspectives. This family of religions tends to have a non-dualistic (monistic) worldview, the idea that behind or within all the multiplicity of forms and forces in this universe there is one unified sacred reality. These religions do have gods that are important—even thousands of them—but often they go beyond the idea of a personal creator God or Gods. They may hold to the idea, for example, that the inner soul of reality or the truth of all reality itself is the sacred ultimate. They generally agree that human existence is part of the process of *samsara*, that is, birth and death over and over in an endless cycle. According to this perspective, the highest goal for humans is to achieve

1

awareness of ultimate reality through practices of discipline, meditation, or devotion, and thereby find liberation from the cycle of rebirth. Whereas Sikhism arose in India and contains many of these ideas, it was also highly influenced by the monotheistic perspective of Islam.

The religions of East Asia, particularly of China and Japan, form a loose family grouping. There are many gods here, in Japanese Shinto and in the Chinese religions, Daoism and Confucianism, together with many popular religious practices. But at their center is an emphasis on harmony with the divine flow of nature and reverence for ancestors and family. Within that harmony, human existence is valued as positive and good. Chinese culture and religion have been very influential throughout the lands of East Asia. In particular, the Mahayana form of Buddhism, from India, has adapted the Buddhist outlook to the East Asian perspective and thus plays a unifying role in the cultural grouping that makes up the East Asian family of religions.

INTRODUCING RELIGION

All religion has to do with fundamental human issues and concerns. Who am I?—the basic question of identity—is crucial to our journey in life. What sense is there in life? How can we find the life that is real and fulfilling? Questions such as these are not mere philosophical problems for academic debate. They reach to the depths of life concerns that are felt, vaguely or forcefully, by all human beings. They deal with the fundamental concern of the *meaning* of human existence. Does life really have any meaning— any *real* meaning—or do we just live and die in a small frame of a pointless, accidental cycle of the universe?

Of course, there are many dimensions of being human, many concerns that are not directly religious ones. We are concerned about our physical makeup, our biological structure, our reasoning capacities, our languages and forms of communication, our historical memories, our forms of society, our psychological makeup, and much more.

But no matter what aspect of human existence we happen to look at, deeper questions of meaning and purpose are close at hand: Why do we happen to function biolog-

ically the way we do? What is the meaning of sex? Why have we evolved into reasoning animals? Is there any sense or direction in our history? What responsibility do we have for fellow humans? In other words, the question of the *meaning* of human existence is met. And wrestling with that question of meaning in its deeper aspects involves us in religious thinking and experiencing.

Religion is not limited to one dimension of human existence. Rather, it has to do with the overall meaning of human existence: Why is *everything* the way it is? What is the rhyme or reason behind all this? What is our purpose in living? Behind all such questions is a fundamental one: Where can we look for that which is ultimately real, that unlimited source from which we derive life and meaning?

It is to that which they feel is ultimately real, the unlimited source, that people within the various religions direct themselves in their many different ways. We designate this focal point of the religions as the "sacred," the ground of ultimate vitality, value, and meaning. The modes of experiencing the sacred, and the responses to this experience, are the forms and expressions that make up the religions of the world.

DIMENSIONS OF RELIGIOUS EXPERIENCE

It would be well at this point to suggest a working definition of what we mean by "religion." Here is a four-part description:

1. Religion is human involvement with what is considered to be the realm of the sacred.
2. It is expressed in thought, action, and social forms.
3. It constitutes a total system of symbols with deep meaning.
4. It provides a path of ultimate transformation.

Human Involvement with the Realm of the Sacred
The first part of the definition of religion suggests a relationship between two levels of experience: the limited human level and the level of that which is felt to be the sacred. Of course, we cannot examine the sacred as if it

were an objective realm of reality; the sacred is not something to be proved or disproved. We must be clear that we are not attempting to define ultimate reality as an objective fact; we are simply investigating how people of different cultures have described their experiences of whatever it is that they consider the ultimate sacred. Still, it is the common experience of many people past and present that there is a sacred realm of reality with ultimate significance, and, further, that the ultimate good in human life has to do with relating to the sacred.

Although the idea of the sacred is distinctive in each particular religious tradition, it is possible to discern some general outlines that resonate across religious boundaries. After all, if there is a shared humanness throughout the different cultures of the world, we should expect some general similarities in the way people describe their experiences of what they consider to be the sacred. Rudolph Otto drew various religious experiences together in an influential study, *The Idea of the Holy*,[1] putting forth the view that

Experience of the sacred takes countless forms in the religions of the world. Here a Hindu woman makes an offering at the River Ganges.

basic to religious experience is a deep sense of the "numinous." This is a term he coined from the Latin *numen* (holy, sacred) to express our basic response to the experience of the sacred even before we develop rational and moral notions about it. Experiencing the numinous as ultimate mystery, people feel a strong sense of awe and reverence, at the same time being fascinated and drawn to the mysterious Other.

Drawing on Otto's perspective, let us make some observations about the experience of the sacred. First of all, bound up with the numinous is an unlimited, primordial, overpowering quality. The sacred is ultimate, the basis of everything else, and nothing can supersede or encompass it. It accounts for everything, and it holds everything together—but it is its own basis without depending on anything else. The sacred, whether expressed as God (Islam), Brahman (Hinduism), emptiness (Mahayana Buddhism), or some other formulation, is felt to be the universal foundation of all truth, reality, goodness, and value.

We encounter the sacred as Mystery, as the Wholly Other that remains completely "other" even when experienced within the human world. It cannot be completely held by humans, either with their hands or with their reason. Words can attempt to describe the sacred, but it is understood that words can only point to the mystery in a symbolic way. Every word refers to a conditioned human reality, but the sacred both encompasses and transcends human realities. For this reason, religions express the experience of the sacred not only by words but also by a variety of other symbolic forms, such as sculpture, ritual actions, meditation, music, dance, silence, and so forth. Bathing in "Mother Ganges" provides a direct, nonverbal sacred experience for Hindus. After the reception of the Eucharist in a Christian church, a moment of silence is often the most appropriate way of responding to the mystery. The stillness of Buddhist meditation brings one into direct touch with the ultimate truth in a way that words can never do.

The experience of the sacred is accompanied with awe and reverence. The sacred cannot be controlled by human design; it bursts the bounds of human understanding and overwhelms with energy and demand. The human response is awe, respect, and submission. For Muslims, for example, washing the body and prostrating oneself in prayer expresses the right human relationship to the sacred. Rudolph Otto called this quality of the sacred the *mysterium tremendum* (terrifying mystery). For the ancient Israelites, the mountain of Sinai was the awesome presence of the sacred; touching it could mean destruction. The image of a god or goddess in Hinduism is full of power so that one should not, for example, take pictures of it.

The experience of the sacred at the same time involves fascination and love; we are compelled and drawn to the ultimate origin of all that is good and true and beautiful, the source of meaning and purpose in life, the fountain of vitality and strength. The sacred is wondrous, marvelous, and compelling. Encounter with the sacred leads to the highest joy, rapture, and love. Buddhists who have experienced awakening describe it as ultimate bliss and rapture. The Muslim pilgrim is drawn to Mecca and the experience of the sacred there as by a powerful magnet. The Hindu worshiper lovingly performs *puja* to the image of the beloved god or goddess.

Since the sacred is the source of ultimate value, the deepest need of human life is to have an ongoing relationship with the sacred. It is this need that is the foundation of the various religions of humankind. Each religion has its own way of providing the context so that the sacred is present to the human community, with the power, value structures, meaning, and purpose that fulfill the religious needs of human beings.

Expression in Thought, Action, and Social Forms

The second part of our definition of religion suggests what goes into the making of that human involvement with the sacred. Since religion is, obviously, a human affair, it necessarily involves human forms or modes of expression. Joachim Wach, in his *Sociology of Religion*,[2] suggests there are three such modes of expression: theoretical (thinking, speaking), practical (doing, acting), and social (fellowship, community). These are the building blocks of religion and they fit together to form a complex, unique universe of meaning, that is, a religion.

The *theoretical* mode of expression comprises the verbal aspect of religion, what is told and described. Religions say things about the most important, basic issues of life: how the sacred is experienced, where the world came from and where it is going, what the goal of human life is, and how we can achieve that. These things are talked about in two basic ways: narrative or story (myth) and theoretical statements about reality (doctrine). All religions have stories or myths that put forth in narrative form the worldview and the important experiences of the sacred on which that religion is founded. Leading thinkers of a religion also express their basic perceptions in teachings or doctrines that generalize from the sacred stories to present the fundamental truths of the religion, providing intellectual guidance to the participants in that religion.

The *practical* level of expression in religion has to do with its visible and performed side: rituals, worship, meditation, ethical conduct, and so forth. Religion is not just mental but also physical, and the acting out, the performance, of the involvement with the sacred is just as important as the stories and the doctrines. Prostrating oneself before the sacred presence, going on pilgrimages, sharing in a sacred meal, chanting texts and prayers, wearing colorful robes, burning incense, observing moral rules, and hundreds of other religious rituals and types of behavior represent the acting out or performance of the religious experience.

Religion is never simply an individual affair but always a group or communal experience involving *social forms*. It is the religious community that carries on the tradition, even before the individual was born and after he or she dies. And it is in identifying with the religious community that the individual finds personal identity. There are different structures of community depending on the type of religious experience, in family or clan, congregations, religious societies, and whole nations. And there are various types of religious leadership, such as queens, kings, priests, sages, prophets, masters, nuns, monks, shamans, and many more. Participation in the social forms of the religious community is what gives continuity of religious experience.

A Total System of Symbols

Taken together, these modes of religious expression form a total worldview, a "map" of human involvement with the sacred, and this brings us to the third part of our definition. Religion guides and gives meaning by presenting a view of the whole order of existence. This religious map of human existence is made up of "symbols"—words, ideas, rituals, pictures, gestures, sounds, social groupings—which evoke the deepest feelings and most important meanings in our lives. These are the means by which a group of people express their perception of what life is all about. To live as part of this community is to share a whole way of knowing the world and one's place in it, a whole way of looking at life and death, and a whole set of assumptions about what is real and true and good. The system of symbols upholds deep-seated attitudes and motivations, providing a complete system of values for human life.

Let us consider a few examples of such symbols. In a Buddhist monastery an ordinary bowl for food becomes a "begging bowl," an important symbol of the spiritual status of the monk or nun on the path toward the ultimate goal of all people in the community. A rooster and a dove are two very common animals, but used by a priest in a Daoist ritual they embody the operational forces of yin and yang and create the balance of sacred power necessary for the well-being of the human community. The act of eating a meal is one of the most common human activities and is often done without any particularly deep meaning. But a Jew sitting at the table celebrating the Passover seder with her family experiences deep religious meaning in that human activity. Similarly, washing oneself is an everyday human activity, but all religions have rituals that express sacred meaning in washing, such as baptism, bathing in a sacred river, or purifying oneself with water before entering a shrine.

We can envision the world view of each religion as a circle with a center. The circle suggests the totality of what the people understand as their existence in the world. It contains their universe of symbols that provides the pattern of life that is their religious path. Within the circle, then, we see the most important symbols of that religion. The meanings that these symbols supply have been told in stories, painted and sculpted in art, sung and played by musicians, expressed in poems and dramas, acted out in rituals and worship, and argued and systematized by theologians and philosophers for centuries.

The various symbols fit together in a circle, for they are all related to each other in such a way as to present a comprehensive and persuasive outlook on life. Above all, the circle of symbols is centered, that is, there is a *central vision* that colors and permeates the whole circle in a pervasive

way. We might suggest, for example, that for Muslims the center is the Holy Book, the Quran, whereas for Christians it is Christ. Buddhism centers on the path to nirvana, whereas the center for Shinto is the exhaustless life of the kami. Many Chinese would put the Dao at the center of their universe of symbols; other Chinese might center their world more on ancestors and family. The symbols closest to the center could be considered the *primary symbols*, those that are most essential to those of that religion. Toward the outside of the circle appear somewhat more *secondary symbols*, those that are more inclined to change when new experiences and challenges arise, those that respond to the needs of the religious communities in different times and places. Of course, people do not always agree on whether a particular symbol is primary or secondary; diverse religious experiences lead to different emphases even within one religious tradition.

We should therefore keep in mind that a religion is not a static, unchanging affair but rather a dynamic organism. Changes and transformations do occur in response to new experiences, new stories, and new challenges. Sometimes what appeared to be a primary symbol to some at one time becomes less important in later ages, whereas a secondary symbol introduced by some new religious experience shifts into a primary position. For example, Indra was one of the most powerful gods for the ancient Aryans, but he shifts to a rather small role in later Hinduism. On the other hand, Vishnu was a minor god for the Aryans, but he rose dramatically to become one of the great gods in Hinduism. In spite of changes in the circle of symbols, however, there is an ongoing basic continuity, flowing outward from the central vision and maintaining the fundamental pattern of faith and life.

As we look at the issues of human life and focus on specific symbols from the religions, we must keep in mind that a particular symbol must always be viewed in its total context. Some of the symbols will, of course, appear quite similar in a family of religions, and rightly so, given the shared history and culture. The word Dao (the "way"), for example, is used by all three religious traditions in China, that is, Confucianism, Daoism, and Buddhism—but with significant differences of meaning. But our task is to see each symbol, each teaching, idea, story, ritual, practice, or community structure, in the light that is reflected from the central vision and from the total pattern of that particular system of symbols.

A Path of Ultimate Transformation

The fourth part of our definition points out that a religion is not only a system of beliefs and expressions about the relation to the sacred; it is also a path, a way of life. Each religion offers something that many humans find essential to human existence: a path to ultimate meaning and transformation.

An important part of religious experience is the realization of the broken or fractured nature of human involvement with the sacred, for from this arises the fundamental troubles and anxieties of existence. This awareness of the human problem is coupled with knowledge of the ideal, ultimate relationship to the sacred. One's religion provides a way of overcoming this fracture, of restoring the bridge to the sacred, of transforming oneself to attain the goal of life as expressed in that particular religion. The path continues throughout one's lifetime, through rituals, symbols, disciplines, study, social relationships, and states of consciousness. Buddhists, for example, follow the Eightfold Path toward the ultimate attainment of nirvana. Christians follow the path of

Christ to overcome sin and attain eternal life. For Hindus the paths of action, worship, and knowledge lead toward spiritual realization and liberation from the cycle of birth and death. Following the life of Torah for Jews is the path toward spiritual perfection. The path is a way of life, a praxis designed to restore wholeness and ultimate meaning to human existence by involvement with the source of life, the sacred. We look at the path toward transformation in more detail later in this chapter.

Comparison and Understanding

A word needs to be added about looking at religion as we are doing here, studying it from the outside, as it were. Whereas many of us know our own religion, none of us belongs to all the religions. Therefore we necessarily find ourselves in the position of being on the outside looking in at the intimate practice of someone else. In looking from the outside, we miss the inner compulsion of commitment and the special meaning that the religion provides for the insider. Further, our view cannot be completely "objective," for our own personal religious beliefs and presuppositions stand in the way and color our perspective.

It is important, then, that we consciously make a deep effort to *understand* these religious traditions of others. To

Chanting the scriptures—symbolic of the ultimate truth—is a very active ritual for these Japanese Buddhist monks.

"under-stand" is to stand under that which gives meaning to the other. It means to stand in her or his religious stance, to look at the universe of religious symbols from the perspective of being on the inside. This is not an easy task, and it is always an incomplete accomplishment. One cannot fully understand Hindu religious experience unless one is a Hindu, and the same is true of Buddhist and Shinto religious experience, as well as all the others.

It is possible to understand at least in an incomplete way, however, if a number of important measures are taken. First, an attitude of respect and openness is necessary, a recognition of the value and importance that the religion has for the other person. Second, a conscious effort must be made to become aware of our own religious presuppositions that color our own views of the religions of others. By becoming aware of our presuppositions, it is possible to "bracket" them to some extent so that they do not hinder us from entering into the worldview of the other religion. Third, it is necessary to refrain, at first, from the important theological task of evaluation, that is, of asking the question of the "truth" of a particular religious idea. Each religion by its very nature makes claims to truth and in doing so also passes an evaluation on the truth of other religions. There is a time and place for responsible theological investigation, evaluation, and challenge to other religions in dialogue. But it is important first of all to understand, and a rush to evaluate and debate truth can stand in the way of understanding. Fourth, a willingness to learn from the other religions and even to grow in one's own understanding is an important component of the process of understanding the religions of others.

There is also a certain value in being able to look at several religions from the outside, as it were, if this is done sensitively and with understanding. By comparing various aspects in different religions, and especially by comparing that which is unfamiliar to elements familiar from one's own religion, it is possible to see universal structures of religion more clearly. We can see recurrent questions and concerns about life and death, and we can survey the persistent themes in the answers provided by the different religions. We can see common practices that give structure to life and society and thus develop deeper understanding of the common human needs that give rise to the various religious traditions of humankind.

BASIC HUMAN CONCERNS AND RELIGIOUS RESPONSES

As we look at each religion of Asia, our ground plan in this book is to take up a number of universal questions and concerns about human existence in relation to the sacred and use them as windows into the fundamental views and practices of each religion. The goal is not to produce a synthesis of answers from all these religions, for each is unique and distinctive. We must be especially careful not to impose outside ideas on a particular religion. Rather, we must try sensitively to hear how each religion frames its own concerns and responses. Still, looking at universal human questions provides opportunities to compare the religions while seeing clearly the unique characteristics of each.

Here is a preliminary listing of the main questions and religious responses to think about as we find our way into the basic dimensions of religion. The questions and responses fall into three general areas:

1. The Sacred Story and Its Historical Context (historical development)
   Who am I? The Sacred Story.
2. The Worlds of Meaning (the main theoretical teachings)
   What's it *all* about? The Sacred Reality.
   What sense is there in life? Creation and Human Existence.
   How can we start living *real* life? The Path of Transformation.
3. Worship and the Good Life (the practical and social aspects)
   How can we find new power for life? Sacred Time, Ritual, and Art.
   How should we live? Social Structure and the Ethical Life.

A brief discussion of these basic dimensions of religion will set the stage for our look at each of the religions in the following chapters.

The Sacred Story and Its Historical Context

One basic human concern is the question of identity: Who am I? When a person tries to answer that question, she starts by telling the story of her life. Although there are many parts of her life story she might emphasize, one important aspect would be her religious identity: "I'm a Hindu." "My family is Buddhist." "I'm a Christian." "I'm Muslim." But what does that mean? It means that a person connects his or her own story with the sacred story, the master story, of his or her religious tradition—with those crucial events or realities of the founding of the religion. To express his identity as a Buddhist, a person tells the story of the Buddha and the founding of Buddhism. To be a Sikh means to tie one's own life story into the master story of the Gurus who founded Sikhism. The story of the founding or the revealing of the religion is of particular concern, because it provides the divine authority for one's religious identity. In this study of the religions we devote considerable attention to the master story and also the historical transformation of each religion. Understanding this question of identity is crucial to developing a sensitive understanding of the ideas and practices of the religion.

Myth and Sacred Story

All religions have master stories telling of decisive events and leaders through which the new truths and practices were inaugurated as the basis of the new way of life. These birth-giving events and leaders are told about in their stories, written about in their scriptures, sung about in their songs, depicted in their art, and remembered in their rituals. They form the central focus, the paradigm, by which the people of that religion express their self-identity.

These sacred stories, or "myths," have a very important function in religion, for they establish the basic outlook and the way of life of the people of that religion. They tell of the central encounters of the people with the sacred, those clear episodes that illumine all aspects of life. Thus these stories, even though they may seem in some cases to refer to distant mythological ages, are understood to be real and true, for they reveal the bridge to the sacred that is essential for human existence. Although they are presented in story form, they provide a kind of map for human life, a model that can be followed so that life can be lived in the fullest way according to the design established by the sacred power. Knowing these stories means that the people know how human life is to be lived in a meaning-

ful way; not knowing the stories or forgetting them would be to live a chaotic, subhuman existence.

But knowing and remembering the sacred story are not just intellectual exercises. To perform the stories—repeating them in words and acting them out in rituals—is actually to become participants in the founding events. It is to reactualize the central happenings so that they become real and powerful in human life today just as they were in the special time told about in the sacred stories.

In sum, the story provides an answer to the question of identity—Who am I?—by making it possible to identify with those events and beings that exemplify in a clear and powerful way the relationship with the sacred that undergirds human life. The master stories may be about human sages and leaders who founded the religion, or they may be about gods and heroes in mythological ages—or both. But in all cases the stories tell about the beginnings, the origins, of the real, authentic way of human life. And thus they tell us who we really are.

In presenting and interpreting the stories of these communities, we rely on scholarly work that has clarified the origins and early history of each of the religions, providing a historical context for the stories. It is our intention, however, to present each story primarily as it is told and interpreted by that religious community. We are, after all, not dealing with history strictly speaking but with *sacred* history. And that sacred history is expressed not by archaeological finds or ancient history books but in the stories told in the worshiping communities.

Change and Transformation in the Religious Tradition

The history of the religious tradition does not end with the sacred story of the beginnings. Each religion is a living organism that changes and develops in new situations and experiences. Understanding this dynamic quality of religious tradition is important, for it is the "passing on" (*traditio*) of the story that finally shapes our religious identity. We receive and interact with the story through the tradition that has brought it to us.

For example, one cannot understand Buddhism in the world today without taking some account of the Mahayana developments and also the various developments in Southeast Asia and in East Asia. And it would be most difficult to understand Chinese religion without considering the rise of religious Daoism, the development of the state cult of Confucius, the importation of Buddhism, and so forth. So it is with each religious tradition. Although in this book we cannot focus extensively on the historical development of each religion, it is important to become aware of the major transformations and the effect they have had on the understanding and practice of the religion.

Worlds of Meaning: Theoretical Teachings

The Sacred Reality

What's it *all* about? Confronted with the maze of human life in a mind-boggling universe, we wonder how we can make sense of everything that is. How does it all hold together? The answer presented in each religion is the sacred, the ultimate reality. Each religion has appropriate terms for this ultimate reality: gods, goddesses, kami, God, Brahman, nirvana, Dharmakaya, Dao, and many more. Without such a vision of sacred reality, religious people feel there would be no center, no order, only a chaos of things and events occurring haphazardly without rhyme or reason. And so since the beginning of human life on this planet, people have always sought after sacred reality as the source and support for this world and human existence within it.

What are some of the ways people think about the sacred? Some religions, especially in the ancient world and among nonliterate peoples of today, have understood the sacred to be experienced in numerous forms and powers. Some speak of an impersonal sacred power that penetrates and interacts with everything. Wherever we turn, in nature and in society, we encounter Power. Often the sacred is personified as gods and spirits, who are immanent in the various aspects of the world: one god shows power in the rain and storm, another in the healing and creating power of the sun, another in pregnancy and childbirth, and so forth. This view, often called polytheism, means power is shared, with no one sacred being having unlimited sway. Many of these religions do have a supreme god who is the primordial creator and has ultimate authority, but this god delegates the functions of the world to other gods and goddesses. This general vision of the sacred can also be found to be widespread within the religions of Asia, such as Hinduism, Buddhism, Daoism, and Shinto. It is generally understood, of course, that such divine beings are not ultimate in power or status.

Another view of the sacred is monotheism, the view that there is one sacred reality, a personal God who created and supports this world and everything in it, with no alternates, no competitors. There is one God and one world, the creation. However, God is not a part of this world. God is transcendent, that is, above and beyond the created world, holy and eternal. At the same time God is present in a personal way to the created world. God encounters us especially in historical events, giving us guidance and challenging us to fulfill the divine will. The three Abrahamic religions are strong advocates of this perspective on the sacred, but it can be found in modified forms in religions like Zoroastrianism, Sikhism, and even special groups within Hinduism and Buddhism.

Still another conception of the sacred is sometimes called nondualism or monism, a broad category of thought and experience with an emphasis placed on the unity of all reality. Nondualism means that there is no real difference between the ultimate reality and the phenomenal world. Monism is the view that all reality is one unified divine reality. There may still be many personal gods, but they may all be understood as facets of the one sacred reality. Within these traditions, it may be emphasized that the sacred is our inner true self; it may be the suchness of reality; it may be the state of ultimate consciousness; it may be the principle that is found in all reality. This kind of perspective on the sacred ultimate is present in some forms of Hinduism, Buddhism, philosophical Daoism, and Neo-Confucianism. Tendencies toward monism can also be found in certain mystical movements in Judaism, Christianity, and Islam, as well as in some philosophical thinkers in the Western tradition, such as Plotinus, Spinoza, and Hegel.

So the sacred can be experienced as many in nature, or one beyond nature, or one and many both in and beyond nature, and more. Depending on which vision is dominant, the religious path to the sacred has distinctive features in each particular religion. The crucial question is, how do we encounter the sacred? Is the sacred found in the forces of nature and society? Is the sacred encountered in history and events? Is the sacred met within as one's real self? Is the sacred experienced as a personal being or as impersonal reality? Is the sacred known as the ultimate truth about reality? In each of the religions, people have opted for a particular vision of the sacred and thus each has a distinctive religious path. Yet people in each religion often explore the other possible perspectives as well to add depth to their own vision and experience.

Creation and Human Existence

What sense is there in life? And why are we here? Why is there so much evil and suffering in the world?

Questions like these are at the heart of all religions, for they pertain to the deepest needs of human life—the need to understand our own existence within the world and society, the need to feel a purpose or destiny, and the need to integrate evil and death into our view of life without despairing.

The religions deal with questions like these especially in their cosmogonic stories, that is, their stories about the creation and maintenance of the world and of humans within it. For it is in knowing the origins of the world that we know its real essence and character.

In the creation stories of the peoples of the world, the origin of the world is attributed to many causes. Often a variety of gods and divine helpers create the world, remaining as ongoing powers within the world. Sometimes the creation of the world is seen as a battle between the various divine forces, and humans get caught up in the conflict. The monotheistic religions insist that the one God is creator of all. Again, especially among the religions of India, the origin and the operation of the world may be viewed as an eternal recurring process, like waves on an ocean, emanating from the sacred reality.

The cosmogonic myths or stories telling of origins also provide important views about the nature of the world and the role of humans within it. Some of the religions of nonliterate peoples teach that the world is controlled by many divine forces, expressing their wills in the functioning of nature; therefore the most important role of humans is to serve and propitiate these gods. The Abrahamic religions teach that because there is one God, the creator and preserver of all things, this world makes sense as a good and purposeful creation. And humans are to assist God to care for this world, fulfilling God's design. Other religions, such as Hinduism and Buddhism, teach that the world as we experience it is somewhat illusory. The most important thing for humans to do is to get in touch with the ultimate reality rather than the illusory world. Again, it is sometimes taught, as in the Chinese religions and in Hinduism, that there is a universal world order or harmony into which everything fits, and humans do best by living their lives according to this order.

It seems that all religions have some view of human failure and imperfection. This follows from their vision of what the ideal is. The ideal human existence is sometimes expressed in creation stories, in descriptions of the origins of the world and of humans. There was an age of innocence, for example, a paradisaical state when people lived peacefully and in harmony. The original human state is looked to as a kind of standard of what we ought to be. And corresponding to that is the realistic view of how things actually are: fractured and estranged because of human imperfection and failure. Of course, the extent to which we are thought to be alienated from the good, ideal state differs in the various religions. But it is commonly accepted throughout the religions of the world that humans are not what they can or ought to be. Of course, much evil happens without our choice. But in our experience we know that people sometimes do things that are destructive and violent. In our own lives we recognize that we sometimes do things that are hateful and ugly, and we fail to do the things we ought to do—why? There is a big shadow of failure and imperfection cast over human existence.

The religions of the world give differing reasons for human failure and evil. Some African tribal religions, for example, have myths of origin in which the first humans live in a paradisaical state with the supreme god, represented by the heavens, close to them on earth. Because of some fault in the humans—like being too greedy for food—the supreme god moves far away, with the result that human life becomes full of pain, death, and evil. The three Abrahamic religions teach that God, although making humans as the crown of creation, also gave them of all creatures a dimension of freedom. And within that freedom comes the possibility and the reality of rebellion, unbelief, and fracturing of the loving relationship with God.

Another way of looking at the human problem is found in Hinduism and Buddhism, where human existence is often seen as a kind of trap. Because of the fire of desire that leads us to cling to false ideas of self, we are trapped in an infinite cycle of material existences full of pain and suffering. We cling to the sensual ego-centered illusions, and by doing so we fall under the causal law of karma: we reap exactly what we sow, experiencing the fruits of our clinging actions. The general view in Confucianism, Daoism, and Shinto is that the highest human good is to be in harmony with the universal order of the cosmos and the flow of sacred powers of the world. When we act in ways to cause disharmony, whether in society or in nature, we experience the resulting fractures and discords as evil and suffering.

Sometimes the problem is put in the form of a question: Is human nature fundamentally good or evil? If human nature is evil through and through, then what else could we expect except violence and destructive behavior any time that humans are free to act unchecked? But some would say that humans are basically good and peaceful by nature. Then the violence and evil must be the result of other forces, such as possession by evil spirits, the corrupting influence of society, or oppression by tyrants. Or human evil may arise from our human tendency to forgetfulness and ignorance.

Is human nature fundamentally good or evil? To put the question thus is certainly an oversimplification, for most religions emphasize human moral responsibility. Somehow humans must be free to make their own choices in decisions of behavior, or they would not be responsible for anything they do. The realities of human existence lead most people to conclude that there is within us a struggle concerning choices about good and evil. Outside forces perhaps influence us; perhaps there are inner inclinations toward good or evil. But finally—in the view of most religions—the choice is authored by the person herself or himself, who bears the final responsibility for it.

What this unsettling state of conflict, ignorance, discord, or sin does, when realized against the standard of sacred design and law for human existence, is to impel us toward some change: repentance, seeking help from sacred powers, following a new path to counter and transform our fractured human existence.

The Path of Transformation and Wholeness

How can we start living *real* life? Where are meaning and peace to be found? How can we be healed?

Questions such as these arise when we come face to face with the existence of fracture, failure, and evil in our lives, knowing at the same time that this is not the way things should be. These are questions about the possibility of transformation and salvation. "Salvation" in all religions means wholeness and health—a transformation away from the fragmentation, alienation, sin, and ignorance we feel in our lives, a movement toward peace, health, and perfection. Transformation as taught in a particular religion responds to the way in which the human problem is understood and experienced. For example, sin must be transformed by forgiveness, pollution by purification, ignorance by knowledge, fracture by healing, and wandering by guidance on the straight path. All religions offer some means by which salvation or transformation can be possible.

Functioning as a means of transformation, a religion provides methods of interaction with the realm of the sacred. This is the ultimate source of life and meaning, and the basic human problem arises when this source is cut off for one reason or another. The first need is some kind of restoration of this contact so that sacred power can transform life.

Although people of all religions agree that it is the power of the sacred that transforms humans, there are different visions as to how this power arises and operates in restoring the relationship. Some religions emphasize human depravity and helplessness; therefore all power and salvation must come from a source outside oneself. A good example of such an approach is Japanese Pure Land Buddhism, which stresses the notion of complete human degeneracy and helplessness in this "age of the end of the Buddhist law." This means that the only hope for humans to escape an endless series of rebirths in the suffering realms is to rely totally on help from the compassionate Buddha, Amida. On the other hand, some religions emphasize an approach to the means of transformation that relies on power within oneself. Also in Japanese Buddhism, Zen adherents say there is no need to look to Amida Buddha for help or salvation. Each person has the transcendent Buddha nature in her/himself and through the practice of meditation each person can awaken to that Buddha reality and reach enlightenment.

A young boy's initiation ceremony among the Parsis in India, a remnant of the ancient Zoroastrians of Persia.

These two opposite extremes are from the same religious tradition, namely, Japanese Buddhism. This would suggest that even within one religion we might expect to find both the "outside power" and the "self power" emphases. And this is the case. In Hinduism, for example, one finds both a tradition of worshiping the gods and relying on their grace, and also a tradition of passing beyond the gods to pure realization of the sacred through discipline and meditation. It is true that some religions speak of themselves more as religions of "grace" (outside power), such as Christianity; and other religions, such as Islam, place more emphasis on human responsibility for action (self power). But the relation to the sacred is always a two-way relation. Even if salvation comes totally from the sacred power, still humans receive it and live it out in human religious structures. And even if the whole emphasis seems to be on one's own power in terms of performing disciplines, still these disciplines draw on deep sources of sacred power. One of the distinctive characteristics of each religion, in fact, is its particular vision of the interaction between human practice and sacred gift.

The means of transformation or salvation that a religion offers will involve all three levels of human expression: theoretical, practical, and social. On the theoretical level, the myth and doctrines of the religion are to be understood and accepted by faith and/or reason, so that the person's whole outlook on life can be transformed. On the practical level, ritual, discipline, and practice are means of transformation. Such activities would include things like praying, baptism, acts of repentance, sitting in meditation, studying, keeping rules of purity, acts of self-discipline, and the like. Means of transformation on the social level would include participating in social structures such as families, congregations, sacred peoples, priesthoods, monasteries, and the like, so that the new way of life can be lived fully as a lifelong practice.

Together, these various means of transformation make up a path to follow. This path of transformation is a dynamic process that goes on throughout life in greater and smaller rhythms. It continually involves a double movement: a distancing and separating from the situation that is fractured and wrong; and a restoration and renewal of the state of wholeness and harmony with the sacred. The movement of separation includes acts such as repentance, vows of abstinence, withdrawal of thoughts from outer things, and rituals of washing and purifying oneself. The movement of restoration and renewal comes through acts such as retelling sacred revelation, feelings of ecstasy in worshiping one's god, receiving assurance of forgiveness, and awakening the mind in enlightenment.

Further, the path of transformation is both a *means* and an *end* in itself. As a means it is a praxis, a method of moving toward a goal: transformation or salvation, restoration of the relationship with the sacred. In one sense, that goal is never fully reached within human life, for the problems of human failure and sin remain until death. For that reason many religions have ideas of the future human state in which the ideal goal is perfectly and completely consummated. There may be some model person who achieves that goal now, such as a saviour, saint, prophet, buddha, arhat, or sannyasin. But for the rest of us, the path is a means toward a goal of salvation or transformation that will be a complete, perfect reality only in a transcendent state or a world or lifetime to come.

However, seen from another point of view, the path of transformation is itself the experience of transformation. There is an "already, even though not yet" quality to the experience in following the path. The path is itself the means we have of experiencing contact with the sacred. Zen Buddhism expresses this most strikingly. Master Dogen insisted that practice (sitting in meditation) and enlightenment (experiencing the Buddha nature) are the same thing, with no difference at all. Other religious teachers would perhaps not identify the path so closely with the transformation it brings. But all would agree that following the path is not just a means to reward in another world to come; the goal of transformation is already at least partially present right now as we follow the path.

Worship and the Good Life

Religion by its very nature is practical and social. Theoretical teachings about the sacred and about life need to be lived, not just believed. And the path provides a structure of life within a religious community. It is never just an individual affair but always involves the person in a larger community of people going on that religious path. The religious community provides daily life with a structure including both sacred time and sacred life. That is, the ordinary time of one's existence is punctuated by special times of worship and festival. And the ordinary living of one's daily existence becomes the arena of the good life in fulfillment of the sacred design for the whole community.

Making Time Sacred through Worship, Ritual, and Art

Where can we find new power for life? How can we live more in touch with what is *real*? These questions and many more like them have to do with our need regularly to renew the meaning and purpose of our lives, day by day, year by year, in family and in community, through worship and ritual.

Mircea Eliade[3] has shown that, looked at in a completely profane or secular way, human life would be a self-contained, closed system with intervention by sacred power logically excluded. There would be no "breaks" to the sacred, no special or strong (sacred) times that can provide centers of meaning and thus give structure and order to life.

Since humans cannot tolerate such a meaningless chaos of existing, we seek out special or strong times. In traditional religions, these are the sacred celebrations, the festivals, holy days, and rituals that periodically punctuate and renew the ordinary day-by-day passage of our existing. Even modern, secularized people who have little use for traditional religious rituals have not transcended the need to have sacred times. Breaks in time, centers of meaning and renewal, are widely sought after in such forms as vacations, national holidays, parties, sports, entertainment, and the like. The purpose of such sacred times is "re-creation," that is, the renewal and enlivening of our otherwise humdrum routine of existing.

Religious communities have found that the power that motivates life needs constantly to be renewed. Life-power tends to run down, to become exhausted and weak. There is need regularly to move into sacred time, the time in which the realities of the sacred story are experienced as new and present once again. Ordinary time is transcended, and the people of *now* become contemporary with the gods and the founders and heroes of the Beginning Time. The rituals and festivals provide a rhythm of periodic renewal.

Rituals and festivals are also sources of orientation for life, centers around which all else makes sense. They establish a pattern of living, derived from the sacred story, that can extend out and sanctify the ordinary hours and days of existing. They make real again the identity shared by the community and the incorporation of the individual within it.

Ritual worship connects the sacred with the common elements of human life. Fundamental to religious ritual is the sense of sacred presence in the most vital areas of human experience: eating, sexuality, birth, death, working, play, family, community, water, earth, sun, and so forth. The materials for ritual celebration stem from these basic elements of the human context. A meal is a most universal form of religious ritual, for example. So also is washing by water, or burying in the earth, or dancing and singing, or offering products of one's labor—the list of religious rituals is as long and diverse as are the vital aspects of human life.

Ritual worship not only incorporates the vital human aspects, but it also "returns" them, now sanctified, to life. By the offering of the first fruits of the harvest, all the harvest is sacred. Through the ritual uniting of a woman and a man, all their sexual life is consecrated. By means of the rites of puberty initiation, boys and girls are incorporated as men and women of the community. Ritual washing means all the body is pure and sanctified. Ritual worship thus transforms human life by lifting it up, connecting it with the sacred, and returning it, now sanctified and empowered, to daily existence.

Ritual celebration of sacred time, as an activity on the path of transformation, has a movement or structure for renewal. First of all there needs to be a *kenosis*, an "emptying out."[4] With the recognition that power has run down and become exhausted comes the need for an emptying out of the old situation, a distancing so that the renewal can take place. This kenosis takes many different forms in religious practice. Among the most common rituals would be those that symbolize washing or cleansing, removal of impurity, confession and repentance, separation from the usual state, returning to a condition of chaos or disorder, and dying.

Once the emptying out has been established, the *plerosis*, or "filling up," follows. Having been brought back to the original state, emptied of all exhausted powers, the renewing power of the sacred can be experienced. Rebirth and new life are symbolized by rituals such as emerging from the waters, putting on new clothes, sharing in a meal, receiving a new name, incorporation into a community, singing and dancing, and the like.

Very often the two movements of kenosis and plerosis are connected by an in-between liminal state (from *limen*, "threshold"). This liminal state can be seen, for example, in puberty initiations. Young boys and girls may be separated from their mothers and removed to the bush (kenosis) before being incorporated back into the community as young men and women (plerosis). During that time in the bush they experience a liminal, threshold state; they are "betwixt and between," having died to their childhood existence but not yet been reborn as adults. In this liminal state they return in a sense to a prebirth existence. Everything may be stripped from them; they may experience ritual death and receive sacred revelations. After this critical threshold experience, they are reincorporated into the community as new, reborn people.

Such a liminal experience can be observed in many rituals and festivals. The New Year festivals of many cultures, for example, typically have a time of cleansing and purifying (kenosis), which leads into a liminal condition of "antistructure" or chaos; finally renewed structure and order are created (plerosis). The Christian ritual of baptism involves a distancing from evil (renouncing the works of the devil), a liminal passage of symbolic death in the waters, and a renewal ritualized by a new name, white garment, and a burning candle. The ritual of pilgrimage, important in Eastern religions, includes symbols of distancing through a long journey, vows, and a special garment. The liminal period covers several days full of intense rituals and experiences. And the pilgrim has a new spiritual and social status upon completion of the pilgimage.

Festivals and Rituals of Passage
Among the most common rituals are those that occur periodically, such as seasonal festivals. They follow the rhythm of the year and celebrate different aspects of involvement with sacred power. Many of these seasonal festivals have some connection with the cycle of sacred power in nature: spring renewal festivals, fall harvest festivals, and the like. In some religions the seasonal festivals are associated with events in the sacred story. For example, the spring festival of Passover celebrates the deliverance of Israel from slavery in Egypt, and a spring festival in Buddhism commemorates the birth of the Buddha. Both of these festivals, although they emphasize events in human history, retain symbolism of liberation of nature's forces from the captivity of winter.

Another very common type of festival occurring periodically is the holy day, a particular day singled out for commemorating and celebrating some aspect of sacred power. These may be lucky or unlucky days determined by the astrological calendar; they may commemorate the birth or death of some great saints or religious founders; they may be critical points in the transitions of the annual seasons, such as the winter solstice; or they may follow a repeating pattern, such as every seven days (Jews, Christians, and Muslims), every nineteen days (Baha'is), or bi-monthly on the lunar pattern (Buddhists). Some rituals recur every day, such as morning devotions for Brahmin Hindus, or even periodically throughout every day, such as the five daily periods of prayer in Islam.

Seasonal festivals and periodic holy days and rituals offer a plenitude of sacred centers in the living of human life, a rhythm of recurring renewal to sustain the identity of the community and of the individual within the community.

Another major type of ritual celebration is that associated with the vital passages of human life, especially birth, puberty, marriage, and death. These "rites of passage"[5] are focused on the individual within the context of the community, serving to transform the person into the new stage of life and to integrate her or him into the community at that new spiritual level. Each of these passages of life is liminal—that is, it involves crossing a threshold from one state of existence to another. Each passage is critical to the full human development of the person and to the welfare of the community, and therefore religious rituals accompany and actualize the passage.

To move from one stage of life to another means first of all to put an end to the old stage. Thus rituals of separation, distancing, or dying are most appropriately used as the first movement in the celebration of passage. The end of an infant's prebirth state may be ritualized by burying the afterbirth, or washing the infant for the first time. Children to be initiated into adulthood are typically separated from their homes and parents as the beginning of their initiation. Carrying a bride-to-be away from her home to the marriage hall shows the end of her state of maidenhood. Funeral rituals typically include the removal of the body from the normal life surroundings.

Separated from the old stage, which is now completed and thus done away with, the person enters into a state of liminality, "betwixt and between." Having moved back to the precreation state, rituals of liminality bring the person into direct contact with sacred power. These include rituals of death and burial, suspension of time and identity, encounter with the ancestors, and so forth. Mother and newborn baby are often confined for a period of time during which various birth ceremonies take place. Children in nonliterate societies die symbolic deaths during their initiation rituals, have their sexual organs cut, or engage in battles with mythical monsters. Marriage passage rites often include a period of betrothal during which the man and woman are neither single nor yet joined as one. In funeral rituals, the newly dead person is often felt to be in an in-between state, and the family and community observe a "wake" or sometimes a lengthy mourning period before the dead one is fully incorporated as an ancestor.

Finally, rituals of rebirth, filling up, empowering, and reincorporation into the community complete the passage. The person has left the previous state, passed over the threshold, and now is recognized and welcomed at the new level of life. The infant is named and thus incorporated into the community. The young people now speak a new language and take their places as adults. The marriage is consummated and rituals of establishing a new home take place. The dead one is welcomed back as an ancestor and is enshrined on the family altar.

Other rituals of passage have to do with spiritual rebirth; they follow the pattern of rites of passage but are not necessarily connected with the physical development of human life. In some societies initiation into secret religious societies follows the pattern of the rites of passage. Religious specialists such as shamans, yogins, priests, or monks and nuns enter into their new spiritual level of existence through passage rituals of ordination or consecration.

Artistic Expression and the Sacred

In our discussion of sacred time and ritual, we need to include some consideration of the arts. In the broad sense we can consider the arts as all human activities and creations that express the aesthetic sense of beauty and meaning, especially the visual, literary, and performing arts. Art is closely tied to celebration and ritual. Religious experience is expressed largely through aesthetic media, for our contact with the sacred must be grounded in our percep-

Expression of the sacred in art: woodcut of Christ on the cross, by Paul Gauguin.

tion (*aesthesis*) of reality. People of the different religions have always known that the sacred is experienced through the things of the world and of human existence. Although interior, direct contact with the sacred is also known, the outer forms through which the sacred is experienced have been lovingly cultivated into artistic forms.

As used in the religions, art forms symbolize the sacred. That is, they point beyond themselves to some dimension of the sacred or of human relationship with the sacred. They are not mere signs or pointers, however. To symbolize the sacred means to share somehow in the sacred reality, to convey the power and the presence of the sacred. A statue of the Buddha on the altar is not itself, wood or stone, that to which Buddhists direct worship. But it conveys the presence of the Buddha to the worshipers and thus participates in the reality to which it points.

Some art is designed mainly to represent the sacred; other art intends actually to "present" the sacred. Art that represents the sacred may be instructional, bringing the sacred to the attention of the people. A drama acting out the story might have the goal of instructing the people. Images and statues on Hindu temples and Christian cathedrals function as a kind of visual narrative of the story of the religion.

Other art more directly *presents* the sacred for a worshipful, transformative religious experience. Use of the arts in worship and ritual is often of this more presentational type, evoking and creating the experience of the sacred. In Hindu puja (worship), the god is invoked into the image and worshiped. The artful ritual actions, objects, and liturgical chanting of the Shinto priest in a shrine festival present the blessing and power of the kami directly to the worshipers. Of course, art can combine both types. The dramatic Jewish Passover meal (seder), for example, educates by narrating the story, but it also creates the religious experience of being present at the great deliverance of the exodus from Egypt.

From the religious point of view, all aspects of human existence have the possibility of being open to the sacred. Therefore religion, especially in worship and ritual, seeks to involve all possible human arts. Since the arts are highly expressive, they can evoke experiences of the sacred at deeper levels than the rational and logical. For example, the various literary arts do, of course, make use of the logical, rational structure of language. But there is a difference between a precise philosophical proposition of faith that attempts to define (and thus limit) the sacred, and a liturgical poetic expression that makes the sacred powerfully present. The great power that people find in the scriptures of their religion is related to the artistic quality of the sacred literature. The aesthetic sound of mantras (sacred formulas) in Hinduism and Buddhism conveys power even if the literal meaning of the words is not understood.

Visual presentations of the sacred and of the sacred story are used in many religions, although there is also reluctance in some religions to portray divine realities in representational visual form. Iconography (representational art) presents essential aspects of the sacred, but it also imbues the sacred with sensuous form—and thus limitations. Painting, sculptures, small figurines, and symbolic abstract designs all serve to evoke senses of the sacred full of aesthetic power and beauty, with form, color, and texture.

The art of music has been found to be a powerful presenter of the sacred in almost all religions. The beautiful sounds of music—gripping rhythm, haunting melody, special qualities of different instruments, reach to deep levels of aesthetic sensibility and express many different aspects of the experience of the sacred. It is particularly powerful when words are wedded to music in sacred chants, mantras, hymns, and the like. The art of music, whether a solitary flute or the ringing Hallelujah Chorus of Handel's *Messiah*, gathers and directs spiritual emotions and evokes the sacred presence like no other art does.

Another art form widely cultivated in the religions is dance, the aesthetic and spiritual expression of body movements. Closely associated with dance would be drama and liturgical rituals. The ritual actions of a Daoist priest very much involve arts of dance and drama, as also the kagura dance in Shinto, the art of ritual prayer in Islam, and dance-drama festivals in Hinduism.

The sense of sacred place is artistically expressed in religions by distinctive forms of architecture. Temples and shrines symbolize the *axis mundi*, the center of the world, providing a center of orientation for all the rest of space. The sacred building is often thought of as a microcosm of the cosmic world. The aesthetic quality of architectural forms expresses essential dimensions of the vision of the particular religion. Soaring Gothic cathedrals reaching toward heaven, Muslim mosques filled with openness and light, Hindu temples with their dark and mysterious inner room, simple wooden Shinto shrines in Japan—all give expression to particular spatial-local qualities of the experience of the sacred.

Since artistic forms can evoke deep feelings with powerful presentations of the sacred, occasionally they can be experienced as destructive or demonic. People can look to the art form itself as ultimate, a situation called idolatry ("worship of an idol") in some of the religions. People in all religions know, however, that the art forms, no matter how beautiful or powerful, are *symbols* of the sacred. They point beyond themselves to the sacred, they convey and present the sacred; but they are not themselves the ultimate sacred.

Each religious tradition chooses special aesthetic forms as the most appropriate, sometimes resisting others as useless, misleading, or even dangerous. We might say that each religion or culture has its own distinctive aesthetic sense, closely related to the deep insights of that spiritual vision. To really understand a culture, we must look at its literature, poetry, dance, visual portrayals, architecture, music, and the rest. For example, the Hindu experience of countless gods within an ultimate unity opens the way for the cultivation of all the arts. And the Muslim reluctance to link God together with likenesses of any thing has led to a restriction on representational visual arts and a flowering of decorative and verbal arts. Arts of some religions are more conducive to meditation, others to celebration and ecstasy. In broad terms, the religions of South and East Asia have stressed intuitional, meditative aesthetic experiences, whereas the religions of the West have often emphasized an aesthetic sense connected with the word, intelligence, and logic. But these differences can easily be overstressed, for the shape of the aesthetic vision is often a matter of emphasis. Even within one religion significant differences can be found.

Sacred Life: Social Structure and the Good Life

How should we live? Where do we belong? What is our responsibility to human society? Religious experience carries with it an imperative to live in a way that conforms to one's religious identity. A person is always a part of a group, a community, and the good life is structured in that community context. Acting according to one's religious

Indians bathing in a religious ceremony at the Pushkar Fair in Rajasthan, India.

identity involves, in many religions, a sense of responsibility and mission to others in the world.

As we saw earlier, each religion has a master story that gives identity and purpose to the religious community and the individual within it. The story tells about the original people, special and sacred. These people are set apart for special identity, for special life, and for a special role in the world. The Japanese Shinto myths, for example, tell how the Japanese islands and the Japanese people descended from the kami (the divine beings). The emperor descended from the most powerful kami, the sun kami Amaterasu. This mythology has supported the sense of the Japanese as a sacred people, with the emperor as the divine head of the nation. Buddhist stories tell how the Buddha, after his enlightenment, gathered a band of disciples into a monastic community of monks and nuns, the sangha. The lay people participate in this religious community by supporting and honoring the sangha. In traditional China, ancient teachings support the strong notion that the clan or extended family is the center of meaning for each individual, and beyond that there are the hierarchically organized village and state within which the individual finds religious identity.

The structure and organization of the religious community are grounded in the sacred history and traditions of the religion. Provision is made for some kind of religious leadership. Sometimes the religious leaders function by virtue of the power of their office, like kings and priests. In other cases, religious leaders are recognized by virtue of their personal charisma and power, such as sages, prophets, shamans, healers, and diviners. The community also has social structures involving clan relationships, congregations, lay groups, secret societies, masters and disciples, apprentices, and the like.

Every society has its traditional roles defined for women and men. Since almost all societies have been structured patriarchally, in almost all religions women have been subordinated to men and have had limited access to leadership roles. This makes it all the more important for us to search out material on women's lives in the different religions and to take note of their important roles (often glossed over by the male-dominated tradition). Further, we need to see the increasingly active leadership roles of modern women in these societies, as they make use of their religious tradition to break out of traditional limitations and help to renew and transform their societies.

The perspective about authentic life for the people is often tied together with stories about a sacred land or territory: the sacred islands for the Japanese, the tribal land and burial grounds for the African tribes, Jerusalem for Jews, the pilgrimage sites and sacred rivers in India, and the like. Sacred space is established by the presence of the sacred, and therefore it is experienced as the center of the world (*axis mundi*), as Mircea Eliade has elucidated.[6] This center functions as the connecting point between the human realm and the divine realms. Once the center is established, it provides orientation and a sense of being at home in the world. Sacred space can be a whole land, or it may be a village, mountain, shrine, temple, altar, or even a house. This is the *real* space that provides meaning and identity. It gives a feeling of rootedness; cut off from it we feel lost in the chaos of foreign, meaningless space.

The Moral Pattern for Authentic Life

The moral pattern for the good life is usually presented in the sacred history, for there we learn what the gods did in the mythological age, or the rules laid down by the ancestors, or the examples provided by the founder.

It is the conviction of people of each religion that this pattern for life is "natural" in a deep sense. It is the way of life that most fits our original nature, as we were intended to be before we turned away or forgot that pattern. Whereas rewards may be promised for living the moral life and punishments threatened for neglecting it, the fundamental motivation for following the ethical guidance of the religion is deeper. This is the model for *authentic* human life, that which harmonizes with the greater spiritual forces and patterns of the cosmos. To many nonliterate peoples, real human life is to do what the gods did in the Time of the Beginning. According to Hinduism, living according to the Code of Manu corresponds to the eternal Dharma (cosmic order), and that is right and brings happiness. The Five Classics, according to Confucianism, express the sacred pattern of life according to the will of Heaven, as exemplified by the ancient sages, and thus studying and following these Classics will bring peace and harmony.

The ethical life has something to do with how we *should* be, and therefore it is based in the religion's vision of creation and human nature. The law of morality is often thought to be an authority outside oneself, usually recorded in scripture and tradition, to which one submits. But the religious teachers also talk about how that law becomes internalized, transformed into the inner motivation for right living, so that one naturally does what is right—thus there occurs a sanctification of life.

It takes practice to live as one ought. Confucius taught that to transform ourselves into people of humanity (*ren*), it is most helpful to take up the discipline and practice of the principles of propriety (*li*). Hindus believe that following the Path of Action, doing one's duty according to one's place in life without desire for reward, is a way of reaching higher spiritual perfection and better rebirths. The thing that makes Jews distinctive from others is their willingness to take up the discipline of the commandments (*mitzvot*)—not for the reward that this will bring, but because the very doing of the mitzvot is itself the good life.

The religious tradition provides guidance in all areas of life. In personal behavior often the stress falls on self-control and moderation. One should not be controlled by the passions and desires, but rather these passions and desires should be controlled and redirected toward transformation of self. The religious tradition also spells out the relation of the individual to others and indicates the right and wrong way of treating others in the various situations. The ethical life is lived for the welfare of the community. In following the code of life, strife and competition are avoided and healing and harmony are promoted. The religions usually teach motivations of compassion and sacrifice, giving oneself for the good of the community.

Technically speaking, "ethics" is the activity of thinking about moral decisions on the basis of the tradition. The religious tradition provides ethical guidance about many or most of the crucial questions in life. But the individual and the community, living in concrete situations with changing circumstances, also continually make ethical decisions about a variety of possible actions. In modern times the ethical decisions have become increasingly numerous and difficult, such as questions of abortion, serving in the military, adopting Western customs, and reforming social injustices. There are a great many burning questions today revolving around changing roles for women and men. Thousands of questions like these face people in all the religions today, and as they think about the possible decisions on the basis of the religious tradition, they are engaging in ethical thinking.

Some religions are tribal, and this means they have little opportunity to express solidarity with humans outside the tribe. People of tribal religious traditions do often have a sense of harmony with the natural world. They promote the welfare and continuation of the world that supports human society, made up of vegetation, animals, and the earth itself, in a kind of primal ecology. A feeling for the sacredness of all human life is also demonstrated among many nonliterate, tribal peoples.

Within the world religions there has developed more awareness of the universality of the human race and of the common human welfare in the world. Thus all the world religions have some vision of the nature and purpose of all humankind and of their own role or mission in the world. In the context of world society, the religions have developed a sense of responsibility for the good of the larger world, especially in areas like social justice, education, and relief for the poor and hungry. In recent times concern for reconciliation and peace-making has come to the fore in many religions. Today people in all religions see the need for peace and harmony between different cultures, especially in view of the drastic threat of modern warfare.

Inherent in every self-conscious religious tradition is the claim to be the truth and thus the ideal way of life. Whereas tribal peoples generally do not attempt to spread their religious practices beyond the borders of their own tribe, all religions that have a sense of universality also have some feeling of responsibility to bring the truth to the rest of the world.

The concern that the truth must be shared with all peoples is especially strong in the so-called missionary religions: Christianity, Islam, and to some extent Buddhism, and also some newer branches of the older traditions, like Bahai, Nichiren Shoshu, and the International Society for Krishna Consciousness. Apart from Buddhism and some of these new religious movements, the religions of the East generally have not actively tried to convince others to convert to those religions. But as the world shrinks and communication between peoples of the globe increases, Hindus, Sikhs, Daoists, and Shintoists are in-creasingly presenting their visions of truth, to be heard and understood by the peoples of the world.

Concern for the welfare of the world, and the realization that other religions also have visions for the world and claims to truth, have led to conversation and cooperation among the religions. Many people today recognize that religions and ideologies have contributed a great deal to the conflicts in the world. In recent years a new movement of dialogue among the religions has become a part of the religious happenings of the world. At the very least, there has developed a widespread sense that peoples of different religions need to work together against the forces of exploitation and violence and secularization that threaten human society today in an unprecedented way.

DISCUSSION QUESTIONS

1. Do you think questions such as "Who am I?" and "What is the purpose of life?" are universal human concerns, or are they the product of modern Western thought?
2. What are some aspects of the experience of the sacred that seem to be shared by people of different cultures and religious traditions?
3. Give some examples of how symbol systems change over time.
4. What is implied in calling religious practices a "path"?
5. How can a story or myth from ancient times still provide identity for people today? Give some examples.
6. What do cosmogonic stories reveal about the way a particular people look at the world and human existence?
7. What is meant by speaking of "salvation" or "transformation" in the various religions?
8. How can participation in sacred times or festivals bring renewal of human life? What do the terms *kenosis*, *liminal*, and *plerosis* mean?
9. How does art represent and present the sacred?
10. Is the good ethical life something natural or unnatural?
11. Do you think a sense of universal truth and mission is something essential to a religion?

KEY TERMS IN THE INTRODUCTION

aesthetic concerning beauty or artistic perception, important for religious expression

cosmogonic related to the creation or founding of the world and of basic human realities

ethics thought and study about moral decisions, on the basis of traditions of right and wrong

free will ability of humans to make moral choices

grace achievement of spiritual goals as given by spiritual powers rather than attained by one's own effort

liminal in ritual, the state between separation (*kenosis*) and restoration (*plerosis*)

monism view that all reality is one unified divine reality

monotheism belief in one almighty God, separate from the world

myth story about sacred beings in the beginning time, telling how existence came to be as it is and providing the pattern for authentic life

New Year Festival important annual festival in many societies, a time of purging out the old year and bringing renewal

path of transformation practice in a religion that changes one from the wrong or inadequate state to the ideal state

plerosis "filling up"; fulfillment or restoration movement of ritual

polytheism belief that many divine powers share in the world's operation

rites of passage rituals connected with the critical changes of life

sacred, the general term for that which is experienced as ultimate reality, the mysterious Other that is the ground of ultimate value and meaning

sacred space space that is made special by connection with the sacred, providing orientation and rootedness for a people

sacred story master story of a religion, providing identity for the adherents (*see* myth)

sacred time special time of ritual and festival, when mythic events are made present once more

salvation reaching the ideal state of wholeness and transformation

supreme god the god with final authority, usually the creator, often associated with the sky

symbols words, pictures, ideas, rituals, and so on, that evoke deep meanings by connecting with sacred reality

temple place of worship in many religions

tradition "passing on" of the sacred story and basic ideas of a religion

understanding "standing under" another's way of thought and life, comprehending it by reference to one's own experience

worship respectful ritual activity in special times, directed toward sacred beings or realities of ultimate value

PART ONE

RELIGIONS ARISING FROM INDIA
Hinduism, Buddhism, Jainism, and Sikhism

INTRODUCTION

Like the Middle East, India has been a fertile spawning ground for world religions. The story of these religions reaches back to the Indus Valley civilization in ancient times and the Aryans who came in from outside to establish Aryan religion and culture in India. From these ancient streams have arisen Hinduism, Buddhism, Jainism, and—much later, after Muslim influence became strong in India—Sikhism. What is the common vision that this group of religions shares?

There is, of course, a close historical and geographical relationship among these religions. Hinduism, Buddhism, and Jainism all took classical shape at approximately the same time in north India. Hinduism does trace its sacred story to the earlier Aryans with their Vedic scriptures, and Jainism reaches back to Parshva (ninth century B.C.E.) and earlier. But certainly one of the most formative periods for each religion was around the sixth century B.C.E. In Hinduism the Upanishads were being composed as the foundation of the Hindu perspective. Siddhartha Gautama was following the way to enlightenment and founding the first Buddhist community. And Mahavira also

was walking the path to enlightenment as the leader of the Jains. There was some interaction among members of these three movements, and they grappled with many of the same issues as they created three distinct paths. It was not until about two thousand years later that Sikhism was founded, but still it grew up in India and drew on the religious vision and practice of Hinduism, shaping that together with Muslim ideas into a distinctive way of life.

For all of them, India has been "Mother India," not only historically but also culturally and spiritually. Most of these religions have been content to stay within the bosom of India, with little attempt to spread and translate their spiritual wisdom into other places and cultures. Only Buddhism has become a missionary religion, losing its status in India but spreading the truth of the Buddha to South Asia, Southeast Asia, and East Asia. Even though Buddhism does not have a lot of adherents in India today, Buddhists still look to India as the sacred source, since their history happened there and almost all their scriptures were composed there.

In their religious thinking, the people of these religions of India tend to start from experience in the world. And their common perception of human existence is that it goes in cycles, lifetime after lifetime, world age after world age. The human individual stands now; but many existences before have brought about the present state of affairs, and many existences to come are being caused by this existence. Furthermore, the whole universe goes in cycles, without beginning or end, in recurrent evolutions and devolutions like the waves on the sea.

One of the big questions that one needs to ask, then, has to do with what is real and ultimately significant. It cannot be the passing phenomena, whether of the world or of oneself. The vision of India says that the real is unified and absolute, forever beyond the changes and cycles of existence. The sacred is generally not seen in personal, historical terms—although, of course, the sacred can be revealed or reflected in such forms. The ultimate sacred reality is impersonal, transcending historical pro-

cesses, not an individual creator God involved personally in the historical events of the world.

The real essence of humans is not our life in this passing world, but rather what connects us with the sacred. Our true nature is somehow to be identified with the ultimate sacred, and the goal of religious practice is to bring this truth to realization. And so each religion teaches its adherents to discipline themselves to withdraw attachments to the passing world, blocking up the causes that will bring about future existences. There are religious practices, especially meditation, to help in seeing the sacred within, leading to spiritual fulfillment and liberation from the cycle.

But perhaps we have said too much already about the common vision, for Hindus, Buddhists, Jains, and Sikhs bring much more to their own visions, interpreting these basic ideas in distinctive ways, developing their own

South and East Asia.

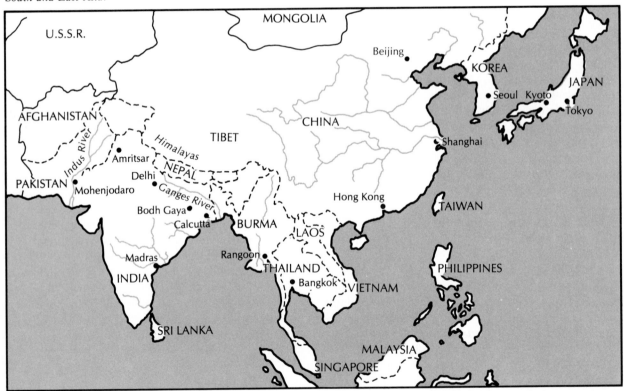

worlds of symbols that guide and structure life. Many of these symbols look similar, of course, as we would expect among closely related religions. But in each religion the symbols reflect the truth of the religious vision in a characteristic way because of the total configuration of the world of symbols.

From India, Buddhism spread widely throughout Sri Lanka, Southeast Asia, and East Asia, and in each of these areas it has developed distinctive forms. But all forms of Buddhism retain a basic continuity with the Buddhist community that first arose in India. In Part I, Buddhism in China and Japan will be discussed only briefly, since those forms of Buddhism will be further explored in Part II, Religions of China and Japan.

CHAPTER 2

Hinduism: Sacred Story and Historical Context

Who am I? To be Hindu is a very broad matter, with few restrictions or exclusions. It almost seems that being a Hindu is the same as being a person of India. As a matter of fact, *Hindu* is a Persian word meaning "Indian." To be Hindu implies accepting and respecting the ancient traditions of India, especially the ancient scriptures (the Vedas), and the social class structure with its special respect for brahmins (the priestly class). Thus, except for several dissenting Hindu groups, the only people of India who are really excluded from this Hindu identity are those who do not accept the authority of the Vedas and the special place of the brahmins—that is, Buddhists, Jains, and Sikhs, together, of course, with Indian Muslims, Christians, and Parsis (the small community of Zoroastrians in India). The Vedas and the social class system—and the sacred realities of which they are a part—provide the center of the Hindu story.

FOUNDINGS: STREAMS INTO THE RIVER OF HINDUISM

Unlike the other religions arising from India and unlike the Abraham religions, Hinduism has no specific founders involved in historical events that gave rise to the religion. The Hindu sacred history places relatively little emphasis on what we normally think of as historical events or persons, and it shows only slight interest in historical sequences. Most things happen in a transcendental kind of timeframe. For example, the events told in the Ramayana Epic take place in the *treta* age, several million years ago, whereas the Mahabharata Epic tells of events in the *dvapara* age, still hundreds of thousands of years ago. The sacred reality is reflected in all these ages and cycles, but it also transcends them. So the stories about the gods and goddesses, the heroes and heroines are not concerned about how they fit in the human history of our age. Hindus have no particular interest in the "historical" Krishna, for example, in contrast to Christian interest in the historicity of Christ. The great kings, heroes, gods, and goddesses the stories tell about are important because they are models of eternal, mythological truth.

So the sacred history is not so much about the founding of Hinduism, but it is about the *foundation* of Hinduism—that is, the sacred realities that form the pattern for Hindu life and meaning. As we look at the Hindu story, we need to provide some historical orientation, which includes events like the migration of the Aryans into India around 1500 B.C.E., the composing of the Upanishads, the development of city-states and the Hindu social order, and the like. But we must take care not to confuse the historical orientation with what Hindu tradition considers to be the real sacred history: the ancient sages hearing and transmitting the eternal Vedas and the legendary and mythological events about gods and heroes described in the Epics. We need the historical orientation, but we also need to understand that the real meaning of the sacred history, for Hindus, is in those events that transcend our historical age.

The Formative Period of Hinduism

The Hindu sacred story highlights the Aryans and their sacred texts as the foundation of Hinduism. We know that the Aryans actually were Indo-European peoples who came into India and eventually became the Hindus. But we also know that there was a great civilization in India before the Aryans arrived, the Indus Valley civilization, which had reached its zenith around 2500 B.C.E. Around 1500 B.C.E. the Aryans, migrating into India from the northwest, superseded this civilization—but in the process some of the indigenous peoples and their religious ideas eventually were absorbed into Hinduism as it developed over a number of centuries. Here—as in the case of the ancient Israelites settling in Canaan—took place a fascinating encounter of two very different cultures: the Indus Valley people were basically agriculturalists, and the Aryans were pastoralists. We do not know much about the details of the encounter, unfortunately, but the resulting creation was the richly textured religion of Hinduism. It seems that other indigenous peoples in India outside the Indus Valley also influenced the development of Hindu religious ideas and practices.

The Indus Valley Civilization

Archaeologists working in the past sixty years have uncovered an amazingly advanced civilization stretching for a thousand miles along the valley of the Indus River, comparable in many ways with the two other great river valley civilizations that existed at this same time, ancient Egypt along the Nile and ancient Sumer along the Tigris and Euphrates rivers. Like them, the Indus Valley civilization lived by agriculture and domestic animals, had developed a system of writing (unfortunately, not enough remains to be deciphered), and built cities. Two of the cities, Mohenjo-Daro and Harappa, are quite large and appear to have been religious and administrative centers. There is a most striking uniformity of culture throughout the whole civilization, from the cities to the several hundred towns and villages thus far discovered, suggesting rigid control by powerful rulers. For example, the cities were all carefully laid out on the same plan, with major streets crossing each other at right angles. Houses were supplied with water and had bathrooms from which water drained out into covered sewers.

Archaeological investigations have turned up a number of things suggestive of the religious vision of these people. One striking point is that they had a great reverence for water and its purifying power. In addition to the bathrooms in individual houses, apparently for ritual purposes, a large bathing tank has been found in the large platform mound of Mohenjo-Daro, flanked by dressing rooms and arcades. It seems they considered water to have important purifying powers, an idea that we find also in later Hinduism.

As befits an agricultural civilization, there appears to have been emphasis on the fertility of mother earth. Many terra-cotta figurines depicting females have been discovered, clearly associated with powers of fertility and the growth of plants. Mythic scenes depicting fertility powers appear on many small personal soapstone seals. There is a series of scenes, for example, portraying an ensemble of goddesses, trees, tigers, and water buffaloes. On one seal there is a horned goddess amid the branches of a pipal tree (sacred in later India), worshiped by a figure on bended knee. The kneeling worshiper presents before the goddess an animal that is a composite of buffalo hindquarters, ram

The Hindu goddess Durga. Goddesses were widely worshiped already in the Indus Valley civilization.

horns and forepart, and a large masklike human face. Lined up in a row are seven figures with tunics, pigtails, curved horns, and bangled arms. It may be assumed that later Hinduism's worship of the great goddesses and perhaps even its emphasis on the cyclical pattern of death and life were influenced by the fertility religion of these ancient people.

Another religious emphasis has to do with male creative powers. Many figurines and seals depict powerful male animals—bulls, tigers, rhinoceroses, antelopes, elephants, and a unicorn-type animal. A two-tiered incense stand is always set before the single-horned animal, showing that these male animals represented sacred power to be worshiped. A number of phalluses, models of the male sexual organ, have been found in the excavations, suggesting some ritual worship of male fertility power. A most fascinating symbol is depicted on several seals: a male person seated in a kind of yoga posture with legs drawn up and heels together, similar to the posture used in yoga meditation in later Hinduism. In one seal the god (we may presume he represents sacred power) is surrounded by an elephant, a tiger, a rhinoceros, and a buffalo, and beneath his stool are two deer. He wears a headdress of two horns, with a plant growing between them. The figure appears to be ithyphallic (with an erect penis). The combination of symbols is striking: fertility of plants and animals, yogic meditation, and male sexual energy. It has been suggested that this god is a prototype of the great god Shiva in later Hinduism, who is known as the great yogin and often symbolized by the *lingam* (phallic symbol).

Worship was probably carried on both in homes and in public shrines. At the domestic level there were no doubt ritual votive offerings involving fertility figurines, bathing, and ritual purity. On the public level, worship was probably associated with the raised platform mounds, perhaps involving animal sacrifices.

These various religious ideas of the Indus Valley civilization have some connections with earlier pre-urban cultures of India and related areas, so they can be understood perhaps as part of a broader cultural complex that was widespread in pre-Aryan times. No historical documentation exists to show the impact these religious ideas had on the development of Hinduism, and certainly Hindus do not usually count the Indus Valley people as part of their

story. But we—looking now from the outside—may surmise that the Indus Valley civilization, along with other pre-Aryan peoples in India, contributed to some of the characteristic Hindu ideas and practices, especially those associated with water, the great goddesses, the cyclic pattern of existence, yogic meditation, and the god Shiva.

Aryan Religion: the Vedic Period

The group of people who migrated into the Indus Valley from the northwest around 1500 B.C.E. called themselves Aryans (noble ones). They were Indo-Europeans, related to all those peoples who migrated in various directions from the original Indo-European homeland, probably in the steppe land that stretches from Eastern Europe to Central Asia. Some of these original Indo-European peoples migrated westward into Europe and became the Greeks, the Romans, the Germanic peoples, the Slavs, the Balts, and so forth. Others of these peoples migrated eastward and became the Persians (Iranians), the Armenians, and the Aryans. The language spoken by the Aryans, Sanskrit, was closely related to the other Indo-European languages, as was their culture and religion. Wherever the Indo-Europeans went, of course, they interacted with indigenous peoples and created distinct cultures and religions.

The Aryans were pastoralists (cattle herders), grouped in a number of tribes each headed by a chieftain. Their society was divided into three classes: the warriors, the priests, and the herders or producers. They were fierce warriors, having domesticated the horse and invented the chariot, and they were skilled in metallurgy and weaponry. After settling in India and replacing or absorbing the declining Indus Valley civilization, the Aryans continued to develop their own traditions for a number of centuries, gradually allowing local, non-Aryan beliefs and practices to enhance the fundamentally Aryan religion.

Although the Aryans did not have a writing system, from early times they composed hymns and ritual verses called *Veda* (knowledge), transmitting them orally in priestly families. Hindus understand the Vedas to be timeless, eternal truths "heard" by the *rishis*, the seer-poets of old; they are the original foundation of Hinduism. Special place is accorded to the four Samhitas (collections), also simply called Vedas. The Rig Veda is the oldest and most important collection, with over one thousand hymns. The

Sama Veda contains verses arranged to be sung by the musical specialist during the sacrifice, and the Yajur Veda supplied short formulas spoken by the priest who performed the physical operations in the sacrificial ritual. The fourth collection, the Atharva Veda, contains incantations for priests to use for various needs like childbirth, illness, securing the affection of a lover, and much more. These Vedic hymns were recited, chanted, and performed as sacred liturgy.

The religion that is expressed in these Vedic hymns and formulas centers on worship of gods by means of sacrifice, petition, and praise. The gods are many, residing in the three realms (sky, atmosphere, and earth), and showing their powers in the various processes of nature. The word for god in Sanskrit is *deva*, meaning "shining" or "auspicious." And that is what the gods are—the powers that create life and growth, that are present in wind, fire, water, speech, consciousness, and all facets of existence. The gods include Dyaus Pitar (god of the sky), Prithivi (earth goddess), Ushas (dawn, daughter of heaven), Surya (the shining sun), Savitar (the sun as generator), Rudra (destroyer and healer), Mitra (the sun), Tvashtar (the heavenly blacksmith), Vayu (the wind), and very many more. As examples of these gods, let us look briefly at four of the most important, namely, Varuna, Indra, Agni, and Soma.

Varuna is god of the vault of the sky, sometimes described as creating the world, whose function it is to guard the cosmic order (called *Rta*). In that capacity Varuna is the god who sees humans in their wrongdoings and catches them in his noose, punishing them with disease. Thus he must be petitioned to remove those offenses.

> For the emperor [Varuna] I will sing a splendid, deep prayer, one that will be dear to the famous Varuna who struck apart the earth and spread it beneath the sun as the priest who performs the slaughter spreads out the victim's skin. He stretched out the middle realm of space in the trees; he laid victory in swift horses and milk in the dawn cows, intelligence in hearts and fire in the waters. Varuna placed the sun in the sky and Soma on the mountain. . . . If we have cheated like gamblers in a game, whether we know it or really do not know it, O god, cast all these offences away like loosened bonds. Let us be dear to you, Varuna.   (RG VEDA 5.85.1–2, 8)[1]

Indra is a god of the atmosphere, the storm god who shows himself in the lightning and thunder. Like Thor among the Scandinavians, Indra is a boisterous warrior god, drinking soma (a hallucinating, invigorating drink) and leading people in battle against their enemies. Many hymns tell of Indra's cosmic battle with the demon Vritra, who has shut up the waters and the sun; after a fierce battle Indra slays him and releases the life-giving forces.

> Let me now sing the heroic deeds of Indra, the first that the thunderbolt-wielder performed. He killed the dragon and pierced an opening for the waters; he split open the bellies of mountains. He killed the dragon who lay upon the mountain; Tvastr fashioned the roaring thunderbolt for him. Like lowing cows, the flowing waters rushed straight down to the sea. Wildly excited like a bull, he took the Soma for himself and drank the extract from the three bowls in the three-day Soma ceremony. Indra the Generous seized his thunderbolt to hurl it as a weapon; he killed the firstborn of dragons.   (RG VEDA 1.32.1–3)[2]

Of the many gods of the third realm, earth, Agni (Fire) assumes special importance as the god of the sacrificial fire. The power of Agni is centered especially in the fire sacrifice, Agni being the sacred power that accepts the offerings and transports them to the realm of the gods. For that reason, Agni is addressed in nearly one-third of the Rig Vedic hymns.

> With praises we worship you, O Fire, king of sacrifices, long-tailed like a horse. May you, O son of strength, be propitious and bountiful to us in your great way. May you, who moves everywhere, O Fire, protect us from mortals far and near who seek to harm us. May you, O Fire, convey our offering of praise to the gods. . . . O Fire, invoked through praises, enter the sacrifice, favor it and complete it.   (RG VEDA 1.27)[3]

Throughout all periods of Hinduism, special importance has been attached to the ritual of fire sacrifice—and thus to the god Agni as the priest of the gods.

Another god of the earth realm who is prominent in the Vedic hymns is Soma, a god whose power is known in *soma*, an intoxicating drink offered to the gods in sacrifice and drunk by the worshipers. "We have drunk the Soma; we have become immortal; we have gone to the light; we have found the gods," a hymn celebrates (Rg Veda 8.48.3).[4]

Soma symbolizes both ecstasy and the special power of consciousness experienced through this divine power.

In the early Vedic conception, then, power for running the world and human existence derives from the gods. How humans live and relate to the gods is important; properly serving the gods results in wealth, long life, many sons, and a happy life after death. The Aryans thought of human life as centered in the *atman* (breath, soul), which lived on after the death of the body. At death the atman, by means of the funeral fire sacrifice, with help from the person's meritorious deeds, is transported to the heavenly realm of the fathers to enjoy the continued blessings of life.

In the early Aryan system, the most important way of serving the gods was by sacrificing to them by means of the fire sacrifice ritual. Daily the head of the household performed domestic sacrifices to Agni and to the sun god, and periodically much more elaborate sacrifices were performed with the aid of the priestly class. The larger sacrifices were performed in the open field. Priests built sacrificial fires, poured ghee and soma on them, and chanted sacred hymns and formulas. The gods were invoked to come and sit with the worshipers on the grass at the holy place, to listen to the hymns and petitions, and to enjoy the ghee and soma. The purpose of the ritual was to promote happiness, health, long life, many offspring, wealth, remission of guilt for wrongdoing, and generally the good things of life.

The basic idea behind the sacrificial cult is the vision of the Vedic seers that humans need to participate in sacred power by sustaining and reinvigorating Agni and the other gods so that the gods will continue their work of creating and bringing blessing to the world and to human existence. Although this Vedic perspective on the centrality of sacrifice underwent development in the next periods, the fact that humans are partners with the gods in continuing the creative processes of the world by sacrifice is a basic presupposition of Hindu thought and ritual. And the Vedic hymns and daily sacrifices are yet today considered essential to the Hindu community, performed by priests and people of the upper classes.

Searching for the One Reality Behind All This

In the story of how Hinduism developed, there is an important speculative period leading from the early Vedic religion toward the classical flowering of Hinduism. We can see beginnings of this speculative period already by about 1000 B.C.E. with some late hymns that were added to the Rig Veda (in Rg Veda Book 10), followed by the Brahmanas, sacrificial manuals and interpretations (ca. 800 B.C.E.), and then finally the Upanishads (starting ca. 600 B.C.E.). In these texts we find important new ideas about sacred reality and human existence. Whereas there is no way of demonstrating the origin of these new ideas, it might be supposed that some of them came about in response to non-Aryan religious ideas and practices.

That something new is happening is evident by a new style used by the seers: they turn to questioning and speculation. "Which god should we worship with sacrifices?" is the refrain of one hymn that attempts to probe the origins of everything and find some one reality behind all the gods (Rg Veda 10.121). No longer satisfied with the traditions about the power of the various gods, the sage speculates that some power prior to the gods is the origin of everything. In a similar way, another hymn even questions the power and the knowledge of the traditional gods: "Who really knows? Who will here proclaim it? Whence was it produced? Whence is this creation? The gods came afterwards, with the creation of this universe. Who then knows whence it has arisen?" (Rg Veda 10.129.6).[5] What the sages are searching for is the sacred center of all, the unified One from which all derives. In their tentative speculations they give different names to this One and describe it in different ways. The poets say that this One is the one life of all the gods, the reality who encompasses all the worlds (Rg Veda 10.121.7, 10). One graphic description envisions the One as a gigantic person (*purusha*) who pervades the whole universe, from whom everything, including all space and all time, derives. Even the gods form part of the one Purusha (Rg Veda 10.90).

This last-mentioned hymn to Purusha shows that, along with the vision of the One, a number of related notions were coming to the fore. It is when Purusha is *sacrificed* that all of the universe comes into existence. The early Vedic idea of the sacrifice reinvigorating the gods is now extended to the whole universe. This primordial sacrifice of the One creates everything (including the gods); this means, by derivation, that each time a priest performs the ritual sacrifice he is repeating this primordial sacrifice and thus creating and sustaining the world.

It is significant that this hymn to Purusha includes the Hindu social order as part of the universe created in the primordial sacrifice. The mouth of Purusha became the brahmins (priestly class), his two arms were made into the kshatriyas (warriors), his two thighs became the vaishyas (merchants, workers), and from his two feet the shudras (servants) were born. This first mention of the basic Hindu social class system in the Hindu sacred texts is noteworthy in that, first of all, it considers these four classes to be part of the cosmic order initiated in the primordial creation. But it also shows that by now the warrior class has lost its superior standing and has been replaced as the top class by the brahmin class. The priests, after all, are the ones who know how to perform the sacrificial rituals that uphold the world and even the gods, and thus their authority is all-important.

Another tendency during this period is the increased emphasis on the importance of knowledge. Finally, the sages conclude, it is not so much the outward performance of the sacrifices that upholds the world and provides blessings, but it is the knowledge of the inner reality. One text from the Brahmanas explains the great public sacrifice known as the Building of the Fire Altar—made of materials collected over the course of a whole year. The text interprets the real meaning of the building in terms of the upholding of the whole universe:

> Indeed, the Fire Altar built here is this world. Its enclosing stones are the waters. Its Yajusmati bricks are the men. . . . The plants and trees are its cement. . . . Yet, verily, the Fire Altar is the air also. The horizon is its enclosing circle of bricks. . . . Yet, verily, the Fire Altar is the sky also, . . . the Sun also, . . . the stars also, . . . the year also. . . . Yet, verily, the Fire Altar is all beings and all gods.

But the interpretation of this ritual makes it clear that the important thing is not just the performance of the ritual; rather, the *inner knowledge* is the power that leads to the world of blessing: "They ascend through knowledge to the place where desires vanish. Neither sacrificial gifts go there, nor do the zealous performers of sacrifices without knowledge. He who is ignorant of this truth does not go to that world by sacrificial gifts and devout practices. It belongs to those with knowledge" (Satapada Brahmana 10.5.4).[6]

Searching for the One, raising the power of sacrifice to cosmic levels, developing the class system with the brah-

mins as supreme, and putting an emphasis on inner knowledge—with these developments some of the basic lines of Hinduism start to emerge. These ideas are worked out more fully in the Upanishads (composed ca. 600–200 B.C.E.), and still more ideas are added to form the foundation of thought for classical Hinduism.

Speculation and Knowledge: The Upanishads

There is no clear break between the Brahmanas and the Upanishads; some of the earlier Upanishads (called Aranyakas, Forest Treatises) were composed as part of the Brahmanas. Hindus consider the Upanishads to be revelation of the same truths as the Vedic hymns and the Brahmanas, and all of these texts are collectively called Veda. The earlier Vedic rituals and sacrifices were being continued by many people. The ritual manuals called Brahmanas had multiplied the sacrificial ceremonies and made them extremely complex and complicated—in keeping with the idea that the order of the whole world is upheld by the proper performing of the ritual sacrifices. But there were some teachers and disciples who continued searching and probing after the inner truth of all reality, the cause of human problems, and the possible solutions offered by knowledge and meditation. The Upanishads resulted from this search. The word *upanishad* refers to teaching passed from a teacher to a disciple sitting near the teacher (*upa*, near; *ni*, down; *sad*, sit), and the setting given in many of the Upanishads is just that: a teacher answering the disciple's questions, a father teaching his son, or a sage instructing an assembly.

Some of the Upanishads talk about ritual and sacrifice, but these acts are both cosmosized and internalized. The Brihad-aranyaka Upanishad, for example, begins with a description of the great horse sacrifice; but then it proceeds to show how this ritual is really an internal act of meditation by which the whole world is sacrificed. The worshiper is instructed to meditate on the dawn as the head of the sacrificial horse, the sun as his eye, the wind as his breath, the year as his body, the sky as his back, the atmosphere as his belly, the earth as the under part of his belly, and so forth. "He [who knows this] wards off repeated death, death obtains him not, death becomes his body, he becomes one of these deities" (Brihad-aranyaka Upanishad, 2.7).[7]

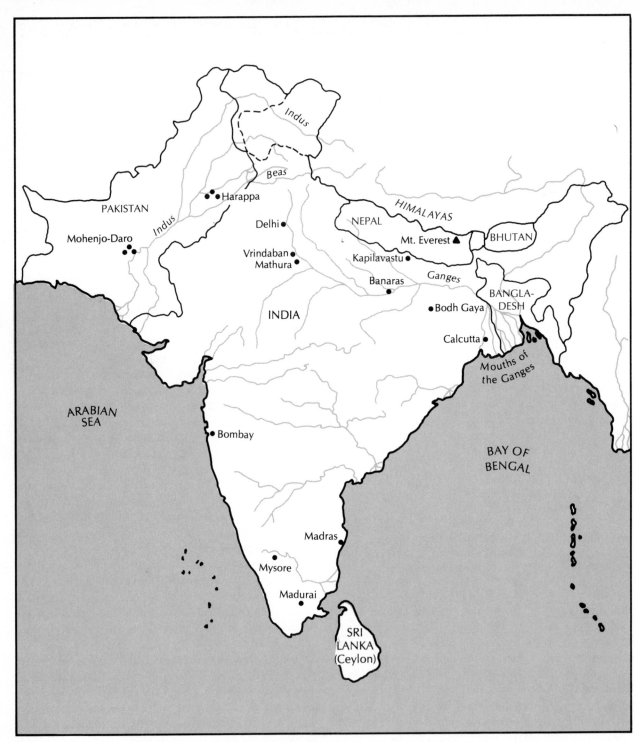

India.

The motivation for this speculation seems to be a new conception that had been developing in some circles, perhaps influenced by the Buddhist and Jain movements. Now, instead of the early Vedic optimistic view of life in this world and the next, there is increasing concern about "repeated death"—that is, death ending not only this life but also the future life. Some way to escape this re-death needs to be found, and this is beyond the power of rituals and sacrifices to the gods. In the Upanishads this idea of re-death was broadened to a cyclical view of human existence: being born in this world is the result of dying in another life, and on and on in a never ending wheel of existence. The way to understand the human problem, according to the Upanishads, is to see that it is *samsara*, an endless round of birth and death.

What causes samsara? Tied together with the notion of samsara is the discovery of *karma*, the law that every action has its effect. Karma literally means "action," and the sages knew from experience that what one does causes consequences to happen. The idea of karma already had religious implications, in the notion that the action of the sacrifice causes results for the gods and for humans. The teachers of the Upanishads related karma to samsara. It is because of the actions that I have done in my previous life that I am born again into this existence. Moreover, the type of karma I have done determines what kind of rebirth I have, whether relatively happy or miserable.

The sages are convinced that there must be a better way, a way to be liberated from the wheel of birth and death.

If all this world, including the gods, is caught up in samsara, where can we turn for that better way? The Upanishads continue the earlier speculation about the One, that which is truly real and the source of all, and the importance of knowledge more than ritual and sacrifice. Although many terms had been used, the Upanishads finally settle on *Brahman* as the designation of the One, the Real. Earlier, the term *brahman* had meant the sacred words used in the sacrificial rituals. Now Brahman is extended to identify that one power, the inner source of all, that which is absolute and eternal and prior to all that is known as samsara.

Further, the sages insist that my true self, the atman, is not what I usually think of as "myself" but is in fact identical with Brahman. If my atman is really the Brahman, it transcends limitation, decay, and death. It is because of my ignorance in thinking of myself as bound up with my body and senses, and because of my desire to perform actions on behalf of this illusory self, that I generate karma and bind myself to the cycle of birth and death. The way out of samsara, then, is a path of knowledge: knowing the real atman, and thus knowing the Brahman, means *moksha*, liberation from the cycle caused by ignorance, desire, and karma.

The means for attaining this liberating knowledge, according to the teachers, is meditation on the atman and the Brahman. No longer the outer rituals and actions, but the inner knowledge leads to the source that brings the power of transformation and transcends the trap of samsara. The Upanishads, and the sages who continued to practice this way of knowledge, devised disciplines and techniques of meditation designed to bring about this transformation and thus final liberation (moksha) from samsara.

Whereas the vision of the Upanishads is complex and the goal practical only for those who are spiritually advanced, the basic ideas of the Upanishads have become the foundation for all aspects of Hinduism. The reality of Brahman and atman, the problem of karma and samsara, the goal of moksha—all Hindus recognize these as fundamental to the Hindu religion.

The texts of the Upanishads complete the sacred writings collectively called the Vedas. All of these texts—the Upanishads, together with the early Vedic hymns (Samhitas) and the Brahmanas, are known collectively as the Shruti (that which is "heard" by the sages), the eternal revelation of the truth. These writings may not be easily understood, but they are the eternal truth, and being a Hindu means respecting them as such and honoring those who study and recite them.

The Many Faces of Classical Hinduism

The Indo-Aryans gradually settled into villages and towns, and a city-state culture developed in north India. Although the records are scanty, it seems northern India was very disunified at this time, made up of some sixteen kingdoms, and the center of developing Hinduism was gradually moving eastward out of the Indus Valley, toward

The Hindu Story: Some Important Dates

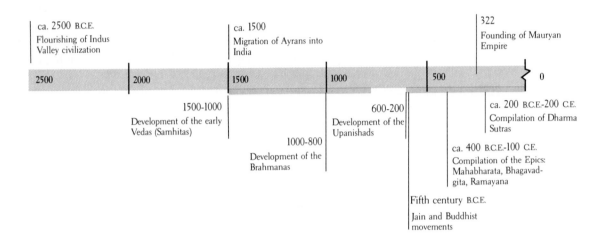

the Ganges River Valley. Starting in the sixth century B.C.E. the Persian Empire established a province in western India, and in the fourth century Alexander the Great invaded western India. Stimulated by these incursions, the Maurya family established a dynasty in north India that eventually grew to include most of central and south India as well. The Mauryan rulers were not especially devoted to the Vedic traditions, often giving their support to non-Vedic groups like Jainism and Buddhism, both of which developed into major movements during the fifth and fourth centuries King Ashoka (ca. 269–232 B.C.E.), in fact became a devout Buddhist and promoted Buddhism throughout his empire and beyond. After Ashoka, the Mauryan Empire broke up into disunity once again, but in the meantime the traditional system of Vedic sacrifices and priestly control lost ground among the people. Finally, after a lengthy period of rival foreign kingdoms in northwest India and regional kingdoms elsewhere, under the Gupta dynasty (320–467 C.E.) there was a return of political unity.

In response to the new situation, a variety of religious tendencies were being developed in the Brahmanical tradition, in this creative period from about 400 B.C.E. to 400 C.E., which is sometimes designated the classical, epic era

of Hinduism. Some of these tendencies go back to earlier ideas and practices; others probably represent non-Aryan forms surfacing in the Hindu synthesis. These tendencies began to focus in a number of directions, later designated as *margas* (paths). These included practical forms of meditation and seeking release from samsara; concerns for the duties of the societal classes and the ongoing life of society; and a flourishing of interest in worship (bhakti) of the gods old and new. Overall this long classical period led to a unification and consolidation of Hinduism.

During this time a great many new sacred writings were composed, expressing the new ideas and practices. To distinguish these new writings from the Shruti scriptures, they are usually referred to as the Smriti (remembered) writings, the Tradition. Major Smriti scriptures composed in this classical period include the Yoga Sutras, especially the Yoga Sutras of Patanjali; the Dharmasutras and the Dharmashastras, especially the Law-code of Manu; and the great Ramayana and Mahabharata Epics, including the Bhagavad Gita. Whereas these scriptures thus have a lower status than the earlier ones and not all Hindus respect them all equally, to many Hindus these writings provide the most immediate guidance in the sacred story of Hinduism.

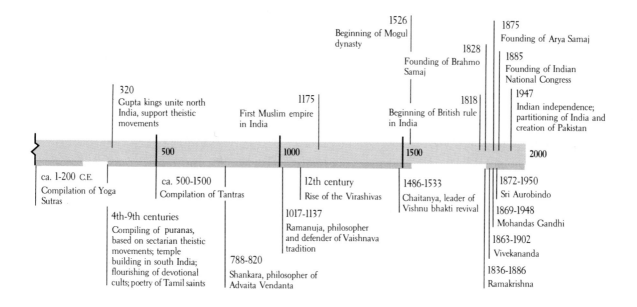

320
Gupta kings unite north
India, support theistic
movements

500

ca. 1-200 C.E.
Compilation of Yoga
Sutras

4th-9th centuries
Compiling of puranas,
based on sectarian theistic
movements; temple
building in south India;
flourishing of devotional
cults; poetry of Tamil saints

ca. 500-1500
Compilation of Tantras

788-820
Shankara, philosopher of
Advaita Vendanta

1175
First Muslim empire
in India

1000

12th century
Rise of the Virashivas

1017-1137
Ramanuja, philosopher
and defender of Vaishnava
tradition

1526
Beginning of Mogul
dynasty

1828
Founding of Brahmo
Samaj

1818
Beginning of British rule
in India

1500

1486-1533
Chaitanya, leader of
Vishnu bhakti revival

1875
Founding of Arya Samaj

1885
Founding of Indian
National Congress

1947
Indian independence;
partitioning of India and
creation of Pakistan

2000

1872-1950
Sri Aurobindo

1869-1948
Mohandas Gandhi

1863-1902
Vivekananda

1836-1886
Ramakrishna

Development of Practices of Withdrawal and Yoga

The practice of withdrawing from the world and practicing asceticism and meditation is ancient in India, mentioned already in the Rig Veda (Rg Veda 10.136). The Upanishads talk about sages like Yajnavalkya who live a detached life as hermits in the forest to practice mental disciplines. These disciplines involve bodily discipline and controlling the mind to realize the true inner atman and reach moksha. A famous image is that of the chariot representing bodily life and the charioteer as the soul; as the charioteer controls the chariot to reach his destination, so the soul should control the various forces of the body, disengaging the atman from its temporary sojourn in a bodily existence (Katha Upanishad 1.3.3–9).

Another technique to reach liberation that developed was called yoga (from the same root as "yoke"). It is by controlling one's attachment to the outer world and withdrawing inward, withdrawing even from mental activity, that liberation can be attained. Classical Hinduism developed many forms of yoga. Indeed, almost every Hindu movement has some form of yogic discipline; physical bodily control, mental discipline, ways of performing actions, even worshiping the gods can all be called yoga.

The best-known form of classical yoga is described in the Yoga Sutra of Patanjali (ca. 200 C.E.?), and these writings have the status of scripture for many. Patanjali devised an eight-step method of discipline and control leading to transformation and liberation. This "royal yoga" as set forth by Patanjali (discussed later) became the basis of one of the later schools of philosophy, and it has guided much of the development in yogic practice ever since.

Compilation of the Dharma Sutras

Another stream of Hindu thought and practice, also reaching back to ancient times, is the emphasis on the eternal order of everything and of human life within that order. In early Vedic times Varuna was looked to as the guardian of this eternal order (rta). In the classical period the eternal order of everything was called Dharma, and sages were busy composing writings that spelled out what this order was all about, especially for society and for the individual within society. These Dharma sutras (Dharma texts) picture an idealized society that is in conformity with the eternal truths of the Vedas. In fact, what Westerners call "Hinduism" is to Hindus simply the "Eternal Dharma." It is true that some tension exists between the goal of moksha, liberation from the world of samsara, and the concern of Dharma, maintaining the good of the social order. But Hinduism is built on that tension, and most religious practices acknowledge the duty both to support the social order and to seek the goal of moksha.

Basic to this vision of Dharma is the idea of karma and rebirth, as taught by the Upanishads. Everyone is born into a particular place in society because of the karma accumulated in past existences. The role of the individual thus is determined by birth, and she or he is expected to perform the actions (karma) appropriate for that particular role. The best known of the Dharma texts is the writing called the Law-code of Manu, traditionally thought to be given by Manu, the originator of humans and the first lawgiver. This extremely influential writing spells out the Dharma especially in terms of class (varna, or color), giving detailed descriptions of the duties of people born as brahmins, kshatriyas, vaishyas, and shudras. These Dharma laws thus consolidated a variety of practices in society, influenced perhaps by the development of Buddhism and Jainism with their monastic/lay structure of society. Probably the periodic disunity in India and the incursions of barbarian peoples into northwest India spurred on these attempts to structure Hindu society in an orderly way in conformity with religious ideas. This idealized varna system later developed into the so-called caste system, in which there are hundreds of subcastes linked with these four classes, and it has continued to exercise great influence over Hindu society. To answer the question, Who am I?, surely requires an identification of one's class and caste, that is, one's place in the Eternal Dharma.

The Ramayana and Mahabharata Epics

An important development in the story of Hinduism is the use of popular stories to convey religious meaning. In fact, for many Hindus, the part of the story they are most familiar with involves the great epics, the Mahabharata and the Ramayana, for these tell the stories of the gods and the heroes of old who provide models for the Hindu way of life. The epics combine interest in the path of knowledge and liberation with support for the values of Dharma and action in society. They also provide a broad foundation for bhakti, that is, worship of the gods. Probably the epics were composed or at least reached their final form between 200 B.C.E. and 200 C.E., although the Hindu tradition sets them in previous world ages, many years

ago. The events described in these epics are not historical in the same sense as the rise and decline of the Mauryan dynasty, for example; rather they are legendary and mythological events. Yet the Hindu tradition considers these events, as ideal types and models of eternal truth, to be a more significant "history" than the confusing, fleeting realm of day-to-day historical events.

The story of the Ramayana epic is the cosmic battle between the great god Vishnu and the demonic forces of evil, and it establishes the paradigm for human conduct according to the notion of Dharma. The main hero of the story is Rama, a prince who is an avatara (incarnation) of the god Vishnu, and his opponent is Ravana, the demon king of the island of Lanka. Rama fought a great war to defeat Ravana and rescue his wife Sita who had been abducted, getting help from a race of monkeys, with the god Hanuman as their chief. In the process Rama set the model for honest and proper conduct, ruling as a righteous king. Even before he became king he showed high ethical qualities, accepting fourteen years of exile rather than question his father's rash promise that gave the kingship to his younger stepbrother. After he had finally established order and a righteous kingdom, he again demonstrated the highest ethical conduct by banishing his pure, beloved wife Sita from the kingdom because some subjects questioned her chastity while she had been under the demon's power. Besides providing a model of Hindu morality and self-control, this story also presents the god Rama as the divine hero to be worshiped. Throughout northern India the cult of Rama is very popular, with a great autumn festival called Ramlila, in which the story of Rama is recited and acted out.

The Mahabharata is an immensely long and complicated epic poem (nearly 100,000 verses long) dealing with conflicts between two related clans in north India in a previous world age. The issues have to do not with good and evil forces but with questions of the dharma of warriors, the goal of moksha, and the importance of devotion to the gods. The heroes of the epic are the five Pandava brothers, who have a conflict with their cousins over who will rule north India. In this rambling, fascinating story, the most famous section is a chapter called the Bhagavad Gita (song of the beloved one). As the two armies prepare to meet on the battlefield, Arjuna, the most renowned warrior of the Pandavas, sees that the ranks of the enemies include relatives,

Rama, divine hero of the Ramayana Epic.

itself to a new body, much like a man discarding old clothes and putting on new ones—therefore one should not grieve over death. Secondly, Krishna explains, action done without desire for its fruits, that is, done simply because it is one's duty, is higher than nonaction. The key is to perform actions without attachment and desires: "When he renounces all desires and acts without craving, possessiveness, or individuality, he finds peace" (Bhagavad Gita 2.71).[8] In this way Krishna synthesizes both paths: seeking liberation and performing one's duty in society.

But the real focus of the Bhagavad Gita is *bhakti*, devotion to one's god. The highest path, Krishna teaches, is the path of selfless action and wisdom through loving and surrendering to Krishna as the supreme Lord. Krishna really is none other than the great god Vishnu, creator and preserver of the whole universe. But, Krishna teaches, from age to age as evil arises Vishnu sends himself forth as an avatara into the world, to destroy evil and establish righteousness (4.5–11). And those who worship him can find the highest liberation: "Keep me in your mind and devotion, sacrifice to me, bow to me, discipline your self toward me, and you will reach me!" (9.34).[9] Women and shudras were excluded from performing Vedic rituals; but everyone including women and shudras can worship Krishna and find salvation in him (9:32). Even those who are devotees of other gods and worship them are really worshiping Krishna! (9.23).

So the Gita presents a grand synthesis of Hinduism and opens the way for a great flourishing of bhakti, devotion to the gods. In this great poem, beloved by Hindus of all persuasions, we see most clearly the foundation for what it means to be Hindu.

The epics describe other gods also, besides Vishnu and his incarnations, Rama and Krishna. The Mahabharata tells of the other great god of classical Hinduism, Shiva, the divine mountain yogin. We saw earlier that perhaps a prototype of Shiva was worshiped in the Indus Valley civilization—a god seated in the yoga position. The epic also refers to the virgin goddess Durga who delights in wine and animal sacrifice and slays the buffalo demon. By the end of the classical period, the Great Goddess, Devi, rises to central importance for many Hindus, representing the creative power of *prakriti* (primal matter or nature). She is worshiped alongside Vishnu and Shiva with the same basic rites.

friends, teachers, and the like, and he is overcome with grief. He drops his weapons and says that it would be better to be killed than to inflict such suffering on others. His charioteer is Krishna, an avatara (incarnation) of the great god Vishnu, who proceeds to teach Arjuna—and all of us—the truth about existence, providing a synthesis of Hinduism that to this day remains the most popular scriptural presentation of the way of Hinduism.

Arjuna really is raising a fundamental question of human life: Is it always best to do one's duty? His duty as a warrior is to fight, but wouldn't it be better for everyone if he did not fight? In answer, Krishna first teaches that, although the body is destroyed, the atman is imperishable and simply takes

As Hinduism moves into the medieval period, the growing bhakti practice tends to cluster around these theistic traditions associated with Vishnu, Shiva, and the Great Goddess. And the great bhakti synthesis really becomes constitutive of mainstream Hinduism from this time on.

So with all these elements of the story—the Upanishads and the Yoga Sutras with their emphasis on meditation and release, the Dharma Sutras outlining the proper way of life in society, and the epics summing it all up and emphasizing devotion to the gods—we can see the general outline of Hindu identity.

TRANSFORMATIONS IN THE SACRED STORY

The master story of any religion is always somewhat openended; the creative events continue to have effect even to the present time. Often, however, there is a sense of closing the age of the sacred story. For example, Muslims consider the source of truth to be the revelation through Muhammad as the final prophet; and Christians determined the limits of the canon of scripture. What happens afterward is historical transformation of the story. In Hinduism, however, the sacred story merges into historical transformations without any clear break. Even after the great epics, sacred writings continue to come forth, expanding the stories of the gods and the possibilities of truth and ritual, at least throughout much of the medieval period (ca. 400–1800).

Medieval Hinduism: Shaping the Sacred Ways

The major developments in the medieval period, shaping the way Hindus think and act, centered on philosophical systems and theistic bhakti movements. A significant but limited movement was Tantrism, focusing on the great goddess and employing ritual techniques to achieve liberation. And a substantial impact came from the Muslim invasion and dominance over much of India during the medieval period.

Rethinking the Vedic Truth: Systematized Philosophical Views

In a dialogue between student and teacher, written by the great philosopher Shankara, the student asks these kinds of questions:

> How can I be released from samsara? Is this suffering indeed my own nature? Or does it result from some cause, my own nature being indifferent? What is the cause? And what will remove it? And what is my own nature? What is ignorance? What is its object? and what is knowledge, remover of ignorance, by which I can realize my own nature?[10]

Such questions have provided the grist for Hindu philosophy for over 2,000 years.

The intellectual underpinnings of Hinduism go back to the sages of the early Vedic hymns and the teachers of the Upanishads, and the quest for intellectual understanding never halted. Eventually six orthodox schools (darshanas, viewpoints) of philosophy came to be recognized (orthodox because they recognize the authority of the Vedas and Upanishads), in addition to unorthodox philosophies like Buddhism and Jainism. Two of these schools (Nyaya and Vaisheshika) were concerned chiefly with cosmology and logic as a means to liberation, and one (Mimamsa) occupied itself with showing how the Vedas are eternal and the Vedic rituals are important for religious duty and attainment of salvation. The most influential schools have been the Samkhya-Yoga pair and the Vedanta school.

We mentioned the practice of yoga earlier, focused on the eight-stage path taught by Patanjali. The Yoga philosophical school with its path toward higher release developed in close relation to the Samkhya school's "map" of the cosmos and the causes of bondage. Samkhya taught a dualism of nature (prakriti), out of which develops the whole person with mind and senses, and pure spirit (purusha), which is the transcendent consciousness. The problem is that the embodied mind mistakes itself for purusha, which causes bondage in the samsara cycle. And so the goal of yogic practice is to disentangle purusha consciousness from the material self and mind and bring about liberation.

The Vedanta school has been very influential in Hindu intellectual developments, continuing to the present day (Mimamsa also continues today among a small number of Brahman ritualists). Philosophers of Vedanta (end of the

Veda) were especially interested in the teaching of the Upanishads concerning the Brahman as the one ultimate reality and the self as identical with Brahman. Vedanta philosophers had disagreements on the nature of Brahman and how Brahman is related to the world—thus there is Nondualist (Advaita), Qualified Nondualist (Vishishtadvaita), and Dualist (Dvaita) Vedanta. But they all agree that knowledge of the Brahman and the atman is of primary importance for liberation. Many Hindus look to the brilliant philosopher Shankara (788–820), of the Nondualist Vedanta school, as an outstanding Hindu thinker. Shankara, from south India, became a sannyasin as a boy and died at an early age, but in those few years he wrote very influential commentaries on the Upanishads and the Bhagavad Gita.

Shankara starts with insistence on the nondual character of reality: there is only Brahman, the ground of being, without qualities, unchanging. Further, Brahman is identical with the eternal, unchanging atman (soul), which underlies all individuals. Moksha (liberation) means the knowledge that one's atman is the eternal Brahman itself. But our problem, according to Shankara, is that we commonly view the world as changing, full of different realities, persons, and things, including our own soul as an individual reality. The way out of this illusion, Shankara says, is not through rituals, actions, or worship, but through knowledge attained through meditation, knowledge that I and the Brahman are one.

This radical nondualism of Shankara has repercussions for traditional Hindu ideas and practices. One is forced to conclude that there really are no permanent individual selves, and that even the samsara cycle and release from it are ultimately illusions. Most radical, perhaps, is the implication that devotion to a god cannot bring liberation—for even the gods must be illusion! And what about the Vedas and Upanishads? Shankara was led to conclude that, in the state of highest knowledge, there are no scriptures. But—and this has been most influential in shaping Hinduism—Shankara allowed that there are different levels of truth, corresponding to one's spiritual development. At the lower levels of truth the scriptures and devotion to the gods can be of benefit for spiritual transformation. But one who reaches the highest knowledge realizes that there is only one Brahman; such a one transcends gods, rituals, Dharma, and scriptures.

Although most Hindus do not actively follow the path of knowledge set forth by Shankara, and later philosophers like Ramanuja disputed his radical nondualism by bringing devotion to God back to center stage, his vision exemplifies the intellectual foundation of the fascinating diversity of what we call Hinduism. How can both an atheistic philosopher and an ardent lover of Krishna—and everyone else in between—all be considered Hindus? Shankara's philosophy shows that there are many levels of spiritual development and each soul proceeds at its own pace toward the goal of liberation.

The Flowering of Bhakti: The Puranas and Sectarian Hinduism

Another important development during the medieval period is the great flowering of devotional cults, a movement that came to dominate all of Hinduism with its gods and goddesses, puja (worship of divine images), temples, festivals, and the like. The new line of kings that reunited northern India in 320 C.E., the Guptas, gave strong support to worshiping the gods, especially Vishnu, raising theism to the level of a state religion, supporting theistic groups and building temples. The gods had always been worshiped in India, but gradually some of the Vedic gods were eased out of prominence, whereas other gods—some perhaps non-Aryan in origin—came to dominate or were combined with Vedic gods. The great epics provided a broad foundation on which bhakti could flourish, and in the centuries following, from perhaps the fourth century to the ninth century C.E., a series of *puranas* (ancient stories) were composed describing the various gods and devotion to them. Many devotional cults sprang up, focused on Vishnu or Shiva or Durga and the gods and goddesses associated with them, and poets and singers never tired of creating a wealth of joyous, ecstatic devotional literature.

In general, most Hindus see their identity intimately connected with these devotional traditions. Some families are traditionally devotees of Vishnu and the gods and goddesses associated with this great god—they are called Vaishnavites. Other families have long been Shaivites, devotees of Shiva and his associated gods and goddesses. Whereas most Hindus follow one of these two great theistic traditions, others devote themselves to the great goddess Durga or, as she is also known, Shakti, Devi, or Kali. Many consider this goddess devotion as part of the

Shaivite tradition. It is important to understand that, whereas bhakti seems to presuppose a great number of gods and goddesses, devotees tend to focus on one of the great gods as the source of ultimate sacred power. To a Vaishnavite, Vishnu is all, the creator, preserver, and destroyer of the universe. Shiva is everything to a Shaivite, and a devotee of the great goddess Durga likewise is "monotheistic" in outlook. At the same time, there generally is a tolerance for the other traditions of bhakti and a sense that God shows herself or himself in many forms.

A number of bhakti scriptures, for example, the Vishnu Purana, the Harivamsa, and the Bhagavata Purana, provide a wealth of material about worshiping Vishnu, his wife Lakshmi, goddess of beauty and wealth, and his delightful avatara, Krishna. Krishna of the Bhagavad Gita, as an avatara of Vishnu, taught Arjuna the essence of the way of Hinduism. The puranas elaborate the story of Krishna greatly, focusing on Krishna Gopala, the lovable baby and young man among the cowherd people of Vrindavana. In festivals devotees performed the stories of Krishna's love affairs with the cowherd girls and especially with Radha, his favorite—stories that demonstrate the highest form of loving God.

The delight of worshiping Krishna and Rama forms the theme of much religious poetry composed by saint-singers throughout the medieval period, as, for example, in Gitagovinda Jayadeva's Love Song of the Dark Lord (twelfth century), one of the world's most beautiful love poems. In the sixteenth century a great revival of Vishnu bhakti swept north India, especially Bengal, led by the famous saint Chaitanya (1486–1533). He introduced the practice of devotees parading around the streets publicly singing and chanting and dancing in praise of the lord. He and his followers established Krishna temples and systematized the theology of Krishna worship. Chaitanya himself was widely regarded as an incarnation of both Krishna and Radha (Krishna's lover) in one body. This tradition of ecstatic Krishna worship has continued to the present and even has been introduced into America through the International Society for Krishna Consciousness (popularly known as the Hare Krishnas).

The story of Shiva in the puranas has quite a different mood from that of Vishnu. There is no connected life story for Shiva, as there is for Krishna and Rama, but there are abundant stories revealing one aspect or another of this great god. Shiva combines all dualities in himself, so the stories tell about his powers of life and death, his passionate pursuits and his ascetic withdrawal, his love and his anger. He is sometimes pictured in images as half-male and half-female, uniting the cosmic generative forces; and his most typical symbol is the lingam (phallic symbol) placed in a yoni (symbol of the female organ). He is the creator and nourisher of existence, but at the same time he is the great destroyer.

Throughout the medieval period, Shaivite movements cultivated the bhakti of this great god in his various aspects. Since Shiva is the great divine yogin, among those devoted to him were a variety of ascetics (sadhus) and yogins. Worship of Shiva became especially dominant in south India, and poets sang praises of him in Tamil. The largest group of Shaivites, the Shaiva Siddhanta, collected their ritual texts in the scriptures called Agamas, holding them to be equal in value to the Vedas. Another important group, Virashaiva, developed in the twelfth century as a kind of countercultural movement, its founder refusing to go through the sacred thread initiation ceremony. Known as the Lingayats because they wear a small stone lingam on a chain around the neck, they protested against the caste system, worship of images, and many other Hindu beliefs and customs. In their poems in praise of Shiva, written in Kannada, they insist on a Shiva monotheism.

Associated with the Shaivite tradition is the worship of Shiva's female aspect called his *shakti*, for Shiva perfectly embodies the divine powers both male and female. This Shakti can be seen as Shiva's energy and power, or Shakti can be personified as the wife of Shiva, under names like Parvati and Uma. Or this Shakti can become the focus of worship in her own right as the Great Goddess, usually under the names of Devi, Durga, and Kali. The relationships of these goddesses to each other and to Shiva is by no means clear in the puranas. What is clear is that both Durga and Kali are ferocious, terrifying goddesses, expressions of the terrible energy and destructiveness of the sacred. The central sacred story about Durga relates how she delivered the world from the vicious attack of the buffalo-demon Mahisha. In the Devimahatmyam (Glorification of the Goddess, probably composed about 400–600 C.E.

An image of the goddess Kali, taken out in festival procession.

and included in the Markandeya Purana), the Goddess Devi emerges fully as the Divine Mother, worshiped by her devotees, the Shaktas.

Perhaps the part of the sacred story most strange to non-Hindus deals with the dark goddess Kali. When battling demon armies, the story goes, Durga became furious and her face turned black as ink; from between her brows emerged the terrible Kali, brandishing a sword and carrying a noose. She wears a garland of human heads and a girdle of severed arms, causing the world to tremble with her bloodthirsty cries and frantic dancing. Yet this terrifying goddess became the focus of bhakti for some groups in Hinduism, especially in Bengal, that find ecstasy and fulfillment in worshiping God also in her destructive aspects. The worship of Kali, the terrifying, destroying mother,

forms an important though difficult to understand strand of bhakti Hinduism.

The Development of Tantrism

Closely related to the worship of the great goddess is a small but significant movement called Tantrism, and to complete the sacred story of Hinduism we must take note of this complicated form that arose in the medieval period. The goal of Tantra is moksha by means of elaborate ritual and yogic practices focusing on the power of the great goddess. Tantra is a vast collection of ideas and practices, expressed in a variety of ritual scriptures. They center on the inseparability of Shiva and Shakti, of male and female, of divine and human, of the macrocosmos and the microcosmos. Since the body is a microcosmos, there is a sacred geography in the body, and through ritual practice it is possible to activate the sacred forces latent in the body, bring about the union of Shiva (passive, pure intelligence) and Shakti (active, creative energy), and achieve a sacred transformation.

The Tantrists distinguish between a right-handed and a left-handed path. The right-handed path is for all Tantrists and employs mantras (sacred sounds), mandalas (cosmic diagrams), and yogic-ritual techniques such as breath control to activate Shakti within to rise and be united with Shiva within. The left-handed path is considered appropriate only for advanced Tantrists, for it includes a special ritual called circle-worship (*cakra-puja*), using elements normally forbidden and associated with the lower bodily senses. These are called the "five M's" (each begins with the letter "M" in Sanskrit) and involve the use of wine, meat, fish, parched grain, and sexual intercourse. It is particularly the use of sexual impulses as ritual yoga to unite the powers of Shakti and Shiva that characterizes this form of Tantra. The orthodox tradition has strongly criticized left-handed Tantra for this seeming perversion of traditional morality. But Tantrists insist that the ritual practice must be done only by advanced adepts in the context of purity, self-discipline, and devotion to the goddess, under the guidance of a Tantric guru, not as gratification of desires but as the redirection of those desires into worship and transformation.

Muslim Presence and Impact in India

During the medieval period, the great expansion of Islam continued on into India. The first Muslim incursions came already in the eighth century; by the thirteenth century Islam dominated north India; and the Muslim Mogul dynasty controlled most of India from the sixteenth until the eighteenth centuries. At first fiercely exclusive in religious practice, Muslim rulers, especially Akbar (r. 1556–1605), developed a toleration for Hinduism and even attempted a synthesis of these religions. Eventually tens of millions of Indians (Hindus and Buddhists) converted to Islam. Many clashes did, of course, occur between these very different religions, with Islam's radical monotheism quite at odds with Hindu bhakti. Muslim invaders of north India in the eleventh century destroyed many Hindu temples in a crusade to wipe out idolatry and establish Islam. And Aurangzeb (r. 1658–1707) of the Mogul dynasty enforced restrictive laws against the Hindus and destroyed famous temples of Krishna, Rama, and Shiva, replacing them with Muslim mosques. But there was also mutual influence. For example, Hindu devotionalism and saints inspired the Muslim Sufis in India, and the Sufis in turn inspired many devout Hindus. In the area of Benares in north India, the poet-saint Kabir (ca. 1440–1518), from a shudra subcaste that converted to Islam, was inspired by Vaishnava devotionalism and composed bhakti poetry that was widely sung in north India. And Nanak (1469–1539), from a Hindu warrior-class family in the Punjab, expressed a loving devotion to the one God in a way that combined aspects of Hindu bhakti with Islamic Sufism. He emerged as the great religious leader Guru Nanak, who combined features of both religions in founding the Sikh religion. By the eighteenth century Mogul power faded and the British entered to take control of India.

The Modern Era: Renaissance and Response to the West

While Christianity had been present in India since the early Christian missionaries went there in the second and third centuries C.E., Christian presence came in a stronger way in connection with Portuguese, Dutch, and English traders starting in the sixteenth century. The British East India Company dominated Indian economic and political life, opening the way to British colonial rule from the nineteenth century until India achieved independence in 1947. Although Christianity remained a small minority in India, less than 3% of the population today, its teachings of love and its demonstration of social responsibility in opening schools and hospitals and caring for the poor had a strong impact on modern Hindu thinkers. Western culture also brought new democratic political ideas, together with modern science and technology.

Two Reform Movements: Brahmo Samaj and Arya Samaj

Western ideas brought to India by the British helped to raise questions among some Hindus about certain aspects of their own tradition, especially the caste system and the sense that the world is the realm of samsara from which the goal is to escape. As Hindus learned Western thought, new ideas began to arise, attempts to reform Hindu society. One of the important early movements of reform was started by Ram Mohan Roy (1772–1833), who had worked for the East India Company. He spoke out against what he considered abuses in the Hindu system, such as polytheism, worship of images, neglect of women's education, and the practice of burning a widow alive at her husband's cremation (called sati or suttee). Influenced by Christianity but unwilling to accept the idea that Jesus was God, Ram Mohan studied the Vedas and Upanishads and found that they also taught a simple monotheism. In 1828 Ram Mohan founded the Brahmo Samaj (Society of Brahman) as a religious society advocating a rational, humanistic religion without all the Hindu rituals and customs. The members of the society would meet weekly to study the Upanishads, pray, and sing hymns.

Later, led by Debendranath Tagore (1817–1905), the Brahmo Samaj broke away from orthodoxy by asserting that reason and conscience, not the Vedas, are the final authority in religion; the truth of the scriptures is to be confirmed by the inner light, which all possess. The society revised the old rituals to excise references to the many gods, and they pressed for laws against child marriage and polygamy. Weakened by divided opinions toward the end of the nineteenth century, the Brahmo Samaj's religious ideas did not carry the day in modern Hinduism, but the society effected a significant change of attitude among Hindus with respect to the unquestioned rule of tradition.

In 1875 the Arya Samaj was founded by Swami Dayananda Sarasvati (1824–1883), representing another attempt to restore the original purity of Hinduism. Dayananda had been a Shaivite devotee, but under the influence of a fiery teacher who accepted only the oldest Vedic scriptures, he came to reject the puranas and all the popular gods of Hinduism, together with image worship and the caste system. In his book, *The Light of Truth*, he held that Hindus should rely on the early Vedas alone (the Samhitas) for all religious truth. Other religions, such as Islam, Christianity, and bhakti Hinduism, have corrupted this pure truth. The early Vedas are also the source of all scientific truth. Further, the caste system made up of numerous subcastes should be abandoned. Anyone can study the Vedas. Women should be educated, widows should be allowed to remarry, and child marriage should be abandoned.

Thus the Arya Samaj moved in somewhat the same direction as the Brahmo Samaj, but it differs in rejecting Western influences and in calling for a return to the early Vedas as supreme religious truth. Advocating Hindu laws for India, the Arya Samaj rejects the modern secular constitution of India and engages in intense opposition to all non-Hindu elements in India—Muslims, Christians, secularists, Communists, and so on. Although the Arya Samaj did not come to dominate modern Hindu thinking, it together with the Brahmo Samaj helped to revitalize Hindu pride in the face of Western dominance and laid the groundwork for a Hindu spiritual revival by reasserting Hindu tradition as the source of value for modern society.

Ramakrishna and Vivekananda

As movements in India revived the sense of pride in India's spiritual heritage, many leading thinkers who had been influenced by the West began to turn to their own heritage for guidance in the modern world. Of the many who contributed to this task, we might single out Ramakrishna Paramahamsa (1836–1886) and his disciple, Swami Vivekananda (1863–1902).

Ramakrishna was a God-intoxicated Hindu who revitalized the Hindu tradition and channeled it into new directions. A temple priest of the goddess Kali who communed with her in trancelike meditation, he also worshiped other gods such as Krishna and practiced the Nondualist Vedanta type of meditation. He also followed disciplines of Christianity and Islam, experiencing visions of Christ and Muhammad; on that basis he came to believe that the ultimate reality may be approached by any tradition of worship. Thus Ramakrishna was able to develop an expansive Hinduism not by pruning it but by incorporating into it Western religious ideas and experiences, remaining all the while devoted to the Hindu tradition. Already in his lifetime he was widely regarded as a great Hindu saint.

One of the disciples of Ramakrishna was Swami Vivekananda who, after Ramakrishna's death, organized the Ramakrishna Order and the Ramakrishna Mission. He came to America to speak at the Parliament of Religions at the Chicago World's Fair in 1893 and excited many with his presentations on Hinduism. Thereafter he traveled about lecturing on Hinduism, founding the Vedanta Society to continue the work of teaching the Hindu tradition in America. In India, the Ramakrishna Mission was dedicated to a wide variety of charitable, missionary, and educational activities for the masses. By his example Vivekananda established a new sannyasin model, a holy man actively engaged in social concerns.

Independence Movement and New Visions: Gandhi and Aurobindo

As the Hindu renaissance represented by these movements brought Indians a new sense of pride and peoplehood, an independence movement arose that, under the leadership of people like Mohandas Gandhi (1869–1948), brought India independence from British rule. The motivation to work for independence came from many sources, of course, including many ultranationalists fighting for a "Mother India" purified from all Muslim and British influences. The man who became the leader, however, was a new kind of religious leader in Hinduism. Gandhi was born in the vaishya (merchant) class and was not particularly learned in the Vedic texts and tradition, studying law in England and working for many years in South Africa before returning to India to lead the independence movement. His favorite Hindu scripture was the Bhagavad Gita, which he felt taught nonviolence and selfless action for the welfare of society, and he was also much influenced by the Sermon on the Mount in the New Testament. Drawing on these religious sources, he developed the philosophy and technique of *satyagraha* (holding to the truth), by

Mahatma Gandhi at his spinning wheel, a symbol of national self-reliance.

which he meant a style of nonviolent resistance that awakens in the oppressors a sense of wrongdoing. It is wrong to seek personal victory over opponents, he taught; one must rather purify oneself of all selfish motivations and act without any violence and without any sense of anger. He was totally confident that this way of love and nonviolence (*ahimsa*) will always win out in any situation.

Gandhi became a kind of sannyasin, establishing a community that lived in simplicity and daily work—his spinning wheel became the symbol of his movement. Living in celibacy with his wife, wearing only the traditional loincloth of the sannyasin, exerting his energy to purify India of the sin of having made one class of people the "untouchables," and bringing the British to their knees in India by nonviolent resistance, Gandhi represented a spiritual moral force drawn from Hinduism that has had great impact not only on India but on the whole world.

Of the many other modern Hindu thinkers who have expressed a new and vital Hindu perspective, we might single out Sri Aurobindo (1872–1950), who lived through the same years as Gandhi but took a somewhat different course. Educated at Cambridge University in England, he

got involved in the nationalist movement in India and was imprisoned in 1910. Discovering through visionary experiences that real human liberation went far beyond the political liberation of India, he chose thereafter to withdraw from the world and established an ashram (retreat) in the French enclave of Pondicherry for the practice of Tantric yoga. In his writings, *The Life Divine* and *Synthesis of Yoga*, he drew on India's ancient wisdom to develop the view that human life can be transformed into the highest forms of spiritual reality by the practice of an all-encompassing discipline of yoga. The divine forces are within us, though we are ignorant of them. If we search within and master these divine forces, making them pervade and transform all dimensions of our life, we will be able to live in the highest possible divine way. Society itself should be reshaped so that it is conducive to this human evolution into the divine life. Although Aurobindo draws on traditional Hindu ideas and techniques, what makes his vision a modern one is the way he integrates individual yogic means with the transformation of social conditions.

Hinduism in the West

Even though Hinduism has never been a missionary religion, the renaissance of Hinduism in India has spilled over to the West, and today many in Europe and America have had contact with the religion of the Eternal Dharma. We noted above the Ramakrishna Mission, which established Vedanta Society centers in various places in America and has for three-quarters of a century been providing Americans with solid knowledge of Hinduism. In recent years a variety of other Hindu movements have been transplanted to the West, including yoga, meditation, and bhakti of various sorts. The two movements most widely known are Transcendental Meditation and the International Society for Krishna Consciousness.

Maharishi Mahesh Yogi studied Shankara's Nondualist (Advaita) Vedanta meditation, but unlike the many other practitioners of this type of meditation he came to America and popularized this system for Westerners. Commonly known as Transcendental Meditation (TM), this practice emphasizes each person's inner divine essence and the creative powers that can be harnessed when this inner source is realized through meditation. TM is a natural process, the Maharishi emphasizes, employing the normal desire of the self to seek joy and happiness. Although some traditional Hindu forms are used, this type of meditation fits well with the American desire for personal success and well-being; by practicing meditation a person can find health and happiness in all areas of life.

A very different form of Hinduism is the Krishna bhakti group known as the International Society for Krishna Consciousness (ISKCON), a movement that has brought Chaitanya's Bengali Krishna worship into the streets of America's big cities. Swami A. C. Bhaktivedanta Prabhupada (1896–1977) became a sannyasin late in life in India and was sent by his master to bring Krishna Consciousness to the West. Arriving in New York City in 1965, he began to chant the names of Krishna in a park and in 1966 opened the first ISKCON center in New York. Soon the movement spread to all parts of the United States and to other countries as well. Prabhupada has also written many studies of the Bhagavad Gita, the puranas, and Chaitanya's writings, through his books making an impact on Western knowledge of Krishna Hinduism. Although there are many lay devotees and many Hindus from India who feel at home at the festivals held in Krishna temples, the devotees who live in the temples and devote their whole lives to Krishna Con-

sciousness form the heart of the movement. Their day begins about 3:45 A.M. and involves a full schedule of personal and corporate rituals, study sessions, chanting in the streets and elsewhere, worship of Krishna and the other deities, and so forth. The Hare Krishnas, with shaved heads and saffron robes, chanting in ecstasy and inviting others to join in the delights of Krishna, have become a familiar touch of Hinduism in the West.

There are many other Hindu-related gurus and movements in the West today. Some of the more bizarre ones get much media attention, whereas others cultivate a traditional type of Hinduism in a Western context. It is clear, both from these new groups in the West and from the vital movements in India today, that Hinduism is alive and well and contributing to the future of humankind's religious experience. Already significant dialogue has been taking place between Hindus and people of other religions, especially Christians and Muslims. In the opinion of some scholars of such matters, Hinduism, because of its expansive conception of religious truth at many different levels, can be a resource for mutual understanding and cooperation between these very different paths we call the religions of the world.

Morning prayer and chanting at the Hare Krishna temple in Philadelphia.

DISCUSSION QUESTIONS

1. Who is a Hindu?
2. Discuss the relationship between the history of Hinduism in the modern Western sense of "history" and the traditional Hindu story as told especially in the Epics. Which is more important to Hindu identity?
3. What were some important features of the Indus Valley civilization, and what influences did this culture have on Hinduism?
4. List the main features of Aryan religion in the period of the Rig Veda.
5. What were the major concerns of the authors of the Upanishads?
6. What major aspects of Hinduism developed during the classical epic era?
7. Discuss the main interests of the religion of the Puranas.
8. Compare the Brahmo Samaj and the Arya Samaj as modern reform movements.
9. What were Gandhi's main ideas and activities? Why did he attract such attention worldwide?
10. What are some main forms of Hinduism in the West?

CHAPTER 3

Hindu Worlds of Meaning

ULTIMATE REALITY IN HINDUISM: BRAHMAN, DHARMA, GOD/GODDESS

What's it *all* about? What is really ultimate, the center of all? Hindus have a long tradition of asking such questions, a tradition going back at least three thousand years. A hymn from Book 10 of the Rig Veda (ca. 1000 B.C.E.) puts it this way:

> Who really knows? Who will here proclaim it? Whence was it produced? Whence is this creation? The gods came afterwards, with the creation of this universe. Who then knows whence it has arisen? Whence this creation has arisen— perhaps it formed itself, or perhaps it did not—the one who looks down on it, in the highest heaven, only he knows—or perhaps he does not know. (RG VEDA 10.129.6–7)[1]

Answering this question, the Hindu traditions have put forth many proposals and experimented with many conceptions of ultimate reality, from the gods of the early Aryans to the modern Hindu's God, Goddess, or gods, from the power of the fire sacrifice to the eternal cosmic order, from the Brahman of the Upanishads to the Shakti of Tantric ritual. In our brief look at these traditions several thousand years in the making, we focus on three prominent answers as to what the sacred ultimate is: Brahman, Dharma, and God/Goddess or gods. These answers, as we by now have come to understand, are not exclusive, of course.

Brahman as the Sacred Ultimate

As noted earlier, the term *brahman* originally referred to the powerful words spoken by a priest in the ritual of fire-sacrifice. The priest who spoke the words was called brahmin, and the manuals about the ritual are the Brahmanas. Increasingly the term *Brahman* was used to refer to the sacred power that pervades and maintains all things. For a major portion of the Hindu tradition, Brahman is ultimate reality.

Brahman as the One Reality

According to the Upanishads, one of the first important ideas about Brahman is oneness, in contrast to multiplicity. A student once asked the sage Yajnavalkya how many gods there are, and Yajnavalkya answered that, as mentioned in a hymn, there are 3,306 gods. "But," the student presses on, "just how many gods are there?" "Thirty-three," is the answer. "Yes, but just how many gods are there?" "Six." "Yes, but just how many gods are there?" "Three." The student is still not satisfied: "Yes, but how many gods are there?" "Two." "Yes, but just how many gods are there?" "One and a half." "Yes, but just how many gods are there?" Finally Yajnavalkya answers, "One," and he explains that all the gods are but various differentiated powers of the One who is called Brahman (Brihad-aranyaka Upanishad 3.9.1–9).[2] Brahman is the one life of all the gods, the one soul of the universe, the one source of all.

As the One, Brahman is primordial, prior to all forms and divisions. Brahman is without qualities and limiting attributes, transcending this universe. Yajnavalkya once was challenged by the renowned Gargi Vacaknavi about his idea of Brahman. Posing a deep mind-puzzle, she asked him to define that across which all reality, all past and present and future, even all space is woven, like warp and woof. "That,

47

O Gargi, is called the Imperishable," he answered. "It is not coarse, not fine, not short, not long, not glowing, not adhesive, without shadow and without darkness, without air and without space, without stickiness, odorless, tasteless, without eye, without ear, without voice, without wind, without energy, without breath, without mouth, without measure, without inside and without outside." The Brahman is the ground of all the universe, Yajnavalkya explained, and further it is the ground of personal existence. "Verily, O Gargi, that Imperishable is the unseen Seer, the unheard Hearer, the unthought Thinker, the ununderstood Understander. Other than It there is naught that sees. Other than It there is naught that hears. Other than It there is naught that thinks. Other than It there is naught that understands" (Brihad-aranyaka Upanishad 3.8).[3] As the ultimate ground of all reality, that from which everything else is derived, the Brahman cannot adequately be described, for any description would have to reduce the Brahman to something else. But the Brahman is the subject of all reality and thus is beyond speech and concepts. Yajnavalkya explains,

> For where there is a duality, as it were, there one sees another; there one smells another; there one tastes another; there one speaks to another; there one hears another; there one understands another. But where everything has become just one's own self, then whereby and whom would one see? then whereby and whom would one smell? then whereby and whom would one taste? then whereby and to whom would one speak? then whereby and whom would one hear? then whereby and of whom would one think? then whereby and whom would one touch? then whereby and whom would one understand? whereby would one understand him by means of whom one understands this All? That Soul (Atman) is not this, it is not that (neti, neti). (BRIHAD-ARANYAKA UPANISHAD 4.5.15)[4]

Although as the ground of reality the Brahman cannot be described adequately, still it can be known directly. For the Brahman is immanent, permeating all things, humans, gods, the physical universe, space, and time. "Verily, this whole world is Brahman" (Chandogya Upanishad 3.14.1). Most importantly, according to the Upanishads, one's own true self (atman) is none other than the Brahman:

> This Soul of mine within the heart is greater than the earth, greater than the atmosphere, greater than the sky, greater than these worlds. Containing all works, containing all de-

sires, containing all odors, containing all tastes, encompassing this whole world, the unspeaking, the unconcerned— this is the Soul of mine within the heart, this is Brahman. Into him I shall enter on departing hence. (CHANDOGYA UPANISHAD 3.14.3–4)[5]

Since the inner atman is really the Brahman, a central path toward liberation in Hinduism, as we see later, is to acquire knowledge of this inner atman, to fully realize, as the Upanishads say many times, that "This Atman is the Brahman" (Brihad-aranyaka Upanishad 2.5.19).

Two Levels of Knowing Brahman

To know Brahman as the ultimate is the goal—but that requires high spiritual understanding. Hindu thinkers have a long tradition of speaking of two levels of truth. One seer, for example, tells of two forms of Brahman, the formed and the formless. The formed Brahman is different from the wind and the atmosphere and thus is personal and worthy of worship. The formless Brahman is the wind and the atmosphere and thus is impersonal, described only by "Not this, not this" (neti, neti) (Brihad-aranyaka Upanishad 2.3.1–6). Generally, the Upanishads describe the Brahman both in personal and in impersonal terms.

The Hindu philosopher Shankara spelled out the two levels of knowing Brahman with characteristic thoroughness:

> Brahman is apprehended under two forms; in the first place as qualified by limiting conditions owing to the multiformity of the evolutions of name and form (i.e., the multiformity of the created world); in the second place as being the opposite of this, i.e., free from all limiting conditions whatsoever.[6]

The Brahman without qualities he called the nirguna Brahman; this is the very ground of existence, prior to any limiting characteristics, which can only be described negatively and known intuitively—the highest truth of Brahman, the ultimate. The Brahman with qualities, the saguna Brahman, is the creative power of the universe, the foundation of the phenomenal world. Shankara considered saguna Brahman to be experienced as God, for whom he used the term Ishvara, the supreme Lord personified as deity; this lord of existence can be described and known and worshiped.

To explain how Brahman is one all-encompassing reality, and yet we experience the world and ourselves as distinct realities, Shankara taught the doctrine of maya (illusion), a word used in the Vedas for divine creative magic. From the point of view of the lower level of knowledge, the empirical world and all that is in it do exist and are really experienced. However, from the point of view of the higher knowledge, the world experienced as made up of distinct entities is an illusory projection superimposed on the one Reality, the Brahman.

To explain this puzzle, Shankara was fond of using the illustration of a snake and a rope. Seeing a coiled-up object lying on a path, one jumps to the conclusion that it is a snake—and one experiences it with all the emotion, fear, and anxiety associated with encountering a snake. It is real. But upon closer examination, it turns out to be a rope coiled up, lying in the path—and now one's subjective experience of it totally changes. It really is a rope. In much the same way, we out of ignorance project our experience of the multiformed world onto the one Brahman. Now Shankara is not arguing that we should treat the world and ourselves and other selves as though they did not exist or have no value. Rather, he wants us to see that this is the way Reality is experienced under the condition of our sense organs and minds—under the conditions of maya. From the viewpoint of the higher knowledge, all these distinct realities, with the associated subjective experiences of them, fade away in the unity of the Brahman. From the viewpoint of *nirguna* Brahman, then, even *saguna* Brahman is the result of maya.

There are of course still other perspectives on the Brahman as ultimate reality in Hinduism. Some philosophers, like Madhva (thirteenth century), abandoned nondualism altogether and went to a dualistic interpretation. He held that the world as empirically experienced, as well as individual selves, are eternally distinct from the Brahman. And the Samkhya school of philosophy argued an ultimate distinction between eternal *prakriti* (the ultimate material principle from which the whole world evolves) and *purusha* (eternal pure consciousness, ultimate self, equivalent to the Brahman).

But we can look to Shankara's nondualism as a very influential perspective on the Brahman as ultimate reality: *nirguna* Brahman as the impersonal, ultimate ground of all with no limiting characteristics; and *saguna* Brahman as creative power of the universe, the foundation of the phenomenal world.

God as Supreme Sacred Reality

Down through the centuries, while philosophers were arguing about Brahman, people continued their worship of the gods. Spurred on by the stories of the gods in the great epics, theistic Hinduism came to be more widely accepted and practiced even by the scholars and philosophers, who developed new interpretations about God (gods) as the ultimate reality.

To Shankara, *saguna* Brahman (personal God) is known at a lower level of truth, but to those Hindu thinkers who are devoted to their god, the argument is equally valid that God is the highest level of truth. The philosopher who argued this most persuasively was Ramanuja (1017–1137), a leading thinker among the Vaishnavites of south India who worked out a theology of Vaishnavism that bridged Shankara's Nondualist philosophy of Brahman and his own devotion to the great god Vishnu. Ramanuja, mainly interested in promoting bhakti, held that whereas Brahman is one unified reality, there is *within* the one Brahman a qualitative distinction between the soul, the world, and the highest Lord. Using the analogy of soul and body, Ramanuja taught that, as body and soul are united and yet different, so the Lord is the soul of one's soul in a personal relationship that includes both identity and difference, so that one's soul can worship its lordsoul. Ramanuja put forth an intellectual system in which God (Vishnu) is the ultimate reality, and worshiping God, therefore, is the highest truth.

So in the great sectarian movements in India, there is a strong and lasting tradition of expressing the ultimate sacred reality in personal theistic terms—as the great God Vishnu, or the great God Shiva, or again as the great Goddess Devi.

The Great God Vishnu

As we know, the Bhagavad Gita revealed Vishnu to be the highest Lord of all, transcending the cycles of samsara, evolving worlds forth from his own essence and absorbing them back again. The theophany (divine manifestation) revealed to Arjuna in Book XI of the Bhagavad Gita stands as one of the most impressive descriptions of God in religious literature. Arjuna prays to see Krishna's divine form, and the resulting vision of Krishna in his "All-Form" as the great god Vishnu is so awe-inspiring that Arjuna's hair stands on end.

Divine image, representing the great gods Brahma, Vishnu, and Shiva.

I see the gods
in your body, O God,
and hordes
of varied creatures:
Brahma, the cosmic creator,
on his lotus throne,
all the seers
and celestial serpents.
I see your boundless form
everywhere,
the countless arms,
bellies, mouths, and eyes;
Lord of All,
I see no end,
or middle or beginning
to your totality. . . .
only boundless strength
in your endless arms,
the moon and sun in your eyes,
your mouths of consuming flames,

your own brilliance
scorching this universe. . . .
You are the original god,
the primordial spirit of man,
the deepest treasure
of all that is,
knower and what is to be known,
the supreme abode;
you pervade the universe,
Lord of Boundless Form.
You are the gods of wind,
death, fire, and water;
the moon; the lord of life;
and the great ancestor.
Homage to you,
a thousand times homage!
I bow in homage to you
again and yet again. (11:15–16, 19, 38–39)[7]

All beings emerge from Vishnu, and he is the dissolution of all. His abode is far beyond the worlds of samsara. Vishnu as the universal lord concerns himself with cosmic stability. He is foremost the creator and preserver of the world, and his consort is Lakshmi, the goddess of wealth and abundance. When the world is periodically threatened by demons he embodies himself in an avatara (incarnation) to restore cosmic order, a factor that has become very important in Vaishnavite theology.

The best-known incarnations of Vishnu are Rama, hero of the Ramayana epic, and Krishna, divine teacher of the Bhagavad Gita. The form of God as Krishna is amply filled out in the puranas, where delightful stories are told about his lovable nature and his exploits as a baby and as a young man among the cowherd people, as we saw earlier. Reflecting on the importance of these incarnations of God, Ramanuja says,

[God's] divine form is the depository of all radiance, loveliness, fragrance, delicacy, beauty, and youth—desirable, congruous, one in form, unthinkable, divine, marvellous, eternal, indefectible, perfect. His essence and nature are not to be limited by word or thought. He is an ocean of boundless compassion, moral excellence, tenderness, generosity, and sovereignty, the refuge of the whole world without distinction of persons. . . . [By his incarnation] he can be seen by the eyes of all men, for without putting aside his [divine] nature, he came down to dwell in the house of

Vasudeva, to give light to the whole world with his indefectible and perfect glory, and to fill out all things with his own loveliness.[8]

For Vaishnavites following Ramanuja's theology, Vishnu is the one supreme reality encompassing all gods.

The Great God Shiva

Many Shaivites have a theistic vision similar to the Vaishnavites, but consider Shiva to the great lord of all, the ultimate One. Yet the theology of Shaivism is quite different from that of Vaishnavism. When we think of what is really central to all existence, what holds everything together, we have to think of evil as well as good, pain and death as well as birth and growth. Divine creativity involves death and rebirth; life coming into this world means life leaving this world. Many in India, strongminded and dedicated to truth as it is really experienced, feel that ultimate reality is best experienced through Shiva and his Shakti (feminine side). Many, of course, worship Shiva and Shakti along with many other gods. For some single-minded visionaries, Shiva is the One, the ultimate form of the sacred.

The stories portray Shiva as the greatest, supremely powerful god. A story in the puranas relates how Brahma the creator god, before creation was complete, met Vishnu and the two argued over who was greater. Suddenly a great pillar of flame shot up out of the darkness below and rose out of sight. Deciding to investigate this pillar, Brahma took the form of a swan and flew upward, and Vishnu took the form of a boar and pushed downward. A thousand years later the two gods returned, unable to find the top or the bottom of the pillar. The sound Om began to come from the pillar, and Shiva himself came forth from the pillar and received the worship of Brahma and Vishnu. The pillar was none other than Shiva's lingam, the infinite source of the whole universe.

Some Shiva devotees have moved toward a Shiva monotheism. For example, the Virashaivites, in their poems in praise of Shiva, often mock other practices and fiercely insist on Shiva as the one god:

> The pot is a god. The winnowing
> fan is a god. The stone in the
> street is a god. The comb is a

god. The bowstring is also a
god. The bushel is a god and the
spouted cup is a god.
Gods, gods, there are so many
there's no place left
for a foot.
There is only
one god. He is our Lord
of the Meeting Rivers.[9]

Shiva is the power connected with the lingam and yoni, the power of yogic meditation, and the dancing divine energy. Central to the theology of Shiva is the encompassing of all dualities—male and female, good and evil, creation and destruction, eroticism and asceticism. As the cosmic generative power, Shiva is the very sap of existence, the vigorous creative power that permeates all life. As the divine model of yoga or the antisocial madman haunting cremation grounds (as in some myths), Shiva beckons people to search for the ultimate truth of liberation from the world. As the divine dancer Shiva expresses the ultimate truth that sacred power is continually creating and destroying the world. In Shiva these opposites are reconciled in a higher unity. Shiva's lingam is the axis of the universe and also extends infinitely beyond, showing that even the temporal and the eternal are united in him, as are manifested existence and unmanifested Brahman.

The Great Goddess: Mother and Destroyer

As we saw earlier, the great goddess has many forms in India, as Shakti, Durga, and Kali, for example, associated with Shiva but also worshiped as the one ultimate by single-minded devotees. Some Hindus came to believe that there is one unified Great Goddess that is revealed in all these diverse goddesses. Although known by many names, she is usually called simply Devi (Goddess) or Mahadevi (Great Goddess). This theological perspective sees the many goddesses all as manifestations of the unifying cosmic sacred principle that is female, powerful, and active, the divine energy from which all creative processes derive. With her great, inexhaustible creative powers, the Great Goddess actively constitutes the material world. So she is the divine mother, guarding and nurturing all her children. But creation also has its destructive side, and the divine mother kills and destroys her creation as well. But this dark, destructive, and bloodthirsty side is seen as a natural part of the total order of the world, with its positive and necessary interaction of creation and destruction, life and death.

The nineteenth-century Hindu saint Ramakrishna, a lifelong devotee of the goddess Kali, expresses this vision of the divine mother as ultimate reality:

> Thus Brahman and Shakti are identical. If you accept the one, you must accept the other. It is like fire and its power to burn. . . . Thus one cannot think of the Brahman without Shakti, or of Shakti without Brahman. One cannot think of the Absolute without the Relative, or of the Relative without the Absolute. The Primordial Power is ever at play. She is creating, preserving, and destroying in play, as it were. This Power is called Kali. Kali is verily Brahman, and Brahman is verily Kali. It is one and the same Reality. When we think of It as inactive . . . then we call It Brahman. But when It engages in these activities, then we call it Kali or Shakti.[10]

Ramakrishna's words show that Hindus can encompass both nondualism and theism in thinking about ultimate reality. The truth of one ultimate Brahman does not prevent the experience of the ultimate in personal forms as god or goddess.

The Eternal Dharma

Since Brahman is the eternal, ultimate, one reality, knowing the identity of the atman with the Brahman leads to moksha, ultimate liberation from the samsara cycle. This, therefore, is held forth by many Hindus as the highest goal. But alongside that basic idea of ultimate reality Hinduism puts forward another perspective on eternal reality, namely, the cosmic order, the Eternal Dharma. What's it *all* about? In the context of living life the way we should, the answer turns out to be Dharma— not the underlying source and essence of reality, not a god to be worshiped, but the eternal order of things to be followed.

The word *Dharma* comes from a Sanskrit root meaning "sustain, support," and in Hinduism it comes to mean the essential foundation of things in general. Originally it was closely related to the Vedic notion of *Rta*, the universal harmony in which all things in the cosmos and in human society have their proper place and function. Dharma is something like the law of nature, eternal and unchanging. Following our dharma means living in accordance with reality. And it has as its correlate the law of karma, the law that there is an unfailing result that comes from every action. The whole world is supported and continues to exist on the foundation of Dharma and karma. The Bhagavad Gita says that even the great God Vishnu has his dharma to fulfill: it is to perform the work (karma) of originating and sustaining the world, and then to absorb it into himself again (Bhagavad Gita 3:22–24). Like all the world, humans also have their dharma, conditioned as we are by our own past karma—the works that follow us from lives lived long ago into our life in the present. The dharma imposed on us in our present class and circumstances is part and parcel of the eternal Dharma.

The eternal Dharma as ultimate stands in a certain tension with Brahman as ultimate. To realize Brahman means moksha, liberation from the world of samsara. But to live according to one's dharma means supporting and sustaining the world. This creative tension is built into the religious paths of Hinduism, and it provides much of the dramatic interest in the stories of the epics and puranas, where the values of Dharma and moksha often conflict.

Shiva Nataraja, the great god dancing out the continual creation, preservation, and destruction of the world.

EXISTENCE IN THE WORLD: DHARMA AND SAMSARA

What sense is there in life? The Hindu vision of the nature of the world and of the situation of humans within it is complicated and varies from one period to another, from one group or community to another. One key idea found throughout most of the traditions is that somehow, behind all this multifaceted world of existence, there is a unitary source from which all evolved in a creative process. The nature of the world and of humans involves two levels or contexts: the phenomenal world and its ongoing process, and the underlying sacred source and its realization. Problems in human existence arise at both levels, because of our ignorance and selfishness. We fail to fulfill our place within the order of things, and we neglect the realization of the eternal source, with the result that existence becomes a wheel of suffering and repeated death.

The World and Human Nature in Hindu Thought

Throughout the three thousand years of Hindu sacred literature, many pictures have been presented of the creation of the universe, its nature and duration, and its dissolution and recreation. And the human role within this picture has been a prime concern of the sages. Finally, we already know, the role of humans is to seek moksha, liberation from the whole conditioned world of samsara. But we need to see that as the ultimate goal, not as the only thing to be said about the world and humans. Whatever the ultimate truth about the world, there is at least a penultimate truth: the world is here, it is real, it functions by the eternal Dharma, the gods work to keep it going, and humans have the duty to contribute to its welfare. There is more to be said, but we can at least begin with that.

Paradigms of the Creation of the World

Pictures of the creation of the world in the sacred texts vary from a mechanistic self-evolving process to a more theistic view of God or gods creating the universe. We have already mentioned the very influential Hymn to Purusha in the Rig Veda, which described the whole universe created from the sacrifice of the gigantic primordial reality, Purusha. From the one sacred, through the power of sacrifice, come all the orders of the universe. We can mention two other well-known paradigms of creation, one from the Upanishads and the other from the Vishnu Purana.

The Upanishads elaborate on the creation of the world from the one sacred reality. One version runs like this:

> In the beginning this world was Soul (*Atman*) alone in the form of a Person. Looking around, he saw nothing else than himself. He said first: "I am." . . . Verily he had no delight. Therefore one alone has no delight. He desired a second. He was, indeed, as large as a woman and a man closely embraced. He caused that self to fall into two pieces. Therefrom arose a husband and a wife . . . He copulated with her. Therefrom human beings were produced. . . . She became a cow. He became a bull. With her he did indeed copulate. Then cattle were born. . . . She became a she-goat, he a he-goat; she a ewe, he a ram. With her he did verily copulate. Therefrom were born goats and sheep. Thus, indeed, he created all, whatever pairs there are, even down to the ants. He knew: "I, indeed, am this creation, for I emitted it all from myself." (BRIHAD-ARANYAKA UP-ANISHAD 1.4.1–5)[11]

Atman (Brahman) is the original solitary reality. This text and others tell how the primordial one desired to be many, and in the heat of that desire evolved itself into many, entering into and becoming this whole creation. The world is multiformed, but its sacred source is still the one dwelling in it all. The whole universe, then, is self-evolved from the primordial Brahman.

Let us, for one more paradigm, turn to a more theistic vision of creation from the Vishnu Purana. Here the great god Vishnu is the supreme lord, identical with Brahman, unified but containing the potential entire universe in his own nature. He unites within himself the primordial forms of spirit (purusha), matter, and time. Stirring himself, he engages in play to create the whole universe with these forms, evolving them into a vast egg resting on the cosmic waters. He enters the cosmic egg as Brahma (the creator) and creates the three worlds of sky, atmosphere, and earth, populating them with gods and all living beings. Then Vishnu becomes the preserver, supporting the world through its great time cycles (for millions of years) until it is exhausted. Now Vishnu becomes the destroyer and burns up the world in a great conflagration, bringing down rain until all is one vast ocean. Vishnu now sleeps on the coiled body of his great serpent (a setting often depicted in art), until he once again creates the world for another world cycle.

Here, in addition to the idea that the whole universe evolves from the one reality, we see that creation is really the "play" of the great god—suggesting both the exuberant divine energy and the temporary nature of the creation. We also learn that creation is a cyclical process of evolution and destruction over and over, a theme firmly set in the Hindu vision. Commonly, this picture of cosmic time cycles has smaller cycles (yugas) set within larger cycles (kalpas). It is said, for example, that the period from the beginning of creation to its destruction is one kalpa, but within each kalpa are 1,000 mahayugas ("great" yugas), each lasting 4,320,000 human years. Each mahayuga is made up of four lesser yugas, which progressively degenerate until a renewal takes place in the new mahayuga. The whole kalpa, made up of 1,000 mahayugas, is called one day of the Brahma, and it is followed by an equally long night of the Brahma in which Vishnu sleeps, until he again creates the universe for a second day of the Brahma. These kalpas continue for a lifetime of the Brahma, which is 100 years of 360 days and nights of the Brahma. Then at last the whole process is reversed until Vishnu alone remains in his primordial state of spirit, matter, and time—until he again decides to play and set the whole cosmic process in motion again.

Humans: Eternal Atman within the Dharma World

What am I, and what is my place within this whole world? The quest for understanding the self is as old as the human race, and Hindus have done their share of speculating on this question. It is important, Hindus believe, to make a distinction between the *real* self and the empirical self that appears to live in this phenomenal world. The empirical self is made up of the physical body composed of the gross elements (earth, water, light, wind, and ether), and it also includes the subtle body made up of the vital breaths, the organs of action, and the organs of knowledge, mind, and intellect. This empirical self seems to be the "real me," for it has all my physical characteristics, and my distinct personality, my habits, my way of thinking also rest in this self. Isn't this the real self?

The wisdom of Hinduism says no. The real self is something other: the atman, eternal and formless, in essence is none other than the Brahman. A famous dialogue in the

Upanishads between a father and son emphasizes this point. The wise father, Uddalaka, instructs his son Svetaketu, who is conceited about his knowledge of the Vedas, but doesn't know the secret, inner truth. Uddalaka tells his son:

> "Place this salt in the water. In the morning come unto me."
> Then he did so.
> Then he said to him: "That salt you placed in the water last evening—please bring it hither."
> Then he grasped for it, but did not find it, as it was completely dissolved.
> "Please take a sip of it from this end," said he. "How is it?"
> "Salt."
> "Take a sip from the middle," said he. "How is it?"
> "Salt."
> "Take a sip from that end," said he. "How is it?"
> "Salt."
> "Set it aside. Then come unto me."
> He did so, saying, "It is always the same."
> Then he said to him: "Verily, indeed, my dear, you do not perceive Being here. Verily, indeed, it is here. That which is the finest essence—this whole world has that as its soul. That is Reality. That is Atman (Soul). That art thou, Svetaketu." (CHANDOGYA UPANISHAD 6.13.1–3)[12]

"That thou art"—this is one of the most fundamental statements of identity. "That"—the Brahman that is the essence of all—is the same as your own true self, the atman. That self is eternal, formless, pure consciousness. That real self is the birthright of all living beings, and knowing it means attaining supreme bliss.

This is the highest self. Yet the lower realities of the self are not unimportant. This real self, atman, is attached to the empirical self made up of physical, mental, and psychological aspects, and it is in this condition that we live out our countless existences. Hinduism teaches that the eternal atman is embodied according to the working of the law of karma. The actions the atman performs in one lifetime, depending on their moral quality, create the conditions for the next embodiment of the atman. "According as one acts, according as one conducts himself, so does he become. The doer of good becomes good. The doer of evil becomes evil" (Brihad-aranyaka Upanishad 4.4.5).[13] The law of karma works neutrally and inexorably metes out the results of one's actions, rebirth after rebirth. There are countless living beings—each one embodying an atman—and countless levels of rebirth, from those in the hells to plants, animals, humans, and gods. One's evil karma may bring rebirth at lower levels, even as an animal or plant; one's good karma may bring rebirth at a higher human level or even as a god or goddess.

This whole process is samsara, the rebirth cycle, which is beginningless and endless. Since, as we saw, there is an eternal Dharma that prescribes the role of all things, every atman within samsara at any given time has its own dharma and thus its own role to fulfill. The dharma involves duties according to sex, caste, and so forth—all this is considered part of the nature of reality and is the basis for the operation of karma. If I am born as a servant, that is the karmic result of my previous lifetimes. In accordance with my dharma as a servant, my actions in this lifetime as a good servant or a bad servant will cause the level of my next rebirth.

The God of the Abraham religions created the world and said, "It is very good." In the Hindu vision, the world, evolved from the primordial One or created as play by the great god, is really neither good nor evil but neutral. On the highest level, the ultimate goal is to seek moksha, liberation from samsara altogether. But on another level, our role is to live the good life according to the Dharma, the eternal law of the world, promoting the welfare of all beings in the interrelated cycle of life.

Samsara and the Problem of Existence

Why do things seem not right? Why is there so much pain and suffering? What's wrong with my life? Whereas to outsiders the idea of living another lifetime after this one might seem attractive, Hindus know that another lifetime—and countless more after that—means more of the same pain and death endlessly. Not that everything about life is unhappy—far from it. The dharma of Hindu householders, for example, includes the duties of pleasure and accumulating wealth. Hindus do not have an unduly pessimistic view of life in the world. But the Hindu tradition does stress the relative, transient quality of life clearly: it is not the lasting, most authentic state of the soul. Seen in the eternal perspective, one searcher discovered, it really is nothing to rejoice about:

Hindu woman feeding a sacred cow. In Hindu thought, all life forms embody eternal sacred reality.

Sir, in this ill-smelling, unsubstantial body, which is a conglomerate of bone, skin, muscle, marrow, flesh, semen, blood, mucus, tears, rheum, feces, urine, wind, bile, and phlegm, what is the good of enjoyment of desires? In this body, which is afflicted with desire, anger, covetousness, delusion, fear, despondency, envy, separation from the desirable, union with the undesirable, hunger, thirst, senility, death, disease, sorrow, and the like, what is the good of enjoyment of desires? . . . In this sort of cycle of existence (samsara) what is the good of enjoyment of desires, when after a man has fed on them there is seen repeatedly his return here to earth? Be pleased to deliver me. In this cycle of existence I am like a frog in a waterless well. (MAITRI UPANISHAD 1.3–4)[14]

The very heart of the human problem, according to Hindus, is ignorance. I don't know who I really am. My true self really is the atman, eternal and identical with Brahman—but I think this living, breathing, thinking, feeling, desiring, socializing body and personality is who I really am. As we saw, the philosopher Shankara provided an astute analysis of our human problem. We commonly view the world as changing, full of different realities, persons, and things. But this arises from *maya* (illusion). Although there is one absolute Brahman, we in the process of maya superimpose false notions on Brahman, notions of separate individual realities and selves. This maya then blinds us so that we react to that illusion as if it is real, and so we live our lives as if we are individual egos in relation to all the separate things of the world. In a cryptic statement, one teacher of the Upanishads said,

> By the mind alone is It to be perceived.
> There is on earth no diversity.
> He gets death after death,
> Who perceives here seeming diversity. (BRIHAD-ARANYAKA UPANISHAD 4.4.19)[15]

If I am ignorant of the unity of the Brahman, that is, if I think of myself as different and see this world as made up of various things, I get "death after death," trapped endlessly in the rebirth and redeath of samsara. Why? Because out of ignorance arises desire, and from desire comes the impulse to selfish action (karma). The law of karma is such that actions performed out of desire have evil repercussions in the next lifetime, bringing a state of suffering and pain for the embodied atman.

Ignorance, desire, karma, rebirth—that is why there is suffering in the world, that is why life isn't what it should be. It is a vicious circle: "He becomes as he desires. By whatever fruit of actions he is made, that kind of action he performs. Whatever actions he does, that [kind of fruit, good or evil] he obtains. . . . 'He who desires [pleasures] comes again to this world to perform actions' " (Brihad-aranyaka Upanishad 4.4.5–6).[16] What one does now, out of ignorance and desire, creates conditions for one's next lifetime under which one will continue to act in ignorance and desire—a vicious circle that is likely to spiral downward. That is why the sages of India have generally regarded samsara as a trap of existence, with the ultimate goal being moksha, liberation from samsara.

But that final goal of moksha requires great spiritual knowledge and perfection, and so at best it is many lifetimes away for most people. And so we ought at least strive to live the good life, doing good deeds instead of evil, so that our karma will create the conditions of a higher rebirth or at least not a lower one. But even knowing that, we find it difficult to get away from selfish actions time after time, desiring other things, experiencing feelings of anxiety and regret when we lose something. How can one keep from despairing over being trapped in samsara? How can one keep ignorance and selfish desires from bringing ever lower rebirths? The Hindu answer is to get on the path of transformation, at the level appropriate to one's spiritual status.

THREE PATHS TO TRANSFORMATION AND LIBERATION

How can we start living *real* life? How can we reach liberation? At first glance the answers to this question given within the Hindu tradition seem almost countless. We find almost every conceivable religious pursuit being practiced by someone or other. One devotes herself to a particular god or goddess; another studies the Vedas and performs sacrifices; another goes on pilgrimages. Then there is another who is deeply skeptical of these practices and prefers speculation and philosophy. One tries to fulfill moral duties and works for the good of the community. Yet another abandons his family and community and wanders about, seemingly uninterested in society and even in the gods. It's a bit confusing! What is the path of transformation for Hindus?

Fortunately, Hindus have traditionally grouped these various ideas and practices into three basic paths (*marga*) of transformation: the path of knowledge (*jnana-marga*), the path of action (*karma-marga*), and the path of devotion (*bhakti-marga*). These three are broad paths and intersect at many points. Typically a Hindu may be following practices associated with all three paths, and the emphasis may change at different points in a lifetime. But each path does have a special focus and structure, and depending on a person's particular spiritual level and progress attention is given more to one or the other of these paths.

The Path of Liberating Knowledge

The theoretical basis of the path of knowledge was first worked out in the Upanishads, although no doubt the roots of this path go back to more ancient times, perhaps even to the Indus Valley civilization. The focus is on self-realization through meditation. Some Hindus consider the path of knowledge to be the highest path toward transformation, because it is the one that can bring the searcher to the final goal of *moksha* (liberation).

Moksha, the Realization of the Real Atman

"Whoever thus knows 'I am Brahman!' becomes this All" (Brihad-aranyaka Upanishad, 1.4.10).[17] So the final goal is to "know" that I am the Brahman. This is what brings moksha, the final and unconditioned release from the bondage of karma and samsara.

We should not be deceived by the simplicity of this answer. Knowledge here is not a merely intellectual knowing but rather a deep, experiential realization of the ultimate ground as one's true self. It far transcends the intellect and the mind, which are aspects of the subtle self involved in the rebirth cycle. The intellect can assist in reaching this knowledge, but eventually even the intellect is transcended in the pure consciousness of the true atman. This knowledge is to be felt, experienced, and lived, knowledge that transforms one's whole being.

How is it that knowledge can be transforming and liberating? We need to recall that ignorance is the root of the human problem. Because I am ignorant of my real atman, I take my empirical self to be my real concern and the focus of my desires. I look upon the other things in this world as separate objects, and I perform action (karma) out of desire to enhance my self, perpetuating the cosmic process that keeps me tied to the samsara cycle. But if I know that my true self is indeed the Brahman, and that the Brahman includes within itself the entire universe, then there is nothing for me to desire for my "self," for I already am all. "If a person knew the soul (*Atman*), with the thought, 'I am he!,' with what desire, for love of what would he cling unto the body?" (Brihad-aranyaka Upanishad, 4.4.12).[18] Since this knowledge destroys all desires and thus all karma, there will be no more rebirths once this knowledge is fully and completely realized.

What is soundless, touchless, formless, imperishable,
Likewise tasteless, constant, odorless,
Without beginning, without end, higher than the great, stable—
By discerning That, one is liberated from the mouth of death.   (KATHA UPANISHAD 3.15)[19]

When the body dies, the subtle self of mind and the vital breaths do not draw together around the self to lead to a new rebirth; the true atman is liberated. "Being very Brahman, he goes to Brahman" (Brihad-aranyaka Upanishad, 4.4.6).[20]

Moksha is described in various ways in the Hindu tradition. Sometimes it is pictured as a dissolving of the atman into the one Brahman. Just as a lump of salt dissolves when thrown into water, leaving no salt to grasp but making the water salty wherever one may taste it, so the atman becomes one with the Brahman. The individuality characterized by the empirical self—the physical body and the traits of mind and personality—comes to an end in the pure oneness of the Brahman. Moksha, however, is not annihilation or extermination of the atman; it is rather expansion, becoming all by transcending the limited self of mortal existence. It is pure bliss, peace, freedom, and joy. It is endless and unlimited.

Mediation and Yoga

To follow the path of knowledge and reach moksha requires a high level of spiritual perfection. Therefore the path of knowledge is necessarily an elite path, although it is beneficial even for those at lower spiritual levels to devote some attention to it. A person who really wants to follow the path of knowledge should take the prior steps of self-discipline and preparation by becoming a sannyasin, a renouncer. By cutting off all ties to this world, by giving up possessions, family links, and all worldly concerns, one will have the freedom necessary to devote oneself to attaining the knowledge that will liberate from samsara.

A most characteristic method practiced on the path of knowledge is meditation, for it is by looking inward that one finds the true self, the atman. Many types of meditation have been developed in India, but in general the process is to withdraw one's consciousness from the outer sensual reality and turn it inward, by stages, until all dualities and conditions dissolve and one experiences the pure, unified consciousness of the Brahman. The

Mandukya Upanishad suggests a four-stage process, based on the mantra OM (in Sanskrit, AUM). OM is often used in meditation, for it is considered the sacred sound that encompasses all sounds and therefore fittingly symbolizes the Brahman. The letter A of AUM corresponds to the waking state, with consciousness turned outward. U corresponds to the dreaming state, with consciousness turned inward but still not unified. M symbolizes the deep-sleep state, which is a blissful, unified, massive consciousness—but still not the final goal. The fourth state, experiencing the real atman, corresponds to the silence that precedes and follows the saying of the mantra AUM. This state is neither cognitive nor noncognitive, it is indescribable and unthinkable. It is the unified, tranquil, blissful experience of the atman as the Brahman. "He who knows this, with his self enters the Self—yea, he who knows this!" (Mandukya Upanishad 12)[21] This universal self is eternal and changeless, and knowing it as one's real self one transcends death and rebirth completely.

Many forms of meditation, especially those involving ascetic disciplines, are commonly spoken of as yoga. We can see the process of reaching knowledge of the Brahman by considering the classical eight-stage yoga practice developed by the ancient sage Patanjali and followed also in the Vedanta school, for these eight stages illustrate the movement from external control to inner knowledge. The first five stages have to do with eliminating external causes of mental distraction. First comes restraint, getting one's life in moral order by abstaining from violence and greed. Second is observance, laying the moral foundation of purity and dedication. External control is perfected in the third, fourth, and fifth stages. Posture involves the proper sitting position to transcend the body. Breath control helps the meditator draw closer to the essence of reality. And withdrawal of senses detaches the mind from the sense-organs so that all powers of consciousness can be focused inward on the source of being.

The final three stages complete the inner rise of pure consciousness. Concentration focuses the mind on a particular object of thought, and meditation stabilizes the mind in an uninterrupted state of contemplation. The final state, trance (*samadhi*), is the culminating experience in which the object of meditation vanishes and the mind swells to encompass a limitless reality. Plural things

A *yogin in meditation.*

and plural souls are no longer recognized; there is only an infinite sense of absolute knowledge, a consciousness of absolute freedom and liberation.

By becoming a sannyasin and following the path of knowledge to these spiritual heights, ultimate transformation can be attained, according to Hinduism. One reaches moksha, the fullest type of existence, and, if that moksha is complete and perfect, when this lifetime ends there will be no more rebirth. Being the Brahman, one attains the Brahman.

The Path of Action

While it might be recognized that the path of knowledge is the path that leads finally to complete moksha, most of us are a long way from that kind of spiritual perfection. Whereas practices like meditation are beneficial, there are other religious pursuits that provide us the most help along the way. Since the human problematic has to do with desire and the resultant action (karma) that binds us in the rebirth cycle at ever lower levels, it makes sense to work toward the lessening of desire and the cultivation of actions that will move us upward in the rebirth cycle. To a great many Hindus, following the path of action (karma-marga) is what Hinduism is all about as a way of transformation.

We learned that karma (action) was the cause of the samsara cycle. How can karma be the basis of a path of transformation? Hindus point out that there are different kinds of karma. Many—probably most—of the actions we do result from desire, from wanting something for ourselves. Action done out of desire or passion produces a "hot" kind of karma that has adverse effects in the future. We become as we desire, the Upanishads teach. This karma will bring fear and anxiety into our lives. And a whole lifetime filled with actions done out of passion and desire will inevitably result in rebirth at lower levels.

But there is another kind of karma, that is, action done without desire, "cool" karma. This kind of karma produces effects, of course, but these are good and beneficial effects. This kind of karma brings peace to life, and it will result in rebirths at higher levels in the samsara cycle. With enough good karma one can even be reborn as a god—though this, of course, is not yet moksha. Eventually, after many lifetimes, a person will reach the level of spiritual perfection in which she or he can follow the path of knowledge and reach ultimate liberation.

So the crucial question is, how can I eliminate action rooted in desire and cultivate action done without desire? The classical Hindu answer is simply to do what is expected of me according to my dharma, my place and role in the eternal order of things. If my karma has caused me to be born as a warrior, I should go about my duty of protecting people, not out of desire or hope for reward, but simply because it's my dharma. If I'm a woman, I should be a good woman; if a slave, I should simply serve others without desiring to be something else. The whole system worked out in the Law-code of Manu, which we discuss later, provides guidance for the path of action: caste, sex, and stage of life make up the essential elements of my dharma, and by performing that role properly, without desiring some reward, I move forward on the path of transformation.

In a sense the path of action is a universal path for Hindus, for everyone is born into it, and most Hindus keep practicing it until the end of their lives. Only some world-renouncers and devotees of certain gods claim to transcend the laws of the Eternal Dharma. The path of action is a way of transformation through discipline, ritual, and morality. Performing one's duty without desire leads to the higher spiritual levels. The Bhagavad Gita teaches:

> He incurs no guilt if he has no hope,
> restrains his thought and himself,
> abandons possessions,
> and performs actions with his body only. . . .
> Always perform with detachment
> any action you must do;
> performing action with detachment,
> one achieves supreme good.   (BHAGAVAD GITA 4.21; 3.19)[22]

The Path of Devotion

There is yet another way. Only few can attain the liberating freedom of the path of knowledge. The path of action does not promise liberation and poses many problems itself, as we see in the great epics where examples of people caught between duty and love abound. Arjuna grieves for his slain relatives and wishes to avoid his duty as a warrior. King Yudhishthira mourns the countless lives sacrificed in the great battles and wishes he could renounce the world. We all know what our duty is; yet desires, longings, and even what appear to be higher values constantly keep us from performing our duty in a completely unattached way. Is there no hope, no other way? Yes, there is: the path of bhakti (devotion).

How Can God Save Us?

Generally in the Hindu system of thought, the gods, though powerful and blessed, are understood to be within the cycle of samsara and therefore not ultimate. From ancient time in India various gods were worshiped for all kinds of benefits. And still today Hindus perform rituals of worship for various reasons, such as worshiping Sarasvati to attain learning and art, Ganesha for success in business, Lakshmi for wealth, and the like. But how can such gods provide salvation? How can they liberate us from the effects of our karma?

We saw earlier how several great theistic movements developed in Hinduism, one centered on Vishnu, another on Shiva, and yet another on the great Goddess Shakti, in each case looking on the great god or goddess as the personal sacred power of the universe. Unlike the descriptions of Brahman in the Upanishads, these great gods are personal and present; they pervade all reality, they are present within the soul, and they can be worshiped and loved. Since, according to devotees, Vishnu and Shiva-Shakti are supreme and in fact none other than the Brahman, they can be sources of saving power, not only bringing limited benefits but transforming us and liberating us from bondage to samsara. It is not only knowledge of the inner Brahman, realized by the spiritually elite, that brings liberation; God, the lover of my soul, to whom I can abandon myself no matter what my spiritual status, can help me to liberation.

Bhakti means to love and devote oneself to one's god, fully and completely. By such self-abandonment, all desires and wants and needs are turned to God rather than to the self. United with the great God of the universe who is also the inner soul of one's heart, one rises above the bondage of karma and finds joy, peace, and ecstasy in the power of the Beloved One.

The Vaishnavite Path of Bhakti

The transforming power of Vishnu can be experienced in different ways by his bhaktas (devotees), whether through his presence in the universe as creator, preserver, and destroyer, or through his avataras Rama and Krishna. The important factor is the love and self-surrender on the part of the worshiper. In the Bhagavad Gita, for example, Krishna emphasizes this self-surrender:

> Keep me in your mind and devotion,
> sacrifice to me, bow to me,
> discipline your self toward me,
> and you will reach me! (BHAGAVAD GITA 9.34)[23]

Our bondage to the conditions of karma—whether high caste or slave, woman or man, pure or sinful—is overcome in the power of God's love. Since Vishnu transcends even the samsara cycle, in loving union with him we too can rise to salvation:

> Even in Brahma's cosmic realm
> worlds evolve in incessant cycles,
> but a man who reaches me
> suffers no rebirth, Arjuna. (BHAGAVAD GITA 8.16)[24]

God is lovable and invites us to love him. The puranas fill out the story of Krishna in the interest of the path of bhakti. A demon king by the name of Kamsa, the story goes, had seized rule of Mathura, and his power threatened even the gods. In answer to their appeal, Vishnu tells of his plan to be born into the world as the eighth son of King Vasudeva and his wife Devaki. King Kamsa, learning of this plan, kills the first six children of Devaki. Her seventh son is an incarnation of Vishnu, Balarama, who is transferred to the womb of Vasudeva's second wife and thus saved. When Krishna is born as Devaki's eighth child, he is exchanged for the newborn daughter of the cowherd woman Yashoda—and thus Krishna and his brother Balarama grow up among the cowherd people of Vrindavana.

Yashoda and the other cowherd people are filled with wonderful joy and love through the presence of the beautiful baby, dark as the lovely blue lotus petal. His playfulness and mischief endear him to everyone—untying village calves, mocking his elders, teasing babies, stealing butter and sweets, playing tricks on the villagers, dancing and sporting with his brother Balarama and the village boys—all of this brings the love of God to the people. How joyful to love God as a baby, as a free and playful child! God is present in spontaneous, tumultuous power, at the same time approachable and adorable. In the child Krishna, we can see that God's very nature is to sport and play, inviting us to share in the divine self-delight.

Child Krishna grows up and becomes young man Krishna—still adorable and beautiful and playful, now irresistible to the gopis, as the young women among the cowherd people are called. When he goes out to the forest and plays his flute, the divine sound is too enticing to resist, and the women leave their chores, husbands, and families and come out to be near Krishna. Krishna dances and plays with all of them, multiplying his form so that each can experience his love. It is a festival of love, full of intoxication, joy, and abandon. One purana describes this great romance:

> Some of the cow herdesses . . . out of fun forcibly took away the flute from the hands of Lord Krishna. Then they pulled his yellow dress. Some passionate girl denuded him of his clothes, took away his yellow garment and then in jest returned it to him. . . . Some danced and sang with Krishna in the centre; others forcibly caused him to dance.

A seventeenth-century temple hanging showing the gopis (cowherd women) searching for Krishna in the night.

Krishna also out of fun, dragged the clothes of some milk-maid, made her naked and then returned the clothes to her.

The scene grows more tumultuous, and Krishna, surrounded by this group of impassioned gopis, makes love to them all, a celebration that even the gods assembled to watch.[25] Among the gopis, Krishna's favorite is Radha, and the stories delight in telling of the many facets of the love affair between the divine lover and his beloved. They are drawn to each other passionately, they grow jealous and quarrel and make up, they consummate their love in ecstasy and abandon and bliss. Krishna plays and delights himself, and Radha and the gopis are drawn into this divine delight. Here all duty and obligation are forgotten, and the gopis and Krishna are drawn together out of sheer divine

passion and delight. Here, some say, is the highest form of loving God. We can love God as a father or mother, as a brother or friend, as a beautiful baby—but to love God as a lover means totally forgetting self and surrendering to the ecstasy of divine joy and delight. And that experience helps the devotee toward transformation and liberation.

The Shaivite Path of Transformation Through Bhakti

Shiva appears to be a very different god from Vishnu, yet his devotees likewise experience transformation and liberation in worshiping him. In Shiva, the creative and the destructive powers of the sacred are held closely together. Shiva is often portrayed as bringing fierce destruction because of his quick temper and outrageous behavior. Sexually attracted to Parvati, daughter of the mountains, he marries her but then practices asceticism and refuses to impregnate her. Parvati has a son Ganesha, born from the dirt she removed from her body while bathing. Ganesha guards the bathhouse, but one day Shiva forces his way in and, enraged that Ganesha tried to stop him, cuts off Ganesha's head with a mighty blow. Parvati's anger now threatens to destroy the world, so Shiva agrees to restore Ganesha's life, taking the head of the first living thing that came by—an elephant—and placing this on Ganesha's body. This is the origin of the extremely popular elephant-headed god Ganesha, worshiped as the bringer of prosperity and good fortune.

Shiva also is described in the stories as the creator and nourisher of existence. He made it possible, for example, for the heavenly Ganges River to descend gently over the Himalayas to water the earth, cushioning the river's descent with his own divine head. Another well-known story tells how the gods and the demons were churning the great milk ocean to obtain the nectar of immortality. They used the great serpent Vasuki as the churning rope and a great mountain as the churning rod, but after a thousand years of furious churning, a terrible poisonous venom began to gush from the thousand mouths of the serpent. Now the lives even of the gods were threatened, so Shiva agreed to accept the poison as if it were the nectar of immortality, saving the gods and all existence from destruction. His supreme power kept him from harm, although the venom left his throat a dark blue color, still seen on artistic representations.

A central story in the puranas is the conflict between Shiva and Kama, the god of desire. As the great ascetic, Shiva is the epitome of chastity; yet he is constantly driven by desire for Parvati. His male powers are evident in that his semen is the seed from which the whole universe arises; yet he retains his seed and refuses to give in to Kama's enticements. A famous passage describes how Shiva destroyed Kama by burning:

> Kama assumed the form of a very subtle creature and entered Shiva's heart. Then Shiva was heated by a desire for sexual pleasure, and he thought of Devi, and his perfection vanished. . . . Then he saw Kama in his heart, and he thought, "I will burn Kama out of my body by means of

withdrawal from worldly objects. . . ." [Kama] shot the arrow of Delusion into Shiva's heart, and in anger Shiva burnt Kama to ashes with the fire from his third eye.[26]

With Kama destroyed, of course, all life and fertility is threatened, and the gods beg Shiva to restore Kama; finally in his desire for Parvati he brings about a revival of Kama.

Based on stories and perceptions like these about Shiva, those devoting themselves to him often involve themselves in yogic austerities and meditation. Worshipers of Shiva may smear ashes on their bodies and haunt cemeteries. They express a deep sense of guilt and pain in separation from Shiva, and they revel in the overpowering holiness of the presence of Shiva. Looking to Shiva as a "madman with moon-crowned hair," devotees transcend themselves in divine ecstasy:

> But me he filled in every limb
> With love's mad longing, and that I might climb there whence is no return,
> He showed his beauty, made me his. Ah me, when shall I go to him? . . .
> Thinking it right, sin's path I trod;
>   But, so that I such paths might leave,
> And find his grace, the dancing God,
>   Who far beyond our thought doth live,
> O wonder passing great!—to me his dancing shewed.
> Ah who could win that which the Father hath bestowed?[27]

Shiva pervades the whole universe as its Atman, and is manifest in it through his Shakti (power, female energy). Therefore, attunement of one's self to this Atman, as it is present in the blissful throbbing waves of divine consciousness in the breast, is the means of ultimate transformation.

Transformation Through the Great Goddess

The Great Goddess (Devi) likewise brings transformation to her devotees. The goddess is worshiped in many forms and localities for a variety of benefits, but there are some who single-mindedly devote themselves to her as a way of salvation. The many faces of the goddess—grace, cruelty, creation, destruction, love, indifference—express the endless energy active at the heart of the world. So worshiping her, through meditation, Tantric rituals, and ecstatic devotion, can bring liberation through her gracious power. Even the form of the ferocious goddess Kali is worshiped by some strongminded ones as the source of salvation. The great Bengali poet Ramprasad Sen (1718–1775) sang the praises of the great goddess—Devi, Durga, Kali—who plays, tortures him, deludes him, brings misery and death, but in the end there is "Grace and mercy in Her wild hair":

I'm sweating like the slave of an evil spirit,
Flat broke, a coolie working for nothing,
A ditch digger, and my body eats the profits.
Five Elements, Six Passions, Ten Senses—
Count them—all scream for attention.
They won't listen. I'm done for.
A blind man clutches the cane he's lost
Like a fanatic. So I clutch You, Mother,
But with my bungled karma, can't hold on.
Prasad cries out: Mother, cut this black snarl
Of acts, cut through it. Let life, when death
Closes down, shoot rejoicing up
Out of my head like a rocket.[28]

The modern Hindu saint Ramakrishna (1836–1886) often sang to Durga-Kali-Shakti in ecstatic trance, as in this example:

Thy name, I have heard, O Consort of Shiva, is the destroyer of our fear,
And so on Thee I cast my burden: Save me! Save me, O kindly Mother!
Out of Thy womb the world is born, and Thou it is that dost pervade it. . . .
Thou art the Primal Power, O Mother! She whose senses are controlled;
The yogis meditate on Thee as Uma, great Himalaya's daughter.
Thou who art the Power of Shiva! Put to death my ceaseless cravings;
Grant that I never fall again into the ocean of this world.[29]

For such devotees, Kali grants the ultimate boon of unconditioned freedom and release from concern over the samsara world; in worshiping Kali one confronts death head on, giving oneself over to her play, singing and dancing with the abandon and ecstasy of liberation.

Ramakrishna not only followed the path of devotion but he brought it together with the path of knowledge. He practiced meditation, and his deepest trances came as he focused on his beloved Kali. Once again we remind ourselves that these three paths of liberation in Hinduism are not exclusive, and it is more than likely that any given Hindu will be following at least two of them at the same time. Within these three paths are possibilities for all people, no matter how high or low spiritually or socially, to move toward transformation and liberation.

DISCUSSION QUESTIONS

1. Outline several prominent Hindu views of ultimate reality.
2. What is meant by different levels of knowing Brahman as proposed, for example, by Shankara?
3. Sketch out some of the main theistic visions, especially those associated with Vishnu, Shiva, and the Great Goddess.
4. Explain the Hindu notion of great world cycles.
5. What is samsara, and how does the Hindu tradition view this condition of existence? What is moksha?
6. Explain the main purpose and process of each of the three major paths of transformation in Hinduism.

CHAPTER 4

Hindu Worship and the Good Life

SACRED RITUALS AND TIMES OF HINDUISM

How can I find new power for life? How can I get in touch with what is *real*? The Hindu answer, at least for the great majority, is to worship—to participate in the exciting, colorful rituals and festivals so close to the heartbeat of Hinduism.

Some spiritually advanced Hindus, withdrawn from the world and approaching the goal of moksha, feel little need for worship of the gods and festivals. Other Hindus would say that everything they do, following the traditional law-codes of Dharma, is worship and piety. But most Hindus acknowledge that worship of the gods, rituals and pilgrimages, festivals, and life-cycle ceremonies are important and spiritually beneficial. Religion is not so much something to theorize about or even to believe; rather, it is a thing to be *done*.

Vedic Sacrifice and Worship of the Gods

One important observation to begin with is the centrality of the notions of pollution and purity in the Hindu way of life. Interaction with the sacred powers is essential for human welfare and spiritual transformation; yet the limiting conditions of human life often make that interaction difficult or even dangerous. The highest gods must be worshiped by brahmins who are in a pure state; polluted by contact with people of lower castes, for example, a brahmin cannot offer the Vedic sacrifices, and the whole community suffers. A woman who is menstruating should not prepare food to be offered to the gods. The ordinary biological processes of the body are polluting, so morning devotions should be preceded by a purifying bath. Rituals, ceremonies, and festivals always begin with the people purifying themselves.

Offering Vedic Sacrifices

The rituals and sacrifices prescribed in the Vedas enjoy great prestige, just as the Vedas themselves do. In earlier times powerful and wealthy individuals hired brahmin priests to perform great public sacrifices offering food and drink to the gods to strengthen them and harness their powers for the welfare of the world and of the people. Equally ancient is the domestic Vedic fire ritual called *agnihotra*, still today performed by pious Hindus twice daily. The man of the household arises at dawn and purifies himself with water. The household fire is worshiped as the god Agni, offerings are made, and ancient prayers are chanted. Raising his arms to the sun god, the man chants this Vedic mantra:

> OM. Earth, Atmosphere, Sky.
> We meditate upon the glorious splendour of the vivifier divine.
> May he himself illumine our minds.   (RG VEDA 3.62.10)[1]

This important ritual destroys the effect of bad deeds, drives away darkness, and harmonizes one's life with the spiritual force of the universe.

Today brahmin priests perform Vedic sacrifices for a variety of purposes. For example, one might see Vedic rituals in drought-stricken villages in rural India in the scorching days of summer, the dry season. The ground is dried up, water is rationed, food is running low, and famine threatens the community. Government agencies are busy sinking deep wells in the drought-afflicted region and bringing water in from elsewhere to avert calamity until, they hope, the refreshing rains of the monsoon season will finally come. But the people of the village are most interested in the group of brahmin priests who go from village to village, spending the whole day chanting Sanskrit mantras from the Vedas and offering fire sacrifice. They are the real "experts" in this crisis, and the people hope and believe that the sacred vibrations set loose in their chanting and their sacrifice will bring rain and benefit to the struggling community. By participating in these Vedic rituals, humans share in the ongoing processes of creation and recreation of the world, nourishing the various gods and spiritual powers so that they will continue to support and uphold the world.

Puja: Celebrating the Powerful Presence of God

Whereas Vedic rituals are restricted to the higher classes (brahmin, kshatriya and vaishya), there are no such restrictions on puja, the acts of worship paid to a god or goddess, usually in the presence of the divine image at a temple or domestic shrine.

The image of the sacred being plays a central role in most puja. The image is made by craftspeople according to the special iconographic tradition for that particular god, and then a ritual calls down the vitalizing presence of the god into the image. All worshipers, of course, know that the image is not the whole manifestation of the god. The god, especially if it is a form of Vishnu or Shiva or the Great Goddess, pervades the whole universe, and the image is simply one local center for the operation of the sacred power.

There are a great variety of images of the gods and goddesses. A most common symbol of Shiva is the lingam (phallic symbol) placed on the yoni (female generative symbol). Another favorite image is the Dancing Shiva. Vaishnavites favor the *shalagrama*, a black stone with fossil

ammonite, or Vishnu reclining on his serpent Sesha, or images of Rama or Krishna. Shaktas might focus on the ferocious image of Mother Kali. The image is carefully and lovingly attended to. Large temples have rituals of putting the god to bed at night, waking the image in the morning, dressing, feeding, and entertaining her or him like a great queen or king, and taking the image out for joyous processions.

Puja at a temple generally begins with purification, invoking the presence of the god, and greeting the god with respect. The goddess (or god) is honored with *kirtana*, which includes offerings of items such as garlands of flowers and clothing, pouring water on the image, marking the forehead of the goddess with sandal paste, circling the goddess with incense, waving lights, singing devotional songs, and playing auspicious music. It is of great spiritual benefit to hold one's hands over the fire that has been offered before the goddess, then to touch the hands to the forehead. The devotees are particularly intent on taking *darshana* (seeing) of the goddess

An eighteenth-century illustration of Shiva puja, worshiping the lingam-yoni image of Shiva.

or god, a ritual accompanied with intense feeling and emotion in the large temples. It is particularly by the ritual "seeing" of the goddess or god, and being "seen" by the god, that the worshiper feels united with the divine power and energy. Another important ritual is the taking of *prasad*, sacred food. The food that was prepared to be offered to the god or goddess is also given to the worshipers, a tangible form of divine grace. By eating the food that the goddess has "eaten," we are accepting the blessing of the goddess and sharing in her power. Puja, especially as done in temples and at festivals, is a joyful, emotional, and exciting event, transforming both the individual and the community. For many Hindus, puja is the central religious activity of their lives.

Festivals and Pilgrimages

The rhythms of sacred time in India come in daily, weekly, monthly, and yearly cycles. Sacred times also have regional emphases, although certain great festivals are celebrated all over India. The same is true of the important practice of pilgrimage to holy places, sacred rivers and mountains, and the like. These are usually set during sacred periods and provide a dramatic experience of sacred time and renewal.

Rituals and Festivals

Depending on individual inclination, and also on caste and family custom, Hindus practice a rich daily series of ceremonies. A pious person rises before sunrise to meditate on the qualities of her god, bathe, and offer puja before eating her morning meal. If he or she is a brahmin, the daily Vedic rite is to be performed twice during the day, at sunrise and sunset, purifying oneself with water, making offerings and reciting mantras to the fire god (Agni) and to the sun god. Orthodox householders of the upper classes perform the five great sacrifices daily: studying the Vedas, offering food offerings to the gods, offering water to the ancestors, giving food to brahmins and students, and offering food to all beings. In modern times many Hindus do not find time for all these rituals. But almost all Hindus observe the ceremonies of purification, bathing in flowing water or pouring water on oneself (never bathing in a closed container, which retains the pollutions). And the rituals of cooking, serving, and eating daily food are carefully observed; the kitchen is the citadel of the household, maintained with ritual purity against intrusions of pollution from the outside. In many families the serving of food is really an act of puja; the food is encircled with drops of sacred water while a mantra is recited. Thus the food is first offered to the god and the family meal becomes a form of prasad, eating food offered to the god.

Many families also have a household shrine, perhaps located near to the pure kitchen area. Images of the gods of special importance to the family are kept there, and worship rituals are performed daily, at least by the devout.

Certain days of the week and of the month, such as the new moon and the full moon, are times for special ceremonies and celebrations. Most characteristic of Hinduism is the annual festival cycle; a typical village in north India, for example, has over forty ceremonial occasions based on the lunar calendar of the year. Hindu religious life passes through seasons with various festivals and fairs, depending on the caste and sectarian affiliation of the community involved. Gods and goddesses all have their special festival times and seasons, far too many to attempt to describe. Here are three brief examples.

One great festival time throughout much of India, coming at the end of the rainy season (September–

Lighting the oil lamps at Divali, the festival of lights.

October), celebrates the triumph of good over evil, remembering especially the goddess Durga's victory over the buffalo demon, Mahisha. In the Belur Math temple in Calcutta (famous because of Ramakrishna's vision of Kali there), for example, a huge statue of Durga is consecrated and dressed, and prayers and songs ask Durga to drive away evil and bless the good. There are gala processions and dancing with lights and music. Another emphasis during this fall festival time is the Ram-lila, celebrating the victory of Rama over the demon Ravana, acted out in dramatic fashion by actors representing the divine heroes and demons, followed by communal celebrations.

Divali, meaning "cluster of lights," comes in October–November and is one of the most festive times of the year. The central ritual is the lighting of row upon row of lamps all over, outside the house and on the roof, as many as possible, for lights symbolize prosperity. Lakshmi, the goddess of prosperity, is a main patroness of this festival, and she is invited to come inside the house to a temporary altar containing symbols of wealth—coins, ornaments, and shells. The people perform puja with sweets and milk, and these are then passed around the family as sacred food. It is a time of housecleaning and refurbishing, a general renewal of life. This festival is especially important to merchants, beginning the new business year.

Probably the most popular festival in north India is Holi, celebrated on the full moon at the beginning of spring (February–March). For days the anticipation of the festival grows as people roam the streets seeking wood and combustibles for the Holi fire—with the accepted rule that everyone must contribute something for the fire. The fire is associated with the story of Prahlada, a virtuous young man who persisted in worshiping Vishnu even though his wicked aunt Holika tried to burn him in the fire. Holika had been given the divine boon of indestructibility by fire, so she held Prahlada on her lap in the flames—but Rama intervened and the lad emerged unscathed, whereas the demoness Holika was destroyed. With the rising of the full moon the great fire flames up, and people of all castes circle it, throwing cakes of cow dung into the flames, shouting obscene phrases of vituperation toward the blaze representing Holika.

The great fire signals the beginning of "Holi play," representing the play of Krishna and Radha, and a carnival atmosphere rapidly develops. Boys run about dousing people with mud and cow dung water; staid women dump buckets of buffalo urine on men's heads; colored water is thrown around on everyone; erotic dances portraying passion and copulation take place; many people drink *bhang* (marijuana) mixed with sweetened milk; and every street reverberates with hymn singing and shouts of Holi joy. Holi is a time of license and frenzy, negating the tight structure and rules of ordinary society, providing a catharsis for high-born and low-born alike. Marriott offers this interpretation:

> The dramatic balancing of Holi—the world destruction and world renewal, the world pollution followed by world purification—occurs not only on the abstract level of structural principles, but also in the person of each participant. Under the tutelage of Krishna, each person plays and for the moment may experience the role of his opposite: the servile wife acts the domineering husband, and vice versa; the ravisher acts the ravished; the menial acts the master; the enemy acts the friend; the strictured youths act the rulers of the republic . . . Each may thereby learn to play his own routine roles afresh, surely with renewed understanding, possibly with greater grace, perhaps with a reciprocating love.[2]

Pilgrimages: Experiencing the Sacred Geography of Mother India

To be a Hindu is to live in India and celebrate the presence of sacred power at the various holy places. Some holy places are naturally beautiful or awe-inspiring sites, such as rivers and mountains; others commemorate the exploits of gods and saints—and often the two types coincide. Like people of other religions, Hindus find it very spiritually rewarding to make pilgrimages to these holy places. A pilgrimage is a passage from the ordinary world of daily life to the world of the sacred. The pilgrimage begins with rituals of separation: shaving the head, putting on special clothes, and physically leaving the familiar neighborhood for a perilous journey. The journey itself represents a liminal, in-between state when the ordinary structures of social life are lifted. People walk in groups with little attention to social status and caste. Hymn-singing, popular religious recitations, and sleeping in makeshift tents all contribute to the sense of crossing the threshold from the profane to the sacred. At the pilgrimage center the pilgrims appropriate the sacred power through rituals and through the very fact of being there, receiving the *darshana* (seeing) of the deity or deities enshrined there. They gain personal merit, derive special benefits such as expiation for wrongdoing or healing. And when they return home they are reincorporated in their own community, with an enhanced personal status.

All over India there are thousands of these sacred places, some visited regularly, some only at certain times—the famous Kumbha Mela festival in Allahabad, for example, is held only once every twelve years, when it attracts millions of pilgrims. Important among the sacred places known as Dhamas (abodes of god) is Mt. Kailasa high in the Himalayas, the celestial abode of Shiva and Parvati. Another is Puri, on a beach on the Bay of Bengal, the abode of Krishna as Jagannath (Lord of the World). The great car festival at Puri commemorates Krishna's journey to Mathura to slay wicked Kamsa. To have *darshana* of the great image on the chariot (a chariot some forty-five feet high and supported by sixteen wheels each seven feet in diameter) provides great power for salvation.

There are also many sacred cities for pilgrims, the most sacred perhaps being Banaras (Kashi), the City of Light. Banaras is especially holy as the residence of Shiva and Parvati, but Vishnu and almost all the gods and goddesses are also present within the circle of this city. And the River Ganges flows through the city. Mother Ganga, the River of Heaven, agreed to flow on earth for the restoring of human life; Shiva caught the Ganges in his hair as she fell so the earth would not be shattered by her torrential force. Coming to Banaras, taking *darshana* of the sacred places of Shiva, Vishnu, and the other gods and goddesses, and bathing in the waters of the sacred Ganges provide great blessing, the salvation of the dead, and the purification of the living. Another of the sacred cities is Mathura, loved by millions of Hindus as the birthplace of Krishna.

Rituals of the Passages of Life

The critical changes in life, such as birth, puberty, marriage, and death, are times when special rituals are needed to bring blessing and renewal. For this purpose Hindus have a series of *samskaras*, rituals of the rounds of life, focused on the individual's life changes but involving the community as well.

Samskaras: Rituals of the Life Cycle

Among the many prebirth rituals, some Hindus observe a "male-producing rite" and a rite for a healthy pregnancy called the "parting of the hair": the husband parts his wife's hair and applies a mark of red cosmetic powder as protection from malevolent spirits. About ten days after birth comes the important naming rite, and at about three years there is the first haircut, leaving only the sacred tuft, which some high-caste Hindus do not cut for the rest of their lives.

The great event for Hindu boyhood (for males of the upper "twice-born" classes) is the *upanayana* (initiation) ceremony. Usually performed when the boy is between eight and twelve, the initiation ceremony is the ritual introduction of the boy to his Vedic teacher (guru), who drapes the sacred thread over the boy's shoulder and chest, to be worn thereafter as the mark of a twice-born Hindu. The boy is now qualified to begin study of the Vedas, having died to the world of childhood and been reborn to the realm of responsibility. The initiation ritual is a joyous family and communal affair.

Another climatic family and communal celebration is marriage (*vivaha*), consisting of a series of rituals symbol-

Elaborate rituals in the Hindu wedding ceremony.

izing this important passage of life. The wedding ceremony has the same kind of importance in a young girl's life as a young boy's initiation into the student stage. Parents arrange a suitable match and solemnize it with a betrothal. On the wedding day, chosen with the help of an astrologist, the bridegroom and relatives go to the bride's house, where brahmin priests conduct the special wedding rituals. Holding the bride's hand before the sacred fire, the groom says, "I seize thy hand for the sake of happiness, that thou mayest live to old age with me, thy husband. . . . The Heaven I, the Earth thou. Come let us marry." The bride places her foot on a stone to symbolize firmness, and the ends of their garments are knotted together. The most binding part of the ceremony is the seven steps, during which the husband says, "May you take one step for sap, second step for juice (or vigor), third step for the thriving of wealth, fourth step for comfort, fifth step for offspring, sixth step for seasons, may you be my friend with your seventh step!"[3] The husband touches his bride over the heart and paints the vermillion cosmetic mark on her forehead. In the evening they go out under the sky to look at the unchanging Pole Star, a symbol of faithfulness in their marriage.

After a person dies, he or she is washed and freshly clothed. Then quickly relatives and friends form a procession with the body to the cremation grounds, led by the eldest son of the deceased. The body is placed on a pyre of wood and the son sets it aflame with an ancient prayer to Agni to convey the soul to the place of the ancestors. The mourners recite verses urging the dead person to join the ancestral spirits, leaving sin behind and avoiding the dogs of Yama. After the cremation the mourners depart without turning around and take a purifying bath before entering their homes. Three days later is the bone-gathering ritual, and the eldest son will take them to the River Ganges or some other water symbolic of the Ganges. The final rituals are the shraddhas, the offering of cakes of rice and water together with the recitation of sacred verses, nourishing the departed on the journey to the realm of ancestors. These rituals continue for twelve days as a symbolic year.

Rituals of Spiritual Transformation

For some few who have reached a high spiritual level of perfection, an important ritual of spiritual passage is the act of becoming a sannyasin, the fourth and final stage of life in the traditional system, the dramatic spiritual break that comes when a person decides it is time to renounce the world. He gives away all his possessions and performs his own funeral rituals, shaves his head, clips his nails, and takes a purifying bath. Performing his householder rites for the last time, he bids farewell to his family and walks away without looking back—never to mention or think of his family and village again. Now he lives as a wandering beggar, roving about freely. To help reach final perfection, the sannyasin may take a guru who gives him the final initiation, tearing off the sacred thread and cutting the tuft of hair—no longer is he bound by rules of caste or duties of social position. Now his one duty is to seek liberation.

The renouncer practices many rituals of meditation and yoga to work toward final liberation. But many Hindus who remain in society also practice these yogic rituals of self-transformation. These are generally individual rituals, often performed under the guidance of a guru, designed to master one's physiological system and tap into the deeper spiritual resources. The rituals are varied, including bodily posture and breath control, ritual chanting of mantras, sitting within a circle of fire, and much more.

Sacred Art in Hinduism

As in other traditional cultures, so also in Hinduism nearly all art is religious to some extent. The monistic vision of Hinduism means that the sacred is present in everything, so the function of art is to help us "see" the sacred. Hinduism is a strongly visual and sensuous religion. The sacred is present in this world and thus all the senses can be means of experiencing it. We see the sacred in the image, we touch the sacred by feeling the image, we hear the sacred sounds, we taste the sacred in the prasad and liquid offerings, and we smell the sacred by means of flowers and incense. Hindu religion is the cultivation of *aesthesis*, "perceiving" the sacred through sensuous forms. Further, Hindu art excels in elaboration and embellishment, to express the divine reality of the world in its full, ideal, perfected form.

The literary arts have been central in Hinduism since the ancient Sanskrit poems of the Vedas, and the art of chanting the sacred sounds is still important. The epics and mythic literature, telling of the deeds of the heroes and the gods and goddesses, have been a vast artistic treasury from which Hindu artists have drawn their inspiration for many centuries. The literary art has flourished especially in devotional poetry, in the poems and hymns of God-intoxicated poets and saints, both in Sanskrit and especially in the vernacular dialects. There is a vast assortment of Sanskrit hymns of adoration and supplication embedded in the epics, puranas, tantras, and other sacred works, or arising independently. Composed all over India, the poems are addressed to forms of Vishnu, Shiva, and Devi, and also many other gods and goddesses. Jayadeva's *Gitagovinda* (late twelfth century) is a Sanskrit masterpiece, unfolding the drama of love between Krishna and Radha. Poet-saints in south India roamed the countryside with Tamil poems in praise of Shiva or Vishna. In north India Hindu bhakti poetry in Hindi and Bengali is widely known. Chaitanya (1486–1533) popularized the practice of singing ecstatic songs in praise of Krishna/Vishnu, and Ramprasad Sen (1718–1775) composed powerful poems to the Great Goddess.

Very characteristic of Hindu art is the sculpture or painting of the gods and goddesses. The creation of an image is an act of religious discipline or yoga on the part of the artist. The artist must see into the divine so that he or she can present the sacred in visual form, that others can take *darshana*—see and experience the sacred presence. The divine image *(murti)* is the instrument that allows the believer to catch a reflection of the deity who transcends what the eye can see but who is present during worship. A most popular artistic creation is the image of Vishnu as he lies sleeping on his cosmic serpent in the period prior to the creation of the world for the new world cycle. The artistic portrayal represents the endless cycle of the worlds, inhaled and exhaled as it were by Vishnu, who is represented as relaxed and serene, the eternal sacred reality.

In another well-known portrayal, Vishnu stands erect, with his four arms (most Hindu images have more than two arms) holding his four main symbols: the conch, wheel, mace, and lotus. The conch, a shell from the deep ocean with its structure spiraling from a single point, represents the origin of the universe. The lotus flower stands for the universe unfolding from the waters of creation.

Ten-armed Ganesha image, from the eighth century.

Time, with its cycle of seasons, is represented in the wheel; and the mace symbolizes powerful knowledge. The four attributes are placed differently in different images (a total of twenty-four varieties), defining the special emanations of Vishnu for the needs of the worshiper.

Another class of iconography includes many images of Shiva, visualizing both his grace and his destructive terror. He is pictured as the great Yogin, as the protector of all animals, as the celestial bridegroom embracing his consort, as the great Lord of wholeness whose right half is male and left half female. Other images portray Shiva as a naked young beggar or, again, an emaciated skeletal god. A favorite image is the dancing Shiva, Nataraja, the great

God simultaneously dancing out the destruction and the creation of the world. He dances in a fiery circle, with a drum and flame in his upper hands—the drum sound symbolizing the beginning of creation, and the flame representing the destruction of the world. His raised foot shows freedom from gravity and all limitations.

Devi, the Great Goddess, the energy and power of all gods, is often portrayed wielding weapons. A widely known image is that of Durga beheading the mighty buffalo demon, her archenemy. Some images show her in divine beauty. Others portray her in a shape of horror as the bloodthirsty Kali, with a necklace of heads and a girdle of severed arms, wielding a bloody sword and holding the severed head of the demon.

Such artistic images, in countless forms throughout India, present the divine realities for us to "see," without words of explanation. Fiercely ascetic and terrifying images, voluptuous and colorful paintings—there is no limitation on presenting the sacred through images in Hinduism.

Another important art form for Hindus is dance drama, in which the actors pattern their movements on the gestures and movements of the gods and goddesses. In the great religious festivals, they perform the lila (play) of the gods to the audience in tangible form, identifying with the divine models they portray. Through this artistic creation the audience is able to experience rasa, the flavor of sacred presence within our human world.

Performances of Ramlila, dance-drama celebrating the life cycle of Rama, are widespread in India. His birth, his coronation, the banishing of Sita his faithful wife, and other aspects of Rama's life are enacted nightly over a period of twenty days. The young boys playing the parts of Rama and his brothers are treated as divine images for the duration of the drama.

Dramas enacting the Krishna stories are very popular in India, with Krishna, Radha, and the cowherdesses (gopis) played by young boys, or, in other cases, young girls. New episodes are presented every day in this lila, culminating in the rasa, the ancient circular dance with Krishna standing in the center and the cowherdesses surrounding. The rasa provides a highly ecstatic experience, and members of the audience prostrate themselves before the young dancers, worshiping them as icons of Krishna and Radha.

A very characteristic Hindu art form is the temple, the sacred architecture that fixes the sacred centers of the world, functioning as earthly dwellings of the gods and goddesses. Hindu temples are designed on the model of the square, reflecting the final perfection and order of divine space in contrast to the temporary, changing earthly spaces. A typical temple has a holy center or garbha (womb), which houses the image from which power radiates. The rest of the temple surrounds that center just as the human body surrounds the inner soul or atman. Many temples have great towers, representing a cosmic mountain to which one might ascend to the presence of the sacred. Other temples lead the worshiper into the depths, to the womb or navel of the cosmos from which the god sends out sacred power.

SOCIETY AND ETHICAL LIFE

How should we live? When one says she is Hindu, this means she belongs to Hindu society by birth, finding her place in that complicated, unchanging structure of society that all Hindus instinctively understand. So important is the Hindu societal system that it was long believed one could not really be a Hindu outside India—that is, outside traditional Hindu society. It is within this society that one finds one's place and knows how to live the good life.

The Structure of Hindu Society

Well known throughout the world is the unique Hindu social structure, the so-called caste system. It is certainly one of the distinguishing marks of Hinduism, rooted in the ancient scriptures and made prolific during the Middle Ages. Though caste discrimination is officially outlawed in modern times, for many Hindus this system still is a powerful and stable structure in their lives.

Origins and Development of the Class System

Whereas the caste system is well known throughout the world, it is often misunderstood. What is sometimes simply called the "caste system" is really made up of two social structures merged together: the varna (color) class divisions and the jati (birth) caste divisions. There are only four (or five) classes (varnas), but over two thousand castes (jatis) in Hindu society. Let us look first at the traditional class system.

As we noted earlier, one reason Hindu social structure is so highly respected and remains unchanged is that its origin is in the eternal Dharma, the order of the world. The four classes, into which all people enter according to their birth, are defined in terms of their religious and social duties.

The brahmins are the highest varna; their duty is primarily to study and teach Vedic learning and preside over the important rituals and sacrifices. The traditional duty of the kshatriya (warrior) varna is the protection of the people and the administration of a beneficial government. Today in India the Rajputs, for example, represent this class. The vaishya (producer) varna is to provide for the economic needs of the community. Today vaishyas are mainly businesspeople. These three upper classes are "twice-born" in that boys go through the initiation ceremony and receive the sacred thread. Thus all three classes are expected to study the Vedas.

The lowest class is the shudra varna, the menials, whose one profession is to serve the upper three. They are often domestic servants, doing work that is forbidden for the other classes. They cannot hear or study the Vedas, but they are permitted to participate in the path of bhakti. Hindu tradition places a fifth class below these four classes, called the untouchables or outcastes, people without varna. These people generally are to live outside the boundaries of cities and perform extremely polluting activities. Untouchables have to avoid contact with people of higher castes lest they pollute them; their occupations include fishermen, hunters, leatherworkers, sweepers, handlers of dead bodies, and the like.

The Structure of Castes (Jati)

Another social structure is superimposed on the class system to make up the characteristic subdivisions within Hindu society. This is the jati (birth) system of castes, subdivided into at least two thousand jatis, some very large, others little more than a group of families in a village. Each jati by tradition belongs to one of the four classes or the untouchable class. A jati is usually characterized by three restrictions on its members: endogamy, commensality, and occupational exclusivity. A jati is al-ways endogamous, that is, one is permitted to marry only within one's own jati—a rule that still today is very widely observed throughout traditional Hindu society. Commensality means eating only with others of one's caste. And these castes are usually occupational groups, following a particular calling that has been handed down over the generations within the families that make up the caste.

One of the primary religious concerns in daily life is to maintain ritual purity, especially for the higher castes, otherwise they cannot perform their religious duties. There are complex rules about contacts between the castes, and settlement patterns are set up to minimize such contacts. When contact must be made, as at a village council meeting, seating is arranged so that the higher castes are elevated and distant from the lower castes.

All this seems very complicated. But Hindus know exactly where they belong in the caste system, and moreover they know how the castes are to be ranked and how people of each caste relate to the other castes. Each of the varna classes contains a large number of castes. There are perhaps hundreds of brahmin castes, for example, engaged in various occupations, and they rank each other, giving rise to the saying that where there are seven brahmins there will be seven cooking fires, each one believing himself or herself higher in the caste system and thus refusing to eat with someone lower.

For all its negative features, especially for the lower castes and the untouchables, the caste system provides a strong sense of security and identity. People know for sure where they belong. Their caste gives them a definite place in society, protects them, and makes it unnecessary for them to compete for higher places. Since it is accepted that one's caste is determined by one's past karma, there is no reason to be bitter about one's lot or to envy others.

Religious Leaders in Hinduism

Even though many brahmins pursue occupations other than being priests, the brahmin class is honored with special religious functions. Those brahmins who become priests have an important function for all in Hindu society, according to the Vedas. Even though some classes and castes cannot hear the Vedas or participate in Vedic rituals, the chanting of the Vedas and the performing of the rituals brings benefit across the board, maintaining the order of the world and society. Some brahmin priests are household priests, that is, they perform rituals and important ceremonies for various families. Other brahmins are temple priests, making their services available for the rituals and festivals centered in the temple for the benefit of the community. Another important function for learned brahmins is in teaching the Vedas.

Religious leaders in Hinduism include many other holy men and women who pursue the higher path of knowledge and who teach others in the many ashrams (retreats) scattered throughout India. The guru or learned person is one who has come to have deep insight into the truth and perhaps has attained a high level of spiritual realization, sometimes even recognized as God-realized or as an incarnation of one of the great gods. The widely revered saint Ramakrishna was one such spiritual master. Sri Aurobindo, a modern religious thinker, also founded an ashram for the study of yoga. In general there is high respect for those holy men and women who leave the world to advance their own spirituality and seek enlightenment. Even if they are simple wanderers seemingly doing nothing of benefit for the rest of society, they are supplying a continuous model and reminder of the high path toward moksha (liberation).

We need to add a word specifically about women's leadership roles in Hinduism. It is abundantly clear, from our discussion so far, that women generally play a subordinate role in Hindu society, and therefore leadership roles tend to be restricted to spheres like family and specifically women's roles and rituals. Yet this is not completely the case. There certainly are some powerful divine models for women's active participation in ultimate matters. There is Devi, the Great Goddess, in all her powerful forms, the energizing power of all the gods, the nurturer and the destroyer together. Radha, beloved of Krishna, and Sita, loyal wife of Rama, provide additional models for virtue and strength of character manifested by women.

There are numerous women gurus and spiritual leaders—even some who have performed priestly roles, much to the consternation of the more traditionally minded. One well-known woman guru in Madras is Shri Jnanananda Saraswati, called Ma ("mother") by her disciples and devotees. She is also called Satguru ("true guru"), in recognition of her high spiritual status as a guru who is also a sannyasin, a fully-realized spiritual teacher.

While there are gender differences between men and women, according to her, they do not relate directly to the attainment of full realization. Charles White reports on the kind of spiritual leadership she provides, for both men and women:

> On March 29, 1979, Satguru granted me a great privilege in allowing me to sit with her on the first of two evenings while she gave *darshan* to her Indian disciples individually or in small, mainly family, groups. In all, I saw and listened to about forty persons during these exchanges. At least for now Ma is able to see personally most of the people who approach her. What an experience of relief this intimate discussion of problems must be to hard-pressed individuals who discover Ma, the loving mother, in the torturing crosscurrents of Indian life! Nevertheless, she does not always say what one would prefer to hear. For Satguru may also be regarded by her disciples as the incarnate goddess, Rajarajeshwari. . . . Her motherliness, therefore, is in a different category altogether from ordinary human motherliness. [4]

Among the many people who took darshan of the Satguru and received spiritual counsel from her were, among others, a young man with job difficulties, a young woman in a deep depression, a middle-aged woman whose daughters-in-law had thrown her out of the house, an athletic young man who worked for the Defense Department, an intellectual who could not bring himself to surrender completely, and a young society girl who rushed in to see Ma Jnanananda between jet flights.

Many women in India today are spiritually accomplished, with education and public life more available to them. For example, in this male-centered society, Indira Gandhi (1917–1984) arose to the highest political and moral leadership as prime minister, internationally known and respected as a compelling leader and spokesperson for India, until her assassination by extremists. As women's lives and women's leadership become more central, the promise of Hinduism as the eternal Dharma, the path that leads toward wholeness and ultimate liberation, will become more practical and available.

Living According to the Dharma

How should we live? Hinduism is suited for people with different temperaments and spiritual abilities; there is a place for everyone, with appropriate duties and ethical requirements. The ethical life is based on the major principles of Hindu society, namely, the class system (varnas), the four stages of life (ashramas), and the four aims of human life (purusharthas). The ethical life based on this pattern is spelled out in the classical writings and commentaries called *Dharma Sutras* and *Dharma Shastras*, the best known of which is the Law-code of Manu. Further, both the Mahabharata and the Ramayana Epics provide a broad and deep foundation for living out these Hindu ethical values.

The Centrality of Dharma for Hindu Ethics

The concept of Dharma, as discussed above, is central to the Hindu understanding of society. Dharma comprises comprehensive precepts having to do with the material sustenance and the spiritual welfare of human society and of the individual.

The Dharma includes universal ethical values that apply to everyone. For example, there are certain acts forbidden to everyone, such as disrespect for one's parents. And there are obligations that are common to all by reason of the human status, such as the obligation to act nonviolently. The Srimad Bhagavatam states, "Avoidance of injury to all beings, love of truthfulness and chastity, abhorrence of stealing, refraining from anger and greed, striving to be of service to all beings—these are the universal duties of all castes."[5]

But for our human life the Dharma touches most concretely where we live and work in society, as it organizes our life through well-defined social classes and through stages of individual life. In its narrow sense, Hindu tradition has often equated the Dharma with *varna-ashrama-dharma*, that is, the ordained duties (dharma) of the four classes and the four stages of life. Our discussion of Hindu ethics can focus on this center field of the Hindu sense of the good life.

Ethical Life Based on the Classes and Castes

How should we live? The first answer is very direct: one should live in the way expected of one in the particular class and caste. The Law-code of Manu spells out in detail the duties of the four traditional classes. The duty of living according to one's class (varna) is commonly extended to include also the obligations, requirements, and prescriptions that belong to the particular occupational caste (jati) into which a person was born. The good life means abiding by the rules of one's caste about marriage, dining, occupation, and clothing. It means above all to avoid polluting the purity of one's caste and of the larger community by wrongful contact with those of other castes.

The ethical vision expressed in the caste system is widely misunderstood by non-Hindus. A chief ingredient in this system is the idea of maintaining caste purity, and it is true that this purity has a hierarchical order, for one brings pollution on his own caste by contact with someone of a lower caste. But it is important to understand that purity is a vital possession of the whole community, not just of one caste. Brahmins do have a special responsibility for maintaining the purity of the community because they study and teach the Vedas and perform the Vedic rituals—an activity of extreme importance for the whole society—and they cannot perform this service if they are polluted by contact with lower castes. But the purity of the community is also maintained by the people of lower jatis, such as the shudras and untouchables who wash clothes, cut hair, carry away garbage, and remove dead animals. The whole community is diminished by a breakdown of purity in its midst, but likewise the whole community is enriched by the purity, solidarity, cooperation, and contribution structured through the traditional caste system.

It is widely recognized by modern Hindu leaders that aspects of the caste system, such as the obligation to engage in the occupation of one's father or the practice of untouchability, seem to be in conflict with the basic Hindu ethical vision. Modern Indian law does not permit discrimination on the basis of caste, and untouchables are permitted to enter temples, sit in movie theatres, and eat in public restaurants. Gandhi took particular care for the untouchables in his movement to reform India, calling them Harijans (children of God) and himself engaging in unclean jobs reserved for the untouchables. Today efforts are being made to help those of the lower castes to improve their lot in modern society. But the Hindu ethical system remains based on the fundamental truth that one's birth is not an accident. It was determined by karmic causes from one's past existences in the samsara cycle. I am where I belong. Therefore the good and noble life consists of living according to my dharma, following the life prescribed for me by my caste.

This is not to say that life is completely free of ethical conflicts. The Mahabharata Epic contains the famous story of King Yudhishthira, who feels bitter inner conflict over his duty as a warrior-king and his higher vision of nonviolence and detachment. Yudhishthira wants to withdraw from life in the world and become a forest-dweller, for he knows that if he continues to live in the world as king he will have to inflict violence and pain on others. But King Yudhishthira did fulfill his duty, encouraged to do so by none other than Lord Krishna, waiting until he had grown old before he finally abandoned the world. So Hindus respect the duties assigned by birth, knowing that the path of liberation ultimately leads beyond duties of class and caste.

The Four Stages of Life

Another key to living the good life is to be observant of the duties and opportunities incumbent in the different stages of life. Hinduism recognizes that the principles that bring a healthy and fulfilled human life change throughout the course of a lifetime, and thus the Dharma scriptures put forth the ideal of four stages of life, at least for males of the higher three classes. In the traditional system, the shudra and untouchable classes do not participate in the movement through different stages of life. Women also did not traditionally move through these stages in a direct way, at least not the student stage. But women certainly share in these stages insofar as they are related to the males in their families. The four stages of life are the stages of student, householder, forest-dweller, and renouncer (sannyasin).

The first stage of life is that of being a student, with the obligations of studying the Vedas, cultivating respect for one's teacher, developing self-control, and learning to be a contributing member of Hindu society. Brahmin boys of eight years of age, and kshatriya and vaishya boys of eleven or twelve, are to begin their student life with the ritual of initiation, after which traditionally they go to study with their teachers. In past times, girls were educated in the home to be wife, mother, and homemaker. The student stage is a rigorous way of life, learning rituals, values, duties, and patterns of behavior. The student is to remain celibate, ritually pure, begging for food, and acting as personal servant to the teacher.

Upon completing the period of being a student, the person moves on to the stage of householder, the keystone of Hindu life and society and an essential stage of personal spiritual development. Some few, it is true, seem spiritually prepared to omit this householder stage and pass immediately to the ascetic rigors of the renouncer stage of life, close to final liberation. But for almost all people, the householder stage is necessary and beneficial. During this major period of one's life, Hindu ethics require a happy, productive, ritually observant way of life. People should marry and raise children to continue the line. As householders they perform the proper sacrifices and rituals, maintain a ritually pure home, and engage in economic and political activity.

In the householder stage the woman's role, according to the Dharma scriptures, is significantly different from the man's role. The wife is subject to the husband and should serve him, not presuming to eat, for example, until after he is finished. At the same time, the husband is required to honor his wife and protect her. The Law-code of Manu states,

> Women must be honored and adored by their fathers, brothers, husbands, and brothers-in-law who desire great good fortune. . . .
> Her father protects her in childhood, her husband protects her in youth, her sons protect her in old age—a woman does not deserve independence.
> The father who does not give away his daughter in marriage at the proper time is censurable; censurable is the husband who does not approach his wife in due season; and after the husband is dead, the son, verily, is censurable, who does not protect his mother. . . .
> The husband should engage his wife in the collection and expenditure of his wealth, in cleanliness, in dharma [religious rituals], in cooking food for the family, and in looking after the necessities of the household. . . .
> Women destined to bear children, enjoying great good fortune, deserving of worship, the resplendent lights of homes on the one hand and divinities of good luck who reside in the houses on the other—between these there is no difference whatsoever.[6]

Deserving no independence and serving her family, on the one hand, and being honored as a goddess on the other—

these are the two sides of the woman's role in traditional Hinduism. The pressure for offspring and for marrying daughters led to marriages involving child-brides. And the notion of self-sacrifice for one's husband sometimes led to the practice of young widows immolating themselves on the funeral pyres of their husbands—becoming thereby *sati* (sometimes called *suttee* in Western languages), a true woman who sacrifices bodily existence for the higher spiritual duty. Modern reforms have mostly put a stop to these practices.

"When a householder sees his skin wrinkled and his hair gray and when he sees the son of his son, then he should resort to the forest."[7] Having reached the end of the productive householder stage, one should go into spiritual retirement and become a "forest-dweller." That is, a man together with his wife retires to a forest retreat (ashram), or at least to quiet quarters within the family residence, to devote themselves to self-discipline, study, and meditation. The responsibilities of home management and business are turned over to the children, though the retirees may still be available for consultation. Abstaining from sex is recommended for this stage, as the withdrawal from householder life becomes more and more complete.

The final stage of life is that of the sannyasin, the "renouncer" who breaks all ties to enter the last part of the path toward liberation. "Having thus passed the third part of his life in the forest, he should renounce all attachments to worldly objects and become an ascetic during the fourth part of his life. . . . He should always wander alone, without any companion, in order to achieve spiritual perfection."[8] Those few who reach this stage of spiritual perfection have dissolved all sense of selfish needs and desires, and therefore, although beyond caste and not involved in society, they demonstrate the highest ethical values as a model for all others.

> He will patiently bear with hard words, despising none, nor out of attachment to the body will he bear enmity to anyone. To one who is angry with him he will not show anger in return, and him that curses him he will bless, nor will he utter any untrue word. . . . By curbing the senses, by destroying affection and hatred, by doing no harm to any living thing, he will conform himself to deathlessness.[9]

Most people will not reach the stage of sannyasin in this existence, but having that model before our eyes helps us to live out our own roles in the proper ethical perspective.

The Four Aims of Human Life

Hindus have traditionally summed up the vision of the good life by speaking of the four aims of human life (*purushartha*). These four good values of life that we should seek after are Dharma, material prosperity (*artha*), pleasure (*kama*), and liberation (*moksha*). This is a well-balanced ethical structure, verified by centuries of experience, designed to balance the concern for good life and happiness with the concern for spiritual development and liberation.

Of course, the balance of these four aims of life differs depending on one's particular stage of life. Fulfilling the Dharma is something that should always be central, for this is the key to how the individual's life in its different stages fits into the total order of reality. Seeking material prosperity is especially important at the householder stage, for involvement in business and politics is the foundation on which the whole society rests. Likewise, seeking pleasure and happiness is most directly appropriate at the householder stage, for without sexual pleasure and physical happiness the life of the family could not go on. Liberation (*moksha*) is understood to be the spiritual goal throughout one's life, but it becomes a more central concern in the forest-dweller stage of retirement, and one who reaches the *sannyasin* stage makes it his total and exclusive concern.

The Hindu Vision for Society and the World

It is sometimes said that Hinduism has no concern for the betterment of society, since it places so much stress on withdrawal from the world of senses and on individual meditation and pursuit of liberation. And it is true that Hinduism never developed the notion of having a mission to the whole world in the sense of spreading Hinduism to all. Yet the Hindu tradition does in its own way display deep concern for the welfare of the whole social order, and some modern Hindus have utilized those resources to improve the lot of all in society. The Hindu values of peace and nonviolence have made an impact on the whole world, and in modern times some Hindu thinkers have taken up the mission of transmitting the spiritual wisdom of India to the rest of humankind.

Worshipers strain to pull huge chariots with Lord Jagannath, Lord of the Universe, during a popular annual festival.

Toward the Betterment of Human Society

One perspective sees all life caught up in endless cycles of samsara, each lifetime determined by the karma of preceding ones, with the final goal being liberation from the whole cycle. This is the perspective of moksha. But another perspective complements this one, the perspective of Dharma. This present order has its own value and importance, and to maintain and promote the Dharma of this world is to enhance the welfare of all beings.

This is why the householder stage is so central, for the proper fulfilment of this role contributes significantly to the preservation and happiness of the whole community. The fact that one of the four aims of life is material success (*artha*), involvement in the economic and political life of the society, shows that working toward the general welfare of all is a central Hindu concern. In fact, all the basic values and duties, such as respect for parents and maintenance of caste purity, prevent social breakdown and corruption and thus work toward the welfare of the whole society.

A major theme of the Hindu ethical tradition is compassion toward others, doing good for the benefit of others. The Mahabharata teaches,

> He succeeds in obtaining happiness who practises abstention from injuring (others), truthfulness of speech, honesty

towards all creatures, and forgiveness, and who is never heedless. Hence one exercising one's intelligence should dispose one's mind after training it to peace towards all creatures. That man who regards the practice of the virtues enumerated above as the highest duty, as conducive to the happiness of all creatures, and as destructive of all kinds of sorrow, is possessed of the highest knowledge and succeeds in obtaining happiness.[10]

In modern times reform movements have drawn on the spirit of the Hindu tradition to better society by doing away with some evils that had developed within the tradition, such as child marriage, widows burning themselves, the subordinate role of women generally, and the cruel lot of the untouchables. Mahatma Gandhi and others worked tirelessly against the evil of untouchability. Gandhi thought the class system, however, could still be the structure of society, for the classes are duties, not privileges, and those of the higher classes are more responsible for the welfare of all. The hallmarks of Gandhi's ethical vision are simplicity, austerity, and nonviolence, and he felt these values could create the good life not only for Indian society but for other societies as well:

> There are two aspects of Hinduism. There is, on the one hand, the historical Hinduism with its Untouchability, superstitious worship of sticks and stones, animal sacrifices and so on. On the other, we have the Hinduism of the *Gita*, the *Upanishads*, and Patanjali's *Yoga Sutras*, which is the acme of *Ahimsa* [nonviolence] and oneness of all creation, pure worship of one immanent, formless, imperishable God. *Ahimsa*, which for me is the chief glory of Hinduism, has been sought to be explained away by our people as being meant for the *sannyasi* only. I do not think so. I hold that it is *the* way of life and India has to show it to the world.[11]

The possibility of reconciliation and peace through nonviolent means and through spiritual discipline and practice, as demonstrated by Gandhi and many others like him, has made a powerful impression on people of other cultures who are searching for a way to reverse the escalation of violence and materialism in the world.

Hinduism's Message for the World

Hinduism is not a missionary religion. It is fundamental to Hinduism to believe that there are many spiritual paths, appropriate to different peoples depending on their own past karma and spiritual perfection, and the idea of converting others to Hinduism does not fit with this. Yet Hindus do believe that the Vedas, as the Eternal Wisdom, present the truth in an ultimate way not found in any other religious path.

In modern times, under pressure from other religions like Islam and Christianity, some Hindu thinkers have attempted to reassert the primacy of Vedic Hinduism. For example, Dayananda Sarasvati, founder of the Arya Samaj, not only rejected many aspects of Hinduism that he felt conflicted with the Vedas but also took an aggressive and militant approach to other religions. He argued that Christian belief was logically inconsistent and that the Quran presents a God unworthy of worship. Some members of this group engaged in attempts to gain Hindu converts from among Muslims.

On the other hand, other modern thinkers, like Sarvepalli Radhakrishnan, have responded to the challenge of Christianity and other religions by seeking out the universalist aspects of these religions that would be in keeping with the Vedantic teachings. Radhakrishnan argued that whereas Hinduism is the ultimate truth of religion, it is a truth that can be universally accepted by all. He brought his Hindu philosophy to the West through lectures and books, teaching that each religion is valid to the degree that it helps its followers achieve spiritual realization:

> If the Hindu chants the Vedas on the banks of the Ganges, if the Chinese meditates on the Analects, if the Japanese worships on the image of the Buddha, if the European is convinced of Christ's mediatorship, if the Arab reads the Quran in his mosque, and if the African bows down to a fetish, each one of them has exactly the same reason for his particular confidence. Each form of faith appeals in precisely the same way to the inner certitude and devotion of its followers. It is their deepest apprehension of God and God's fullest revelation to them. The claim of any religion to validity is the fact that only through it have its followers become what they are.[12]

Some Hindu groups today, such as the International Society for Krishna Consciousness, take the stance that Hinduism is the exclusive highest truth, and they bring it to the West as part of their commitment to this truth. Other modern Hindu thinkers follow the tradition that truth is found in many paths. Convinced that Hinduism still is the highest of these many paths, many Hindus do feel a responsibility to help peoples in the rest of the world to become acquainted with the ancient wisdom, come to understand it, and incorporate its basic truths into their lives also. The world society will become enriched, they feel, more spiritual, and more peaceful if the perspective of Hinduism is better understood and appreciated.

DISCUSSION QUESTIONS

1. Why do the Vedic sacrificial rituals have such great prestige, even though people of the lower classes cannot perform them?
2. What is puja, and why is it so central to many Hindus?
3. What kind of religious experience is darshana? How is this important in activities like festivals, pilgrimage, and art?
4. Explain the class (varna) and caste (jati) systems and how they fit together in Hindu society.
5. Discuss how the story of King Yudhishthira (in the Mahabharata) illustrates the tension often expressed in Hinduism between doing one's duty (dharma) and seeking liberation (moksha).
6. Explain the four stages of life and the four aims of life, taking note also of the experiences of women.

KEY TERMS IN HINDUISM

Agni Vedic god of fire

Aryans Indo–European people who migrated into India

ashrama a stage of life in Hinduism; also a hermitage or place for meditation

atman in Hinduism, the soul or self, considered eternal

avatara descent or incarnation, especially of the great god Vishnu, as Krishna or Rama

Bhagavad Gita important Hindu scripture containing Krishna's teaching to Arjuna

bhakti devotion, self-surrender to one's god

Brahma designation for the creator god in Hindu thought

Brahman Hindu term for ultimate reality; the divine source and pervading essence of the universe

Brahmanas ritual commentaries, part of the Vedas

brahmins (brahmans) highest ranked, priestly class in Hindu society

darshana the ritual act of being granted the "seeing" of a sacred image, person, or place

Devi Goddess, sometimes meaning the Great Goddess, often under many other names

Dharma in Hinduism, the cosmic order, social duty, and proper behavior

Divali autumn festival of lights and good fortune in India

Durga great, fierce Hindu goddess, a form of Devi

Gandhi leader of the Hindu independence movement emphasizing spiritual preparation and nonviolent resistance (1869–1948)

Ganesha son of Shiva, popular elephant-headed Hindu god who overcomes obstacles and brings good fortune

guru spiritual guide and master

Holi popular festival in northern India with a carnival atmosphere

Indra Vedic storm-warrior god

Indus Valley Civilization urban-agricultural civilization that flourished in the third millennium B.C.E. and left influences on Hinduism

jati "birth"; one's caste or closed social group as determined by birth in India

Kali goddess of death and destruction in Hinduism, a form of Devi, the Great Goddess

karma "action," law that all deeds and thoughts, according to one's intentions, will have set consequences

kirtana devotional group worship through song and dance

Krishna avatara of the great Hindu god Vishnu; hero of the Bhagavad Gita and popular god in Vaishnavite devotional movements

kshatriyas the classical warrior class in Hindu society

lingam the phallic pillar that symbolizes the great Hindu god Shiva

Mahabharata one of the two great epics of Hinduism

mantra sacred word, formula, or verse

maya appearance, illusion, term to indicate that which prevents one from seeing truly

moksha liberation from bondage to samsara and karma; the goal of Hindu spiritual practice

nondualism view that ultimate reality and the phenomenal world are not different

Path of Action (karma-marga) Hindu path toward liberation based on acting according to Dharma, without desire for the fruits of action

Path of Devotion (bhakti-marga) Hindu path toward liberation based on devotional practices directed toward one's god

Path of Knowledge (jnana-marga) Hindu path toward liberation based on knowledge, emphasizing meditation

puja ritual worship of the image of a god by offering food, flowers, music, and prayers

Puranas late Hindu scriptures that developed from popular theistic devotional movements

Rama avatara of Vishnu, divine hero of the Ramayana

Ramanuja Hindu philosopher and advocate of the Vaishnavite bhakti tradition (ca. 1017–1137)

Ramayana story of Rama, one of the two great epics of Hinduism

rebirth in the religions of India, belief that after the death of its body the soul takes on another body

Rig Veda the earliest and most important collection of Vedic hymns

Samhitas "collections" of early Vedic hymns and verses; there are four collections: Rig-Veda, Sama-Veda, Yajur-Veda, and Atharva-Veda

Samkhya one of the classical schools of Hindu philosophy stressing an absolute distinction between matter and spirit

samsara the rebirth cycle of existence

samskaras rituals performed at the critical changes and passages of life

sannyasin one who has renounced the cares and concerns of the world; the fourth stage of life in Hinduism

Shakti divine energy, personified as a goddess; female aspect of a god, especially of Shiva

Shankara great philosopher of Advaita (nondual) Vedanta (788–820 C.E.)

Shiva the great ascetic Hindu god symbolized by the lingam; focus of the Shaivite devotional movement

Shruti "that which is heard," the eternal truth, that is, the Vedas

shudras classical servant class in Hindu society, the fourth class

Smriti "that which is remembered," the tradition, that is, the scriptural writings after the Vedas

Tantrism movement in Hinduism (and Buddhism) using initiation, rituals, imagination, and sexual symbolism as spiritual practices leading toward liberation

Upanishads secret teaching; collection of teachings about the self and ultimate reality that makes up the last part of the Vedas

vaishyas the classical producer-merchant class in Hindu society

varna "color," term for the classes in the classical system of Hindu society

Varuna Vedic god of the heavens

Vedanta "end of the Vedas"; influential school of philosophy based especially on the Upanishads

Vedas most important scriptures of Hinduism, the Shruti; they consist of the Samhitas, Brahmanas, Aranyakas, and Upanishads

Vishnu great Hindu god manifested in avataras, including Krishna and Rama; focus of the great Vaishnavite devotional movement

Yoga techniques of spiritual discipline for overcoming bondage to samsara, often emphasizing breathing and meditation exercises; one of the classical schools of Hindu philosophy

yoni a circular sacred image representative of the female reproductive organ, often associated with the lingam

CHAPTER 5

Buddhism: Sacred Story and Historical Context

uddhism, born in India but grown to become the light of much of Asia, shares many things with Hinduism. But the wisdom taught by Siddhartha Gautama turned Buddhism in a different direction, leading Buddhists to reject the idea of the eternal Brahman and atman (self), the authority of the Vedic scriptures, the caste system of society, and even for the most part the importance of worshiping the gods. Not unlike Christianity's turn away from the Jewish tradition and the Muslim turn from the Jewish and Christian traditions, Buddhism turned from the Vedic tradition to create a spiritual perspective very much like its sister Hinduism in so many ways—but so different in still more crucial ways. Buddhists and Hindus today can certainly recognize a family resemblance between themselves. But like relatives who have long gone in different directions, the things held to be most important are those things that are different.

THE STORY OF THE BUDDHA

Who am I? To be a Buddhist, to be on the Path of the Buddha, means to derive one's identity from the story of the Buddha, Siddhartha Gautama, who lived about 2,500 years ago in India.

Unlike Hinduism, Buddhism is a "founded" religion; a particular person and the things he did and said are the foundation of the religion. In that sense Buddhism is like Judaism, Christianity, and Islam, with the story of the founder at its heart. Whereas the Buddha was not divine or a prophet of God, he was like these founders in the sense of being the teacher and the model for the lives of his followers.

An important difference with those other founded religions is Buddhism's special sense of history in relation to ultimate reality. The fact that God is revealed in historical events and works through persons is important to Judaism, Christianity, and Islam, and thus the historical events and persons take on a special significance. Like Hinduism, Buddhism sees the historical events of this particular world age as fairly insignificant in the context of the great world cycles of samsara. Whereas Siddhartha Gautama's lifetime 2,500 years ago is indeed crucial as a model and guide, it is not necessarily the complete focus of revelation and truth. The Buddha existed many lifetimes before this, for example, and there have been other Buddhas. Historical events are part of the story; but equally important are mythological stories and revelations of eternal truth.

We must, of course, make use of scholarly historical research to provide orientation in the beginnings and development of Buddhism, but our primary interest is to understand how the sacred story is understood by Buddhists themselves as a central paradigm giving meaning and identity. Even after the master story of Siddhartha Gautama, the Buddha, some important transformations took place in Buddhism, especially in the rise of Mahayana Buddhism. And we need to look briefly at the historical shaping of the Buddhist way beyond India, the land of its birth, as Buddhism developed in unique ways in response to different local cultures. The forms of the path that developed in Sri Lanka and Southeast Asia, and also in China, Japan, and Tibet are significant for understanding what it means to be a Buddhist today.

The Sacred Biography of the Buddha

The Buddha lived in northeast India in the sixth century B.C.E., at the time when fellow sages were composing the Upanishads and thus helping to create Hinduism. This was an age of social and political instability, as small communities were giving way to larger political states. At this time some sixteen small independent states existed in north central India, but within a century after the life of the Buddha, only one empire, the Magadha, would rule this whole area. This was a most creative period, for at the same time the early Jain leaders were developing their religion, and there were other movements with new interpretations of the Vedas.

Important religious figures in this northeastern part of India were wandering ascetics who had withdrawn from society and lived in the forests. These hermits (*shramanas*) stood in a certain tension with the Brahmins, who represented the Indo–Aryan establishment. They often went about in groups, following a recognized teacher, practicing austerities, and discussing various theories about the truth of human existence. The ideas they were discussing were those found also in the Upanishads: karma, samsara, rebirth, the relation of the soul and the supreme reality, liberation, and the like. It was a time of searching, experimenting, and debating about the ultimate truths of human existence.

Among these wandering ascetics we find Siddhartha Gautama (and also Mahavira, leader of the Jains). Siddhartha searched for the truth for some years, experienced a great awakening, and became the Buddha, or "enlightened one"; then he taught a community of disciples for some forty-five years until he died. His life was in many respects not unlike that of other holy men of his time. But this teacher was different, as attested in the sacred biography. In his career, Buddhists believe, the ultimate truth for all human existence is found.

We do not know for sure when the first scriptures of Buddhism were composed or written down; Buddhist tradition says they were transmitted orally by disciples from the parinirvana (passing away) of the Buddha. The most important biographical accounts of the Buddha's life were not written until about five hundred years later, such as the very influential one by Ashvaghosha (ca. first century C.E.). Thus it is not possible to unravel the "historical" details from mythological elements. We cannot find the historical Buddha any more than the historical Jesus or the historical Moses. But the important thing is to see the sacred story as Buddhists understand it, and for that reason the legendary and mythological materials are as important as the historical facts. The story is more than just a history of certain people. It reveals the true path of life.

The Birth of the World Saviour, the Buddha

Siddhartha was born about 563 B.C.E. in a tribe in northeast India called the Shakyas, who also used the traditional name of Gautama. So Siddhartha is often simply called Gautama or Shakyamuni (wise one of the Shakyas). His parents were royalty, King Shuddhodana and Queen Maya of Kapilavastu (in present-day Nepal). There he grew up, married, and had a child, until his spiritual experiences led him to go forth at about age twenty-nine to become a wandering ascetic, searching for the truth. A story not unlike many others of his time—but this one was different, as the tradition makes clear. The life of the Buddha, like other great religious founders, is larger than life. That one human lifetime is connected with transcendental power and meaning. The birth of Siddhartha comes as the result of aeons of preparation, and his lifetime and teachings have ramifications for people of all times and places.

Reaching beyond the boundaries of human finitude, many stories tell of the previous lifetimes of the Buddha in which he achieved merit and wisdom leading finally to Buddhahood. For example, the Buddha told his disciple Ananda about a wise and compassionate prince named Mahasattva who lived in the remote past. One day, strolling in a forest, he came upon a tigress surrounded by seven small cubs. The tigress was exhausted from giving birth to the seven cubs and was weakened by hunger and thirst. Mahasattva realized that if she found no fresh meat and warm blood, she would die, so he resolved to sacrifice his own body, which, he reasoned, was doomed to perish in the end anyway. Taking a vow to sacrifice himself to win enlightenment for the welfare of the world, he threw himself down in front of the tigress. But she was so weak that she could do nothing, so he cut his own throat with a sharp piece of bamboo. Finally, when she saw his body covered with blood, she ate up all his flesh and blood and was strengthened. Concluding this story, the Buddha told Ananda: "It was I, Ananda, who at that time and on that occasion was that prince Mahasattva."[1] So through many lifetimes the Buddha-to-be grew in compassion and perfected himself in wisdom.

But finally the decisive moment came. After a lifetime in the Tushita heaven, he decided to enter the womb of pure Queen Maya of Kapilavastu to be born one final time as a human and to reach Buddhahood. In a dream Queen Maya saw four guardian angels carry her away to the Himalayan Mountains and purify her. Lying on a couch, she saw a superb white elephant approach and seemingly enter her body so that she conceived. At the conception of the Buddha the world shook, the blind, deaf, and lame were healed, all fires in hell went out, flowers fell from heaven, and many other signs appeared showing an event of world significance had happened. When the time came for Maya to give birth, she went out to the beautiful Lumbini grove, accompanied by many attendants. She gave birth standing up, and four angels placed the baby on a golden net. The young child stood, took seven steps, and said, "I am born to be enlightened for the well-being of the world; this is my last birth."[2] Learned Brahmins who were present saw the auspicious signs on his body and said that he was certain to become either the perfectly enlightened one, or else a universal monarch.

> Should he be a great, earthly sovereign, he will rule the entire world with courage and righteousness, leading all kings, as the light of the sun leads the lights of the world. If he seeks deliverance by living in a forest, he will acquire true wisdom and illumine the entire world.[3]

The Going Forth

Siddhartha's mother Maya died seven days after bearing him, and King Shuddhodana married Maya's sister Prajapati, who brought up the young prince as his foster mother. His father the king, of course, wanted him first to be a mighty king and then, perhaps, retire to the forest in his old age. From the sages he learned that if Siddhartha

saw four special sights he would abandon his life in the royal warrior family and withdraw to the forest. What are the four sights? He was told that they are four realities of human existence: a decrepit old man, a diseased man, a dead man, and a hermit monk. Wanting Siddhartha to become a great world ruler, the king ordered that none of these sights should be allowed near him, surrounding him instead with luxury, pleasure, and martial training. He built three beautiful palaces for Siddhartha, and he arranged for him to marry the lovely maiden Yashodhara, who in time bore him a son, Rahula.

The gods knew that the time for Siddhartha's enlightenment was drawing near, so they intervened, according to the story. When Siddhartha was out on an excursion in his golden chariot, the gods created an old decrepit man, and Siddhartha exclaimed, "O charioteer! Who is this man with gray hair, supported by a staff in his hand, his eyes sunken under his eyebrows, his limbs feeble and bent?" And the charioteer had to explain old age to Siddhartha, who then asked, "Will this evil come upon me also?" And the answer: "Advanced age will certainly come upon you through the inescapable force of time, no matter how long you may live."[4] The young prince sat looking at the old man for a long time, disturbed that this human process of old age indiscriminately destroys beauty and strength, and yet people in the world are not changed from their selfish pursuits by such a sight. Again, on a second excursion, the gods created a diseased man, and then thirdly a dead man, with the same shattering effect on Siddhartha. Finally he saw a hermit monk, one who has withdrawn from the world and thus is in some way above all this. And Siddhartha moved toward his own decision to withdraw to the forest and devote himself fully to searching for the truth.

But, as we all know, such decisions are not made without a struggle between conflicting values and loyalties. Siddhartha was now twenty-nine, with a wife and a son, heir to the throne of the kingdom. His father, sensing Siddhartha's inner struggle, attempted to persuade him that his duty was to fulfil the role of a householder first before withdrawing from the world in his old age. But Siddhartha countered with a metaphor that has become famous in Buddhist literature: "It is not right to hold by force a man who is anxious to escape from a burning house."[5] The king made one final attempt to keep Siddhartha from going forth to become a wandering hermit, providing the most pleasurable entertainments with dancing girls and lovely music. Siddhartha was unmoved, and as the night wore on all the women fell asleep in distorted postures and shocking poses— "some with their bodies wet with trickling phlegm and spittle; some grinding their teeth, and muttering and talking in their sleep; some with their mouths open; and some with their dress fallen apart so as plainly to disclose their loathsome nakedness."[6] Seeing all this the prince was filled with disgust and determined to go forth that very night. He bid a silent farewell to his sleeping wife Yashodhara and son Rahula. Mounting his faithful horse Kanthaka, with his servant Channa he rode to the edge of the forest, the gods having opened the palace gates that had been secured tightly by orders of his father. He cut off his hair and beard and put on the robe of a monk in place of his princely robes, instructing Channa to bring his hair and jeweled sword back to his father. Thus took place the crucial turning point in the Buddhist story, the Great Renunciation.

Unlike Christianity's founder Jesus, who was born in poverty, Siddhartha was born and grew up in riches, luxury, and power. But it is precisely these things—which we all strive for—that keep us from seeing the real nature of human existence. When Siddhartha did finally see human existence as it really is, stripped of the veneer of luxury and pleasure, he realized that the princely life was an illusion and he cast it aside, going forth to search for the truth as a forest monk.

The Attainment of Enlightenment

For the next six years Siddhartha wandered about, begging for his food and searching for the truth. He followed two teachers who taught him yogic knowledge and techniques, but, although he quickly mastered these disciplines, after a time he came to feel that this was not the path to the ultimate truth he was seeking. Then for a time he practiced the path of extreme self-mortification, like that followed by Mahavira and the Jain monks, fasting and depriving himself of even the bare necessities of life in an attempt to attain victory and release. Five other ascetic monks were attracted to his struggle, and they practiced fasting and other disciplines with him. However, near starvation, Siddhartha came to an important realization: "This is not the way to achieve passionlessness, enlightenment, liberation. . . . How can it be reached by a man who is not calm and at ease, who is so exhausted by hunger and thirst that his mind is unbalanced?"[7] Mind and body are united in this search; weakening the body means weakening the mind also. So Siddhartha resolved to follow the "middle path," avoiding the extremes of riches and luxury, on the one hand, and self-mortification, on the other.

At just that moment, inspired by the gods, a cowherd woman named Sujata brought milk-rice and offered it to the Buddha-to-be. He accepted it, bathed himself, and ate it to nourish himself for his attainment of enlightenment. The five monks abandoned him because it appeared he

The Buddha pointing to the earth. From a twelfth-century stele with scenes from the life of the Buddha.

had given up the search, but Siddhartha went alone to sit crosslegged in meditation under a wisdom (*bodhi*) tree at Bodh Gaya, making the mighty resolution, "Never from this seat will I stir, until I have attained the supreme and absolute wisdom!"[8] The struggle was on. Representing the forces of passion and death, the god Mara (Death) entered the picture, to attempt to thwart the attainment of Buddhahood. Mara is the god of worldly desires; seeing that Siddhartha was passing beyond his control, Mara brought his battle legions to overwhelm the monk, frightening even the gods. But all his awesome powers were rendered harmless by the strength of Siddhartha's meditation. Now Siddhartha pointed to the earth, calling upon it to be witness to his merit and his right to achieve Buddhahood, and the earth responded with such a deafening roar of assent that all Mara's hosts were scattered and defeated.

The greatest event in human history was taking place, and the gods and all of nature were waiting in anticipation. Siddhartha continued in the power of his meditation, and on the night of the first full moon he attained Buddhahood. In the first watch of the night he reviewed all his former existences, and then he turned his compassionate mind toward the sufferings of all beings in the unending wheel of rebirth. In the second watch of the night he attained the divine eye by which he saw the entire world as in a spotless mirror, with all beings impelled by their deeds to undergo repeated death and rebirth; and he grew in compassion. Siddhartha turned his meditation in the third watch of the night to the real nature of this world, understanding the causes of all rebirth, suffering, and death, beginning with ignorance and yearning for existence, and thus he also perceived the path leading to the cessation of all this.

> He knew what was to be known : he became a Buddha
> awoke from his meditation and saw a self nowhere in the world
>   gained the highest peace by the eightfold noble path
> I have attained this path : I have fulfilled this path
>   which the great seers followed
>   (who knew the true & the false)
>   for the benefit of others
> And in the fourth watch, when dawn appeared
>   and the whole world was tranquil

> He gained omniscience : the imperishable state
> & the earth trembled like a drunken maiden when he was enlightened
> the heavens shone with his success
>   and kettledrums sounded in the sky[9]

Turning the Wheel of the Dharma

For some time the Buddha stayed there at Bodh Gaya, looking into his own mind and knowing he had found freedom. But now the question arose as to whether this enlightenment should be shared with others. It seems the Buddha was thinking at first that humans would not be able to understand his teaching. But the god Brahma came and pleaded with him, persuading him that some beings would understand. The Buddha surveyed the whole world with his Buddha eye, and he had compassion for all living things, deciding to teach this way of liberation to the world. Making his way to Sarnath near Banares, he sought out the five ascetics who had earlier abandoned him and preached to them, turning the wheel of the Dharma (truth). He told them that the two extreme ways of life, living in luxury and practicing total self-mortification, were useless; it is the "middle path" that leads to enlightenment. Then he proclaimed the four noble truths:

> The Noble Truth of suffering (*Dukkha*) is this: Birth is suffering; aging is suffering; sickness is suffering; death is suffering; sorrow and lamentation, pain, grief and despair are suffering; association with the unpleasant is suffering; dissociation from the pleasant is suffering; not to get what one wants is suffering—in brief, the five aggregates of attachment are suffering.
> The Noble Truth of the origin of suffering is this: It is this thirst (craving) which produces re-existence and rebecoming, bound up with passionate greed. It finds fresh delight now here and now there, namely, thirst for sense-pleasures; thirst for existence and becoming; and thirst for non-existence (self-annihilation).
> The Noble Truth of the Cessation of suffering is this: It is the complete cessation of that very thirst, giving it up, renouncing it, emancipating oneself from it, detaching oneself from it.
> The Noble Truth of the Path leading to the Cessation of suffering is this: It is simply the Noble Eightfold Path, namely right view; right thought; right speech; right action; right livelihood; right effort; right mindfulness; right concentration.[10]

The vision of life and its goal of transformation expressed in these four truths is profound, and we look at it more closely later. The Buddha retained the Indian view of life as samsara, a series of deaths and rebirths caused by karma. He saw that this whole existence involves "suffering," that is, discontent, frustration, and the anxiety of being death-bound. He had seen that all this suffering arises from clinging, grasping, holding onto the self. But he had also experienced the liberation that comes when clinging is totally done away with and thus suffering ceases—this liberation he called nirvana, which means ending the samsara cycle and reaching complete freedom. And the way to reach this, he taught, was the noble eightfold path, a lifetime of disciplines focused on knowledge, ethics, and meditation, designed gradually to root out all clinging and bring about the transformation of existence, the attainment of nirvana, the imperishable and absolute state beyond all this.

The Buddha's teaching differed from the teaching of the Hindu Upanishads particularly in his doctrines of impermanence and no-self. There is nothing, he taught, that is permanent and absolute, not even Brahman, that which Hindus consider to be ultimate reality. Rather, everything is in a state of constant flux and change, birth and death, and therefore there is nothing to hold on to. Further, there is no permanent, eternal atman (self). I cling and crave because I mistakenly suppose that I have a permanent self; the goal of the path is to come finally to the full realization that there is no self to cling to, and with that realization comes the peace and freedom of nirvana. It is this new Dharma that the Buddha proclaimed.

Founding the Sangha

The five hermits accepted the Buddha's Dharma and were ordained as the first monks, and with that the Buddha created the sangha, the community following the path to enlightenment. A tradition says the Buddha went to Kapilavastu and preached the Dharma to his father, who was overjoyed, and even went to the heaven where his mother dwelt and preached the Dharma for her and the gods there. He spent the rest of his long life, some forty-five years, traveling about northeast India, teaching the Dharma and gathering many disciples into the community of the sangha. When he had a community of sixty enlightened monks (Pali: bhikkhus), the Buddha sent them out as missionaries to travel about and bring the Dharma to all beings, and many converted to this path. The Buddha accepted all classes of people without regard to race or social status, thus breaking away from the Indian caste system. On urging from Ananda he also accepted women into the sangha in a separate order of nuns (Pali: bhikkhunis), with his foster mother Prajapati and her attendants as its first members. As he organized the sangha into a monastic community, he established the main guidelines for monastic life, including the basic precepts like chastity, having no possessions, begging for food, and nonviolence toward all living things. Whereas the early monks were basically wanderers, the Buddha did establish the custom of retreats during the summer monsoon season, often gathering in caves in northern India. Eventually the conversions got so numerous that the Buddha gave the monks permission to ordain new monks wherever they went, and thus the sangha spread as a kind of republican society of monastic communities in various places.

The Buddha also accepted lay adherents to the path—kings, princes, merchants, and others, teaching them to observe the basic moral precepts and attain merit by supporting the monastic community. He also insisted that the monks and nuns teach their lay supporters and help them live meritorious lives. So the sangha has four divisions: monks (bhikkhus, nuns (bhikkhunis), laymen, and laywomen.

With the founding of the sangha the Buddhist identity is complete. All Buddhists down to the present day have expressed this identity by saying the formula that is used for entry into the Buddhist community: "I take refuge in the Buddha, I take refuge in the Dharma, I take refuge in the Sangha."

The Death of the Buddha: Parinirvana

After a long, full lifetime of teaching, the Buddha knew the end of his human existence was near. He said to Ananda and the other monks,

I am old now, Ananda, and full of years; my journey nears its end, and I have reached my sum of days, for I am nearly eighty years old. . . . So, Ananda, you must be your own lamps, be your own refuges. Take refuge in nothing outside yourselves. Hold firm to the truth as a lamp and a refuge, and do not look for refuge to anything besides yourselves.[11]

Statues of the Buddha and the monks that formed the sangha, with a prostrate worshiper in front, from Pagan, Burma.

Ananda wept at the prospect of the teacher leaving him, but the Buddha told him not to grieve, reminding him that it is in the very nature of things that we must sever ourselves from all things near and dear to us. After ascertaining that none of the monks had any doubts or perplexities about the Buddha, the Dharma, the sangha, or the path, the Buddha spoke his last words: "All composite things must pass away. Strive onward vigilantly."[12] And in the midst of his final meditation he passed into parinirvana, complete liberation without any ties remaining to pull him back for another lifetime in samsara. At the passing of the Buddha, the earth shook, thunderbolts crashed, rivers boiled with water, and the tree over the Buddha's couch showered his golden body with flowers.

The grief-stricken laypeople of the area, the Mallas, honored the Buddha's remains for six days. Then they carried his body on a bier to a great funeral pyre, and fire consumed all but his bones. The bones and other relics of the Buddha were kept in golden jars and taken to the village hall, where they were venerated for seven days. Rulers of the neighboring regions also wanted relics of the great teacher so they could establish shrines, and after some resistance the Mallas allowed the relics to be divided into eight parts and taken by the kings of the region, who built stupas (memorial mounds) over them. The relics provide a sense of the ongoing presence of the Buddha who is beyond existence in the state of parinirvana.

The Tripitaka: Word of the Buddha

The Buddha had told the monks that the Dharma would be their leader, and so they looked especially to his sayings and teachings as the source for the Dharma. During the first rainy season retreat after the Buddha's parinirvana, the story says, five hundred arhats (monks who had achieved nirvana) assembled in the First Council at Rajagrha and collected the sayings and teachings of the Buddha so that the Dharma might abide. Since Ananda was the one who heard him speak most often, they asked Ananda to recite the Buddha's sayings. So Ananda recited the words that the Buddha spoke in his sermons and dialogues (the *sutras*). Another monk, Upali, recited the various rules that the Buddha had given to regulate the life of the monks and nuns (the *vinaya*). Thus arose two of the main parts or "baskets" (*pitaka*) of the scriptures, the Sutra (Pali: Sutta) Pitaka and the Vinaya Pitaka, containing the Dharma of the great teacher. Somewhat later, disciples produced a set of scholarly treatises on points of doctrine, the Abhidharma (Pali: Abhidhamma), also considered to derive from the word of the Buddha. These three sets of writings are the Tripitaka (Pali: Tipitaka), the "Three Baskets," the scriptures of Buddhism. Scholars of today think the formation of the scriptures was a longer and more complicated process than the tradition says. The sayings were passed on orally by different groups, interpreted and added to, and eventually written down in the Pali language centuries later. But what the Buddhist story emphasizes is that the Dharma of the scriptures derives directly from the word of the Buddha.

In the story of the Buddha, then, one finds the paradigm for what it means to be a Buddhist. The Buddha, the

The Buddhist Story: Some Important Dates

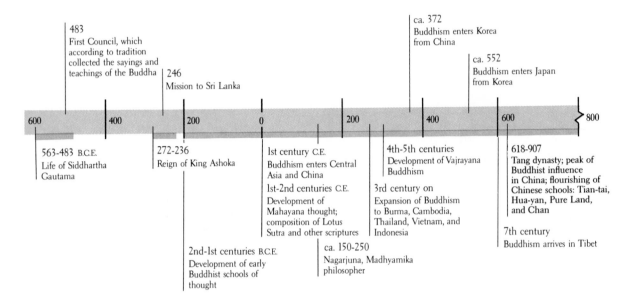

Dharma, and the sangha are not just historical artifacts to be researched and reconstructed; they are living realities in which all Buddhists of all ages can participate. Further, the life story of the Buddha is in a real sense the life story of every Buddhist, showing how the path proceeds from ignorance and worldly attachment to knowledge, detachment, and complete liberation.

HISTORICAL TRANSFORMATIONS: SHAPING THE BUDDHIST WAY

The story of Buddhism, although it centers on the historical life of Siddhartha Gautama, is actually very open-ended. The ultimate truth can be expressed in many other persons and realities. For example, as we noted earlier, the Buddha himself had many previous lifetimes. And there have been other Buddhas in the great aeons of the past and there will be other Buddhas in the future. So the story could be expanded greatly as Buddhism developed in its various historical transformations. Because of its great influence on the identity of many Buddhists today, especially those of East Asia, we will need to look particularly

at the expanded version of the story that took place in that movement known as Mahayana.

Ashoka, the Second Founder of Buddhism

For two centuries Buddhism spread mainly in the Ganges Valley area of eastern India. But in the middle of the third century B.C.E., it burst forth and spread throughout India and southward to Sri Lanka. One of the primary agents of this expansion was the great King Ashoka (r. ca. 272–236 B.C.E.), one of the most important rulers in Indian history and a zealous Buddhist. At the beginning of the third century B.C.E., the Maurya dynasty was engaged in extending control over much of India. The third Maurya king was Ashoka, who conquered Kalinga in northeast India, the last area to be subdued. But in the process the extensive bloodshed and destruction filled Ashoka with remorse, and he began to study the Dharma of Buddhism. He became a lay follower and even lived in a monastic community for a while, giving up the royal pastime of hunting because of the Buddhist precept not to harm living things.

Some five years after the bloody conquest of Kalinga, Ashoka proclaimed the new policy of the peaceful

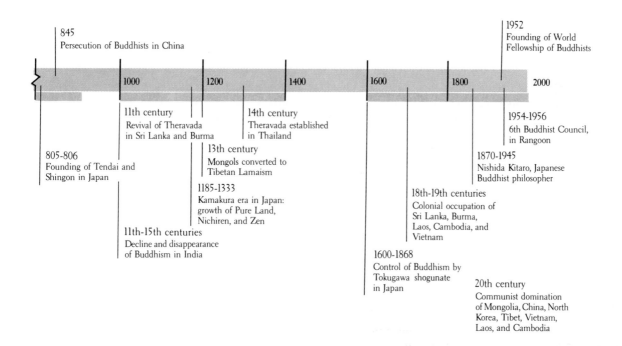

845
Persecution of Buddhists in China

1952
Founding of World
Fellowship of Buddhists

1000   1200   1400   1600   1800   2000

11th century
Revival of Theravada
in Sri Lanka and Burma

14th century
Theravada established
in Thailand

1954-1956
6th Buddhist Council,
in Rangoon

805-806
Founding of Tendai and
Shingon in Japan

13th century
Mongols converted to
Tibetan Lamaism

1870-1945
Nishida Kitaro, Japanese
Buddhist philosopher

1185-1333
Kamakura era in Japan:
growth of Pure Land,
Nichiren, and Zen

18th-19th centuries
Colonial occupation of
Sri Lanka, Burma,
Laos, Cambodia, and
Vietnam

11th-15th centuries
Decline and disappearance
of Buddhism in India

1600-1868
Control of Buddhism by
Tokugawa shogunate
in Japan

20th century
Communist domination
of Mongolia, China, North
Korea, Tibet, Vietnam,
Laos, and Cambodia

Dharma conquest. In a series of fourteen edicts engraved on rocks throughout his empire, he proclaimed that all people are his children and that they should live by basic Buddhist precepts: they should do no injury to any living things, they should be obedient to parents and elders, reverent to teachers, and the like. He abolished animal sacrifice and regulated the slaughter of animals for food, provided for the welfare of the common people, built thousands of stupas, supported the monastic communities, and worked to have the developing sects of Buddhism recognize and tolerate each other. King Ashoka is fondly remembered by Buddhists as the "second founder" of Buddhism, establishing the model of the Buddhist layperson and the Buddhist state, complementary to the ideal of the sangha monastic community.

One of Ashoka's edicts says he sent Dharma-envoys to the Greek rulers of Syria, Egypt, Macedonia, Cyrene, and Epyrus, although these missionaries apparently did not have much success. Closer to home, however, in addition to spreading the rule of Dharma throughout India, Ashoka sent his son Mahinda and his daughter Sanghamitta as missionaries to Sri Lanka, and the two of them converted the king and the women of the court to Buddhism. Buddhism was on the way to becoming a world religion.

Theravada and Mahayana

In the course of its development, Buddhism came to be divided into two main branches: Theravada (Path of the Elders) and Mahayana (Greater Vehicle). Through complex historical developments, Theravada came to be dominant in South Asia and Southeast Asia, whereas Mahayana spread through the lands of East Asia. A third branch, Vajrayana (Diamond Vehicle) or Tantric Buddhism, was accepted in Tibet.

In the first three or four centuries after the Buddha's death, there was much debate over basic questions of teaching and practice. By 200 B.C.E. reports indicate the existence of seventeen or eighteen "schools," each with a particular way of interpreting the path taught by the Buddha. One was the group that called itself Theravada, claiming to follow closely and to transmit the original teachings of the Buddha. Another early group was known as the Mahasanghikas (Great Sanghites), who admitted lay followers and nonarhat monks to their assemblies and taught that a transfigured Buddha exists with endless life beyond the world, appearing at different times and places. They also, of course, claimed that they carefully preserved the teaching of the Buddha.

All of these groups further splintered and eventually died out, with the exception of Theravada. The Theravadins established themselves in Sri Lanka, preserved the Buddhist scriptures in their Pali form, and have continued to exist to the present. Some of the teachings of the Mahasanghikas were taken over and continued in the Mahayana movement that developed.

Contrasting them with Mahayana, all these early Buddhist schools were sometimes called Hinayana (Lesser Vehicle). Since this can be considered a derogatory term, it has become customary in modern times to replace it with Theravada, the one group among all these that continued to exist. In general, it may be said that Theravada did maintain the central teachings of early Buddhism, with its structures of monastic orders and lay supporters, whereas Mahayana was more open to new ideas and practices.

Pressure for these changes came from several sources. In the sangha the arhats (enlightened monks) tended to form an elite guild and insisted only they knew the true Dharma, alienating many other monks and laypeople, so in some communities there was a movement to include all, even laypeople, as equals on the path. The influence of Hindu bhakti (devotional) movements began to be felt, with many people desiring ways of expressing devotion and worship, even though they were Buddhists. And the philosophical searching and speculation characteristic of thinkers in India led some Buddhists to explore the nature of reality in a more systematic, philosophical way, contributing new perspectives on the original Buddhist vision. These tendencies came to fruition in Mahayana Buddhism.

During the second and first centuries B.C.E. Mahayana ideas were being formed, and new scriptures, now in Sanskrit, were written expressing these ideas. The expanded story came to incorporate new conceptions of the sangha, the scriptures, the ideal saint, and the Buddha.

The Great Sangha and New Sutras

A major Mahayana innovation was to open the path to all people, monks and lay alike. The word Mahayana means "greater vehicle" or "greater course," and one implication of this new name is that the narrower concept of the arhat as the one reaching the goal was being broadened to include others, even laypeople. All can be equally on the path toward achieving Buddhahood. Of course, Mahayana communities continued to recognize monastic discipline as especially important in cultivating the higher virtues, but the path was thought to be within the reach of those who chose not to withdraw from the world and become monks or nuns. In contrast to the Greater Vehicle, the traditional form of Buddhism was designated as Hinayana, the Lesser Vehicle, since it offered salvation only to the few.

The Theravadins in turn criticized the Mahayanists for developing these new ideas rather than relying only on the Dharma of the Buddha. The new writings composed in Sanskrit by Mahayana were not just commentaries on the older Pali scriptures; they were claimed to be the secret teaching that the Buddha himself had given to his most advanced disciples. Mahayana thus taught a kind of progressive revelation of the truth; to those with lesser understanding the Buddha had revealed the preliminary truth embodied in the Tripitaka, the scriptures of Theravada, but to those with deep understanding he revealed the full truth, which was passed on orally and eventually written in the Mahayana sutras. All of these are still "word of the Buddha." Important early texts of Mahayana include writings like the *Sadharmapundarika* (Lotus), *Prajnaparamita* (Perfection of Wisdom), and the *Sukhavati* (Pure Land) sutras. In the following centuries a great number of additional sutras were added to the Mahayana corpus, filling out and refining the new understandings of the Buddha and the path.

The Course of the Bodhisattva

Mahayana is really the "great course" of the bodhisattva (Buddha in the making). It was one of the main innovations of Mahayana to teach that the Great Course leads directly to Buddhahood, whereas the Lesser Course (Theravada) leads only to arhat-ship. Theravada, it is true, had an idea of the bodhisattva path toward liberation, but they associated it with a few special beings like Gautama. But Mahayana began to teach that the course of the bodhisattva is the higher path that leads to Buddhahood and which, further, is for all to follow, open even to laypeople. In a significant shift of focus, Mahayana Buddhists started looking not to the arhat, who reaches nirvana with great discipline and effort, as the supreme spiritual model. Rather, Mahayana Buddhists began focusing on the course of the bodhisattva, an enlightened being who reaches nirvana but voluntarily remains in the samsara existence, rebirth after rebirth, for the purpose of helping others.

Some bodhisattvas are celestial beings, living in the heavens and working to help and save all beings. These bodhisattvas can be worshiped and prayed to for help, bringing the element of bhakti into Mahayana Buddhism. One such heavenly bodhisattva is Manjusri, who appears to humans in dreams. Hearing his name subtracts many aeons from one's time in samsara, and those who worship him are protected by his power. Another widely worshiped bodhisattva is Avalokiteshvara, who is described in the Lotus Sutra as an omnipresent saviour rich in love and compassion, taking many different forms to help living beings. Those who worship him and call on his name will be saved from all dangers, whether drowning in water, bound in prison, or burning in a fire. He grants women their desire for a daughter or son. In China and Japan the names Guan-Yin and Kannon are used for this bodhisattva, whose images are often represented as a compassionate woman, a "goddess of mercy."

The Mahayana Conception of Buddha

The Mahayana group also expanded the conception of who or what the Buddha is. They emphasized that the Buddha is really the eternal power of the Dharma, and that this "Dharma Body" of the Buddha is transcendent and universal, yet forever active in the world. The Dharma Body has lived for countless ages in the past and will continue to live forever in the future. This Dharma Body is the only real body of the Buddha; it is ultimate reality.

But the Dharma Body has various manifestations for the welfare of living beings, such as the human form, Siddhartha Gautama. And important manifestations are the heavenly Buddhas who preside over Buddhalands in which all the inhabitants are assured of attaining enlightenment. Moreover, some of these heavenly Buddhas can also be worshiped by people still living in this world, sharing merit with them so that they can be saved from a variety of sufferings and ultimately be reborn into one of the heavenly Buddhalands.

Mahayana Schools: Madhyamika and Yogacara

As Mahayana thinkers speculated on the meaning of these new ideas about bodhisattvas and Buddhas, a new philosophical perspective emerged to become characteristic of the Mahayana approach, formulated especially by the Madhyamika school and its famous thinker, Nagarjuna (ca. 150–250 C.E.) The Madhyamika thinkers came up with the dramatic new idea that, since all things in the world come into existence as a result of causes and conditions, they do not have an independent existence and thus are "empty" (shunya). This whole phenomenal world of samsara is empty. Taking this one step further, the Mahayana thinkers proposed that nirvana also is empty, since it is devoid of all definitions and discrimination. This means that the phenomenal world of samsara and the realm of nirvana are both empty, and thus they may be equated with each other. Rather than seeing nirvana as the opposite of samsara, nirvana is to be understood as the realization that all things are really empty and therefore there are no dualisms. One who understands this fully is enlightened and realizes the Buddha-nature within himself or herself.

Nagarjuna is famous for his logical reduction-to-absurdity method to show that every concept contains contradictions in itself and therefore is unreal, proving that the whole phenomenal world is empty or unreal because it is based on contradictory relations. The purpose of this method, he points out, is to free our minds of all theories and enable us to realize the unconditioned truth, beyond all words and concepts.

The other important Mahayana philosophical school, Yogacara, focused on how the mind creates and experiences the illusory world as real. With its slogan, "Mind only," this philosophical school worked out a complex theory that the experienced world is nothing but a perceptual construct. They identified emptiness with what they called the "storehouse consciousness," the basis of all existence. Later philosophers of this school equated the storehouse consciousness with "the womb of the Buddha" (*tathagatagarbha*), that is, the womb from which all Buddhas are born. Further, it is the embryo Buddha nature that is present in all things. This idea implies that all beings possess Buddhahood and that the goal is to realize that Buddhahood. If that is so, then many possible paths toward realizing that Buddhahood open up, from meditation and yogic practices to devotion and worship of the Buddhas. And in fact, especially in China, many Buddhist schools developed to cultivate the different paths toward realizing Buddhahood.

Buddhist Tantra: Vajrayana

Yet another form of Buddhism developed in India, influenced by Tantric aspects of Hinduism, which used many rituals, mantras (sacred words), mandalas (sacred diagrams), ritual sexual intercourse, and the like, to achieve realization of Buddhahood. Eventually the Tantric Buddhists produced new scriptures; these are manuals for rituals and meditations designed to lead directly to the realization of Buddhahood. These Tantras purported to come directly from the Buddha passed on secretly to his most advanced disciples, and they were written in a kind of code language so the uninitiated would not understand. Called Vajrayana (Diamond Vehicle), this form of Buddhism greatly extended the Buddha pantheon by adding many new Buddhas, bodhisattvas, feminine consorts, gods, and goddesses, representing the whole cosmos. Tantrists also believed that this sacred cosmos is replicated in the human body, that is, all these Buddhas and bodhisattvas reside within us, so with the proper rituals and meditation one can visualize or identify with these powers and realize Buddahood. Vajrayana, later influential especially in Japan and Tibet, thus developed a path by which one could achieve Buddhahood even within this very lifetime.

Great Expansion of Buddhism in Asia

Unlike Hinduism, Buddhism from early times on considered the Dharma to be the truth for all living things, and therefore one of the important duties in following the path is to make it possible for others to share in the benefits of that Dharma. Buddhism spread to several major cultural areas and in transforming them was itself transformed, taking on a distinctive flavor in each region. First Buddhism spread throughout India and to Sri Lanka at the time of King Ashoka. Then with the Indianization of Southeast Asia it also became dominant in those lands. Since the Theravada form of Buddhism was strong in India during these expansions, those lands became Theravada countries, with indigenous cults and traditions still in place. When the expansion to Central and East Asia took place, Mahayana was in the ascendency, so East Asia emerged predominately Mahayana.

Within India itself, Buddhism remained fairly strong in most regions up to the seventh century, but over the next centuries a slow decline set in. By about the thirteenth century Buddhism had virtually disappeared from the land of its birth. One element in the demise of Indian Buddhism was perhaps the extent to which monastic Buddhism, with landed estates and royal grants, had grown unresponsive to the needs of the people. The general populace found their needs met more by theistic Hinduism and increasingly turned in that direction, incorporating some Buddhist worship and piety into popular Hinduism. Another factor in the weakening of Buddhism in India was the onslaught of outside invaders. Beginning with the White Hun invasions of the sixth century, the Buddhist monasteries of northwest India were devastated. Later Muslim invaders and Muslim rulers continued to demolish Buddhist temples and monasteries, along with Hindu temples. Hinduism, depending on village brahmins and devotional cults, survived, but Buddhism, focused on the monastic communities, weakened and eventually disappeared. But by this time Buddhism had already become the light of many other parts of Asia beyond its homeland.

Expansion to Sri Lanka and Southeast Asia

Beginning when King Ashoka's son and daughter converted the rulers of Sri Lanka, Buddhism has flourished there for over two thousand years, the longest continuity of Buddhism anywhere. At times there has been Mahayana influence in Sri Lanka, along with Hindu cults, but Theravada eventually became dominant. Sri Lanka boasts a tree said to have grown from a shoot of the tree of Bodh Gaya under which the Buddha reached enlightenment; the tree shoot was brought to Sri Lanka by King Ashoka's

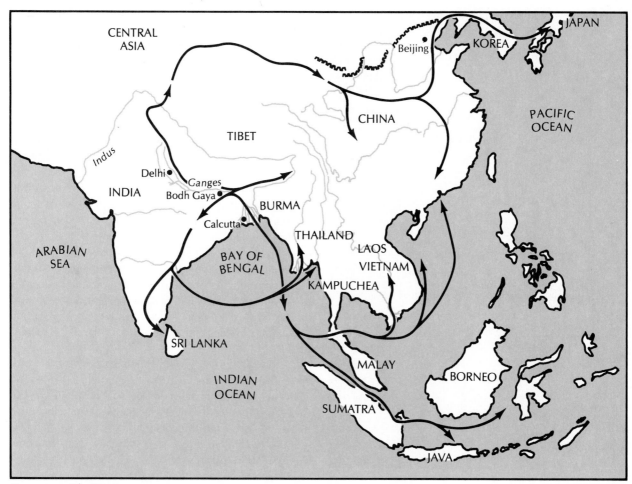

Expansion of Buddhism.

daughter. And a special temple in Kandy houses a tooth of the Buddha. From the beginning the sangha was strongly supported by the rulers of Sri Lanka. Buddhist kings were patrons of Buddhist art and learning, and they built many temples and monasteries, even helping to regulate the affairs of the sangha.

Since Burma provided a trade gateway for India to Southeast Asia, Indian merchants were bringing Buddhism with them into Burma already in the third century B.C.E., and some monks were also sent by Ashoka. Over the next centuries Buddhist influences continued, and

gradually Burma became a flourishing center of Buddhist life. For a while Mahayana and Tantric influences were strong, but during the period of the Pagan kingdom, King Anawrahta (1040–1077) turned to Sri Lanka for inspiration, and thus Burma became a thriving center of Theravada Buddhism, retaining a pure form of Theravada ordination and tradition. Lay Buddhism in Burma took on a special character by adopting local cults of spirits (*nats*), so that side by side with the monastic community are found shamanistic practices involving women possessed by *nats* healing people and providing benefits for them.

Ruins of the great Buddhist monument at Sukhothai, Thailand.

A mixture of Mahayana Buddhism and Hinduism spread into Cambodia, Thailand, and Laos from about the fourth century C.E. onward. Theravada did not come to Cambodia until the twelfth century, when it supplanted both Mahayana and Hinduism. The Thai states developed in the thirteenth century and accepted Theravada from Burma, although Thai kings used Hindu law and Brahmanical ceremonies. The first Laotian state developed in the fourteenth century and the Khmer missionaries from Cambodia introduced Theravada Buddhism, which became the official religion of Laos. Vietnam, though a part

of Southeast Asia, received strong influence from China and has been predominantly Mahayana in orientation. Indonesia was Hinduized by the fifth century C.E., but Buddhism was also introduced and existed side by side with the cult of Shiva. At Borobudur on the island of Java was built the greatest and most glorious of all stupas, in the shape of a great mandala in stone representing the pilgrim's search for enlightenment.

Characteristic of the development of Buddhism in Sri Lanka and Southeast Asia is the interrelationship between the monastic community and the laypeople. The monks and nuns pursue the path toward nirvana, of course, and the laypeople carry on householder life in the cities and in rural areas. But each group lives in a certain dependence on the other. The monks need the support of the laypeople in terms of food, buildings, security, and the like. The laypeople need the services of the monks in terms of teaching, chanting scriptures, and providing spiritual power for the community. In some of these lands it has been customary for boys to spend at least some time as novices in a monastery before going on to adult secular life in society.

Development of East Asian Buddhism

As early as the first century C.E. Buddhist monks and laypeople made their way along the silk routes into central Asia. For a time both Theravada and Mahayana flourished in central Asia, until Buddhism was stamped out by Islam around the tenth century C.E. Scholars today are only beginning to recover the impressive achievements of Buddhists in central Asia, including temples, sculptures, and important translations of Indian Buddhist texts.

From central Asia monks and missionaries brought Buddhism to China, where in its Mahayana form it rose to become one of the three great religions of China, along with Confucianism and Daoism. Buddhism contributed to many transformations in Chinese society and religious thought, and in the process Buddhism itself took on characteristic Chinese forms. Particularly important was the development of special lineages or "schools" of Chinese Buddhism, each with important writings and practices. The Tian-tai school, for example, focused on the Lotus Sutra, and Hua-yan made the Garland Sutra its principal scripture. Eventually two Buddhist schools became the most widespread in China. There was Pure

Land, which centered on the worship of the compassionate Buddha Amitabha and promised rebirth in the Pure Land paradise; and Chan (meditation) Buddhism, which worked out methods of awakening to one's innate Buddhahood through emptying the mind in meditation. These Chinese schools of Buddhism will be discussed further in Part II.

From China, Buddhism spread to Vietnam, Korea, and Japan, with the result that these cultures became predominantly Buddhist. Vietnam was influenced both from India and from China, but it was Chinese Mahayana especially in the Chan form that finally prevailed. Later Pure Land Buddhism came to dominate village-level Buddhism in Vietnam, whereas the monasteries remained predominantly Thien (Chan).

Buddhism was brought to the northern part of Korea in 372 c.e. by a Chinese monk, spreading throughout the rest of the land by the sixth century. Korean religion had been a form of shamanism, which still survives today as a cult of spirits. When Buddhism came in, the common people were much attracted to Pure Land Buddhism with its promise of salvation in the next world. During the eighth and ninth centuries, Chan (in Korean, Son) was introduced from China, and this became the most popular form of monastic Buddhism in Korea. The Buddhist scriptural canon was printed in Korea two times, as Korean Buddhism made a particularly important contribution to the spread of Buddhism. The wooden blocks from the thirteenth century printing are still preserved, and a new printing is being made from them.

From Korea Buddhism spread to Japan; around the year 550 Korean kings sent gifts of Buddhist sutras and Buddha images to the Japanese emperor. Buddhism in Japan was first adopted by the court and ruling families as a means of unifying the nation, but later it became an important part of popular Japanese life. Important schools of Buddhism developed in Japan, as in China, continuing their vitality up to the present time. Tendai (the Japanese form of Tian-tai) and Shingon (esoteric or Tantric Buddhism) became widespread foundational Buddhist movements in Japan's classical Heian era (974–1185). And in the upheavals that accompanied the beginnings of the feudal period in Japan, Pure Land and Zen (the Japanese form of Chan) became widely popular, together with the movement founded by the charismatic Japanese Buddhist leader, Nichiren. Japanese Buddhism is discussed in more detail in Part II.

The Special Shape of Tibetan Buddhism

In the seventh century c.e., Buddhist missionaries from India began to press northward to a new region in central Asia, the isolated Himalayan mountains of Tibet. The indigenous religious practice of Tibet was called Bon, and it focused on many spirits good and hostile. Shamans went into trances to communicate with these spirits, and the people offered animal sacrifices. Since during this period Tibet also had contact with central Asia and China, Chan Buddhism was successful in Tibet for a while, but at the same time the Tantric form of Buddhism, Vajrayana, was being imported from India. Toward the end of the eighth century the Tibetan king staged a remarkable international debate between Chinese Chan monks and monks from India. According to the Tibetan version of the story, the Chinese were defeated and expelled from the country, after which Tibet definitely turned toward India and Tantric Buddhism. The specific type of Buddhism created in Tibet in the interaction between Indian Tantrism and Tibetan culture is called Lamaism, from the term *lama*, which means a spiritual master.

Under support from the kings, Indian missionaries entered Tibet to teach, translate Sanskrit scriptures into Tibetan, and found monasteries. One missionary remembered in a host of legends was Padmasambhava, who arrived in Tibet in 747 and used his Tantric powers to subdue all the Bon demons who were hostile to Buddhism; after being subjugated, they were included in the Tibetan Buddhist pantheon as protectors of Buddhism. Under royal patronage Indian and Tibetan monks translated a vast number of scriptures into Tibetan, virtually creating the Tibetan literary language in the process. Many monasteries were established where scholar-monks practiced the disciplines of monastic life and mastered the classical Vajrayana doctrines. And countless wonder-working Tantric yogins wandered about, not concerned with monastic disciplines, often married and with families.

Tibetans, with their background in the popular shamanistic religion, accepted Tantric Buddhism from India but shaped it in their own way, enriching the pantheon with

An esoteric paint-on-cotton rendering of the Buddha Ratnasambhava, from the Himalayan region.

Lamaist saints, Tibetan gods and goddesses, demons, local heroes, and the like. The pantheon included many female figures, such as the bodhisattva Tara who became a kind of universal protectress worshiped by both monks and laity. Monks and nuns participated in popular Buddhism, but they also cultivated esoteric practices involving yogic meditation and Tantric rituals, with the goal of transforming the consciousness into the absolute Buddha reality. The religious specialists were the lamas, the highest spiritual authorities, often thought to be living gods, and under their direction the disciplines and rituals were practiced.

A significant event was the conversion of the Mongol leader Kublai Khan (1216–1294) to Lamaism, and several centuries later the peoples of Mongolia, northern China, and southern Russia also came to follow Lamaism. An important reform movement beginning in the fifteenth century was called the Gelukpa (partisan of virtue) sect, also known as the Yellow Hats, named after their hats in contrast to the red hats of the traditional Buddhist groups and the black hats of the Bon priests. Tsong-kha-pa (1357–

1419), founder of the Gelukpa sect, advocated a return to the traditional Buddhist monastic life and also a modification of some of the Tantric magical practices. His third successor, his nephew Gendun Truppa, was recognized as an incarnation of the bodhisattva Avalokiteshvara and is counted as the first Dalai Lama, spiritual leader of Lamaism. Since lamas are recognized as incarnations in a continuing series, after the death of a Dalai Lama a search party goes out to find the new Dalai Lama, who will be an infant born forty-nine days later (the period of the intermediate stage). The searchers are guided by the dying lama's indications and other pertinent signs, and once the right child is found, he is brought to Lhasa to be educated for his role while regents rule temporarily. The present Dalai Lama is the fourteenth in this line.

Buddhism in the Modern Era

Developments in the modern era have often been disruptive to Buddhism as to other religions. Even before the modern era, as we saw, Buddhism disappeared in its motherland India. Then starting in the mid-sixteenth century, Western mercantilism, imperialism, and missionary work posed challenges to the other traditional Buddhist societies. In Sri Lanka, for example, the Portuguese attempted to convert the people to Catholicism, destroying Buddhist temples and relics and executing monks found wearing the yellow robe. And the challenges of rationalism, science, and secularism have affected Buddhist peoples as well as those of the Western religious traditions.

In the twentieth century, communism has proven to be a drastic challenge to Buddhism, as Communist governments now dominate the area that has for centuries been the heartland of Buddhism: China, Mongolia, North Korea, Tibet, and the Southeast Asian countries of Vietnam, Laos, and Cambodia. Mongolia, taken over by a Soviet-inspired Communist government in the early 1920s, replaced Buddhist teaching with Communist ideology and stripped the Lamaist leaders of their power. In China the Maoist procedure was to close the monasteries and force monks and nuns to return to secular life, gathering the remnants of Buddhism into a state-run Chinese Buddhist Association. The Chinese conquest of Tibet caused great disruption in this traditional Buddhist culture, which had not even experienced a period of modern-

Buddhist monk ringing the monastery bell at Eiheiji Temple in Japan.

ization; the Dalai Lama and thousands of others fled the country, and apparently the Chinese took over the administration of the monasteries with serious curtailment of Buddhist activities. It appears that the Communist governments in Southeast Asia have also seriously weakened the Buddhist institutions.

Revitalization of Buddhism Today

Yet there is a sense of revitalization of Buddhism today. Facing the challenge of Western influences and Christianity in the late nineteenth and twentieth centuries, Buddhists in various lands have responded with a revival of Buddhist activity, especially in the area of scholarly work. To meet the challenge of modern secular values, Buddhist scholars have retrieved the sources of their own traditions and are reformulating Buddhist doctrines to meet modern questions. Some Buddhist thinkers, such as Japanese philosopher Nishida Kitaro (1870–1945), have tried to relate Buddhist ideas with Western philosophical and scientific modes of thought. Other thinkers have stressed the relevance of Buddhist teachings for creating a just and peaceful society.

Within Buddhist lands there have been Buddhist reformers who have redirected the monastic life toward constructive religious and social roles. And much attention has been given to an increased activity of the laypeople in Buddhist affairs, through education, religious activities, and lay Buddhist associations. Interest in the revitalization of worldwide Buddhism is seen in the founding of the World Fellowship of Buddhists in Sri Lanka in 1952 to unite Buddhists of all nations. And in connection with the 2,500th anniversary of the Buddha's enlightenment, a two-year-long Sixth Great Council of Buddhism was held in Rangoon in the 1950s. There are even signs in the People's Republic of China that the newly issued policy of freedom of religion will assist a revival of Buddhist leadership.

In motherland India there are some first inklings of a revival of Buddhism. Small groups of Indian intellectuals have been attracted to Buddhism because it suits their ideas of social reform and rational spirituality. Refugees from Tibet live in communities in India, continuing some of the traditions of Tibetan Buddhism. And in 1956 the leader of Maharashtra's untouchables led 600,000 of his followers to a mass conversion to Buddhism, partly in protest against the caste system of Hindu tradition. Since then the number of Buddhist converts has doubled and constitutes a significant presence of Buddhists in India.

Another significant aspect of Buddhism today is its expansion in the West. Thriving communities of immigrant Buddhists have been established especially in such places as Hawaii and California, but increasingly in other areas as well. Many of these are organized into the Buddhist Churches of America and follow the Japanese True Pure Land school. But more recently immigrants from other parts of Asia—Korea, Thailand, Vietnam, and others—have strengthened the Buddhist presence in the West.

There are also significant numbers of Westerners who have become Buddhist. This trend started especially with the writings of D. T. Suzuki, who interested many in Zen Buddhism, leading to the establishment of many Zen centers in the larger American cities. Then in the 1960s came a surge of interest in Tibetan Buddhism and the establishing of centers for studying and practicing this more esoteric form. Now there are a variety of other Buddhist traditions represented as well. The most significant development, perhaps, is the ordination of Western successors to Asian Buddhist masters, indicating a basis for the continuation of the fledgling Buddhist community in the West.

DISCUSSION QUESTIONS

1. According to the traditional Buddhist story, what was Siddhartha's early life like? Why did he decide to go forth to seek the truth?

2. Describe Siddhartha's attaining of enlightenment. What was the role of Mara and of the gods?

3. What was the content of the Buddha's first sermon given at Sarnath near Banares?

4. How, according to tradition, was the Tripitaka compiled?

5. Why is King Ashoka called the second founder of Buddhism?

6. What important new ideas came to expression in the Mahayana movement?

7. Outline the expansion of Buddhism in Asia and account for its virtual disappearance in India.

8. What are some special characteristics of Tibetan Buddhism?

9. What have been some major problems for Buddhism in the modern period? What are some indications of Buddhism's revitalization today?

CHAPTER 6

Buddhist Worlds of Meaning

THE ULTIMATE: DHARMA, NIRVANA, BUDDHA

What's it *all* about? What is really ultimate in our existence? Buddhists, like Hindus, do not fall back on a simple single answer like God. God and gods, like everything else, are part of the samsara cycle and therefore cannot be ultimate. One of the central Buddhist teachings about reality is that everything is impermanent and conditioned; there is nothing, even God, that is eternal and absolute. Does this mean, then, that Buddhists have no ultimate reality at all? Some have suggested this, speaking of Buddhism as a philosophy rather than a religion.

But such a view would be misleading, for Buddhists for many centuries have found ultimate meaning and transformation in the path of the Buddha. What is really ultimate? The Buddhist Three Refuge formula gives us some help, for that to which a person goes for refuge must have something to do with the ultimate. According to the Three Refuge formula, a Buddhist goes for refuge to the Buddha, to the Dharma, and to the sangha. The Dharma is the transcendental absolute truth, and the sangha focuses toward the experience of nirvana, the unconditioned state of liberation. Whereas the Buddha as a human being is not ultimate, his example of reaching enlightenment and his role as teacher and guide are so central that we need to consider the Buddha within the concept of ultimate reality.

The Ultimate as Unconditioned Truth

It might appear to someone on the outside that Buddhists worship the Buddha as sacred reality. They build temples dedicated to the Buddha, perform rituals before statues of the Buddha, revere relics of the Buddha, and the like. Buddhist religious rituals and festivals can be as colorful and dramatic as any other. But, Buddhists insist, they are not worshiping the Buddha or any other object as ultimate reality, for the Buddha is beyond existence in the unconditioned state of nirvana, and all other objects of worship are conditioned and limited like everything else. Whereas it is beneficial to bow before a statue of the Buddha or invoke a guardian goddess, these objects of devotion are not ultimate and unconditioned. What then *is* ultimate and unconditioned? It is the Dharma as the truth of reality, and nirvana as the unconditioned state.

The Ocean of Dharma

Before the Buddha died, he counseled Ananda and the other disciples on what they should hold fast to: "So, Ananda, you must be your own lamps, be your own refuges. Take refuge in nothing outside yourselves. Hold firm to the truth [Dharma] as a lamp and a refuge, and do not look for refuge to anything besides yourselves."[1] The Dharma is to be found in the word of the Buddha transmitted in the scriptures. Of course, the scriptures themselves are conditioned, but the Dharma is not. It is the eternal truth that transcends even this world age, taught by all the Buddhas and known directly by those attaining enlightenment.

99

The word *dharma* was taken into Buddhism from the broader traditions of India, where it came to mean, as in Hinduism, the universal ordering principle that penetrates everywhere and is operative in everything. As such it is equated with things as they really are, and so the word *dharma* in Buddhism comes to mean ultimate truth, the knowledge of what really is. It is this truth that was realized by the Buddha when he reached enlightenment. Dharma is the truth about the way existence *really* is: the truth about the nature and function of the world, and the truth about liberation from the bondage of samsara. The story of the Buddha's enlightenment reveals the basic content of this Dharma. It tells how he saw the whole chain of his previous existences and then he saw the whole universe as in a mirror, with the operation of the law of karma and rebirth. He perceived the Four Noble Truths about reality. Finally, according to Ashvaghosha's account of his enlightenment, he realized the principle of "dependent arising" (*pratitya samutpada*) as the last step to enlightenment and release from samsara.

"Dependent arising" is essentially a doctrine of causality, showing the interconnectedness of everything. There is no god who causes everything; but it is also false to assert that everything happens randomly by chance. Rather, the truth is that everything and every event are caused by something prior in an interrelated process. Every condition contributes to the next, but it is itself conditioned by countless other determining conditions. This universal truth is often expressed in the abstract statement: "When that exists, this comes to be; on the arising of that, this arises. When that does not exist, this does not come to be; on the cessation of that, this ceases."[2]

Dependent arising is thus the most real knowledge about the world, and it is often simply equated with the Dharma—whoever sees one sees the other, and understanding it is tantamount to enlightenment. Since this Dharma was realized and taught by the Buddha, the Dharma is also often equated with the teaching of the Buddha. At the Deer Park in Sarnath, the Buddha first preached the truth and "turned the wheel of the Dharma."

The Dharma is not simply some mechanical law about reality. It is a transcendental principle immanent and operative in the world, real, valuable, and normative; at the same time it is infinite and eternal. The Dharma is alive in a sense; how well the sangha lives out its vocation in the world has an effect on the Dharma. When unhappiness and trouble come upon society, it is assumed that the ruler and the sangha have disrupted the Dharma by unfaithfulness. When the future Buddha Maitreya arises, Dharma will be stirred up again so that humankind will again know and live the truth. When monks chant scripture for the laypeople, they are unleashing the power of the Dharma for the benefit of the people.

The Dharma is a central aspect of ultimate reality to Buddhists. It is not a supernatural being or god. But, as unconditioned truth, the Dharma takes on a character of awesomeness, protection, and deliverance. It should not only be respected but worshiped and sought as a refuge. The hall of meditation in a monastery is often called the Dharma hall, the seat where the teacher sits is the Dharma seat, and the rule of King Ashoka is the reign of Dharma.

The Unconditioned State of Nirvana

Closely related with the Dharma is the unconditioned state of nirvana. The importance of the Dharma is that it leads to nirvana; fully realizing the Dharma means achieving nirvana. Nirvana is not a place like heaven or the

A Sri Lankan sculpture of the Buddha in the meditation posture.

realm of the gods, for all of these are part of samsara and thus conditioned and impermanent. Nirvana is freedom from samsara and therefore is a permanent, unconditioned state. The Buddha speaks:

> There is, monks, an unborn, not become, not made, uncompounded, and were it not, monks, for this unborn, not become, not made, uncompounded, no escape could be shown here for what is born, has become, is made, is compounded.[3]

As in this description, nirvana is often described negatively, for it is unlike anything else in our human experience. But how can such a negative idea be thought of as ultimate reality? The fact that nirvana is often described in negatives has led some outsiders to think of it as annihilation or as unreal. But this is a misunderstanding, for the Buddhist tradition applies many positive concepts to nirvana. Edward Conze draws from various texts some of the things that can be said in describing nirvana; in the texts we are told

> that Nirvana is permanent, stable, imperishable, immovable, ageless, deathless, unborn, unbecome; that it is power, bliss and happiness, the secure refuge, the shelter and the place of unassailable safety; real Truth and the supreme Reality; that it is the *Good*, the supreme goal and the one and only consummation of our life, the eternal, hidden and incomprehensible Peace.[4]

Such descriptions contain many attributes that Jews, Christians, or Muslims might apply to God, and they show that nirvana does function as ultimate for Buddhists. Yet nirvana is not in any sense like God, for it is not a sacred power outside oneself, operating in the world. Nirvana is a reality experienced within, as it were, a state of unconditioned freedom.

Still, nirvana is real. It is eternal, absolute, unconditioned, and ultimate. Therefore, it is highly to be desired and looked to by every Buddhist as the supreme goal of human existence, even though it may be thousands of lifetimes away.

Emptiness and Suchness

Mahayana Buddhists go further in their view of the unconditioned real. Reflecting philosophically on the ultimate qualities of nirvana, they tend to emphasize positive terms like "emptiness" (*shunyata*) or "suchness" (*tathata*). Early Buddhism taught that everything is a conglomeration of elements or "dharmas"; the chariot, for example, is only the sum of its parts and therefore not real, although its parts are real. A distinction was then made between all these dharmas or conditioned things, and the one *unconditioned* dharma, namely, the state of nirvana. But Mahayana teaches that emptiness (shunyata) is actually the common predicate of all dharmas, whether conditioned or unconditioned. Emptiness means the absence of "own-being," that is, something existing through its own power and having an immutable essence. So emptiness is really the same thing as the truth of dependent arising. But Mahayana points out that not only are all conditioned dharmas (that is, the phenomenal world of samsara) empty, but also the unconditioned reality of nirvana is empty. This leads to the conclusion that, since both nirvana and samsara are empty, there is no essential difference between them. Nirvana is samsara.

The fact that emptiness is a predicate both of nirvana and of samsara means a revaluation of living in the world. Nirvana is not a state found by fleeing from this world, but it is experienced precisely within this world. There is a nirvanic quality that can be experienced in life if we but awaken to it, because of the emptiness that characterizes all reality. Nirvana is precisely awakening to emptiness, seeing the world as it really is in its "suchness."

So among Mahayanists, especially in East Asia, emptiness is considered a positive and powerful basis of reality. It is true that "emptiness," especially to Westerners, may sound like a lack or a deprivation. But actually it is more the supreme affirmation or fulfillment, for emptiness is really the co-dependence, the cooperation of all. Emptiness is actually the womb (*tathagatagharba*, womb of the Buddha) that gives birth to all reality, the creative source of all that is. In more direct terms, it is the silence that surrounds and supports every sound, the stillness that is the foundation of all movement, the pure consciousness that is the ground of all thought.

So, what's it *all* about? The Dharma. Nirvana. Emptiness. These terms together, all basically undefinable, point to the shape of the ultimate reality in Buddhism.

Going for Refuge to the Buddha

Along with the Dharma and nirvana, it seems that the Buddha has always had some place within the Buddhist idea of ultimate reality. It should be clear by now that the Buddha is not God, although he did live as a god in one of the heavens in a previous existence. He is not "supernatural" in the sense of a power that comes from beyond to save people. The Buddha was, in his final lifetime, a human being like the rest of us humans, and he remained a human being for forty-five years after becoming the Buddha, until he died and reached the state of parinirvana, beyond existence and nonexistence. His great achievement was done at the human level, and thus it is a goal that all living beings can reach, since all living beings have the possibility of being born at the human level.

The Perfections and Powers of the Buddha

Still, as a human being the Buddha was "supernormal," for he achieved all those supreme spiritual qualities that are far beyond the capabilities of most. Over countless lifetimes he reached the ten perfections, achieved miraculous powers, and attained complete omniscience, not to mention various other higher powers. Yet all these attainments and powers, which might appear to outsiders as possible for God alone, do not make the Buddha a god. Rather, they make him, still a human being, into the Tathagata, the "one who has arrived there," the victorious one, the very embodiment of the Dharma.

A statue of the Buddha Shakyamuni in the posture of turning the wheel of the Dharma.

To put the Buddha in the proper perspective, we need to remind ourselves that there have been and will be other Buddhas in the infinite cycles of the rise and fall of the universe. And they will all reach the same perfections and powers and teach the same Dharma. The story of Siddhartha Gautama is the story of a being who, through a long series of lifetimes as a bodhisattva, made such spiritual progress that becoming a Buddha was inevitable, and he was born as a human at the time and place of his own choosing, to achieve the great breakthrough and become the Buddha, the world saviour to whom Buddhists in our world-age go for refuge.

So then, it is appropriate to chant in devotions every day, "Adoration to him the blessed one, the worthy one, the fully enlightened one." Whereas Buddhists know that the Buddha is not alive today as a god or saviour, the powers he achieved are real and present in our world, symbolized by his images and relics, present in his words and teachings, experienced in meditation, and actualized in those who follow his path.

The Mahayana Vision: Dharmakaya and Heavenly Buddha

Mahayana Buddhists go much further than Theravadins in their visions of the Buddha reality. The ultimate reality seen in the Dharma, in emptiness, and in the achievement of the Buddha are brought together in the Mahayana notion of "Buddhahood," expressed especially in the Three Body doctrine. The doctrine of the Three Bodies of the Buddha, as worked out by philosophers of the Yogacara school, is a way of formulating the dimensions of ultimate reality in terms of Buddha. There are three "bodies" (*kaya*) or dimensions of "Buddha": the Dharma Body (Dharma-kaya), the Bliss Body (Sambhoga-kaya), and the Transformation Body (Nirmana-kaya).

The idea of Buddha now moves far beyond the historical human Siddhartha Gautama, the teacher. The Buddha is really the eternal power of the Dharma. The Dharma Body of the Buddha encompasses all aspects of ultimate reality. Just as the Dharma is universal, eternal, and ultimate, so also is the Buddha. Just as nirvana is unconditioned and absolutely free, so is the Buddha. The Buddha is the same as suchness and emptiness. It is the Buddha-source identified as the Womb of the Tathagata, innate to all living beings, irradiated by the pervading power of Buddhahood. Mahayana, with its notion of a supermundane, universal Buddha essence, brings into Buddhism something like Brahman in Hinduism—an underlying ultimate reality. The Dharma Body is the fundamental Buddha-essence, which permeates and supports all things.

The human form of Buddha (Transformation Body) now is seen as a kind of magical-appearance body by which the everlasting Dharma Body of the Buddha showed humans in our age the path to enlightenment. Siddhartha was really an apparition that took on the characteristics of human life and reached enlightenment as a model and guide to other living beings in this age. Likewise the Buddha reality has shown itself through Transformation Bodies in countless other ages and worlds.

Further, it makes sense that the Dharma Body, characterized by eternal, all-powerful compassion, should create bodies in all times and places in the universe, to respond to the needs of living beings everywhere. And so Mahayanists believe that the universe is filled with heavenly Buddhas (the Bliss Body of the Buddha) who use all kinds of means to lead all living beings to enlightenment and salvation, functioning almost like gods and saviours. There have been, according to the Lotus Sutra, an infinite number of Buddhas saving people, hundreds of trillions of kinds.

One of the most widely worshiped of the heavenly Buddhas is Amitabha (Unlimited Light). Countless aeons ago, Amitabha was a monk named Dharmakara who decided to become a Buddha. He was taught by the Buddha for ten million years and practiced meditation for five aeons, concentrating all the qualities of Buddhahood on the creation of one Buddhaland, the Pure Land. He vowed that his Buddhaland would contain no evil destinies, that all those reborn there would be destined for nirvana, and that all who meditate on him could share in his merit and thus attain rebirth in this paradise. After practicing as a bodhisattva for a trillion years, Dharmakara became the Buddha Amitabha, presiding over the Pure Land of the West, sending out unlimited compassion to all who call on him.

Another important heavenly expression of ultimate Buddhahood is Mahavairocana (great Shining Out), widely worshiped as the sun Buddha. One view is that Mahavairocana is actually the cosmic Dharma Body of the earthly Buddha. Important especially in Tantric Buddhism, Mahavairocana's body is really the whole cosmos, and his mind and power permeate the universe.

Some Buddhists of the Pure Land school and the Tantric school look to Amitabha or Mahavairocana as the ultimate reality, virtually identical with the Dharma Body of the Buddha, and thus express a kind of monotheism or cosmotheism. But most Buddhists recognize that these countless Buddhas are not themselves the ultimate reality, but they are manifestations of the ultimate in various times and places to lead people to salvation. We need to understand that since truth is experienced at different levels, Buddhism can tolerate the worship of these heavenly Buddhas and much more, including bodhisattvas, gods, goddesses, and a variety of local spirits. And this is true both in Mahayana and in Theravada lands. For the common people these various divine forces are direct sources of help and salvation. For the spiritually advanced, these forces are but expressions of the universal Buddha nature or are simply divine beings operating within the samsara existence.

EXISTENCE IN THE WORLD

What is this world all about anyway? The origin of the world is not so important to Buddhists as the nature of the world and of ourselves. The Buddha said, "The first beginning of beings wandering and running round, enveloped in ignorance and bound down by the fetters of thirst is not to be perceived."[5] Questions about origin and purpose could imply a beginning and an end, and Buddhists think more in terms of a beginningless, endless process. Of more concern is the question: what is the nature of reality and what is one's own nature? Long wrestlings with these questions have produced both deep intellectual speculations and single-minded practices.

The Nature of the World

Origin of the World and of Humans

Buddhists like Hindus think of the universe as virtually endless both in time and in space. One illustration, for example, says that the amount of time this universe has existed is innumerable times greater than how long it would take to wear down to sea level a vast high mountain by touching it lightly with a piece of soft Banaras silk once every one hundred years. And texts talk of hundreds of trillions of worlds, so that our earth is but a small point in the vast canvas of the universe.

The Buddhist traditions agree with the Hindu view that there are periodic creations and destructions of the universe, like the rhythm of waves on the sea. As the various worlds are destroyed and evolve again, beings are born from one into another because of karma. The Buddha told a story about this process in which he skillfully rejected the idea of creation of the world through the god Brahma.

There comes time, my friends, sooner or later, . . . when the world is dissolved and beings are mostly reborn in the World of Radiance [one of the heavens]. There they dwell, made of the stuff of mind, feeding on joy, shining in their own light, flying through middle space, firm in their bliss for a long, long time.

Now there comes a time when this world begins to evolve, and then the World of Brahma [a lower heaven] appears, but it is empty. And some being, whether because his allotted span is past or because his merit is exhausted, quits his body in the World of Radiance and is born in the empty World of Brahma, where he dwells for a long, long time. Now because he has been so long alone he begins to feel dissatisfaction and longing, and wishes that other beings might come and live with him. And indeed soon other beings quit their bodies in the World of Radiance and come to keep him company in the World of Brahma.

Then the being who was born first there thinks: "I am Brahma, the mighty Brahma, the Conqueror, the Unconquered, the All-seeing, the Lord, the Maker, the Creator, the Supreme Chief, the Disposer, the Controller, the Father of all that is or is to be. I have created all these beings, for I merely wished that they might be and they have come here!" And the other beings . . . think the same, because he was born first and they later.

And it might well be that some being would quit his body there and be reborn in this world. He might then give up his home for the homeless life; and . . . he might attain such a stage of meditation that with collected mind he might recall his former birth, but not what went before. Thus he might think: "We were created by Brahma, eternal, firm, everlasting, and unchanging, who will remain so for ever and ever, while we . . . are transient, unstable, short-lived, and destined to pass away."

"That," said the Buddha, "is how your traditional doctrine comes about that the beginning of things was the work of the god Brahma."[6] So the idea of creation of the universe by Brahma is an illusion. Really, the world and all living beings, including the gods, go on through successive stages of evolution and devolution, without beginning, without end.

According to the Buddhist tradition, the beings reborn on earth in this process begin to eat an earth essence and thus become dependent on subtle morsel food, their bodies becoming more substantial. Then they start eating rice-pap sort of food, and male and female characteristics appear, and soon they indulge in sexual acts. Finally the earth-human society evolves to include the idea of private property with individual rice plots, stealing, and violence—and our human historical era begins.

The Real Nature of the World and of Humans

Like all the peoples from India, Buddhism accepts the basic idea of karma and samsara. There is a wheel of existence, both for the whole world and for the individual, and it is propelled by karma. But what is distinctive about the Buddhist view is the emphasis on *impermanence, no-self,* and *dependent arising* as doctrines about the nature of the world.

What is there to really hold on to in this world? Nothing. For there is nothing that is permanent, lasting, and absolute. Everything is impermanent, in a process of flux, coming into being and passing out of being endlessly. Even the gods, even the world itself, come and go. Even Brahman, central to Hindu belief as absolute reality, cannot be an eternal, unchanging reality. Whatever exists is a stream of becoming. A beautiful, fragile blossom is often used to exemplify this view. It blooms in beauty momentarily, but then it is driven to the ground by the rain or wilted by the sun. That is not particularly tragic or to be regretted; that is the nature of existence.

One aspect of the doctrine of impermanence regards one's own self. What is the real self? From Hinduism we learned that inward of the empirical self is the real atman, eternal and indestructible, which is embodied in existence after existence but itself does not change. The Buddha says there is no atman (*an-atman*), no permanent reality we can call the self. Rather, that which we call the self or the person is really a changing process made up of a series of five aggregates combined together for a lifetime. This process of aggregates includes physical matter, sensations, perceptual activities, impulses to action, and bits of consciousness. These aggregates come together for a lifetime, constantly changing, and they dissipate when the lifetime ends. Where, beyond these aggregates, asks the Buddha, do you see a permanent self? There is none.

For understanding the nature of the world, it is important to remember the central Buddhist teaching about dependent arising, which shows the interconnectedness of everything. Everything is conditioned by other things, but it is false to assert that everything happens randomly by chance. Thus there is some continuity even in this world of change. For example, is an old man the same person as he was when he was a baby? On the one hand, he obviously is not, for everything about him has changed since babyhood. On the other hand, he still is the same because of the common stream of conditions that has made him what he is.

So it is the idea of dependent arising that makes it possible to understand how there can be rebirth cycles and yet no permanent self. Hinduism teaches that the eternal atman passes from one lifetime to the next. The question for Buddhism is: what is it that goes through the rebirth cycles if there is no atman? The answer is that *nothing* goes through the rebirth cycles. Rather each rebirth is caused by the previous existences in a chain of causation. It is like touching the flame of one candle to the wick of another and lighting it. Nothing is passed from the one candle to the next; there is no "candle-soul" or substance transmitted, yet the first burning candle is the cause of the burning of the second candle. It is the heat from the first flame that combusts the second candle, and likewise it is the karma from one lifetime that "combusts" the next lifetime.

Whereas the highest truth about the world consists in these doctrines of impermanence, no-self, and conditioned arising, there is still ample reason to carry on life in the world in a constructive, beneficial way. That I am no real self is the highest truth, to be realized by those reaching high spiritual perfection. Yet "my" life-process goes on, interrelated with all other living beings, and further teachings about reality provide guidance on the ideal way to live. One important idea is the interrelationship of all

things: all beings are one in the ocean of life. What affects one affects all. Another important facet of reality is the nature of karma. As explained by the Buddha, the law of karma has a volitional aspect; it is not the working of a merely mechanical fate, but it involves will and desire. I am who I am now because of past existences, but every moment I have the freedom to perform moral rather than immoral actions, thus changing the flow of karma and my own future existence.

As we have seen, Mahayana Buddhists have additional things to say about the nature of the world and human existence. Since the essence of all reality is the Buddha nature, the very truths of impermanence and no-self point to this. That is, the samsara cycle of birth and death is Buddhahood; all things interpenetrate all else, and all are the Buddha nature. What is thought to be the self is illusory, but one's true nature is Buddhahood. So the goal in life is to realize the Buddhahood of the world and oneself. Whereas Mahayanists share the fundamental Buddhist outlook on the world, these additional doctrines give a somewhat different color to their view of the goal and the problematic of human existence.

The Human Problem: Clinging

The evolutionary cycles of the world, the stream of karma and rebirth, the impermanence of all things—these are neutral facts of existence. That's the way things are. So what's the problem?

The Truths of Suffering and Clinging

The problem, the Buddha said in his first sermon, is *dukkha*, suffering (the first Noble Truth). All existence is permeated with suffering. The Buddha was not a grim-faced doomsayer or even overly pessimistic about human life. He allowed that people do experience moments of happiness and joy. But there always is that sense of anxiety and uneasiness, knowing that we are going to lose what we have, knowing that finally we will lose even our selves in death. So the problem is a matter of how we experience our existence, constantly fearful of losing what is important to us.

Why do we feel this kind of suffering and anxiety? It is because of clinging, answers the Buddha (the second Noble Truth). We try desperately to cling and hold on to things like happiness, to life itself, to ourselves. But the truth is that there is nothing to cling to, since everything is passing, so we lose what we try to hold on to, and in the process we experience suffering.

Buddhists have gone to great lengths to illustrate these truths of suffering and the cause of suffering. Once, according to a poem by Ashvaghosha, a relative of the Buddha named Nanda became a monk but was about to leave the order because of his longing for his wife. The Buddha took him to the paradise of King Indra, a heaven of indescribable beauty where beings who had built up much merit as humans now live happily as gods, perpetually young and free from suffering. Beautiful celestial nymphs reward all who come to this paradise by virtue of their previous austerities. Seeing the ravishing beauty of the nymphs, Nanda forgot his wife, and the world of humans seemed to him no better than a cemetery. So, having seen this paradise, Nanda resumed his austerities in order to reach this reward. But his fellow monk Ananda warned him that living in paradise is only temporary, and that one day the gods there also will fall to be reborn on earth—and just think of the tremendous suffering they will feel because of the great delights and pleasures they will finally be losing! "It is better, therefore," Ananda counseled, "to strive for final release. Even the dwellers in heaven, with all their might, come to an end. No intelligent man would set his heart on winning the right to a brief stay among them."[7]

Trapped in Ignorance

Why is it that we are trapped in an existence in which we are constantly desiring and therefore constantly suffering? To account for the arising of these conditions, Buddhists apply the principle of dependent arising to human existence. They picture a series of twelve causes of becoming, each cause conditioning the next cause. Frequently these twelve causes are pictured in the form of a twelve-spoked wheel, since there really is no beginning or end to the process. The hub of the wheel, the driving force, is made up of hatred, delusion, and greed. And the twelve groups of conditions are:

1. Ignorance, causing volitional actions
2. Volitional actions, causing consciousness
3. Consciousness, causing personal existence
4. Personal existence, causing the mind and the senses
5. Mind and senses, causing mental and sensorial contact
6. Mental and sensorial contact, causing sensations and feelings
7. Sensations and feelings, causing craving
8. Craving, causing grasping
9. Grasping, causing new becoming-forces
10. Becoming-forces, causing rebirth
11. Rebirth, causing aging and dying
12. Aging and dying—causing ignorance again

And the wheel rolls on and on. Buddhist art has developed a graphic form of this wheel, held in the claws and mouth of the demon Death.

The wheel of existence leads to the six realms or destinies of rebirth. The most degrading realms of rebirth are the hells (age-long but not eternal punishment), next the realm of the hungry ghosts, then the realm of animals. Fourth is the human realm, fifth that of the demigods, and the highest realm is that of the gods. Remember that even the gods, when their traces of karma run out, suffer death and lower rebirth, because they lack sufficient merit—and losing their heavenly joys causes indescribable suffering. Only in the human realm can virtue and wisdom be increased, to proceed toward the goal, to transcend the wheel entirely.

So the whole wheel of life is really a trap, founded especially in ignorance, the delusion that I am a self and therefore I need things for myself. "I am—therefore I want." Our faint stirrings of morality, compassion, and goodness are quickly swallowed up by delusion, desire, and anger, and the wheel of selfish existence rolls on.

To stop this wheel of existence takes something more than struggle and selfish desire—it takes getting on the path of transformation.

THE PATH TO NIRVANA AND BUDDHAHOOD

How can we start living *real* life? Where are meaning and peace to be found?

Paradoxically, the Buddha taught that the only way to find real life is to withdraw from life as we normally perceive it, to work toward cessation of those attachments that keep existence going. Some therefore have thought of

Buddhism as a negative, world-denying religious path designed to lead to extinction. But that is to misunderstand Buddhism. The path leads to cessation of attachments so that true life and meaning can be experienced—that which is called nirvana or Buddhahood.

Nirvana and the Noble Eightfold Path

The human problem, as we saw, is depicted in terms of suffering caused by craving or clinging in a universe that is characterized by impermanence. At the heart of the problem is human ignorance and the illusion of a permanent self. The Buddha described the human problem only to show the way out, the means of conquering and reaching liberation.

The Noble Truth of Nirvana

In his sermon at the Deer Park in Sarnath, after enunciating the first truth that human existence is suffering and the second truth that the cause of suffering is craving, the Buddha presented the third Noble Truth: "The Noble Truth of the Cessation of suffering is this: It is the complete cessation of that very thirst, giving it up, renouncing it, emancipating oneself from it, detaching oneself from it."[8] The suffering and frustration of our existence can be removed! It is removed by eliminating that which causes it, namely, craving. All craving can be eliminated by removing all the conditions on which it depends. The conditions on which craving depends are, we remember, depicted in the twelve-spoked wheel of existence: ignorance, wrong intentions, impure consciousness, the illusion of self, and so forth. Eliminating these conditions, and thus eliminating craving, will bring cessation of suffering. And this is the state of nirvana.

Nirvana is not the extinction of existence, nor is it a state to be experienced only after death. Nirvana (blowing out, cooling off) is the experience of full life and meaning achieved by eliminating all forms of grasping and attachment. It is complete freedom from conditions and limitations, permitting life to be lived in the full richness of the present moment, without fear or anxiety. Since the causes of bondage have been eliminated, one who attains nirvana will not experience further rebirths in the samsara cycle; the liberation is complete.

It sounds simple. But as we all experience over and over, eliminating craving is an awesome thing, and even the most painful results of our craving do not induce us to give up that craving. How can this state of nirvana be attained?

The Noble Eightfold Path

The Buddha was more concerned with practical spiritual results than with philosophical speculations about existence. He thought of himself as a physician or therapist. He showed people their symptoms (suffering), made a diagnosis of what causes the suffering (craving), made a prognosis that suffering can be stopped by stopping the cause (nirvana), and finally gave the prescription: the Path.

Not all the Buddha's disciples were satisfied with this practical approach. The monk Malunkyaputta felt the Buddha had left unanswered a whole set of important questions, like whether the world is eternal, whether it is infinite, whether the self and the body are identical, and whether one who reaches nirvana exists after death. So he challenged the Buddha, saying that he would leave the monastic life unless the Buddha would answer these questions. The Buddha reminded Malunkyaputta that he had never promised to answer such questions, and further he pointed out that the questions rested on so many assumptions and distinctions that they could not be answered in a lifetime. But, most important, these questions are simply beside the point.

> It is as if, Malunkyaputta, a man had been wounded by an arrow thickly smeared with poison, and his friends and companions, his relatives and kinsfolk, were to procure for him a physician or surgeon, and the sick man were to say: "I will not have this arrow taken out until I have learned whether the man who wounded me belonged to the brahmana, kshatriya, vaishya, or shudra class; the name of the person who wounded me and the clan to which he belongs; whether he was tall, short, or medium in height; whether he was black, yellow, or brown; what village, city, or town he was from; what kind of wood the bow was made from; what kind of material the bow-string was made of; what kind of arrow it was, and with what it was feathered; what kind of sinews it was bound with; and what kind of point it had." That man would die, Malunkyaputta, without ever having learned this.[9]

This kind of speculation does not profit, nor does it have to do with the fundamentals of the religious path.

Whether the world is eternal or not, there still remain birth, old age, death, and suffering. The important thing is to get on the Path.

The noble Eightfold Path sets forth a whole way of life leading progressively to higher levels of spiritual transformation. It consists in:

1. Right understanding ⎫
2. Right intention   ⎬ Wisdom
3. Right speech   ⎫
4. Right action   ⎬ Moral conduct
5. Right livelihood   ⎭
6. Right effort   ⎫
7. Right mindfulness   ⎬ Contemplation
8. Right concentration   ⎭

These eight norms are not separate steps, as if one followed the other in succession. Rather one should cultivate a way of life in which all eight norms are followed together, for each supports all the others. The eight are traditionally grouped in the three basic axioms of the path, namely Wisdom, Moral Conduct, and Contemplation.

First, Wisdom involves both some basic understanding of the nature of existence and also the intention to act in accord with this understanding. **Right understanding** would include knowing the four noble truths of existence, the doctrines of impermanence and no-self, the teaching of the conditionedness of all existence, and the like. Whereas understanding deepens as we follow the Path,

Monks chanting Buddhist sutras, at Eiheiji Temple in Japan.

some understanding is necessary to reverse our ignorance and motivate us to start on the path in the first place. This leads to the **right intention** of freeing ourselves from the conditions of craving by cultivating the virtues of selflessness, goodwill, compassion, and love for all beings.

Next, Moral Conduct results directly from Wisdom. **Right speech** is telling the truth, speaking in kindly and friendly ways, and saying only what is helpful. **Right action** means not killing or hurting living things, no stealing, and no wrong sexual activity; positively it fosters the welfare of all living beings. **Right livelihood** involves avoidance of occupations that bring harm to others, accepting only those occupations that promote peace and well-being.

Finally, Contemplation is made possible when all the other norms are in place, and it involves a steady discipline of mind that leads to awareness and insight. **Right effort** means achieving a strong will that prevents and gets rid of wrong states of mind and creates and develops wholesome states of mind. **Right mindfulness** means being carefully aware of what goes on in the body and in the mind, attentively mindful of all sensations, feelings, and thoughts. And finally **right concentration** is the attainment, through meditation, of higher stages of mental awareness by direct insight and enlightenment. Here all sense of self and selfishness drops away, and ignorant grasping is replaced by peace and total freedom. The "I am" conceit is rooted out, and nirvana is experienced.

As we can see, there are a great many practices and disciplines that make up the Buddhist path of transformation. There are steps here both for the beginning layperson and for the advanced nun or monk. And there is plenty to occupy oneself with for a lifetime—or for many lifetimes. But among all these steps and disciplines, it is most characteristic of the Buddhist path of transformation to consider meditation to be the final means toward reaching nirvana. There are different types of meditation, of course, as Buddhists point out. One type, for example, involves concentrating and focusing the mind on an object or idea, leading to the calming of the mental processes and even to higher states of trance and supernormal psychic experiences. Whereas this type of meditation can be useful, the movement of meditation that leads toward nirvana involves developing insight and awareness, for finally it is "seeing" reality as it *really* is (the truth of dependent arising) that brings the nirvanic experience. So the Buddha taught *vipassana*, "insight" meditation, an analytic method based on mindfulness, observation, and total awareness of reality as it is.

The Buddha suggested that such insight meditation might profitably deal with four areas of life: the body, the feelings, the mind, and intellectual subjects. For example, the meditator might simply become totally aware of the bodily breathing process, watching and observing every minute aspect of breathing-in and breathing-out. Or again, the meditator might observe and become mindful of sensations and feelings. A Buddhist scholar, Walpola Rahula, explains the process and the goal:

> First of all, you should learn not to be unhappy about your unhappy feeling, not to be worried about your worries. But try to see clearly why there is a sensation or a feeling of unhappiness, or worry, or sorrow. Try to examine how it arises, its cause, how it disappears, its cessation. Try to examine it as if you are observing it from outside, without any subjective reaction, as a scientist observes some object. Here, too, you should not look at it as "my feeling" or "my sensation" subjectively, but only look at it as "a feeling" or "a sensation" objectively. You should forget again the false idea of "I." When you see its nature, how it arises and disappears, your mind grows dispassionate towards that sensation, and becomes detached and free.[10]

So also through meditation one becomes totally aware of the operation of the mind, knowing the mind with lust as being with lust, the mind without lust as being without lust, the mind with hate as being with hate, the mind without hate as being without hate, and so forth, through all states of mind, cultivating total awareness and with it the cessation of attachment and clinging. Further, one may meditate on the truths about reality—the Four Noble Truths, the five aggregates, and so on. By becoming totally aware and thus seeing reality directly as it is, one facilitates the cessation of clinging and false sense of self, moving toward the experience of nirvana.

Arhats and Laypeople on the Path

Following the Path is a lifelong affair, indeed, a many-lifetimes affair for all but the most spiritually advanced. Because of the disciplines involved, to follow the Path

fully one must leave society and become a nun or monk. Among the monastic community various levels of attainment are also recognized. At a high stage of spiritual perfection a monk or nun is recognized to be a "stream-winner," destined to have only a limited number of rebirths before reaching nirvana. Higher yet are the "once-returner," who will experience only one more rebirth, and the "nonreturner," who will achieve nirvana in this lifetime. The final stage is the arhat (worthy one), one who has already achieved nirvana and lives the completely enlightened, free life. Even for the monks and nuns at lower spiritual levels, the goal held out is victory over the world, the elimination of the illusion of self, the attainment of nirvana.

What about the laypeople in Buddhism? How can they follow such an elite religious path? Is there no hope for them? In Theravada Buddhism, it is true, the laity cannot expect to reach the goal of nirvana without eventually becoming a monk or nun. But laypeople can still get on the path and cultivate at least generosity and moral conduct. Besides deepening their understanding and intention, such disciplines also build up merit to counterbalance their store of bad karma. Merit can bring about more favorable rebirths; sufficient merit can even bring about rebirth as a god. The final goal of such merit, of course, is a lifetime in which the pursuit of nirvana will be possible. But that may be a long way off, and in the meantime it is better to be reborn in a happy state than in a despicable state. Some Theravadin laypeople do practice meditation, of course.

The Mahayana Enlargement of the Path of Transformation

Whereas Mahayana Buddhists accept the basics of the path as described above, their expanded vision of the sangha and the Buddha allows for additional possibilities on the path. Nirvana is understood as realizing one's Buddhahood, and this path is open to laypeople as well as monastics. The model to follow on the path is the bodhisattva rather than the arhat. And new possibilities of help from heavenly Buddhas and of realizing the inner Buddha-nature make this a much broader path of transformation. Yet it still is, we must remember, the same path of the Buddha.

Becoming the Buddha: The Broad Path

Since Mahayanists believe the Dharma Body of the Buddha is the source and essence of all reality, the goal of the path can be rephrased in terms of realizing one's Buddha-nature. Further, since Buddha-nature (or nirvana) is not a state apart from this life but is in fact identical with the samsara world, the goal is to awaken to the Buddha-nature of this very life. The basic problem, for Mahayanists as well as Theravadins, is ignorance. We do not see the real Buddha-nature, and instead we cling to our illusory nature—and we suffer in this lifetime while creating an equally suffering future lifetime by our karma. How do we start living the real Buddha life?

The place to start is certainly the discipline of the Eightfold Path. But since the emphasis is on realizing the Buddhahood of all beings, the path stresses the awakening of the thought of enlightenment and the cultivation of compassion. Monastic disciplines are still important, but even laypeople can attain the realization of Buddhahood. In a significant shift on the path of transformation, Mahayana Buddhists do not look to the arhat, reaching nirvana with great discipline and effort, as the supreme spiritual model. Rather, the Mahayana path is really the course of the bodhisattva.

Inherent in Buddhism from the beginning was an emphasis on compassion, the sense of oneness with all living beings. But monastic religion seemed to some to place a great emphasis on striving for individual salvation. The arhat is one who perfects himself or herself through spiritual disciplines, roots out all clinging, and finally attains nirvana, liberation from the sufferings of the rebirth cycle in which all other beings are trapped. Whereas the arhat cultivates compassion as a virtue, the ultimate goal is release. But the bodhisattva, according to the Mahayana story, is a great being who aeons ago grasped the thought of enlightenment and took vows to work incessantly for the welfare and salvation of all living things, thus starting on the bodhisattva course. Through countless lifetimes the bodhisattva cultivates the ten perfections, eliminates all defilements, and reaches enlightenment and supreme Buddhahood. But having reached the goal, the bodhisattva delays entering into nirvana, continuing in the rebirth cycle in order to work for the salvation of all beings, in accordance with the bodhisattva vow.

An important factor in the idea of the bodhisattva is the Buddhist notion of merit, which is built up by moral, selfless deeds. The bodhisattva builds up a tremendous amount of merit in his long course, especially in voluntarily being reborn in samsara even after reaching enlightenment. And this merit can be transferred to others in need, delivering them out of physical distress and even helping them to rebirth in one of the paradises. One such bodhisattva vow says:

I shall be the inexhaustible treasure of all the needy. I shall be in the vanguard with all kinds of means (for them). I shall give up all enjoyments in which by nature the ego is involved. I shall give up the merit that leads to all the three worlds and I shall do so for fulfilling the desires of all beings and without expecting any return. Nirvana is the renunciation of everything. My mind desires Nirvana. If everything is to be given up by me, it is better that I make a gift of everything to living things. I am the light for those who need light; the bed for those who need a bed; and the servant of those who need service. I am all these to all.[11]

The bodhisattva may be born in the world, appearing as an ordinary person, to help others. "Although the son of Jina [the conqueror] has penetrated to this immutable true nature of dharmas, yet he appears like one of those who are blinded by ignorance, subject as he is to birth, and so on. This is truly wonderful. It is through his compassionate skill in means for others that he is tied to the world."[12]

The Mahayana scriptures record many bodhisattva vows, put forth as a model to guide all beings on the path of transformation. Here is another such vow:

A Bodhisattva resolves: I take upon myself the burden of all suffering. . . . And why? At all cost I must bear the burdens of all beings, in that I do not follow my own inclinations. I have made the vow to save all beings. All beings I must set free. The whole world of living beings I must rescue, from the terrors of birth, of old age, of sickness, of death and rebirth, of all kinds of moral offense, of all states of woe, of the whole cycle of birth-and-death, of the jungle of false views. . . . I must not cheat all beings out of my store of merit. I am resolved to abide in each single state of woe for numberless aeons; and so I will help all beings to freedom, in all the states of woe that may be found in any world system whatsoever.[13]

The bodhisattva pursues a path of transformation based on the cultivation of compassion, of sharing merit with others, as the highest virtue that finally transforms one. The path of the bodhisattva is a model for all, showing the infinite transformations ahead on the path and the shape of the final goal.

Two Ways on the Path

Because of the idea of the universal Buddha-nature, in Mahayana there can be a number of approaches toward this path of transformation. It is possible, on the one hand, to practice meditation and see directly into one's Buddha-nature and the Buddha-nature of all reality. On the other hand, the compassionate nature of the Buddha reality makes it possible to receive help along the path from various bodhisattvas and Buddhas who are dedicated to the salvation of all beings. Frequently the path can be a combination of these two impulses.

Meditation plays an important role for many on the Mahayana path, as in Theravada. Practices of meditation are especially important in some East Asian Mahayana schools such as Tian-tai (Tendai in Japan) and Chan (Zen). A special emphasis in Mahayana meditation is the realization of emptiness, that is, seeing the nirvanic quality of all reality. In Chan meditation, for example, it is felt that the main barriers to experiencing one's innate Buddha-nature are the mind-blocks that we normally place in the way. The mind is ever active, like a monkey flitting about from tree-limb to tree-limb, and so it creates a secondary dualistic reality that blocks the mind from seeing directly the Buddha reality. Therefore, by emptying the mind in meditation the dualistic barriers are overcome and one "sees directly" the Buddha-mind. After all, if one's real nature is the Buddha-nature, then transformation occurs by overcoming the illusion of separate selfhood and awakening to the Buddha-nature within. In this sense, one can "become Buddha" even within this very body and life—that is, awaken to one's innate Buddha-nature and thus live life in a transformed way. And this awakening is available for all people, not only for monks and nuns, for all people equally possess the Buddha-nature.

The meditation practices of Tantric Buddhism have often focused on the potential each person has for realizing the inner Buddha-nature through ritual practices. In

Statue of a bodhisattva, probably Avalokiteshvara, from thirteenth century Nepal.

Tibetan Buddhism, for example, one important ritual technique is visualization. Since the cosmos is filled with Buddha-nature, it is possible through ritual meditation using sounds, movements, and pictures to visualize and so mentally create that cosmic Buddha reality and to identify oneself with it. In this way, one is transformed ritually and becomes one with the cosmic Buddha nature.

The strong Mahayana ideas about the universal Buddha essence, the virtue of compassion, and the model of the bodhisattva mean that the path of transformation can include reliance on power from Buddhas as well as self-power for transformation and salvation. If one cannot follow the holy path of discipline and meditation to reach nirvana, and if one cannot even build up sufficient merit to hope for a better rebirth, there still is another way: one can rely on the power of the merciful Buddhas and bodhisattvas for help and salvation. This path has become very popular in East Asian Buddhism, both for laypeople and for monks and nuns.

This view is often associated with the notion that the world has degenerated progressively over the different ages and we now live in an age of increased evil and suffering. So the question is, how can I, sinner that I am and living in this degenerate age, have assurance of salvation from these lifetimes of suffering and evil? The Pure Land school would answer: have firm faith and recite the powerful name of Amitabha Buddha. If people practice this as a discipline and make it the center of life, they will receive spiritual assurances and growth in this life and salvation in paradise in the next life. Most Pure Land Buddhists acknowledge that rebirth in the Pure Land is not yet Buddhahood—but those reborn there will never again be born at lower states of woe, and they will achieve Buddhahood in just a few more lifetimes. Nichiren Buddhists in Japan believe that, since the Lotus Sutra is the supreme truth and contains all Buddha power, reciting the title of the Lotus Sutra enables one to receive the power of Buddhahood; it brings great blessings to the individual and to the whole community.

How can this "easy path" still be called Buddhism? Behind this path is the basic vision of Mahayana: all beings are one in the ocean of life, and merit achieved by one can be shared with others. Through faith the mind and heart lie open to the presence of the Buddha power. Reciting the sacred name actualizes that power and transforms us, breaking the bonds of past karma and bringing us to realization of the Buddha-nature. In these Mahayana Buddhist schools the path of salvation is not a matter of an individual struggling on her own merits to

reach liberation; it is rather a path in which the individual can tap into the communal resource of saving power made available through the supreme Buddha Power.

We see, then, that the path of transformation in Buddhism is multicolored. There is the nirvanic path followed by Theravada monks and nuns, leading to arhatship. But the laypeople follow the karmic path of building up merit for better rebirths. In some Mahayana schools the path of Buddhahood-realization is followed, through meditation and ritual. And still other Mahayana Buddhists follow the salvation-through-saving power path. Though they seem quite different, one can still recognize the basic Buddhist accents in all of them.

DISCUSSION QUESTIONS

1. Discuss the ultimate as unconditioned truth. What is signified by "dependent arising"?
2. What is nirvana? What is emptiness (shunyata)?
3. What is the Mahayana doctrine of the Three Bodies of the Buddha?
4. Explain the doctrines of impermanence and no-self. How can there be rebirth if there is no-self?
5. What, according to Buddhism, is the basic problem in human existence?
6. Explain the workings of the Noble Eightfold Path, showing how it leads toward nirvana.
7. In Mahayana, what are the two general ways toward realizing Buddhahood?
8. What is a bodhisattva? How would you recognize one?

CHAPTER 7

Buddhist Worship and the Good Life

WORSHIP AND RITUAL

How can we find new power for life? How can we get in touch with what is real? Buddhists feel these needs as do people of other religions, and the answer lies in ritual practices and observance of sacred times.

Buddhism has a strong sense of individual mindful effort as the means of transformation, and with that has always gone a relativizing attitude toward worship and ritual. The goal of ultimate transformation, that is, nirvana, can be reached only by individual discipline and mindful meditation, not by acts of worship or ritual directed toward sacred beings. Certainly worship cannot provide forgiveness or expiation for sins. Bad karma can be diminished only by discipline and meritorious action.

Yet there still are many reasons and goals for worship and ritual in Buddhism, even for the spiritually advanced monks and nuns. Many rituals are commemorative, remembering and respecting the Buddha and the great saints of the past. Rituals can also be expressive, a way of showing emotions of thankfulness, respect, and devotion to the Buddha, the Dharma, and the sangha. Performing such rituals can guide people in their practice of the path, and they can help to create the refreshed and peaceful mental attitude necessary for mindful meditation and meritorious action.

Many Buddhists believe that worship and ritual are also instrumental in bringing about blessings in life and even inner spiritual transformation. Worship can be beneficial in concerns like health, wealth, rainfall, coping with crises, passing through stages in life, and the like. And worship can contribute toward happy rebirths, because of the merit involved in making offerings to the Buddha and also because worship creates a favorable mental state—and it is the mental state at death that largely determines the nature of one's next existence. Sacred rituals like ordination as a monk, chanting the scriptures, and making pilgrimages can help to bring about important inner spiritual transformation.

Central Rites and Ceremonies of Buddhism

The Structure of Buddhist Ritual

For all the variety of ceremonial in different places of the Buddhist world, there are several basic rites that Buddhists perform no matter where they are. They always include some form of giving or offering in worship. Making offerings with the proper attitude and motivation serves to bring merit, and it is especially appropriate to show homage to the Buddha, the monks, and the spirits by making offerings of lighted candles, flowers, water, and food. Of course, the Buddha does not need or receive these offerings, for the state of parinirvana is beyond all this. But making the offerings brings merit for the future and blessings for this life; it reminds one of the Buddha and his teaching so as to better contemplate his attributes; and it helps on the way toward selflessness and compassion.

Another rite that all Buddhists perform is bowing before the Buddha image, the pagoda in which Buddhist relics are kept, or other symbols of the Buddha or bodhisattvas. A person may bow to the rosary and to the cushion used for meditating. And parents may bow to their ten-year-old son who has just been initiated as a temporary novice monk. This ritual of bowing is not that of a humble sinner petitioning a holy God for pardon and blessing. Rather, it shows respect for the Buddha, the Dharma, the sangha, parents, teachers, and all beings on the path. By bowing a person experiences the truth of no-self, symbolically turning away from self-centeredness to the real Buddha-nature of compassion and love.

Buddhists also use words of prayer, devotion, commemoration, and petition. A widely used Buddhist common prayer runs like this:

> I beg leave! I beg leave! I beg leave! By act, by word, and by thought, I raise my hands in reverence to the forehead and worship, honor, look at, and humbly pay homage to the Three Gems—the Buddha, the Law, and the Order—one time, two times, three times, O Lord [Buddha]! . . . By this act of worship may I be free from the four States of Woe [in hell, as an animal, a ghost, a demon], the Three Scourges [war, epidemic, and famine], . . . the Four Deficiencies [tyrannical kings, wrong views about life after death, physically deformed, dull-witted], and the Five Misfortunes [loss of relatives, wealth, health, proper belief, morality], and may I quickly attain Nirvana, O Lord![1]

Buddhists often recite the Three Refuges and other important formulas, and monks and priests spend much time chanting words of scripture. In words of worship they share merit with all others, especially wishing love for all beings:

> May all creatures, all living things, all beings, all persons, all individuals, all males, all females, all Aryans, all non-Aryans, all gods, all mankind, all spirits be free from enmity, from care, and from oppression. May they all live happily. May they all be free from trouble and adversity. May they all enjoy prosperity. May they all help themselves through the law of karma.[2]

Meditation, of course, is one of the central practices of Buddhism, especially for monks and nuns but also for spiritually advanced laypeople. Whereas meditation is not necessarily a part of all Buddhist worship and ritual, typically it is done in a context of worship. Before Buddhists sit to meditate, they bow to the image of the Buddha and perhaps to images of bodhisattvas and other masters, and they chant scriptures together. After meditating they offer incense and bow again. Whereas meditation takes one beyond outward ritual to the higher truths, the ritual context is beneficial for calming the mind and developing the proper will and intent.

Universally used objects of worship include images of the Buddha and bodhisattvas. For some centuries after the Buddha's death no images of him were used. Instead people paid homage to symbols of the Buddha such as an empty throne, a pair of footprints, a wheel, or a lotus plant—symbols still used in Buddhist art. Later Buddhists began using images of the Buddha, and today people will almost always turn to such an image as they worship. Other widely used objects of worship include relics of the Buddha, such as the famous Buddha tooth at the temple of Kandy in Sri Lanka, and also the stupas and pagodas in which the relics have been kept. Homage is paid also to monks and nuns and to the yellow robe they wear.

The great stupa at Sanchi. The gateway has important early Buddhist artistic depictions.

Daily Rituals and Worship

Traditional, pious Buddhists usually have a small shrine in their home, perhaps a simple shelf with a small Buddha image and a vase for offering flowers. The first act in the morning and the last act in the evening is worship, offering fresh flowers and/or food offerings, lighting a candle, bowing, reciting prayers, and sometimes saying the rosary of 108 beads.

Monks and nuns, on the path toward victory, of course, have a much more demanding ritual schedule throughout the day. Many of the common daily activities are accompanied with rituals of devotion and homage to the Buddha and the other sacred realities. From 3:00 A.M. in the morning until 10:00 P.M. at night there is typically a busy schedule of chanting scripture, meditating, making offerings to the Buddha and to other monks, saying prayers, reciting the Three Refuges and the monastic rules, listening to talks on the Dharma, participating in the communal tea ceremony, and much more. Even daily work like gardening and cleaning can be ritual opportunity for spiritual transformation, as practiced especially in the Chan (Zen) monasteries of China and Japan.

Holy Days and Festivals

The rhythm of renewal follows a regular pattern on certain days of the month and the year, with variances, of course, in different Buddhist lands.

The Uposatha Holy Day

Although Buddhists do not have a weekly holy day like Saturday or Sunday for communal worship, many do observe a similar type of regular holy day (*uposatha*). This rhythm is based on the lunar calendar, with the days of the full moon and the new moon, together with the eighth day after each. On these days the monks have special observances, and these are appropriate times for laypeople to visit the monastery or the temple for worship. This is not something required as a religious duty, and there is no demerit in not observing this worship—many good Buddhists only keep this day occasionally. But there is merit and benefit in going to the monastery or temple to show respect to the monks and the priests, hear them chant scripture, give offerings, receive the precepts, and listen to

instruction. Even if one does not understand the words the monks are chanting, there is spiritual blessing just by being in their presence and honoring them. This is an opportunity for laypeople and monastics to meet together and share spiritual benefit.

These holy day observances provide an opportunity for some devout laypeople to live temporarily according to the rules of monastic life. A person who has a job and a family normally takes only the five precepts for laypeople (to refrain from taking life, from stealing, from wrong sexual relations, from wrong speech, and from drugs and liquor), but on this holy day the person can take some of the additional precepts followed by monks and nuns and stay overnight in the monastery, practicing the discipline of a novice monk, before returning to normal householder life the next day.

The Great Annual Festivals

Perhaps not a lot of Buddhists participate in the uposatha holy day, but the great annual holy days and festivals are central to the rhythm of religious life, providing occasions for all the people to gather at the temples and holy places. These annual festivals often commemorate events in the life of the Buddha or the great bodhisattvas and celebrating them provides an opportunity to get in on the sacred story and make it real once more. Other festivals have to do with the seasonal changes in monastic life and with the veneration that is due for the ancestors. Among the most important and most widely celebrated festivals are the New Year's festival, the Buddha's birthday, the beginning of the Rainy Season Retreat, the presentation of robes to the monks, and the Ullambana festival celebrated in China and Japan.

In Theravada countries, the New Year comes at the end of the dry season and the beginning of new life in nature, falling in the month of April. It is a time of cleaning up, washing away the demerits of the past, and starting afresh. The first two days are celebrated in a carnival-like atmosphere as a water festival—for water cleans away the old and the dirty. Besides the spiritual cleansing, it is great fun to douse each other with water! The third day of the festival is a time for rededication to the Buddhist path, worship at the temples, taking the precepts, and giving offerings. It is especially meritorious on this festival, as on other festivals, to set animals and fish free into enclosures or ponds where they will be safe from harm for the rest of their lives. Since the release of the animals is accompanied by a monk or priest reciting the Three Refuges and the Precepts, the animals become "children of the Buddha" and have increased advantage of better rebirths.

The birthday of the Buddha is a joyful celebration, observed on the last full moon in May in Southeast Asia and on the eighth of April in China and Japan. Besides the usual worship activities, this festival is marked by the ritual of washing the Buddha image—a ceremony based on the tradition that the Buddha was bathed with scented water poured down by the gods after he was born. Another important ceremony is the procession of Buddha images, amidst the cheering and shouting of the people setting off firecrackers, burning incense, scattering flowers, and the like. Children love this festival—on this day they can dress up in their finest clothes, themselves little Buddhas.

In Theravada communities the beginning of the Rain Retreat is an especially important sacred time. The practice of the Rain Retreat goes back to the Buddha's time in India, when monks gathered in caves during the rainy season for intensified spiritual practice. When the Rain Retreat begins, the monks and nuns dedicate themselves to study and meditation, and the laity present specially prepared candles to the monastery to burn throughout the retreat. Other special offerings of food, money, and items of personal use are also made to the monks, and the senior monk leads the laypeople in the recitation of the precepts and the prayers. During the month at the end of the Rain Retreat (October–November), the laypeople perform the ritual of presenting newly made yellow robes to the monks, together with other elaborate gifts. High government officials also participate in these ceremonies, showing that the continued presence of the monastery is essential for the welfare of society. Pagodas and houses are decorated with lamps during this time, and crowds of people throng the streets at night during this festival of lights.

A most popular festival in China and Japan is the Ullambana festival (All Souls' festival) for ancestors, which will be discussed in Part II. There are many special festivals held in sacred places in addition to these widely observed festivals. For example, the Temple of the Tooth in Kandy, Sri Lanka, has a big ten-day celebration in August, featuring a procession of great elephants carrying the precious relic of the Buddha's tooth. Temples celebrate the birthdays of special Buddhas and bodhisattvas. Pilgrimage to the sacred places often takes place in the context of festivals.

Rituals of the Changes of Life

Buddhists, like other humans, have special rituals for the critical passages in life. Less concerned with birth and growth than with spiritual transformation and death, emphasis in Buddhism is especially on the rites of initiation and funeral rites.

The Rites of Passage

All over the Buddhist world, families and communities observe many prebirth and birth rituals. Some rituals ensure safety during pregnancy, and others are directed to the health and welfare of the baby: the first head-washing, placing into the new cradle, naming, and so forth. These rituals are observed according to local tradition with little Buddhist context, although monks may bring blessing to the family by their presence. Likewise, the variety of wedding rituals has little reference to Buddhist concerns, and Buddhist monks and priests do not usually attend the actual wedding ceremony. They, of course, may be invited to chant sutras for the safety of the new home and to be fed by offerings from the family. Buddhists recognize that birth, growth, sexuality, and happiness in life are important, and it is all right to perform rituals dedicated to those gods and spirits who provide these blessings. But the world is transitory, and the deeper Buddhist truth teaches one to keep all this in perspective by cultivating detachment and preparing for a holy death.

Much more important, as far as Buddhism is concerned, are the rites of passage that focus on the higher truths. In many Theravada communities the ritual of initiation for a young boy is one of the most important events of community life. The initiation corresponds to a puberty rite of passage, but its meaning is a spiritual transformation: the young boy becomes a novice monk for a temporary period. Typically this ceremony is carried out amid great festivities, the family inviting many relatives and friends for a joyful celebration complete with food, songs, dancing, and the like, in honor of the young prince decked out in his finest. In some communities an ear-boring ceremony is performed for young girls at the same time, although this ceremony does not indicate spiritual passage in the Buddhist sense. It is after all these festivities, when most of the guests have left, that the real ceremony takes place. Some monks assemble, the boy's head is shaved, and he takes the vows of the monastic life. Now he spends the night in the monastery and, when he goes out begging the next day, even his parents bow to him to honor his elevated spiritual state. After a few days or weeks the boy may return to normal life, but now he is spiritually an adult and may reenter the monastery again sometime in the future.

All things are impermanent. So Buddhists believe they should keep death in mind always, and funerals are times to remember most directly the transitory nature of existence. Buddhists also believe that a person's rebirth is determined at least in part by her state of mind immediately before death, so preparation for death is vitally important. And if the departed person is reborn in one of the states of woe, as a hungry ghost or in one of the hells, it becomes important for the descendants to offer prayer and merit to ease the sufferings and make deliverance possible.

To help the dying person to a peaceful, unattached, calm state of mind, Buddhist devotions are recited at the death bed, and monks may come to recite sutras. Pure Land Buddhists recite the name of Amida Buddha over and over, on the basis of Amida's vow to save all beings who recite his name. After death the body is washed and the head shaved. Many friends and relatives come to call, and on the day of the funeral a Buddhist service is held in which the priests chant scriptures and burn incense. Then the body is taken in a procession to the crematorium or to the burial ground, and the memorial tablet may be taken back to the house and placed in the household shrine. A variety of rituals during the funeral may offer food to hungry ghosts, keep the soul of the deceased from returning to the house, and transfer the merit of the monks to the departed one. After the funeral, regular rites are held on the seventh day and at regular intervals thereafter, including annual anniversaries of the death. Although rites for the dead differ widely among areas such as Burma, Tibet, and China, they all symbolize that this most critical pas-

sage of life is taken seriously and affects everyone, the living as well as the dead. Hope for a favorable rebirth is a central concern. Yet at the same time, Buddhists believe we should think of the higher truth that our own life with its karma causes rebirth and that ultimate liberation from the rebirth and redeath cycle is the final goal.

The Great Spiritual Passage of Life

These natural passages of life have spiritual importance. But the highest and most beneficial passage is that critical step of leaving normal life with all its cares and clingings, passing through the narrow passage to become a mendicant to follow the higher path of the Buddha. Ordination into the monastic life is therefore a very important community affair, and those who bear its expense build up a considerable amount of merit. Some Buddhist communities, especially in China, traditionally had a tonsure ceremony that preceded ordination. The candidate was accepted by a spiritual master, who performed the head-shaving ceremony and thus established the candidate as a trainee, learning the discipline to be a monk or nun. In Theravada lands, it is customary for ordination as a novice to come before full ordination. The novice takes the Three Refuges and the Ten Precepts in the "going forth" ceremony.

Full ordination (*upasampada*) as a monk or nun is a drastic step and not to be taken lightly. The candidate must be at least twenty years of age, and much training and preparation are involved. For the ordination ceremony there must be an assembly of at least ten monks. The candidate, head shaven and dressed in a yellow robe, petitions the assembly for admission to the sangha. The candidate is questioned to ascertain that he or she is free from certain diseases, is of free birth, debtless, exempt from military service, at least twenty years old, and furnished with parental permission. The candidate then kneels and asks the assembly for ordination. Silence indicates assent, and the interrogation is repeated a second time. The proclamation is made: "If any approves, let him be silent. If any objects, let him speak." If silence follows three repetitions of the proclamation, the tutors announce that the candidate has received ordination, noting down the date and the hour of the ordination into the sangha, since seniority is determined not by age but by time of ordination. Then the new monk or nun is given an exhortation to the effect that from now on his four reliances are to be alms for food, old rags for clothing, the shade of a tree for shelter, and cow's urine for medicine.

Art in Buddhism

With its focus on escaping the world and reaching nirvana, it might seem that Buddhism would hardly be conducive to art's sensuous, earthy aspects. For example, monks and nuns vow to wear no ornamentation and to go to no shows or music. But Buddhism, like most other religions, does harness the various human creative activities to produce art expressive of the Buddhist vision of life. Though the emphasis is on enlightenment and nirvana, the path proceeds *through* human life with its many activities and arts. And the aesthetic expressions that most deeply and compellingly express the real meaning of human life are those that arise from the creative power of one who has awakened to the Truth by following the path.

Since the Dharma rests on the word of the Buddha, it is fitting that Buddhists have always cultivated the literary arts. From the very beginning up to the present the sacred words have been memorized, recited, reiterated, elaborated, written, chanted, and sung with an enormous inlay of artistic power and creativity. The narrative art has been especially important: the creation of stories about the previous lives of the Buddha, elaborations on the events in the Buddha's life, stories about many other Buddhas and bodhisattvas, and stories about saints to provide inspiration and a model to follow. Poetry is another characteristic Buddhist literary art, for the sense of oneness with nature and the immediacy of insight into the truth can be especially well expressed in a poem. From the earliest disciples of the Buddha come poems like this, from the collection called Songs of the Nuns and Songs of the Elders:

> I am thin
> I am sick & weak
> but leaning on my stick I go
> climbing the mountain
> I lay aside my robe
> turn my bowl upside down
> lean against a rock
> & smash the mass of darkness

Poems of early Buddhist nuns often describe their own very vivid personal experience that guided them to take up the nun's life:

> I was drunk with my beauty
> with my form & with my fame
> I was still with youth
> I despised other women
> I adorned this body
> for the delight of fools
> I stood at the whorehouse door
> like a hunter laying a snare . . .
> today I went to beg for alms
> shaven & dressed in robes
> I sat at the foot of a tree
> & attained to nonthinking
> all bonds are loosed
> human & heavenly
> I have destroyed all drunkenness
> I have become cool : quenched[3]

Poetry is a favorite art form in all cultures penetrated by Buddhism, in their various national languages. In Tibet, for example, the great poet Milarepa (1052–1135) is said to have composed 100,000 verses, expressing how his life experiences crystalized his enlightened sense of impermanence—contributing greatly to the Buddhist arts and also to the Tibetan national cultural heritage.

Probably the most characteristic Buddhist art form is the Buddha sculpture, omnipresent wherever there is a temple, shrine, or altar. In the early centuries Buddhists refrained from creating images of the Buddha, possibly reflecting the transcendence of the Buddha, plus the practical consideration of educating the people not to worship him as they were accustomed to worship Hindu gods. The Buddha's presence was symbolized by motifs such as the throne of enlightenment, the begging bowl, his footprints, or the Bodhi tree under which he sat to attain enlightenment.

Beginning around the first century B.C.E. or C.E., artists began creating statues of the Buddha, illustrating different qualities of Buddhahood. The statues would be standing, seated, or reclining in the parinirvana symbolism, often with several of the thirty-two auspicious marks that designate a Buddha—such as elongated earlobes, wrinkles on the neck, or gold skin coloring. Many statues are truly colossal in a variety of media, chiseled in cliffs, cut in stone, cast in bronze, or modeled in clay. Most typical is the Buddha seated in meditation, legs crossed, on a throne, depicted in various local Indian, Thai, Chinese, Tibetan, etc., styles. Such local styles concretely indicate the universality of the Buddha presence.

Of particular importance are the hand gestures (*mudras*) on the statue. Of the many gestures, these might be mentioned: the mudra of the fulfilling of the vow, with the palm lowered and turned outward in a gesture of offering; the mudra that grants the absence of fear, with the hand raised, palm facing outward; the mudra of appeasement or teaching the Dharma, hand raised, palm outward, with thumb touching the end of the index finger; the mudra of touching the ground, with right hand pointing downward; and the mudra of concentration, with the hands in the lap.

Buddhist art includes sculptures and paintings also of the heavenly Buddhas and bodhisattvas of Mahayana, and also monks, masters, and guardian gods. One significant type of painting is the mandala, a symbolic depiction of the whole universe emanating from the cosmic Buddhas.

Architectural expressions of Buddhism include the early stupas, royal burial mounds that housed the relics of the Buddha and many other artistic symbols. These memorial stupas developed to incorporate cosmic symbolism, such as the egg-shaped dome and the vertical axis or pillar. As a symbol of the Buddha's presence, stupas became objects of devotion, and later they were enclosed in a large hall, also providing shelter for worshipers. Shelters for monks and nuns were also added, and throughout the Buddhist world are found large temple compounds, with fitting architecture to serve the needs of both the monastics and the laypeople.

A grand expression of Buddhist architecture is the great stupa at Borobudur in Java, from the eighth century. It is a giant mandala in stone, representing the Buddhist cosmology, with its five square terraced galleries and its three upper circular terraces set with many perforated stupas and crowned by a solid stupa. The pilgrim path, representing the search for enlightenment, is adorned with more than two thousand sculptures. The Buddhist temple takes many forms, influenced by the different indigenous cultures, from the pagoda form in southeast Asia to the massive temples of China and Japan, complete with statues of Buddhas, bodhisattvas, and arhats.

The Sri Mahatat Temple in Bangkok, Thailand.

BUDDHIST SOCIETY AND THE GOOD LIFE

How should we live? To be Buddhist is to take the Buddha's story as one's own, to find one's place in the community of those on the path of the Buddha, that is, the sangha, following the ethical precepts given by the Buddha.

The Structure of Buddhist Society

The Sangha as Monastic Community

In one sense the sangha is restrictive, focused in the community of monks and nuns. But in another sense it is wide open, open, that is, to all who genuinely search for the truth. Buddhism rejected the caste system of Hinduism and accepted people of all classes and castes and of both sexes into the sangha. The major requirement is that people enter voluntarily and in good faith, willing to dedicate themselves totally to seeking enlightenment.

The main purpose of the monastic community is to strive for nirvana. This means that the social ideal for monks and nuns is radical world renunciation, for nirvana can be achieved only by the extinction of all attachments to the world and its vanities. It might seem that the sangha monastic community, the ideal social order for Buddhists, is antisocial in its very essence. The monk or nun rejects many normal social values, begs instead of works, does not marry or have a family, and cannot participate in politics or defense of the community. If all people joined the sangha, there could be no society!

But the sangha does have a most constructive role in society. First of all, its very presence is a constant reminder to all Buddhists of the ultimate goal of the Buddhist path—to transcend attachment to the world and reach nirvana. Only a small percentage of the people in society join the monastic community, of course. It is estimated that in the 1950s somewhat under one percent of Thailand's population were in the monasteries. There may be about five percent of Burma's population who are monastics.[4] But for all of the laypeople the monastic life represents the final goal of the path. Further, the monks and nuns perform valuable spiritual services for the laypeople, even though all recognize this is not their primary func-tion. For example, the temple-monastery complex contains halls where the laity can participate in the ceremonies and school buildings where the local boys and girls can be instructed. Monks and nuns regularly chant scriptures and perform rituals at the temple and at people's homes. The basic idea is that some of the purity and merit built up in the monastic life can be channeled into the community for the benefit of all.

Although the Buddha made it clear from the beginning that caste, class, and gender differences are of no import on the path, it is abundantly clear that women, even nuns, have generally been subordinate to men and have had minimal opportunity for religious leadership in Buddhist societies. Some of this subordination is surely cultural, somehow in-bred in the cultural practices of India, Sri Lanka, Thailand, China, Japan, and all the other societies that embraced Buddhism. Yet the fundamental Buddhist perspective places women equal with men on the path. The Buddha formed an order of nuns equal to the monks. Some nuns achieved renown for their learning and their skill in teaching the Dharma, and an early collection of poems of the nuns preserves poems of some seventy women. Yet for various reasons nuns have always been subordinate to monks, and over the years nuns' orders have lapsed, especially in Theravada countries. The idea even gained ground in some circles that women have to be transformed into men or be reborn as men in order to reach Buddhahood!

Yet there are many positive models for women's leadership in the Buddhist tradition. Divine figures include the feminine form taken by the great bodhisattva Avalokiteshvara in East Asia, that is, Guan Yin in China and Kannon in Japan. A popular Buddhist sutra tells of Queen Srinala, portrayed as an ideal layperson and esteemed teacher, teaching others about the *Tathagatagarbha*, the inner Buddha-nature that all carry within themselves. The order of nuns, with its checkered history, has had a strong impact on culture and political affairs in the various Buddhist countries. Holy women, as enlightened and highly respected *siddhas* (spiritual leaders), have been fairly common in Tibet. Today there are many educated and able Buddhist women sharing in religious leadership in many ways. There are new attempts to revive and strengthen the orders of nuns, for example, and numerous women have become Zen disciples and masters. It was a woman roshi, for example, Jiyu Kennett Roshi, who founded Shasta monastery in America.

The Role of the Laypeople in Buddhist Society

Buddhist laypeople are not following the *nirvanic* goal; rather, they pursue the *karmic* goal of a good life and better rebirths. Along with living according to Buddhist moral precepts, one of the most important roles of the laity is to support and maintain the sangha, making it possible for the monks and nuns to strive for nirvana. Supporting those who are on the monastic path brings a good deal of spiritual merit. It might be said that, whereas in some other religions the clergy serve the people and help them reach transformation and salvation, in Buddhism the people serve the monk and nun to help them attain nirvana. In the process, the people build up merit for their own benefit and better rebirths.

We might use the simile of a sports team and its followers to explain the relationship of the sangha and the laypeople. The real team is the sangha, struggling for victory on the field of the Dharma. The laypeople are the supporters of the team, cheering them on, supporting them so that they can devote themselves fully to the struggle, and reaping the benefits of having a victorious team in the community.

Religious Leadership

Religious leadership in Buddhism is again bound up with the monastic community, although there are popular religious specialists and lay leaders outside the monasteries that are also important to laypeople.

Like Hinduism, Buddhist society focuses on the religious adept, the virtuoso who, like the Buddha, has experienced the truth at a high level and can thus be a model and illumination for others. It is, of course, within the monastic community that these religious leaders are found. The social structure of the monastery is hierarchical, from the young novice at the bottom to the abbot of the monastery at the top. Seniority is determined by how many years the person has worn the monk's robes. The abbot and the senior monks provide leadership for the monastery. For the laypeople, the monks and nuns pro-

vide spiritual leadership by instructing, performing ceremonies, and chanting scripture. Especially in Mahayana communities the ordained monks are often thought of as "priests" as they serve the local people in various ways.

Of particular importance, especially in the Mahayana tradition, is the "master" who founded the spiritual lineage and who passed on his authority to designated Dharma successors. The head of a monastery will be recognized as a Dharma successor of the founder, and he in turn may choose one or more monks to be his successors. The relationship between master and disciple is like that between parent and child, forming an important social structure within Buddhism.

Outside the realm of "official" Buddhism, there are in some Buddhist lands additional religious specialists who perform a variety of rituals and exorcisms, dealing with the spirits and gods who affect the immediate welfare of the people. This has nothing to do with the goal of nirvana, so generally monks and nuns pay little attention to such things. But for the people involved with concerns of birth and sickness, marriage and wealth, such religious specialists can offer immediate help and benefit.

The Buddhist Vision of the Good Life

So how should we live? Since the doctrine of no-self is fundamental to the Buddhist conception of existence, the ideal way of life would be one that demonstrates as little sense of self as possible. This may sound like a negative approach to life, but really it aims to bring out the fullest potential. This task is not easy, of course, and Buddhism offers many guidelines and practices to help one move toward that kind of good life. It is recognized that not everyone is at the same grade of spiritual development, however, and so the ethical life needs to be expressed at different levels. Whereas it is the same ethical life, the forms it takes differ somewhat for the monastic life and for the life of lay householders.

The Life of Love and Compassion

Among the many traditional subjects for meditation in Buddhism is one that has to do specifically with relationship to others, that is, with ethics. This meditation is on the four

Buddhist monks at Myoshinji Temple in Kyoto, Japan.

"sublime states," which are (1) boundless love, (2) boundless compassion, (3) sympathetic joy, and (4) limitless equanimity. These four states give expression to the way Buddhists cultivate their own inner life with respect to others, and so they reflect the Buddhist ethical vision. They all spring from the enlightened wisdom that knows there is no separate self and that all beings exist in interdependence.

Boundless love (*metta*) is related to friendliness. But many of our experiences of friendly love are intertwined with feelings of need, dependency, lovability of our friend, and so forth. Buddhists cultivate love that is unconditioned and unlimited, based on the knowledge that all are one in the ocean of life. The well-known sutra on boundless love states that one should direct her thoughts by reflecting in this way:

May all beings be happy and secure; may their minds be contented.

Whatever living beings there may be—feeble or strong, long, stout, or medium, short, small, or large, seen or unseen, those dwelling far or near, those who are born and those who are yet to be born—may all beings, without exception, be happy-minded!

Let not one deceive another nor despise any person whatever in any place. In anger or ill will let not one wish any harm to another.

Just as a mother would protect her only child even at the risk of her own life, even so let one cultivate a boundless heart towards all beings.

Let one's thoughts of boundless love pervade the whole world—above, below and across—without any obstruction, without any hatred, without any enmity.

Whether one stands, walks, sits or lies down, as long as one is awake, one should maintain this mindfulness. This, they say, is the Sublime State in this life.[5]

If one has anger in one's heart, one takes it out on all, regardless of who or what they are. So also, when one's mind is filled with thoughts of boundless love, that love radiates out to all, regardless of who they are or whether or not they are deserving of love.

The second sublime state, boundless compassion (*karuna*), is the intense fellow-feeling one should have for all living beings who suffer pain, anxiety, ignorance, and illusion. It was Siddhartha Guatama's compassion that led him, after achieving enlightenment, to devote the rest of his life to teaching the way to liberation for the benefit of all beings suffering in the ocean of life. Compassion is knowing that when one living being suffers, we also suffer, for we are not separate from any being but are one with all. Mahayana Buddhists have raised this sublime state of compassion to a supreme virtue as displayed by the bodhisattva who takes a vow to devote him- or herself unceasingly to bearing the sufferings of others and sharing merits for the salvation of all others. Out of compassion the bodhisattva vows:

All creatures are in pain, all suffer from bad and hindering karma. . . so that they cannot see the Buddhas or hear the Law of Righteousness or know the Order. . . . All that mass of pain and evil karma I take in my own body. . . . I take upon myself the burdens of sorrow; I resolve to do so; I endure it all. I do not turn back or run away, I do not tremble. . . . I must set them all free, must save the whole world from the forest of birth, old age, disease, and rebirth, from misfortune and sin.[6]

Of course, this is the vow of the highly perfected bodhisattva! But then all Buddhists are "Buddhas-in-the-making" (bodhisattvas), and so these sentiments of compassion can be cultivated by all.

Whereas compassion is sometimes thought to dwell on the negative aspects of human existence, sharing the suffering and pain of all, the third sublime state of sympathetic joy moves one to seek out the prosperity and happiness of others and rejoice with them. Strangely, this is difficult to do, for in selfish inclination people seem more ready to gloat over the misfortunes of others. However, when the sense of our needy, grasping self is extinguished, we no longer need to feel superior and therefore can genuinely not only promote the welfare of others but join in sympathetic joy in their material and spiritual happiness.

The final sublime state, limitless equanimity, is in the mind of some Buddhists the culmination of these four states. It expresses that sense of nonattachment to self and to world that the arhat achieves by following the path of transformation and rooting out all desire and clinging. In terms of the ethical life, equanimity is that fundamental sense of impartiality that makes it possible to treat all others equally with love, compassion, and joy, with no aversion to them and no desire to win their approval. Unthreatened by the evil vibrations of others, not seduced by the bribes or temptations offered by others, one can radiate love, compassion, and joy to all beings equally.

Ethical Steps on the Path

These four sublime states portray a high-minded ethical vision of selflessness and giving. But is it practical? Who can live according to such principles in the real world? Buddhism is above all a practical religion, and the emphasis is on the actual practice of these ideals. There are many scriptures that spell out practical guidance and concrete disciplines for the good life. The Dhammapada, for example, offers over four hundred statements to give direction in how to live. here are three samples:

"He abused me, he beat me, he defeated me, he robbed me"; the hatred of those who harbour such thoughts is not appeased.

One should not pry into the faults of others, into things done and left undone by others. One should rather consider what by oneself is done and left undone.

Conquer anger by love, evil by good; conquer the miser with liberality, and the liar with truth.[7]

To get a feeling for the practical dimension of Buddhist ethics, we can concentrate on the Five Precepts, recited often and respected as a model for life by all Buddhists.

The Five Precepts are:

> To refrain from taking life;
> to refrain from taking what is not given;
> to refrain from wrong sexual relations;
> to refrain from wrongful speech; and
> to refrain from drugs and liquor.

Through these precepts Buddhist ethical ideals are put into everyday practice.

The principle to refrain from destroying life is especially central to the Buddhist vision; this is the principle of nonviolence (*ahimsa*), shared in common with Hinduism and Jainism. The concept of not taking life and not harming life does not apply only to human life but also to animal life, and so it has always been the Buddhist principle to refrain also from killing animals, even for food, thus making vegetarianism the ideal way of sustenance. It is true that, given the reality of the natural world order with its continual struggle for existence, some provision has been made in Buddhism for laypeople to eat meat and even for monks and nuns to eat meat if it is received as a gift—provided that they did not see the killing of the animal and that the animal was not killed for their sake. But the positive side of the principle is important: one should do all possible to promote and support the well-being of fellow humans and of all living beings, assisting them, whether near or far, to live with honor, dignity, and security. It is particularly meritorious to save animals from harm and death by setting them free in a safe place.

To refrain from taking what is not given, that is, stealing, of course, means also to avoid all forms of cheating or dishonest dealings to gain an advantage over others.

Rather, putting away selfish motivations, one should share with them and promote ways in which they can lead a peaceful and secure material life.

When Buddhism teaches to refrain from wrongful sexual behavior, it does not mean that everyone should totally avoid sex. That is true, of course, for monks and nuns on the higher path of perfection. But the Buddha had many lay followers also. It is expected that lay householders should indeed marry and have sexual intercourse in a rightful way. But the sexual impulse is one of the most powerful human drives, and therefore it can easily upset one's self-control. It can lead one to take advantage of others, harming both them and oneself.

To refrain from wrongful speech goes far beyond just avoiding lies and only telling the truth. It does, of course, mean to avoid all falsehoods, because they are always harmful to others and to oneself as well. The Buddha said that there is no evil that will not be done by one who is not ashamed to lie. But right speech means also to refrain from all slander and recriminations that would bring about hatred, enmity, and disharmony among people. It means to avoid all abusive, harsh, rude, and impolite language, for this is offensive to others. And it means to stay away from all gossip, all disparaging of others, and all idle and useless babble. Avoiding these kinds of wrong and harmful uses of words, one's conversation with others will deal with the truth, with that which is friendly, pleasant, meaningful, and beneficial to others.

To refrain from drugs or liquor is important, for these tend to cloud the mind and make insight and awareness difficult, thus hindering one's progress on the path. Further, intoxication can lead to reckless behavior and violence of various kinds to others, thus leading to the breaking of the other precepts.

These Five Precepts form an ethical guide to the kind of profession and social involvement that would be consistent with the virtues of love and compassion. Obviously one should avoid any activity that, directly or indirectly, brings harm to others. This would obviously include professions that have to do with harming and killing people, such as making or trading in arms and lethal weapons, serving in military forces, or even supporting the making of weapons and military actions by our taxes. Occupations having to do with killing animals are also to be avoided—

slaughtering animals, hunting, working in leather, and the like. Since intoxicating drinks and drugs are harmful to the minds and lives of people, one should avoid activities that promote or use such harmful materials. It is not justified to claim only to be a middleman or to argue that what others do with what one has produced is not one's responsibility. To earn wages by engaging in activities that contribute to causing harm to living beings is inconsistent with the Five Precepts. Rather, one's personal livelihood should at the same time be service for the welfare of the community of living beings.

These Five Precepts are practical, down-to-earth principles for leading the good life of compassion, love, and fulfilment. In the wisdom of the Buddha, however, they are at the same time steps along the way to transformation. The more we practice these disciplines, the more we root out clinging and become self-giving and loving.

The Ethical Life for Monks and Nuns

The Buddhist path of transformation is such that one becomes a nun or monk to pursue the higher stages—and thus there is a higher ethical life also, that of the mendicant. The basic principles of boundless love, boundless compassion, sympathetic joy, and limitless equanimity are the same, simply intensified in practice. The main difference is that the monk or nun has gone beyond society and practices a high level of detachment from those material, economic, and social attachments that characterize life for laypeople. Yet the presence of these mendicants within society helps to set the ethical tone for the community: they are the conquerors, near to the goal, and their lifestyle is the model to approximate whenever possible.

The ethical life of monks and nuns is characterized first of all by the Ten Precepts, which they take at their ordination as novices. The first Five Precepts are taken by laypeople also, but they are intensified by monks and nuns. The Ten Precepts are to refrain from (1) taking life, (2) taking what is not given, (3) sexual misconduct, (4) lying, (5) drinking liquor, (6) eating after noon, (7) watching shows, singing, and dancing, (8) using adornments of garlands, perfumes, and ointments, (9) sleeping in a high bed, and (10) handling gold and silver. These basic principles are elaborated in the Vinaya scripture as the rules of discipline for monks and nuns. Over two hundred rules define categories of offenses, prescribe punishments, and regulate the conduct of the monks and nuns. The two dominant ethical concerns are not harming life and sexual continence, but many other matters are dealt with as the code defines the proper mendicant life-style.

The code defines four most serious offenses that warrant expulsion from the order: sexual intercourse, theft, intentionally killing a human being, and falsely claiming spiritual attainments. Many rules deal with improper sexual conduct; for example, a monk is put on probation if he intentionally ejaculates, touches a woman, speaks suggestively to a woman, urges a woman to gain merit by yielding to a monk, or serves as a go-between in arranging a meeting between a man and a woman. Other serious offenses meriting probation include false accusations against another monk, causing divisions in the monastic community, and refusing admonishment from other monks. Some offenses require forfeiture and expiation, such as accumulating more than one begging bowl or buying articles with gold or silver. There are quite a few offenses that require expiation, such as lying, stealing another monk's sleeping place, digging in the ground, destroying any vegetable, taking animal life, drinking liquor, or going near an army drawn up for battle. Whereas many of the rules seem trivial and quaint, taken together they shape a life-style designed to facilitate the rooting out of clinging and desire and to promote love and compassion for all living beings.

The Dharma Model for Society and the World

With the highest ideal being withdrawal from society and the world, how does Buddhism have anything to offer for the betterment of human society? The Buddha likened life in the world to a burning house from which one should escape as soon as possible. Isn't it the position of Buddhism just to let the house burn itself down?

Of course, Buddhism, like all religions, has a vision for the betterment of society. It is true that much attention in the scriptures is given to the role of the monks and nuns, and little is said about laypeople and their lives in society. But from the beginning the Buddha did have lay disciples and he did give them guidance on life in society.

The Buddhist Model for Society

The earliest Buddhist societal reform was the sangha itself. Whereas Indian society was stratified into the different classes, the Buddha accepted people from all classes to be in the sangha. He argued that biologically all humans are of one species, and therefore the different classes were simply convenient designations for different occupations. When some brahmins tried to maintain the superiority of their class, he asked, "Do the brahmans really maintain this, when they're born of women just like anyone else, of brahman women who have their periods and conceive, give birth, and nurse their children, just like any other women?" And he went on to assert that people from all classes can equally live the high spiritual life. He asked his questioner,

And if [a person] avoids grave sin, will he go to heaven if he's a brahman, but not if he's a man of the lower classes?
No, Gautama. In such a case the same reward awaits all men, whatever their class.
And is a brahman capable of developing a mind of love without hate or ill-will, but not a man of the other classes?
No Gautama. All four classes are capable of doing so.[8]

The Buddhist view of ranks in society is summed up in this passage:

No brahman is such by birth.
No outcaste is such by birth.
An outcaste is such by his deeds.
A brahman is such by his deeds.[9]

Essential to the Buddhist vision for society is the fundamental principle that all types of people are equal and that honor depends not on circumstances of birth but on moral and spiritual achievement.

But what about life in family, in community, in society? Doesn't Buddhism downgrade the importance of this, so that it really has nothing to offer except the advice to escape the burning house? In one important discourse the Buddha set forth great respect for family and social life, saying that one should "worship" parents, teachers, wife and children, friends and counselors, slaves and servants, and ascetics and brahmins. There should in fact be mutual honor and care and help from children and from parents, from students and from teachers, and so on. With respect to the relation between husband and wife, the Buddha taught:

Sunday services at Chua Giac Minh, a Vietnamese Buddhist temple in Palo Alto, California.

A husband should serve his wife . . . in five ways: by honoring her; by respecting her; by remaining faithful to her; by giving her charge of the home; and by duly giving her adornments. And thus served by her husband . . . a wife should care for him in five ways: she should be efficient in her household tasks; she should manage her servants well; she should be chaste; she should take care of the goods which he brings home; and she should be skillful and untiring in all her duties.[10]

The Buddha occasionally spoke about the needs of material, economic life. He clearly stated that poverty is the cause of immorality and crime; this cannot be suppressed by punishment, but rather the economic condition of the people needs to be improved. When a layperson asked him how laypeople can improve their welfare, the Buddha told him that there are four things conducive to welfare. First, a person should be skilled in his profession. Second, he should protect the income that he has earned righteously. Third, he should have good and helpful friends. And, fourth, he should spend reasonably, in proportion to his income, not hoarding

and not being extravagant. But along with this, of course, the person should cultivate spiritual values, keep the precepts, be generous, and develop wisdom.[11] Wealth is not bad, according to Buddhism; in fact, proper care for economic security can be conducive to a peaceful and spiritually minded society.

What about political power and the necessary force to keep order in society? The Buddhist scriptures do not say a lot about states and government, but one text does put forth these ten duties of the king: he should be generous, of high moral character, sacrificing everything for the good of the people, honest, gentle, austere, free from hatred, nonviolent, patient, and not opposing the will of the people.[12] A government based on these principles would surely create a happy, peaceful nation! Actually, the great Buddhist King Ashoka (r. ca. 272–236 B.C.E.) put many of these principles into practice as he ruled according to the Buddhist Dharma, treating people with forgiveness, extending his kindness also to animals. One of Ashoka's edicts states: "For this is my rule—to govern by Righteousness, to administer by Righteousness, to please my subjects by Righteousness, and to protect them by Righteousness."[13] Describing how painful his earlier bloody conquests were to him now, Ashoka publicly declared that he would never draw his sword again for any conquest; from now on the only conquest would be that by righteousness. At the zenith of power, Ashoka renounced war and violence and turned instead to nonviolence and peace.

Following Ashoka's model, Buddhists often are pacifists, not abandoning the world to its self-destruction but seeking to conquer violence and terror by kindness and righteousness. Today Buddhists are at the forefront of movements for peace in the world. The fact that it was a predominantly Buddhist country, Japan, that experienced the only military unleashing of nuclear terror so far has further motivated Buddhists to promote world peace by nonviolent means. The Buddhist aim would be to create a society in which the ruinous struggle for power and supremacy is renounced and where hatred is conquered by kindness.

Spreading the Dharma to the World

The missionary nature of Buddhism derives from the Buddha himself, from the compassion he felt after his enlightenment as he surveyed the whole world and saw suffering, ignorant beings everywhere. He preached the first sermon and began the turning of the wheel of Dharma. And when there were sixty enlightened monks, he sent them out to proclaim the Dharma for the benefit of all, out of compassion for the world, for the welfare of humans and of gods. The human condition analyzed in the Dharma is universal, and the path put forth in the Dharma is universal—so the motivation to bring the Dharma to others naturally arises out of the Buddhist sense of compassion.

This does not mean that Buddhists are intolerant of other peoples' beliefs and religious practices. They acknowledge that many of the world religions recognize something of the fundamental problem of human ignorance and clinging, and the religions also incorporate many elements of the path of transformation in their own various ways. On one of his rock edicts King Ashoka engraved this message, referring to various sects within India:

> The Beloved of the Gods [King Ashoka] . . . honors members of all sects. . . . But he does not consider gifts and honors as important as the furtherance of the essential message of all sects. This essential message varies from sect to sect, but it has one common basis. . . . Whoever honors his own sect and disparages another man's, whether from blind loyalty or with the intention of showing his own sect in a favorable light, does his own sect the greatest possible harm. Concord is best, with each hearing and respecting the other's teaching.[14]

Not all Buddhists, of course, demonstrate this religious tolerance toward others as stated by King Ashoka, especially when threatened by aggressive members of another religion. But with their emphasis on love and compassion, and with their insight that it is finally the mind, not faith, that brings one to liberation, Buddhists have generally chosen the style of spreading the Dharma by rational explanation, practical advice, and personal example.

One important consideration for the spread of the Buddhist Dharma is the flexibility Buddhism allows in matters that religions traditionally focus on. There is plenty of room in the Buddhist cosmology for gods and goddesses, demons and devils, ancestors, nats, shen, gui, kami, and whatever other spiritual beings people believe they have to deal with to live a happy life. As Buddhism spread from people to people, it left many of the traditional religious practices intact—for finally they have little importance, positively or negatively, for the Buddhist path of liberation. Let the nat wives, the shamanesses, the exorcists, and the ritualists ply their trade and deal with the supernatural world for the material welfare of the people. The path of liberation is a different matter, and when one advances far enough in the Dharma she will find herself beyond these gods and spiritual beings. Different concerns arise, of course, when religious claims for ultimate liberation and salvation are made on the basis of worshiping God, as in world religions like Judaism, Christianity, and Islam. And so some Buddhists of today have entered into dialogue with members of other religions, showing respect and tolerance, yet affirming the ultimacy of the Dharma.

DISCUSSION QUESTIONS

1. With the Buddhist idea of only the unconditioned truth as absolute, what is the meaning of worship, ritual practices, and images of the Buddha?
2. Describe several great annual festivals of Buddhism.
3. Describe the ordination ritual (upasampada). Why is this so important in Buddhism?
4. Explain what the sangha is, and how there can be both nirvanic and karmic goals on the path.
5. What are the Five Precepts?
6. What basic principles of Buddhism do you think would be helpful for the betterment of human society?

KEY TERMS IN BUDDHISM

Amitabha   Buddha of infinite light presiding over the Western paradise; Amida Buddha in Japan

arhat   a perfected saint who has reached nirvana and will be released from samsara at death

Ashoka   great Buddhist king in India (r. ca. 272–236 B.C.E.), the "second founder" of Buddhism

bhikkhu, bhikkhuni   Pali terms for Buddhist monk and nun

Birthday of the Buddha   important festival celebrated in May (Southeast Asia) or April (China and Japan)

Bodh Gaya the place where Siddhartha Gautama attained enlightenment

bodhisattva being who is to become fully enlightened; in Mahayana, one who reaches enlightenment but vows to continue rebirths in samsara to assist others

Buddha "Enlightened one"

Chan school of meditation Buddhism in China, influential in the arts (Zen in Japan)

Dalai Lama leader of Tibetan Lamaism

Dependent Arising (pratitya-samutpada) central Buddhist teaching that everything is conditioned by something else

Dharma in Buddhism, truth; the teaching of the Buddha; *dharmas* also refer to the constituents of all phenomena

Dukkha "suffering," characteristic of all conditioned reality as stated in the First Noble Truth of Buddhism

Eightfold Path the fundamental path toward nirvana as taught by the Buddha

Emptiness see **shunyata**

First Council of Buddhism held at Rajagrha shortly after the Buddha's parinirvana, where, according to tradition, the Buddha's sayings were recited and compiled

Five Precepts the basic moral precepts of Buddhism, to refrain from destroying life, from taking what is not given, from wrongful sexual behavior, from wrongful speech, and from drugs and liquor

Four Noble Truths basic teachings presented in the Buddha's first sermon: the truths of suffering, of the cause of suffering, of the overcoming of suffering, and of the path to follow

Four Sights sickness, old age, death, and a wandering hermit; seeing these motivated Siddhartha Guatama to seek enlightenment

Hinayana "lesser vehicle," term applied to those Buddhist sects that arose in the first four centuries after the Buddha's death; of these sects, Theravada still survives today

Impermanence basic Buddhist doctrine that change is characteristic of everything that arises

karma "action," law that all deeds and thoughts, according to one's intentions, will have set consequences

karuna Buddhist ideal of compassion

Lamaism derived from Lama, "master"; the special form of Buddhism in Tibet

Lotus Sutra important early scripture of Mahayana Buddhism

Madhyamika early school of Mahayana Buddhism that emphasized *shunyata* (emptiness)

Mahavairocana the great sun Buddha

Mahayana the "great vehicle," form of Buddhism that arose in India beginning in the second century B.C.E. and eventually spread to East Asia

mandala painting of the sacred cosmos used especially in the Tantric Buddhist ritual and meditation.

Nagarjuna important philosopher (ca. 150–250 C.E.) of the Madhyamika school of Buddhism

nirvana "blowing out" the fires of life, liberation from suffering and rebirth, the spiritual goal of Buddhist practice

no-self (an-atman) the basic Buddhist doctrine that there is no permanent, absolute self

ordination (upasampada) important Buddhist ritual marking the beginning of life as a monk or nun

parinirvana full nirvana; complete liberation attained at the death of a Buddha

Pure Land popular Buddhist school that worships Amitabha and looks to the Pure Land paradise

samsara the rebirth cycle of existence

sangha the assembly of Buddhist monks, nuns, and laity

Shakyamuni a title of the Buddha: the wise one of the Shakya clan

shunyata "emptiness," Mahayana Buddhist teaching that all things are devoid of any substantial or independent reality

skandhas "heaps" or aggregates; the Buddhist teaching that a person is really a changing process in five aggregates

stupa memorial Buddhist shrine or reliquary

Tantrism movement in Buddhism (and Hinduism) using initiation, rituals, imagination, and sexual symbolism as spiritual practices leading toward liberation

Tathagata title for the Buddha meaning the "Thus Come One," that is, the perfected one

Theravada an early Hinayana sect that survives today; term generally used for Buddhism in South and Southeast Asia

Three Body Teaching Mahayana doctrine of three dimensions of the Buddha: the Dharma Body, the Bliss Body, and the Transformation Body

Three Refuges the Buddha, the Dharma, and the sangha; many Buddhist prayers and declarations begin with the Three Refuge formula

Tipitaka   *See* **Tripitaka**

Tripitaka   (Pali: *Tipitaka*) the scriptures of the Pali Canon, meaning "Three Baskets"; they include the Vinaya Pitaka, the Sutra Pitaka, and the Abhidharma Pitaka

Ullambana   Buddhist festival in China and Japan worshiping the souls of ancestors and providing for souls temporarily released from purgatory; called Obon in Japan

Uposatha   fortnightly Buddhist holy day when meetings for prayer and meditation are held

Vajrayana   Diamond Vehicle, the Tantric tradition of Buddhism, represented especially in Tibet

Vinaya   texts containing rules for Buddhist monastic life and discipline

wat   monastery complex of buildings in Southeast Asian Buddhism

zazen   "sitting in meditation," central practice in Chan (Zen) Buddhism

Zen   *See* **Chan**

CHAPTER 8

The Path of the Jains

SACRED STORY AND HISTORICAL CONTEXT

Who am I? To call oneself a Jain means to follow the teaching and model of the Jinas, the "conquerors." The Jinas, also called "Ford Builders" (*Tirthankara*), are those who have conquered by reaching liberation from the wheel of existence and who show the way across the ocean of suffering. The most recent Jina in our world cycle is Mahavira, whose story, though 2,500 years in the past, provides in a very direct way the model of life for Jains.

At the beginning of his study of the Jaina path, Padmanabh Jaini presents this story of a modern follower of Mahavira:

It is August, 1955. On the holy mount of Kunthalagiri, in the state of Maharashtra in India, an old man called Santisagara (Ocean of Peace) is ritually fasting to death. He is the *acarya* (spiritual leader) of the Digambara Jaina community; now, after thirty-five years as a mendicant, he is attaining his mortal end in the holy manner prescribed by the great saint Mahavira almost 2,500 years earlier. Santisagara has owned nothing, not even a loincloth, since 1920. He has wandered on foot over the length and breadth of India, receiving food offerings but once a day, and then with only his bare hands for a bowl; he has spoken little during daylight hours and not at all after sunset. From August 14 until September 7 he takes only water; then, unable to drink without help, he ceases even that. At last, fully conscious and chanting the Jaina litany, he dies in the early morning of September 18. The holiness and propriety of his life and the manner of his death are widely known and admired by Jainas throughout India.[1]

Shocking perhaps to many outside India, this ascetic manner of life and death is greatly admired in India, and not only among the Jains. To understand this path, we need to look to the Jaina sacred story.

Mahavira Becomes the Jina for Our Age

Jains conceive of the universe as a vast structure subject to endless cycles of time, each cycle consisting of a progressive half-cycle and a regressive half-cycle. Twenty-four Jinas (Tirthankaras) will arise in each half-cycle as teachers, leading others to attain liberation. The first Tirthankara of our present half-cycle was Rshabha, who established civilization, taught the path, and lived approximately 600,000 years. The twenty-third Tirthankara was Parshva who lived in the middle of the ninth century B.C.E. and established an order of mendicants. Mahavira was born as the twenty-fourth and last Jina of our cycle, no more to come for many thousands of years. Whereas Jains pay worship to all twenty-four Tirthankaras, it is Mahavira who is the most recent Jina and thus the most important model for following the path.

The Sacred Life Story of Mahavira

The stories about Mahavira differ slightly between the two main sects of Jainism, the Svetambaras (white-clad, that is, clothed), and the Digambara (sky-clad, that is, unclothed). But the general outline of his life is accepted by all, centering around the five auspicious moments that Jains still celebrate: his conception, birth, renunciation, enlightenment, and final death (nirvana). Mahavira (Great Hero) is said to have been born in 599 B.C.E. at Kundagrama near modern Patna. Stories about his birth make it clear that this child was intended for a high destiny. For example, his mother had a series of dreams involving things like a white elephant, the rising sun, and an enormous heap of jewels, dreams that are still celebrated in ritual and art. Within the womb, the Jina-to-be showed the virtue of *ahimsa* (nonviolence), lying still lest his kicks should cause his mother pain. Like the Buddha, he was born to royal parents of the kshatriya (warrior) caste and lived in wealth and luxury. The second of two sons, he married and had a daughter (the Digambara sect says he remained a bachelor) and, even though he wanted to renounce the world, he fulfilled the duties of a householder until both his parents died. When he was thirty, certain gods appeared and urged him to make the great renunciation: "Awake, reverend lord of the world! Establish the *dharma-tirtha* (teaching of the holy path) for the sake of every living being in the entire universe; it will bring supreme benefit to all."[2]

The Great Renunciation is celebrated as a glorious occasion, as it is for all renunciants in Jaina communities even today. The story says Mahavira was adorned with garlands by the gods and carried on a palanquin to a large park. There he fasted, renounced all possessions, removed all his clothing, pulled out his hair by hand, and set forth on the mendicant path. The Svetambara sect says he wore a loincloth for thirteen months until it accidentally caught on a thorn bush and was pulled off, after which Mahavira went about unclad.

He joined a group of hermits for a while, but then he came to believe one must practice a more severe form of asceticism to win release, and he went wandering about and practicing extreme austerities for the next twelve years. He begged only for the most minimal food, and often he practiced complete fasting, that is, abstaining from both food and water for long periods of time, sometimes as long as a week. Further, he was convinced that a most essential practice was ahimsa, nonviolence toward every living thing. The scriptures report, for example:

> Ceasing to inflict injury on living beings, abandoning concern for the body, and having perceived the true nature of

the self, the Venerable One, houseless, endured the thorns of the villages [that is, the abusive language of the peasants]. . . . Once when he [sat in meditation], his body unmoving, they cut his flesh, tore his hair, and covered him with dirt. They picked him up and then dropped him, disturbing his meditational postures. Abandoning concern for his body, free from desire, the Venerable One humbled himself and bore the pain. Just as a hero at the head of a battle is surrounded on all sides, so was Mahavira there. Undisturbed, bearing all hardships, the Venerable One proceeded [on the path of salvation].[3]

He walked carefully to avoid stepping on living things, moving not at all during the four-month rainy season when the paths teemed with living things. Insects and other things gathered on his body and caused pain, but he did not wash or scratch so as to avoid hurting them. In the cold he sought out cold places to meditate, and in the heat he sat in the sun.

After twelve years of the harshest self-deprivation, Mahavira reached the highest enlightenment (*kevela*), the infinite, supreme, omniscient state, and thus he became the twenty-fourth and final Jina of the present world cycle.

Jina Mahavira and the Jaina Community

Digambara stories say that after his enlightenment Mahavira was completely free from all defects of human existence—hunger, thirst, disease, and so forth. He engaged in no mundane activities but sat in omniscient meditation in a special hall created by the gods. Disciples were attracted to his victorious nature and the Jaina community was thus established. Other stories from the Svetambara sect say he preached to the gods, then converted three brahmin priests who were offering a Vedic sacrifice. These were Indrabhuti Gautama and his two brothers, who with their 1,500 followers were taken into the new order. Soon eight other brahmins were converted, completing the inner circle of eleven chief disciples (*ganadharas*), who with their followers swelled the Jaina order to over 4,000.

Whereas Mahavira primarily demonstrated for his followers a way of life to reach liberation, some basic teachings about the nature of reality and human existence guided his followers. Although the soul has knowledge, bliss, and energy, because of past actions the soul becomes enmeshed in karmic matter, which leads to embodiment

Colossal statue of Bahubali, with crowds gathered around at a huge festival.

Death of Mahavira and Life of the Community

When he was seventy-two years old, Mahavira passed into nirvana as the result of voluntary self-starvation, thus becoming fully liberated, forever free of rebirth and embodiment. He "cut asunder the ties of birth, old age, and death, became a siddha, finally liberated."[4] And thus he became the model for all Jains ever since, including Santisagara in 1955.

All eleven of Mahavira's chief disciples attained enlightenment either during the master's lifetime or shortly thereafter. His closest disciple, Indrabhuti Gautama, was so deeply attached to his master that he could not attain this goal. On the last day of his life Mahavira exhorted Indrabhuti not to linger on the path:

> As a dewdrop clinging to the top of a blade
> of Kusa-grass lasts but a short time,
> even so the life of men;
> Gautama, be careful all the while!
> You have crossed the great ocean; why do
> you halt so near the shore? Make haste
> to attain the other side;
> Gautama, be careful all the while![5]

Mahavira died that day soon after giving this exhortation, and Indrabhuti attained enlightenment also that very day.

The Jain story says that when Mahavira preached, his words took on a divine sound, and this divine sound was translated into the scriptures by the chief disciples, especially Indrabhuti, who passed them on through oral transmission. The main scriptures are called the Angas (limbs), giving Mahavira's teaching on conduct for monks and nuns, false doctrines to avoid, basic teachings, and exhortations for the laity. Many secondary scriptures arose after the time of the chief disciples, and Jains also composed numerous commentaries and philosophical writings interpreting the teachings of the enlightened Jina.

Historical Transformations in Jainism

The Great Division: Digambaras and Svetambaras

Shortly after the time of Mahavira, a difference of opinion arose over a number of points, leading to a schism into

at the level appropriate on account of the past actions. Fettered with karma of passion and desire, the soul commits more such actions, leading to more and more rebirths. Every soul passes through tens of thousands of incarnations, ranging from fire, mineral, air, and vegetable bodies to animal, human, and god bodies. In most of these existences the soul experiences great suffering, and so the goal of liberation from the whole cycle is the most important thing, according to Mahavira's teaching. The path toward liberation involves an awakening of knowledge, faith in liberation, and conduct that will lead finally to that liberation.

two major sects. One group insisted that being real monks meant going totally unclad as Mahavira had done, for clinging even to a loin cloth is a form of attachment. This group, called the Digambaras (sky-clad), also insisted that women could not be allowed into the monastic life; they can become monks and reach enlightenment only after rebirth as men. The other group is called the Svetambaras (white-clad), holding that it is not important whether one is clad or unclad, as it was not important to Mahavira. The Svetambaras allowed women into the monastic community and felt they also could reach enlightenment. In fact, according to the Svetambaras, the nineteenth Tirthankara, Malli, was a woman.

The split between these two groups happened when one part of the community fled southward in the face of a great famine about 360 B.C.E. After twelve years they returned, but they found that the other group had prepared an official recension of the sacred texts containing many things that were unacceptable. Furthermore, the "northern" monks had taken up lax habits like the wearing of clothes. So the southern group, the later Digambaras, considered themselves the "true" Jains and eventually wrote their own stories about Mahavira.

Other points have accumulated to divide the two groups. Digambaras think a Jina, who has omniscient cognition, cannot engage in worldly activity and bodily functions, whereas the Svetambaras hold that he can. Svetambara monks carry small begging bowls and beg for food door to door, not entering the houses to eat. But Digambara monks receive food offerings only in their upturned palms, and they may enter a house and eat if they have gone there only to beg. Eventually the two communities also became separated geographically, the Digambaras moving to the south and the Svetambaras to the west. The schism between the two groups has not lessened through the centuries, although there have been attempts at cooperation in modern times.

Jains and the Culture of India

Jain monks and nuns have tried to strike a balance between perpetuating orthodox faith and practice, on the one hand, and fruitful intercourse with Hindu society, on the other. Adopting elements of Hindu ritual and worship, Jains incorporated worship of Hindu gods like Rama and Krishna, with appropriate adjustments to Jain values, in addition to the twenty-four Jinas whom they worship. They took over the use of ritual offerings, mantras, and holy fire. Also, rituals of the passages of life were adapted from Hindu models. Over the course of centuries they erected over forty thousand temples, many renowned for their architectural beauty.

To be a Jain means above all not harming any living thing—thus there are some occupations that Jains must avoid, occupations that involve taking life or making profit from the slaughter of living things. So Jains have generally been restricted from being soldiers, butchers, exterminators, leatherworkers, or even farmers. Because of this, Jains have tended to enter commercial professions, where their reputation for honesty and morality have made them quite successful and generally wealthy. They have also made significant contributions to the public welfare by founding institutions such as public lodgings, public dispensaries, and schools. They have established libraries and contributed to Indian literature and philosophy.

The basic principle of nonviolence has become firmly embedded in Indian tradition, also in Hinduism and Buddhism, partly because of the persistent Jain adherence to this principle of ahimsa. Mahatma Gandhi, who successfully put this principle into practice in modern times in the movement leading to India's independence and brought it into the moral recognition of the whole world, acknowledged that he had been strongly influenced by Jains, especially the saintly layman Raychandbhai Mehta.

WORLDS OF MEANING

Ultimate Reality: Eternal Universe, Liberation

What's it *all* about? What is really the center that holds everything together? Jainism is decisively atheistic, somewhat like the Upanishads and early Buddhism. Yet—as we have learned in India—there is not just one way. Jains also worship the Jinas and a number of gods.

Jains do not believe in a creator god or supreme being. Rather, the world process operates according to its own innate laws, in world cycles of evolution and degeneration without beginning and without end. In a sense we could say that ultimate reality is this eternal universe, with its laws of operation and its constituents of space and time, matter and infinite individual souls. What is really central and permanent on the Jaina path is the pure state of blissful omniscience achieved by the soul that reaches complete liberation from the embodied condition of samsara. But even this liberation process is controlled by the laws that are inherent in the universe.

In a sense, then, ultimate reality is the truth taught by those Jinas who attained this state of omniscience and liberation. According to the laws of the eternal universe, in each world half-cycle there will arise twenty-four Jinas, conquerors, who attain complete omniscience and thus can teach the truth for others to follow. Our world age has already seen its twenty-four Jinas, the last one being Mahavira, and, with increasing degeneracy until the end of our age, no one will even be able to attain enlightenment (the last one who did so was a saint who lived shortly after Mahavira). So it is proper to worship and venerate the Jinas, not as "gods" who hear our prayers and save us, but as conquerors whose souls now enjoy the bliss of eternal liberation and omniscience. The other gods worshiped for various benefits are souls who have attained rebirth in the god-realm but who still must in some future rebirth become humans in order to achieve liberation.

Karmic Matter and Eternal Souls

What is this world all about? The Jain view of the world resolutely rejects any creator or any beginning or end to

the process of the universe. Jain writers through the ages have raised deep questions about a theistic idea of creation:

> If God created the world, where was he before creation? If you say he was transcendent then, and needed no support, where is he now? . . . If he is ever perfect and complete, how could the will to create have arisen in him? If, on the other hand, he is not perfect, he could no more create the universe than a potter could. . . . If out of love for living things and need of them he made the world, why did he not make creation wholly blissful, free from misfortune? . . . Know that the world is uncreated, as time itself is, without beginning and end, and is based on the principles, life and the rest. Uncreated and indestructible, it endures under the compulsion of its own nature.[6]

The Jaina Universe and Human Existence

The Jain view of the world and human nature is very complex. Jains envision the universe, eternal and uncreated, as a vast three-dimensional structure, often pictured as a man or woman with arms and legs apart, with three levels. The lower level contains 8,400,000 hells, the middle level houses worlds in which humans and animals live, and in the upper level live the gods, who are always young and beautiful. Crowning the whole structure, beyond the celestial realms, is the crescent-shaped abode of the liberated souls. Surrounding the cosmic structure is absolute nothingness. The complex physical structure of the universe is further complicated by the idea that the middle regions are subject to endless time cycles. Each cycle contains a progressive half-cycle followed by a regressive half-cycle. The progressive half-cycle moves through six stages from an extremely unhappy to an extremely happy stage, and the regressive half-cycle moves through six stages from extremely happy to extremely unhappy. Only in the middle portions of each half-cycle—when conditions are neither extremely happy nor extremely unhappy—can beings be moved to seek enlightenment. As mentioned above, twenty-four Jinas are said to arise in each half-cycle.

All existing things, besides time and space, can be divided into matter and souls. Space contains an infinite number of immaterial, eternal souls whose essential nature is pure consciousness, bliss and energy. But all these souls—except those who have attained liberation and dwell in the pure state in the highest realm—are embod-

Jain saddhus (holy men), two with cloths over their mouths to keep from doing injury to organisms with air bodies.

mied in matter and always have been so. Existence in an embodied state is accompanied by desire, which causes more karma to accumulate, leading to further defilement and endless embodiments in the cycles of rebirth (samsara). The possibilities of rebirth are enormous, from the crudest life forms to the most exalted gods. And these are not mere possibilities. Jains hold that in the vast world cycles every soul already *has* been born in all these states and will continue in virtual endless repetition of these rebirths. The four main categories of birth destinies are as gods, humans, hell beings, and animals and plants. These four categories have from earliest times been illustrated in Jain art by the swastika-shaped wheel of life. The animal-plant category is almost infinite, including even microscopic creatures with only the sense of touch and single-sense organisms whose body is air, water, fire, or earth. It boggles the mind: I have already existed as all these beings.

The Bound Soul: Karma

Why is my soul bound like this? The Jain view of karma and how it affects the soul is distinctive among the religions, for Jains see karma as a subtle form of matter. The universe is filled with tiny imperceptible particles of material karma, floating about freely until attracted to an embodied soul. Because of its defilement, the soul's inherent energy creates vibrations that attract the karmic particles. Because of the passions of desire and hatred the soul is "moistened" and the karmic particles stick to it, clouding its pure consciousness, giving rise to more desire and hatred, which attracts more karma, and on and on.

The influx of karma leads to an actual change in the soul, like drinking wine involves an actual alteration in one's internal chemistry. Some forms of karma cause the soul to become confused and desirous, other karma obstructs the qualities of the soul, and still other types of karma bring about embodiment and determine the precise type of embodiment (whether the soul will be born human or plant, male or female, etc.) and also the duration of that embodiment. The effect of the karma depends on the type of act that attracted it. For example, if greed leads to robbery, the attracted karma will eventually cause loss of one's own possessions; and if I slander someone else, the karma I attract will cause me to be slandered sometime in the future.

The rebirths caused by the accumulated karmic matter adhering to the soul include not only the relatively pleas-

ant life of humans and the blessed life of the gods, but also the untold lifetimes spent as hell-beings and as incarnations in animal, plant, even air and water bodies. The intense sufferings experienced by the soul in these unimaginable vast numbers of lifetimes is portrayed with deep feeling by the young prince Mrgaputra as he begs his parents to allow him to take up the life of a mendicant to cut the bonds of suffering once and for all:

> From clubs and knives, stakes and maces, breaking my limbs,
> An infinite number of times I have suffered without hope.
> By keen-edged razors, by knives and shears,
> Many times I have been drawn and quartered, torn apart and skinned.
> Helpless in snares and traps, a deer,
> I have been caught and bound and fastened, and often I have been killed.
> A helpless fish, I have been caught with hooks and nets;
> An infinite number of times I have been killed and scraped, split and gutted.
> A bird, I have been caught by hawks or trapped in nets,
> Or held fast by birdlime, and I have been killed an infinite number of times.
> A tree, with axes and adzes by the carpenters
> An infinite number of times I have been felled, stripped of my bark, cut up, and sawn into planks.
> As iron, with hammer and tongs by blacksmiths
> An infinite number of times I have been struck and beaten, split and filed. . . .
> Ever afraid, trembling, in pain and suffering,
> I have felt the utmost sorrow and agony. . . .
> In every kind of existence I have suffered
> Pains which have scarcely known reprieve for a moment.[7]

When we remember that one can only seek liberation when born on the human level, we realize that, passing up the chance in this lifetime, it may be millions of lifetimes before we again are born as humans. That's why Jains—laypeople as well as monks and nuns—are intent on following the path of transformation.

The Path of Liberation

How can we reach liberation?

The Jain view of the human problem, as we saw, is quite bleak: eternal souls trapped for millions of lifetimes because of karmic matter, born in material bodies mostly at lower levels full of suffering. The path of transformation, then, consists of a process of purifying the soul, eliminating the karmic matter so that the soul can move upward toward the highest state of enlightenment (*kevela*) and ultimate liberation. There is no possibility that this can be accomplished in this lifetime, for according to Jain doctrine we are now in the degenerate part of this half-world-cycle when no one can any longer reach enlightenment. Still, the consequences of passing up this human lifetime with no strenuous efforts at purifying the soul would be drastic, trapped ever again at lower rebirth levels. So there is strong motivation to follow the path, not only for monks and nuns, but also for laypeople.

Jains reject the idea that a divine power from outside can help the soul, and they also reject the idea that the soul is hopelessly trapped with no possibility of changing its fate. Rather, the soul, even in its defiled state, retains certain capacities that can change the effect of the karmas, especially the central capability to start, under certain conditions, in the direction of knowledge and liberation. The soul has an innate tendency toward self-improvement, and time and again it progresses to higher states only to fall back again because of onrushing karmas. But, Jains believe, a moment can come when two factors coincide: the soul both is in a relatively pure state, and it encounters a set of outside conditions that activate the energies of the soul toward liberation—the outside conditions could be, for example, an encounter with a Jina or his image, or hearing the Jain teachings. That transforming event completely redirects the soul toward moksha so that, no matter how many lifetimes it may take, it never falls back; the bonds of samsara begin to unravel, and ultimate liberation is assured.

Once started on the ladder upward, the soul progresses fourteen rungs (stages of purification) until it reaches ultimate liberation and pure consciousness at the top of the universe. Every embodied soul dwells at the first stage (ignorance) until the great shift occurs, the first awakening when the soul, blind until now, has its first glimpse into its true nature. The soul achieves certain attainments of knowledge and energy that eliminate masses of accumulated karmas, melting away like ice before a flame, and the soul, with growing insight and energy, eventually reaches the fourth stage on the ladder, the state of true insight. The significance of this stage is that the soul now is irreversibly on the path to moksha. It will fall back to lower stages, for the deluding

karmas have been suppressed but not entirely eliminated yet. But even in falling back the soul retains true insight and will eventually make its way upward again. It is said that the soul that has reached true insight will remain in bondage no longer than the time it requires to take in and use up one-half of the available karmas in the universe—which may seem a tremendous time but really is tiny compared with what the soul has already gone through! Before reaching this stage of true insight, following the religious path is not possible. But to progress beyond the fourth stage requires voluntary restriction of activities tying one to the material world, and for this purpose the Jains have two paths, that for laypeople, and that for mendicants.

The path for Jain laypeople is ascetic, actually a modified and simplified version of the mendicant path. Central to the path are the "restraints" that govern behavior, including the five restraints of nonviolence, not lying, not stealing, refraining from illicit sex, and nonpossession or nonattachment. In addition to their ascetic disciplines, laypeople participate in rituals such as worshiping the Jinas, keeping holy days, and going on pilgrimages. Laity are also expected to visit and venerate the mendicant teachers, fast, give alms, and, ideally, die a holy death in fasting meditation. Laypeople can progress spiritually until their religious disciplines are almost as rigorous as the monks' and nuns'.

To be a Jain monk or nun means basically to observe all the restraints and other disciplines on a path of total renunciation, in contrast to the "partial" renunciation of the laity. In the case of nonviolence, for example, nuns and monks extend this principle to *all* living things, even one-sense beings. They thus cannot dig in the earth, bathe or walk in the rain, light or extinguish fires, fan themselves, or touch a living plant—for all of these activities harm delicate one-sense beings who have earth, water, fire, air, or vegetation as their bodies. A monk or nun possesses only things like a begging bowl, a whiskbroom, scriptures, and a loincloth (Digambara monks renounce even those). By observing all the restraints in a radical way, they reduce activities in the world that would generate the influx of karmas and the rise of fresh passions. Rigorous meditation techniques are used to attain deeper insight, and finally, after a lifetime of such severe disciplines, the monk or nun may attain the highest spiritual state of enlightenment. But even then the last step remains to be taken: elimination of those activities that accrue to embodiment. Just before death the enlightened one ideally enters a trance in which he or she stops all activities of mind and body, including even heartbeat and breathing, so that the soul, now freed from all embodied activity, may at the moment of death dart upward to liberation at the top of the universe.

We who are still a long way from such perfection and bliss can take comfort in remembering that even those most exalted souls at the top of the universe were once trapped in bondage just as we are.

WORSHIP AND LIFE

Ritual and Worship Among the Jains

How can we find new power for life in our everyday existence? Jains have always taken a skeptical attitude toward ritualism and worship of the gods. Still, the Jain tradition recommends that people worship the five worshipful ones,

Two unclothed Jain monks with lay Jain devotees.

perform the rites of the life cycle and the festivals, and above all engage themselves in prayer and meditation. There is, of course, considerable difference between the worship life of mendicants and that of laypeople, but it is a difference of degree, not of substance.

Jains are sometimes called atheistic, and to some extent that is true, as they do not accept an ultimate creator god to whom they should direct their worship. How then can one worship, and who does one worship? It is beneficial to practice the ritual of worship directed to the "five worshipful ones." These are not gods, of course, for Jains believe that final perfection can happen only at the human level. These worshipful ones are humans who have reached perfection or are well on the way toward perfection. The first category is that of the Arhats, that is, the Jinas or Tirthankaras who have conquered and who are no longer to be seen in their embodied state; statues of these Jinas are installed in temples to remind Jains of the spiritual attainments for which they are adored. The second category is that of the Siddhas, the perfect liberated souls who live in eternal bliss but who, therefore, cannot easily be imaged or even imagined. The other three types of worshipful ones are the true ascetic aspirants: the masters, the teachers, and the spiritual guides who are worthy of veneration. These great ones can be worshiped—not that they hear prayers and grant favors, but because it elevates one's soul to dwell on their ideal perfection.

It is not wrong for the common people also to worship gods and goddesses who control and protect various aspects of human existence. This kind of worship can be distracting, of course, since these gods are not ultimate. Yet many Jains do find it helpful to worship, for example, the guardian gods of the regions, Sarasvati the goddess of learning, and the spiritual guardians who are attendants of the Jinas.

Daily worship (puja) for Jains involves bathing in the morning and repairing to the temple, standing respectfully in front of the statue of the Jina, reciting sacred formulas, and making some offerings of food or flowers. They may also say the rosary of 108 beads and devote a few minutes to the study of the scriptures. If more time is available, such as on festival days, devotees may bathe the image of the Jina with pure water and make more elaborate offerings, symbolizing the desire to attain eventually to the status of the Jina. Jains might conclude the daily worship with this prayer for peace:

May Lord Jinendra bestow peace on the land, the nation, the city and the state, and welfare on all the citizens, may the rulers and administrators be strong, law-abiding and righteous, the rains be timely and adequate, all the diseases and ailments disappear, no one in the world be afflicted with famine or scarcity, with theft, loot, plunder and devastation, nor with epidemics, even for a moment: Peace to all!!![8]

Jains observe many fasts and festivals along with visits to temples and pilgrimages to holy places. Since the practice of austerities is important, there are various fasts, such as the important fast of Paryushana, which lasts for eight to ten days in the month of Bhadra. On these days all the people assemble at the temple in the mornings, perform worship and study, and fast to their abilities—some taking no food at all for these days, others eating only once a day. It is especially important during these fast days to prevent any animal life from being taken. Other festivals include events like the nine-day saint-wheel worship done twice a year by Svetambara Jainas, the birthday of Lord Mahavira (the only festival commonly celebrated by all sections of the Jain community), the day of worshiping the sacred books, and great Indian festivals such as Divali observed by Jains along with Hindus.

Holy places for the Jains are the beautiful temples built for the worship of the Jinas. In these temples laypeople can come near to the statue of the Jina, just as some in ancient times encountered a living Jina sitting in omniscient glory. The image can be a tangible aid to visualization of this sacred being, stirring up the soul for awakening. The most renowned temples are the lovely marble temples of Vimalasaha and Vastupala.

Rituals of the passages of life observed by traditional Jains are many—one listing for Digambaras adds up to fifty-three ceremonies from cradle to nirvana, beginning with the conception ceremony between husband and wife, and ending with the ceremony of achieving final deliverance.[9] Many ceremonies surround birth, naming, and tonsure of the child. The initiation ceremony comes at about eight, when the child adopts the cardinal virtues and becomes a student. The marriage ceremony, of central importance in the life of a householder, is generally similar to the Hindu rite. A person on her deathbed offers final prayers, does repentance, abstains from food, and dies in meditation. The body is cremated and the ashes thrown into a river, while the family meditates on the transitory nature of life. No days in honor of the dead person are

Jain saddhus worshiping at the foot of the huge statue of Bahubali at Shravanabelogola, India.

observed. In cases when the dying person has taken the vow of *sallekhana* (fasting to death), the end is considered especially laudable and a model for the survivors.

For sacred times and rituals, Jains have created art and architecture that ranks in the foremost of the cultural heritage of India. The most distinctive contribution is in the area of icon-making. Innumerable images of Jinas have been created of all kinds of materials, to be consecrated in temples and worshiped by the faithful. These sculptures—sometimes colossal in size, radiant in selfless contemplation, often unclad, epitomizing the perfection of the saint who has conquered—provide the main focus for Jain worship and pilgrimage. Jain temples with their richly carved and sculptured pillared chambers have contributed significantly to Indian architecture and art. The way of Jainism, leading far beyond the world, still is grounded in the basic stuff of this world through ritual, art, and architecture.

Society and Ethics

The Jain Sacred Community: Mendicants and Laity

How should we live? The good life means to live as one of those on the Path of the Jina, the Conqueror.

The Jain community, which Jains believe to be the oldest continuous religious community in the world, has never grown large by standards of the other religions—there are some 2,600,000 adherents in India today according to the 1981 census. Yet Jainism did survive in India, whereas the other non-Vedic movements (like Buddhism) did not.

One reason for the vitality of the Jain community has been the close association of the monks and nuns with the laypeople. Monks and nuns do not withdraw to monastic centers of learning far removed from the laypeople. Rather they stay in close contact and in effect simply practice a more radical and austere form of the same path that the laypeople are following. The role of the laity is to support the monastic community.

It is interesting that the number of women in monastic life has always been very high, more than men. Buddhism also, of course, allowed women into the mendicant life, but orders of Buddhist nuns have been very small in number, and today only the Chinese order of nuns still exists.

According to a 1977 census, there are approximately 1,590 monks and 3,972 nuns among the Jains.[10] Many of the nuns are widows, but the numbers still show a striking participation of women in the highest levels of the path to liberation.

Whereas the role of women in Jainism thus differs from Hinduism, the Jains have adopted some aspects of the Hindu social caste system, especially the caste of Jain-brahmins. However, Jains interpret the origin of the castes not as stemming from the eternal order of things, as in the Hindu understanding, but as simply necessitated by events. Rshabha, the first king and the first Jina of our world half-cycle, originated the organization of human society. All humans belonged to a single *jati* (birth), but Rshabha, while still a layperson, took up arms and became a king to curb the excessive lawlessness, thus establishing the kshatriya caste. As he invented new means of livelihood and various arts and crafts, the vaishya and shudra castes also arose. Finally, Rshabha's son Bharata arranged a kind of "ahimsa test" for the people. He scattered the courtyard of his palace with fresh flowers and sprouting grain, and then he invited the people to a festival. Those who were careless in their vows of nonviolence walked on the flowers and grains, whereas the most virtuous refused to enter the place lest they harm the living things. Those then were honored by Bharata, given the sacred thread, and called divine brahmins. Those of the shudra class generally have been excluded from the full mendicant life, but they can perform nearly all the lay ceremonies and can attain to a quasi-mendicant status.

How does one become a Jain monk or nun? The distinction between advanced laypeople and the mendicants comes about with the formal assumption of the great vows in the *diksa* (initiation) ceremony. The new monk or nun casts off all lay possessions and abandons his or her former name. The relationship between the laity and the mendicants is demonstrated in the initiation ceremony, which is supported financially by laypeople. Besides renouncing everything (even a loincloth in the case of a Digambara) and receiving a whiskbroom for gently removing insects, Jains enter the mendicant status by slowly pulling hair from the head in five handfuls. On the day following the initiation there is great excitement as the new monk goes begging for the first time. The householder who provides these alms is considered to earn great merit.

The Jain View of the Good Life: Nonviolence

The Jain vision of the good, ethical life is strongly shaped by the underlying idea of karma, which attaches to the soul through certain types of deeds. The Jinas are the conquerors who by strenuous self-discipline, asceticism, and meditation, mastered the flesh, annihilated all karmic forces, and attained the highest spiritual perfection. The path they taught is for everyone to follow, and it involves the same kinds of self-discipline and asceticism practiced by the Jinas. Perhaps the best way to approach an understanding of Jain ethics is to consider the five vows or restraints taken both by laypeople and by mendicants—the laypeople observing them less strictly, the mendicants observing them with stringent completeness. The five vows are nonviolence, abstaining from falsehood, nonstealing, celibacy, and nonpossession.

Of these vows, the one that stands in the forefront of Jain ethics is nonviolence (*ahimsa*). In fact, nonviolence is the driving principle in almost every aspect of Jain conduct. It is intentional violence toward living organisms that causes karmic matter to adhere to the soul, so the most important ethical principle would be to abstain from such violence in any form. Violence is understood to be doing any kind of harm or injury to any living organism—including the billions of microscopic organisms of one or two senses. A distinction is made between violence done with intention and nonintentional violence; intention here means through selfish motivation but also through pleasure, wantonness, or avoidable negligence. It is permitted for laypeople to harm one-sense organisms (such as vegetable life), for the obvious reasons of providing food for society, but they are strictly enjoined from harming animals and thus practice vegetarianism. Monks and nuns avoid doing harm to all organisms, even to one-sense organisms. For example, they carry a whiskbroom to clear the path so they do not inadvertently step on microscopic creatures, and they strain their water before they drink it. Some orders of monks and nuns even wear a cloth over their mouths so they do not harm air bodies (one-sense organisms that have the air as their body) by sudden rushes of air while breathing.

Nonviolence is not just something negative. One Jain saint, Samantabhara, said that nonviolence is the highest bliss known to beings in the world. Violence not only causes pain to other beings but it results in calamity for oneself in this world and in future existences. But nonviolence brings blessings and bliss. It means showing benevolence toward other beings, feeling joy at the sight of virtuous beings, showing compassion toward the suffering, and displaying tolerance toward the ill-behaved. The Jain path is really the path of total nonviolence.

The second vow, speaking truthfulness, is related to nonviolence, since all lying is motivated by the passions and damages the soul. Further, particular care should be taken not to use any speech acts, even if true, that cause harm or damage to living beings. This requirement, of course, may lead to complicated situations. For example, when asked by a hunter where a deer is, a layperson should probably mislead the hunter rather than cause destruction to the deer by her speech. Nuns and monks, of course, must observe this vow perfectly and thus could only keep silence in the face of the hunter's question.

The third vow is not to steal, that is, not to take anything not given, since doing so always arises out of greed and causes violence. Necessarily, then, a person should not engage in any activities involving gain at the expense of others, such as substituting inferior goods for the original, using underhanded measures, accepting stolen goods, and the like. Even finding and keeping something that has been lost by another person is wrong.

The fourth vow, celibacy, means for the layperson to refrain from all illicit sexual activities, practicing moderation in sexual behavior strictly within marriage, and avoiding all types of sexual thoughts or contacts with persons besides one's spouse. As laypeople progress toward higher spiritual development, they may late in life take the more stringent vow of complete celibacy. Monks and nuns, of course, avoid all sexual feeling, since that is always accompanied by the passions, and all sexual contact, since that always causes violence and slaughter for the microscopic organisms dwelling in the generative organs.

The fifth vow is nonpossession or nonattachment, and for monks and nuns that means giving up all possessions entirely, even clothing, as we noted, for monks of the Digambara sect. Merely thinking about possessions is damaging to the soul. For laypeople, some possessions are necessary for the welfare of society in general, but one should not be attached overly to one's possessions. Rather, people should impose restrictions on themselves so as to check their greediness; once they have the amount of possessions they need for a decent life, they should voluntarily refrain from further acquisitions.

Jainism thus envisions a human society based on the central principle of nonviolence with its related corollaries. Whereas ethical practice is primarily directed toward the end of perfecting the soul and finally reaching liberation, Jains have always been concerned about the welfare of the whole society and of the entire ecological sphere with its countless billions of living organisms. Some modern Jain thinkers have pointed out that the basic Jain principles of nonviolence can make a great contribution to world society. The Jain ethical vision has an answer to the modern problems of racism, economic inequality, the inadequacies of both capitalism and communism, the disastrous destruction of our ecology, modern sexual exploitation, overpopulation, intolerance, and above all warfare.

Jains are not missionaries out to convert the world. But leading thinkers clearly articulate for all thinking people the universal benefit of following the Jain principles, as in these words of Jyotiprasad Jain:

> And, it is today, more than ever, when suspicion and distrust are vitiating the atmosphere of international peace and brotherhood, when the world is filled with fear and hate, that we require a living philosophy which will help us to discard them and recover ourselves. Such a living wholesome philosophy, bearing the message of love and goodwill, ahimsa and peace, internal as well as external, personal as well as universal, is the Jaina philosophy of life. It is this system of Jaina religion, thought and culture that stands for the highest and noblest human values, moral elevation and spiritual uplift, eternal and universal peace and happiness.[11]

DISCUSSION QUESTIONS

1. What is a Jina or Tirthankara?
2. Describe how Mahavira became a Jina. Why is his story, of all the Jinas, of particular importance to the Jains?
3. Describe the two major groups within Jainism.
4. What is the Jain conception of the universe?
5. Describe the particular Jain notion of the working of karma.
6. What insights into the Jain perspective do you find in the poem by young prince Mrgaputra?
7. How does the soul move upward on the path of transformation?
8. Describe the practice of nonviolence (ahimsa) as observed by a Jain monk or nun.

KEY TERMS IN JAINISM

ahimsa "nonviolence," one of the most important Jain principles; also emphasized in Buddhism and Hinduism

Angas main scriptures of the Jains

Digambara "sky-clad," renouncing the use of clothing; one of the two major groups among the Jains

Diksa initiation ceremony for Jain monks and nuns

Jina "conqueror," Jain idea of one who has reached total liberation; see also **Tirthankara**

karma Jain idea of subtle form of matter that clings to the soul because of the soul's passion and desire, causing rebirths

kevela the highest state of enlightenment, according to Jainism

Mahavira the twenty-fourth and last Jina of the present world half-cycle, who lived from 599 to 527 B.C.E.

Parshva the twenty-third Jina of the present world half-cycle, who lived in the mid-ninth century B.C.E.

restraints the Jain vows of nonviolence, not lying, not stealing, refraining from wrong sex, and nonpossession or nonattachment

Svetambara "white clad," accepting the use of clothing; one of the two major Jain groups

Tirthankara "ford builder," Jain idea of one who has reached total liberation and shows the way across the ocean of suffering; see also **Jina**

Worshipful Ones in Jainism, beings (not gods) who can be venerated because they have reached perfection or are well on the way, such as Jinas and masters

CHAPTER 9

The Way of the Disciples: The Sikhs

Sikhism, beginning in the sixteenth century C.E., is the youngest of the major religions to arise in India, and it was influenced by the interaction of Hinduism with Islam, that strongly monotheistic religion from the outside of India that seems so opposed to the Hindu vision of life but that became such an important factor in Indian culture and religion. In a remarkably fertile religious and intellectual climate, spiritual forces from these sharply contrasting religions were drawn together in Sikhism, the path of the disciples of the Gurus. Sikhism provides an Indian way, still within the worldview of samsara and rebirth, to find salvation by union with the one God, through love experiencing the person of God dwelling within and responding with the heart to the voice of the Divine Guru.

SACRED STORY AND HISTORICAL CONTEXT

Who am I? To be a Sikh means to be a "disciple," a disciple of the Guru. And who is the Guru? Of course, it is Guru Nanak and the other gurus, ten in all. But then the Guru is also the Holy Book, the Adi Granth. In the final analysis, God is the Guru. The identity of Sikhs is tied up with the sacred story about the Gurus, the Holy Book, and God.

Nanak and the Other Gurus

The time for the founding of this new religion of India came when Islamic spiritual influence became strong in India and, in Hinduism, the great Vaishnavite bhakti movement was popular. This movement had begun in the Tamil country in the south, but in the fourteenth and fifteenth centuries it spread all across north India and had much contact with Islam. These devotees maintained that Vishnu is the one and only divine reality, though known by many other names, and that the best way to salvation is by singing God's name and approaching God in love. The Muslim Sufis in India were cultivating a similar path of mystical love and devotion to God, with emphasis on the master who guides the devotional meditation.

Among the Vaishnavites an important predecessor of Nanak, the founder of Sikhism, was the poet Kabir (1440–1518), who rejected the authority of the Vedas and combined Hindu and Muslim ideas in his syncretistic approach. He taught that all should worship the one God, that images and rituals such as pilgrimages provide no help, and that the simple love of God that captures the heart is sufficient to free one from the wheel of rebirth. The path of Kabir is still followed by groups in India called the Kabirpanthis. And Sikhs look to Kabir for spiritual inspiration—many of his hymns and verses appear in the Adi Granth.

Nanak Becomes the Guru

Nanak was born in 1469 in the village of Talwandi near Lahore (in present-day Pakistan) to a Hindu kshatriya (warrior) family. His father was a revenue officer for the Muslim overseer of the village, and Nanak received a Hindu upbringing along with considerable exposure to Islam. Whereas Sikhs consider Nanak's writings in the Adi Granth to be the only completely authentic information about him, they have many other popular stories about his life. He was a precocious youth, a poet by nature, more given to meditation and searching for religious truth than to the business affairs his father tried to interest him in. In this heavily Muslim area he explored Islam as an alternative to Hinduism, and he took every opportunity to talk with holy persons of any sect. Eventually he was married and had two sons, and he worked for a while for a Muslim official in the nearby town of Sultanapur. He became close friends with a Muslim family servant, Mardana, who played the rebec, a stringed instrument, and together they sang the hymns that Nanak composed, gradually attracting a small community of seekers.

When Nanak was thirty came a crucial, intense religious experience that transformed his life. One morning after bathing in the river he disappeared in a forest and experienced being carried up to God's presence, where he was given a cup of nectar and a divine call:

> This is the cup of the adoration of God's name. Drink it. I am with you. I bless you and raise you up. Whoever remembers you will enjoy my favor. Go, rejoice in my name and teach others to do so. I have bestowed the gift of my name upon you. Let this be your calling.[1]

Emerging from the forest three days after he disappeared and had been thought drowned, Nanak was silent for one day, and then he said, "There is neither Hindu nor Mussulman [Muslim], so whose path shall I follow? I shall follow God's path. God is neither Hindu nor Mussulman and the path which I follow is God's."[2]

Now Nanak was a guru, one who drives away darkness and teaches enlightenment, giving voice to the word of God who is the true Guru. The story says he pursued his divine calling by spending many years traveling about India, often accompanied by Mardana, teaching and singing evangelistic hymns in marketplaces, street corners, and open squares. One tradition says he and Mardana even traveled to Mecca, Medina, and Baghdad. To emphasize his pronouncement that there is neither Hindu nor Muslim, on one occasion he wore a Hindu dhoti (lower garment) and a mango-colored jacket with a white sheet over both, a Muslim hat, and a necklace of bones, and on his forehead he had a Hindu saffron mark. Later in his life he adopted the common garb of a householder, to show, perhaps, that his religious path did not mean abandoning the world.

After many years of traveling, in about 1521 Nanak decided to settle down with his family, establishing a religious center in Kartarpur, a village whose residents were Sikhs. Then he devoted the rest of his life to teaching and serving this community. His teachings revolved around God as the sole reality who is formless and beyond all conceptions, whose self-manifestation is the whole creation so that in a sense everything is in God. Yet the transcendent, unknowable God is experienced as personal through love and devotion. One of the most important passages in the Adi Granth, the first part of the Japji (recited by Sikhs in every morning devotion), was composed by Nanak immediately after his enlightenment experience. It well expresses his experience of God:

> There is one God,
> Eternal Truth is His Name;
> Maker of all things,
> Fearing nothing and at enmity with nothing,
> Timeless in His Image;
> Not begotten, being of His own Being:
> By the grace of the Guru, made known to men.[3]

The primary problem in human existence, Guru Nanak taught, is separation from God through ignorance and self-centeredness. The soul is capable of pure union with God, but in self-centeredness it turns to the world as something separate from God and allows itself to be dominated with passions and pride. The soul that is trapped in evil will have to endure countless rebirths, sufferings, and deaths. But the way to union with God is revealed by the guru, through whom God's word reverberates. By meditating on this word and on God's name, disciples are given

God's grace and favor and enabled to hear his voice and open their hearts to salvation.

Since the true path is an inward preparation of the heart to receive and experience God, Nanak rejected the traditional Hindu and Muslim rituals and scriptures. And since all beings are God's creation, he rejected discriminations on the basis of sex or caste. The path Guru Nanak taught includes techniques and disciplines for preparing the heart, particularly singing God's praises (*kirtan*) and meditating on God's name, repeating it so that the divine sound fills one's whole being: "Repeating [the Name] of the True God means engrafting [Him] in the *man* [soul]."[4]

The Ten Gurus and the Sikh Community

Before his death in 1539, Guru Nanak named Lehna, a former devotee of the goddess Durga, to be his successor as head of the Sikh community, renaming him Guru Angad (part of me), implying that Angad did indeed possess Nanak's own spirit. Henceforth God's word would continue to come through the gurus, leading the community to union with God. For a succession of ten gurus, the position of guru continued to be central to the Sikhs, because the gurus were vehicles through whom God's message was expressed. When the third guru, Amar Das, began collecting the Sikh scriptures, he included not only hymns of Guru Nanak but also hymns composed by Guru Angad, himself, and a number of non-Sikhs such as Kabir, for they all were regarded as transmitting the voice of God. This holy book became known as the Adi Granth (Original Collection) and is also often called Granth Sahib (Sacred Collection), itself called Guru.

The third guru also created a system of Sikh parishes and established rituals and festivals for Sikh observance in place of Hindu celebrations. Ram Das, the fourth guru, enjoyed the favor of the tolerant ruler Akbar, and set up the village Amritsar near a pool of water that had been especially beloved by Nanak. Amritsar became the religious center for Sikhs and their most holy city. Now the guruship became hereditary. Under the next guru, Arjan, the Sikhs began to build the Golden Temple at Amritsar. The hymns of the first four gurus and other inspired hymns and poems were gathered into the final, authoritative edition of the Adi Granth and this was enshrined in the Golden Temple, to be from that time the central focus of Sikh faith and worship.

But now political adversity comes into the story. The Muslim successors to Akbar were less tolerant and began persecuting non-Muslims, and Arjan had to choose between accepting Islam or death. Choosing death, he became the first Sikh martyr (1606), followed later in martyrdom by the ninth guru, Tegh Bahadur (1675). These martyrs have also become an important part of the Sikh sacred story and are remembered in festivals.

Yet another important component of the story comes under the tenth guru, Gobind Singh. Part of a male Sikh's identity is his long hair, dress, and his name Singh; and when Sikhs worship together they glorify the *Khalsa*.

A Sikh reading at the Golden Temple at Amritsar.

What is this all about? Already in the time of Guru Arjan, the Sikh community began to realize that it needed to develop military preparedness to defend itself, and the gurus were trained as military leaders. The tenth guru, Gobind Singh, in preparation for a momentous struggle for Sikh survival, founded the khalsa military society in 1699. According to the traditional story, Guru Gobind addressed an assembly of Sikhs on New Year's Day and stressed the seriousness of the times and the need for strength, unity, and loyalty to the guru. With his sword uplifted, he called for five volunteers to come forward to die for the Sikh cause to show their loyalty and conviction. After a fearful silence, one Sikh came forward and was led into the guru's tent. Guru Gobind emerged with his sword dripping with fresh blood and asked for more volunteers. One by one four more brave Sikhs came forward and were escorted into the tent. In a dramatic climax, Guru Gobind emerged from the tent with all five Sikhs still alive; he had substituted a goat for the sacrifice of the five men.

Now Guru Gobind performed a ceremony of initiation of the Five Beloved Ones, as they are called. Mixing nectar in water with a two-edged sword, he gave them to drink of it and sprinkled it over them, initiating them into the khalsa (pure) Order. Then he himself received initiation from them. As the physical sign of the khalsa all vowed to wear the five K's: uncut hair *(kais)*, a comb *(kangha)*, a sword or dagger *(kirpan)*, a wrist guard *(kara)*, and short pants *(kachha)*. The uncut hair was to be kept in a topknot under a turban.

After these first members, the guru threw open membership in the khalsa to everyone of all castes, including women. Men entering the khalsa adopted the common surname Singh (lion), and the women took the name Kaur (princess). And the guru set up a special code of discipline, prohibiting tobacco, eating meat of animals slaughtered in the Muslim way, and sexual contact with Muslims, but enjoining regular singing of the guru's hymns and congregational worship with men and women participating on a equal basis. Thousands of men and women were initiated on that founding day, and afterward people of all castes eagerly entered the khalsa. Although, of course, not all Sikhs became members of the khalsa, it did sustain the Sikh community through times of grave crisis, and still today the ritual of initiation, accepting the

prohibitions, and wearing the five K's are important aspects of Sikh identity.

Guru Gobind's four sons died in the struggle with the Muslim forces, and Gobind fled to south India where he was assassinated by a fanatic. But before he died he declared that the line of gurus ended with himself, the tenth guru. From now on, he decreed, the Adi Granth would be their Guru. From that time onward, except for a couple of small Sikh sects who retained human gurus, Sikhs have looked to Guru Granth Sahib, the Holy Book, for God's word.

Developments, Struggles, Transformations

Religious Developments in Sikh History

As time went on and the Sikh community spread, more congregations were established, and in every locality they erected *gurdwaras*, buildings for worship and meeting together. Often these included a kitchen area *(langar)* where a free common meal would be served for all. This, together with the worship gatherings in which men and women participated together without priests and without class distinctions, served to maintain the sense of unity and equality in the Sikh community.

Although maintaining Guru Nanak's emphasis on a religion of the heart rather than ritual and pilgrimage, Sikhs did adopt many of the festivals of Hinduism in northern India, together with traditions and lore from the Hindu epics. Guru Gobind Singh produced a supplement to the Adi Granth, called the Granth of the Tenth Guru, not considered as sacred as the Adi Granth but still used widely for edification. Along with his own hymns, Gobind included much material from the Hindu epics, especially about the gods Rama and Krishna and their renowned exploits. He also included stories about the great goddess Durga and her victories over evil. Such heroic material could be used especially to instill bravery in the khalsa to stand firm in their faith and fight against the enemies of the Sikhs.

After the death of the tenth guru, the hostility between the Sikhs and the Mogul rulers continued to increase, and members of the khalsa took to the hills to carry on guerrilla warfare for the survival of the Sikh community. The Sikhs emerged victorious in the area of Lahore, and a Sikh kingdom was set up under Ranjit Singh (1780–1839) that controlled most of the Punjab area. But the British had taken the place of the Mogul Empire, and a period of running battles between the Sikhs and the British led ultimately to the complete surrender of the Sikhs to British control. Because the British treated them with fairness and justice, the Sikhs turned out to be loyal subjects, serving with bravery and distinction in the armies through which the British maintained their control of India.

But the longstanding desire for freedom and an independent Sikh state could not be entirely suppressed, and the Sikhs tended to join the movement for India's independence from the British. However, they were devastated by the decision to partition their homeland, the Punjab, between the newly created Muslim state of Pakistan and India. With immense suffering, two and a half million Sikhs had to leave their homes and move across the new border to India, leaving behind rich farms and sacred places such as the birthplace of Guru Nanak.

The Sikh Community Today

Today Sikhs still make up the majority in the Punjab in India. Whereas the Sikh community has maintained a strong sense of unity, several divisions did develop in the course of history. Today the Singh group (the khalsa) makes up the great majority of Sikhs. A small order called Udasi is inclined toward asceticism and celibacy, going about in yellow robes with begging bowls, often with shaved head and no beards. The Sahaj-dhari group, also clean-shaven, is a nonkhalsa group that refused to go along with the militant stance of the tenth guru. Within the large Singh group there are some differences as well. One faction takes a rather militant stance and carries martial implements. Another faction leans toward contemplation and scholarship.

The vision of a Sikh state has always been a part of Sikh belief. Many Sikhs have been working toward and demanding a Sikh-dominated state in the Punjab, a demand that in recent years has caused considerable violence and bloodshed, even at the Golden Temple. The Sikh community has not been able, to date, to unify itself on the question of what course to take within the extremely complicated politics of India. A Sikh has been president of India; but others advocate violent uprising against the Hindu-dominated government.

Another problem Sikhism faces today, like all the major religions, is the lure of secularism and the loss of tradition. Many young people abandon the khalsa emblem of unshorn hair, and there is some tendency, especially among Sikhs living outside of strong Sikh settlements, to lapse back into Hindu society. To combat these tendencies, Sikh leaders promote a revival of Sikh tradition, stressing those features that are unique to the Sikh heritage. In general, Sikh identity appears strong today. Sikh hospitals, educational institutions, and social relief agencies are flourishing in India. There have been recent celebrations of the quincentenary of Guru Nanak (1969) and the tercentenaries of Guru Gobind Singh (1966) and Guru Tegh Bahadur (1975), resulting in conferences and publications.

Sikhism is a world religion today, with perhaps fourteen million adherents in various parts of the world. Some twelve million live in India, but there are about one million living in thriving Sikh communities in the United States and Canada, and around half a million Sikhs live in England.

WORLDS OF MEANING

The Sacred Ultimate: God

What's it *all* about? What is really the center that holds everything together?

For Sikhs, as for Jews, Christians, and Muslims, the answer is God. Guru Nanak and the other gurus certainly were influenced by the radical monotheism of Islam. But the "monotheism" of Sikhism is born of India, counting also Vaishnavite theologians and poets among its sources, signaled by Guru Nanak's important teaching that God is neither Hindu nor Muslim.

At the heart of the world's existence is the one God, who is immortal, unborn, self-existent, omniscient, formless, and totally beyond human conceptions and categories. God is the creator of the universe and transcendent far beyond it. At the same time, the universe is an emanation from God's being, a manifestation of God's own essence, so in a sense we can say that God is in everything and everything is in God. The world exists within the

Sikh leaders at the Golden Temple of Amritsar. Recent conflicts have brought bloodshed and violence to this holy shrine.

unity of God, and even the Hindu gods can be seen as manifestations of the supreme one name: "He, the One, is Himself Brahma, Vishnu and Shiva; and He Himself performs all."[5] God rules over the world in the samsara cycles of existence and even over the law of karma.

But God is not simply like the Hindu Brahman, impersonal and beyond conception. God is personal, being revealed to the human heart through the word in all creation and especially through God's name, Nam, the dimension of God that can be known and loved by humans. "The Name is the total expression of all that God is and this is Truth. *Sati Nam*—His name is Truth."[6] Sikhs believe that before the creation God lived alone in formlessness. But when God became manifest, God first formed Godself into Nam and then created nature. Nam is not different from God; Nam is the total expression of all God is, sustaining everything with the divine presence. Thus God is the true Guru, granting self-revelation through the creation, and through grace enabling humans to hear the divine voice. Persons who thus open their hearts to God's

presence and follow the path will ultimately attain nirvana, absorption into God's being like water blending with water. In this way the Sikh experience of God as ultimate reality blends monistic and monotheistic, impersonal and personal dimensions.

Divine Creation and Human Nature

In thinking about the creation of the world and human nature, often we encounter two opposite views: belief in one creator God who creates humans for a single lifetime, or belief in world cycles with karma and rebirth as the human lot. The first is characteristic of the Abrahamic religions, and the second is typical of the religions arising from India. We have already been chastened in holding this assumption too strictly, for we found within Hinduism groups believing in one creator God. Now in Sikhism we have a religious perspective that specifically combines elements of both these views.

The Divine Creation: World and Humans

What is this world all about? Just as Sikhs combine the ideas of a transcendent, impersonal God and an immanent, personal God, so also they combine views of the world as God's creation and the world as an emanation of God's being. God, formless and eternal, created all existence, and God sustains all forms of existence by dwelling in them. Originally there was darkness everywhere with only the Omnipotent One existing in abstract meditation. Then God willed, and from the word expressing the divine will the universe came into existence as a hot nebula spinning out the planets.

> Through uncountable ages,
> Complete darkness brooded
> Over utter vacancy;
> There were no worlds, no firmaments.
> The Will of the Lord was alone pervasive;
> There was neither night nor day, nor sun nor moon
> But only God in ceaseless trance. . . .
> When He so willed, He shaped the Universe;
> The firmament He spread without a prop to support it.
> He created the high gods, Brahma, Vishnu and Shiva.
> And Maya the goddess, the veil of illusion,
> Who maketh Truth dark and increaseth worldly attachment.
> To some, to a chosen few, the Guru revealeth the Lord's Word.
> The Lord creates and He watcheth His Creation;
> He made the heavenly bodies,
> Our Universe in the endless space,
> Above, below and around it.
> And out of the Unmanifested, Unmovable ground of His Being,
> To us and in us, He made Himself manifest.[7]

God creates the universe and dissolves it time and again in divine play. God sustains nature with Nam, God's own presence, and delights in it all:

> God created Himself and assumed Name
> Second besides Himself He created Nature
> Seated in Nature He watches with delight what He creates.[8]

The universe is real, but it is not eternal and has no independent existence. God creates both good and evil, but the overall existence of the world is good and beneficial, and accordingly Sikhism does not advocate asceticism or withdrawal from the world. God also preserves the world according to the divine will or norm expressed in the orderly functioning of existence. In accordance with the divine norm, the Adi Granth says, we are born and we die, and everything, ahead and behind, is pervaded by this norm.

What is one's real self? Human souls are part of the creation emanating from God, like sparks arising from the fire. God is infinite, but the soul is finite and has its own individuality; yet it is deathless. It takes bodily form according to the will of the creator, and it gives consciousness to the body. Mind and intellect are the outer coverings of the soul; it is through the mind and intellect that the soul controls the working of the bodily senses. It is the soul that is conscious of truth or falsehood, that determines virtue or sinfulness. The soul is the basic link with God, as the receptacle of God's love. When the body dies the soul leaves and continues forever, transmigrating to other bodies in the rebirth cycle in accordance with karma. There are heaven and hell into which one can be reborn, although these are not eternal or ultimate, and we can be reborn as animals or plants. At death the soul leaves the body and appears before the God of justice. Depending on its karma, it may be sent to be reborn as an animal, a bird, or an insect. It may be sent to heaven or hell. Or it may be sent to be born again as a human being for its further development. The goal of the Sikh religious life is to attain final nirvana, that is, total union of the soul with God, thus transcending heaven and hell and the rebirth cycle, enjoying uninterrupted bliss forever.

The Human Predicament

Although the world and humans were created by God and thus are not essentially evil, our self-centeredness and pride lead to attachment to the pleasures and concerns of the world. The result of this is separation from God and all the manifold human sufferings, including the endless cycle of rebirths.

The main human problem is the ego, that is, self-centeredness, which arises because we are enveloped in *maya*, delusion, which also is part of God's creation. It is not inevitable that humans give in to self-centeredness. Sikhs do not believe in a predestined course of the soul nor do they hold to the belief that the soul is basically evil. The soul and the world are both good and pure. If the world is seen as God's creation, it is like a beautiful gem; and if the soul is pure, it reflects God's purity and love. But most of us give in to self-centered tendencies and turn our attentions to the pleasures of the world rather than to God. And the curse of the self-centered person is separation from God. "God, the Incomprehensible, is within us, but not perceived, for the screen the 'ego' hangs in between."[9] We fill our souls with self-love rather than love for God, and such a soul is trapped by the passions into a life of sin and evil.

> Those who do not cherish the Lord's Name
> Wander, deceived and bewildered;
> Without such cherishing of the Lord's Name,
> Without the love of His Eternal Being,
> Man can have no destiny except remorse and anguish.[10]

Such a person suffers further deprivation of God's love and grace, sinking ever deeper into a life of fear and anxiety. Yama, the lord of death, uses the evil tendencies to snare those who are separated from God and lost in the world; their lot is the endless cycle of rebirths.

> O Self-love, Self-will, thou root of births and deaths,
> Thou soul of sin, thou makest a man to
> Estrange friends and increase the enmity of enemies:
> He thinketh ever of heaping up more wealth,
> And his soul exhausts itself in deaths and rebirths
> And suffers uncountable delights and agonies.
> Thou makest man to lose himself in error's dark wood,
> And thou strikest him mortally sick with covetousness.[11]

Such wanderings can stop only when we meet a true preceptor, a guru, who will guide us onto the path of transformation.

The Path of Transformation

How can we start living *real* life?

The human problem is selfishness, which makes one love the world rather than God, causing one to be separated from God. The answer? In Guru Nanak's words,

> What keepeth me in my detachment
> Is meditating on the Ungraspable One,
> Through the One Divine Word
> God is made real to us,

> And the saints destroy the flames,
> Of attachment to the little self.[12]

Nanak repeatedly rejected the need for various religious practices like sacrifices, pilgrimages, fasting, and the rest. Rather the path is essentially an inner discipline aimed at opening the heart to God's presence. The heart needs to be purified so it can resonate to God's name.

Sikhs believe that God's name reverberates throughout creation as the revelation of God's own being. It is the means through which God can be known, and it reveals the path leading to union with God. It comes first of all through God's grace, awakening our minds and hearts. Guru Nanak said, "*Karma* determines the nature of our birth, but it is through grace that the door of salvation is found."[13] Every person has the capability to hear and respond to this name, for it is the revelation of God's personal being whom we can know and love. By focusing on the divine name we enter into a personal relationship with God. But how can we, selfish and forgetful, hear and respond to God's name?

Sikhs believe that to get on the path of transformation it is necessary to hear the word of the guru, for it is through the gurus that God channels grace to humankind. A modern Sikh scholar explains:

> To be communicable, the Supreme Being chooses one of his created men to be his vehicle and speak to humanity through that chosen vehicle in a language that man can understand. "He places himself in the Guru," the specially chosen form, says Guru Nanak. . . . They [the gurus] only proclaimed what was inspired in their holy beings by the Master as a command or communication. The voice thus received was recorded in human language and it, so preserved, became the eternal Guru. The voice "vibrates in the pages of the Guru Granth."[14]

The ten gurus were illuminated by the inner truth of God's word, and by their perfection they were able to be illuminators of that truth to bring others to salvation. After the death of the tenth guru, the truth that the gurus illuminated was understood to be merged into the Adi Granth. The path of transformation is above all to focus on the word of the guru, for that word inspires and transforms human life:

> And as music has a strange fascination for the mind, the Guru's Word is to be sung to fire one's mind with an ex-

perience that sinks in the soul, and turning the usual, habitual tide of the mind, makes the soul experience the nature of God within one's emotional self. Yea, and then this God-nature will outflow into secular activity as well, deflect man's mind from his immediate environs and personal pulls and passions, and yoke it to the service of the others in order that the Name, the all-pervading Spirit, is seen through all creation.[15]

Thus the path involves honoring, reading, singing, and meditating on the words of the gurus as they are written in the Adi Granth.

Achieving this realization naturally affects the way people live their lives. They control their desires and their sense of ego, not withdrawing from the world but seeing it as God's creation and God's revelation. As people advance in spiritual perfection and purity of mind, they deepen their piety, knowledge, effort, and fulfillment, until finally they attain to God-realization, entering into union with God's own true, formless being. The realm of birth and death, even the realm of heaven and hell, are left behind in this eternal bliss.

> They who think on Thee, they who meditate on Thee,
> In this dark age have their peace.
> They who think on Thee: they are saved, they are liberated;
> For them death's noose is broken.
> Those who meditate on the Fearless One
> Will lose all their fear;
> Those who have worshipped the Lord,
> In the Lord they are now mingled.[16]

A yogin once asked Guru Nanak how it was possible to live in this maya world of materialism, and still become one with God. Guru Nanak gave two examples. A lotus flower cannot exist without water, yet it remains unaffected by the water, always rising above the surface. And a duck cannot live without water, yet since it never gets its wings wet, it never drowns in the water. In the same way, the Guru said, a person cannot live without the maya world of material; yet a person through praise and prayer can enshrine God's name within oneself, thus crossing the ocean of the world in communion with God. In this communion is bliss, peace, and everlasting joy, a taste of the heavenly elixir.

WORSHIP AND LIFE

Ritual and Worship Among the Sikhs

How can we find new power for life? The Sikh answer is love, God's love, experienced and expressed in service, ritual, and worship. The active love and worship of God, focused on the divine revelation in the Adi Granth, God's presence in the gurdwara, and God's word brought through the gurus, characterize the Sikh religion. The proper way to relate to God is in prayer, submission, study of God's word, thankful praise, and a life-style that reflects this love.

Worship starts with the word of God, which is experienced concretely in the Adi Granth. Daily worship at home means reading and meditating on the sacred word, the Adi Granth, which is kept in a special room of the house. Devout Sikhs rise before sunrise and bathe, followed by saying prayers, reciting scriptures, and concentrating on the name of the Lord. When the day is done, they again recite prayers and scriptures before retiring for the night.

Worship also means visiting the gurdwara, daily, perhaps, and participating in worship there—this is the heart of the Sikh religion. Since there are no priests or ordained worship leaders in Sikhism, each person is free and em-

Sikhs preparing holy water for ritual use.

powered to perform the rituals of worship. The central object of worship is the Granth Sahib, the Holy Book, which is placed on a low cot and draped in embroidered silks with a royal awning above. People remove their shoes and cover their heads when entering the gurdwara. Often they bring some flowers and copper or silver coins to deposit before the Holy Book. They walk solemnly to the Holy Book, bow and perhaps touch their foreheads to the edge of the sheet covering the Book. Then they move back to sit on the carpeted floor with the rest of the congregation.

The pattern of worship in the gurdwara consists of two main activities: reading and explaining the scriptures, and singing the hymns (kirtan). Both men and women read from the Holy Book. Often there are trained musicians who lead the faithful in the devotional music, which is a valuable means of lifting the soul to communion with God. After the prayers, Sikhs receive karah parshad, a sacred food made of flour, sugar, and ghee.

Generally Sikhs observe the usual festivals of northern India, such as Holi and Divali. There are also specifically Sikh festivals commemorating the birthday of Guru Nanak, the martyrdom of the fifth Guru Arjun, and the like. In celebrating a festival, the Holy Book is placed in a decorated palanquin carried on a flower-bedecked lorry. The joyful procession is led by men marching with drawn swords, and many enthusiastic and gaily dressed devotees participate, some in singing parties, others as sword-stick performers, and the like. Often the festival includes a common meal for the worshipers at the kitchen (langar) of the gurdwara.

Sikhism does not approve of excessive ritualism. Still, there are commonly observed ceremonies relating to the main passages of life. Some Sikhs follow the tradition of reciting the first five verses of the morning prayer in the ears of a newborn child. In the naming ceremony, the Holy Book is opened and the child is given a name starting with the first letter of the first word on the top of the page. Religious instruction is provided privately or at the gurdwara, and the first day when the child learns to read the Granth Sahib is a day of great festivity. When Sikh boys and girls come of age they are formally initiated into the order of the khalsa. Five Sikhs perform this ritual before the congregation, stirring sugared water (amrit) with a steel double-edged dagger accompanied by the recitation of sacred verses. The holy water is poured into the cupped hands of the initiates and they drink of it, and it is then sprinkled all over their bodies.

A Sikh marriage takes place in the gurdwara before the Adi Granth. The main ceremony is circling the Adi Granth four times accompanied by the singing of special verses. After each round the couple bow down before the Holy Book. After the fourth round the marriage is complete.

When a Sikh dies, the body is bathed and dressed in the emblems of the faith and taken in solemn procession to the crematorium. No wailing is permitted, only recitation of the holy word and the distribution of food to the family and mourners. A short period of mourning is observed, and on the last day family and friends assemble in the house for singing hymns and reciting the Adi Granth.

The worship life of Sikhs gives expression to the love of God in a variety of art forms. Shunning sculpture because of the worship of images in India, Sikhs celebrate the artistic beauty of nature in its manifold forms. Since the word of God is central, the literary arts have been highly cultivated, especially that of religious poetry, with the powerful poems of the gurus taken as models. Another art beloved by the Sikhs is music, used in singing the sacred songs to uplift the soul. Guru Nanak spoke:

In the house in which men sing the Lord's praises
And meditate upon Him,
In that house sing the songs of praise
And remember the Creator;
Sing the song of praise of thy fearless Lord,
Let me be a sacrifice unto that song,
By which we attain everlasting solace.[17]

A Sikh writer explains the importance of the art of music in this way: "Music carries an individual above the mundane and helps in merging the not-Self with the Self. By music the soul is lifted into an almost mystic union with God."[18]

Society and the Good Life

Sikh Society: Khalsa and Gurdwara

How should we live? A Sikh should live as befits one who belongs to the Panth (path), the Sikh community of believers, disciples of the gurus.

Many Sikhs think of themselves as part of the khalsa, the special form of the Panth founded by Guru Gobind. Their salutation to one another is, "The khalsa belongs to God; victory to Him!" Historically, the khalsa is the community founded by the tenth guru to keep the Sikhs in military readiness and bravery, but it has become a symbol of belonging to the Sikhs, an identity expressed concretely by the uncut hair and turban worn by men. Although there are birth rituals for Sikhs, the real entrance into the Sikh community is through the initiation into the order of the khalsa held when the individual comes of age.

The Sikh community differs from the other religions arising from India in having no priests, mendicants, or other holy persons as worship leaders. It is an egalitarian community, and any person with reasonable proficiency in the Punjabi language, including women, can conduct congregational services and act as readers of the Adi Granth.

Leadership in the Sikh community is found in the committees formed to manage the gurdwaras (temples). These are local autonomous bodies, elected democratically. These groups not only manage the temples but run many educational institutions and publish religious literature, playing a leading role in political developments as well. But there is also a central authority that decides on the major issues that affect the larger Sikh community. This group is made up of the leaders of four major gurdwaras in India, including especially the one at Amritsar. The decisions of this central authority are binding upon the Sikh community.

The Sikh Vision of the Good Ethical Life: Self-realization

In answer to the question, How should we live?, Sikhs could answer in the words of Guru Nanak,

> Men of contentment serve their Lord and dwell upon the True One.
> They do not put their feet in sin; they do good deeds and practise Dharma.
> They loosen their sensual bonds and eat but sparingly.
> And the Grace of God is heaped upon them.[19]

Love of God and the guru is the basis of the good ethical life, leading to happiness, grace, and self-realization. And that good life is the natural life, following the highest law

that is in the human heart. "Act according to the Universal Will that is written within one's Self," said Guru Nanak.[20]

The primary human problem that stands in the way of the good life is the ego, that is, attachment to self apart from God. Sikhs believe that one's present life has been shaped by karma in past existences, and further that the Will of God controls all existence. However, even though much of our existence is beyond our ability to control, we do have a realm of free will in which we can cultivate the love of God and follow the guidance of the guru in order to break our attachment to selfishness. The good life is seen as the way to move away from ego to the union of the self with God and thus complete self-realization. This means cultivating concrete virtues and avoiding attachments to sins and vices, thus becoming a true Sikh.

There are, of course, springs of action that hinder the moral life; these are concupiscence, anger, covetousness, attachment, and pride, the "evil ones and thieves" that continuously steal away our virtues. Against these vices Sikhism does not advocate extreme asceticism or withdrawal from social relations. Rather, recognizing one's place in God's Will, one should cultivate the central virtues. Guru Nanak said that "as many are the vices, so many are the chains round one's neck. One removes vice with virtue, for virtue is our only friend."[21]

Heading the list of virtues would be wisdom, as the foundation for the good life, and truthfulness, as a fundamental quality growing from the love of God and one's fellow humans. Another central human virtue is justice, regarding all others as equal to oneself, respecting their rights, and not exploiting them. Sikhs further emphasize the virtue of self-control, living one's life in moderation and governing the lower impulses by the higher, not through extreme asceticism but through moderation: eating less, sleeping less, and talking less, as Guru Nanak suggested. A related virtue would be contentment, that is, accepting both success and failure calmly.

Still one more characteristic virtue in the Sikh view of the good life is courage. Sikhs are enjoined to be fearless and unflinching in standing in their faith, no matter what the suffering. Beginning with Guru Gobind Singh, the tenth guru, the virtue of courage was extended to taking arms and struggling on the battlefield in the cause of righteousness: "When the situation is past all remedies, it is righteousness to take to sword."[22] Such militant courage is to be used only when all other avenues are closed and together with the other virtues of justice and love. The virtue of courage is embodied especially in the khalsa with its code of discipline and the symbolic wearing of the sword.

But how does one apply these virtues concretely to life in family and in society? Sikhism teaches that all should perform the duties associated with their particular station in life. Further, all should observe the duties of right livelihood, not depending on the charity of others and not being dishonest in trade. They should help the needy, regarding such help as an act of service to the guru. Extramarital sexual relations are immoral, and intoxicants and narcotics are forbidden.

As part of their vision of the good life in human society, Sikhs reject the Hindu caste system in favor of the principle of universal equality. One concrete symbol of this social equality is the characteristic Sikh institution of the community kitchen (langar), where people of all sorts sit together and partake of the same food without any distinction between the high and the low. Further, women are to be accorded equal status and respect with men, conducting worship services, leading Sikh armies, voting in elections, and the like. Guru Nanak said,

Of a woman are we conceived,
Of a woman are we born,
To a woman are we betrothed and married,
It is a woman who is friend and partner of life,
It is woman who keeps the race going. . . .
Why should we consider woman cursed and condemned
When from woman are born leaders and rulers.
From woman alone is born a woman,
Without woman there can be no human birth.
Without woman, O Nanak, only the True One exists.[23]

To realize human brotherhood, Sikhs are taught to do away with slander of others and all enmity toward them. In a positive sense they are to practice altruism toward all, involving themselves in social service for the poor and needy—for in serving humanity one is serving the guru and serving God. Sikhs point to the example of Bhai Ghanaya, whose duty on the battlefield was to bring water to the thirsty soldiers. But he was found bringing water to the

Hindus and the Muslims as well as the Sikhs, so the Sikhs complained to the Guru that he was helping the enemy. When the Guru asked him about his actions, Bhai Ghanaya explained, "O true King, I do not see who is a friend and who is a foe. I see your image in every one of them alike. I saw that they were all your Sikhs and none else and so I served water to every one of them."[24] When by the grace of the Guru our heart is filled with divine light, there is no enemy, and none is "other."

In the Sikh vision of the good life for the world today, peoples of all nationalities and religions are considered equal. The tenth guru proclaimed:

Let it be known that mankind is one, that all men belong to a single humanity. So too with God, whom Hindu and Muslim distinguish with differing names . . . There is no difference between a temple and a mosque, nor between the prayers of a Hindu or a Muslim. Though differences seem to mark and distinguish, all men are in reality the same.[25]

All religions originated with good intentions and are like different roads leading to the same destination. Sikhs feel they should not enter into arguments about the truth of other religions. Rather the gurus encourage the cultivation of a rational attitude, finding out for oneself what is right and what is wrong. In doing so, Sikhs believe one will find that the path taught by the ten gurus is the highest path of self-realization.

A modern Sikh thinker, Taran Singh, has interpreted the khalsa in such a way as to transcend a narrow sectarian view. There is one universal Spirit, he holds, who belongs to all people, whatever their color, country, caste, or religion; there are no privileged people or superior faiths. He writes,

The doctrine of the Khalsa or the Universal Brotherhood of the Pure, proceeds from the doctrine of the all-pervasive and indivisible ultimate Reality. The Wonderful Lord manifests himself in a wonderful drama . . . of the cosmos and creation. In fact all the actors in this cosmic play are Khalsa or Pure; they are all saints and no sinners. . . . So the brotherhood of the Pure is the brotherhood of the entire humanity.

And those initiated Sikhs who make up the actual khalsa are to be seen as an ideal society of humankind who have a mission to perform: "It is a society of humanity so that they might transform the world into the Kingdom of Heaven."[26]

DISCUSSION QUESTIONS

1. Relate the beginnings of Sikhism to developments in India in the fourteenth and fifteenth centuries C.E.
2. What was the experience that transformed Nanak and made him a guru?
3. What is the role of the ten gurus in Sikhism? Why is the Adi Granth also called Guru?
4. Describe the special Sikh form of monotheism. How is this similar to, or different from, the monotheism of the Abrahamic religions?
5. How do the Sikhs maintain both the idea of God's creation of the world and belief in samsara and rebirth?
6. According to the Sikhs, what is the major human problem? What is the main movement on the path of transformation, and what is the spiritual goal?
7. Describe worship at a gurdwara.
8. What is the khalsa?
9. Describe some basic points of ethics in the Sikh view.

KEY TERMS IN SIKHISM

Adi Granth "original collection," the sacred scripture of the Sikhs; *see also* **Guru Granth Sahib**

Arjan the fourth guru and first Sikh martyr (d. 1606)

Gobind Singh the tenth and last Sikh guru, who founded the Khalsa

Golden Temple important Sikh gurdwara at Amritsar

gurdwara temple and meeting place for Sikhs

guru leader and guide for Sikhs; besides the ten Gurus, God and the Adi Granth are also called Guru

Guru Granth Sahib "Sacred collection," the sacred scriptures, with the title guru; another name for the Adi Granth

Kabir a poet (1440–1518), an important predecessor of Guru Nanak, founder of Sikhism

karah parshad sacred food used in Sikh worship assembly

Khalsa a major military-type group within Sikhism, founded in 1699 by Gobind Singh, the tenth guru, with a special code of discipline

kirtan Sikh practice of singing hymns in worship of God

langar Sikh community kitchen

Nam the Name of God, the total divine presence in the world

Nanak founder (1469–1539) of Sikhism and the first guru

Sikh "disciple," that is, one who follows the gurus

Singh surname taken by men who join the Sikh Khalsa

Word of God in Sikh thought, God's presence that reverberates throughout creation, channeled especially through the Gurus

PART II

Religions of China and Japan

INTRODUCTION

East Asia is a tremendously diversified cultural area, with many different ethnic and linguistic groups. Moreover, it has a mind-boggling number of people—perhaps one-fourth of the world's five billion plus people live in the area of East Asia! The peoples of East Asia have the same human experiences as others on this planet, and they ask similar questions about human existence, finding the answers in their long experience. Their answers fall in many ranges, for they have seriously experimented with many world visions, philosophies, and ways of life. These traditions are called by different names—Confucianism, philosophical Daoism, religious Daoism, Mahayana Buddhism, Shinto, and many new religions. But there is some commonality of vision underlying all this, even in the divergent practices and teachings.

A complete study of the religions of East Asia would include many peoples, such as those of Korea, Mongolia, Tibet, the Philippines, even Vietnam. We concentrate our investigation here on the dominant traditions of China and Japan, for these are representative of East Asia and have been most influential throughout the whole area.

The family of religions that we find in China and Japan is perhaps not as closely knit historically as those arising in India or the Abrahamic religions (Judaism, Christianity, and Islam). Even within China the vast land and the variety of ethnic groups promoted a diversity of religious traditions, and Japan developed in isolation until Chinese influence began to infiltrate in the sixth century C.E. East Asia embraces religious traditions of three totally different origins: Confucianism and Daoism arising in China, Shinto arising in Japan, and Buddhism imported from India.

Yet it is still possible in a certain sense to speak of the religions of China and Japan as a family of religions, for they do share important historical developments and religious ideas. Historically, China had developed a great civilization by the second millennium B.C.E., and its Confucian and Daoist religious traditions were passed on later to Japan and the rest of East Asia to become the heart of the common East Asian vision. And Mahayana Buddhism, though originally foreign to China, was accepted and transformed into a Chinese religion, and this also was shared with Japan and the rest of East Asia to form another major component. So the common history is largely a matter of Chinese civilization, developing stage by stage, moving outward to permeate the rest of East Asia with its culture, written language, and a common religious outlook, tempered, of course, by the indigenous traditions such as Shinto in Japan.

But what are some main elements of that common East Asian religious vision? A good word to start with is *harmony*—the functioning harmony of a cosmos filled with sacred forces. There is a close interrelationship of the human and natural orders, and the sacred forces—gods, kami, spirits, yin-yang forces—stand at the heart of the sacred ecology. This is one unified world—no transcendent God or eternal world outside this unified sacred cosmos. We are a part of this one world together with all the sacred forces and all of nature, and our highest good comes in maintaining harmony and balance within it.

The natural social links to family, community, and nation are key arenas of religious involvement for the peoples of China and Japan. The family in particular is the realm of sacred power most directly and concretely affecting one's existence. And the family is founded on the ancestors, so worship of ancestors is a most characteristic form of religious expression. Many gods and spirits are associated with the home and most religious rituals are based in the family. The pattern of family relationships is also the basis for one's relationship to the community and to the nation as a large sacred family.

The religions of China and Japan are typically "this worldly," in the sense that some transcendent world or a future life after death is not the center concern. It is true that Mahayana Buddhism did bring into East Asia a concern about the fate of the souls of the dead. But the strongest emphasis is on the good, balanced life here and now. The world is good and beautiful, human nature derives from positive sacred forces like Heaven and the kami, and the religious path means to achieve and enhance the potential life of sacred harmony in the world and in human society. There is no sharp division, then, between sacred and secular parts of life, between spiritual and humanistic concerns, for all are joined together in balance.

We should note that one strong common factor throughout East Asia is the worldview of Mahayana Buddhism. Though originally a foreign religion from India, Mahayana Buddhism was thoroughly transformed into an East Asian religion, itself transforming East Asia at the same time. The key concepts of shunyata (emptiness) and the universal Dharma Body of the Buddha have permeated the culture and the arts of China and Japan in very fundamental ways, in a creative union with the Chinese

notion of the Dao as the source and support of all reality.

Founded on these common ideas, the cultures of China and Japan demonstrate a profound appreciation for ritual and for the aesthetic quality of life. Important aspects of life tend to be highly ritualized, for ritual helps to create and sustain harmony. Art is united with religion, for it is in the good and beautiful material of human life that the fullest expressions of the religious vision can be created. And it is not only the product of art but the process of artistic creation—the "way" of art—that is considered important in East Asian religions.

As with the other families of religions, it is tempting to put great emphasis on the common elements, for this provides a basic arena in which to compare and understand these particular religions. But this can be misleading if it covers up the fact that each tradition has its own special shape and integrity. Among the religions of China and Japan the interplay between common elements and distinctive traditions is somewhat complicated. First of all, the Chinese religious traditions form their own unity, and the Japanese religious traditions also make up a unified culture. But within China it is important to recognize the distinctiveness of the separate traditions: Confucianism, philosophical Daoism, religious Daoism, and Mahayana Buddhism. And yet actual Chinese religion as practiced by the people consists of a synthesis of these traditions and includes many common popular religious practices as well. The situation is similar in Japan. Shinto is the indigenous tradition, still alive and well today, but Mahayana Buddhism also receives the allegiance of most Japanese; and Confucian values and popular religious practices are also part of Japanese religion as it is lived in local communities.

Because Buddhism is detailed in Part I, we devote more of our attention here to the Confucian, Daoist, and Shinto traditions of China and Japan.

CHAPTER 10

China: Sacred Story and Historical Context

Who am I? To be Chinese is to be from one of the most ancient societies on earth, to respect the ancestors and the land. Called the Middle Kingdom, this ancient great people and vast land were felt to be the reflection on earth of the mandate of Heaven, the society of the cultivation of the perfect human.

For many Chinese, the three paths—Confucianism, Daoism* (Taoism), and Buddhism—are one story. Traditional Chinese honor the teachings of Confucius and strive to attain that ideal; they respect the practice of harmony with nature shown by Lao-zi (Lao Tzu), legendary founder of Daoism; and they take inspiration from the deep insights into human existence and liberation taught by the Buddha. This is the Chinese way—the way of harmony. Still, each of these three traditions has its own story and its devotees in China, each tradition putting forth a total vision of sacred reality and human existence.

The Chinese story begins in very ancient times with great kingdoms and ideal rulers. Important classical writings were produced that have guided Chinese thinking ever since. The story includes the diversification of the tradition in the forms of Confucianism and Daoism, and

the coming of Mahayana Buddhism fills out the religious universe of the Chinese people.

Each of the three great traditions underwent centuries of growth and decline and revitalization, interacting with each other and contributing to the common popular religion of most of the Chinese people. But in this diversity of traditions and schools there remains a striking unity, based on a common written language, an overriding sense of the centrality of the family, an abiding concern for the harmony of the Dao, common classical writings, and an overall sense of this vast group of peoples as one national family.

Because the Chinese religious traditions are so intertwined, we treat their beginnings together in this chapter, looking at the later historical developments and transformations in the next chapter.

THE BEGINNINGS OF THE CHINESE STORY

The beginnings of the Chinese story go back to far ancient China, long before Confucius and Lao-zi. China is one of the oldest continuous civilizations in the world, and thus this story is the accumulation of wisdom over many, many centuries. Confucius and Lao-zi did not start totally new traditions—they simply reshaped and revitalized what had long been present in China.

---

*The pinyin spelling of Chinese names and terms, widely in use today, will be adopted here. The older Wade-Giles spelling, still used in many scholarly works and in some of our quotations, will be given after the first use for key terms. We will use the name Confucius in its very familiar Western form.

The Ancient Rulers and Their Ancestors

Humans have lived in China for hundreds of thousands of years. Near Beijing important discoveries of so-called Beijing Man have been made in caves, the human culture of Homo Erectus dating from about 500,000 years ago. Humans here had learned the use of fire, used tools and hunted big game animals, and had developed speech and social structures. After the last glacial period, abundant evidence of Neolithic culture is found in China, agricultural peoples who lived in villages, made coarse pottery, used the stone-bladed hoe for agriculture, and kept domestic animals like pigs, horses, and cattle.

Chinese traditions tell the story of important sages who lived during the third millenium B.C.E., namely, the Three Sovereigns and the Five Emperors. The Three Sovereigns domesticated animals, instituted family life, and invented agriculture. Heading the list of the Five Emperors, Huang Di, the Yellow Emperor, is traditionally seen as the symbolic ancestor of all Chinese people. Appropriately, he and his court are credited with inventing many of the cultural boons so important to later Chinese: writing, music, medical arts, wooden houses, carriages, bronze mirrors, silk cloth, weapons, and the like. The last of the Five Emperors is said to have founded the first Chinese dynasty, the Xia (Hsia, ca. 2200–1750 B.C.E.). Although archaeological work has not substantiated the existence of the Xia dynasty as such, it is clear that there was a fountainhead of culture in this period, whose people knew the art of casting bronze, the cultivation of the silkworm, the use of the wheel, and perhaps the value of written symbols. Surely they venerated their ancestors, and they paid great concern to the fertility of the earth and the presence of many sacred powers of nature.

The History of the Shang Rulers

History—that is, ancient life known from written materials and supported by archaeological evidence—begins in the Shang period (ca. 1751–1111 B.C.E.). Shang kings mastered neighboring tribes in northeast China and marched to northwest China to incorporate the Xia alliance. Under the Shang rulers, important features of Chinese culture developed: ceramics, carving, bronze casting, the chariot, architecture, the feudal system, the calendar, and the art of writing. Most important to the story are the religious forms that found expression during the Shang era.

The Shang rulers established a kind of theocracy with themselves as divine rulers who worked for the welfare of their people by worshiping the gods, the ancestors, and especially the high god, Shang Di. All the forces of the world—sun, wind, rain, rivers, and earth—are gods to be worshiped and served. But they are all part of the pantheon presided over by Shang Di, the "Lord Above," who can be worshiped only by the Shang ruler—perhaps being the ruler's primordial ancestor. The hierarchy of the ruler and his people is reflected in the hierarchy of the supreme god and the lower gods and goddesses, and that establishes a central dimension of Chinese religious tradition: the pattern of social ranks and divine ranks making up the total order of nature and society.

Besides structuring the hierarchy of the gods and of society, the story of the Shang kings establishes the model for two additional basic tendencies in Chinese religion. The Shang kings worshiped their ancestors, and they performed divination rituals to understand the will of their ancestors and of the forces of nature.

Worshiping the ancestors was a very elaborate affair, and for the Shang rulers it involved establishing a royal genealogy and a well-organized ritual cycle. Further, it was important for each king to become an ancestor when he died, and so elaborate burials were performed, including burial of carriages, utensils, ritual vessels, jewelry, weapons, food, and the like. Even wives and slaves, with their chariots and horses, were buried alive with their master, to continue the total royal life into the next world when the ruler would be an ancestor. The practice of burying wives and servants with the dead ruler was stopped later, with clay representations sometimes substituted; but the important truth that the ancestor continues to live and rule in an effective way is a long-time heritage of Chinese religion.

In order to determine the will of the ancestors and the operation of the various forces of nature, the Shang rulers consulted divination experts, just as some Chinese have continued to do up to the present time. Their favored form of divination was to use bones and shells heated in a fire and plunged in water, the cracks being read by experts and the answer inscribed on the bones. These oracle inscriptions—nearly 100,000 examples from the Shang capital city—represent the first clear use of Chinese writing in pictographs and ideographs, appropriately designed as an operational method of achieving harmony with the forces of nature.

The Everlasting Ideal: Zhou Society

A rebellion by the Zhou tribal alliance brought down the Shang kingdom in the eleventh century B.C.E. and inaugurated the Zhou dynasty (ca. 1123–221 B.C.E.), whose early ruler created a realm remembered ever after as a model for the ideal Chinese society. It was the evils of the Shang nobility that brought about the rebellion of the Zhou family, we are told by the early Zhou writings, *The Classic of History*, *The Classic of Poetry*, and inscriptions on bronze vessels. A new religious consciousness had evolved, which held that the supreme God cannot merely be a patron deity of a ruling tribe. Rather, the supreme God, which now is called Tian (Heaven, *T'ien*), is a universal righteous God for all. Heaven will give its mandate to rule only to a righteous king governing a righteous state, taking the mandate away from unrighteous rulers and peoples. Morality is of the essence before Heaven, and the welfare of all humans and all nature equally before Heaven becomes a prominent theme in the tradition.

Bronze ritual vessel from the late Shang period, decorated with designs of birds, dragons, serpents, and fish.

Without pity *T'ien* has brought destruction on Yin [Shang], since Yin has lost its mandate to rule, which we of the house of Chou have received. I do not dare to affirm that what we have established will continue forever in prosperity. Yet, if *T'ien* assists those who are sincere, I would not dare to affirm that it will end in misfortune.[1]

The Duke of Zhou developed the notion of the moral mandate and righteous rule into a complete feudal political system, with the king as "Son of Heaven," and the whole Zhou society was stratified hierarchically according to the relationship with the royal family. Here is the pattern that later generations looked to as the ideal human society.

The Zhou rulers developed ceremonialism to a degree perhaps unknown in many other cultures. Why do Chinese put so much emphasis on ceremonies, rituals, bowings, and the like? Performing the proper reverential ceremonies (*li*), according to the ancient sages, is an expression of cosmic order. The ceremonies make connections with the larger forces of existence, especially with the ancestors, so that the people continue in their blessing. From the ancient Classic of Songs we read this description of a ceremonial sacrifice for the ancestors in the early Zhou era:

We proceed to make fermented liquor and to prepare viands for the offerings and for sacrifice. We seat the representatives of the dead and urge them to eat. Thus we seek to increase our bright happiness. We with grave looks and reverent attitude choose our sacrificial victims without blemish, oxen and sheep, to serve in the autumn and winter sacrifices. Some slay the animals; others attend to the cooking; some put the meat on stands; some arrange it for sacrifice. The master of ceremonies stands at the temple gate to await the arrival of the ancestor spirits. The sacrifice is all ready in brilliant array. The ancestor spirits arrive and accept our offerings. Their filial descendant receives their blessing. The spirits reward him with happiness and long life. Some reverently tend the fires, whilst others place in position the great stands [for the meat]. The queen reverently sets out a large number of smaller dishes. The guests and visitors draw near and a toast is drunk. All the ceremonies are meticulously observed; each smile, each word in perfect decorum. The personators of the ancestor spirits arrive and promise every blessing and ten thousand years of happiness. We have done all within our power and performed the rites without error.[2]

Ancient Religious Ideas: Yin–Yang and the Five Elements

The personal wills of the ancestors and the gods of nature are important, of course. But there are also impersonal forces that shape everything humans are and do, as discovered by the Zhou sages. These are forces that are powerfully helpful and productive when they are in harmony, but they cause destruction and death when they are out of harmony. One of the most significant discoveries in the Chinese story is the bipolar activity of the yin and yang forces. All reality is made up of the interaction of two polar forces: yin forces of darkness, femininity, coldness, wetness, and passivity; and yang forces of brightness, masculinity, heat, dryness, and activity. Keeping these forces in harmony brings benefits and happiness, but disharmony causes disaster and suffering.

The Chinese also discovered by the early Zhou period that all reality operates through the five elements, which are qualities that act and transform things. These are water, fire, wood, metal, and earth, all operational qualities that cause things to be the way they are.

To deal with these forces of the gods, the ancestors, yin and yang, and the five elements, people in the early Zhou period continued the practices of divination they inherited from the Shang peoples. The system of divination that now came to be widely used is the system of trigrams made up of broken and unbroken lines (e.g., ☰ and ☷), the unbroken lines representing yang and the broken lines representing yin. Each trigram has its own referent in cosmic forces operating in this particular context. By placing one trigram on top of another, a system of sixty-four hexagrams is developed, each with a special operational meaning. Commentaries on these hexagrams are written in the *Yi Jing* (*I Ching*), the Classic of Changes, begun during the early Zhou period and certainly one of the most influential books in all of Chinese history. Still today people consult the *Yi Jing* for guidance on all sorts of matters.

FOUNDINGS: THE STORIES OF CONFUCIUS AND LAO-ZI

Some of the most important religious developments come when bad times overtake the stable institution that seems to be the religious ideal. In ancient Israel, for example, when King David, King Solomon, and their successors reached the highest power, adversity set in and prophets arose to bring about a far-reaching religious transformation in Israel. So, too, in China, the ideal Zhou kingdom fell onto bad times, and in the ensuing questioning and searching, there was a great period of religious transformation in which the most important Chinese religious traditions were founded.

Anarchy and Search in the Middle Zhou Period

Troubles for the Zhou rulers started around 800 B.C.E. when their power dwindled with the emergence of a number of independent states headed by powerful princes. The struggle for supremacy among these states continued for five centuries until the rulers of the Qin (Ch'in) state emerged victorious and unified China under a dictatorship in 221 B.C.E.

A striking picture of the situation in the eighth and seventh centuries is given in some of the poems in *The Classic of Poetry*, reflecting the suffering and disruption felt during these times. If the rulers are really ruling according to the Mandate of Heaven, why are all these misfortunes and wars occurring? Is Heaven really the moral force that oversees all rulers and all nations?

> I raise my eyes to August *T'ien*, but it does not pity us. It sends down great afflictions without respite. There is no stability in the land. Officers and people alike suffer.
>
> Oh, great far-spreading *T'ien*, whom we call father and mother! Though guiltless, on me these troubles fall. Great *T'ien*, you are too stern. I have examined myself and am without fault. Great *T'ien*, you send down afflictions, but I am blameless.
>
> Vast, far-spreading *T'ien* does not extend its virtue but sends down death and famine to destroy the land. Pitiful *T'ien* now strikes terror without rhyme or reason. It is right that sinners should be punished for their crimes, but why should innocent people be overwhelmed with ruin?[3]

The poets lamented the fact that people look to Heaven but find no clear guidance. With the questioning of the traditional beliefs came a tendency toward a more rationalistic and humanistic interpretation of life.

The middle and late Zhou periods, in spite of the troubles of society, are remembered as the classical age of ancient China, for many creative developments took

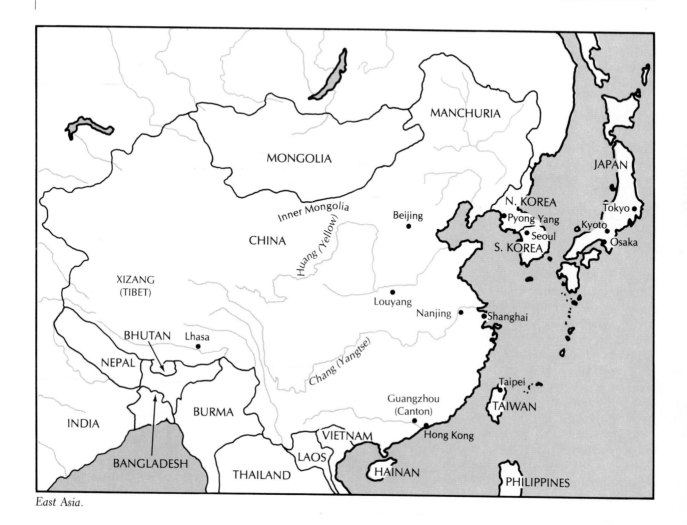

East Asia.

place. The laws were written down for the first time, and there were important advances in agriculture and production. The earlier classical writings of poetry, history, and divination were read and memorized by statesmen and scholars. Teachers set up schools to train boys for public office or instructed small groups of disciples in their homes. Their teachings had to do with the ancient traditions, but they also took up the burning religious, political, and social issues of the day. The words of some of these teachers were remembered and written down by their disciples. Among these teachers were sages and leaders like Kong-zi (K'ung-fu Tzu, that is, Confucius) and Lao-zi, along with Mo-zi (Mo Tzu), Meng-zi (Meng Tzu or Mencius), and Zhuang-zi (Chuang Tzu). The important religious traditions of China—later known as Confucianism and Daoism—developed from these foundations.

The Story of Confucius

The man whose teachings transformed Chinese society and guided the Chinese state and educational system for the past two thousand years was of fairly obscure birth and was not widely recognized in his own lifetime. His disciples carried on his teachings after him, transforming it in the process, and eventually in the Han period his philosophy of life was enshrined as the official way of Chinese thought and the Confucian cultus became the state religion of China. The heart of the story is the vision of life articulated in the Confucian tradition. But the life story of Confucius himself is also important.

The Life of Confucius

Although there is a biography of Confucius from several centuries after his lifetime, supplying a detailed ancestry that makes him a direct descendant of the Shang royal house, contemporary records say little about his background. The collection of his sayings, the Analects, does not give much biographical information about his life. We know nothing for sure about his parents, for they are never mentioned in the materials from Confucius' time, leading to the supposition that he was orphaned at an early age. We do know of a daughter and a son, but from the early sources we know nothing about his wife.

He was born in the small state of Lu in the northeast part of China in the year 551 B.C.E. Confucius said of himself that he was of humble status and he owned little personal property. Yet all the traditions suppose that he came from an aristocratic ancestry, and he certainly was well educated and had leisure time to pursue such arts as music and archery. In his day there were many members of formerly wealthy aristocratic families who were not able to maintain their high social status, for there were not enough government positions available for all of them. According to Meng-zi, Confucius was once a keeper of stores and once he was in charge of pastures. One of his disciples said that Confucius did not have a regular teacher, so perhaps he was largely self-taught. It is clear, however, that he excelled in learning the classical writings of the past.

Like most educated people of his day, Confucius aspired to political office, and there are persistent traditions that he was a minister in the state government of Lu for a time. His special goal was to restore the culture and religion of China as under the ideal reign of the Duke of Zhou. His service in public office, however, was not recognized, and he was repeatedly rebuffed in his attempts to attain responsible public positions for which he felt he was suited. He turned to teaching to make his great contribution to Chinese culture. Confucius, perhaps because of his own background, had developed a sympathy for the common people, and when he set up his own school he resolved never to turn away an aspiring student no matter how poor he was.

Confucius had a full life teaching in his state of Lu and seeing his disciples attain government positions so as to shape culture and society. But in his fifties he was frustrated and disillusioned with the lack of moral leadership in the state, and he decided to leave and journey to other states to instruct rulers and attempt to find a way of putting his principles into practice. Although he was respected and well received by many rulers, and even offered a position here and there, he did not find the kind of moral commitment and understanding necessary to revitalize the ideal Zhou rule and society.

Finally Confucius was invited back to the Lu state, after a decade of wandering, when he was nearly seventy. Outwardly it perhaps seemed that he had failed, for no ruler had heeded him and put his ideals into practice. But these journeys and challenges contained the sparks of the future, when other Confucianists would journey and teach and create a society that would use this fundamental vision as the standard of culture and religion.

After several years with his disciples back in Lu, Confucius fell sick and died. We do not know the details of his death, but the Analects (the collection of his sayings) tell about an earlier sickness when his disciples feared he was dying. His disciple Lu Yu was agitated that the master was dying and suggested that sacrifice and prayer be offered. Confucius dryly commented, "Is there such a thing?" When his disciple quoted the ancient classics to support such prayer, Confucius said simply, "My prayer has been for a long time" (Analects 7.34). His life was his death prayer.

Death in Chinese society is a very important communal affair, and the mourning rituals—up to three years of mourning—are a high priority for the family. Although they were not his family, Confucius' closest disciples observed the three years of mourning after his death. He is like the sun and the moon, one disciple said (Analects 19.24); he was the uncrowned king, in the eyes of later generations.

The Way of Life According to Confucius

Perhaps we do not know a great deal of certain facts about the life of Confucius. But then the most important dimension of the Confucian story is not the life of Confucius but the way of life that he taught as recorded in the

A Manchu period portrait of the great sage Confucius.

Analects. Many Chinese have found identity in following the Way of Confucius.

The way of life that Confucius walked and taught to his students was not a new, revolutionary change from the traditional Chinese way. He felt that the main problem was a breakdown in morality and values resulting from turning away from the standards of the early Zhou society. Now rulers usurped power and oppressed their subjects, ruling by laws and punishments, and the people responded with violence and hatred. So Confucius taught that the people needed to return to the basic principles of virtue as these were enacted by the Duke of Zhou and the other virtuous rulers of the early Zhou period, who followed the Mandate of Heaven and presided over realms of peace and harmony.

What does it take for people to transform themselves into people who live in peace and harmony? Confucius articulated an important goal, that of *ren (jen)*, humane goodness. Like so many ideographs among the written Chinese characters, *ren* is most expressive: the sign for a person plus the sign for two—that is, two persons in harmonious interaction, representing society in harmony. Confucius felt that all humans have the capability for this basic goodness. The reason people act selfishly and harmfully toward others is the influence of social anarchy and immorality of the rulers. How can this be turned around so that the people can become people of *ren*?

People need a discipline, Confucius taught, and the best discipline is the deliberate cultivation of the tradition of the ancient sages. That is the key to harmony and peace and prosperity. By studying their words and modeling one's actions after their actions, a person can become humane like they were. So Confucius led his disciples in studying the classics, writings traditionally held to stem from the sage-kings of earlier times. Some traditions say Confucius even had a hand in writing or at least editing these classics, which form such an important part of the Chinese tradition. The heart of the Confucian scriptures has always been the Five Classics. As they took their final form in later times, these include the Classic of History (*Shu Jing*), recording words and deeds of the ancient sage-rulers from the prehistoric Yao period to the early Zhou period. The Classic of Poetry (*Shi Jing*) is a collection of some three hundred poems dating mostly from early Zhou times, exemplifying the quintessence of moral virtue and poetic beauty. The Classic of Changes (*Yi Jing*) is a book of divination that includes interpretations and commentaries explaining the patterns of the universe. A sacred text on ritual is the Classic of Rites (*Li Jing*), giving detailed accounts and interpretations of the rituals of the ancient sage-kings, plus additional philosophical teachings. And the fifth classic is the Spring and Autumn Annals (*Chun Qiu*), a record of events in Confucius' native state of Lu between 722 and 481 B.C.E., together with several commentaries. There apparently was a sixth classic, the Classic of Music, which is no longer extant.

In transmitting and perhaps editing these classics, and in leading his disciples into a path of self-transformation based on their study, Confucius established the model of a life of study that has been so influential in providing the shape of the Chinese way.

The key principle in the sages' way of life, Confucius taught, is *li*, a word that means "propriety" or "respectful ritual." This word originally referred to the sacrifices and rituals directed toward the ancestors, actions filled with respect and performed with great care and thoroughness. The heart of propriety is filial piety directed toward parents and ancestors. But Confucius showed how this attitude of respect can permeate all actions; we can practice propriety as we live our daily lives, performing the proper rituals and ceremonies as an outer discipline so that we transform ourselves inwardly into people of *ren*. Confucius saw a close relationship between ritual and human goodness, as illustrated in this dialogue:

> Yen Yuan asked about humanity. Confucius said, "To master oneself and return to propriety is humanity. If a man (the ruler) can for one day master himself and return to propriety, all under heaven will return to humanity. . . . Do not look at what is contrary to propriety, do not speak what is contrary to propriety, and do not make any movement which is contrary to propriety." (ANALECTS 12.14)[4]

The purpose of practicing propriety, Confucius taught, is to establish the proper relationships in family and in society. As these outer relationships are in order, so the inner nature is also in order.

In teaching the discipline of study and the practice of rituals to transform people toward humaneness, Confucius knew he was putting forth a way of life that had its foundation in sacred power. He spoke of his practice as the Dao (way), a term used from earlier times to designate the way of the universe. To follow the Dao means to be in harmony with the ancestors and spirits, with the forces of yin and yang and the five elements. Yet Confucius was not overly interested in what we might think to be the "religious" aspects of the Dao, that is, the gods, spirits, and natural forces. His concern was human life in family and society, not invocation of gods and spirits. Once a student asked him about worshiping gods and spirits, and his answer was: "If we are not yet able to serve man, how can we serve spiritual beings?" And when the student asked about death, Confucius replied: "If we do not yet know about life, how can we know about death?" (Analects 11.11).[5]

The gods and spirits should not be the focus of attention; much more important is the transformation of human society into a society characterized by humaneness.

But this is not to say that Confucius had no vision of the sacred in relation to human life. He was deeply religious in his conviction that Heaven as the supreme moral authority ruled over all through its decree or mandate. And he believed that his own way was in harmony with the mandate of Heaven, although he preferred to leave the demonstration of that to the real evidence of his life. Once, when he was in danger, he said: "If (my) Way is to prevail, it is (Heaven's) Mandate. If it is to be stopped, it is (Heaven's) Mandate. What can Kung-po Liao do about (Heaven's) Mandate?" (Analects 14.38).[6]

So it is that through Confucius' teaching and life the Way of Heaven became a central part of Chinese identity. Even Chinese who do not call themselves Confucianists still follow his model in studying the classics, practicing the traditional rituals, cultivating the proper family relationships, and striving to live together in peace and harmony according to his teachings.

Disciples of the Confucian Way

Many of Confucius' disciples went on to become important government officials, for Confucius was particularly concerned with educating the superior person who could lead the people with virtue and propriety and thus help them develop their humanity. As these disciples passed on the teachings of Confucius, they also developed and shaped them. Two new writings in the Confucian tradition were produced that had a great effect and became part of the story, helping to shape Chinese identity ever since. These are the Doctrine of the Mean and the writings of Meng-zi.

The Doctrine of the Mean (*Zhong Yong*), attributed to Zi Si (Tzu Ssu), a grandson of Confucius, teaches that the Way of Heaven that prevails throughout the universe also underlies the moral nature of humans. Our nature has been imparted to us by Heaven. Therefore we can develop this Heaven-given nature, assisting in developing the nature of others, even reaching the point of assisting in the transformation process carried on by Heaven and Earth. The Doctrine of the Mean set forth the very influential image that humans can become a unity with Heaven and Earth in the nourishing and transforming process of the Way.

Meng-zi (ca. 372–289 B.C.E.) is said to have studied under disciples of Zi Si, and he has been accepted by many as the chief interpreter of the Confucian tradition. His writings rank second only to Confucius in their importance for shaping the Confucian way of life. Meng-zi established the philosophy that humans in their original nature are "good," and from this he drew the principle that all political and social institutions exist for the benefit of the people. We are to serve Heaven, Meng-zi taught, by fulfilling human nature and living the good moral life. "He who knows his nature knows Heaven. To preserve one's mind and to nourish one's nature is the way to serve Heaven."[7] Meng-zi followed the lead of Confucius in teaching a humanism rooted in the Way of Heaven—a humanism that for many centuries has been a foundation of the Chinese way of life.

Lao-zi and the Beginnings of Daoism

The Dao has long been a central concern of Chinese. In the experience of Confucius, the Way is realized especially in social relations, in the family structures, the ruler-subject relationships, and the like. But there were others in this fertile middle Zhou period who took a sharply different approach to harmony with the Dao. These Daoists (as they later came to be called) felt the Way of Confucius was too artificial and structured. Real harmony with the Dao is to withdraw from the structures of society and experience the natural rhythms of the universe itself. Daoism later developed institutions of priesthoods and rituals that identify it as a particular religion of China. But as a philosophy of life, complementing Confucianism as its polar contrast, the vision of Daoism has greatly influenced many Chinese people.

The Story of Lao-zi and the Dao De Jing

Who was Lao-zi, the founder of Daoism? There are legends about his life, although some suspect these legends are collective representations of many sages who protested against the tight structuring of society by withdrawing to the mountains as recluses, to practice methods of harmonizing with nature. Details of his life are rather scanty. Even the great historian Si-ma Qian, writing in the mid-second century B.C.E., despaired of writing an accurate biography of Lao-zi. And that is properly so. For one who attunes himself so completely with the flow of the Dao as did Lao-zi passes beyond the limitations of human history.

But the legend has its importance. Lao-zi was born about 604 B.C.E., it is said, making him an older contemporary of Confucius. He was conceived sixty-two years before this at the time when his mother had admired a falling star. When time came for his birth, his mother gave birth while leaning against a plum tree, and he was able to speak when he was born. Since his hair was already white, he was called Lao-zi, "Old Master."

Later Lao-zi became palace secretary and keeper of archives for the court of Zhou at Louyang. Many knew of his wisdom and the spiritual depth of his meditative practices and came to be his disciples. The story reports that even Confucius came to visit Lao-zi in 517 and was overwhelmed by his deep insight and spirituality.

But by the time he was 160 years old, Lao-zi had become disgusted with the way people lived in the world, and he decided to withdraw from society to pursue the higher virtues in the mountains of the west. As he departed through the Han-gu Pass, riding a chariot drawn by a black ox, the keeper of the pass recognized him as a sage and prevailed upon him to write his wisdom in a book. Lao-zi responded by writing down the 5,000 characters of the book called the *Dao De Jing* (*Tao Te Ching*) and then he departed for immortal sagehood.

These legendary stories of Lao-zi's life do not connect with historical events very well. He appears to be representative of the approach developed by a group of recluse thinkers, especially in the fourth and third centuries B.C.E., who resisted the Confucian structures of society and advocated instead a simple nature mysticism. Whereas Lao-zi is an important character, it is not so much the legend of his life as the sacred writing associated with him, the *Dao De Jing*, that has profoundly shaped Chinese life and thought.

This short text with its vision of living in harmony with the flow of the Dao has been a most influential book in Chinese history. People of almost all religious schools in China have gone to it for inspiration. And its influence has not been limited to China—no book except the Bible has been translated into Western languages as often as this text! It is, of course, a special book of those who call themselves Daoists, the ones who follow the Dao.

Lao-zi, the legendary founder of the Daoist philosophy. Stone rubbing from the Ming Dynasty.

It operates everywhere and is free from danger.
It may be considered the mother of the universe.
I do not know its name; I call it Tao [Dao].   (CH.25)[8]

Everything in the world is produced by this universal Dao, so all of nature has an inherent harmony and balance in its natural process.

Since the Dao is the source of all, the greatest human good is to be in harmony with the Dao. And people get in harmony with the Dao not by following rules of propriety or structuring their activities in society, but by *wu-wei* (no action). That is after all how nature itself operates: passively, quietly, in a natural rhythm. The tree grows, water flows, winter changes into spring—all without effort or striving. And so the Daoist sage will follow that pattern of no-action and nonstriving, withdrawing from the activities of society, harmonizing the inner self with the flow of the Dao.

In weakness and passivity there is strength, the Dao De Jing teaches. The softest things in the world overcome the hardest things. Water washes away mighty mountain cliffs. The sage who attunes with nature, who does not use aggression and violence, who seeks not reward and position, who lives spontaneously without rules and plans, who accepts weal and woe with equanimity—such a one is kingly and free. "Being one with Nature, he is in accord with Dao. Being in accord with Dao, he is everlasting and is free from danger throughout his lifetime" (ch. 16).[9]

Daoist Freedom and Creativity: Zhuang-zi

Nearly as important as Lao-zi in the formation of the Daoist story is Zhuang-zi (ca. 369–286 B.C.E.)—and his life is almost as legendary and obscure. It appears that he was a government official at one time, but probably he lived most of his life as a recluse doing, apparently, some very unconventional things. The traditional story counts him as the main successor and interpreter of Lao-zi and, most importantly, the author of the very influential book called the *Zhuang-zi*. It is from Zhuang-zi's stories and parables more than anything else that we have derived our image of the free, unimpeded, nonconventional, roaming Daoist saint. Zhuang-zi thus plays a significant role as a model for the Daoist way of life.

Zhuang-zi was not concerned with good government or society; he proposed no plan to remake the world to improve the human situation. Rather, he used his great lit-

The title, ~~Dao~~ De Jing, means "Classic of the Dao and its Power." It puts forth a vision of the Way that stands in sharp contrast to the Confucian notion of the Way of Heaven. The Dao is the sacred principle immanent in nature, that which is the source of all and that to which all returns. In a typically cryptic statement the *Dao De Jing* describes the Dao:

There was something undifferentiated and yet complete,
Which existed before heaven and earth.
Soundless and formless, it depends on nothing and does not change.

erary skills to advocate emancipation from the shackles of conventional values and thought and a total identification with the very process of nature, namely, the Dao. Our conventional way of thinking tells us that some things are good and others evil, that pleasure is different from pain, that life is desirable and death is undesirable. But the Dao encompasses all forms of existence without such distinctions and dualities. To be in tune with the Dao is to transcend ordinary judgments and emotions and attain absolute happiness by understanding the real nature of things. The Dao, embracing all things, is in a constant process of change and transformation. Rather than reacting to these changes with pain or pleasure, the wise one accepts them as the natural process and goes along with them.

Zhuang-zi delighted in shocking conventional wisdom by extolling creatures that (by ordinary values) were ugly, misshapen, or useless; to Zhuang-zi, they display the freedom and naturalness of the Dao. He told a story about a horribly deformed man, Zi-yu, who had a hunched back, internal organs on top of his body, and his shoulders higher than his head. But when asked whether he disliked this condition, Zi-yu replied,

> No, why should I dislike it? Suppose my left arm is transformed into a cock. With it I should herald the dawn. Suppose my right arm is transformed into a sling. With it I should look for a dove to roast. Suppose my buttocks were transformed into wheels and my spirit into a horse. I should mount them. What need do I have for a chariot? When we come, it is because it was the occasion to be born. When we go, it is to follow the natural course of things. Those who are contented and at ease when the occasion comes and live in accord with the course of Nature cannot be affected by sorrow or joy. This is what the ancients called release from bondage. (CH. 6)[10]

Living with the Dao frees one from the limitations imposed by normal, conventional life. In act, Zhuang-zi told stories about the ability of Daoist sages to fly through the air above the clouds, avoiding all harm, achieving miraculous longevity, and otherwise transcending normal human limitations. So one is freed from the conventions imposed by social life, laws and rules, ceremonies and etiquette, and all other forms of artificiality. Providing an alternative to the dominant Confucian philosophy of life, Zhuang-zi has embedded in Chinese tradition a vision of

spontaneity and naturalness that has given a special shape to culture, art, and religion.

Development of Religious Confucianism and Daoism

The teachings of Confucius and Meng-zi, on the Confucian side, and of Lao-zi and Zhuang-zi, on the Daoist side, are very important to the Chinese religious perspective; but they do not yet represent completely what average Chinese think of as Confucianism and Daoism. There is something more to these religious ways, something more involving temples, altars and shrines, gods and spirits, rituals and festivals. Moreover, the story is the story of the three Ways, and we have not yet mentioned the founding of the third Chinese Way, Buddhism. It was during the Han dynasty (202 B.C.E.–220 C.E.) that beginnings were made in the direction of a more specifically religious orientation of these Ways, and we include some of these key developments to conclude our look at the story of the founding of Chinese religion.

Confucian Triumph and the Cult of Confucius

For some centuries after the time of Confucius, the Confucian approach to the humanization of society existed as one philosophy among others. There was the Daoist alternative, of course. Another important alternative to Confucianism was the movement founded by Mo-zi (ca. 471–391 B.C.E.), who lived soon after Confucius and taught an approach to life that rejected certain Confucianist principles. Mo-zi held a strong belief in a righteous God (Heaven) who loves all people impartially. The evils of the day, Mo-zi taught, are directly caused by the fact that people do not love one another altruistically but only selectively and partially—as exemplified by the Confucian notion of filial piety with its concern directed mainly to one's own family and clan. This kind of unequal treatment of others must be replaced by "universal love," loving all others as oneself, equally and impartially, showing the same respect for their lives and possessions as for one's own. Mo-zi was strongly against war and violence, and he taught that the highest good is that which benefits people, gaining for his movement the

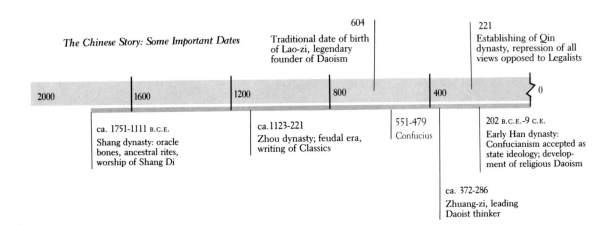

The Chinese Story: Some Important Dates

604
Traditional date of birth
of Lao-zi, legendary
founder of Daoism

221
Establishing of Qin
dynasty, repression of all
views opposed to Legalists

2000   1600   1200   800   400   0

ca. 1751-1111 B.C.E.
Shang dynasty: oracle
bones, ancestral rites,
worship of Shang Di

ca.1123-221
Zhou dynasty; feudal era,
writing of Classics

551-479
Confucius

202 B.C.E.-9 C.E.
Early Han dynasty:
Confucianism accepted as
state ideology; develop-
ment of religious Daoism

ca. 372-286
Zhuang-zi, leading
Daoist thinker

name Utilitarianism. Mohism had many devout followers for several centuries and provided strong competition to the Confucian vision of human life.

Another significant alternative to mainline Confucianism grew up within the Confucian tradition itself, stemming from Xun-zi (Hsun-Tzu, ca. 300–238 B.C.E.). Xun-xi turned away from the perception of the fundamental goodness of humans to take the more realist position that humans by nature are basically inclined toward evil. Consequently, he advocated a strict system of discipline so that people's natural evil inclinations might be overcome and peace and order might exist. He also rejected all superstitious beliefs about supernatural powers and taught a naturalistic understanding of the world and of the value of rituals and ceremonies. Some of Xun-zi's ideas found expression in the school of the Legalists, who advocated a system of authoritarian government with strict laws and punishment to enforce order. These Legalists managed to gain control of the state of Qin (Ch'in), and eventually it was the Qin rulers who conquered the other Chinese states and established a unified empire in 221 B.C.E. The Qin Empire lasted only a few years, but it enforced a uniform order by the repression and wholesale slaughter of all opponents. It was, in fact, made a capital crime to discuss Confucian writings and principles, and books representing all views opposed to the Legalists were burned.

Here was a profound crisis for the Confucian tradition, as well as for the other non-Legalist schools of thought.

But the story tells how some scholars, at risk to their lives, managed to save some of the classic writings so that the ancient wisdom was not lost in this book-burning frenzy. The Qin dynasty fell rapidly, to be replaced by the Han dynasty (202 B.C.E.–200 C.E.). The first Han rulers continued to be of the Legalist persuasion, although without the violent excesses of the Qin rulers. But now Confucian scholars managed to revive their teachings and work out a complete cosmological basis for a unified state under an emperor who served as the representative of Heaven, channeling the cosmic forces and providing harmony in society. The turning point for Confucianism came when Emperor Wu-di (r. 140–87 B.C.E.) ascended the throne and, realizing the need for well-educated officials, ordered scholars to appear for interviews. Among some one hundred scholars to be interviewed was Dong Zhong-shu (179–104 B.C.E.), who convinced the emperor to practice the teachings of Confucius only and dismiss all other theories and scholars. Emperor Wu appointed Dong to be the chief minister of the state, and soon he established doctoral chairs for the classics, thus making Confucianism the state ideology. Later Dong convinced the emperor to found a national university for which fifty of the most talented students in the classics were selected. Now all state officials had to pass civil service examinations in the Confucian classics, ensuring that Confucianism would remain as the official state ideology and thus as the leading component in the Chinese identity—a position it held until the beginning of the twentieth century.

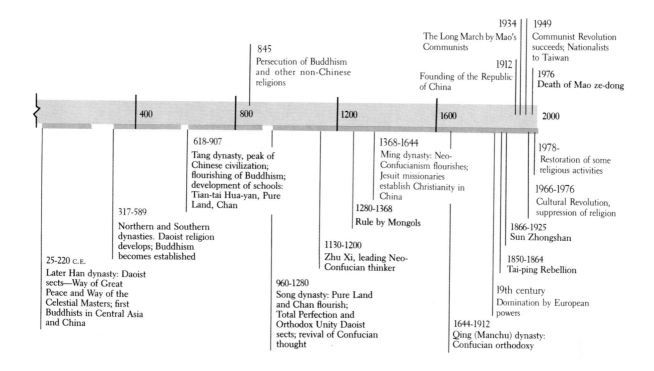

845
Persecution of Buddhism and other non-Chinese religions

1934
The Long March by Mao's Communists

1949
Communist Revolution succeeds; Nationalists to Taiwan

1912
Founding of the Republic of China

1976
Death of Mao ze-dong

400   800   1200   1600   2000

618-907
Tang dynasty, peak of Chinese civilization; flourishing of Buddhism; development of schools: Tian-tai Hua-yan, Pure Land, Chan

1368-1644
Ming dynasty: Neo-Confucianism flourishes; Jesuit missionaries establish Christianity in China

1978-
Restoration of some religious activities

1966-1976
Cultural Revolution, suppression of religion

317-589
Northern and Southern dynasties. Daoist religion develops; Buddhism becomes established

1280-1368
Rule by Mongols

1130-1200
Zhu Xi, leading Neo-Confucian thinker

1866-1925
Sun Zhongshan

1850-1864
Tai-ping Rebellion

25-220 C.E.
Later Han dynasty: Daoist sects—Way of Great Peace and Way of the Celestial Masters; first Buddhists in Central Asia and China

960-1280
Song dynasty: Pure Land and Chan flourish; Total Perfection and Orthodox Unity Daoist sects; revival of Confucian thought

19th century
Domination by European powers

1644-1912
Qing (Manchu) dynasty: Confucian orthodoxy

Together with this intellectual triumph of Confucianism went a new emphasis on the rituals and ceremonies associated with Confucianism and the state. State-supported temples for Confucian ceremonies were established all over China, Confucius' home became a national shrine, spirit-tablets of Confucius and his disciples were venerated in elaborate rituals, and the so-called state cult of Confucius was born. Soon new versions of the texts began to assert the semidivine status of Confucius, and eventually Confucius even came to be considered a god in the popular religion of China.

Through all of this, the very broad range of teachings, rituals, education, and social structures that bears the name Confucianism had become the central focus of the Chinese cultural tradition.

The Beginnings of Religious Daoism

The philosophical Daoism of Lao-zi and Zhuang-zi is not the complete story of Daoism. There were other streams of practice that merged with those basic Daoist insights to produce that broad, complex religious tradition

that we can call religious Daoism. All of these streams were in existence in pre-Han times, although the full development of religious Daoism complete with its writings, priests, and sects took many centuries.

The common denominator of these Daoist streams is the concern about long life and immortality. Lao-zi and Zhuang-zi already made some statements about the freedom from human limitations that can be experienced by getting into complete harmony with the eternal Dao. Around this central notion there began to draw together many popular practices and beliefs cultivated from ancient times by shamans, mediums, and diviners, all rooted in the fundamental idea that humans can get in tune with the larger spiritual forces of our universe. The so-called hygiene school emphasized breathing exercises and various methods of controlling the bodily processes of decay as a way of prolonging life. A search was on to use the five elements in such a way as to produce an elixir of life, a movement that later became known as alchemy. And expeditions were organized to sail across the seas and find the Isle of the Blest, where it was believed there grew a plant that could renew a person's life and vitality. The emperor of the Qin dynasty already sent out such expeditions, and they continued in the Han period.

This search for immortality began to extend also to the common people, and it combined with the ancient interest in gods and spiritual beings. For example, around the year 3 B.C.E. a popular religious movement erupted centered on a mother goddess named Xi Wang-mu (Queen Mother of the West). All over China people turned to her with singing and dancing, believing that by worshiping her and wearing charms with her name written on them they would be able to avoid death. As these movements spread, other gods, goddesses, spirits, and Daoist immortals (sages who were thought to have become immortal) came to be included in the powers who could grant long life and immortality. One Daoist group called itself the Way of Great Peace (Tai Ping Dao). Their leaders functioned as both priests and military officers, and their chief god was Lord Lao, that is, Lao-zi, author of the Dao De Jing, now worshiped as a god and as the creator of the world. They had a sacred book, the *Scripture of Great Peace*, which revealed how to restore good government, encourage peace, and bring good health and long life to the people. Another group in western China during the later Han period was the Way of the Celestial Masters (Tian Shi Dao), which set up its own state ruled by a Master of Heaven with priest-officials as assistants. They also worshiped Lao-zi as a god.

These communities, worshiping Lao-zi and other gods and immortals and centering on rituals performed by priests on the basis of sacred texts, were the forerunners of religious Daoism. Here the philosophy of Lao-zi and Zhuang-zi was taken over and put in concrete form through rituals, priests, techniques for attaining immortality, and community forms. Religious Daoism developed many more scriptures, organizations, rituals, and techniques over the next centuries, but its basic role in the Chinese story was already established: the philosophy of Daoism combined with rituals, gods, priests, and a search for long life and immortality.

The Beginnings of Chinese Buddhism

So we have the Way of Confucius and the Way of Daoism. But when traditional Chinese think of who they really are,

Buddhism became one of the major religions of China; here is a modern Chinese monk at the Big Wild Goose Pagoda in Xian.

the Way of the Buddha also plays a part, and so we should include the beginnings of Chinese Buddhism in the foundational history. The acceptance of Buddhism came gradually, over a number of centuries, and it was the Mahayana form of Buddhism that most connected with the Chinese story.

A tradition says that Han emperor Ming (58–75 C.E.) had a dream in which he saw a golden man, taken by his wise men to be the Buddha; so he dispatched envoys to northwest India to bring back scriptures and teachers. We know that already in the first century C.E. Buddhist monks and laypeople made their way along the silk routes into Central Asia (through present day Afghanistan) and on into China. For a time Buddhism flourished in central Asia until stamped out by Islam around the tenth century C.E. But from central Asia monks and missionaries went to China, and Buddhism came to be firmly planted in China and rose to become one of the three great religions of China, along with Confucianism and Daoism. This remarkable development—a religion from India being adopted by the Chinese and from the Chinese also by the Koreans and the Japanese—led to rich new transformations of Buddhism.

How did it come about that such a foreign way of thinking came to be so important in China? It is not easy to answer that, for there were things about Indian Buddhism that the Chinese people could not understand or accept. What was most problematic about Buddhism as it arrived in China was the monastic system: monks and nuns leaving their families, not working but begging for their food, taking the vow of celibacy and thus cutting off the family line. Traditional Chinese society strongly advocated the centrality of the family and the individual's duty to respect and care for parents and to continue the family by marrying and having children. Chinese values affirmed living in society, seeking happiness, and working productively for the good of all. Buddhist monks were accused of being lazy and idle because they went about begging and did nothing for the welfare of society. The notion that life is suffering and that worldly pleasure should be renounced also seemed strange to the Chinese, as did the "no-self" teaching of Buddhism. And Chinese scholars pointed out that Buddhism was a foreign, barbarian philosophy, not mentioned in the Chinese classical writings.

And so Buddhism was not widely accepted at first in China. But the incursion of Buddhism continued. Mahayana scriptures were brought in and translated into Chinese, and gradually the Chinese came to understand what Buddhism was about, transforming it in the process to fit better into the Chinese worldview. The upheaval that came with the end of the Han dynasty (220 C.E.) led many Chinese to turn away from Daoism and Confucianism and embrace Buddhism. From the fourth to the sixth centuries C.E., Buddhism consolidated its place and then became, for a time, the most powerful and vital religious force in the country.

The appeal of Buddhism was manifold and soon outweighed the initial negative reactions on the part of the Chinese. The disunity and warfare surrounding the end of the Han dynasty induced many to turn to the relative security and peace of the Buddhist monasteries, escaping among other things serving in the armies. And Buddhism in China showed itself not to be opposed to the importance of family life. By becoming a monk or nun, a child could actually fulfill a great amount of filial piety, praying for the family, accumulating merit for the welfare of the ancestors of the family, erecting pagodas to perpetuate the memory of the parents, chanting scriptures for their welfare, and performing the funeral rituals and the rituals for the release of the ancestral souls from purgatory. The monasteries in China tended to be like settled communities, supported by landholdings, serving as art centers, hostels, retreats, and centers of life. Although joining a monastery meant leaving one's family, it was like becoming part of a new family, especially in the son–father relationship with one's Buddhist master.

When Buddhism came to China, it brought important new ideas about human existence that were enlightening to the people of China. The Chinese traditions had virtually nothing to say about life after death or the causes of one's present existence, and here Buddhism was influential. The law of karma, for example, helped to explain why people were born in particular circumstances, whether slave or king. And the Buddhist doctrine of samsara helped people to understand that there are rebirths for all in future existences, on many different planes. In addition, Buddhism supplied a great variety of conceptions about Buddhas and bodhisattvas, heavens, and hells. The cult of Buddhas and bodhisattvas could be added to other popular Chinese cults, and the idea of rebirth in the heavens was not unattractive. The Mahayana notion that each person possesses the Buddha-nature and is capable of salvation appealed to the common people. Buddhism from India contributed great scriptures and works of art to enrich Chinese culture and religion.

One way in which Buddhism was transformed in China was through the translation of Buddhist scriptures into Chinese. At first Theravada scriptures were translated, but as time went on the great Mahayana texts of India were translated into Chinese or—scholars think some of them may actually have been composed in China—attributed to a translator. The high regard the Chinese have for the ancient classics led them to respect these translations and seek more. At the same time, putting Indian texts into Chinese inevitably meant coloring those ideas by Chinese vocabulary and concepts. Perhaps the greatest translator was Kumarajiva (344–413), who translated or revised translations of most of the popular Mahayana sutras and treatises from Nagarjuna's school, thus introducing the very important philosophy of emptiness into Chinese thought. Kumarajiva's translations are still in use today.

DISCUSSION QUESTIONS

1. What were the main religious activities of the Shang rulers (in the Shang dynasty)? What was the origin of writing?

2. How did the beginnings of Confucianism and Daoism reflect the social situation in the middle Zhou period?

3. Explain the basic Confucian ideas of *ren*, *li*, and study of the tradition.

4. It is sometimes said that Confucius' ideas were humanistic, not religious. How would you define the matter?

5. What does the *Dao De Jing* put forth as its basic perspective on the world?

6. What were some of Zhuang-zi's major contributions to the Daoist tradition?

7. How did Confucianism triumph and become the leading ideology of the Chinese state? What is the "state cult of Confucius"?

8. What were the streams that went into the making of "religious Daoism"? How were these related to the ideas of the *Dao De Jing* and *Zhuang-zi*?

9. Discuss factors that worked for and against the Chinese acceptance of Buddhism.

CHAPTER 11

Transformations in Chinese Religious History

The shape of Chinese religion reaches its fullness with the triumph of Confucianism as the state ideology and cult, the rise of religious Daoism in its popular forms, and the acceptance of Buddhism as one of the foundations of the Chinese story. So by the end of the Han period or not too long afterward, the main components of Chinese identity are in place. But Chinese tradition, like the Dao itself, is dynamic, changing and restructuring itself with the flow of time. Religion in Chinese history, from the end of the Han period up to the present, is characterized by the persistence of ancient ideas and practices and the continual interaction of the great religious traditions.

After the disintegration of Han rule around 220 C.E., China entered into a period of political disunity until the end of the sixth century. During this time Buddhism gathered in acceptance and vigor, and Daoism was also in ascendancy, whereas Confucianism was gradually eclipsed. A high point of Chinese culture came in the Tang (T'ang, 618–907) and Song (Sung, 960–1280) eras, when there was a brilliant flowering of literature, art, and philosophy that signaled China as perhaps the greatest world civilization of the time. Winds of change came with the Mongols ruling all of China in the Yuan era (1280–1368). Chinese rule was temporarily reestablished with the Ming dynasty (1368–1644), and Neo-Confucian orthodoxy won the day. But now European influences started to penetrate China with the first Jesuit missionaries and all that followed, opening up contact with the West that was to continue unbroken. The Revolution of 1911 destroyed imperial China and disrupted its traditions, although the traditional religions continued in some form in the Republic of China (since 1949 confined to Taiwan). The disruption of all the religious traditions has been much more drastic in the People's Republic of China, controlling the mainland since 1949.

FLOURISHING OF THE RELIGIONS IN POST-HAN CHINA

Buddhist Expansion and Crystalization

The Golden Era of Buddhism in China

Part of the reason for Buddhism's great success in China was its acceptance by various emperors, such as Emperor Wu of the Liang dynasty (r. 502–549), who abolished Daoist temples and built Buddhist ones and who himself entered a monastery as a lay servitor. The Sui emperors (581–618) and the Tang emperors (beginning in 618) continued imperial support of Buddhism. The emperors were particularly attracted to the intellectual systems of the Buddhist schools, which could serve as a unifying ideology.

The whole Chinese cultural landscape was being made over under Buddhist influence. Thousands of monasteries and shrines were built, tens of thousands of people became monks and nuns, and often the monasteries had huge land holdings. Elaborate Buddhist rituals came to supplement the Confucianist and Daoist ones, and Buddhist festivals such as the Lantern festival, the Buddha's birthday, and Ul-lambana (All Souls' Day) came to be universally observed. Monasteries became social centers for money lending, medical care, serving also as hostels and retreats. Buddhist influence fostered literature and art, with particularly significant contributions in Buddhist sculpture.

Schools of Chinese Buddhism

Very important and characteristic of Chinese Buddhism was the development of a number of different schools or "lineages" that took place during the seventh century. Mahayana teachings had opened the way for a variety of different practices to reach the goal of liberation, whether by help from Buddhas and bodhisattvas or by one's own discipline and meditation—and many combinations in between these two paths. And it had produced many scriptures, purporting to be the Buddha's own word, explaining these paths. Why there are so many scriptures and paths was easily explained: the Buddha uses skillful means and thus teaches different doctrines and practices to suit the condition of the audience. So monks and nuns could devote their attention to one or several of the great scriptures and develop a school that would specialize in certain teachings and practices. Whereas some ten such Chinese Buddhist schools are recognized, a number were of relatively minor importance, and only two continued past the persecutions at the end of the Tang period, that is, Pure Land and Chan (Ch'an). Two others did contribute a great deal to Chinese thought, however, and also to Buddhist developments in Japan: Tian-tai (T'ien-t'ai) and Hua-yan.

The Tian-tai school, founded by Zhi-Yi (538–597) at the monastery on Mount Tian-tai, can be seen as a synthesis and harmonization of all Buddhist teachings and practices. According to this school, the great mass of scriptures taught by the Buddha can be classified into five periods in which the Buddha taught the different scriptures. In the earlier periods he taught the Theravada scriptures and then, when the people were more enlightened, the elementary Mahayana scriptures; finally in the last period he taught that all paths leading to salvation are united in the one path as taught in the Lotus Sutra, which is the full and perfect teaching.

The Hua-yan school devoted its attention mainly to the Garland Sutra, teaching that the absolute reality and the temporary phenomenon are completely interfused with each other and that all phenomena interpenetrate each other. Thus every thing or event in this passing world is a manifestation of the absolute, which means that everyone possesses the Buddha-nature and thus each is related to all other beings. Both Tian-tai and Hua-yan, harmonizing many basic strands of tradition, deepened the Mahayana sense of the Buddha-nature as a universal reality present in all beings.

The cultural climate of China lent itself to the creation of more simple and direct versions of Buddhism, which had greater appeal to the masses than the complex philosophical teachings of Tian-tai and Hua-yan. The inspiration for both these new forms, Pure Land and Chan, came from India, of course, but as they developed in China they took on special Chinese characteristics and greatly increased the popular appeal of Buddhism in China. They surfaced strongly in the Tang era partly as reformist reactions against the increasing worldliness of the powerful monastic establishment.

Amitabha Buddha, the compassionate heavenly Buddha who created the beautiful and peaceful Pure Land paradise and assisted living beings to be reborn there, had been known in China from earlier texts, and meditation on Amitabha was practiced in monasteries. In the Tang era, Dao-chuo (562–645) and his disciple Shan-dao (613–681) began to preach salvation in the Pure Land solely through the power of Amitabha, open to all who recite his name orally with a concentrated and devout mind. By saying Amitabha's name over and over with faith in his vows to save all beings, even sinful people could hope for rebirth in the Pure Land paradise. It is easy to understand that the Pure Land school appealed directly to the common people with its simple but effective teachings and practices, and its influence also permeated the other schools. Here was a form of Buddhism that could spread through the populace and be practiced in independent communities and societies outside the monasteries. Pure Land Buddhism soon became the most popular form of Buddhism in China and was taken also to Japan, where some centuries later it likewise became immensely popular. As it developed, Pure Land Buddhism became a characteristic form of East Asian culture.

The other distinctively Chinese school of Buddhism is Chan (meditation) Buddhism, likewise simple and direct and popularly supported. Chan is a unique creation of Chinese Buddhism, yet it draws on the early Indian practices and texts that emphasize meditation. Meditation was, of course, practiced in all the schools but as only one aspect of many disciplines of study and ritual. Chan's achievement was to make meditation the one practice to be almost exclusively pursued to reach enlightenment. In this sense it was a reform and simplification, somewhat parallel to the Pure Land movement.

According to Chan tradition, the founder of this school was Bodhidharma, an Indian meditation master who came to China around 470 C.E. When Emperor Wu of Liang asked him what merit he had earned by his donations and temple building, Bodhidharma answered, "No merit at all." Banished by the emperor, Bodhidharma went to north China and settled in a mountain temple, where he spent nine years sitting in meditation gazing at a wall, it is said, until his legs fell off. He also, the story says, cut off his eyelids so that his gaze would not falter. Among the successors of Bodhidharma, the most famous was Hui-neng (638–713), known as the sixth patriarch, who supposedly was illiterate but demonstrated a flair for the direct, sudden awakening taught in Chan. His legendary career provided a model for Chan life, and all later masters claim to be descended from him. Two schools of Chan eventually became particularly influential, Lin-ji (Lin-chi) and Cao-dong (Ts'ao-tung), differing on whether enlightenment should come suddenly or as a gradual process.

Chan is characteristically Chinese in the way it brings Buddhism into contact with Chinese ideas and practices, especially those of Daoism. The emphasis on meditation carries with it a certain anti-intellectual tendency, for, according to Chan, thoughts and concepts cloud the mind and therefore the mind must be emptied so that we can see directly into our Buddha-nature. In order to empty out the mind and see the truth directly, relationship with a master is crucial, for there is a special transmission of the truth outside the scriptures that goes from mind to mind, without words. Sayings and dialogues of the masters were collected and came to be used as themes for meditation. These "public documents" (*gong-an*; Jap. *koan*) were used to show that ordinary logic must be transcended in order to see directly into one's real nature.

Bodhidharma, the legendary founder of Chan Buddhism in China, crossing the Chang (Yangtze) River on a reed.

This school of Buddhism first became influential in the Tang era, advocating group meditation in the context of disciplined communal life in a monastery. Monasteries were established in remote areas, and frugality and shared work characterized the communal life. Whereas Chan did not become a "popular" movement in the sense of great numbers of people joining the monasteries, it did achieve widespread support among the people of China. The Chan form of Buddhism is distinctively a creation of China, and in the stories about the masters, the iconoclastic attitude toward rituals and doctrines, the practice of meditation to realize Buddhahood, and the poems and paintings by Chan artists, we find some basic shadings of Chinese identity.

The golden age of Buddhism was glorious—but brief. Although it enjoyed wide support from all levels of society, there remained opponents among the Confucianists and Daoists, some of whom thought of Buddhism as a "foreign" religion. And the relative independence and growing wealth of the monasteries were often seen by the rulers of the state as a distinct threat. Finally in 845 an ardent Daoist emperor, Wu-zong (r. 840–846), ordered the suppression of Buddhism, leading to the destruction of some 4,600 monasteries and 40,000 temples and shrines, and forcing some 260,500 monks and nuns to return to lay life. Wu-zong died the next year and the order was rescinded, but Buddhism never regained its former prestige and position. The only schools that survived the persecution were the popularly supported Pure Land and Chan schools, and they did continue to exercise considerable influence on Chinese culture.

A new development in the Song era (960–1280) was the emphasis on the compatibility of the two Buddhist schools. In the monasteries both meditation and recitation of Amitabha's name came to be employed together as two techniques toward achieving the same end of emptying the mind and reaching awakening. Another important development was the growth of lay Buddhist societies, including both men and women, both gentry and commoners, who devoted themselves to good works and recitation of the Buddha's name.

The Maturing of Religious Daoism

The search for long life and immortality continued to dominate the Daoist movement throughout the period of disunity following the Han era and also during the Tang and Song periods. Sometimes patronized by the rulers, Daoist masters perfected a great variety of ritual techniques for the controlling of the forces of the cosmos, reversing the forces of decay and establishing the forces of renewal. Great scriptures were revealed, written down, and memorized for use in the rituals. Many sects developed, founded by recognized masters based on a particular scripture, and each sect developed its own ritual experts or priests.

Neo-Daoism in Philosophy and Life

Before following the growth of religious Daoism, we might note that interest in the more philosophical aspects of Daoism was revived in the period after the fall of the Han dynasty. Daoist philosophers like Wang Bi (226–249 C.E.) and Guo Xiang (d. 312) wrote commentaries on the *Dao De Jing* and the *Zhuang-zi*, talking about the Dao as nonbeing or vacuity, the primal source of all the myriad things of the world. Interestingly, they thought of Confucius as the greatest sage because he, unlike the Daoist writers, did not talk about the mysterious operations of the Dao and thus exemplified vacuity.

Other Neo-Daoists were more romantic and practical in their approach, mainly poets and painters who tried to practice the Dao in a life of freedom and ease without conforming to conventions. Since they wanted all their talk to be pure, aesthetic, and in harmony with nature, this group is sometimes called the Pure Conversations movement. Well known are the Seven Sages of the Bamboo Grove, who refused office, sought enjoyment of life and freedom from cares, glorified drinking wine, and lived in complete harmony with nature.

These Neo-Daoist attitudes and styles had a profound effect especially in the shaping of Chan Buddhism, as is clear in the well-known Chan saying: "Here is a miracle of Dao! I draw water, I chop wood."[1] And this philosophical Daoism continued to influence thinkers, artists, and poets in China. Theories of aesthetics came to be based in the notion of the resonance of the Dao, which gives rise to artistic inspiration and expression. The artist meditates, gets his spirit in tune with the Dao, and spontaneously lets the artistic form create itself.

Religious Daoist Experts: Interior Gods and Alchemy

The rise of religious Daoism has many facets, but a central focus is on the *qi* (*ch'i*), the primordial breath or substance from which humans like all nature evolve. The qi comes ultimately from the Dao, and it is present especially in the cosmic gods, the astral bodies of the universe, and the other manifestations of nature. The problem is that under the conditions of our existence our vital breath becomes stale and exhausted, and thus our life becomes weak and short. Religious Daoism consists of the various techniques for renewing and restoring that vital qi, so that long life and even immortality may be achieved.

The human body is a microcosm of the great cosmos of nature, and so within each organ of the body there reside gods, and furthermore the great Dao forces of the cosmos can be called down and actualized within the human body. Daoist specialists developed ritual techniques by which they could visualize these interior gods of the body and the cosmic bodies and planets as they descend into the body, purifying and preserving the vital organs.

Carrying over the interest from ancient China in the five elements and how these can be used to promote long life, Daoist experts cultivated various techniques for creating substances to be ingested into the body to renew the vital breath. The science of alchemy developed, based on the idea that the ingestion of gold and other chemicals can renew the vital breath and prolong life.

But there were also the "inner elixir" techniques for renewing and prolonging life. Ritual techniques were developed by Daoist priests involving breathing techniques and gymnastics. By special breathing and bodily exercises the breath could be circulated through the various zones of the body to nourish the vital powers. At the same time, it was felt that much care should be given to diet, especially avoiding grain foods that, coming from the yin earth, nourish the three "worms" or principles of death in the body. Some advanced adepts practiced ritual techniques of sexual intercourse, the idea being that the forces of yin (female) and yang (male) nourish each other and thus restore the vital forces.

Development of Daoist Sects

Something new happened in the rise of religious Daoism—there developed communities or congregations of Daoists led by priestly authorities, something unheard of in the Chinese tradition up to this point. The Yellow Turbans who followed the sacred text called Classic of Great Peace, whose rebellion brought on the end of the Han dynasty, was one of the first such group religious movements.

The most important Daoist religious group movement was the Way of the Heavenly Masters (Tian-shi Dao), which established a state in northern Sichuan that was organized like a church, having a Celestial Master at its head and local parishes under the authority of "libationers" or priests. The first Heavenly Master was Zhang Dao-ling (died between 157 and 178 C.E.) who received revelations from Lao-zi, now thought of as a god, and instituted various communal rituals. Since almost all sects of religious Daoism trace themselves in some manner back to Zhang Dao-ling, he is often considered the "founder" of religious Daoism. Faith-healing was practiced in this sect, based on the idea that sickness was caused by sin, and therefore repentance, confession, and good deeds were part of the healing process. Documents inscribed with the sins and the penances were transmitted to the rulers of Heaven, earth, and the waters, to ensure healing and blessing. This communal Daoist movement had a strong emphasis on moral, virtuous living as part of the requirement for healthy, long life. Following this, one of the characteristics of religious Daoism in general has been the emphasis on the practice of moral virtues in addition to the rituals and ceremonies.

During the Tang era (618–907) Daoism received considerable support from some of the emperors, enabling it to flourish and develop. Emperor Gao-zong (r. 649–683) conferred on Lao-zi the title of emperor, thus confirming Lao-zi's divine status and claiming him as a royal ancestor. The political power of Daoism reached its zenith with the suppression of Buddhism and other non-Chinese religions in the 840s.

The most important Daoist order during the Tang era was the Mao-shan sect, based on Mao-shan Mountain where many temples were built, scriptures edited, and disciples trained to be priests. There, under the direction of a hierarchal priesthood headed by "masters of doctrine," they carried on ritual activities of purgation and cosmic renewal, calling down the gods of the stars and practicing ritual meditation. Their outstanding leader was Si-ma Cheng-zhen (647–735), who authored many works and was well known for his calligraphy. He emphasized ritual meditation focused on "emptiness," for, he wrote, "only the heart which has been emptied can be the dwelling place for the Dao."[2]

Among the many new sects of Daoism that developed in the Song era (960–1280), two were lasting and are still influential in the twentieth century. A scholar named Wang Zhe (1113–1170) became the founder of the Quan-zhen (Total Perfection) sect in northern China. Wang ex-perienced two mysterious encounters with Daoist immor-tals that led him to dig a grave and live in it for three years, after which he lived in a thatched hut for four years before burning it down and setting out to start the new Daoist order. He selected seven disciples who lived as eccentric ascetics, but they attracted lay followers from all classes, including women. Influenced by Chan Buddhism, this sect spiritualized some of the ritual practices. Wang taught celibacy and sitting in meditation to control the mind and the will and to nourish one's nature and life force. As the first Daoist sect to base itself in monasteries, the Total Perfection sect aimed for a rigorous life of simple monastic discipline, including celibacy and abstinence from wine and meat. Founder Wang stressed practices of inner al-chemy and self-perfection as well as Confucian and Bud-dhist doctrines, teaching the unity of the three religions.

One of Wang's disciples made a three-year trek to visit Chinggis Khan at his central Asian court in 1222, ensur-ing the continuation of imperial support for this Daoist sect even into the time of the Mongol rule. For a while the Total Perfection sect was favored over Buddhism by the Mongol rulers, but a conflict developed when the Daoists started to teach that the Buddha was one of the eighty-one transformations of Lao-zi. After a series of debates Khu-bilai Khan ordered the Daoist Canon burned and the Daoist priests returned to lay life, and the sect went into a long eclipse. But as late as the 1940s, the seat of the sect, the White Cloud Monastery of Beijing, retained influence over the monastic Daoist priests of China.

The other major Daoist sect that came to influential status during the Song era was the Zheng-Yi (Orthodox Unity) sect, which was a continuation of the Way of the Heavenly Masters of earlier times. Its patriarchs were be-lieved to be descendants of Zhang Dao-ling, and they based their headquarters at Dragon-Tiger Mountain (Lung-hu Shan) in Jiangxi (Kiangsi) Province. The thirty-sixth generation Heavenly Master, Zhang Zong-yan, was invited to the capital by the emperor in 1277 to perform a "Grand Offering of the Entire Heaven," and shortly after that the emperor appointed him head of all Daoists in southern China. Then in 1295 the emperor decreed that

Heavenly Master liturgical texts be used throughout the empire, and since then this sect has generally had the highest influence in ritual and liturgical matters. Under the first Ming emperor, toward the end of the fourteenth century, the Heavenly Masters were put in charge of all Daoist affairs.

In contrast to the celibate monks of the Total Perfection sect, the priests of the Orthodox Unity sect do not live in monasteries nor do they restrict themselves to a vegetable diet. They hand down their esoteric ritual arts in their fam-ilies. Since they marry and live with their families, they are sometimes called "fire dwellers," that is, living by the fam-ily hearth. This sect of the Heavenly Masters continues to the present day, although the Heavenly Master in 1949 had to leave the Dragon-Tiger Mountain and flee to Taiwan, where he set up the organization of religious Daoism.

Other Daoist sects arose in the Song era and afterward, and many of the sects contributed new works to the bur-geoning Daoist Canon. The compilation of the present Daoist Canon was commissioned and completed by 1447, under the Ming emperors. The emperors brought the growing sectarianism under control by decree of the court, limiting to three the monastic centers authorized to grant licences of ordination, without which the local Daoist masters were forbidden to practice. But popular, unautho-rized Daoist movements continued to rise and spread throughout the Ming (1368–1644), Qing (Ch'ing) (1644–1912), and even modern periods. This created a polariza-tion between the traditional classical orders and the pop-ular Daoist priests of local origin. The traditional orders were given the title "orthodox," whereas the popular groups were called "heterodox."

The Resurgence of the Way of Confucius: Neo-Confucianism

Confucianism, of course, remained a strong component of Chinese government and family life, the main founda-tion for morality, social custom, and status even after the fall of the Han dynasty. But as a vital religious force it was eclipsed by Buddhism and religious Daoism for many cen-turies, as the best philosophical and religious thinkers of China devoted themselves to Buddhism, and Daoism attracted government support because of its expertise in rituals of health and long life. To be sure, there were a few Confucian philosophers in this period, such as Han Yu (768–824), who reasserted the central Confucian theme of the goodness of human nature and sharply attacked both Daoists and Buddhists for belittling humanity and human relations. But in general there was not much fresh thinking in Confucianism from the fourth to the tenth centuries.

However, suddenly in the eleventh century, during the Northern Song dynasty, a series of important thinkers appeared who attempted to revive Confucianism as a philosophical vision of life. They were influenced by Buddhism and Daoism, but they turned back to Confucian sources to articulate a new philosophy of life, focused on positive human nature, family life, and social reform. Neo-Confucianism arose vigorously in the Song era, became dominant in the Ming era, and controlled Chinese thought throughout the Qing era down to the twentieth-century revolutions.

The Northern Song Masters and Zhu Xi

The beginnings of a Confucian revival can be seen in the Tang era, centered in the class of people known as "literati" (ru). The Tang government kept a huge bureaucracy to administer its vast empire, and the examination system required that higher status in the government was won by those who mastered the study of the Confucian classics. In the following Song era these literati established themselves as dominant in the political and intellectual spheres. Many of the literati, of course, got caught up in the expediency of government politics, but there was a minority who devoted themselves to study and teaching in an attempt to recover the ancient Confucian ideal of the "noble man," the one who perfects his moral qualities.

Actually the Neo-Confucians went further than the noble man ideal, cultivating themselves to become "sages" like the ancient sages who had revealed the truth of the Way in the classics. The true sage, they believed, reaches the ultimate of true humanity by complete identification with the nature of all things. This is possible, they believed, because the heavenly principle is universal, possessed both by the self and by all things. One who meditates on that universal principle becomes more wise,

Confucius, the Buddha, and Lao-zi. Despite the occasional conflict between leaders of these three religions, there is a long-standing Chinese vision of their unity.

mature, and in control, so that he can help to bring order and harmony to family, society, and government.

In the eleventh century there was a group of outstanding Confucian thinkers who worked out a Neo-Confucian cosmology and metaphysics based on redefining concepts from the Confucian classics. For example, Zhou Dun-yi (1017–1073), sometimes considered the real founder of Neo-Confucian philosophy, taught that the Great Ultimate (tai ji) generates yin and yang, which, through their alternation, give rise to the five elements, which in turn produce the myriad of things, of which humans are the most intelligent. But the many are actually the one reality, and the one is differentiated in the many. Zhang Zai (1020–1077) identified material force with the Great Ultimate, functioning through yang and yin; he also redefined the gods (*shen*) and evil spirits (*gui*) as positive and negative spiritual forces involved in the expansion and contraction of material force. Zhang is famous for his short essay *The Western Inscription*, which he inscribed on a panel in the western window of his study, reflecting on the ethical implications of the doctrine that all creation is united by the universal underlying principle. He wrote in part:

> Heaven is my father and earth is my mother, and even such a small creature as I finds an intimate place in their midst. Therefore that which extends throughout the universe I regard as my body and that which directs the universe I consider as my nature. All people are my brothers and sisters, and all things are my companions.[3]

A key idea of these early Neo-Confucianists is that of "principle" (*li*). The Cheng brothers (Cheng Hao, 1032–1085, and Cheng Yi, 1033–1107) based their teaching entirely on principle, which they conceived of as self-sufficient, extending everywhere, and governing everything. It is that by which all things exist, and it is possessed by everyone and all things, binding all together into a unity. The principle is one, but its manifestations are many. Since the one principle is identical with all things and with one's mind and nature, moral and spiritual development comes through the investigation of things and through the cultivating of one's nature and mind.

These basic Neo-Confucian ideas of the Northern Song masters were synthesized and organized by Zhu Xi (Chu Hsi, 1130–1200). He taught that the whole universe is but one principle, the Great Ultimate, which is prior to form and which contains all principles and is the source of all principles. At the same time each phenomenon has its own defining principle. Zhu Xi explained this by using the metaphor of the single moon that is reflected in many lakes and rivers; everything has the Great Ultimate, yet the Great Ultimate remains one. But, according to Zhu Xi, principle never exists in isolation but always is attached to material force (*qi*), that which exists within form.

Now humans have principle as their original nature, good and humane. But principle needs to be attached to material force to be actualized, and this aspect of human nature is often characterized by selfish desires, clouding principle and leading to evil results. Therefore it is important, Zhu Xi taught, for humans to cultivate themselves to rectify the mind and penetrate to the underlying principle. The way to self-cultivation is through intellectual learning, meditation, and the investigation of things, both in the external world and within oneself.

Other Neo-Confucian thinkers put more emphasis on the mind as morally self-sufficient, innately endowed with knowledge of the good and ability to do the good. This Mind School of Neo-Confucianism, represented especially by Wang Yang-ming (1472–1529), has as its central thesis the view that principle and mind are one. Since the mind, which innately contains all principles, is the master of the body, to cultivate oneself one need only follow the impulses of the mind's innate knowledge. Thus, Wang argued, the way to self-cultivation is not through the investigation of external things, as Zhu Xi taught, but through the cultivation and extension of the innate knowledge of the mind, through inner moral and spiritual cultivation.

The idealistic concern for awakening the moral consciousness of the mind, as put forth by Wang Yang-ming, continued to have influence in later generations of Neo-Confucianists, but Zhu Xi's more rationalistic concern for the ordering principle tended to remain dominant. The Manchu rulers, who conquered China in 1644 and inaugurated the Qing dynasty, affirmed Zhu Xi's Neo-Confucianism as the orthodox ideology of their reign, and so it remained until the onslaught of Western imperialism and the revolutionary forces of the twentieth century both brought down imperial rule in China and put the whole Confucianist tradition in jeopardy.

Persistence and Transformation of Popular Religion

The Chinese story revolves around the three religions as they developed to their full space by about the end of the Song era—Buddhism, religious Daoism, and Confucianism (both in the state cult and in Neo-Confucianism)—continuing more or less in that form down to the modern era. But we should not neglect a vast area that overlaps with these three religions but includes much more—Popular Religion. The popular religious tradition goes back as far as the records go, and it includes a great variety of religious activities practiced by the whole population except those who specifically opted out, that is, the strict Confucian scholars, Buddhist monks, orthodox Daoist priests, and state officials in their public roles.

In ancient times most Chinese shared in religious activities like ancestor worship, exorcism, use of spirit mediums, divination, sacrifices to spirits, and belief in ghosts and demons. These activities were based in family, clan, and village, and they continued effectively even as the great religions developed. By the end of the Song era, the various strands of popular religion came together and incorporated Buddhist and Daoist ideas about karma and rebirth, Buddhas and bodhisattvas, and gods and spirits, forming the more-or-less coherent popular religious system that has continued to the present day, at least in Taiwan and Hong Kong.

Although popular religion does also promise salvation from hell and favorable rebirth, generally it has focused on practical, immediate human concerns like protection of property, health and long life, expulsion of evil spirits, obtaining favor from the gods, peace and harmony in the home, good livelihood, repose of ancestors, and the like. For these benefits, the most important sacred powers are the ancestral spirits and the popular gods. These powers bring benefits and protection in life and in death.

Most of the gods of popular religion were originally human beings who were gradually deified over time as more and more people recognized their power and efficacy. The gods have a reciprocal relationship with the humans: they understand the needs of the worshipers, and they need the offerings and recognition of the worshipers if they are to keep their position as gods. New gods are recognized as their power and fame is effective; but gods can also be demoted and forgotten if their benefits no longer are felt. Under Daoist influence, the gods of popular religion were organized into a bureaucratic system with each one having a particular function, like protecting fishermen, bringing children, causing rain, protecting the village, and so on. The Jade Emperor presides over the gods, parallel to the emperor in the human realm, and the Jade Emperor appoints the various gods to their offices, promoting them for effective help but also demoting them when their effectiveness fails.

The popular gods maintain order over and against the vast array of demons and ghosts that can bring sickness and death. These demons (*gui*) usually are spirits of the restless dead who died unjustly or who were not cared for by their descendants, and they need to be expelled by a spirit-medium or a Daoist priest in the name of a powerful god. Harm can also come from ancestors who have been aggrieved, and harmony can be restored by a medium communicating with the ancestor to learn what the family should do to make amends.

Popular religion has always been carried on in the midst of the family, village, and city neighborhood, and so there are usually no full-time specialists. The temples are run by local people who have other jobs. Some people have special talents as spirit-mediums, spirit-writers, healers, and the like, and Daoist priests and Buddhist monks can also be employed to perform special rituals. Popular religion is associated with a rich cycle of annual festivals, funeral rituals, and rituals of geomancy (*feng-shui*), the process of locating the proper place for a house or a grave.

These activities of popular religion have given a special character to most Chinese families and communities, even as the people also pursued Confucianist, Daoist, and Buddhist practices. In modern times popular religion has been questioned in some areas and is ranked as superstition in the People's Republic, but it still is a significant factor in Taiwan, Hong Kong, and some overseas Chinese communities.

WESTERN INCURSION AND REVOLUTIONARY CLIMATE

One major foreign influence that transformed traditional China was, of course, Buddhism; but Buddhism was indigenized and contributed much to the shape of Chinese religion. More disruptive were the incursions of religions and ideas from the West, followed in the nineteenth century by foreign imperialism in China. The upheaval in traditional Chinese society culminated in the Revolution of 1911, ending two millennia of imperial rule and inaugurating the Republic of China. More disruption followed the Communist takeover of the mainland, with the result that Chinese religion today is somewhat minimal in the

Chinese pilgrims pray at a Buddhist shrine on Heng Mountain in Hunan Province.

People's Republic, although it is still alive in other Chinese communities.

Foreign Religions and Western Domination

We should note that other foreign religions besides Buddhism did play a part in China's religious history. During the Tang period, for example, Zoroastrianism and Manicheism (teaching a cosmic dualism) came into China as a result of contact with Persia, and they dealt some influence on Daoism and Buddhism.

During the Tang and Song periods, increased Muslim dominance of the western edges of China led to the presence of a significant Muslim community in northwestern China. When the Mongols established the Yuan dynasty in China (1280–1368), Muslim merchants, soldiers, and religious leaders settled throughout China, and numerous Chinese converted to Islam during this period. But Muslims maintained the purity of their faith, refusing to blend it with other Chinese religions, and adherents of Islam tended to be from minority non-Han tribal groups, lumped

together as the Hui peoples. Generally they retained their own language and culture, thus maintaining a separate religious and ethnic identity. Today Muslims total some twenty-five million people in China. In general they have been given a good bit of autonomy under the Communist government. Whereas they, like other religious groups, suffered during the Cultural Revolution, they have revived quickly and today practice their religion actively. Yet, because they have stood aloof from the syncretistic tendencies of the traditional Chinese religions, the overall impact of Islam on Chinese religion has been limited.

There is also an interesting though brief story of Jewish presence in traditional China. During the Song dynasty a Jewish community was established in Kai-feng, and an impressive synagogue was built there in the style of a Chinese temple. But cut off from contact with other Jews, the small Jewish communities in China eventually lost their identity and were totally assimilated.

Traces of Christian presence in China go back as far as the Tang period, when Nestorian Christians came to China. And in the thirteenth century the pope at Rome dispatched Franciscan monks overland to China, during the time when the Mongols ruled all of central Asia and

Marco Polo had made Europe aware of China. But with the fall of the Mongol dynasty the Ming rulers closed the door to foreigners, and the fledgling Christian communities died out.

The real beginning of Western Christian impact on Chinese culture came with the Jesuit mission in the sixteenth and seventeenth centuries. Around 1500 Portuguese traders came to southern China, and Christians started entering China especially from the Spanish Philippines. The newly founded Jesuit order devoted itself to a missionary-scholar approach, both in Japan and in China. The first Jesuit missionary in China was Matteo Ricci (1552–1610), who went to China in 1582 and set out to learn the ancient Chinese writings, accommodating Christianity to the best of classic Chinese culture. The Jesuits took on the role of Chinese literati, wrote works in Chinese, and proved helpful to the Chinese rulers by providing maps and Western learning in science and astronomy.

The Jesuits found acceptance in the scholarly, governmental circles partly because they tried to integrate Christianity into what they considered the best of Chinese culture. They made Christianity acceptable to many Chinese by, for example, using the Chinese words Shang Di and Tian for God in the Christian sense, adopting the ceremonies of respect for Confucius, teaching that Confucian ethics were consonant with Christian faith, and interpreting the ancestral rituals as acceptable within the Christian understanding. But before long rival religious orders attacked the Jesuit methods of accommodation, accusing them of not imposing fasting and not teaching that Confucius was in hell. After much discussion of this so-called rites controversy, the pope at Rome finally decided against the Jesuit position, leading to the breakdown of the Jesuit relationship with the Chinese emperor and the suppression and expulsion of Christian priests.

Around the beginning of the nineteenth century came English and Dutch traders to China, and with them the first Protestant Christian missionaries arrived. These missionaries tended to work with the working classes, not the literati. The Western presence was fortified by military power, which forced the Chinese to open up ports and allow foreigners to travel in the interior and teach Christianity. By the end of the nineteenth century, there were some 2,000 Christian missionaries in China. Some mis-sion groups, like the China Inland Mission in particular, began to adapt more to Chinese customs and carried on much educational and medical work, which had a considerable impact on Chinese society. But the close association with Western imperialism and the general failure to recognize the drastic changes in modern China kept Christianity from gaining wide favor, and the revolutionary movements of the twentieth century turned against the Christian movement.

Revolutionary Movements and Communist Society

Responding to the West and to Christianity, China was gripped by new religious movements, rebellions, and revolt against its own traditional imperial system. An early response to Christian influence was the Tai-ping Rebellion in the middle of the nineteenth century. A farmer boy named Hong Xiu-Quan, influenced by Christian pamphlets, had visions of ascending to heaven where he learned that Confucius had confused the people and that he himself was the Father's son next younger to Jesus. Hong organized a religious movement based on some Christian ideas, baptizing, throwing out the ancestral tablets, and destroying shrines and temples. The movement drew on the centuries-old peasant frustration with the old hierarchical system; they advocated an egalitarian social structure, equality of the sexes, and the redistribution of land. In 1851 Hong proclaimed himself the Heavenly King of the Heavenly Kingdom of Great Peace (Tai-ping Tian-guo). The movement grew rapidly and started to attack armies in Beijing and elsewhere, but in 1864 the whole group, now 100,000 strong, was defeated and massacred. But the rebellion had devastated China and almost toppled the Qing dynasty.

The winds of change blew strongly as the twentieth century began. The abortive Boxer Rebellion in 1899–1900, a vast antiforeign movement that tried to drive out Western influences and attacked Christian missions in the name of Chinese gods, was symptomatic of the growing conflict between traditional values and the impact of the West. The imperial government, humiliated by defeat at the hands of the Japanese in 1894–1895, was not able to stem the growing tide of dissatisfaction. Reforms were attempted, such as abolishing, in 1905, the long-standing Confucian examinations for government service. But it was too little too late, and the Qing government fell in the 1911 revolution, the final end of many centuries of imperial rule.

Whereas the majority of Chinese continued their traditional religious practices, many intellectuals turned to Western ideas and philosophies, including Marxism. The leader of the revolution and of the republican government that followed, Sun Zhong-shan (Sun Yat-sen) (1866–1925), had received a Western, Christian education, as did his successor as leader of the Nationalist party, Jiang Jie-shi (Chiang K'ai-shek). Sun and Jiang followed a kind of modern, liberal Protestantism; Jiang even promoted the revival of ancient Confucian virtues during his leadership of the Nationalist government. Other leading intellectuals were influenced by the antireligious attitudes of Western liberal thinkers like John Dewey and Bertrand Russell and took a strong stand against all traditional religion. The famous May 4, 1919, student protest, for example, demanded a New China based on humanistic liberal principles, free of all old literature, education, and religion.

But Western liberalism could not control the spirit of anarchy that had developed, and in 1920 a group of Marxists secretly formed the Communist party. The Communists cooperated for a number of years with the Nationalist party, but by 1928 an irrevocable split had occurred. Jiang Jie-shi led the Nationalist government, relying on rural landlords and the urban business class, whereas the Communist party built support among the peasantry. The Nationalists began a notorious "bandit extermination" campaign against the Communists, but under the leadership of Mao Ze-dong (1893–1976) the Communists escaped to the north in the famous Long March of 1934, creating a mythology that supported Mao's domination of the Chinese Communist party. In the chaos following World War II, Mao and his followers successfully carried through a revolution and established the People's Republic of China in October 1949, sweeping Jiang's forces out of the mainland and into an exiled Nationalist government on the island of Taiwan.

The religions of China have been subjected to disruption under Maoist rule unlike any previous period in Chi-

A scene from the Cultural Revolution—Red Guards chatting at the entrance to Sun Zhong-shan's mausoleum near Nanjing.

nese history. The constitution of the People's Republic does establish the freedom both to support and to oppose religion. In practice, however, sharing the Marxist attitude that religion is an instrument that oppressive overlords use to pacify and exploit the energies of the people, the Chinese government mounted a series of campaigns to turn people's loyalty away from the traditional religions to support the new Chinese order. People were encouraged to "struggle against Confucius," for that system of thought supported the old hierarchical state. Popular Daoist practices were denounced as superstitions, not to be tolerated in the modern society. For a time state-controlled Buddhist and Christian associations were tolerated. But during the so-called Cultural Revolution, which began in 1966, all religious institutions were subjected to intense persecution by fanatical Red Guards in the struggle to rid China of the "four olds": old habits, old ideas, old customs, old culture. The Red Guards invaded homes to expose people practicing religion and to destroy religious art, scriptures, and literature. Temples and churches were closed, images destroyed, leaders returned to lay life, and books burned. All over China there was an attempt to get rid of everything that looked like a remnant of the "bad old days" before the 1949 revolution. It seemed that the thousands of years of religious tradition in China had come to an abrupt end.

Coinciding with the attack on the traditional religions, there grew up a new "religion" in China: the cult of Maoism. The philosophy of Marxism, as has often been pointed out, has some of the characteristics of a religious philosophy, with its call for repentance, conversion, and unconditional commitment, and also with its view of history moving toward the consummation of a classless society. In China, communism took over some of the traditional religious forms: Mao has been revered almost like a state deity, and national holidays are celebrated complete with popular music, art, drama, parades, and banners to create the atmosphere of a sacred state. During the Cultural Revolution, Maoism went further in taking on many of the characteristics of a religious cult. Some people looked to Mao almost as a god, and young people carried the "bible" of his sayings around, studying, memorizing, and reciting his teachings. It was in the intolerant furor of this cult of Mao that the excesses against everything having to do with the "old" religions and institutions were carried out.

The Cultural Revolution came to an end with the death of Chairman Mao in 1976 and with the downfall of his wife and three other leaders (the Gang of Four) who tried to continue these policies. Though traditional religious ideas had been drastically shaken and reduced in influence, they were not dead. Under more moderate leadership, China entered into a new phase in which more relaxed and practical programs have been emphasized in order to attain the "Four Modernizations": science, agriculture, industry, and defense. Along with all this has gone a liberalization of government policies toward religion. Hundreds of churches, temples, and

mosques have reopened, and the government is even paying back rent for the religious buildings that were confiscated during the Cultural Revolution. A few seminaries, monasteries, and religious training centers have been opened, and priests and ministers are again available, though in comparatively low numbers, to serve Buddhist and Christian needs. Sacred scriptures are being published, and religious scholars again publish writings about religious subjects.

Reports from China today indicate a general flourishing of Christianity, free from control of foreign churches and dedicated to the socialist ideals of the new China. In addition to overflowing churches in some of the cities, there are countless "house church" groups throughout China guided by lay leaders. The revival of Buddhism has not been as dramatic but nonetheless is apparent as some temples are again busy, priests chant sutras and perform rituals, and some monasteries and training centers again have accepted young people for training. Islam, as a recognized ethnic group in China, did not suffer as drastically during the Cultural Revolution and has managed to continue its religious practices somewhat outside the mainstream of Chinese social and political life.

Religious Daoism has not shared very much in the general revival of religion, partly because many of its practices are still looked upon as superstitions harmful to the new society. Likewise, Confucianism, that is, the whole religious, ethical, and literary tradition based on the Confucian Canon, has been deeply damaged by the persistent Maoist attack on this backbone of Chinese "feudal" civilization. Whereas scholars again can study and write about the classics, there seems little likelihood that the Confucian philosophy will again become the guiding vision of thinkers in modern China. There is some evidence on the popular level of a renewed interest in religious practices like ancestor worship and funeral rituals. And certainly attitudes of respect for the family and for elders, loyalty to the community and the nation, and the acceptance of reciprocity as the basis of human relations continue in present-day China, evidence that deeply based religious attitudes persist even in drastically changed conditions.

It must still be said that religious activities take place only on a small scale in the People's Republic of China today, and that the vast majority of the people simply no longer seem interested in religion. Their concern is for good jobs, education for their children, modern appliances, and working to better Chinese society. Whether the basic human religious questions and concerns will again play a part in their lives appears to be an open question.

The religious situation in Taiwan, Hong Kong, and among the overseas Chinese is quite different, of course. The religious practices differ greatly from place to place, and modernization affects religious ideas and practices as elsewhere in the world. But in general traditional religion still flourishes, based in a strong family system and community support of temples, monasteries, festivals, and various popular religious rituals.

DISCUSSION QUESTIONS

1. Describe the major Buddhist schools or lineages in China during the Tang period. Why were Pure Land and Chan able to survive the persecutions of 845?

2. What were the most important Daoist sects or orders during the Tang and Song periods? Which have survived to modern times?

3. Explain the development of Neo-Confucianism.

4. Why must we include a category such as "Popular Religion" in addition to Confucianism, Daoism, and Buddhism in China?

5. Sketch the history of Islam and Judaism in China.

6. How did Christianity rise to become influential in the sixteenth and seventeenth centuries? What caused its subsequent decline?

7. What was the Tai-ping Rebellion?

8. What were the roles of Sun Zhong-shan, Jiang Jie-shi, and Mao Ze-dong in twentieth-century events?

9. Discuss the status of traditional religion during the four decades of the People's Republic of China.

CHAPTER 12

Chinese Worlds of Meaning

THE SACRED ULTIMATE IN THE CHINESE VISION

What's it *all* about? Where do we look for the absolute center, the real? Chinese people know about these questions, having learned them from the sages of ancient times. "Is Ti [Lord] going to order the rain within the fourth month?," asks an oracle inscription in one of the earliest written texts in China. Ancient skeptics raised questions: "Now the people in their peril look to T'ien [Heaven], but find no clear guidance." Others affirmed that there is a sacred center of all: "T'ien loves the whole world universally. Everything is provided for the good of mankind."[1] These ancient ideas were refined in the Confucian teachings and in philosophical Daoism. Religious Daoism and popular religion have continued the emphasis on a multiplicity of sacred beings all working together in cosmic harmony.

The Supreme Sacred Power: Heaven

The early Chinese worldview was naturalistic. The whole universe was felt to follow the basic laws of cyclical processes, growth and decline, and the bipolar operation of the forces of yin and yang. In a sense, the world itself was ultimate reality, operating in harmony and following the natural laws without any supreme creator or law-giver. This "universism" has remained central to Chinese experience and has colored all thinking about sacred beings and powers. But, as we saw earlier, there was belief in a supreme being from early times on, called Shang Di (Ruler Above) or Tian (Heaven), and these terms have figured centrally in the Chinese conception of ultimate reality ever since.

Shang Di, as worshipped by the rulers of the Shang dynasty, was not the ultimate or unlimited god over all, of course, but did function as the power of conspicuous importance that controlled nature and brought both good and evil on the Shang rulers. Although Shang Di may have been the special god of the Shang rulers, perhaps even thought of as the high ancestor of the ruling house, this was not just a tribal god. Shang Di had control over all the natural forces and over human welfare, bringing the benefits of rain, military victory, and building cities, but also the punishment of drought, defeat, and ruin of cities. The texts show that Shang Di was felt to have divine personality and intelligence, could issue orders to the wind and rain and other natural forces, and could bring things and events into being.

Beneath Shang Di there was a full pantheon of gods of nature—Sun, Moon, Wind, Rain, Earth, Mountain, River, and gods of the Four Directions—functioning as divine subordinates of the supreme god. In addition, all the ancestral gods of the house of the Shang rulers were members of Shang Di's pantheon. The deceased kings of the Shang dynasty were worshiped especially as mediators to approach and obtain Shang Di's approval. It seems that deceased queens were also worshiped as accompanying Shang Di, and perhaps even the ancestral dukes, ministers, and diviners found their place among the ancestral gods. The sacred powers of nature and of human ancestry were linked in harmony around the center provided by the supreme god.

Heaven as Universal Moral Authority: Tian

Tian (Heaven), as worshipped by the rulers of the Zhou dynasty, was assimilated to Shang Di and was conceived as the all-powerful, all-knowing, purposeful god who sent down blessings or disasters in accordance with divine pleasure or displeasure with the people. When kings prospered, it was believed that they had received the mandate of Heaven; in the case of corrupt or unworthy rulers, Heaven would withdraw the mandate and the ruler would fall.

Texts from the Classic of Poetry and the Classic of History describe Tian:

> Be reverent! Be reverent! *T'ien* has revealed its will. Its mandate is not easy to preserve. Do not say that *T'ien* is far distant above. It ascends and descends, concerning itself with our affairs, and daily examines all our doings.
>
> *T'ien* inspects the people below, keeping account of their righteousness, and regulating according to their span of life. It is not *T'ien* who destroys men. They, by their evil doing, cut short their own lives.[2]

Here there is a strong emphasis on the universal moral authority of Heaven along with the notion of Heaven as an impersonal governing authority. When we live in accord with Heaven's will, we prosper, but when we go against that will, our lives are short and bitter.

Chinese ideas and feelings about Heaven are colored by the sayings of Confucius, who emphasized this universal moral power. Confucius had a strong belief in the mandate of Heaven, and he was convinced that he had a sacred mission that had been conferred on him by this purposeful supreme power. To Confucius, Heaven was the guardian of humanistic culture. Once, mistreated by the people of Kuang, he said,

> Since the death of King Wen [founder of the Zhou dynasty], is not the course of culture in my keeping? If it had been the will of Heaven to destroy this culture, it would not have been given to a mortal [like me]. But if it is the will of Heaven that this culture should not perish, what can the people of K'uang do to me? (ANALECTS, 9.5)[3]

Some leading thinkers continued to emphasize the personal character of Heaven as a supreme being to be loved and worshiped. Mo-zi (late fifth century B.C.E.) described Heaven as the father who loves all people equally, who accepts sacrifices from all and is concerned about the moral conduct of the people. Others emphasized more the impersonal qualities of Tian. Xun-zi (ca. 300–238 B.C.E.), for example, denied that Heaven acts in response to human actions or pleas. Rather, Tian is simply the operation of the physical universe according to its inherent laws.

Since these ancient thinkers, many have continued to ask the question whether Heaven is personal and interactive with humans or whether Heaven operates impersonally and naturally. For example, the Neo-Confucianist Liu Yu-xi (772–842 C.E.) summed up both positions and proposed his own theory about the mutual interaction of Heaven and humans:

> There are two theories about Heaven today. Those who are bound by what is obvious say that Heaven and man really influence each other. Calamities will surely descend on us because of our sins, and blessings will surely come when induced by good deeds. If we are in distress and cry out, we will be heard, and if we keep our suffering to ourselves and pray, we will be answered. There seems to be definitely someone who rules them. Hence the theory of silent recompense wins.
>
> On the other hand, those who are bigoted about what is hidden say that Heaven and man are really different. Lightning hits animals and trees without anyone committing any sin, and the spring nourishes flowering bushes without selecting any good deeds to reward. . . . It seems there is no one who rules us. Hence naturalism wins.
>
> Therefore I have written "A Treatise on Heaven" to bring the argument to its final conclusion. For everything that is included in the realm of physical forms and concrete objects, there are things it can do and things it cannot do. Heaven is the largest of things with physical form and man is the best among living things. What Heaven can do, man cannot, and what man can do, there is some that Heaven cannot do. Therefore I say that Heaven and man mutually overcome each other. The explanation is this: The way of Heaven lies in producing and reproducing, and its function is expressed in strength and weakness, whereas the way of man lies in laws and regulations and his function is expressed in right and wrong.[4]

As suggested by this example, the Neo-Confucianists did a lot of speculating on the nature of Heaven, the powerful reality that somehow is involved in controlling human existence.

The importance of Heaven can be seen in the emperor's practice, continued down to the twentieth century, of making special sacrifices to Heaven and to the ancestors and other gods. One part of the prayer offered to Heaven by the emperor on the festival of the winter solstice reads:

> Thou madest heaven; Thou madest earth; Thou madest man. All things with their re-producing power, got their

Temple of Heaven in Beijing.

The Chinese Vision of the Way of Nature: Dao

The ancient conception of the Dao, or the way of nature, has also played an important part in Chinese views of ultimate reality. Dao has many meanings, but as ultimate reality Chinese think of Dao as the source and origin of everything and also as that power that maintains harmony and balance in the world. This eternal Way of the universe can be thought of at many different levels, as evidenced by the fact that all the religious traditions of China have focused in one way or another on this reality. But it is the texts of philosophical Daoism that have most deeply explored this dimension of ultimate reality.

Dao as the Undifferentiated Source of All

Chinese thinkers and searchers from early times have talked of a primordial source of all reality, itself undivided and prior to all the multiplicity of things that make up our existence. The famous passage in Chapter 25 of the Dao De Jing, in its mysterious, cryptic language, sets forth this understanding:

> There is Something undifferentiated and yet complete in Itself,
> It existed before the birth of heaven and earth.
> Soundless and formless,
> Independent and unchanging,
> Pervasive and invincible.
> It can be regarded as the Mother of the Universe.
> I do not know Its name.
> I name It "Tao," only when I was forced to give It a name.
> I regard It simply "Great,"
> For in greatness, It produces.
> In producing, It expands;
> In expanding, It regenerates. . . .
> The way of man follows after the law of Earth.
> The law of Earth follows after the law of Heaven.
> The law of Heaven follows after the law of Tao.
> The law of Tao follows after Its own naturalness. [6]

being. O Te [Heaven], when Thou hadst separated the *Yin* and the *Yang*, Thy creating work proceeded. Thou didst produce, O Spirit, the sun and the moon and the five planets. . . . I, Thy servant, venture reverently to thank Thee, and, while I worship, present the notice to Thee, O Te, calling Thee Sovereign. Thou hast vouchsafed, O Te, to hear us, for Thou regardest us as a Father. [5]

Heaven, whether personal god or naturalistic power, has an important role in holding everything together for human benefit. And according to the traditional Chinese conception, the emperor as the representative of humans shares in the responsibility of nourishing the process of life with sacred power.

So Dao is one, prior to all differences. Nothing produced Dao, nor is it limited or affected by anything. Whereas everything else is dependent on Dao, Dao only follows its own nature. It is that eternal, primordial reality that contains within itself the inexhaustible source and creativity of the whole universe. It is the "mother" of all and operates within everything, pervasive and invincible, producing all and regenerating all.

This rich description of Dao in the Dao De Jing uses many terms and qualities that might be ascribed to God in the monotheistic Abraham religions, although it is said that Dao contains all within itself and is immanent in all—far different from the monotheistic concept that the creator is transcendent beyond the creation. But Daoists hold that such terms and qualities are only pointers to a deep, mysterious reality that cannot be grasped by word or concept. It is important that Lao-zi's 5,000-character description of Dao in the Dao De Jing begins with the assertion that such a description is impossible:

> The Tao that can be told of is not the eternal Tao;
> The name that can be named is not the eternal name.
> The Nameless is the origin of Heaven and Earth;
> The Named is the mother of all things.[7]

Once Dao is named and described, it is limited and thus no longer primordial Dao. Zhuang-zi once said:

> The fish trap exists because of the fish; once you've gotten the fish, you can forget the trap. The rabbit snare exists because of the rabbit; once you've gotten the rabbit, you can forget the snare. Words exist because of meaning; once you've gotten the meaning, you can forget the words. Where can I find a man who has forgotten words so I can have a word with him?[8]

Dao is immanent in heaven and earth and all things as the undifferentiated stuff out of which all namable things are articulated—but Dao in itself can only be known intuitively by getting one's mind and whole being in harmony with the movement of Dao.

Dao operates as the inner law of all things, even the most common and insignificant, as we see in this dialogue in the Zhuang-zi:

> Tung-kuo Tzu asked Chuang Tzu, "What is called Tao—where is it?"
> "It is everywhere," replied Chuang Tzu.
> Tung-kuo Tzu said, "It will not do unless you are more specific."
> "It is in the ant," said Chuang Tzu.
> "Why go so low down?"
> "It is in the weeds."
> "Why even lower?"

> "It is in a potsherd."
> "Why still lower?"
> "It is in the excrement and urine," said Chuang Tzu.
> Tung-kuo gave no response.[9]

So Dao, prior to everything, operates in even the most insignificant realities. How does it operate? Not through power and coercion, not through commands or absolute structures, but simply as the innermost universal way of nature. "Dao invariably does nothing, And yet there is nothing that is not done" (ch. 37).[10] The Dao is really the operation of the way of the universe in its totality.

> The Great Tao flows everywhere.
> It may go left or right.
> All things depend on it for life, and it does not turn away from them.
> It accomplishes its task, but does not claim credit for it.
> It clothes and feeds all things, but does not claim to be master over them.   (CH. 34)[11]

Zhuang-zi describes the Dao as the final harmony and unity of all realities, all forms, even all gods:

> Tao has reality and evidence but no action or physical form. It may be transmitted but cannot be received. It may be obtained but cannot be seen. It is based in itself, rooted in itself. Before heaven and earth, Tao existed by itself from all time. It gave spirits and rulers their spiritual powers. It created heaven and earth. It is above the zenith but it is not high. It is beneath the nadir but it is not low. It is prior to heaven and earth, but it is not old. . . . The Great Dipper obtained it and has therefore never erred from its course. The sun and moon obtained it and so they have never ceased to revolve. The deity K'an-pi obtained it and was therefore able to enter the high K'un-lun mountains.[12]

Not only those who call themselves Daoists but most Chinese have been deeply impressed by this vision of Dao as the source of existence. Even as many adhere to other views of ultimate reality, these views somehow cohere with the worldview represented by Dao.

The Daoist Gods of the Prior Heavens

To the thinkers and experts of religious Daoism, the abode of the transcendent, eternal Dao is most associated with the stellar constellations, the Prior Heavens, and in these Prior Heavens there are great gods who are exempt from the changes that take place in the visible world (the Posterior Heavens). The great gods are one with the eternal Dao and thus are the source of life, primordial breath, and blessing for our visible world.

At the summit of the gods are the Three Ones, headed by Tai Yi, the original one divine reality. These are the "three primordial breaths," whose origin is described in an early religious Daoist text:

> The *Tao* gives forth a subtle breath
> The colors of which are three:
> *Hsuan* [dark], *Yuan* [primordial], *Shih* [origin].
> The *Hsuan* is blue-green, and formed the heavens.
> The *Yuan* is yellow and made the earth.
> The *Shih* is white, and is the *Tao* [of man].
> From the center, the three breaths rule heaven and earth.[13]

In present-day Daoist rituals, these Three Pure Ones or Three Heavenly Worthies are Yuan Shi, the Primordial Lord of Heaven, Ling Bao, the Lord of Earth, and Lord Lao, the Lord of Humans. The Three Heavenly Worthies head a pantheon of gods that includes the Five Primordial Spirits, the Five Great Mountains of China, and many more deputies and helpers.

In the Daoist conception of reality, these great gods are not only resident in the Prior Heavens. Since our world and our human body make up a microcosm (small cosmos) corresponding to the macrocosm (great cosmos), these gods are also present within our world and within our body. For example, the Lord of Heaven is also Lord of the head and the primordial breath; the Lord of Earth is also Lord of the chest and the spirit; the Lord of Humans is also Lord of the belly and the seminal essence. The power that originates in the primordial Dao is very present and active in the several spheres of our existence. Since favorable activity of these gods is essential for human happiness and success, people look to the Daoist experts to summon and revitalize these powers within the community.

The Gods of Popular Religion

Some Daoist texts identify one of the Three Heavenly Ones as the Jade Emperor; other texts seem to think of the Jade Emperor as another sacred being. In any case, popular religion in China has looked to the Jade Emperor as the supreme arbitrator over life in this changing, human world—perhaps as the deputy of the Lord of Heaven in administering the heavenly bureaucracy and in governing the world of humans. It is widely believed among traditional Chinese that the Jade Emperor is the head of the heavenly court, and that he has many helpers and deputies to govern our world. There is, for example, the god of Tai Shan, the great mountain of the East, who is the Jade Emperor's regent on earth. Then there are the city gods (the Gods of Moats and Walls) who have been given the administration of particular villages and cities. Another important local god is Tu Di Gong (T'u Ti Kung), the earth god, guardian of the local community in all its fortunes and misfortunes. Then there are important household gods, including especially Zao Jun (Tsao Chun), God of the Cooking Stove, who keeps the ledger of good and bad deeds committed by the members of the family and, in general, looks after the welfare of the home.

All these deputy gods, it is believed, come to the Jade Emperor's court once a year to report and hand in accounts of their administration over the past year. And then they are promoted or punished accordingly, for their beneficial administration must harmonize with the work of the human emperor and the local administrators. If the larger good of human society is not served, the fault must lie somewhere within these human and divine bureaucracies.

Worshipers at the temple of Wong Tai Sin in Kowloon; Wong Tai Sin, a shepherd boy, became a god who provides good health and success in business.

Where did all these gods come from? Well, many (probably most) were originally humans who died and as ancestral spirits displayed such power and benefit that they were promoted to the ranks of the higher gods. The simple test of divine status is efficacy—does this god really come through with beneficial power or not? This approach is very practical-minded. When sacred power from a particular deceased human is experienced by many in the community and beyond, clearly an important god is in the making, for the gods are channels of sacred power as it is dispersed for the welfare and growth of the human community.

As important among the divine powers, we should mention two outstanding gods who are worshiped all over the Chinese communities, Ma-zu (Ma Tsu) and Guan Yin (Kuan Yin). Ma-zu is a favorite goddess, "Old Granny." Her story is especially important, for it illustrates how a human soul becomes a most universal, beneficial channel of sacred power. The story originates on an island in south China, where a teenaged girl showed special powers in communicating with and helping fishermen at sea. She knew when her father and brothers were experiencing a horrible shipwreck, and she flew to them in spirit to save them. She carried her brothers to safety in her arms but lost her father, for she was carrying him in her mouth and had to open her mouth in reply to a question from her mother. She died as a young woman, but soon other fishermen experienced her assistance, and then still others, until before long all across southern China, Ma-zu was revered as a most efficacious sacred power. Eventually even the emperor recognized her powers and she was raised to the status of Imperial Consort of Heaven—certainly a high position in this whole realm of sacred beings. Ma-zu provides much help in the practical circumstances of life—childbirth, healthy children, happy marriages, and much more.

Gods can make their appearance from many different directions, and Guan Yin is one who came in from Buddhism. As the great Bodhisattva Avalokiteshvara in India, this sacred being was widely known for saving and helping people, and in China the power continued and increased. Now known as Guan Yin, the Lord Who Looks Down (a translation of the Sanskrit name), this bodhisattva has become one of the most widely worshiped gods in China. The compassion and mercy of this bodhisattva have come to be expressed in feminine symbols and images, and many think of Guan Yin as the great goddess of mercy who grants help in the most critical areas of life.

Ma-zu, Guan Yin, and many more—Chinese people know that these gods, goddesses, and spirits are not ultimate and universal in their power, but they represent the ways, the avenues in which the ultimate Dao shows effective presence within daily human existence. These sacred powers are tangible and real elements of the operating everyday universe, and to stay in harmony with them is a most important practice of life.

The Inner Principle of All: Neo-Confucian Metaphysics

What really holds everything together? The Confucian tradition made important intellectual advances in China during the Song era, and this Neo-Confucian philosophical attitude became central to the vision of ultimate reality held by many Chinese. What we call Neo-Confucianism was really known as the school of "Principle," that is, the underlying Principle that holds everything together, and thus it is precisely what we are looking for in this investigation, ultimate reality as Chinese understand it. The theory of principle (li) attaches itself to the earlier views, incorporating the concepts of Heaven and Dao. These terms flow together in the Neo-Confucian notion that all is principle and that the mind itself reflects and resonates with this principle.

We can take Zhu Xi's (1130–1200) synthesis of Neo-Confucian thought about ultimate reality as representative, though, of course, there were alternate ideas and emphases in some of the other thinkers. As the very source of all Zhu Xi posits the Great Ultimate (tai ji), another term used from ancient times. The Great Ultimate transcends time and space. It is both the sum total of the principles of all things and also the highest principle within each. As the repository for all actual and potential principles, the Great Ultimate is present in the universe as a whole and in each thing individually. Zhu Xi explained this relationship in this way:

> The Great Ultimate is merely the principle of heaven and earth and the myriad things. With respect to heaven and earth, there is the Great Ultimate in them. With respect to the myriad things, there is the Great Ultimate in each and

every one of them. Before heaven and earth existed, there was assuredly this principle. . . . Fundamentally there is only one Great Ultimate, yet each of the myriad things has been endowed with it and each in itself possesses the Great Ultimate in its entirety. This is similar to the fact that there is only one moon in the sky but when its light is scattered upon rivers and lakes, it can be seen everywhere. It cannot be said that the moon has been split.[14]

So the real center of all, that which holds all together, is ultimate principle, both transcendent and completely within all things.

But how can we understand principle within each individual thing? Zhu Xi made a distinction between principle and "material force" (*qi*). Principle is eternal, unchanging, indestructible, and incorporeal. On the other hand, material force is transitory, changing, destructible, and corporeal. Yet these two do not exist separately. Principle needs material force to adhere to, and material force needs principle as its essence. Understandably, someone asked Zhu Xi which came first, principle or material force. Principle has never been separated from material force, Zhu answered, even though if we talk about origins we would have to say that principle is prior.

But what about the Lord Above and Heaven? What about gods and spirits? In answer to questions like these, Zhu Xi consistently interpreted all such ideas as simply the operation of principle. One questioner referred to passages in the classics about Heaven's creative activity and said: "I ask whether these and similar passages mean that there exists above the blue sky a real master and governor; or whether, Heaven having no mind, it is Li that is responsible." Zhu Xi's answer was direct: "These passages have all the same meaning—it is Li [principle] alone which acts thus."[15] Thus in its view of ultimate reality Neo-Confucianism has effectively excluded the idea of a personal creator God who rules over all. Finally it is principle that holds things together and keeps the world running.

The Chinese Buddhist Vision of the Ultimate

If the Chinese perspective on the ultimate is not too complicated already, we should add that many Chinese also have accepted the Mahayana Buddhist view of ultimate reality as emptiness and as the Dharma Body of the Buddha (discussed in Part I). Many distinctive Chinese ideas associated with the sense of cosmic harmony and the Dao have colored Buddhist views of the ultimate in China. The Hua-yan school, for example, articulated a complicated teaching about the interpenetration of the transcendental Dharma (suchness) and the dharmas of the conditioned world of rebirth, so that all phenomena enter into and are identical with each other. To illustrate this, one great Hua-yan master placed a Buddha image illuminated with a lamp in the middle of a hall, setting up mirrors in all the ten directions (the four cardinal directions, the four intermediate directions, and up and down). Each mirror thus reflects the Buddha image—and each also reflects the Buddha image as reflected in all the other mirrors, showing the interpenetration of all reality infused with the Buddha nature.

Chan Buddhism perpetuated the basic Mahayana conceptions of the ultimate and presented them in direct, forceful form in China: nirvana as nondifferent from samsara, the Buddha essence of all reality, and the Dharma Body (equated with the Dao) as universal. The second patriarch of Chan in China, Hui-ko, is reported to have taught:

> The deep principle of the True is "utter nondifferent." From of old, one is confused about the Gem and thinks it is a piece of tile. When suddenly "oneself" wakes up, there is the real jewel. Ignorance and wisdom are the same and without difference. Know that the myriad things are all identical with suchness. When you regard the body and do not distinguish it from the Buddha, why go on to seek [nirvana] without the remainder?[16]

In characteristic Chan language, the message is that ultimate reality is no different from the suchness of life in every moment as we live it.

So the Chinese tradition puts forth a number of important answers to the question about what is ultimate, what really holds everything together. One may believe in the Lord Above, Heaven, as the power that runs the world. Or one may look to the Dao of nature as the center of all. Again, one may find that the great gods of the Prior Heavens, together with their deputies on earth, provide the real center and support for existence. Or, one may take the view that all these forces are really the natural, impersonal functioning of Principle. Finally, there is the Buddhist view of ultimate reality as the Dharma Body of the Buddha and as emptiness. The truth of the matter is that many Chinese have held to all these views in varying degrees. Chinese religious thought has produced many creative visions of ultimate reality on the basis of these fundamental patterns.

COSMOS AND HUMANITY

So what sense or meaning is there in life? What is this world all about anyway? Ancient Chinese thinkers spent a great deal of time speculating and arguing on precisely questions like these, and their positions have influenced Chinese religion ever since. There are ancient myths of the creation of the universe and of humans within it. And there are philosophical theories about the origin of all and about how the sacred forces operate together in this world. All these stories and theories point to a cosmology in which humans are closely interwoven with the various aspects of the world in the harmony of the sacred power that is within, not outside, nature.

Origin of the Cosmos and Human Nature

The Pan Gu Myth of the Origin of the Cosmos

One ancient myth about the creation of the cosmos has special standing in the Chinese tradition: the Pan Gu myth. Stories about Pan Gu are well known in Chinese popular tradition. The ancient myth, from a third century C.E. text, goes like this:

> Heaven and Earth were in the chaos condition [*huntun*] like a chicken's egg, within which was born P'an-ku [perhaps "coiled-up Antiquity"]. After 18,000 years, when Heaven and Earth were separated, the pure *yang* formed the Heaven and the murky *yin* formed the Earth. P'an-ku stood between them. His body transformed nine times daily while his head supported the Heaven and his feet stabilized the Earth. Each day Heaven increased ten feet in height and Earth daily increased ten feet in thickness. P'an-ku who was between them daily increased ten feet in size. After another 18,000 years this is how Heaven and Earth came to be separated by their present distance of 90,000 *li* [roughly 50,000 kilometers].[17]

Another version of the myth about this cosmic person, from a sixth-century C.E. text, tells that after Pan Gu died he was transformed into the universe. His breath became the wind and the clouds, his voice the thunder, and his eyes the sun and moon. His blood became the rivers, his flesh the soil, his hair and beard the constellations, his skin and body hair the plants and trees, and his teeth and bones the metals and stones. And the parasites on his body, impregnated by the wind, became human beings.[18]

The origin of all things in a condition of chaos, called Hun-dun, is an ancient and widespread Chinese idea. It is, of course, found in other religious traditions also, such as the ancient Babylonian and Hebrew stories of the creation of the cosmos from a condition of chaos. Hun-dun is the great void, the undifferentiated, formless, watery source that through a process of differentiation engendered our universe. A recently discovered text from ancient China gives this striking description of primordial chaos:

> In the beginning of the ancient past,
> All things were fused and were identical with the great vacuity.
> Vacuous, and blended as one,
> Resting in the [condition of] one eternally,
> Moist and chaotic,
> There is no distinction of dark and light. . . .
> From ancient times it [Dao] had no form,
> It penetrated greatly but was nameless.[19]

This chaos is beyond all categories, characterized by flexibility, simplicity, and spontaneity, with inexhaustible potency to create the cosmos. As an eternal reality, it underlies the cosmos as the perpetual source of regeneration.

The Pan Gu myth describes chaos as a chicken's egg, a notion that is widespread in ancient China and also in many other cultures. Early Chinese writers likened the universe to an egg, with the heaven enclosing the earth from without as a shell does the yolk of the egg, the earth being the yolk suspended in the midst of heaven. The symbolism is appropriate, for the egg contains creative potentiality, with all the aspects of life already present, ready to evolve and burst out. All the multiplicity of things, all opposites, even yin and yang, are united in this source of creativity.

The cosmic person, Pan Gu, is engendered and nurtured within chaos to become the universe itself. There is no creator god here, working from the outside, as in the Hebrew creation story. Rather creation grows organically from within as that which is born in the chaos-womb grows to become the universe. There is a complete unity between the producer and that which is produced; the chaos-source evolves itself into the universe, still of the same essence. There is a continuing process of transformation, as Pan Gu grows and Heaven and Earth become established. The transformation continues with the death of this cosmic Person. Pan Gu, the macrocosm (great universe), becomes all the various aspects of the world, so that each part of the world is organically linked to the whole.

Here is a self-evolved world. The original chaos is completely unified with the resultant world in a continuous process of creation and regeneration.

The World Process: Dao, Yin-Yang, and Five Elements

Lao-zi and later Daoist thinkers identified the primordial chaos as none other than Dao. They held that Dao is not only the origin of all but the inner source of the continual transformation of the whole universe. That process involves generation and evolving forth; it also involves devolving and returning to the source, the "uncarved block," the Dao.

How does the Dao operate? The Dao De Jing says,

> Tao produced the One.
> The One produced the two.
> The two produced the three.
> And the three produced the ten thousand things.
> The ten thousand things carry the yin and embrace
> the yang, and through the blending of the material force
> they achieve harmony.   (CH. 42)[20]

Chinese cosmological views have always given an important place to the forces of yin and yang in understanding the nature and operation of the world. A widespread view of how the world originated is that Dao, in the great primordial chaos, engendered a separation between the finer and brighter elements, which became Heaven (yang), and the coarser and darker elements, which became earth (yin). From yang come fire and the sun, from yin water and the moon—and so on in the total operation of the

Working in the rice paddies; the sense of the rhythms of nature is prominent in Chinese religious thought.

world, the Dao functioning in the interaction of yin and yang. All of this is closely related to human welfare and happiness:

> Therefore the Yin and the Yang are the great principles of Heaven and Earth. The four seasons are the great path of Yin and Yang. Likewise, punishment and reward in government are to be in harmony with the four seasons. When punishment and reward are in harmony with the seasons, happiness will be produced; when they disregard them, they will produce calamity.[21]

As we see from the four seasons, the Dao operates in yang–yin cyclical processes of rise and decline. We can also understand the Dao as the operation of the five elements or forces. The five elements are wood, fire, earth, metal, and water, but these are identified with many other sets of five: planets, weather, seasons, cardinal directions, sense organs, tastes, viscera, moods, and so forth. These are dynamic operational agents that are continually moving in cyclical changes from one to the other. Each element has its time to rise, flourish, decline, and be taken over by the next. The relationships are complicated processes of mutually producing, conquering, and transforming. Thus, for example, wood conquers earth, metal conquers wood, fire conquers metal, water conquers fire, earth conquers water. In this whole cyclical process an ecological balance is maintained. For example, over-forestation would be stopped by forest fires, which would be stopped by rain. On the other hand, water can produce forests faster than metal cuts the trees down. This ecological balance is extended into all facets of personal, social, and political life.

The Human Position in the World

Where do we come from and why are we here? The Pan Gu myth, describing how everything in the world came from different parts of the cosmic Pan Gu, tells how the parasites on Pan Gu's body were impregnated by the wind and became human beings. This may seem to be a rather modest view of human origins and of human function in the world, unlike the view in the three Abrahamic religions that humans were made specially as the crown of creation to be God's representative over all. Actually, the point of the Pan Gu story of human origins does not seem to be that humans are parasites on the world. Rather, humans are

from the same one source as the whole universe, organically related to the rest of nature. Humans are not masters of the universe, but they are evolved from the same source and share the common process of life with all.

The Pan Gu myth is important, but it is especially the classics and the writings of the Confucian and Daoist philosophers that define the nature of humans and their position in the world. There is general agreement that human nature is intricately related to all the sacred forces inherent in the universe. One of the clearest statements of human nature is in the Book of Rites: "Humanness is consistent of benevolent virtue of Heaven and Earth, the co-operative union of Yin and Yang, the joint assembly of ghost [gui] and spirit [shen], and the finest breath contained in the Five Elements."[22] Human nature is the finest cooperative product of the universe itself, containing the basic substance and elements of the universe.

This passage from the Book of Rites refers to "the joint assembly of gui and shen" within human nature. Chinese traditionally conceive of two souls within humans, appropriately, since humans are the "cooperative union of yin and yang." One soul is the yang soul (hun), which comes from Heaven, the realm of pure yang. The other soul is the yin soul (po), from the pure yin source, Earth. The yang dimension is also thought of as the spiritual aspect, and the yin as the physical aspect, of a person. During life yin and yang are united, but at death they again separate. The yang soul, stemming from Heaven, becomes shen, a spiritual being or god. The yin soul is gui, an earthy spiritual force to be returned to its original source, the earth, in burial. If the qui is not properly buried and cared for by descendants, it may become an unhappy wandering spirit, or "ghost."

Thus we see that human nature is a microcosm of the great universe itself. Human nature reflects all those powers writ large on the cosmic scale, now active and focused on the human scale. Many philosophical texts delight in spelling out the correspondences between the human body and the forces of Heaven and Earth, yin and yang, and the five elements. One text says,

> The roundness of the head imitates Heaven, and the squareness of the foot imitates Earth. Like Heaven has four seasons, Five Elements, nine divisions and 360 days, human beings also have four limbs, five viscera, nine orifices

and 360 joints. Like Heaven has wind, rain, cold, and heat, human beings also have the qualities of accepting, giving, joy and anger. Therefore gall corresponds to clouds, the lung to vapor, the spleen to wind, the kidneys to rain, and the liver to thunder. Thus human beings form a trinity with Heaven and Earth, and the human mind is the master.[23]

The suggestion here that humans form a triad with Heaven and earth is an important idea in the Chinese view of human nature and makes it clear that humans have an important role to fill. Philosophical discussions of human nature inevitably come to that question of what special role humans have in the universe.

According to Lao-zi and Zhuang-zi, human beings have received the special quality of "virtue" (de) from the Dao, the life principle inherent in each individual. Therefore, humans simply need to discover that virtue within and live according to it.

For Confucius and his followers, the ideal human position in the world could best be characterized by the concept of ren, "humaneness," a notion that puts strong emphasis on interrelationship between people, in kindness and morality. It is this morality that makes humans different from animals; humans have the Heaven-given qualities of love or commiseration, righteousness, propriety, and wisdom; and they have the potential of fulfilling these qualities. Dong Zhung-shu (178–104 B.C.E.), a great Confucianist who synthesized the ideas of yin–yang, five elements, and Dao within Confucianism, had a bit to say about the high position of humans in the universe.

> Of the creatures born from the refined essence of Heaven and Earth, none is more noble than man. Man receives the mandate from Heaven and is therefore superior to other creatures. Other creatures suffer troubles and defects and cannot practice humanity and righteousness; man alone can practice them. . . .
>
> The highest humanity (ren) rests with Heaven, for Heaven is humaneness itself. It shelters and sustains all creatures. It transforms them and brings them to birth. It nourishes and completes them. Its works never cease; they end and then begin again, and the fruits of all its labors it gives to the service of mankind.[24]

In this Confucianist interpretation is summed up the high Chinese view of the role of humans in the world, to be in union with Heaven and earth not only physically but also spiritually and thus help to maintain harmony in the universe through moral life.

The Realities of Human Existence in the World

Why do things seem so uncertain and confused? Why is there so much evil and suffering in the world? What keeps us from living the way we should? Since ancient times Chinese philosophers have debated questions about why humans seemingly do not reach their full potential in their own nature and in society. Sometimes, usually among Confucian thinkers, the discussion focuses on the question of whether humans are good or evil by nature, seen within the social context. Those inclined toward the Daoist vision see the problem more in terms of humans trapped in artificiality and conventional strictures instead of living in full harmony with the Dao. Buddhists emphasize the problems of ignorance, desire, and karma. Those concerned about our relation to the gods and spirits feel that problems arise because humans forget them or fail to make use of their power of renewal. Whichever view is chosen, there is consensus on one thing: we humans do not live the full life of happiness, because we are out of harmony with the sacred power(s) at the heart of our existence.

Life in Community: Are Humans Good or Evil by Nature?

It is not hard to see that things are not right in the world. True, there have been eras of relative peace and harmony—Chinese thinkers often took a nostalgic look back to the early Zhou period (starting ca. 1100 B.C.E.) as a time when sage-kings ruled according to the mandate of Heaven in an era of peace and prosperity. But even that peaceful era was short-lived. Both Confucius and Lao-zi lived in a time of upheaval and anarchy. At no time could it be said that humans reached their full potential in peace and prosperity.

Chinese thinkers of all persuasions have offered theories as to why humans fail to live up to their possibilities. There are many possible theories, but it is characteristic of Chinese thinking that good and evil behavior is seen as a human problem, not something that is determined by divine forces, whether god or evil power. Of course, humans do interact with many spiritual forces, and hungry wandering spirits can cause suffering and misfortune. But in the final analysis the human problem of failure lies within humanity itself, in the individual, in society, or in both.

It is a time-honored view in China to consider human nature as essentially good and positive, in spite of the reality of evil and suffering in human society. This was the view suggested by Confucius and articulated clearly by Meng-zi. Confucius based his whole approach on the educability of human beings, including the common people whom he accepted in his school. He held that it was lack of moral leadership and the attempt to rule by laws and penalties that prevented the people from developing a sense of honor. It is not that people by nature are hurtful and cruel; it is the anarchy of society and especially the greed and brutal power of rulers that turn human behavior to negative and harmful directions.

Meng-zi articulated clearly the basic notion that humans are essentially good by nature but turn to evil because society and its leaders fail to cultivate and nourish that goodness of nature. All people have four intrinsic virtues: the feeling of commiseration, the feeling of shame, the feeling of courtesy, and the sense of right and wrong. Famous in this discussion is Meng-zi's parable of a child falling into a well:

> Why I say all men have a sense of commiseration is this: Here is a man who suddenly notices a child about to fall into a well. Invariably he will feel a sense of alarm and compassion. And this is not for the purpose of gaining the favor of the child's parents, or seeking the approbation of his neighbors and friends, or for fear of blame should he fail to rescue it. Thus we see that no man is without a sense of compassion, or a sense of shame, or a sense of courtesy, or a sense of right and wrong. The sense of compassion is the beginning of humanity [ren]; the sense of shame is the beginning of righteousness; the sense of courtesy is the beginning of decorum [li]; the sense of right and wrong is the beginning of wisdom. Every man has within himself these four beginnings, just as he has four limbs. Since everyone has these four beginnings within him, the man who considers himself incapable of exercising them is destroying himself. [25]

These four beginnings are motivations and possibilities that are inherent in everyone. Starting with commiseration, these originating impulses in human nature motivate us to become humane, righteous, proper, and wise.

But, Meng-zi holds, these beginnings of goodness need to be nurtured and developed—and for many people that fails to happen. It seems that what we call evil in human nature is really due to lack of completion and development of the innate goodness. Meng-zi explains:

> Can it be that any man's mind naturally lacks Humanity and Justice? If he loses his sense of the good, then he loses it as the mountain lost its trees. It has been hacked away at—day after day—what of its beauty then? However, as the days pass he grows, and, as with all men, in the still air of the early hours his sense of right and wrong is at work. . . . Indeed, if nurtured aright, anything will grow, but if not nurtured aright anything will wither away. [26]

So evil does not arise within human nature but comes, in a sense, from without, from lack of nourishing by society. The tendency of human nature is to do good, Meng-zi said, like water flowing downhill. Of course, you can interfere and splash water uphill, but this is due not to the nature of water but to the force of circumstances. Similarly, humans may be brought to do evil, but that is because something has been forced onto human nature. Lack of nourishment of our good nature, corrupting influences from outside—from these arise the human problematic of evil and suffering.

But there is an alternate way of looking at the problem, and this was best articulated by another disciple in the Confucian tradition, Xun-zi (ca. 300–238 b.c.e.). Xun-zi, taking a "realist" position, held that human nature is essentially selfish and hateful, and any kind of goodness can only be acquired by training or enforced through laws and punishment. Heaven—which to Xun-zi is a mechanistic force without moral qualities—produces a human nature that loves profit, envies and hates, and strives and plunders selfishly. Xun-zi wrote,

> The nature of man is evil; his goodness is acquired. His nature being what it is, man is born, first, with a desire for gain. Second, man is born with envy and hate. If these tendencies are followed, injury and cruelty will abound and loyalty and faithfulness will disappear. . . . Hence to give

rein to man's original nature and to yield to man's emotions will assuredly lead to strife and disorderliness, and he will revert to a state of barbarism. (CH. 23)[27]

If left to itself, our evil human nature would destroy any goodness in our civilization. Yet, for all his pessimistic view of human nature, Xun-xi was optimistic that humans could be reshaped through the laws and training produced by the sages.

Since Meng-zi and Xun-zi seem to hold opposite positions, it is inevitable that there might be a view of human nature somewhere between the two. Some later Confucianists argued that both Meng-zi and Xun-zi were right; human nature is partly good and partly evil. If the good aspect is cultivated and nourished, the goodness increases; but if the evil aspect is cultivated, the badness increases. One thinker put it this way: "Man's nature is a mixture of good and evil. He who cultivates the good in it will become a good man and he who cultivates the evil in it will become an evil man."[28] This view suggests that Meng-zi and Xun-zi were perhaps not as far apart as might appear at first glance. The basic problem is still a genuinely human one: evil tendencies (whether from society or from human nature) often grow and spread, whereas good tendencies (whether from human nature or from society) often wither and diminish. And the struggle goes on not in the cosmos but on the stage of human life in society. The Confucian path of transformation is designed to reverse that human situation so that humaneness and righteousness prevail.

Life in Nature: The Problem of Artificiality and Coercion

There is still another position on the question of whether humans are good or evil by nature. One thinker challenged Meng-zi by claiming that there is no distinction between good or bad in human nature: "The nature of man may be likened to a swift current of water: you lead it eastward and it will flow to the east; you lead it westward and it will flow to the west. Human nature is neither disposed to good nor to evil, just as water is neither disposed to east nor west."[29] Perhaps asking whether human nature is good or evil is the wrong approach, for that very judgment is artificial and may in fact contribute to the

problem. Perhaps our basic problem is that we pass such judgments about good and evil!

This is the general approach to the human problem taken by philosophical Daoism. It is artificiality and coercion that lie at the root of our problems in the world. The Dao by nature grows and wanes, operating in everything in harmony, and the good life is always to be in complete harmony with the Dao. But our human tendency is to try and take charge of our lives, change things in accordance with our own strategies, and force structures onto nature and ourselves. We judge wealth and power to be good, and we judge poverty and weakness to be evil— and we spend our lives struggling for one and trying to escape from the other. But in doing so we are alienated from the harmony of Dao.

Zhuang-zi stated the problem with his characteristic flair for imagery:

> The duck's legs are short, but to stretch them out would worry him; the crane's legs are long, but to cut them down would make him sad. What is long by nature needs no cutting off; what is short by nature needs no stretching. That would be no way to get rid of worry.[30]

It is in going against the givenness and spontaneous fitness of nature that we experience suffering, frustration, and defeat. All of our problems come from trying to force things in artificial, unnatural ways.

Where does this human tendency come from? Lao-zi and Zhuang-zi do not really say whether it is inherent in human nature or whether it stems from institutions of society. Probably even these distinctions are false and misleading. Nature itself is the operation of Dao, and evil embodies all that resists pristine nature through coercion, artificiality, and intellectual skill. However they originate, these tendencies at least are promoted by social institutions such as laws, education, ceremonies, rules of morality and etiquette, and the like. This means that the people who do the most to worsen our human problems are the law-enforcers, the teachers, and the ritualists—all of them imposing restraints on what should be natural and free.

Of course, this perspective of philosophical Daoism pertains most directly to those following the path put forth by Lao-zi and Zhuang-zi. But the same basic notion flows over into the more widespread religious Daoist view of the human problem: we are out of balance with the cosmic forces that support and sustain us. These forces are the great gods of the stellar constellations, managing the operation of yin–yang and the five elements. Through neglect and ignorance we often live out of harmony and bring deprivation and evil upon ourselves. In popular religious understanding, these forces are the gods and goddesses that make up the pantheon of the state and the local community; they are the ancestral spirits that oversee the family and dispense weal or woe in accordance with our harmony with them. One need only look at one's failures and frustrations, conflicts and tragedies to recognize that the general disharmony with Dao and yin–yang is reflected in daily life in family and community.

Chinese Buddhist Views of Human Existence

In bringing to China ideas of karma arising out of ignorance and desire, the wheel of existence, rebirth, and so forth, Buddhism contributed much to the Chinese conception of human nature and the human problem. We can briefly note several tendencies in Chinese Buddhist thought regarding the human problem, one that emphasizes ignorance of the Buddha quality of human nature, one that sees this world-age as especially degenerate, and one that focuses on the horrors of the purgatory that awaits humans after death.

The Hua-yan, Tian-tai, and Chan schools emphasized the classical Mahayana doctrine of the universal Buddha-nature that all people possess, holding that it is human ignorance that keeps us from seeing this Buddha-nature and thus remaining trapped in suffering. A clear statement about human nature and the human problem comes from the fifth patriarch of the Hua-yan school, Zong-mi (780–841):

> The Doctrine of the Manifestation of the Dharma-nature . . . preaches that all sentient beings possess the true mind of natural enlightenment, which from time immemorial has always been there, clear and pure, shining and not obscured, understanding and always knowing. It is also called Buddha-nature and Tathagata-garbha (Store of the Thus-come). From the beginning of time, it has been obscured by erroneous ideas without knowing its own (Buddha-nature), but only recognizing its ordinary nature, loving it and being attached to it, accumulating action-influence, and suffering from the pain of life and death.[31]

One tendency that developed among some Chinese Buddhists was to view the present world-age as particularly degenerate compared to earlier ages, thus making it much more difficult to follow the disciplines of the Buddhist path. An old Buddhist teaching about the Three Ages of the Dharma was popularized and influenced many. Basically, the first age, the first 500 years after the lifetime of the Buddha (some held it was 1,000 years), was the age of the Perfect Dharma, when the Buddha's Dharma was correctly preached and human minds were clear, so that many could follow the holy path to nirvana. The second age (the next 1,000 years) declined into the age of the Counterfeit Dharma, when minds were clouded and following the holy path was much more difficult. But then comes the Age of the End of the Dharma, in which all humans have become so degenerate in intellect and will that it is no longer possible to follow the former disciplines to reach the goal of enlightenment. Since Chinese Buddhists generally dated the Buddha's death as having occurred in 949 B.C.E., the feeling arose among some Buddhists that the world had entered into the Age of the End of the Dharma in the year 552 C.E. Consequently, it was now extremely difficult if not impossible for humans to make progress on the path. Not all Buddhists agreed that human nature had degenerated to this extent, but those who did started advocating new, simpler solutions to the human problem, such as the Pure Land path.

Chinese popular imagination was fascinated by Buddhist ideas about bad karma accumulated during one's existence and rebirth in purgatories and hells, and lurid descriptions of the horrors of those purgatories abound in popular literature. Buddhist notions of purgatory were expanded by Chinese notions of trial and punishment for the guilty. One popular tract first issues a plea for the sinners to repent, and then presents a portrait of what is in store for them if they do not. Here is the general policy:

> The Judges of the Ten Courts of Purgatory then agreed that all who led virtuous lives from their youth upwards shall be escorted at their death to the land of the Immortals; that all whose balance of good and evil is exact shall escape the bitterness of the [worst three of the Six Paths], and be born again among men; that those who have repaid their debts of gratitude and friendship, and fulfilled their destiny, yet have a balance of evil against them, shall pass through the var-

ious Courts of Purgatory and then be born again amongst men, rich, poor, old, young, diseased or crippled, to be put a second time upon trial. Then, if they behave well they may enter into some happy state; but if badly, they will be dragged by horrid devils through all the Courts, suffering bitterly as they go, and will again be born, to endure in life the uttermost of poverty and wretchedness, in death the everlasting tortures of hell. Those who are disloyal, unfilial, who commit suicide, take life, or disbelieve the doctrine of Cause and Effect (i.e., karma) . . . are handed over to the everlasting tortures of hell.

After a long description of the most horrid punishments imaginable, the tract reflects on the foolishness of human nature, illustrated by those shades who, having passed through the purgatories and through the Terrace of Oblivion (where they are caused to forget all that has happened to them), now rejoice at the prospect of being born again as humans:

> Yet they all rush on to birth like an infatuated or drunken crowd; and again, in their early childhood, hanker after the forbidden flavours. Then, regardless of consequences, they begin to destroy life, and thus forfeit all claims to the mercy and compassion of God [the Jade Emperor]. They take no thought as to the end that must overtake them; and finally, they bring themselves once more to the same horrid plight. [32]

THE PATH OF TRANSFORMATION

How can we start living the life that is *real?* How can we find power for renewal and transformation?

The portrayals of the human problematic in the Chinese traditions, against the background of the human potential for goodness and happiness, help to set the stage for the Path of Transformation, the kind of praxis that leads to renewal of harmony with Dao, the gods, the spirits, and the innermost sources of life.

Confucianism: Transformation Through Study and Ritual

The Confucian tradition, disdaining as it does some of the usual religious practices like calling on the gods for help, has sometimes not been considered a religious path at all but rather a kind of philosophy for improvement of self and society. Are these questions, having to do with the search for real life and renewal, even applicable to the concerns of Confucianists?

Of course they are, for these are basic, universal human concerns. Confucianists are just as concerned as anyone else about real, authentic life and self-transformation. The emphasis is not on life after death or salvation through help from the gods, it is true. But perhaps for that very reason there is a very strong emphasis on achieving the life that is truly human and fulfills our full potential for peace, harmony, and happiness—according to the design of Heaven. Confucianism is clearly a path of spiritual transformation, stressing both the intellectual pursuit of education and study and also the practical and social pursuits of ritual behavior and propriety. We look more closely

Decorated steles in a Confucian temple in Beijing.

at the Confucian rituals and ethical actions later; here we want to understand the theoretical basis of the path: how can study, ritual, and moral behavior be the basis of self-transformation, the path to real life?

Transformation Through Study and Moral Cultivation

Confucius was above all an educator, and those following in his tradition have always stressed the path of study and education as the means toward transformation. The human problem, as we have seen, is that our fundamentally good nature gets stunted for lack of nourishment and even misdirected by the anarchy that tends to rule in society because of selfish rulers, repressive laws, and wrongful social relationships. But we have the potential to realize our humanness and become noble people, if we have noble teachers and rulers, if we allow ourselves to be educated, if we study our own nature and the nature of things as determined according to the will of Heaven. This means using the intellect for education, study, and moral self-cultivation.

Confucius taught that the sage-kings of old had deep insight into the will of Heaven and perfected their own humanity in harmony with Heaven. Therefore the classics that tell about their sayings and their lives can mediate that wisdom and perfection to those who read and study these sacred writings, for through such study and education one's human goodness can be nourished and perfected.

In a famous passage in the Analects, Confucius points to the way of learning as a lifelong process of self-cultivation:

> At fifteen, I set my heart on learning. At thirty, I was firmly established. At forty, I had no more doubts. At fifty, I knew the will of Heaven. At sixty, I was ready to listen to it. At seventy, I could follow my heart's desire without transgressing what was right (2.4).[33]

There is no quick fix here, no sudden conversion and transformation. The path is a long, gradual movement of study and learning, awakening the inner knowledge of the will of Heaven and growing into that will so that the very springs of motivation are in complete harmony with it. So study is not just for knowledge's sake, but for inner cultivation and growth in realizing the will of Heaven—thus becoming a true Noble Person.

The study of the classics actually involves all the major liberal arts, providing a thorough humanistic education. The six disciplines are based on the Six Classics, and they include study of poetry for refinement of thought and expression; study of history for understanding the tradition and refining moral judgment; study of ritual for understanding propriety; study of music for inner transformation; study of politics for social transformation; and study of cosmology to harmonize with the sacred forces. By such study and practice it is possible to cultivate the innate human capabilities to become good and noble and superior; and such noble persons can then lead and guide others to become humane and good.

The Neo-Confucianists developed the path of study into a total system of moral and spiritual self-cultivation, and to many Chinese this Neo-Confucian model of the path has been their highest aspiration. Learning and knowledge cross over into transforming the will and mind and personal life, and this strength of personal character influences the whole social setting of the family, the community, and even the world. One of the most important descriptions of this path of self-cultivation is in the Book of Great Learning:

> The Way of learning to be great consists in manifesting the clear character, loving the people, and abiding in the highest good. . . . The ancients who wished to manifest their clear character to the world would first bring order to their states. Those who wished to bring order to their states would first regulate their families. Those who wished to regulate their families would first cultivate their personal lives. Those who wished to cultivate their personal lives would first rectify their minds. Those who wished to rectify their minds would first make their wills sincere. Those who wished to make their wills sincere would first extend their knowledge.

So all the good expressions of character depend on steps of self-cultivation that finally rest on extending one's knowledge, as the very first movement. The text continues:

> The extension of knowledge consists in the investigation of things. When things are investigated, knowledge is extended; when knowledge is extended, the will becomes sincere; when the will is sincere, the mind is rectified; when the mind is rectified, the personal life is cultivated; when

the personal life is cultivated, the family will be regulated; when the family is regulated, the state will be in order; and when the state is in order, there will be peace throughout the world.[34]

Here are eight steps toward the transformation of human society in the world! The last three have to do with family and society—reflecting the importance of parents, teachers, rulers, and others on the path of transformation. But the focal point still is the cultivation of personal life. The text goes on to say, "From the Son of Heaven [the emperor] down to the common people, all must regard cultivation of the personal life as the root or foundation. There is never a case when the root is in disorder and yet the branches are in order."[35]

So the important question is, how can one cultivate personal life so as to become a noble person? The text lays out some basic steps, namely, investigation of things, extension of knowledge, the will becoming sincere, and the rectification of the mind. These form the heart of the path of transformation, leading to the moral and spiritual cultivation of personal life. The investigation of things means to study the nature of the world and of oneself, arriving at true understanding of the underlying moral principles of the universe. In this process the will becomes sincere, resolving on the goal with calmness and unflagging determination. The path of transformation specifically involves rectification of the mind, becoming one with the whole universe by understanding its principles and looking upon the whole cosmos as one's own self. All of this adds up to cultivation of personal life, that is, self-discipline and practice with diligence and zeal, in study, meditation, and cultivation of moral virtue.

Transformation Through Ritual

In addition to the mental disciplines of study and extension of knowledge, the Confucian path places great emphasis on the practical disciplines of self-transformation. In some religions, such as Judaism and Islam, ritual and ethical behavior according to God's law play a major part in the path of transformation. Confucianism does not think in terms of God's law, but it finds ritual and ethical behavior (propriety) in society to be powerful instruments of self-transformation. Both ritual and the rules of propriety, in fact, correspond to the patterns immanent in the whole of reality.

It is important to understand that what we are calling ritual and ethical behavior both are the same one word in Chinese: li (not the same word as li meaning principle). As the inherent ritual pattern of the universe, li is followed and practiced both in the various traditional rituals and in one's proper roles in family and society.

In traditional China there were rituals for almost every purpose—sacrifice to the ancestors, political occasions, family events, great public occasions, receiving a guest, and so on. And many great thinkers have written about the meaning of ritual, following the lead of the Classic of Rites, the ancient text that describes many rituals and also provides important ideas about the meaning of the rituals. Chinese have always thought of ritual as closely connected with the underlying principles of the whole universe. In ancient China, for example, rituals of divination were used to connect with the sacred powers of the world and even to direct and control them. Thus, by performing ritual correctly, we are harmonizing ourselves with the forces of Heaven and earth.

One Confucian thinker who wrote a lot about ritual, Xun-zi, has this to say about the origin of ritual:

> Rites (Li) rest on three bases: Heaven and earth, which are the source of all life; the ancestors, who are the source of the human race; sovereigns and teachers, who are the source of government. . . . Hence rites are to serve Heaven on high and earth below, and to honor the ancestors and elevate the sovereigns and teachers.

So ritual has both a cosmological origin and a social origin. It issued forth from Heaven and earth as part of the very principle of the universe. And it also was transmitted by ancestors and shaped by teachers and rulers.

Indeed, it is ritual that upholds and unifies the whole realm of the world, as Xun-zi writes:

> It is through rites that Heaven and earth are harmonious and sun and moon are bright, that the four seasons are ordered and the stars are on their courses, that rivers flow and that things prosper, that love and hatred are tempered and joy and anger are in keeping. They cause the lowly to be obedient and those on high to be illustrious. . . . Rites— are they not the culmination of culture?[36]

Therefore ritual can effect the great transformation of harmonizing us with the world, so that we humankind do become, as the classics state, a trinity with Heaven and earth. Through rituals our innate goodness is nourished and we conform ourselves more and more into the pattern of Heaven and earth, becoming people of humanity.

Moral Cultivation Through Propriety in Society

Confucius taught that we can become people of humanity (ren) especially by practicing the rules of li, "propriety" (the same word as ritual). Here the focus is on relationships in society, in accordance with the will of Heaven, transforming ourselves by practicing and fulfilling our proper roles.

The Confucian tradition talks about the "rectification of names," that is, transforming oneself so as to practice one's proper roles in family and society. Confucius said, "Let the prince be the prince, the minister be minister, the father father and the son son" (Analects 12.11).[37] Each person is related to all the others in society, so each needs to fulfill the particular role and duty that she has. Much of the breakdown in society today results from people not fulfilling their proper roles, usurping the roles of others, rulers looking after their self-interest, teachers misleading students, and all the rest. Many people do not live according to their proper role in family and society—they usurp the authority of their elders, they fail to respect and obey the rulers, they consider themselves above their teachers. To transform ourselves into our potential human goodness, we need the discipline and practice of rectifying our social roles, Confucius taught. We need to discipline ourselves to live as a father, a son, a sister, a ruler, a subject. Only in this way will we be able to inject humaneness (ren) into our lives and into our relation with others. "Without knowledge of the rules of propriety," Confucius said, "it is impossible for one's character to be established" (20:3).[38]

What makes this pursuit of ritual and propriety a religious path is the deep sense that the elaborate systems of ritual and the rules of propriety are based in the pattern originating in the cosmic principle of the universe, according to the mandate of Heaven. "Without knowing the Mandate [of Heaven], it is impossible to be a superior man," Confucius said (20:3).[39]

The Daoist Path of Transformation

How can we start living *real* life? Where do we find power for life and immortality, beyond failure and death? The Daoist tradition is very much concerned with these questions, and it proposes one fundamental answer: get into harmony with the Dao!

The basic human problematic from the Daoist perspective, as we recall, is forcing our lives against the flow of Dao, engaging in the human tendency of artificiality, judging others, planning strategies, forcing people into roles, and generally struggling selfishly against the stream. This is what causes evil and misery, war and violence, sickness and early death.

So what can one do to transform all this? The path offered by those of the Daoist persuasion consists of ideas, disciplines, and practices to lead to harmony with Dao and with all the spiritual forces that operate within our universe. In the words of Lao-zi,

> Being one with Nature, he is in accord with Tao.
> Being in accord with Tao, he is everlasting,
> And is free from danger throughout his lifetime. (CH. 16)[40]

According to philosophical Daoism, the way to ultimate transformation involves the practice of inaction, meditation, and withdrawal from society. Religious Daoism offers many more rituals and practices that restore the powers within our bodies, call down the great cosmic gods, all together balancing yin and yang forces to bring blessed life and immortality. Some scholars have held that philosophical Daoism and religious Daoism are very different modes of religious practice. The understanding we will follow, on the contrary, will see these two movements as basically related paths. One emphasizes harmony with Dao through personal meditation and experience; the other looks to gods and other sacred forces to establish the balance needed for blessed life and immortality.

The Path of Transformation According to Philosophical Daoism

The kind of existence that can be attained, according to Lao-zi, Zhuang-zi, and other Daoist thinkers, is one beyond all limitations, hindrances, and finite borders. We can become transcendental, realizing our body as part of the universe. That means we need have no worries or anxieties, for the real truth transcends normal knowledge and moral principles. Invincible and immortal, we can live fully in tune with Dao.

The most important movement on the path of transformation, according to the Dao De Jing, is to practice "no action" (*wu wei*). This seems like a contradiction in terms—how can you practice no action? Of course, what the path prescribes is a way of life in which nothing is done against the course of nature, no actions are forced, no mental concepts are imposed on the Dao, and judgments about good and bad or desirable and nondesirable are completely avoided. The Dao in itself is neither good or bad, neither right or wrong, so there is no need for actions on our part to resist or change the natural transformations. The course of the Dao is simply the natural, universal course of the Dao—and our highest good is to be in harmony with that Dao just as it is. That calls for a life in which we dedicate ourselves to disciplines and practices that open us up toward the Dao—disciplines of nonstriving, noncontrol, nonstructure, and nondirection. Never do anything that is against the natural flow of Dao—that is the basic meaning of wu-wei, no-action. Stated positively, it means to do everything in accord with the flow of Dao.

This kind of life requires practice. And the Daoist texts put forth a program designed to cultivate the no-action type

Workers crossing the Yellow River near Louyang. Daoist philosophy cultivates harmony with the flow of nature.

of life: withdrawing from society, living simply, cultivating one's inner nature. Early Daoists were hermits and recluses, following the Dao in the mountains and valleys, through winter and summer, alone and in groups, practicing the discipline of no-action. Central to this is meditation, emptying out the plans, structures, and strategies of the mind so that the natural flow of Dao might fill the whole being. An important text in the *Dao De Jing* says:

> Attain complete vacuity,
> Maintain complete quietude.
> All things come into being,
> And I see thereby their return.
> All things flourish,
> But each one returns to its root.
> This return to its root means tranquility.
> It is called returning to its destiny.
> To return to destiny is called the eternal (Dao).   (CH. 16)[41]

What is proposed here is a type of meditation that empties the mind of all ideas and concepts that limit and restrain, so that the mind can directly experience the flow of Dao, the rise and return of all things to the root and source of all. Through such meditation we can harmonize ourselves with the Dao so that we are not affected by change, by feelings of good and bad, even by death. By being one with the Dao we can live totally freely and spontaneously, letting everything happen as it will.

This path of transformation does not involve study and learning, for such activities only serve further to cloud over our minds so that we cannot open ourselves to the flow of Dao. Nor does this path mean learning our proper roles in society, for such structures only increase artificiality and coercion. Rather the ideal path would be that of a mountain hermit, roaming about freely and carelessly, fully attuned to the rhythms of nature, acting only in full harmony with the flow of Dao. It is possible to follow this path without becoming a mountain hermit, of course, but the method of withdrawing from societal structures and meditating in harmony with nature is still important even for those who remain in society.

Since words and concepts do not help on the path of Dao, it is misleading to offer too many rationalized explanations. Fortunately, Zhuang-zi was a great storyteller, and through these stories we can develop some sensitivity for what it means to practice no-action and follow the Dao. Once, Zhuang-zi said, Prince Wen-hui's cook was cutting up a bullock. "Every touch of his hand, every shift of his shoulder, every tread of his foot, every thrust of his knee, every sound of the rending flesh, and every note of the movement of the chopper was in perfect harmony." Prince Wen-hui was impressed and praised him for his perfect skill, but the cook replied:

> What your servant loves is the Tao, which I have applied to the skill of carving. When I first began to cut up bullocks, what I saw was simply whole bullocks. After three years' practice, I saw no more bullocks as wholes. Now, I work with my mind, and not with my eyes. The functions of my senses stop; my spirit dominates. Following the natural markings, my chopper slips through the great cavities, slides through the great cleavages, taking advantage of the structure that is already there. . . . A good cook changes his chopper once a year, because he cuts. An ordinary cook changes his copper once a month, because he hacks. Now my chopper has been in use for nineteen years; it has cut up several thousand bullocks; yet its edge is as sharp as if it just came from the whetstone.

Now the prince understood and said, "Excellent. I have heard the words of this cook, and learned the way of cultivating life" (ch. 3).[42] This way of cultivating life is the way of no-action, that is, not scheming and forcing things but working spontaneously with one's spirit in harmony with the Dao. That approach brings success and happiness in life; in fact, one completely in tune with the Dao overcomes the normal human limitations, as Zhuang-zi says somewhat playfully:

> Let me try speaking to you in a somewhat irresponsible manner, and may I ask you to listen to me in the same spirit. Leaning against the sun and the moon and carrying the universe under his arm, the sage blends everything into a harmonious whole. He is unmindful of the confusion and the gloom, and equalizes the humble and the honorable. The multitude strive and toil; the sage is primitive and without knowledge. He comprehends ten thousand years as one unity, whole and simple. All things are what they are, and are thus brought together. (CH. 2)[43]

The Path of Religious Daoism

There is no sharp division between the path of transformation as understood in philosophical Daoism and that in religious Daoism. Religious Daoism starts from the basic perspective of Lao-zi and Zhuang-zi and offers a path that relates more concretely to the human concerns of health, material happiness, well-being of family and community, and even immortality. Whereas the path of philosophical Daoism is mostly a private pursuit of individuals, the path of religious Daoism is a community concern and focuses on experts and priesthoods, temples and festivals, for the welfare and transformation of the community. Still, the priests and experts follow the path for their own personal transformation, for only in that way can they share the transforming power with others. The path of religious Daoism really operates at two levels, then: the level of the expert or priest and the level of ordinary people in the community.

The Daoist view of the human situation holds that our problems arise because we are out of balance with the cosmic forces that support and sustain us. Religious Daoism sees these forces as the great gods of the stellar constellations who manage the operation of yin–yang and the five elements, related also to the ancestral spirits and the gods and goddesses of everyday life. So how can one start living *real* life? The basic answer is to follow the path that restores one's balance with these cosmic forces.

An important theory in understanding the path of religious Daoism is the microcosm–macrocosm relationship. The macrocosm or "great cosmos" is the Dao operating through the gods of the stellar constellations, yin–yang, and the five elements. The microcosm or "small cosmos" is our limited world, our local temple, and even our human body, a small-scale replica of the great cosmos. This means that the regions of the temple and of the human body correspond to the regions of the cosmos. And the forces of the cosmos are also present within the temple and the human body, or they can be called down to inhabit them.

The path of the Daoist adept or priest is first of all a path of study and discipline, for it is necessary to memorize the spirit registers and the appropriate rituals for summoning the gods. Typically a priest would pass this knowledge and expertise on to one of his sons—the rule being one priest in each generation of the family. So through a long discipline of study and practice the Daoist priest becomes adept at the rituals, able to summon the great powers into this realm and into his own body to bring about renewal and transformation.

In ancient times the path included the practice of alchemy, creating a kind of gold-dust fluid to drink for the purpose of nourishing the inner forces and prolonging life. More important for Daoists today, the path includes various practices of bodily exercises and meditation designed to nourish the life-forces. It is believed that the most important elements in the body are the breath, the spermatic essence, and the spirit. These are present throughout the body but are especially concentrated in the three Cinnabar fields, namely, the head, the heart, and just below the navel. These three fields are also the special realms of the Three Pure Ones, the great stellar gods that inhabit the body. The processes of yin and yang are also at work in the body, for the yang soul came from Heaven and the yin soul from earth. As life goes on, yang gradually is used up and yin increases, leading to an imbalance. And finally breath, seminal essence, and spirit are dissipated in death.

The path followed by the Daoist adept is designed to reverse this process, to renew the heavenly yang forces and thus restore vitality to breath, seminal essence, and spirit. There are methods of inner contemplation in which the One Dao is meditated upon; and through a visualization technique the Three Pure Ones are summoned into the three fields of the body to bring renewal. There is also visualization of the gods who dwell in each point and each organ of the body, and visualization of the heavenly bodies and planets that also descend into the body. Further, there are breathing techniques, gymnastics, and dietetics to free the body of impurities, clear the channels of circulation throughout the body, and nourish the primordial breaths. One important practice is guiding the breath through the different fields of the body to nourish the vital forces.

Since it is only the Daoist priests who know the names and characteristics of each of these spiritual forces, together with the elaborate techniques for summoning them to provide renewal, this is a path of transformation that is followed by the priests and adepts, not by the common people, even though they also reap benefits from it.

But what about the average person? Does she have no path of transformation, no way to find the life that is whole and blessed with harmony? Of course, an important part of the religious path for the common people is relying on the priests and experts for their services, in the great festivals, critical life events such as marriages and funerals,

and times of sickness and other need. The priests and experts can restore the balance of sacred forces by exorcising the evil spirits and calling down the great gods to renew life force and restore harmony. In this respect religious Daoism resembles other religions, such as some forms of Christianity or Hinduism, in which there is reliance on the authority of ritual experts to effect the desired transformations. For example, only those with proper training and authority can say the Christian mass or chant the Hindu Vedas for the desired transformation. So, too, in religious Daoism, one part of the path for laypeople is to respect and rely on these ritualists and experts in the Dao.

But laypeople themselves have appropriate involvement on the path, for the sake of maintaining a balance of sacred forces in their personal lives, in family, and in community. These practices go beyond religious Daoism strictly speaking, including Buddhist and Confucian elements together with long-held local folk traditions. The popular religious path has many variables, but it centers around the cult of popular gods and goddesses, the ancestral cult, and personal spiritual cultivation.

Whereas the priests summon the great cosmic gods of the Prior Heavens that bring renewal and harmony to the universe, there are other powers in our world that have a lot do with health and happiness in our lives, and when we are out of balance with these powers we suffer in various ways. So people can go to the local temple and worship the gods who have demonstrated their power and importance. For example, Guan Yin, a Buddhist bodhisattva of great mercy, is to many people a compassionate mother, the giver of children, and a source of help in time of need. The Jade Emperor, a Daoist cosmic god, is also the supreme god to whom all the local gods report. The path of the laypeople means invoking and worshiping these gods and many more, so that the sacred balance may be maintained in their personal lives.

The theory of the ancestor cult is rooted in the conviction that the souls of the dead ancestors continue existence after death, and that the original family relationship remains in full force, with the ancestors possessing even more spiritual power than they had in life. The dead and the living are mutually dependent on each other, the living providing sacrifices and care for the graves, the ancestors providing blessings. To maintain harmony in this reciprocal relationship, people need carefully to fulfill the requirements for proper funerals and graves, offer continuing sacrifices to the ancestors, and observe the seasonal visits to clean and repair the graves. In all of these activities, the family and clan maintain and renew a sense of wholeness and cohesion, bound together in the love and remembrance of the ancestors.

Buddhist Paths of Transformation in China

The path followed by average Chinese people has been significantly influenced by Buddhism as by the other Chinese religions. We discussed (in Part I) the basic Buddhist path, but we need to take note of the important Chinese contributions to the shaping of the Mahayana path of transformation. We can focus on the two major schools, Pure Land and Chan.

Worship of Buddha Amitabha (Amita) was known from early times in India, but the main emphasis had been on the discipline of meditation, since the early Pure Land sutras talked of concentrating on Amita as a meditative discipline. But as some Chinese Buddhists adopted the idea that the world had now entered into the degenerate Age of the End of the Dharma, they began to seek new solutions that did not depend on the ability to practice the disciplines. Two major new ideas were introduced by the Chinese Pure Land masters to make this path more appealing and more usable by the common people. Amita's original vows were interpreted to mean that simply reciting the name of Amita with faith in one's heart is sufficient to attain rebirth in the Pure Land through Amita's power. And, based on the Mahayana emphasis that all living beings possess the Buddha-nature, the Chinese Pure Land masters taught that even those who have committed evil deeds and atrocities can be reborn in the Pure Land if they sincerely desire it. Here is a Chinese path of salvation open to everyone, and as a result Amita became very widely worshiped in China.

The path of transformation offered by the Chan school focuses almost exclusively on meditation, with many similarities to Theravada and early Buddhism in this regard. Becoming totally aware of the true nature of reality is what brings transformation. But meditation in the Chan school is based on Mahayana principles—that all reality is the universal Buddha-nature, that nirvana is not different from samsara, and that one's original nature is the Buddha-nature. Through meditation it is possible for anyone, learned or unlearned, to awaken to this true Buddha-nature. Scriptures and orthodox doctrines are not necessary, for the Chan masters held there was a special transmission of the truth outside doctrines, a direct transmission from mind to mind. The basic path was simply to strive constantly to have no notions but to see directly into one's nature.

Therefore the master–disciple relationship was crucial in the Chan path; in private interviews the master would teach and provoke the disciple, until finally, at a critical moment, the disciple would experience a spontaneous awakening to the Buddha-nature. Stories about these master–disciple encounters were later collected and became a characteristic part of Chan literature. A typical example is the story told about Lin-ji Yi-xuan (d. 867). Lin-ji went to talk with Master Huang-bo, asking him the real meaning of Bodhidharma coming from the West (a standard question in Chan interviews). Immediately Huang-bo struck him. Lin-ji came back to visit the master three times, but each time he received blows. Finally, on Huang-bo's advice, Lin-ji went to visit another master, Da-yu, who asked him what Huang-bo had taught him. Lin-ji answered, "When I asked him for the real meaning of Buddhism, he immediately struck me. Three times I put this question to him, and three times I received blows. I don't know where I was at fault." But Master Da-yu cried out, "Your master treated you entirely with motherly kindness, and yet you say you do not know your fault." Upon hearing this, Lin-ji was suddenly awakened and stated, "After all, there isn't much in Huang-bo's Buddhism!"[44]

It appears that Chan was influenced considerably by the Daoist path of meditation and cultivating freedom of living in the world. Chan emphasized that one need not try to escape from the change and flux of the world. The path itself is enlightenment and freedom. The Buddha-nature is universal and can be realized without any special searching, in the commonness of daily existence. Often-quoted words of Master Lin-ji Yi-xuan make this point in a dramatic way:

> Seekers of the Way. In Buddhism no effort is necessary. All one has to do is to do nothing, except to move his bowels, urinate, put on his clothing, eat his meals, and lie down if he is tired. The stupid will laugh at him, but the wise one will understand. . . .

Buddhist monks at a temple in Beijing in 1966.

Seekers of the Way, if you want to achieve the understanding according to the Law, don't be deceived by others and turn to [your thoughts] internally or [objects] externally. Kill anything that you happen on. Kill the Buddha if you happen to meet him. Kill a patriarch or an arhat if you happen to meet him. Kill your parents or relatives if you happen to meet them. Only then can you be free, not bound by material things, and absolutely free and at ease. . . . My views are few. I merely put on clothing and eat meals as usual, and pass my time without doing anything. You people coming from the various directions have all made up your minds to seek the Buddha, seek the Law, seek emancipation, and seek to leave the Three Worlds. Crazy people! If you want to leave the Three Worlds, where can you go? "Buddha" and "patriarchs" are terms of praise and also bondage. Do you want to know where the Three Worlds are? They are right in your mind which is now listening to the Law.[45]

The path in the Chan tradition is not a matter of striving to escape the samsara world and achieve nirvana. The path itself is enlightenment.

DISCUSSION QUESTIONS

1. Reflect on the nature of the Dao as the source of all existence.
2. What is the difference between the Daoist gods of the "Prior Heavens" and the gods of popular religion?
3. What are some basic implications about the world to be drawn from the Pan Gu myth?
4. How do yin and yang and the five elements operate as part of the world process?

5. What does it mean to say the human body is a "microcosm" of the great universe itself?
6. Review the discussion in the Confucian tradition about whether humans are basically inclined to good or evil. Which view becomes dominant?
7. What view does Daoism (the Dao De Jing and Zhuang-zi) put forth as to the nature and problem of human existence?

8. How can study be transformative? How can ritual and the practice of social propriety be transformative?
9. Explain the Daoist principle of nonaction (wu-wei). How can this be transformative?
10. Describe the path of transformation as taught in Pure Land and Chan Buddhism.

CHAPTER 13

Worship and the Good Life in China

RITUAL RENEWAL AND WORSHIP

How can we find new power for life, new meaning in our everyday existence? Ritual has always been very important in Chinese society—after all, one of the ancient texts is the Classic of Rites. Confucian thinkers have taught and written a lot about the proper practice of ritual and what it means. From time immemorial Chinese have ritualized all facets of family life and life within the state's political community, and there are frequent colorful and spectacular Daoist rituals and folk festivals. Since the religious traditions of China are so interwoven, it is not possible to draw sharp distinctions between the rituals of the different traditions in all cases. We look first at what are generally recognized as Confucian and as Daoist rituals, and then we consider the more general festivals and rituals of the life cycle. Although we speak of Chinese ritual and worship in the present tense, it should be remembered that this applies more directly to pre-Maoist China and to Chinese communities in Taiwan, Hong Kong, and overseas.

Worship and Ritual in the Confucian Tradition

Confucianists traditionally placed a strong emphasis on ceremony and ritual. The term "ritual" or "propriety" (*li*) as used by Confucius goes back to the ritual sacrifices offered to the ancestors. Confucian scholars thoroughly investigated the function of ritual to show how it serves to transform and renew life. In fact, as we saw, ritual is a cosmological principle.[1] Performance of ritual helps to uphold the whole universe, to stay in communion with the ancestors, and to harmonize human society.

Ritual in the Family and the Cult of the Ancestors

The Confucian emphasis on ritual is most apparent in aspects of family and community life that have to do with the principles of hierarchy and reciprocity. It is through ritual that the relationship is maintained between parent and child, between ancestor and descendant, between friend and friend. Perhaps the most important rituals are those that hold the family together in proper order, that is, the rituals expressing and cultivating filial piety. The idea of reciprocity, of mutual dependence of younger and elder, of living and dead, is basic to these ritual actions.

Each traditional home will have an altar on which the ancestral tablets are kept and also where images of the gods important to the family are worshiped. Incense is offered on the table before the altar daily, usually by a woman of the house. On important occasions, the central ritual actions in worshiping the ancestors and the gods include offerings of food, offering of spirit money, acts of reverence such as kowtowing (prostrating oneself), and prayers. Since the ancestors are kinspeople, they are offered food in much the same form as the family's guests. The table in front of the altar is set with rice bowls, chopsticks, spices

211

and condiments, and fully prepared dishes hot from the stove, including cooked rice. Food offerings are also made to the gods in the home, and on certain occasions meals are offered to the homeless spirits—but these are always placed outside the house. Paper spirit money is also sometimes offered at the altar, usually silver for ancestors and gold for the gods. Kowtowing before the ancestors and the gods is an essential act of reverence, and the number of kowtows depends on the status of the spirit being worshiped—a person may kowtow four times before ancestors, for example, only twice before the Stove God, and a hundred times before Lord Shang Di. Further, kowtowing is done in the proper order in the family hierarchy.

Here are some excerpts from a description of family worship during the ancestor festival of the seventh month, in a town in southwestern China in the early 1940s.

> The dishes offered on this occasion are all elaborately prepared and contain chicken, pork, fish, and vegetables. Each dish is topped with flower designs. If the household worships as one unit, all dishes, together with at least six bowls of rice, six cups of wine, and six pairs of chopsticks are laid on the offering table in advance. Members of the household then kowtow one after the other before the altar. . . .
>
> They kowtow before the altar, the elder before the younger, and men before women. The usual number of kowtows appears to be four, but often individual members perform this obeisance five, nine, or even more times. . . .
>
> When the offerings and homage at the family altar terminates, the same dishes are taken by a male member of the household (or branch of the household) to the clan temple. There the food is briefly offered at the main altar, and the male who delivers it kowtows a number of times. After this, the offering food is taken back to the house, and all members of the household come together to feast on it. . . .
>
> After the meal the *shu pao* (burning the bags) ceremony begins. Each bag contains a quantity of [paper] silver ingots and bears the names of a male ancestor and his wife, of the descendants who are providing the bag for them, and the date on which this is burned, together with a brief plea entreating the ancestors to accept it. . . .
>
> A big container with some ashes and a bit of fire is placed in the middle of the courtyard just outside the west wing of the house. A young member of the household then kneels on a straw cushion beside the container, facing the west wing. The rest of the household may be sitting or

standing around him. All the bags are heaped beside the kneeler. He first picks up the bag for the most ancient lineal ancestor, reads slowly everything that is written on it, and then puts it on the fire. . . . After all bags are burned, the ashes are poured into a stream which finally carries them into the lake.[2]

Worship in the Community and the State

Beyond the family, the Confucian principle of ritual permeates community and government life. At the local level, officials, magistrates, and governors perform rituals for the harmony and happiness of the community. And at the highest levels, up until the twentieth century, the emperor and the supreme officials performed rituals directed to Heaven and earth and the royal ancestors, for the harmony and welfare of the whole people.

An example of worship in the state cult would be the emperor's sacrifice to Heaven at the winter solstice, during the longest night of the year. The emperor and his officials arose before dawn and climbed to the top of a great stone altar south of the city (the direction of yang). The ancestors and other gods were represented by inscribed tablets on the altar, and food was placed before them. A young red bull (a symbol of yang) was offered to Heaven, and wine, incense, and silk were presented together with music from bells and drums. It was important that all the ritual be done well on the emperor's part, so that Heaven and the ancestors would do their part and assist in the rebirth of yang and the coming of spring once again, for the benefit of all nature and society.

In traditional China, officials were assigned by the imperial government to have charge over a particular locality, and it was each official's job to worship the spiritual powers for the welfare of his territory. Important in the local capital was the Confucian temple, whose main hall contained the spirit-tablets of Confucius and other sages. Sacrifices were held here twice yearly, in midspring and midautumn, with the city magistrate as the chief celebrant and the senior officials in attendance. At dawn sacrifices were placed before the tablet of Confucius, including a roll of silk, chalices of wine, bowls of soup, other food dishes, an ox, a pig, and a sheep. The officials lined the sides of the courtyard below the hall, and six ranks of young students in traditional costume postured with long wands tipped with

The Altar of Heaven in Beijing.

pheasant feathers. Drums and an orchestra playing an ancient melody accompanied the ceremonies, as the celebrant made each offering, together with kowtows and hymns of praise. An observer marked that

> . . . it is in reality one of the most impressive rituals that has ever been devised. The silence of the dark hour, the magnificent sweep of the temple lines, with eaves curving up toward the stars, the aged trees standing in the courtyard, and the deep note of the bell, make the scene unforgettable to one who has seen it even in its decay. In the days of Kubilai the magnificence and solemnity of the sacrifice would have required the pen of a Coleridge to do it justice. The great drum boomed upon the night, the twisted torches of the attendants threw uncertain shadows across the lattice scrolls, and the silk embroideries on the robes of the officials gleamed from the darkness.
>
> The flutes sounded, and the chant rose and fell in strange, longdrawn quavers.
>
> "*Pai*," and the officials fell to their knees, bending forward till their heads touched the ground.

"*Hsin*," and they were erect again.

> Within the hall, the ox lay with his head toward the image of Confucius. The altar was ablaze with dancing lights, which were reflected from the gilded carving of the enormous canopy above. Figures moved slowly through the hall, the celebrant entered, and the vessels were presented toward a silent statue of the sage, the "Teacher of Ten Thousand Generations." The music was grave and dignified, and the sound of the harsh Mongolian violin was absent. The dancers struck their attitudes, moving their wands tipped with pheasant feathers in unison as the chant rose and fell.
>
> It would be hard to imagine a more solemn and beautiful ritual, or one set in more impressive surroundings. . . .[3]

At the local level, town officials go out on every new and full moon to worship and burn incense to Tu Di, the local earth god, and to pray for the welfare of the people, so that the reciprocal relationship will be maintained and harmony and prosperity will continue. One simple but typical prayer to the earth god reads:

> *Wei!* The efficacy of *shen* [the earth god] extends so far as to transform and sustain, to preserve and protect all [within these] city walls. *Shen* defends the nation and shelters the people, and all we officials rely upon him completely. Now, during the mid-spring (or, mid-autumn), we respectfully offer animals and sweet wine in this ordinary sacrifice. Deign to accept them.[4]

Worship in Religious Daoism and Popular Religion

Just as some aspects of worship and ritual are linked with Confucian ideas and principles, we can identify other kinds of rituals more specifically with religious Daoism. Of course, the line between religious Daoism and the more general popular religious rituals and festivals is indistinct and there is no particular need to separate them rigorously. Some of the rituals are performed specifically by priests or experts for their own transformation, but most of them are to help and benefit the people whom the priests serve. Reciprocity is also a principle of Daoist religious ritual, the mutual exchange of gifts and benefits between people and gods, the setting up of a reciprocating contract or relationship.

Summoning the Gods: Cosmic Renewal

Daoist priests are recognized primarily by the level of their command of the sacred powers. The people are also served by exorcists, those who are familiar with the local gods and can use rituals to bring their power to bear on evil spirits that cause sickness and ill fortune. Daoist priests (dao shi), in addition, are familiar with the great gods of the universe, knowing their names and their characteristics, able to summon them when needed. Daoist priests chant scriptures and use written formulas, ritual implements, and ritual dances to accomplish what is necessary for repulsing evil spirits and obtaining boons from the higher gods. In addition, the priest makes use of internal rituals such as meditation, visualization, and ritual breath control.

The rituals used by Daoist priests have a long history, going back to the methods for attaining immortality practiced by the Heavenly Master sect and other sects from the later Han era on. The rituals are based on the belief that the Daoist's body is a microcosm of the great cosmos, and that therefore the great gods of the stellar constellations can be summoned into the body to supply power of renewal. Today the main ritual that still contains the purely Daoist rituals is the Jiao (Chiao), the Rite of Cosmic Renewal, performed in Taiwan by Daoist priests to renew a particular community's covenant with the highest gods. Jiao are held at different intervals depending on the community, and they may last from one to as many as seven days, although three days is the most likely duration.

What makes the Jiao different from the many other popular rituals and festivals is that the powers addressed are not the gods of local popular religion but the Three Pure Ones, the threefold primal expression of the Dao. The Three Pure Ones receive only "pure" offerings (wine, tea, cakes, and fruit), in contrast to the meat sacrifices offered to the popular gods. And they are worshiped by the Daoist priests inside the temple, unseen by the people who carry on their own popular religious rituals outside in the community during this festival. Occasionally the two celebrations come together when the Daoist entourage emerges to perform some rituals for the people, but essentially what goes on inside the purified temple is something that can be done only by qualified Daoist priests: summoning the great gods and renewing the whole community through the primordial power of the Dao. The people's participation is in the form of contributions and support for the Daoist experts.

To prepare for the Jiao the temple is sealed except for one door, and the gods of the people are removed from their places of honor along the north wall and placed on the south, to prepare for the coming of the Three Pure Ones and the other Heavenly Worthies from the realm of pure yang. The temple area is set up as a model of the Prior Heavens, with scrolls representing the Three Pure Ones on the north wall and other important gods represented on the east and west wall. In the center is an altar at which the priests stand, with a brass bowl on the east side giving forth yang sounds when struck and a hollow wooden sphere on the west side to give forth yin sounds when struck. The chief priest stands in the center, while acolytes to the east and west chant the liturgy alternately, representing the alternation of yin and yang in the universe. The vestments worn by the priests are symbolic of the powers of the universe, including the flame-shaped golden pin on top of the chief priest's crown, showing that he is lighted from within by the eternal Dao.

The rituals performed by the priests are very elaborate and complicated. They include summoning all the spirits to attend and then the very dramatic ritual of purifying the sacred area, sealing it off so no forces of yin can enter. Perhaps some sense of the intense religious drama can be felt in Michael Saso's description of a Jiao in which he participated (as a Daoist priest):

> The chief Taoist and all present are then purified by the reciting of prayers that penetrate deeply into every part of the body. . . . Through the purificatory cleansing of the ritual, all three of the microcosmic sections of the body, with eight orders of spirits in each, corresponding to the three times eight or twenty-four cosmic realms, are filled with the *Tao*. . . .
>
> The Taoist then calls upon the orthodox spirits of the seven Pole Stars to come and fill the body; he asks specifically that the three Pole Stars of the Dipper's handle, which control man's destiny, come and fill the three realms of the body, upper, middle and lower, in order to give birth to, nourish, and protect the "Tao-life" conceived within. It is specifically into the Taoist's body that the spirits are called; and with the Taoist as mediator, they are infused into the bodies of all those present.

Next the Taoist performs a sacred dance called the "Steps of Yu," based upon the nine positions of the magic square called *Lo Shu*, dragging one foot behind the other, imitating the lame pace of *Yu* when he stopped the floods, . . . with the same efficacy that *Yu* the Great had when he paced around the nine provinces of the ancient empire, ordering nature and stopping natural calamity. . . .

Now the climax has been reached, as the Taoist begins to trace another heavenly dance step, that of the seven stars of the Great Dipper, in the center of the area. He summons the exorcising spirits of the north to close all entrance to the sacred area from spirits of malevolence, *Yin*, or death. Next, he summons all the heavenly spirits [and a long list of all the great sacred powers] to assemble now at once in the sacred area, right at the devil's door, and seal it forever.

Taking the great sword in his right hand, the Taoist then draws a circle on the floor, three revolutions from left to right, that is, clockwise, going toward the center. Then over this he draws another circle, this time from right to left, counter-clockwise. Over these two concentric circles he then draws seven horizontal lines, representing heaven, and seven vertical lines, representing earth. By thus sealing the Gate of Hell, that is, the northeast position, the primordial breath of earth and the seminal essence of wood can no longer flow away, but they with the *Tao* (spirit) can now be kept within, that is, in the Yellow Court of the center. Finally, he draws the character for demon, *"Kuei,"* in the center of the figure, and runs it through with the sword, spraying the purifying water on it from his mouth. The Gate of Demons is now sealed, with primordial breath, semen, and spirit kept within, and the evil influences of *Yin* locked without. The sacred *T'an* area having been purified, the members of the entourage are filled with the orthodox *Yang* spirits of the heavens, the five elements are now in their life-giving order bearing *"Yang,"* and the liturgy of the encounter with the spirits of the Prior Heavens may begin.[5]

The liturgy goes on with continuous reading of scriptures, offerings to the heavenly guests, and lighting of the new fire of yang. As physical rituals are performed by the assistants, the chief priest performs internal meditation, summoning the great gods of the universe, visualizing within himself the process of restoring the universe to the pristine vigor of yang. The high priest has special audiences with the Three Pure Ones to make them present, and finally he brings the Three together in the center to offer them a great banquet accompanied by a heavenly ritual dance. Then the petitions of the whole community are sent off to the assembled gods by burning the paper slips on which they were written. Finally, the priests go outside the front of the temple and present the petitions of the community to the Jade Emperor and the other gods who rule this changing world. The whole community has now been renewed through the powers of the heavenly world of pure yang.

In addition to these essential Daoist rituals, the Jiao contains many rituals promoting the welfare of the people. The presence of the ancestors is especially felt, for they have been invited to attend by the Daoist priests, and there is a great procession to float paper lanterns in the rivers, to summon the souls from the underworld. After the presentation of the petitions to the Jade Emperor outside the temple, a twenty-four-course banquet is laid out for the ancestors and the orphan spirits, and the Daoist priests come out to perform the ritual to release all souls from hell. The great celebration that follows is a fitting conclusion to the Rite of Cosmic Renewal; meantime, the Daoist priests alone in the temple send off the gods to the realms from which they came.

Rituals of Exorcism and Divination

Whereas the Jiao, held only occasionally, is the special time for the advanced Daoist priests to perform their highest role, much more common are the other rituals that the priests and exorcists perform for the service of the people in their everyday needs. The most important needs are illness, bad luck, and death, already experienced or anticipated. The Daoist priest, for example, will perform a brief ceremony for one in need, presenting a written memorial calling on the gods in charge, in exchange for offerings, to cause good fortune to come to the one named in the memorial. The memorial is read and then transmitted to the gods by burning. Mediums offer the service of communicating with the dead for various purposes, and both exorcists and priests perform rituals to deliver souls imprisoned in hell.

A most important occasion for Daoist ritual, of course, is a time of sickness. A Red-head Daoist priest on Taiwan, for example, in curing a child's sickness, first computes from the daily almanac the relative yin and yang influences for the child, depending on the date of birth, and then he determines the cause of illness (both natural and supernatural). The Daoist then summons the various gods at his command. On a piece of yellow paper he draws a talisman and signs it with a special seal. Lighting a candle, he recites an exorcistic mantra such as this:

> I command the source of all pains in the body—
> Muscle pains, headaches, eye sores, mouth sores
> Aching hands and aching feet
> [insert the particular ailment of the child]—
> With the use of this magic of mine,
> Here before this Taoist altar,
> May all demons be bound and captured,
> May they be chased back into Hell's depths.
> "Ch'iu-ch'iu Chieh-chieh"
> You are sent back to your source!
> Quickly, quickly, obey my command![6]

The priest casts the divination blocks, and once he receives a positive answer from the blocks the talisman is burned. Water with some of the ashes mixed in it is given to the child to drink, along with a prescription for medicines the priest thinks will cure the natural causes of the illness.

Some forms of exorcism pit the priest or exorcist against the power of the evil spirits causing the trouble. A major source of trouble is the soul of a person who has died violently or tragically and thus becomes a wandering spirit, and in such cases dramatic rituals of exorcism are needed. For example, a child drowned in a village pond in Taiwan and, since it happened while the image of the chief god of the village was away for a different village's festival, people thought an angry ghost had pulled the child in. But now the child's spirit would also become very harmful, having died so tragically. So the village leaders prepared an exorcism using divination chairs. These are small chairs each held by two bearers. Gods descend on these chairs and cause them to move about, sometimes violently, providing instructions on how to perform the exorcism by tracing out characters on a tabletop with one of the protruding arms. In this ritual, a local god became present on one chair and instructed the people to avoid speaking bad words to each other, since the death had caused disharmony in the village; furthermore, they should keep their children away from the fish pond. Then a second chair was possessed by the chief village god, who gave them instructions for the exorcism.

The two gods would go into the pond to drive out the "bad thing" (avoiding the word "water ghost," which should not be spoken), and the people should stay away so that it would not lodge in their bodies. The wielders of the chair were instructed to carry spirit money signed by one of the gods—who proceeded to cause the arm of the chair to dip in ink and make a blot on sheets of spirit money that had been laid out on the table. The anthropologist's report becomes vivid:

> The men stuffed these into their pockets and left in a great hurry for the fish-pond, following the two wildly swinging divination chairs, which fairly dragged their wielders along the road. Upon arrival at the pond the chairs ran madly about the perimeter of the pond, then hurled themselves and their bearers into the water, where they circled the pond several times more swinging up and down into and out of the water to drive out the bad thing. At the same time the onlookers shouted high-pitched shouts, hurled burning firecrackers over the pond, and threw handfuls of sesame seeds into the water. The shouting, the rain of sesame seeds, and the continual and ubiquitous explosions of firecrackers were all calculated to terrify the ghost, and added to this were the chairs of the gods ploughing through the water, hot on the trail of the startled ducks. When the gods climbed out at one bank, they would leap in wildly elsewhere and beat the water with renewed vigor.[7]

The key force for the exorcism is the command from the village god to the ghost—in this case conveyed rather dramatically to that ghost.

As seen in this example, rituals of divination are important in many Chinese ceremonies, for it is through divination that communication is established with the spirits, gods, and sacred forces. They can make their will known through a divination chair held by two bearers writing on a table, as we have just seen. Again, they can speak through a Y-shaped stick suspended above a shallow tray of sand, handled by a stick-wielder possessed by a particular god, scratching out characters that are "read" by a trained expert. Much of the revelation received from the gods comes through such spirit-writers.

There are other forms of divination based on reading the forces of yin and yang. The system contained in the Yi Jing (Classic of Changes) has been used continuously in China since ancient times. This system began as eight trigrams, consisting of all the possible combinations of three broken lines (yin) or unbroken lines (yang). This developed into sixty-four hexagrams by placing one trigram on another, working out all the possible combinations of six broken or unbroken lines. These patterns can be divined in various ways, such as by throwing coins to determine the yin or yang character of each line. The Yi Jing then is consulted, for it contains judgments and commentaries on each of the hexagrams, helping people understand how the universal forces are operating and how to stay in harmony with them.

Another example of rituals of divination is the practice of *feng-shui* (wind and water), which is the science of reading the interaction of the yin–yang forces at a particular place, to determine the best location and shape of a house or an ancestral grave. The geomancer (feng-shui expert) ritually determines where the yin and yang "breaths" are pulsating, finding the outlines of the azure dragon (yang) and the white tiger (yin) in the landscape and devising the best way to retain the breaths in maximum harmony and vitality. To accomplish this, trees are often planted behind the house to counteract evil exhalations and a freshwater pond placed in front.

But much worship and divination need not involve Daoist priests or experts. Anyone can go to the temples to visit the local gods, give offerings to them, and seek their help. After all, they are in their position as gods because they have shown that they can provide benefits to the people as they worship them. The whole community—people and gods—are bound up in a reciprocal relationship. The gods are housed in temples, their official residences, lesser gods first and then the principal god in the center. The temple doors are open at all times, and people can go in at any time to bring personal problems to the gods. The worshiper lights several sticks of incense and places them in the brazier on the altar. She bows before the altar to show respect, sometimes burning paper spirit money or offering different kinds of food. Then she consults the god about her personal problem or question, and for this she can use rituals of divination to see what the divine answer is so that she knows what course of action to take. One simple ritual is to throw

Worshipers at the Wong Tai Sin Temple in Kowloon lighting joss sticks; some are shaking bamboo containers to obtain a numbered stick by which their fortune can be told.

two divination blocks on the floor before the altar. The blocks are rounded on one side and flat on the other (like the halves of a banana that has been split lengthwise). A flat side down signifies yin in the ascendancy, and a rounded side down signifies yang in the ascendancy. So it is when one rounded side and one flat side are up together that yin and yang are in harmony—and that is an affirmative answer from the god. Another method of divination is to shake numbered sticks out of a vase, taking the first stick to fall out to the attendant, who matches the number with a slip of paper and interprets one's destiny for the occasion from what is written on the paper.

Buddhist Influences in Chinese Worship and Ritual

Buddhist rituals and worship in the home and at temples or monasteries, as described in Part I, have been a part of Chinese worship life for many, even those who also participate in Confucian and Daoist rituals. In popular religious practices, Buddhist rituals and prayers, for example, those dedicated to the great bodhisattva Guan Yin, mingle together with other non-Buddhist rituals. Some temples have room for Buddhas and bodhisattvas along with Confucian and Daoist deities, so rituals can be directed to whichever one or ones are appropriate for the current need. Among people more specifically committed to the Buddhist path, many have altars in their homes, near the shrine that holds the ancestral tablets, and they offer incense to the Buddha image and recite sutras. In addition to worship in families and in temples, some join lay societies that meet together regularly for worship, reciting favorite Buddhist scriptures or chanting Buddha Amita's name, sometimes six or seven hours a day.

Ritual and worship at Buddhist monasteries in traditional China developed some characteristic Chinese forms. The ritual of tonsure symbolizes the beginning of life as a novice monk. In the presence of other monks and novices, the master and the candidate prostrate themselves before the Buddha image and offer incense. Then the candidate hands a razor to the master, saying, "I, your disciple, today beg Your Reverence to be the Teacher who shaves my hair. . . . I wish to renounce lay life as your

dependent." After admonishing him about the meaning of shaving his head, the master cuts off his hair and the novice changes into a monk's gown.[8]

Full ordination in Chinese Buddhism involves elaborate rituals. According to the traditional pattern, after a training period of several weeks at the ordaining monastery, a first ordination is held in which the ordainees recite the Three Refuges and the Ten Precepts. After a night of penance, followed by ritual bathing, they process to a secluded ordination platform and accept the monastic vows collectively, then go up to the platform in groups of three to be examined and accepted as monks or nuns by the three ordination masters. A week later they recite the "Bodhisattva Vows," which impose a commitment to lead all sentient beings into nirvana before attaining it themselves. A special feature of Chinese Buddhist ordination is the ritual of burning "incense scars" into the scalp at the end of the ordination ceremonies. Cones of moxa are placed on wax on the novice's head and then lighted by a head monk. As the cones burn down into the scalp other monks or nuns hold the novice to help control the pain, and all chant prayers until the ordeal is over—and the new monk or nun is branded for life.

Buddhist rituals are most fully practiced in the monastic setting, and Homes Welch has provided a detailed description of the daily ritual routine in a Chan monastery.[9] The monks are awakened at 3:00 A.M. to wash and march to the great shrine hall to recite morning devotion to the accompaniment of a liturgical orchestra of monks sounding a handchime, wooden fish, bell-and-drum, cymbals, and hand-gong. The liturgy consists of scriptures, poems of praise to the Buddha, the Three Refuges, and reciting the Buddha's name. Then the monks recite Buddha Amitabha's name while processing in a serpentine course around the shrine hall and in the courtyard. At breakfast an acolyte takes seven grains of rice from a bowl in front of a Buddha image and places them out for the hungry ghosts, after which the monks eat in silence, meditating on the debt they owe to those who provided the food. After visiting the latrines, the monks join in circumambulation, a rapid walking or "running" while swinging their arms, meditating all the while.

At 7:00 A.M. they go to the meditation hall, sitting in exact order of rank. They sit erect in silence with crossed legs, while a meditation patrol observes carefully. If someone dozes, the patrol goes before him and strikes him with the incense board on the upper part of the back as a reminder. At 8:00 there begins another cycle of "running" and then sitting in meditation. At 9:00 they go to the refectory for some rice and then, back at their seats, are served tea, the first of three teas served to them during the day. There is a "noon meditation" period, followed by yet another meditation period, lasting until 2:00. Then comes another meal, after which the monks may go to the apartment of the abbot or an instructor for discussion about their progress. Around 3:00 comes the afternoon worship in the great shrine hall, the liturgy including the reading of the Pure Land sutra. For about two hours the monks have a rest period in the meditation hall, but then comes the longest and most important meditation period of the day, lasting an hour and a half. At 8:00 a meal is served to them in their seats, followed by "running," an exhortation by the abbot, and still another period of sitting in meditation, ending at 10:00 with lights out.

During special intensive training for seven weeks starting on the fifteenth of the tenth month, the daily regimen is much stricter, with monks leaving the meditation hall only for meals and once a week to bathe. Their running and sitting cycles add up to fifteen hours a day.

In addition to their monastic rituals, the monks are often called on to perform rituals of chanting scripture on various occasions for laypeople, especially for funerals and for anniversaries of deaths.

Sacred Times in the Chinese Traditions

Although much of the worship and ritual in China depends on the specific needs of the people, one major need is to have regular times for renewal of life—that is, seasonal festivals, special holy days, sacred times that occur periodically to revitalize life and the bonds with family, ancestors, and community.

Birthday Festivals of the Gods

One of the favorite days of communal celebration is the birthday festival of the god, whether this is one of the great gods traditionally worshiped throughout China or one of the local gods worshiped especially by the people of the local community. Widely celebrated with great excitement, for example, are the birthday festivals of the Jade Emperor (ninth day of the first lunar month); Lao-zi (fifteenth of the second month); Bodhisattva Guan Yin (nineteenth of the second month); Ma-zu, the goddess of seafarers and Consort of Heaven (twenty-third of the third month); the Buddha Shakyamuni (eighth day of the fourth month); Guan Gong, the warrior-protector (twenty-fourth of the sixth month); and Confucius (twenty-seventh of the eighth month). But each community also celebrates the birthday of its own local Tu Di, the earth god, and the other important gods of the village or community.

These divine birthday festivals have colorful processions in the city streets, packed with sightseers and worshipers. There are offerings of food, lighting of candles and incense, and burning of spirit money. The honored god is carried in a large sedan chair, with firecrackers to announce his or her coming and a band playing traditional music. Multitudes join in the parade, dressed in court clothes and carrying placards. People hail the god as she or he passes by, holding infants in arms to be blessed and protected. All such festivals include standard theatricals or operas to entertain the gods as well as their human audiences.

The festival of the Buddha's birthday, unlike the other birthday festivals, is completely Buddhist in orientation. A small image of the Buddha is placed in a basin of fragrant water with flower petals. Worshipers ladle dippers of water over the image in honor of the gods bathing the Buddha immediately after his birth.

New Year's Festival and Other Annual Festivals

The New Year, of course, has important symbolic meaning for all peoples as the renewing of time and of life that has run down in the course of the past year. In China the New Year's Festival has long been the most important and elaborate of all the festivals. The Chinese New Year, fixed according to the lunar calendar, comes in late January or early February, a time of renewal and celebration before the start of spring planting. Events begin ten days earlier with housecleaning and closing of business offices. About a week before New Year's eve, the God of the Cooking Stove, Zao Jun, is sent off to heaven to report to the Jade Emperor on the behavior of the family members for the past year. It is traditional to take his printed image from the wall and smear his mouth with syrup before sending him off by burning, so that he will only tell sweet things. He returns home on New Year's eve, when a new picture is pasted up over the stove, to be present for the main event of the New Year festival: the family feast on New Year's eve, when important rituals of family bonding are held.

On New Year's eve, the family members worship Heaven and earth, the tutelary gods of the home, and the family ancestors. At the conclusion of these rites, all family members who can possibly be there—but no outsiders—join in the family feast. Then, to show respect for the living elders, each family member comes forward in order of precedence to kowtow to the family head and his wife. Firecrackers are set off, and on New Year's day and several days afterward courtesy visits are made to relatives and friends. The season ends at the full moon (fifteenth day of the first month) with a celebration of light called the Lantern Festival.

Two other major annual festivals are the Dragon Boat and the Mid-Autumn Festivals. The Dragon Boat Festival ("double fifth," i.e., fifth day of the fifth lunar month), popular in south China, features dragon boat racing and

Worshipers and onlookers at a Buddhist temple in Hangzhou.

making triangular-shaped rice dumplings wrapped in bamboo leaves. These rituals are said to be connected with the story of a third-century B.C.E. poet and official who, when a corrupt king refused to accept his advice, committed suicide in a river. The rituals have to do with searching for his body and nourishing his spirit by throwing rice into the river. The festival also has to do with the summer solstice that occurs about this time, the high point of yang and the beginning of its displacement by yin. The Mid-Autumn Festival (fifteenth of the eighth lunar month), celebrating the autumn harvest as in many cultures, features enjoyment of the beauty of the harvest moon and round sweet pastries called "moon cakes."

Two other main festivals have to do primarily with honoring the ancestors: the Qing Ming (Ch'ing Ming, pure and bright) Festival on the third of the third lunar month (early April), and the Feast of Souls on the fifteenth of the seventh lunar month (late August). For the Qing Ming Festival, the people bathe in flowing streams to wash away the dirt and harmful forces that have accumulated during the winter, and they put out all old fires for three days before starting new fires by rubbing two sticks together—the rebirth of spring yang power. Most importantly, family members process out to spend the day at the ancestral graves, cleaning the tombs, offering food to the ancestors, and renewing family ties with a joyful, hearty picnic feast.

The Feast of Souls (Ullambana) was influenced by Buddhist ideas of souls in purgatory. The souls of the ancestors are worshiped on the fifteenth day, when family members give offerings and sometimes burn spirit money and other paper equipment for the comfort of the dead souls. But during the whole month it is believed the gates of purgatory stand open and the souls from purgatory—the hungry ghosts—wander about before being sent back to purgatory on the last day of the month. Out of compassion for their plight and in recognition that one's own ancestors might be suffering in purgatory, families set out offerings of food for them. During this festival many rituals are performed by Buddhist monks (and Daoist priests, to a lesser extent). In the great services in the middle of this month, the monks recite the Chinese Buddhist scripture which tells how the monk Mu-lian descended to the deepest hell to rescue his mother from her miseries there, and how this festival was instituted to save the ancestors, at least temporarily, from the tortures of purgatory. The ritual is called "ferrying across [to salvation] all [souls]," and the general population joins in the extensive ceremonies associated with this ritual of universal salvation.

Rituals of the Life Cycle in China

Since the family is the locale of meaning in an individual's life, the rituals connected with the important passages in a person's life—birth, puberty, marriage, and death—are, as in most cultures, closely connected with the family. And since the family is focused on the ancestors, these rituals are performed with close attention to the ancestors.

Not much attention is paid to individual birthdays in China—the real birthday for everyone is New Year's day when everyone is counted a year older—and so there are no particularly important religious rituals associated with birth. There are, of course, customs having to do with propitiating hungry ghosts that could cause harm during pregnancy and birth. And, naturally, offerings are made to the ancestors, the God of the Cooking Stove, all the gods in the family shrine, and the local patron god.

After years of education involving training both for livelihood and for carrying on the family traditions socially and ritually, young people enter into adulthood. Years ago there were special ceremonies of initiation, giving a new adult name and cap to a man in a "capping" ceremony, and providing a special hair-do and new clothes for a woman. In recent times the special coming-of-age ceremonies tend to be celebrated just before marriage.

As befits the strong emphasis on family and ancestors, the two most important celebrations in a lifetime are at marriage and death. A traditional Chinese marriage consists essentially in the ritual transfer of the bride from her own patrilineal group to that of her husband-to-be, accompanied by exchange of gifts and agreements between the two families. They will consult a diviner to make sure the horoscopes of the couple are compatible and to set an auspicious date for the wedding ceremony. Then they formalize the engagement with exchange of gifts and visits of the young man and woman to their future parents-in-law. Gifts from the bridegroom's family go toward the woman's dowry, especially to buy furniture and other items for the

new household. On the day of the wedding the woman's dowry is sent to the man's home in a procession through the streets. The groom's family hires a special red sedan chair to be sent to the bride's house to receive the bride, the groom himself riding in a blue sedan chair. This ritual leave-taking is full of the symbolism of separation, as shown in this description from Taiwan:

> The arrival of the groom and his party to claim the bride quickens the pace of activity. . . . The go-between then calls the couple to the family altar to bow first to the gods and then to the girl's father's ancestors. At this point the sedan chair . . . is carried into the living room, and parents and daughter begin to exchange the ritual formulas of farewell, wishing each other long life, wealth, happiness, and for the bride, many sons. By this time mother and daughter are weeping uncontrollably. . . . The chair is closed, and the bearers carry it out of the house. The house doors are quickly slammed behind the bride's chair to prevent the wealth of the family from following the bride. Her brother spits or throws water on the departing chair to indicate that just as spilt water cannot be returned to the container, so the bride cannot return to her natal home.[10]

When the sedan chair procession arrives at the groom's home, the couple bows before the gods of Heaven and earth, the God of the Cooking Stove, and the ancestors, indicating that the bride is now part of her husband's lineage. Then the couple pays respects by kowtowing before the groom's parents, uncles, aunts, older brothers and sisters-in-law, and any other senior relatives. A great many guests have been invited, and the feasting may go on for several days.

Death rituals represent the culmination of life—the safe passage to ancestral status, with the soul secure in the family grave (the yin soul) and in the tablet kept on the ancestral altar (the yang soul). These funeral rituals are the most serious and protracted of all traditional Chinese rituals, and they are described only in brief outline here. Chinese are well aware of death and begin to prepare a proper coffin and a grave long before, though the actual duty of making funeral arrangements falls on their sons. When a person is near death, he or she is moved into the main hall of the home, where the ancestral tablets are kept. When the person dies, the body is covered with a coverlet red on top and white (the color of death) on the bottom, and food offerings are placed at the feet. The family don mourning garments and wash the body; and they send out cards announcing the death to relatives and friends, who come to wail and mourn. A soul-tablet is made with the name of the deceased and set up by Daoist or Buddhist priests to receive the prayers of the mourners. The grave jacket (longevity jacket) is put on the body, the corpse's mouth may be filled with rice, and the deceased is placed in a coffin together with paper spirit money. The family is in no hurry to remove the body from the home; they may wait weeks or even months for the auspicious day chosen for taking the coffin out for the final funeral rites.

After the coffin is taken outside, sacrifice is offered to the deceased and the coffin is sealed. Then the funeral procession is organized with a banner, musicians, and many symbolic palanquins. Most important is the sedan chair for the soul-tablet, followed by Daoist or Buddhist priests and then the coffin itself, carried by four or more pallbearers. The oldest son walks behind the coffin, followed by the other sons and all the rest of the mourners. The mourning clothes typically are of sackcloth, with different colors and types showing different relationships to the deceased. At the grave the soul-tablet is placed on an altar and the coffin is lowered into the pit. The filial son kneels with the soul-tablet, and it is dotted with a brush dipped in vermilion ink, signifying that it is now the actual residence of the soul of the deceased. This soul-tablet is carried home by the eldest grandson, seated in the sedan chair; finally the tablet is placed in the main hall to join the other ancestors.

Mourning continues for quite some time, showing proper respect and ensuring that the deceased person's soul will be in a beneficial relationship to the family as an important ancestor. The intensity of mourning and the length are determined by how closely one is related to the deceased; traditionally there were five degrees of mourning. First-degree mourning is for the sons, daughters, and spouse of the dead person, lasting from two to three years, in which they eat simple food and wear coarse clothing. Others are to observe mourning in a lighter tone; for example, the great grandsons wear clothes of joyous colors showing that the lineage of the dead ancestor will continue on.

Ritual and Art in Chinese Religions

As in all cultures and religions, art forms have always been intricately bound up with religious expression in China. Since the goal of religion in China is the fullest harmony with the natural forces, art enters in to express and perhaps even to create that harmony. Further, since our human existence is a microcosm of the great cosmic processes, artistic endeavors can imitate those sacred processes on our human scale.

Each of the great religious traditions of China had significant influence in the development of the aesthetic perspective and interest of the Chinese people. For example, the Daoist sense of letting the innermost truth of the sacred process of nature express itself became a key principle of art. Confucianism, especially Neo-Confucianism, put emphasis on self-cultivation and self-transformation through the disciplines of study and ritual. From this view, the artistic pursuit itself can become a way of life that transforms oneself. And Chan Buddhists brought the experience of spontaneity, emptiness, and the universal Buddha-nature to add its distinctive flavor to the arts—they can become ways of enlightenment.

Many art forms developed in China under the direct influence of these three religious traditions. For example, sculptures and paintings of Daoist gods and immortals, as well as buddhas and bodhisattvas, were created in great numbers, so that they seem almost as numerous as worshipers in China's many temples. Stories told by Buddhist monks eventually gave rise to the full-length Chinese novel, the most famous of which is *Journey to the West*, a series of tales about a famous Chinese Buddhist monk's pilgrimage to India. Through the trials of this journey he and his companions (a monkey, a pig, and a water monster) eventually attain spiritual transformation and receive heavenly ranks in reward for the merit achieved on their difficult journey.

The ancient Chinese emphasis on ritual led to the full cultivation of the aesthetics of movement, dance, drama, chanting, clothing, and especially music. The ancient texts particularly extol the art of music—meaning music and dance together—as expressive of full human emotions. Xun-zi had this to say about the art of music:

This is the symbolism of music: the drum represents a vast pervasiveness; the bells represent fullness; the sounding stones represent restrained order; the mouth organs represent austere harmony; the flutes represent a spirited outburst; the ocarina and bamboo whistle represent breadth of tone; the zither represents gentleness; the lute represents grace; the songs represent purity and fulfillment; and the spirit of the dance joins with the Way of Heaven.

The drum is surely the lord of music, is it not? Hence, it resembles Heaven, while the bells resemble the earth, the sounding stones resemble water, the mouth organs and lutes resemble the sun, and the scrapers resemble the myriad beings of creation.[11]

The ideal music-dance performance evokes and expresses various human qualities as well as cosmic features. In fact, it helps assure the harmonious working of the whole universe.

Chinese poetry is known as far back as the *Shi Jing*, the Classic of Poetry, an anthology containing 305 poems dating from between 1100 and 600 B.C.E. The poems cover a great variety of subjects, but some are addressed to royal ancestral spirits, and many are concerned with Shang-di or Tian in relation to human experience. The tradition of songs and hymns dedicated to the various deities continued throughout the Zhou and Han eras. After the Han period, many poets tended to be syncretistic, drawing their inspiration and imagery from all of the religious traditions. The three greatest poets of the golden age of Chinese poetry, the Tang era (618–907), are said to represent, respectively, the three great religious traditions. Du Fu (712–770), the Sage of Poetry, wrote poems with a strong emphasis on Confucian ideals of morality and compassion. A favorite image for him was the phoenix, the bird of fire and a powerful yang symbol, appropriate for the Confucian perspective. Li Bo (701–762), the Immortal of Poetry, adopted a Daoist view of life, embracing naturalism—a favorite image is the moon reflected on the water at night. He fully indulged in the sensual pleasures of life, but his poems are full of Daoist mythology and a yearning for the realm of the immortals. Wang Wei (701–761), the Buddha of Poetry and also a renowned landscape painter, used some of his poems for direct Buddhist teaching. In other poems he conveys more subtly an overall Buddhist vision of human existence, a contemplation of nature with the sense both of tranquility and of sadness.

Architecture in China, as we already noted in discussing the technique of feng-shui, has been greatly influenced by ideas about the sacred cosmic forces, especially yin and yang, and the sense that the human space is a microcosm of the great cosmic order. Temples, often combining popular religion with Daoist, Confucianist, and Buddhist shrines and images, typically have their major halls built on a north–south (yin–yang) axis, with other halls on parallel north–south lines or on east–west lines. The whole compound is surrounded by an outer wall, and there is a high, decorated main gate (often a triple-gate) opening from the south, where creative yang influences come from. The main halls have their back to the north, the direction of baleful yin influences. As one progresses from the south into the compound, there usually are inner gates, and then comes the main hall in the central position—where the main god's throne and altar are set, facing south. There are halls of lesser importance to the sides and back of the main hall, balancing each other in a configuration of harmony, all reflecting cosmic order.

This same sacred temple space is illustrated in Beijing's famous Forbidden City, the capital of the Ming and Qing dynasties. First, the whole city of Beijing was built in a balanced concentric pattern, with outer walls enclosing the entire city, an inner square walled area marking the limits of the imperial city, and within that yet another very large inner walled area, the Forbidden City. The main gate of the Forbidden city, Tiananmen Gate, opens from the south, and all the main halls are on the north–south axis. The imperial throne halls are in the center, with the imperial palaces behind. This was not only the center of government but the ceremonial center of Chinese religion, with the emperor maintaining the harmony of the gods and sacred forces for the benefit of all the Chinese people.

Temples that are specifically Buddhist follow the same architectural patterns, with the particular Buddha image and attendants enshrined in the main hall in the posture of the Chinese emperor. These temple compounds typically include multistoried pavilions dedicated to individual Buddhas and bodhisattvas, sutra repositories, storage rooms for temple treasures, ceremonial gates, lecture halls, and residences for monks and nuns. Characteristic Buddhist architecture in China includes also the towering pagoda, a form imported from India. These pagodas loom over the lower Chinese buildings (the tallest pagoda in China is over 67 meters) to give a definite signal of the presence of Buddhism, with its foreign origins, in the midst of Chinese society.

A striking Chinese art form is monochrome ink landscape painting (plain black ink against a plain white background). Early Daoist painters strove to capture the authentic spontaneous forms of nature, and later Chan Buddhist painters brought the ink landscape painting to a peak of naturalness and simple harmony. One of the main principles of Chinese painting was called "Spirit Resonance and Life Movement," and painters interpreted this to mean being filled with the creative power of nature (Dao) so that it could be expressed in spontaneous brushstrokes that were not so much skills of the painter but movements of the Dao itself. A few comments Su Shi (1036–1101) made about Yu-ko (d. 1079) help us see the attitude:

> When Yu-k'o painted bamboos he was conscious only of the bamboos and not of himself as a man. Not only was he unconscious of his human form, but sick at heart he left his own body, and this was transformed into bamboos of inexhaustible freshness and purity. . . .
>
> In his earlier years Yu-k'o painted his bamboos whenever he found some pure white silk or good paper. He grasped the brush quickly, brushing and splashing with it freely. He simply could not help (doing) it. . . .
>
> Painters of to-day draw joint after joint and pile up leaf on leaf. How can that become a bamboo? When you are going to paint a bamboo, you must first realize the thing completely in your mind. Then grasp the brush, fix your attention, so that you see clearly what you wish to paint; start quickly, move the brush, follow straight what you see before you, as the buzzard swoops when the hare jumps out. If you hesitate one moment, it is gone. Yu-k'o taught me thus.[12]

To paint bamboo, one should first sit down and meditate, harmonize one's spirit with Dao, become a bamboo—then pick up the brush and let the bamboo paint itself!

This Daoist approach to painting was further shaped by Confucianists into a way of self-cultivation and by Chan Buddhists into a way of enlightenment. Chan painters in

Seven Pines, *by Dang-Ze-Hua from the Yuan period (1280–1368).*

particular influenced the Chinese theory of painting with Chan ideas of spontaneity and emptiness. The effortlessness and sudden insight of Chan meditation are reflected in the quick, spontaneous creation of a painting. And Chan painters sometimes made use of empty space more so than brushstrokes, reflecting their experience of the "emptiness" of reality. Reality is formless, and thus the function of what has form in the painting is to help one experience formlessness.

SOCIETY AND THE GOOD LIFE

How should we live? One who is Chinese belongs to a huge, multiethnic grouping of peoples speaking a variety of dialects, yet unified around Confucian traditions of the family and the nation. The good life consists in fitting into this society at appropriate places and observing the moral principles taught in the religious traditions.

The Structure of Chinese Society

Sometimes it is said that in the Asian religions, in contrast to the Abraham religions, the individual is not important, for only the group has value. That is, of course, not true. The individual is very important in China, so much so that rituals of individual life passages such as marriage and funerals are the focus of much attention. And personal, individual self-transformation is the goal of the path as set forth in Daoism, Neo-Confucianism, and the different schools of Chinese Buddhism. The value and the religious needs of the individual are surely not forgotten in China!

Yet the individual is seen in balance with the larger community in Chinese society. Individual worth and meaning are closely tied to roles within the social nexus of family, local community, and nation. What meaning would a person have if he cut himself off from these reservoirs of meaning to move out as an "individual" into some new world? The key to Chinese social tradition is that full personal worth and belonging comes with the cultivation of fellow-humanness—in family, in community, in nation.

Family-ism, the Heart of Chinese Society

In China, religious affiliation is not primarily a matter of belonging to a particular religion or a denomination (although there are such things in China, too), but it centers on the family or clan. We have already seen how the cult of the ancestors has formed the basis of Chinese society both historically and theoretically. In practical terms, the ongoing life of the ancestors and their continued influence comes in the arena of the family, as each family elder who dies becomes a *shen* and is enshrined in the spirit-tablet on the family altar. Within the family, the virtue of filial piety is all important, and it is this virtue that underlies all the different roles of the various individ-

uals within the family structure—the head of the family and his wife, the oldest son and his younger brothers, the daughters, the sons-in-law and daughters-in-law, the oldest grandson, the other grandchildren, the various uncles and aunts, and the rest. All have their proper roles in the family structure, and by fulfilling this role each individual realizes personal fulfillment.

The family structure is based on the patrilineal clan or lineage, those who share a common surname and a shared descent from common ancestors, usually supported in written proof in geneological records. Within this larger clan, the individual households revolve around a male of the older generation who was a part of the original household, one who "shared the stove" of the house. The family is multigenerational. And those who have died are present as ancestors, and those yet unborn are present in potential in the lives of the young people who cultivate their bodies and grow up to marry and produce offspring who will carry on the family and its life. The sons will keep the family surname and continue the family into the next generation. The daughters are brought up in order to be transferred into other lineages through marriage contracts.

The family thus is the primary focus of meaning and identity for all members. The worst imaginable tragedy is to be cut off from the family with its network of obligations and support; this would be to lose all meaning and purpose while living and to become a "hungry ghost" after death.

The National Family

The Confucian tradition built on the family structure with its central value of filial piety and, in fact, extended the basic structure to the larger community groupings, to the village or town, and especially to the nation. The family is the prototype of all these concentric circles of human relationships. A filial son will certainly also be a good citizen, and a ruler or superior who lives as a good parent will also be an ideal ruler. During the long successions of dynasties in China (from the third century B.C.E. up to the twentieth century), the state was conceived as a "national family," with the emperor fulfilling the role of "father" and the guiding principles being filial piety and paternal love. As the head of the national family, the emperor was concerned both with the welfare of the people and with the spiritual welfare of the national ancestors.

Along with this ideology of the national family, the Confucian state also developed a centralized bureaucracy based on the principles of ceremonials (*li*) and penalties. Under the emperor there was a large bureaucracy made up of Confucian scholars from the gentry, chosen on the basis of an examination in the Confucian classics.

Even though the national family was considered sacred, this is not completely a "chosen people" ideology. The emperor, called the "Son of Heaven," was thought to be given a mandate from Heaven to rule as long as he kept order and prosperity for his people. He therefore was held responsible both for mismanagement in government and also for natural disasters that befell the nation. If disasters occurred, it was believed that the mandate of Heaven was being taken away from the emperor.

There are other religious communities besides the family and the state, certainly. The village or town is an important social unit, with respected local leaders performing the important rituals on occasions of community festivals. The people of the community unite in support of the local temples, and often there are special gods whose duty it is to guard the community and bring prosperity to its people. Further, there are special voluntary religious groups, such as Buddhist monasteries or nunneries, lay Buddhist associations, and the various orders of Daoist priests.

Religious Leaders in China

Religious leaders correspond to the major social groupings in China. Perhaps most important of all is the head of the family, the one responsible for continuing close communion with the ancestors, governing the activities of the family, presiding over the important family rituals, and so forth. It is imperative that the head of the family have a wife to perform many of the important household rituals. And many duties fall to the oldest son, who in a special way is the representative of his grandfather and thus is very important for carrying on the worship of the ancestors and the family well-being.

In the traditional feudal hierarchy in China, those responsible for governing at the different levels also had corresponding roles of religious leadership. The village elders, the city administrators, and the province governors all had specific roles to play in the local and state cults. They were ranked in a hierarchy just as the gods are accorded different ranks. At the top, corresponding to Heaven and earth, is the emperor, the father of the nation and the only one empowered to perform the essential rituals that bring renewal and harmony to the whole land.

Among the other important religious leaders are the Confucian scholars, the literati, who attained their leadership by virtue of mastering the classics and passing state examinations, who also presided at important Confucian rituals, often connected with the state cult. Then there are the various types of ritual specialists, especially the Daoist priests, who go through long training in the secretive scriptures and rituals and receive an ordination rank depending on how extensive their command of the spirit world is. Today there is generally recognized a distinction between the monastic Daoist priest who pursues the Daoist disciplines for his own transformation, and the "fire-dwelling" priest, that is, one who has a family and serves as a ritualist for the community. In Taiwan today, those fire-dwelling priests who can perform the great festivals in the "orthodox" way are sometimes called Black-head priests (from their black headdresses), whereas the priests performing the more popular rituals and exorcisms are called Red-head priests. Finally, there are also Buddhist monks and nuns who pursue their own spiritual growth but who also have special spiritual powers that they can share for the benefit of the laypeople in chanting scriptures, saying prayers, and the like.

Women, as is clear from our discussion here, have always had subordinate roles in Chinese society, starting from the Confucian patriarchical image of the family, with excesses like footbinding to assure the marriageability of the family daughters. We need to point out, of course, how Chinese women did take a strong role in family life and how Daoism in particular places high value on the feminine side of human activity. There are some powerful divine models for women in the Chinese religious tradition, starting with the Queen Mother of the West, worshiped by Daoists as the source of immortality, the Queen of all Immortals. And there is Ma-zu, the fisherman's daughter who became a goddess after death and eventually was elevated to the rank of Consort of Heaven, rescuing those in need in all places and circumstances. Still another model is Guan Yin, the most widely worshiped deity in all of China, manifesting the great compassion of the bodhisattva, most appropriately depicted in feminine form.

There is the fascinating story of Empress Wu Ze-tian (625–705) of the Tang dynasty, the only woman to hold the title and absolute power of emperor. She skillfully used both Confucianism and Buddhism, even to the point of understanding herself as a bodhisattva in female form. Individual women have gained fame as Daoist masters and adepts, and a number of famous alchemists were women. Buddhist nuns were very influential in political and cultural affairs in China. Many nuns were widely known as great teachers who gave lectures on the Buddhist sutras to groups of nuns and large congregations of laypeople. Some wrote commentaries and treatises on Buddhist doctrines. They acted as spiritual guides to the emperor and other members of royal families. There are even instances of nuns who publicly debated famous monks—and defeated them. Women often provided strong leadership in the revolution in China and still do in the People's Republic today.

A type of religious leader that cuts across religious traditions in China is the "master," one who has reached a high level of spiritual achievement and who takes a small number of disciples. Unlike a teacher who simply passes information to students, the master imparts something of himself, his secret insights, and his special disciplines to the disciples. And he remains in that master–disciple relationship with them as long as they live. Great masters established "lineages" that continued for many generations as the conduit for transmitting advanced spiritual insights and practices. In modern times abbots of Buddhist monasteries, Chan masters, and Daoist chief priests still fulfill this important religious role of master.

The Confucian Vision of the Good Moral Life

How should we live? We saw earlier how Confucianism sees Heaven (Tian) as the ultimate moral authority by whose mandate all human decisions and actions are measured—not as an external law-giver and judge but as the cosmic law that is also inherent in our human nature. We also saw that Confucianists have generally considered human nature as basically good and positive, so that living according to our moral nature is possible. The famous opening passage of the Doctrine of the Mean sums it up succinctly:

That which is bestowed by Heaven is called man's nature; the fulfillment of this nature is called the Way; the cultivation of the Way is called culture. The Way is something that may not be departed from even for one instant. If it could be departed from, it would not be the Way.[13]

What does it mean to cultivate the Way in day-by-day situations? The place to start is by molding all one's actions to the principle of filial piety. Moving out from there, the same basic attitude of respect and reciprocity is extended to all others through acts of propriety (*li*) as the humanizing force in social relationships.

In spite of the practical bent of Confucian principles, they are not based simply on utilitarian motivations. It is true that the influential thinker Mo-zi, or at least his disciples, advocated a form of utilitarianism: "Any word or action that is beneficial to Heaven, spiritual beings, and the people is to be undertaken. Any word or action that is harmful to Heaven, spiritual beings, and the people is to be rejected."[14] And that kind of practical test of moral actions—whether they bring good and happiness to the people—is often used to evaluate a ruler's actions. But Confucius spoke strongly against doing a moral action simply because of the reward that would be received: "The gentleman understands what is right; the inferior man understands what is profitable" (Analects 4.16).[15]

The Good Life of Filial Piety

Confucius often described the ideal moral life as the life of humaneness (*ren*), that is, fully displaying one's innate human goodness in relationship to others. The very root of that humaneness, he taught, is in filial piety (Analects 1.2). The Chinese character used for filial piety (*xiao*) is very illuminating, made up of the graph for old person, supported by the graph for son placed underneath it. And that means, according to the Classic of Filiality,

In serving his parents the filial son is as reverent as possible to them while they are living. In taking care of them he does so with all possible joy; when they are sick he is extremely anxious about them; when he buries them he is stricken with grief; when he sacrifices to them he does so with the utmost solemnity. These five [duties] being discharged in full measure, then he has been able [truly] to serve his parents.[16]

Out of all crimes and wrongs, there is none worse than being unfilial—in traditional China such a crime, in fact, could be punished by death. To get some feeling of the kind of total devotion that filial piety calls for, here are some examples from a long list of instructions in the Classic of Rites. First of all, sons and sons' wives, on the first crowing of the cock, should proceed to where their parents are.

> On getting to where they are, with bated breath and gentle voice, they should ask if their clothes are (too) warm or (too) cold, whether they are ill or pained, or uncomfortable in any part; and if so, they should proceed reverently to stroke and scratch the place. They should in the same way, going before or following after, help and support their parents in quitting or entering (the apartment). In bringing in the basin for them to wash, the younger will carry the stand and the elder the water; they will beg to be allowed to pour out the water, and when the washing is concluded, they will hand the towel. They will ask whether they want anything, and then respectfully bring it. All this they will do with an appearance of pleasure to make their parents feel at ease.[17]

Among the primary obligations of filial piety is the duty to marry and have offspring, so that the ancestral sacrifices can be continued and the family line will not die out. But beyond the duty to honor and support parents, perform the sacrificial rites for the ancestors, and produce offspring to continue the family, filial piety is a moral virtue that permeates how one lives all of life. Meng-zi lists some of the things that are unfilial:

> There are five things which in common practice are considered unfilial. The first is laziness in the use of one's body without attending to the support and care of one's parents. The second is chess-playing and fondness for wine, without attending to the support and care of one's parents. The third is love of things and money and being exclusively attached to one's wife and children, without attending to the support and care of one's parents. The fourth is following the desires of one's ears and eyes, thus bringing his parents to disgrace. And the fifth is being fond of bravery, fighting, and quarreling, thus endangering one's parents.[18]

The last point is interesting: in what way do bravery and fighting endanger one's parents? Getting oneself killed or maimed is, in effect, to cut off filial service to one's parents. A dead son will not get married to produce offspring. Even to be maimed in some part of the body is to do dishonor to the parents who gave one's body in a state of wholeness. Therefore a pious son "avoids climbing to great heights, he avoids going near precipices, he avoids cursing or laughing incautiously; he avoids moving in the darkness; he avoids climbing up steep slopes; he fears to dishonour his parents!"[19] What a person does with his personal life is no private matter; reckless sports, brawling, even careless accidents are slaps at one's parents.

Filial piety thus forms the heart of practicing the good ethical life. And it extends beyond considerations of parents and family to the other areas of life. "Filiality begins with serving of our parents, continues with the serving of our prince, and is completed with the establishing of our own character."[20]

The Good Life of Propriety

But what about the rest of life besides considerations of parents and family? What are the basic ethical principles having to do with community, business, politics, and the rest? In a sense these principles are derived by extending the respectful, serving attitude of filial piety to embrace all other relationships. At the heart of his ethical system Confucius put the practice of rites (li), usually translated as "propriety" when it refers to social relationships. As we have seen, this word originally was used for the sacrificial rites offered to the ancestors. The Confucian tradition held that even Heaven and earth are upheld by li as a cosmological principle, and so it makes sense to pattern social relationships after this: one should always treat others with respectful reverence.

To get a feeling for what the traditional Chinese mean by respectful reverence, here is a description of how one should receive a guest.

> Whenever (a host has received and) is entering with a guest, at every door he should give place to him. When the guest arrives at the innermost door (or that leading to the feast-room) the host will ask to be allowed to enter first and arrange the mats. Having done this, he will come out to receive the guest, who will refuse firmly (to enter first). The host having made a low bow to him, they will enter (together). When they have entered the door, the host moves to the right, and the guest to the left, the former going to the steps on the east, and the latter to those on the west. If the guest be of the lower rank, he goes to the steps of the host

(as if to follow him up them). The host firmly declines this, and he returns to the other steps on the west. They then offer to each other the precedence in going up, but the host commences first, followed (immediately) by the other. They bring their feet together on every step, thus ascending by successive paces. He who ascends by the steps on the east should move his right foot first, and the other at the western steps his left foot.[21]

Such attention to ritual detail may seem extreme, also to modern Chinese, but the idea is that social relationships are nourished in proper balance and harmony through these rituals.

When asked exactly what were the essential ingredients of the principle of propriety or respectful reverence, Confucius stated that it all was based on reciprocity (*shu*) and loyalty (*zhong*) (Analects 4:15). In explaining these basic principles, the Analects give two versions of a golden rule:

> What I do not want others to do to me, I do not want to do to them. . . . A man of humanity, wishing to establish his own character, also establishes the character of others, and wishing to be prominent himself, also helps others to be prominent. (5:11; 6:28)[22]

The first statement is expressed negatively and the second positively, but both together show that propriety is really the expressing of mutual, reciprocal relationships of trust, loyalty, and respect, in which one is actively concerned for the well-being of the other.

Confucian thinkers have generally defined these reciprocal relationships in a hierarchical scheme, for there needs to be an orderly structure so that trust, loyalty, and respect can prevail, avoiding confusion and anarchy. And where there is structure, there is superior and inferior, older and younger. Such hierarchy does not mean arbitrary power, for the superior in each case must show the appropriate moral virtues. Of course, there are many types of human relationships, but Confucian thinkers since Meng-zi have talked about the five basic human relationships, that is, five fundamental patterns into which all social relationships fit so that the proper forms of propriety can be practiced. These five paradigmatic relationships are father–son, husband–wife, elder brother–younger brother, ruler–subject, and older friend–younger friend. In each of these relationships there is a particular quality of propriety

that is to be shown. The son is to show filial piety to the father, for example, and the wife should show obedience to the husband. The younger brother shows respect to the older brother, the subject shows loyalty to the ruler, and the younger friend should show deference to the older friend. But these are reciprocal relationships, so the appropriate virtues should also be shown from the superior party: the father should show kindness, the husband caringness, the older brother nobility, the ruler benevolence, and the older friend humaneness.

Within this structure the moral principles can be brought into daily life, for these reciprocal relationships provide the basic patterns for all social involvement. For example, the father–son relationship is the pattern for parents and children and also for ancestors and descendants. And the ruler–subject relationship is the pattern for all cases where one is in authority and the other is under that authority. And all of this, Confucius teaches, corresponds with the will of Heaven for living the good life in human society.

Live the Best Life at Your Place

Confucianism has a positive, life-affirming outlook. One should not withdraw from society in favor of some higher, purer spiritual pursuits. Political and economic involvement is necessary and good, and wealth and success do not corrupt the morally superior person. Physical needs and desires are not evil and should be fulfilled through the proper social means for food and provisions, clothing, and sexual relations with one's spouse. Always the guiding principle is the welfare of the family and the community.

The ethical philosophy expressed in the Doctrine of the Mean might be summed up as doing one's best according to one's place in life.

> The superior man does what is proper to his position and does not want to go beyond this. If he is in a noble station, he does what is proper to a position of wealth and honorable station. If he is in a humble station, he does what is proper to a position of poverty and humble station. If he is in the midst of barbarian tribes, he does what is proper in the midst of barbarian tribes. In a position of difficulty and danger, he does what is proper to a position of difficulty and danger. He can find himself in no situation in which he is not at ease with himself.[23]

Jade carving depicting sages of ancient China; they each taught their vision of the good life.

The Confucian ethical vision has a strong interest in the leaders and rulers of society, for these people set the tone for all the rest. An evil ruler will fail to promote the goodness of the people and will create anarchy and disaster, but a good leader will educate and nourish the moral nature of the people. One of Confucius' sayings hits this point directly:

> Lead the people with governmental measures and regulate them by law and punishment, and they will avoid wrongdoing but will have no sense of honor or shame. Lead them with virtue and regulate them by the rules of propriety (li), and they will have a sense of shame and, moreover, set themselves right   (ANALECTS 2.3).[24]

There were Legalists in ancient China who tried to rule the people with strict laws and punishment, based on the theory that people are evil by nature. But the Confucian tradition advocates the power of moral action as the key principle for social and political ethics.

The Daoist Perspective on the Good Life

The good life seen from a Daoist perspective has quite a different hue from that of Confucianists, though it is not as fully articulated. The thrust toward withdrawal, no-action, and meditation tends toward a more quietistic and carefree type of life, at least for those looking to philosophical Daoism. A fundamental principle of religious Daoism would be the need to maintain a balance in all activity; giving in unduly to the senses can lead to an exhausting of life powers and an unhealthy imbalance.

No-Action as a Basis for Living

Whereas the Confucian approach has definite principles of right and wrong, good and evil in human behavior, it is characteristic of the Daoist view to take a relative position on such issues, as we saw. To a duck, short legs are good, but to a crane, long legs are good. Making judgments about right or wrong is forcing something artificial on the natural process. Thus the fundamental Daoist approach to the good life would be to do everything in the natural way, freely and spontaneously, without artificiality or coercion. That is, no-action should be one's basic principle. This does not necessarily mean withdrawal to a life of reclusion and quietism, although some Daoists have done that. In family and in community, in work and in play, it means to always act spontaneously and naturally, not according to plans or schemes or strategies.

This approach to the good life works best, it is true, at the personal level, although even then it may strike others as bizarre or even immoral. The Seven Sages of the Bamboo Grove (ca. 210–263 C.E.) were notorious because they flaunted customary mores to live their lives freely and spontaneously. They dropped out of politics, lived impulsively, and had drinking parties in which they drank wine from a common bowl on the floor, sharing it even with pigs. One of them, Liu Ling, liked to go around naked in his house, scandalizing others when they came to visit.

But to them he replied, "The whole universe is my house and this room is my trousers. What are you doing here inside my trousers?"[25]

Of course, Daoism does not advocate simply giving in to every whim, but cultivating a style in which the natural events of life are not stifled through emotional judgments about good and bad but are simply accepted and lived for what they are. A good example of this approach to life is Zhuang-zi's behavior when his wife died. A friend came to offer condolences, but he found Zhuang-zi squatting on the ground and singing, beating on an earthen bowl instead of performing the mourning rites. The friend was scandalized and rebuked him: "To live with your wife, and see your eldest son grow up to be a man, and then not to shed a tear over her corpse—this would be bad enough. But to drum on a bowl and sing; surely this is going too far!" "Not at all," replied Zhuang-zi.

> When she died I could not help being affected by her death. Soon, however, I remembered that she had already existed in a previous state before birth, without form or even substance; that while in that unconditioned condition, substance was added to spirit; that this substance then assumed form; and that the next stage was birth. And now, by virtue of a further change, she is dead, passing from one phase to another like the sequence of spring, summer, autumn and winter. And while she is thus lying asleep in eternity, for me to go about weeping and wailing would be to proclaim myself ignorant of these natural laws. Therefore I refrain. (CH. 18)[26]

One should not let emotional judgments about good and bad stand in the way of living the natural life.

Of course, Daoism does provide certain guidance about ideals and virtues in life. Here is a description of the kinds of virtues the ancient Daoists held:

> Not to be encumbered with popular fashions, not to be dazzled by the display of things, not to be unfeeling toward other men, and not to be antagonistic to the multitude; to desire peace in the world for the preservation of the life of the people; to seek no more than is sufficient for nourishing oneself and others, thus setting one's heart at peace—these were some of the aspects of the system of the Tao among the ancients. . . . To be impartial and nonpartisan; to be compliant and selfless; to be free from insistence and prejudice;

> to take things as they come; to be without worry or care; not to rely on one's wits; to accept all and mingle with all—these were some of the aspects of the system of the Tao among the ancients. (ZHUANG ZI, CH. 33)[27]

Many of the virtues and ideals listed here have to do with relationships with others, even though the emphasis is on the individual's style of life. Like Confucianism, Daoism is also concerned with how leaders and rulers should live their lives for the benefit of their people. But, in contrast to the Confucian ideal of a ruler who leads with the rules of propriety, the Daoist notion of a good ruler is one who lets the people develop naturally. Already in the *Dao De Jing* is this statement about the good ruler:

> Govern the state with correctness.
> Operate the army with surprise tactics.
> Administer the empire by engaging in no activity.
> How do I know that this should be so?
> Through this:
>> The more taboos and prohibitions there are in the world,
>> The poorer the people will be.
>> The more sharp weapons the people have,
>> The more troubled the state will be.
>> The more cunning and skill man possesses,
>> The more vicious things will appear.
>> The more laws and orders are made prominent,
>> The more thieves and robbers there will be.
> Therefore the sage says,
>> I take no action and the people of themselves are transformed.
>> I love tranquility and the people of themselves become correct.
>> I engage in no activity and the people of themselves become prosperous.
>> I have no desires and the people of themselves become simple. (CH. 57)[28]

A leader who uses laws and punishments, weapons and force, even cunning and strategy will inevitably rule by force and coercion, thus doing injury to the natural flow of life. A leader who follows the Daoist vision will rule through no-action, that is, practicing the virtues of Daoism and thus allowing the people also to live freely and spontaneously.

It is true, of course, that most rulers in Chinese history have been Confucianists!

Religious Daoism: A Life of Balance

In that large realm of Chinese life that we have associated loosely with religious Daoism, the people, of course, follow moral principles derived both from Confucianism, especially with regard to the family, and from the philosophical Daoist texts. The scriptures of religious Daoism do put forth some principles for the good and wholesome life, arising from the Daoist view of the balance of sacred forces in the universe and in the body. Some of these principles have to do with the ancient notion that certain types of food nourish the yin processes of the body and should be avoided, and others come from the idea that certain types of actions use up the vital forces of the body and should be avoided. One Daoist text states, for example:

> When the five organs are ruled by the heart [mind] and are not perverse, then a regulated will overcomes, and does that which is not evil. When a regulated will overcomes and does not do evil, then seminal breath and spirit flourish, and life breath is not dissipated. When seminal breath and spirit flourish and life breath is not dissipated, then there is order. . . . When ear and eye are seduced by sensual pleasure of sound and color, then the five organs are shaken and unstable. When the five organs are shaken and unstable, then breath and blood [will] overflow and are wasted, never resting; when breath and blood overflow and are wasted, never resting, then seminal breath and spirit gallop forth unbridled and are not kept within.[29]

There is an ancient tradition in one form of religious Daoism that the inner gods will be beneficial for renewal only if the adept practices virtues and good works. So some Daoists did good deeds like repairing bridges, endowing orphanages, and caring for the poor and sick. Still today, in preparation for a Daoist festival, the people of the community will give attention to alleviating their wrongdoings and to doing good deeds, such as giving money to repair temples, giving alms to the poor and the crippled, and presenting offerings of food to the hungry ghosts who flock about on the last day of the festival. The underlying motivation is that of maintaining harmony and balance among the forces that affect the lives of all. When someone suffers, whether through poverty or as a hungry ghost, all the people are responsible in some way, and the baleful effects of that suffering are felt also in their lives. When people help those unfortunate ones, the benefits of that are also shared because of the enhanced harmony and peace that results.

Patterns and Paradigms for World Society

The religions of China, except for Buddhism, have traditionally been seen simply as Chinese religions, of benefit specifically for those varied peoples who came to call China their sacred land. In theory both Confucianism and Daoism are universal religions, that is, the basic principles apply to the whole world and even the whole universe, although the Chinese have not attempted to draw other peoples of the world into the Chinese religions. In modern times attempts to reform and better Chinese society have often included breaking the hold of the traditional religious system, especially of Confucianism. But there are modern thinkers who believe the traditional wisdom of China has some important things to contribute to the peace and welfare of the whole world.

Throughout the centuries, the Chinese religious traditions have held up the ideal of harmony and balance in the universe and in society. And the model structure for living that harmony is the family. The lineage, the community, even the state have been structured after the paradigm of the family. Within the paradigm of the family, the notion of reciprocal relationships is central; when conflict arises, when injustices become apparent, when needs change, the whole structure works toward reconciliation so that the harmony can be restored.

This model was extended to all of society in China, operating slowly to bring reforms and changes, all the while maintaining harmony and balance. The big question is whether it can continue to work today. The heavy blows against this Confucian-based ideal have been modernization and the Communist movement in China, both purporting to liberate the people from the shackles of tradition. The future of the traditional models of society is indeed clouded in China, although in Taiwan, Hong Kong, and overseas communities the pattern has remained more intact. But, at least according to some observers, the basic paradigm of family, reciprocity, and reconciliation to maintain harmony still plays a central role even in the People's Republic of China. Maoism has been described as a quasi-religion, patterned very much after

The Great Wall of China, symbol of the unification of China during the Qin dynasty (ca. 210 B.C.E.).

the Confucian tradition, with Mao taking the part of the sage-father, and the state (or the party) as the family. However the new China develops, it appears that the ideals of reconciliation and harmony will always play a key role.

With nearly a quarter of the world's population, China is a not-so-small world in itself, and with its own problems there has been little time to think of responsibility for the rest of the world. But since ancient times the theme of a "grand unity," not just of humanity but of the whole universe, has fascinated Chinese thinkers, and these visions can still excite imagination today and suggest an enduring world message of China's wisdom. Here are three passages based on the Confucian vision, one from the time of Confucius, one from the Song era, and one from the twentieth century, representing the Chinese vision of the great unity.

In this passage from the Classic of Rites, these words were purportedly spoken by Confucius:

> The practice of the Great Way [Dao], the illustrious men of the Three Dynasties—these I shall never know in person. And yet they inspire my ambition! When the Great Way

was practiced, the world was shared by all alike. The worthy and the able were promoted to office and men practiced good faith and lived in affection. Therefore they did not regard as parents only their own parents, or as sons only their own sons. The aged found a fitting close to their lives, the robust their proper employment; the young were provided with an upbringing and the widow and widower, the orphaned and the sick, with proper care. Men had their tasks and women their hearths. They hated to see goods lying about in waste, yet they did not hoard them for themselves; they disliked the thought that their energies were not fully used, yet they used them not for private ends. Therefore all evil plotting was prevented and thieves and rebels did not arise, so that people could leave their outer gates unbolted. This was the age of Grand Unity. [30]

Another passage famous in Chinese tradition is the Western Inscription by Zhang Zai (1020–1077), which he inscribed on a panel of his west window:

> Heaven is my father and Earth is my mother, and even such a small creature as I finds an intimate place in their midst. Therefore that which fills the universe I regard as my body

and that which directs the universe I consider as my nature. All people are my brothers and sisters, and all things are my companions. The great ruler [the emperor] is the eldest son of my parents, and the great ministers are his stewards. Respect the aged. . . . Show deep love toward the orphaned and the weak. . . . Even those who are tired, infirm, crippled, or sick; those who have no brothers or children, wives or husbands, are all my brothers who are in distress and have no one to turn to. . . . He who disobeys [the Principle of Nature] violates virtue. He who destroys humanity is a robber. . . . But he who puts his moral nature into practice and brings his physical existence into complete fulfillment can match [Heaven and Earth]. . . . In life I follow and serve [Heaven and Earth]. In death I will be at peace.[31]

Kang You-wei (1858–1927), making the following radical proposals based on Confucianism, was actually considered a Confucian reactionary because he advocated restoring Confucianism as the state religion.

Having been born in an age of disorder, and seeing with my own eyes the path of suffering in the world, I wish to find a way to save it. I have thought deeply and believe the only way is to practice the way of Great Unity and Great Peace. . . . The Way of Great Unity is perfect equality, perfect impartiality, perfect humanity, and good government in the highest degree. . . . My way of saving people from these sufferings consists in abolishing [the] nine spheres of distinction. First, do away with the distinction between states in order to unify the whole world. Second, do away with class distinctions so as to bring about equality of all people. Third, do away with racial distinction so there will be one universal race. Fourth, do away with the distinction between physical forms so as to guarantee the independence of both sexes. [So also he advocates doing away with all other distinctions, and with restrictive social institutions including marriage, nations, private property, and taxes!]. . . . In the Age of Great Peace, there are no emperors, kings, rulers, elders, official titles, or ranks. All people are equal, and do not consider position or rank as an honor either. Only wisdom and humanity are promoted and encouraged.[32]

In spite of its idea of a Great Unity, the Confucian vision has fallen on hard times in the modern secular, liberated, Marxist-oriented world of China. Daoism is also in deep trouble, because many religious Daoist practices are considered superstitious and thus anti-modern. But the message of Daoist philosophy has also been heard by many in the world today—through the many translations of the *Dao De Jing*, through overseas Chinese who still consult the Almanac and the Yi Jing, through people who are interested in arts like tai qi. This is hardly the kind of missionary outreach that is done in Christianity and Islam. It is rather people in the Western world discovering a vision of the world and a practice of harmony that fascinates and compels them—not to become Chinese, but to accept something of lasting value from that ancient wisdom.

DISCUSSION QUESTIONS

1. Describe the various rituals by which the family maintains relations with the ancestors.
2. What goes on in the Daoist Jiao festival? Describe both the actions of the Daoist priests and the community celebration outside the temple.
3. In an exorcism ritual, who are the main antagonists?
4. Outline the daily rituals in a Chan monastery.
5. Show how Chinese monochrome ink landscape painting was especially expressive of Daoist and Chan ideas.
6. What are the main aspects of filial piety?
7. What are the five basic patterns of reciprocal social relations, according to the Confucian tradition?
8. How does Zhuang-zi's behavior when his wife died illustrate Daoist perspectives?
9. What advice do Confucianism and Daoism have toward bettering government?

KEY TERMS IN CHINESE RELIGION

Note: Chinese terms are given in the pinyin spelling, with the Wade-Giles spelling in parentheses.

Analects compilation of the sayings of Confucius

Chan (Ch'an) school of meditation Buddhism in China, influential in the arts (Zen in Japan)

Confucius, Kong-zi (K'ung-fu Tzu) teacher whose philosophy of life become dominant in Chinese culture

Cultural Revolution the period from 1966 to 1976 in China during which fanatical Red Guards attempted to destroy all forms of "old" religion and culture

Dao (Tao) "way," Chinese term for the indefinable source of all reality; the way of nature

Daoist Canon vast secretive sacred writings produced in religious Daoism

dao shi (tao shih) Daoist priest

Dao De Jing (Tao Te Ching) "Classic of the Dao and Its Power"; earliest and very influential text of Daoism

divination various techniques of reading and interpreting the operation of the sacred forces of nature and of the ancestors

feng shui geomancy, the Chinese art of reading forces of yin and yang so as to determine the most beneficial location for graves and houses

filial piety, xiao (hsiao) primary Confucian virtue of respect toward parents and ancestors

Five Classics the heart of the Confucian scriptures, including the *Shu Jing* (Classic of History), the *Shi Jing* (Classic of Poetry), the *Yi Jing* (I Ching, Classic of Changes), the *Li Jing* (Classic of Rites), and the *Chun Qiu* (Spring and Autumn Annals)

Five Elements Chinese idea of five modes of energy in the universe that mutually influence each other: wood, fire, earth, metal, water

Guan Yin (Kuan Yin) Bodhisattva Avalokiteshvara, widely worshiped in China as a god/goddess of great mercy (Kannon in Japan)

gui (kuei) malevolent spirits in Chinese popular thought

Han Dynasty Period in China (from ca. 202 B.C.E. to 220 C.E.) during which Confucianism became the state ideology and cult, Buddhism made its entry, and religious Daoism developed

Hua-yan (Hua Yen) a Chinese school of Mahayana Buddhism based on the Garland Sutra

Jade Emperor supreme god in Chinese popular religion

Jiao (Chiao) important festival in religious Daoism, the Rite of Cosmic Renewal

Lao-zi (Lao Tzu) legendary author of the Dao De Jing and founder of Daoism

Legalists school of thought in China that emphasized the need for law and order

li rites, propriety; the Confucian code of ceremonial behavior

literati, ru (ju) learned Confucian scholars

Mandate of Heaven in Chinese religion, the expression of Tian's moral will, especially in granting prosperity to virtuous rulers and cutting short evil ones

Mao Ze-dong (Mao Tse-tung) leader (1893–1976) of the Communist movement and of the People's Republic of China

Matteo Ricci first Jesuit missionary to China (1552–1610)

Ma-zu (Ma Tsu) widely worshiped goddess of Chinese seafarers; known as the Queen of Heaven

Meng-zi (Meng Tzu; Mencius) leading thinker after Confucius, whose writings have shaped the Confucian tradition

Neo-Confucianism revival of Confucian thought in the eleventh century C.E., with emphasis on the underlying principle of all things

No Action, wu-wei basic Daoist principle of not doing anything contrary to the flow of nature

noble person, jun-zi ideal Confucian goal, a noble person defined by moral character

Pan Gu (P'an Ku) in Chinese tradition, mythic primordial person out of whom the whole universe developed

Principle, li neo-Confucian concept of the underlying source of all phenomena

Pure Land school of Buddhism focusing on worship of Amita Buddha, with hope of rebirth in the Pure Land paradise

Qing Ming (Ch'ing Ming) "clear and bright" festival; spring festival of visiting and renovating ancestral tombs in China

rectification of names Confucian program for the development of a moral society by properly structuring social relationships

Religious Daoism general term for the variety of Daoist practices related to priests, scriptures, and techniques for prolonging life

ren (jen) humaneness, an important ideal in Confucianism

Shang Di (Shang Ti) supreme god worshiped by the Shang rulers in ancient China

shen in Chinese religion, benevolent and honored spirits, including ancestors

Son of Heaven title of Chinese emperor

spirit writing in Chinese religion, writing on a tray of sand or on paper by a spirit who moves the pen

Tai-ping Rebellion (T'ai P'ing) abortive popular movement in the middle nineteenth century in China, based on religious ideas, attempting to change the hierarchical structure of society

Three Ages of the Dharma Buddhist teaching of increasing decline and degeneracy in humans' ability to follow the Buddhist path: the Age of the Perfect Dharma, the Age of the Counterfeit Dharma, and the Age of the End of the Dharma

Three Pure Ones designation for highest gods summoned by Daoist priests

Tian (T'ien) "heaven," from ancient times in China considered an ultimate power that rules especially through the moral order

Tien-tai (T'ien T'ai) a school of Mahayana Buddhism in China, based on the Lotus Sutra

Tu Di Kong (T'u Ti Kung) local earth god in Chinese religion

Ullambana Buddhist-oriented All Souls' festival

yin and yang Chinese idea of polarity of forces in the universe; yin is the passive, earthly force, and yang is the active, heavenly force

Xun-zi (Hsun Tsu) important Confucian thinker (ca. 300–238 B.C.E.) who advocated a realistic understanding of the human inclination toward evil

Yi Jing (I Ching) the Classic of Changes, an ancient Chinese divination manual based on sixty-four hexagrams (each of six unbroken and broken lines)

Zao Jun (Tsao Chun) God of the Cooking Stove in Chinese religion

Zhou Dynasty (Chou) long dynasty (ca. 1123–221 B.C.E.) during which the classics were compiled and Confucianism and Daoism developed

Zhu Xi (Chu Hsi) leading thinker of the Neo-Confucian movement (1130–1200 C.E.)

Zhuang-zi (Chuang Tzu) important early teacher of Daoism, whose writings have been very influential for the Daoist movement

Japan: Sacred Story and Historical Context

Who am I? To be Japanese is to find one's real identity in the story of Japan, that is, the religious and cultural heritage of the land and the people of Japan.

Japanese religious identity is complicated, made up of perhaps half a dozen important religious traditions from earlier times. Some of these traditions have developed institutional forms, but Japanese characteristically find no problem in sharing in a number of religious traditions simultaneously. The life story of a typical person can illustrate this. When the person was born, his parents took him to the family Shinto shrine to dedicate him to the kami (gods, sacred beings) traditionally worshiped by the family. He goes to the shrine on New Year's Day and other holidays, and he was married in a Shinto wedding ceremony. But the wedding date was determined in accordance with lucky and unlucky days according to the Daoist calendar. In his family relationships he strives to uphold the Confucian virtue of filial piety toward parents and relatives, and his associations in school and business build on the Confucian attitude of loyalty. He has studied Christian teachings and especially respects Christian morality, finding the Christian idea of love even for the poor and downtrodden a most commendable attitude for modern society. He likes the local festivals, legends, and other activities of his hometown, folk religious practices unique to his region and dating from who knows when. He turns to Buddhism as he remembers his parents and ancestors who have died. His intellectual commitment is to the Buddhist vision of life and the final goal of liberation and the peace of nirvana.

Shinto, Daoism, Confucianism, Christianity, folk religion, Buddhism—a Japanese person often is involved in the sacred stories of all of these. Since we discussed the major traditions like Confucianism and Buddhism in previous chapters, here we pay particular attention to the Shinto tradition of Japan. It should be kept in mind that "Shinto" (shen-dao, "way of spirits") is a word taken over from Chinese to designate the indigenous religious practices of Japan. It was not an organized religion but included both the traditions of the ruling family and the various practices throughout the different localities of Japan. Today the Association of Shinto Shrines is an organization that includes the main part of those who consider themselves Shinto, but generally various local folk practices and new religious movements are also included in this designation.

THE STORY OF THE JAPANESE PEOPLE

Although the early Japanese did not have any system of writing to record their sacred stories, they did pass them on orally generation by generation in the different clans and communities. In early Japan there was no organized religion, so the stories about the kami and the origins of the people varied from place to place. Many of these stories were never written down, whereas others were collected

237

and shaped into larger narratives that focused on the imperial clan and the important families and localities. These stories have provided the origins of a general national story for many generations of Japanese. The sacred stories about the kami go back to the Time of the Beginnings and tell of the creation of the world, moving without a break into the origins of the land of Japan and the sacred people.

The Prehistoric Heritage of Japan

To provide some orientation, it is helpful to set the stories of the kami and the people into historical context. The very late development of writing in Japan means that essentially everything before the eighth century C.E. is in the prehistoric period. The first Japanese writings—the Kojiki (712) and the Nihon Shoki (720)—were written in Chinese characters under considerable influence from Chinese civilization and the political developments of the imperial rule in Japan.

Origins of the Japanese: Hunters and Rice Planters

The Japanese story goes far back into prehistoric times in Japan, to the Jomon period (ca. 4500–250 B.C.E.) when the early humans in this land lived by hunting and fishing. Since the Japanese islands are bounded on all sides by seas, a somewhat unified cultural sphere developed. Some people in the ancient period perhaps had matriarchal societies. They lived in pit dwellings and made pottery with a rope pattern. They placed flexed bodies decorated with red ochre in burials, indicating some hope of a passage to the afterlife. They had a special sense for the power of the sun, building many stone circles used apparently for rituals related to the sun. The kami associated with the sun, we know from the myths, is a dominant kami in the Japanese story. Other religious ideas are indicated by ritual objects similar to ones found in China, especially curved beads, swords, and mirrors—symbols of the emperor later on. They also made ritual use of phallic stones, clay masks, and fertility figurines. Whereas we do not know a lot about the religious vision of these stone-age ancestors of the Japanese, we can recognize some later Japanese ideas and practices having their origins in this dim past.

But new migrations of people came into Japan during the Yayoi period (ca. 250 B.C.E.–250 C.E.), and now an important new development becomes central: wet-rice cultivation. Later it is taken for granted that growing rice is the heart of the Japanese way of life, and many festivals and rituals have to do with planting and harvesting rice. Traditional Japanese religion, associated with the cultivation of rice, is concerned with fertility, growth, birth, and renewal. In the communal religion of the Yayoi peoples, we can discern the origins of the Japanese way of life. Probably the Japanese language was developing in this period, and the artistic expressions of the people show many of the aesthetic characteristics of later Japanese art. These people are Japanese.

Some of the descriptions in the records of Chinese dynasties are illuminating about the people in this formative period. We are told that men tattooed their faces and decorated their bodies with designs, and women wore their hair in loops. They enjoyed liquor and practiced a form of divination to tell whether fortune will be good or bad. Whenever they went on a sea voyage, they would select a man who did not comb his hair, rid himself of fleas, or wash his clothes, also abstaining from meat and lying with women. This man behaved as a "mourner," and he would be rewarded if the voyage met good fortune or killed if ill fortune occurred. Earlier these people of "Yamatai" had been ruled by a man, but after much warfare they accepted as their ruler a woman, Pimiko, who remained unmarried and practiced magic. When she died a great mound was raised in her honor, and over a hundred attendants followed her to the grave, according to the Chinese account.

Such glimpses into ancient Japanese society show that communication with the kami through divination and reliance on shamans and shamanesses were part of Japanese religion from very ancient times.

Clans, Shamans, and the Imperial Rule

The formation of Japanese society and religion was completed in the Kofun (tomb mount) period (ca. 250–550 C.E.), characterized by the large mounds that served as tombs for rulers and their attendants. Possibly there were new migrations of peoples from the continent and from the southern islands of the Pacific Ocean during this era, and the people

A figurine from the late Jomon period.

constituted many large families and clans. Before long one clan attained dominance over the others, and this became the imperial clan. The head of this clan was the ruler, the emperor—and gradually traditional Japanese society made up of emperor and people took shape. The head of each clan served as priest of the kami of the clan, and the emperor, as head of the whole people, was recognized as high priest of the kami for the sake of all the people.

As the imperial clan established its rule, a new cultural impetus developed. The emperors built huge mound-tombs for their burials, and the art produced for these tombs is strikingly Japanese in character. Of particular significance are the *dogu*, clay representations of animals and people, which were placed in the tombs to accompany the deceased ruler. Archaeological evidence makes it clear that by the end of the prehistoric period the imperial family was firmly in place in this area of Japan, ruling over a people whose religion and culture is the fountainhead of Japan as we know it from the historical period. The mythology recorded in the Kojiki and the Nihon Shoki seems to reflect the religious ideas and practices of this formative period, at least from the point of view of the imperial clan.

Sacred Nation: The Story of the Kami

The Japanese sense of identity as a people in this sacred land was influenced by traditions of interaction with the kami of the land—the kami of the mountains, the rivers, the rice fields and the rest of nature, together with the kami of ancestors and families. The story has many local variants, but an important part is told in the Kojiki and Nihon Shoki in the mythologies about the kami who created the world and the land. The story includes the origin of the imperial family and of all Japanese from the kami. It tells how sacred government spread over the land and how many festivals and rituals originated. The myths establish the basic Japanese way of looking at nature, the land, the kami, and the people.

Izanagi and Izanami: Creating the Land and Culture

Among the kami generated on the Plain of High Heaven in the beginning time, Izanagi and Izanami are most important because they are the ones whose creative power brings forth the land and Japanese civilization. The myths tell how Izanagi and Izanami, descending to the Floating Bridge of Heaven, stir up the brine below and thus create an island to which they then descend to give birth to the various kami of the world. The whole world is interpenetrated with kami power—the myths talk of eight hundred myriads of kami on the Plain of High Heaven, to say nothing of the kami of earth.

Why do Japanese have so much concern for purity? Why do they venerate the sun kami as special among all the kami? Why do they celebrate festivals at shrines with prayers, music, dancing, and the like? These are age-old traditions that provide a special identity, and they have models in the sacred story.

When Izanami died (after giving birth to the kami of fire) she went to the underworld. Izanagi descended there to try and bring her back, in his impetuousity breaking in to see her in her state polluted by death, which made her rather angry so that she pursued him. Escaping from her, now Izanagi needed to purify himself from the pollutions of the underworld, so he washed in a river, purifying and exorcising the evil from himself. Thus was established the model for purification rituals.

Finally when Izanagi washed his left eye, Amaterasu (Heaven Illuminating Kami, that is, Sun Kami) was born, and from washing his right eye and his nose, Tsukiyomi (Moon Kami) and Susanoo (Valiant Raging Male Kami) were born. Izanagi rejoiced at these kami of the sun, moon, and storm, and he gave his necklace to Amaterasu and entrusted her with this mission: "You shall rule the Plain of High Heaven." To Tsukiyomi he gave the mission of ruling the night, and to Susanoo the rule of the seas. Thus it is that Amaterasu, the sun kami, born in this sacred land, became the ruler of all the heavenly kami.

The narrative goes on to tell of the conflict that developed between Amaterasu and Susanoo, her boisterous storm kami brother. Amaterasu withdrew to the rock cave of heaven, so that now constant night began to reign on the Plain of High Heaven and in the Central Land of Reed Plains, with cries rising everywhere and all kinds of calamities occurring. So the eight hundred myriads of heavenly kami held a great festival. They set up a sasaki tree and hung strings of curved beads, a large mirror, and white and blue cloth in its branches. They presented offerings and intoned prayers. And Kami of Heavenly Headgear performed a shamanistic dance on a bucket, exposing her breasts and genitals and entertaining the kami so that the Plain of High Heaven shook with kami laughter. Intrigued by the raucous festival, Amaterasu was enticed out of the cave, and the Plain of High Heaven and the Central Land of Reed Plains were illuminated once more. Following this model, Japanese perform festivals of entertaining the kami at the shrines, so that the blessing of kami power will continue.

The Divine Descent of the Imperial Family

In the beginning times, the story says, the kami of the earth were unruly, so from time to time heavenly kami were sent down to pacify and subdue them. Finally the Central Land of Reed Plains was subdued, and Amaterasu decided to send down her descendants to rule the land. To her grandson Ninigi she gave the commission: "The Land of the Plentiful Reed Plains and the Fresh Rice-Ears has been entrusted to you to rule. In accordance with the command, descend from the heavens." Then Amaterasu gave Ninigi the three symbols of divine rule: the myriad curved beads, the mirror, and the sacred sword, saying, "You have this mirror as my spirit; worship it just as you would worship in my very presence" (Kojiki chs. 38–39). Then came the great descent: Ninigi pushed through the myriad layers of the trailing clouds of heaven until he stood on an island by the Heavenly Floating Bridge. Then he descended from the heavens to the peak of Mount Takachiho to inaugurate kami rule on earth. Emperor Jimmu, the legendary first emperor, was the great-grandson of Ninigi.

According to the traditional way of thinking, all emperors of Japan are direct descendants from this line, descendants of the great kami Amaterasu, and thus they are fit to rule the land and people. Other myths say the Japanese people are also descended from the kami. Many people today, of course, do not understand these myths in a literal, factual way. But the myths do say something important about land, people, and emperor: all are bound together in the sacredness of Japan.

People and Kami in Communion

In early times, as the story tells it, life centered on family, clan, hunting, planting and harvesting rice, the people responding to the goodness of the kami in the rhythm of the seasons, the beauty of mountains and forests, and the fertility of the land. The head of the family or clan acted as a priest for the kami of the clan, worshiping and honoring the kami at a shrine on a hill or in a forest. The shrine probably had no building, at least in early times, but a rope boundary was stretched around the sacred space and the kami was called down to be present there to receive gifts of prayer and food and to give blessings to the people. The chieftain of a large clan would sometimes set up a special pure house near the shrine and appoint a female relative to be priestess for the kami, communicating with the kami through shamanistic trances and providing information for the chieftain.

The story tells how the emperor, chieftain of the ruling clan, at first worshiped Amaterasu, his kami ancestor,

Worshipers ascending to the ancient Inner Shrine at Ise, where Amaterasu is enshrined.

right in the imperial palace. But Sujin, the tenth legendary emperor, was not at ease living with such awesome power in the palace, so he established a special shrine for Amaterasu to reside in and appointed Princess Toyosukiiri to act as high priestess. Later, at the time of the next emperor, the sun kami revealed this wish: "The province of Ise, whose divine winds blow, is washed by successive waves from the Eternal Land. It is a secluded and beautiful place, and I wish to dwell here."[1] So the shrine for Amaterasu was built at Ise, the most important shrine in all of Japan for the worship of the sum kami, the divine ancestress of the emperor.

All of Japan was dotted with shrines for worshiping the kami, both the kami of the various clans and also many other kami of various localities, of mountains, trees, waterfalls, rice fields, and the like. Each community had seasonal festivals at these shrines, during which the kami came to provide their powerful presence for the people and grant blessings so the rice crops would grow and the people would be healthy and prosperous. When calamities struck, great purification ceremonies would be conducted to rid the community of the pollution and restore purity for the continued blessing that comes through the kami.

The Coming of Buddhism and Chinese Culture

In the sixth century C.E., this early Shinto world was penetrated by a very different religion and culture, a way of looking at existence that seems nearly contrary to the early Shinto vision. Buddhism, with its view of the passing nature of this world and the goal of nirvana, made its appearance in Japan, together with Chinese culture such as Confucianism, Daoism, scriptures, art, and writing. Now the story of Japan was transformed and drastically redirected—yet that story goes on, as the Japanese absorbed Buddhism and the other aspects of Chinese culture while continuing the main lines of their traditional society.

Sacred Buddha Image and Scriptures

In 552 C.E., according to the Nihon Shoki, a provincial king in Korea sent gifts to Emperor Kimmei, and among these gifts were a Buddha image and Buddhist scriptures. Of course, something was known about Buddhism before this, since Korean immigrants had recently come to Japan. But now for the first time the Japanese emperor, father of the people and high priest of the kami, was confronted directly with the claims for the superior power of this new teaching of the foreign Buddha. Along with the gifts the Korean king sent this message:

> This [Buddhist] Law is superior to all other teachings. It is difficult to understand and to comprehend, and even the wise Duke of Chou and Confucius had no knowledge of it. However, this Law will bring about boundless rewards and blessings, and enable men to attain supreme enlightenment. To have this wonderful Law is like having a treasure which would bring about everything one asks for according to his wish, because everything one asks the Buddha in prayer will be fulfilled without fail. Therefore, from India in the distant west to Korea in the east everyone upon receiving the Law pays utmost respect to it.[2]

Now the Japanese leaders were in a dilemma—they who had always looked to Amaterasu and the kami as the divine forces who bring all good and blessing in the world. They had never seen this mysterious kami in seated position with eyes closed, so contrary to the Japanese tradition of not making images or statues of the kami. And they had never used any form of writing, so they could not understand these mysterious scriptures.

Emperor Kimmei was overjoyed at this gift, but he was undecided about what he should do, so he consulted his three trusted ministers, saying, "We have never seen such a dignified face as that of the Buddha which has been presented to us. Should we worship [the Buddha]?" Soga no Iname felt the superiority of the Chinese culture should determine the answer: "How can [Japan] refuse to worship the Buddha, since all the nations in the west without exception are devoted to Him?"[3] But the other two ministers were from the Mononobe and the Nakatomi families, both hereditary priesthood families, and they saw a potential risk. Since it has always been the custom of the emperors to worship the Japanese kami, they argued, should a foreign kami be worshiped instead, it might incur the wrath of the kami of our nation. In this dilemma, Emperor Kimmei compromised, giving the Buddha image to Minister Soga to worship privately as an experiment. Soga was overjoyed; he enshrined the Buddha image in his house and began to follow Buddhist disciplines and practices in worshiping the Buddha. This was a momentous step—a court minister worshiping the foreign kami, the Buddha. Shortly after this a pestilence prevailed in the land, and the Mononobe and Nakatomi ministers petitioned the emperor, saying that this pestilence broke out because their advice had not been followed; now happiness could only be secured by throwing the Buddha image away. So the emperor ordered the Buddha image to be thrown into a canal—whereupon a sudden fire swept away the great hall of the imperial palace! Thus the dilemma of how to respond to the power of the Buddha continued to rage in the land of the kami.

But the attraction of the new religion was not to be denied, even as the question of its relation to the traditional way of Japan was unresolved. The next year people reported hearing Buddhist chants coming like thunder from the sea, together with a great light from the west.

Investigating this, they found a piece of shining camphor wood floating on the water, and the emperor ordered an artist to make images of the Buddha from this wood. In the following years more Buddhist images and scriptures came from Korea, and also Buddhist monks and nuns who could teach the Buddhist disciplines, meditation, making of images, and building of Buddhist temples. The Soga family continued its dedication to Buddhism. Soga no Umako, son of Soga no Iname, worked tirelessly for the acceptance of Buddhism and for Japanese to study the Buddhist scriptures and disciplines. Gradually the teaching of this "foreign kami" attained a foothold among the leading families of Japan.

Transformation of Japan Through Buddhism and Chinese Culture

One of the most brilliant rulers in Japanese history, Prince Shotoku (573–621), who administered the nation as prince regent, was a key figure in the Buddhist transformation of Japan. Shotoku continued the traditional worship of the kami, issuing an edict saying that all ministers should pay homage to the kami of heaven and earth from the bottom of their hearts. But Shotoku also studied Buddhism and Confucianism and attained deep understanding of both. In 604 he issued the famous Seventeen Article Constitution, in which he advocated the Confucian virtues of harmony, propriety, and loyalty to the emperor. But most importantly, he stated in this constitution: "You should sincerely venerate the Three Treasures, namely, the Buddha, Buddha's Law, and the Buddhist Order, which are the final refuge of [all creatures] and have indeed been venerated by everyone at every age."[4] Prince Shotoku was strongly committed to the Buddhist teachings and even gave lectures on the Buddhist sutras. For this he has won veneration in the sacred story as the founder of Buddhism in Japan. Through Prince Shotoku the transformation was realized that set Japanese culture firmly on three foundations: the kami way, Buddhism, and Confucianism. The relationship among these foundations has been debated through the centuries and still today. But Japanese life and culture are shaped by these traditions.

As Japan moved into the Nara period (710–784), with the capital no longer shifting about with each new emperor but now set permanently at Nara, Buddhism and

Chinese culture became ever more an integral part of the Japanese story. The city of Nara was laid out in the style of the current Chinese capital city, for example. And the structure of government with bureaucracies and systems of ranks was modeled after the Chinese pattern.

The Confucian influence from China was perhaps not as direct as that of Buddhism but still it was pervasive, in its emphasis on social harmony through a system of hier- archical relationships in which the subordinate one is loyal and benevolent. The Japanese sense of family was reinforced with the Confucian notion of filial piety. And Confucianism supported the traditional respect for the emperor as the head of the leading family by its notion of loyalty of subjects to rulers. One difference retained in Japan was that the emperor, equated with Heaven in the Chinese Confucian view, ruled not only according to mandate of Heaven but according to his descent from Amaterasu. Whereas Chinese emperors could be deposed if they lost the mandate of Heaven, the traditional Japa- nese story makes the imperial line permanent and eternal.

The influence of Daoism from China was subtle but extensive. Following the Chinese bureaucratic model, the Japanese government set up a Bureau of Divination, offi- cially incorporating Daoistic practices of divination for determining auspicious dates for government activities and interpreting good and bad omens. Gradually ideas and practices from religious Daoism merged with tradi- tional Japanese ideas of kami and nature and filtered into all the Japanese religious traditions.

The importation of Buddhism by means of monks and nuns, images and scriptures, masters and searchers, con- tinued strongly in the Nara period, when the first impor- tant Buddhist philosophical schools developed in Japan. Important for the story is the increasing acceptance of Buddhism first by the nobility and the imperial court, followed by a general turn to Buddhism also by the com- mon people of the land. Wandering shamans and charis- matic leaders adopted the new Buddhist vision and be- came evangelists for the new teaching. One shamanistic Buddhist priest, Gyogi, had no education or ordination but because of his zeal and ability to unify the people around Buddhism was made archbishop of Buddhist priests in Japan. In 752 Emperor Shomu decided to build a great Buddhist temple in Nara as the central temple for all Japan, and he enlisted Gyogi and others to raise money from the common people for erecting a colossal statue of Lochana, the Sun Buddha (Vairocana) there.

But what about the sun kami, Amaterasu? What did the imperial Ancestress feel about this foreign sun deity? The story says that the emperor sent Gyogi to inquire of Amaterasu at the Grand Shrine of Ise, and the august Ancestress communicated that the Sun Buddha Lochana was really a manifestation of the kami and could be wor- shiped as identical with the sun kami, Amaterasu. Since the protection provided by the Buddha was now consid- ered important, the emperor also set up temples in all the provinces where monks and nuns could live and pray for the welfare of the nation.

Thus the sacred history was transformed to include both Confucianist virtues and Buddhist worship. The Jap- anese story is based on relationship to the kami. But it is also the story of Confucius, and it is especially the story of the Buddha who came to the Japanese land.

The great statue of the Sun Buddha at Todaiji Temple in Nara.

HISTORICAL TRANSFORMATIONS OF THE JAPANESE WAY

After the formative periods in the prehistoric and Nara eras, the Japanese tradition has seen many historical transformations. These have resulted both from internal developments and from political and social changes, especially pressures on Japan from the outside.

Transformations Along the Way

The Japanese path, now accepting Buddhism and Chinese culture as part of the story, widened and deepened during the Heian (974–1185), Kamakura (1185–1333), and Muromachi (1333–1600) periods. One of the chief characteristics of Japanese history is the periodic influence that came from the Chinese mainland. Japanese people responded—usually scores of years later—to religious and cultural developments in China, and the shaping of the Japanese way was closely related to these influences. Some powerful religious personalities came forth during these times to provide dynamic leadership and founded Buddhist movements that transformed religious life in Japan.

Firming Up the Foundations: The Heian Period

When the capital city was moved to Heian (Kyoto) in 794, a classical period of refinement and deepened religious understanding commenced, under imperial courtly rule. The emperor was the nominal ruler, but real power was held by the Fujiwara family, which cultivated a courtly style of elegance and taste well illustrated, for example, in Lady Murasaki's *Tale of Genji*, a masterpiece of early Japanese literature. Much of the stimulus for culture came from two new Buddhist schools imported from China, Shingon and Tendai. Each established an important monastic center in Japan and acted as a wellspring for Buddhist education and the transmission of culture.

A young monk named Saicho (767–822) studied at the Tian-tai (Jap. Tendai) monastery in China and upon his return to Japan established a Tendai monastery at Mt. Hiei near Kyoto. Tendai in Japan actually included practices from some of the other schools, like Chan, Pure Land, and Tantric Buddhism. The Tendai monastery on Mt. Hiei flourished for a number of centuries and became a center for many of the later developments in Japanese Buddhism.

The founder of the Shingon school, Kukai (773–835), is considered to be one of the most gifted and brilliant religious leaders in Japanese history. Trained first for government service, Kukai spent years in austere Buddhist practices. He studied the Tantric (esoteric) form of Buddhism in China and advocated these practices for the Japanese people, greatly influencing the emperor and others of the court from his monastery at Mt. Koya. The Shingon practices included the use of mantras (sacred formulas), ritual gestures (mudras), mandalas, and other forms of meditation and ritual. Kukai excelled in the arts and literature, and he established a special school that gave instruction in both religious and secular education. His writings describe the development of all religions through ten stages, with Shingon as the highest level; and he taught the doctrine of becoming a Buddha in this very body through the Tantric practices. Shingon became a kind of national religion for Japan, and literature and the arts were widely promoted under Kukai's influence.

Now that Buddhism was firmly established as a central factor in the Japanese way, Shinto also went through some new transformations. In earlier times Shinto was simply a variety of folk beliefs and practices loosely held together by the leading clans and their mythologies. Now there was an attempt to create a more self-conscious Shinto tradition based on the ancient way of the kami. Imperial edicts called for the people to be pure, bright, and upright, in accordance with the kami way, and a work on history as transmitted in a Shinto priestly family was compiled, the *Kogoshui* (Gleanings from Ancient Accounts). Rules were put forth regulating the shrines and priests and designating a number of important shrines as "specially privileged," receiving support from the court. Now Shinto, at least as represented by the larger shrines and their priesthoods, was becoming an institutionalized religion.

But important internal transformations of Shinto were also occurring. Shinto priests were not oblivious to the powers of the Buddha and of Chinese culture. The feeling eventually developed that the kami themselves could benefit by the help of the Buddha, and in some shrines Buddhist chapels were set up and Buddhist scriptures recited before the presence of the kami. These popular attitudes were reinforced by ideas that the kami were "protectors of the Buddha's Law." Therefore kami were enshrined in Buddhist temples. Before long the idea developed that Buddhahood was the "original essence" of the kami, and so the kami could be worshiped as manifestations of the Buddha, some of them even given the title *bosatsu*, bodhisattva.

As Shinto was transformed by Buddhist influence, Buddhism was also being influenced by the Japanese traditions, especially the this-worldly attitude of the Shinto way. Many people took to a path that combined ideas and practices from both Shinto and Buddhism. For example, popular religion featured many shamanistic men and women who went about healing and helping people, using rituals and practices from both Shinto and Buddhism. Some, called *yamabushi* (literally, those who sleep in the mountains), underwent spiritual disciplines in the mountains to acquire sacred power, and they used that power in healing and exorcisms for the people. Typically they based their practice in esoteric Buddhist rituals. But they also practiced Shinto rituals of purification and abstinence and made retreats to Shinto holy mountains.

During the later Heian period the worship of Amida Buddha grew rapidly in Japan, permeating both the Tendai and the Shingon schools and becoming very popular with the aristocrats. Shamanistic Buddhists like Kuya (903–972) took the gospel of Amida to the masses, teaching them to sing the Nembutsu, "Praise to Amida Buddha," to a popular tune. Also extremely popular among the common people was the Bodhisattva Jizo (Ksitigarbha), who had taken a vow not to attain Buddahood until the last soul was redeemed from hell. Since fear of suffering in hell was very real, especially among the peasants, Jizo was a good figure to which to turn in anxiety and distress, for he mediates on behalf of the souls destined to descend to the lower world, particularly the souls of infants and children who die. The worship of Amida Buddha and of Jizo was not confined to any particular school or locality, being absorbed into the general religious system of the people.

Salvation in Uncertain Times: the Kamakura and Muromachi Eras

Rule by the aristocracy of the imperial court came to an end in the twelfth century with the rise of the *samurai* (warrior) classes and the new feudal system in which landed barons called *daimyo* with their samurai retainers and vassals vied with one another for power and control. The strongest military leader, Minamoto Yorimoto (1147–1199), moved the center of power to Kamakura and ruled as *shogun* (military dictator). The imperial house continued to exist and to exercise ceremonial leadership, but the real power from now until the nineteenth century was in the hands of such feudal shoguns.

The collapse of the aristocratic culture of the Heian era and the outbreak of more or less continual fighting between the various daimyo brought a new sense of uncertainty and despair among the people. How can we find order and meaning in life? How can we be delivered from this passing world and attain assurance of salvation in the next world? Such questions were foremost to the people of the Kamakura period in these uncertain times.

The Buddhist traditions that came to the fore in this period had already been present in Japan for some time, but now they resonated to the new urgency of the situation. In the eyes of many, this was a particularly degenerate age. The old Buddhist idea of the three ages of the Dharma, which had already played a significant role in China, now became popular in Japan. The feeling developed that the third age, the Age of the End of the Dharma, had begun in Japan about the year 1052—a feeling corroborated by the collapse of Heian society and the upheavals inaugurating the feudal era in Japan. In this third age of the Dharma, many felt, it was no longer possible to reach salvation by the traditional path. So people were looking for new assurances of deliverance and salvation, which the older practices seemingly could no longer provide. The new schools that developed in this period are clear expressions of a Japanized Buddhism, emphasizing salvation and enlightenment through simple faith and practice.

Worship of Amida Buddha, popular already in the Heian era as part of the Tendai system, now became the only way to salvation in the eyes of many. Honen (1133–1212), considered the founder of the Pure Land sect in Japan,

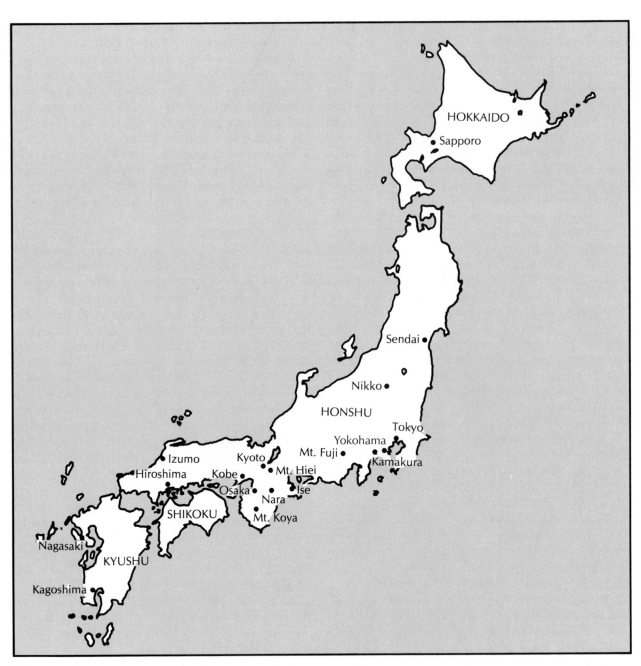

Japan.

declared, "It is clear that for ordinary mortals living in this contaminated world there is no way to reach the Pure Land except by depending on the saving power of Amida."[5] Honen was one of the most persistent advocates of the path of salvation by calling on Amida's name with the words, "Namu Amida Butsu." This formula of praise to Amida, called the Nembutsu, should be said over and over with firm faith in Amida's vows to save all beings. The Pure Land sect became a movement devoted to the exclusive worship of Amida Buddha for the gift of rebirth in the paradise of the Pure Land.

Shinran (1173–1262), one of Honen's disciples, laid even greater stress on the total inability of humans in this degenerate age to move toward salvation by one's own merit or efforts. The highest path is simply to accept the gift of salvation promised through Amida's vow to save all beings and, out of thankfulness, to chant Amida's name and rely completely on his grace. To emphasize that humans can have no merit in this degenerate age, Shinran gave up monastic life, married, and raised a family— starting the tradition of married Buddhist priests in Japan. The sect founded by Shinran, the True Pure Land, became very popular in medieval Japan and has continued to be the religious practice of a large segment of the Japanese people down to the present day.

A similar answer to the question of salvation was provided by Nichiren (1222–1282), a humble fisherman's son who became, in the eyes of many, "the pillar of Japan, the eye of the nation, and the vessel of the country." Nichiren was convinced that the woes Japan was experiencing resulted from the abandonment of the true Buddhist path. The true path is the teaching of the Lotus Sutra; this is the supreme teaching of the Buddha Shakyamuni, revealing the one and only way to salvation both for individuals and for the whole nation. Now, Nichiren felt, the different Buddhist schools had abandoned this pure and simple truth, and because of that Japan was suffering various misfortunes. To return to the true path people need only to take on their lips the name of the Lotus Sutra through the formula, "Namu myoho rengekyo" (Praise to the wondrous truth of the Lotus Sutra). Nichiren himself was identified as an incarnation of a bodhisattva, and he made it his mission to save Japan from the political and social evils that he felt came from wrong Buddhist teach-ings. He condemned the other Buddhist schools, caused great difficulty for the government, was twice exiled, and narrowly escaped execution. But he received considerable recognition when the Mongol invasion that he predicted actually occurred, and many were attracted to his simple religion and his vision of Japan as an earthly Buddha-land. Nichiren's zeal and his straightforward path appealed to many in this broken age, and the Nichiren sect grew to a large movement. Through the centuries Nichiren Buddhism has been a special Japanese form of Buddhism, and today many people in Japan belong to Nichiren groups.

Not all people were looking for salvation through sacred power that comes to us from outside, whether from Amida Buddha or from the Lotus Sutra. Some in this turbulent period were looking to Buddhist roots for something that would transcend the disorder and anxiety and restore calmness in the heart. And they found this in the practice of Zen (Chin. Chan) Buddhism. The Zen meditation type of Buddhism was known in Japan in the Nara and Heian periods along with the other forms of Chinese Buddhism, but the impetus for developing Zen as a separate school in Japan came from fresh importations from China. Eisai (1141–1215) is credited with bringing Zen anew to Japan; he found favor with the military rulers and emphasized the nationalistic value of Zen, as in his tract, "Propagate Zen, Protect the Country." It was Dogen (1200–1253) who provided the intellectual foundation for Zen in Japan. As a Tendai monk, he was bothered at an early age with the question that if all living beings have the Buddha-nature, then why does one have to engage in religious practices to gain enlightenment? His search took him to China, and when he returned he established a monastery where he taught the single practice of *zazen* (sitting in meditation). It is not by "other power" that one is saved, Dogen taught; rather it is through self-power, simply sitting in meditation, that one reaches enlightenment. Since one already possesses the Buddha-nature, all one has to do is awaken to that nature.

Dogen founded the Soto (Chin. Cao-dong) Zen sect in Japan, which advocates "gradual enlightenment," that is, an unhurried, purposeless, nonstriving practice of zazen, which gradually deepens one's experience of enlightenment. The other main school that developed is Rinzai (Chin. Lin-ji), the "sudden enlightenment" school.

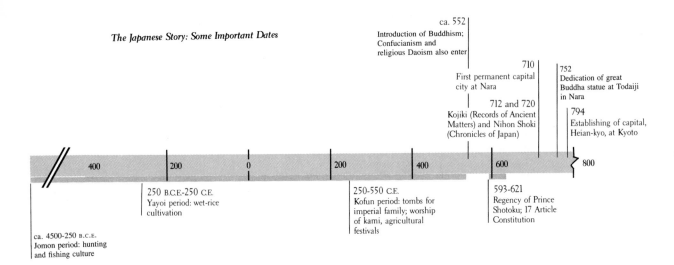

The Japanese Story: Some Important Dates

ca. 552
Introduction of Buddhism;
Confucianism and
religious Daoism also enter

710
First permanent capital
city at Nara

752
Dedication of great
Buddha statue at Todaiji
in Nara

712 and 720
Kojiki (Records of Ancient
Matters) and Nihon Shoki
(Chronicles of Japan)

794
Establishing of capital,
Heian-kyo, at Kyoto

400   200   0   200   400   600   800

250 B.C.E.-250 C.E.
Yayoi period: wet-rice
cultivation

250-550 C.E.
Kofun period: tombs for
imperial family; worship
of kami, agricultural
festivals

593-621
Regency of Prince
Shotoku; 17 Article
Constitution

ca. 4500-250 B.C.E.
Jomon period: hunting
and fishing culture

Rinzai masters typically gave their disciples koans, Zen questions and riddles from the sayings of the Chinese masters. The disciple would concentrate on this koan, eventually experiencing a sudden breakthrough, an awakening.

Zen monasteries in Japan practiced an austere mode of life with heavy emphasis on meditation as the path to enlightenment. Critical of the "easy paths" of Pure Land and Nichiren Buddhism, Zen adherents cultivated a strong-minded approach to the spiritual life that brought calm and control in the midst of the troubles of the age. There is no need to rely on the Buddha from far off or to long to be reborn in the Pure land of the West. The Pure Land is right here; the Buddha is within oneself! Anyone, taught Dogen, even women and common people, can sit in meditation and realize Buddhahood.

Of course, the common people were not drawn to Zen as they were to Pure Land and Nichiren, but one important class did find the Zen approach most attractive—the samurai. This newly rising class of warriors and military lords found meaning in the discipline, self-reliance, strong commitment, and mental control involved in Zen practice. Zen's strong sense of enlightenment directly within the pursuits of the ordinary world gave strong im-

petus to martial arts like swordfighting and archery, and it likewise contributed greatly to other traditional arts like poetry, classical Noh drama, and the tea ceremony. Although the total number of Zen adherents during these times was perhaps never large, through the important Zen monasteries and the dedication of the warrior class and artists Zen had a transforming effect on all Japanese society and culture.

Zen provided a new avenue for Confucianism to permeate Japanese society—now the Neo-Confucianism of the late Song period in China. With emphasis on loyalty to superiors and self-transformation through discipline and study, Neo-Confucianism combined with Zen to provide a foundation for the "Way of the Warrior," or *bushido*. Samurai became retainers of a particular daimyo master and dedicated themselves with total loyalty to that master, practicing military discipline as a kind of spiritual training. Bushido placed a heavy emphasis on bravery, duty, and being fearless to meet death in the service of one's lord.

Shinto continued to be an important influence during the medieval era, existing both in its local popular forms and in the amalgamation with Buddhism. For the first

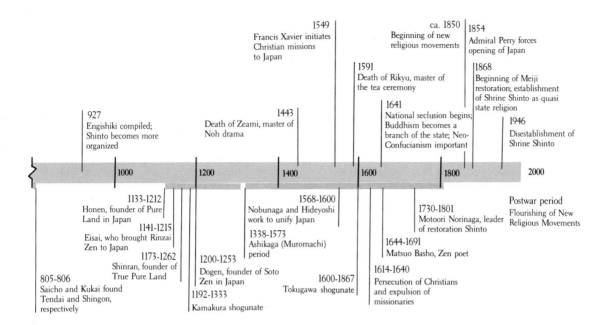

927
Engishiki compiled;
Shinto becomes more
organized

1443
Death of Zeami, master of
Noh drama

1549
Francis Xavier initiates
Christian missions
to Japan

1591
Death of Rikyu, master of
the tea ceremony

ca. 1850
Beginning of new
religious movements

1641
National seclusion begins;
Buddhism becomes a
branch of the state; Neo-
Confucianism important

1854
Admiral Perry forces
opening of Japan

1868
Beginning of Meiji
restoration; establishment
of Shrine Shinto as quasi
state religion

1946
Disestablishment of
Shrine Shinto

1000   1200   1400   1600   1800   2000

1133-1212
Honen, founder of Pure
Land in Japan

1141-1215
Eisai, who brought Rinzai
Zen to Japan

1173-1262
Shinran, founder of
True Pure Land

805-806
Saicho and Kukai found
Tendai and Shingon,
respectively

1200-1253
Dogen, founder of Soto
Zen in Japan

1192-1333
Kamakura shogunate

1568-1600
Nobunaga and Hideyoshi
work to unify Japan

1338-1573
Ashikaga (Muromachi)
period

1600-1867
Tokugawa shogunate

1614-1640
Persecution of Christians
and expulsion of
missionaries

1644-1691
Matsuo Basho, Zen poet

1730-1801
Motoori Norinaga, leader
of restoration Shinto

Postwar period
Flourishing of New
Religious Movements

time in Japan, leading thinkers tried to articulate the Shinto basis of the Japanese way, acknowledging the contributions made also by Confucianism and Buddhism but beginning the intellectual process that eventually attempted to separate Shinto from Buddhism.

This cultural synthesis involving Shinto, Buddhist, and Confucian religious traditions formed the basis for the aesthetic pursuits that blossomed in the Muromachi era (1333–1600). So much of what we consider to be typically Japanese cultural forms in architecture, literature, and the other arts grew out of this synthesis. Main elements were contributed by the different religious traditions: the sense of the purity, beauty, and goodness of nature; the realization of spiritual realities through art forms; and the experience of self-cultivation and transformation through the artistic practice. Such elements as these combine in the Japanese *geijutsu-do*, the "way of art." Among the arts widely practiced as spiritual aesthetic paths were poetry, painting, Noh drama, calligraphy, the tea ceremony, flower arranging, gardening, and even martial arts like sword fighting and archery. The heritage from the medieval religio-aesthetic synthesis has been a strong factor in shaping Japanese identity.

The Coming of the West and the Modern Period

The first real encounter with the West and with Christianity came in the middle of the sixteenth century, near the close of the Muromachi period. The unification of Japan under the Tokugawa shogunate together with the reaction against Christianity and foreign influence had its effect on the Japanese religious traditions.

Unification, Christian Impact, and Reaction
The close of the Muromachi period was signaled in the gathering strength of three military dictators who finally unified Japan during the last thirty years of the sixteenth century: Nobunaga, Hideyoshi, and Tokugawa Ieyasu. The long medieval period of wars and conflicts ended when Tokugawa Ieyasu (1542–1616) established the Tokugawa Shogunate, instituting a peaceful period for Japan from 1600 to 1867.

By the time Oda Nobunaga (1534–1582) came to power, the various Buddhist groups had attained considerable land and even military power in Japanese society, and there was also much fighting between the Pure Land

and the Nichiren groups, each with its own army of soldier-monks. With power, of course, came a tendency toward political involvement, and a power struggle ensued between Nobunaga and the Buddhists, especially the Pure Land group. In several attacks Nobunaga massacred tens of thousands from this sect. The violence of these events considerably weakened the influence of the Buddhist groups, at least for a while.

But the religious situation during the unification of Japan was complicated by the intrusion of a new foreign religion: Christianity. European explorers and traders began to arrive in the 1540s, and the Jesuit missionary Francis Xavier arrived in 1549, followed by other Jesuit missionaries and priests of the Franciscan and Dominican orders. Christian and European influence rose sharply for half a century and then just as sharply declined and virtually disappeared in the Japanese reaction that led to the closing of Japan. But the Christian story, so foreign to Japan, touched and contributed to the Japanese story.

The Society of Jesus, formed by Ignatius Loyola in 1540, sent forth an army of Christian monk-soldiers into the Asian world. Pursuing a policy of accommodation to the best of the local cultures, Frances Xavier and other Jesuits attempted to convert the Japanese feudal leaders to Christianity, with some success for a time. Following the lead of certain feudal lords, tens of thousands of people took over the Christian vision. The spread of Christianity

Himeji Castle, typical of castles in Japan dating from the medieval period.

was aided perhaps by Nobunaga's hostility toward the organized Buddhist groups.

But suspicions about the connections of Christians with the foreign European powers soon surfaced, and Nobunaga's successor Hideyoshi (1537–1598) turned against the Christians and instigated the first persecutions, to be followed by the more systematic attempts by the early Tokugawa rulers to control and wipe out the European-Christian intrusion. There were heroic martyrdoms and even a peasant-based revolt of some 37,000 people, mostly Christian, in Shimabara in 1637–1638, who stood against government forces for several months before being massacred. Finally the Tokugawa authorities enforced their ban on all Christian priests and Christian activities. Responding to the threat of foreign intrusion and domination, they closed Japan to Western contact and influence, and the Christian century was over. The ban on Christianity was enforced by requiring all people to register with their local Buddhist temples, and reports of continuing involvement in Christianity were investigated and the offenders punished. A number of Christian families and groups in more remote areas did manage to continue practicing Christianity in secret; some groups of these "Hidden Christians" still existed two hundred years later when Westerners again were permitted into Japan.

Neo-Confucianism and Resurgence of Shinto

Whereas the Tokugawa government made Buddhist temples into the guardians of the state against Christianity, the ideological leanings of the regime were toward Neo-Confucianism. A strict separation of the classes of society was developed, with duties assigned to each: the samurai, the farmers, the artisans, and the town merchants. But changes were coming, and before long the samurai class became relatively nonproductive, the farmer-peasant class became impoverished, and the merchant class rose to create a flourishing urban culture with new religious and artistic dimensions. In the Genroku era (ca. 1675–1725), this new urban world of art and pleasure was called the "Floating World" (*ukiyo*), made up of a lively interaction of painters, playwrights, performers, and geishas, supported by the flourishing merchants. Novels and bunraku (puppet theater plays) on themes of love and townspeople's life were widely popular. The novels, *The Life of a Man*

Who Lived for Love and *Five Women Who Chose Love*, both by Saikaku, and *The Love Suicides at Sonezaki*, a bunraku play by Chikamatsu, suggest the sort of themes that caught the interest of the merchant class. Japan was entering into the modern era, even though its social structures were still based in the medieval world.

Neo-Confucianism inspired Japanese scholars to go back to the original classics of China. But before long scholars were also going back to the Japanese classics, and the Shinto Restoration movement was born. Earlier medieval scholars had begun to resist the dominant theory that kami were reflections of the original Buddha reality; they suggested instead that the kami represented the sacred essence, and the Buddhas were but reflections of this original reality. Now a School of National Learning developed to promote the study of original Shinto writings and to attempt to restore an authentic Shinto way purified of foreign (Buddhist) influence.

A leading scholar of the National Learning movement was Motoori Norinaga (1730–1801), who came from a merchant-class family. He had training in Pure Land Buddhism and Confucianism, but he became interested in ancient Shinto as the source of the special Japanese spirit. So he devoted his life to the study of the ancient Japanese way, as set forth in the Kojiki and the Nihon Shoki, and also early poetry like the Manyoshu collection. He argued, for example, that the Kojiki provided the best and universal principle for Japan and for humankind. And he advocated the restoration of a "natural," pure Shinto based on the ancient texts. Motoori further articulated the unique Japanese outlook on life in aesthetic terms, as *mono-no-aware*, a "sensitivity to things," which he explained as an emotional, aesthetic openness to both the beauty and the pathos of life. The Shinto Restoration movement exerted much influence on the political scene and helped to create the climate that led to the restoration of imperial rule.

The Meiji Restoration and Nationalistic Shinto

Internal pressure from Restoration Shinto and from peasant uprisings combined with pressure from the West to bring great changes: Japan was opened to the West, the Tokugawa regime fell, and imperial rule was restored in 1867 under Emperor Meiji. The Meiji Restoration combined two quite different tendencies. On the one hand, Japan became a modern nation and adopted many Western forms of government and education, including freedom of religion. On the other hand, the government attempted to restore a kind of "pure" Japanese society on the basis of the classic Shinto texts. The emperor was thought of as the father of the nation. And Shinto was separated from Buddhism and taken over under the administration of the state. So that there could be freedom of religion and still universal participation in Shinto, the government declared that state Shinto was not a religion but rather the cultural heritage of all Japanese. Even Buddhists and Christians were expected to participate in Shinto rituals to show their loyalty to the emperor and the nation.

In the rising tide of Japanese nationalism, especially in the 1920s and 1930s, the government used the educational system to teach the Shinto mythology as the basis of its claim to the divine origin of Japan and its manifest destiny to rule Greater Asia. There were dissenting voices to this misuse of the Shinto tradition, but they were considered unpatriotic and dealt with harshly. After the defeat of Japan in World War II, the Occupation Forces insisted on the complete disestablishment of Shinto, removing government support of the shrines and making Shinto simply one religion alongside Buddhism and Christianity in Japan. The emperor remained as the symbolic head of the nation, but he renounced the nationalistic use of the Shinto traditions.

Religion in the Post-War Period

Today Japan is a very modern, technologically advanced nation. The people are highly educated and outwardly very Westernized. Secularization has played a big role in Japan in recent years, and many people find it unimportant to participate in the traditional religious activities. Modern urban life does not lend itself to the family and clan-centered focus that was the heart of so much of the religious activity in the past.

This does not mean that religion is dead in Japan today—far from it. After the great disruption caused by its disestablishment after the war, Shinto was stabilized and continues to find support in the local communities. The Association of Shinto Shrines sees to it that priests are ed-

*Priests and worshipers observing the Mifune Boat Festival
in Kyoto. Such Shinto festivals attract large crowds of
worshipers and sightseers in modern Japan.*

ucated in the Shinto traditions and rituals, assigning them
to shrines as needed. Although many smaller shrines do not
have resident priests, they still can be administered by local
people and served by priests from time to time. Even
though many people no longer keep a *kamidana* (household shrine) in their homes, they visit the shrines on festival
days and participate in Shinto community activities.

Buddhism still holds the intellectual allegiance of most
Japanese, even though they may not actively take part in
Buddhist activities. Many who are quite secular still turn
to Buddhism in times of crisis or when a family member
dies. The major sects of Japanese Buddhism today, based
in the schools of Tendai, Shingon, Pure Land, Nichiren,
and Zen, appear to have weathered the crises of post-war
Japan: defeat, economic loss, westernization, secularization, growth of "New Religions." Large numbers of people
still look to Buddhist temples and priests for guidance in
life crises and for comfort and ritual when death strikes in
the family. The intellectual life in Japanese Buddhism has
been particularly lively, and numerous Japanese Buddhist
scholars have contributed significantly to the revival of
Buddhist scholarship in the world. Many Japanese schol-

ars working out of the Buddhist intellectual tradition have
achieved international reputation, such as the founder of
the famous Kyoto school of philosophy, Nishida Kitaro
(1870–1945), as well as his leading successor, Nishitani
Keiji (1900–), and many others. Buddhist scholars and
leaders are also much engaged in dialogue with leaders of
other religions and with movements seeking peace
throughout the world.

One of the most striking developments in Japanese religion in the modern period has been the emergence of
many "New Religions," which have captured the imagination of a good portion of the Japanese people. While it
is difficult to be precise, it is estimated that as many as thirty
percent of Japan's population participate in one way or
another in the activities of these New Religions. They represent one of the most vital sectors of Japanese religion
today. Some of these started in the nineteenth century, but
most are more recent movements, and the real spurt of
growth has come in the post-war period. In a sense, these
are not really "new" religions, for they generally adopt elements from the traditional religions and combine them in
new ways. Some draw mainly on Shinto traditions, others
stem from Buddhism, and still others draw from a variety
of traditions, including Christianity. In fact, one characteristic of many New Religions is their syncretistic
character—their main teachings and practices typically
come from a number of religious traditions and, in addition, often draw on modern science and technology as well.

A central characteristic of the New Religions is a
strong, charismatic founder or leader who has new rele-
vatory experiences. Another characteristic is their emphasis on concrete, this-worldly benefits and goals, especially
healing from sickness and success in life. They have simple teachings and practices, and above all they offer a
caring community in which people, lost in the frustrations
of modern life, can find identity and meaning.

These New Religions run the whole range of traditional
religious emphases in Japan. One movement that has
many Shinto and shamanistic elements is Tenrikyo,
founded by a farmwoman, Nakayama Miki (1798–1887),
through whom a monotheistic God spoke, providing a
narrative of the creation of the world and establishing
rituals to bring humankind back to God. Many groups
have arisen from Nichiren Buddhism, among them Soka

Gakkai, a lay movement that emphasizes chanting the name of the Lotus Sutra for immediate health, happiness, and success in life. Yet another type is represented by P. L. Kyoda (Perfect Liberty Order), which advocates a balanced life and graceful rituals in keeping with its slogan, "life is art."

An event of considerable significance in the Japanese religious world was the death of Emperor Hirohito, who ruled as emperor for 64 years (1925–1989). His period as emperor encompassed great events and drastic changes—the emergence of Japan as a great power, the total defeat in World War II, the astounding resurgence of Japan to world leadership. The funeral rituals for the emperor, some of a civil, international flavor, others of a specifically Shinto nature, certainly marked the end of an era. Now the new emperor, Akihito, has been enthroned with the traditional Shinto rituals; civil calendars in Japan now mark the new era proclaimed by the emperor, Heisei—"Achieving Peace."

So the Japanese sacred story still goes on today, with many changes and transformations. It is difficult to predict the future in the Japanese context. Certainly the story of the traditional religions, Shinto and Buddhism, will continue, and perhaps renewal and revitalization will take place. And just as certainly the widespread secular attitudes of many people will continue and perhaps grow. Less certain is the future story of the New Religions, whose growth has stabilized after the great surge in the early post-war period. Perhaps these religions will mature, enter into associations with others, and become a continuing part of the Japanese religious story.

DISCUSSION QUESTIONS

1. What are the half-dozen religious traditions that share in making up the identity of many Japanese?
2. In what ways has the mythic tradition about the creation of the world and the rule of Amaterasu provided identity for the Japanese people?
3. What does the story about the first introduction of a Buddha image into Japan reveal about the early Japanese reaction to Buddhism?
4. What was Prince Shotoku's importance for Buddhism in Japan?
5. Outline the teachings of three Buddhist sects that developed in the Kamakura period. What concerns did they have in common?
6. What might account for the success of Christianity in the sixteenth century in Japan? And why was it soon banned?
7. What were the concerns of the leaders of the Shinto Restoration movement in the Tokugawa period?
8. What are some main characteristics of the so-called New Religions of Japan?

CHAPTER 15

Japanese Worlds of Meaning

SHINTO VIEWS OF ULTIMATE REALITY AND HUMAN LIFE

As we seek to understand the Japanese perspective on the central human questions about ultimate reality, existence, and the path of transformation, we will look first at the Shinto worlds of meaning. Then we will take up the Buddhist view once again, specifically to identify how Buddhists in Japan have shaped the Japanese world of meaning—and have in turn been shaped by it.

What's it *all* about? What is really the meaning and purpose of life? Where do we look for the power that transforms us? The basic Shinto answer to questions like these centers on the kami and our relationship to the kami.

Reality as Myriads and Myriads of Kami

The word *Shinto*, modeled after Chinese terms, means in native Japanese terms the "Way of the Kami" (*kami no michi*). This refers primarily to Japanese religion as a way of life according to the will of the native kami. But the Japanese people have never given much concern to working out theoretical doctrines about kami nature. It was not until the Shinto Restoration movement in the Tokugawa era that Shinto theoreticians articulated basic teachings about the nature of the kami. More important to Japanese understanding are the ancient myths about the kami preserved in classical texts like the Kojiki and Nihon Shoki, and the numerous other stories and beliefs passed on in the various shrines in Japan.

Myths About the Kami: Generation of Sacred Life

Are the kami eternal, or where did they come from? The myths are not really about whether the kami are related to some eternal transcendent being or principle. Rather, the emphasis is on the generation of kami as a continuous rhapsody of sacred life, from an indescribable and inexhaustible source.

The myths telling the origin of the kami begin quite simply with the primordial chaos and a spontaneous generation of a series of kami:

> In the time of the beginning of heaven and earth, on the Plain of High Heaven there came into existence first Lord of the Heavenly Center Kami, then High Generative Force Kami, and then Divine Generative Force Kami. These three kami came into existence as single kami, and their forms were invisible. When the world was young, resembling floating oil and drifting like jellyfish, something like reed-shoots sprouted forth, and from this Excellent Reed Shoots Male Kami and Heavenly Eternal Standing Kami emerged. These two kami also came into existence as single kami, and their forms were invisible. These are the Separate Heavenly Kami. Then there came into existence Earth Eternal Standing Kami and Abundant Clouds Field Kami. These two kami came into existence as single kami, and their forms were invisible. Next there came into existence the Clay Male and Female Kami, Post Male and Female Kami, Great Door Male and Female Kami, Complete Surface Kami and his spouse, Awesomeness Kami; and Izanagi and his spouse, Izanami. These are the Seven Generations of the Kami Age. (KOJIKI, CHS. 1-2)

The kami sprang forth without progenitors, independently, in some mysterious generation out of the fertile,

254

primordial, divine chaos. The last pair, Izanagi and Izanami, became the bearers of sacred life as they created the first land and descended to it to begin the creation of everything.

For understanding the kami nature, it is important to realize that everything that Izanagi and Izanami gave birth to is called kami—rivers, sea, wind, trees, mountains, plains, and fire. They overflowed so much with kami power that they spontaneously generated many more kami from their tears, blood, purification water, and so forth, in complete continuity with the originating kami.

Japanese generally make a distinction between the Kami of Heaven—such as those in the myths discussed so far—and the Kami of Earth. The Kami of Heaven are the powerful kami of the Plain of High Heaven, headed by Amaterasu, connected with the greater forces of nature such as the sun, moon, wind, and the like. The Kami of the Earth are those myriads of kami who are resident in all facets of nature throughout the earth, usually associated with certain localities.

The myths provide a large canvas of kami activity on earth, with stories about various kami of the different regions and their interaction with the people. Already in the Age of the Kami, Susanoo, too unruly for the Plain of High Heaven, was forced to descend to the region of Izumo, and Susanoo's descendant O-Kuninushi (Great Land Master Kami) held sway in the Izumo region and finally agreed to accept the rule of the descendant of Amaterasu. But the divisions between the Kami of Heaven and the Kami of Earth are not rigid. Even the sun kami herself, though she rules the Plain of High Heaven, is in close relation to the people; the stories tell how the emperor enshrined his august Ancestress in the shrine at Ise. Ever since that time the emperor has performed special ceremonies of worship to Amaterasu at Ise for the welfare of the whole people.

Nature and Role of the Kami

These myths in the Kojiki and Nihon Shoki, and many stories and rituals associated with the kami at the thousands of shrines throughout Japan, provide a general view of the kami. Japanese have a personal, intuitive sense of the kami as the center of existence, without trying to define fully who or what they are. Still, there are some basic ideas that can be expressed about the nature of the kami and especially about their role in our world.

Scholars have often attempted to find the etymological meaning of the ancient word kami, but there are no theories that have gained widespread consensus. The only way to understand the word is to pay attention to how the people feel and act toward the kami. Perhaps the best definition was given by the famous Shinto scholar Motoori Norinaga (1730–1801), who wrote,

> The word kami refers, in the most general sense, to all divine beings of heaven and earth that appear in the classics. More particularly, the kami are the spirits that abide in and are worshipped at the shrines. In principle human beings, birds, animals, trees, plants, mountains, oceans—all may be kami. According to ancient usage, whatever seemed strikingly impressive, possessed the quality of excellence, or inspired a feeling of awe was called kami.[1]

So kami are defined principally by the awesomeness and striking impressiveness that they demonstrate, calling forth feelings of respect, fear, and appreciation of beauty and goodness.

Thus anything that seems imbued with kami quality is thought of as kami. This can include the qualities of growth, fertility, and productivity; various natural phenomena and objects, such as wind and thunder, sun, mountains, rivers, trees, and waterfalls; animals such as the fox and the dog; and ancestors, especially the ancestors of the imperial family. Further, kami can include the guardian spirits of the land and of occupations; the spirits of national heroes; and even spirits that are pitiable and weak, such as those who have died tragic deaths.

Unlike conceptions of the creator God in the Abrahamic religions, and unlike Indian and Chinese conceptions of transcendent gods or eternal principles, Shintoists believe the kami, even the Kami of Heaven, to be entirely immanent within the forces and qualities of the world. They are not preexistent beings who create the world and then stand above it. Rather the kami are the inner power of all nature, constituted from the sacred nuclei of the world itself. As such, they are the forces that bestow and promote all life, growth, and creativity.

Some distinction in rank among the various kami can be made, but only in terms of how they contribute to life

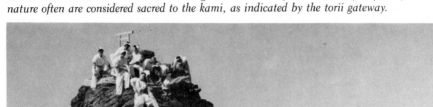

The so-called "Married Rocks" at Futamigaura in Mie Prefecture. Beautiful spots of nature often are considered sacred to the kami, as indicated by the torii gateway.

and growth. There is some tendency to think of the Kami of Heaven as superior, with Amaterasu having the leading position of all the kami. Yet even Amaterasu is not absolute in her power and authority. She pays her respects to other kami and consults them; and even though Japanese revere her, they also worship other kami and go to them for concerns that fall under their functions. And certainly there are kami that are inferior, such as kami of flora and fauna, who also need to be respected and appeased with religious rites when their domain is impinged upon. The kami who are negative and destructive are also respected, those who bring vengeance and calamity on humans. For these kami, too, are manifestations of life-power, turned to the destructive side, and they also are worthy of reverence and worship.

The kami sometimes communicate important knowledge to those who worship them. It was taken for granted in ancient Japan, for example, that the kami communicated their will to the clan leader and to the people through oracular means, usually through a shamanistic priestess. This revelation was kept and passed on as important truth for the family and community. For example, when a special spate of calamities struck, Emperor Sujin inquired of the kami through divination. A powerful kami spoke through the "kami-possession" of Princess Yamato-totohimomoso: "Why is the emperor worried over the disorder of the nation? Doesn't he know that the order of the nation would be restored if he properly venerated me?" This kami identified himself as Omononushi-no-Kami, the kami who resides in Yamato, and further designated a particular man to be his chief priest.[2]

Under Buddhist influence there was some tendency in medieval Shinto to look for some kind of kami essence or principle that could be compared to the Buddhist notion of the universal Buddha-essence. Some, for example, thought of the kami as local reflections or forms of the Buddhas, all of whom really go back to the one Buddha-reality. Later some Shinto scholars, as we saw, held that the Japanese kami are really the "original essence" and the various Buddhas are the reflections of this. And there was a tendency to regard one particular kami, such as Heavenly Center Lord Kami, the first kami to be generated in the mythological account, as the supreme original kami who existed before the creation of the world. But today Shinto leaders reject any notion of a supreme creator kami, affirming instead the independent dignity of each kami in the Shinto pantheon, still giving the central position, of course, to Amaterasu.

What holds it all together? Monotheistic religions have one absolute God, and monistic or nondualistic religions have some one principle that holds everything together in a unified whole. It is sometimes said that a polytheistic religion necessarily understands the world in a fragmented way, with the different aspects of the world under the domain of different gods. But Shintoists believe that the myriads of kami function together in complete harmony so there is no division of the cosmos against itself. The kami generate all life, growth, happiness, creativity, also all suffering and destruction. The way of the kami is a cosmic harmony.

The Shinto Perspective on the World and on Humans

How can we make sense out of this world and our lives? Why are things so filled with confusion and violence? Questions about the meaning of life and the cause of evil and suffering have been felt by the Japanese long before atomic bombs exploded over Japanese cities. Buddhist views of the nature of the world and human existence are of course widely accepted by the Japanese. But the ancient Shinto tradition also has a particular vision of the world and of humans, a vision that still today forms part of the Japanese way of looking at human existence.

A World Replete With Kami

The world in its essence is good, pure, and beautiful, as we learn from the myths and from the unsystematized traditions.

This is because the kami are good, pure, and beautiful, and the world originated from them. The Shinto myths of the creation of the world really do not tell how the world was created; rather they tell how the kami of everything in the world came into existence, and that is equivalent to the origination of the things themselves. We are told how the kami of the mountains were born, how the kami of forests came into existence, how the kami of sun, moon, and storm were engendered. In this vision there is no such thing as neutral matter that makes up the world; all operates in the will and activity of the various kami.

The main cosmology assumed in the early myths is a vertical, three-layered one, consisting of the Plain of High Heaven, the Manifest World, and the World of Darkness. The Plain of High Heaven is the locale of the spontaneous generation of the first series of kami, but how the Plain of High Heaven itself originated is not told. The unformed world is described as "resembling floating oil and drifting like jelly-fish," and some of the kami were born from reedlike shoots that sprouted from the floating chaos.

The beginnings of the Manifest World came when Izanagi and Izanami, from the Floating Bridge of Heaven, stirred the brine below with their Heavenly Jeweled Spear and, when they lifted the spear, the brine dripping from it heaped up and formed an island. Descending to the island, they had sexual intercourse and bore as kami-children the Great Eight-Island Land (Japan) and then the other lands and the various kami of all other things. But when Izanagi gave birth to the kami of fire, she was badly burned and died, now descending to the World of Darkness, the abode of the dead. Even in her death more kami came into existence from her vomit, feces, and urine—all these things are highly charged with kami power.

The overall sense we get from the myths of creation is that the whole world is replete with kami essence, symbolized by the phrase, "800 myriads of kami." This is a kami-saturated cosmos, for all the kami are immanent within the world. There is no such thing as nature in distinction from the sacred power, as is the case in monotheistic religions. An early poem from the *Manyoshu* expresses this feeling:

> Between the provinces of Kai and Suruga
> Stands the lofty peak of Fuji.

Heavenly clouds would not dare cross it;
    Even birds dare not fly above it.
The fire of volcano is extinguished by snow,
    and yet snow is consumed by fire.
It is hard to describe;
    It is impossible to name it.
One only senses
the presence of a mysterious kami.[3]

Furthermore, the world gradually progresses from chaos to order, from confusion and conflict to harmony and unity, as the kami engender the whole world and then bring it all into peaceful functioning under kami rule. All things, organic and inorganic, fit together in this divine harmony—humans, animals, mountains, rivers, forests, and so forth. The whole universe is essentially a sacred community of living beings, all together contributing to the development of inexhaustible kami power. This-worldly values are not negated in Shinto, for there is no need to transcend the Manifest World for a different kind of world. This world—the only world for humans—is inherently good, pure, and beautiful.

Humans as Children of the Kami

Unlike the creation stories of the Abrahamic religions, the creation of humans does not receive special attention in the Japanese myths. Humans are "children of the kami," just like the mountains, rivers, animals, and all the rest. There really is no sharp line separating humans from kami, for in a sense all humans have the kami nature. After death humans can be thought of as kami, though this term is usually reserved for great and important ancestors. Since humans received life from the kami, they have that kami essence within themselves. They are originally pure and clean.

The meaning and purpose of life is implied in the truth that humans are children of the kami. Owing life to the kami, humans should show gratitude by contributing to the continuing evolution of the kami-based world.

The Reality of Human Existence: Pollution and Failure

Why do we fail to live in harmony and happiness? For all its optimism, Shinto does know of human failure and inadequacy. Whereas this does not stem from the essence of human nature, it still is real and often felt in our lives. Where does it come from?

The Shinto tradition is realistic about life in this good and beautiful world. The myths of origins describe how the world evolved slowly from chaos, as even the originating kami experienced failure and suffering in the process of generating this world and humans within it. Izanagi and Izanami failed in their first attempt at producing kami-land offspring, giving birth to a leech-child because of a ritual failure when Izanami spoke before Izanagi. And the dark scepter of death and the World of Darkness rose up when Izanami gave birth to the kami of fire; she died amid vomit and feces and descended to the underworld, where she was seen by Izanagi with maggots squirming around her body amid great pollution. Failure and death, it appears, are bound up with the generation of life.

As the world evolves through kami-generation, a persistent theme in the myths is the unruliness of many aspects of the world. This is symbolized already by Susanoo, the storm-kami brother of Amaterasu. Whereas Amaterasu represents the purity and sovereignty of the sun, Susanoo rages against her, plays dirty tricks, and instigates Amaterasu's withdrawal into a cave, which brings about a disastrous darkness over the whole world. The kami of the Plain of High Heaven depose Susanoo—to, of all places, the Central Land of the Reed Plains (the human world, specifically Japan), where he and his descendants continue their unruly ways and are only gradually pacified so that finally Amaterasu's grandson Ninigi can descend to inaugurate kami-rule on earth. The world evolves toward peace and harmony—but unruliness, failure, suffering, and death are always present in the process.

To get a picture of the realistic Shinto view of human existence, we can turn to the ancient ritual prayers (Norito), to the prayer for the great exorcism to be celebrated on the last day of the sixth month, to purify the whole nation from defilements. Included in the prayer is this statement illustrating human existence in a realistic way:

> With the increase of the descendants of the heavenly kami, various offences were committed by them. Among them, the offences of destroying the divisions of the rice fields, covering up the irrigation ditches, opening the irrigation sluices, sowing the seeds over the seeds planted by others, planting pointed rods in the rice fields, flaying living animals or flay-

ing them backwards, emptying excrements in improper areas, and the like, are called the "offenses to heaven," whereas the offences of cutting the living or the dead skin, suffering from white leprosy or skin excrescences, violating one's own mother or daughter, step-daughter or mother-in-law, cohabiting with animals, allowing the defilements by creeping insects, the thunder or the birds, killing the animals of others, invoking evils on others by means of witchcraft, and the like, are called the "offences to earth."[4]

This interesting listing of the various offenses among the descendants of the heavenly kami (that is, the nobles and officials of the land) seems to indicate that people have always been the same, greedy, selfish, unruly, and thoughtless of others. That's just the way humans are—and that's why, of course, the Great Purification was necessary every year.

But the Shinto view does not find evil and offense as something inborn in human nature. This listing of offenses is realistic, but there is no idea here of some original, innate sinfulness. Shinto texts do talk of offense or sin, but the word for this, *tsumi*, really means defilement or pollution, as well as sickness, error, and disaster. These offenses are harmful because they bring pollution, and pollution stands in the way of life, harmony, and happiness. Since the kami are pure, they dislike impure deeds, and thus our pollution hinders the flow of blessing and life from the kami.

There are some suggestions in Shinto tradition that even evil happenings stem from the kami, that is, the evil and violent kami. When Izanagi fled from the World of Darkness, he brought pollutions with him, and from these pollutions were born the Kami of Great Evils. To counteract this evil, the Kami of Great Good were also born at the same time. Some Shinto thinkers have interpreted these kami as the origin of all evil and all good events in the world. The great Shintoist Motoori Norinaga explained it like this:

It goes without saying that every event in this world is willed by the kami. There are various kinds of kami, noble and humble, good and evil, and just and unjust. Among the events there are some which may be regarded as unreasonable or unjust; these are operated by evil kami, such as the events which cause troubles to the nation and harm to the people. The evil kami is one who came out of the nether world with the great kami

Izanagi when he [returned from there and] purified himself. Although the heavenly kami attempt to overcome the power of evil kami, they cannot always restrain him. There are certain reasons, established already during the divine age, why evil is mingled with good.[5]

Norinaga's reason for emphasizing this is to advocate the Shinto attitude of accepting evil and death as part of life without resorting to foreign teachings (as in Buddhism and Christianity) that deny death by hoping for some kind of life after death. There is nothing sadder than death, Norinaga noted; but the authentic human emotion, knowing death is caused by evil kami, is to weep and mourn, respecting and pacifying the malevolent kami. Other Shinto thinkers like Hirata Atsutane (1776–1843) have held that the Kami of Great Evils are those who hate pollution and therefore become violent and rough when there are pollutions and wrongdoing. In other words, kami do not originate evil, but they do become rough and violent when humans commit defilements and pollution.

The Shinto tradition sees human nature as originally pure but also imperfect and limited. Humans are not at war with kami, there is no fall into sin, and evil is not a cosmic force overpowering us. But evil and pollution are accumulated in the ordinary course of living, like dirt and dust. Since humans are finite and imperfect, they do sometimes act with a black heart rather than with a bright pure heart; they make errors and mistakes, bringing pollution and shame upon themselves, hindering the flow of life and happiness from the kami. These pollutions affect not only the individual but also the whole community, for relation to the kami is always a social affair, and almost all offenses are social offenses.

Consequently, what humans need to move toward better and fuller life is the path of purification.

The Shinto Path of Purification

The Pure and Bright Heart

How can we start living the life that is *real?* Where do we find sacred power to give meaning and goodness in life? The Shinto tradition has not worked out theories of how people become transformed and in harmony with the kami. Rather it is in myths, rituals, and poems that we understand the path of purification. The primordial model for purification is Izanagi, who was polluted when he visited Izanami in the world of darkness. He bathed in a stream, washing his body with water and thus cleansing the pollution from himself. In a certain sense all pollution originates in the world of darkness, and people repeat Izanagi's act of purification every time they purify themselves with water or by other means.

Something of a theory of how pollution is done away with is found in the Great Purification Ritual of the sixth month. According to the Norito (ancient prayers), this is a national, communal purification to cleanse all Japan from pollution. In this ritual the defilements of the nobles and officials are transferred to narrow pieces of wood and sedge reeds, which are then thrown into the river and carried out to the sea. When this exorcism is performed, the liturgy says, the kami of the various river shoals and the kami of the ocean depths cooperate in carrying the pollution from the river to the sea and to the distant ocean depth. Then the kami of the ocean depths swallow the pollution and blow it away to the world of darkness from which it originally came. "And when the offences are thus lost, it is announced that from this day onward there is no offence remaining among the officials of the sovereign's court and in the four quarters of the land under heaven."[6]

Hundreds of thousands of people visit Meiji Shrine in Tokyo on New Year's Day, purifying themselves for the new year.

Pollution comes from the world of darkness, and the kami assist in cleansing the world by returning pollution to the world of darkness.

But Shinto teaches that outward purification of the body and community should be accompanied by inner purification, a cleansing of the heart that restores it to its original uprightness. Very frequently in imperial edicts, poems, and other Shinto literature, terms like "the bright and pure heart" or "the honest and sincere heart" are used. The Shinto scholar Kitabatake Chikafusa (1293–1354) quotes a revelation from the kami that says, "Fast and prepare yourself purely and fairly with a bright, red heart and not a dirty, black heart."[7] Chikafusa explains that the true way of purity consists in discarding one's own desires and keeping oneself lucid and clear in any situation, just as a mirror reflects objects—alluding to the bright mirror of Amaterasu, the sun kami, that she transmitted to her grandson Ninigi when she commissioned him to descend and establish kami rule on earth.

The Path of Dedication to the Kami

Purification of the body and a bright and pure heart are required before coming into the presence of the kami. Further transformation comes from worshiping the kami through rituals of dedication, as people offer sprigs of the sacred sasaki tree and other offerings, present music and dance, and read the solemn prayers. The prayers are permeated with praise of the kami, petitions for protection and blessing, dedication to the will of the kami, and vows to live an upright pure life.

Shinto believers do not try to formulate a theory of what happens when one comes into contact with the kami. But as one approaches the kami, the inner heart changes with a sense of awe and reverence and a strong feeling of appreciation and gratitude. This feeling was well expressed by a fourteenth-century Buddhist priest by the name of Saka who made a pilgrimage to worship the kami at the shrines of Ise and found the experience so transforming that he shed tears of gratitude:

> When on the way to these shrines one does not feel like an ordinary person any longer but as though reborn in another world. How solemn is the unearthly shadow of the huge groves of ancient pines and chamaecyparis, and

there is a delicate pathos in the few rare flowers that have withstood the winter frosts so gaily. The crossbeams of the Torii or Shinto gate way is without any curve, symbolizing by its straightness the sincerity of the direct beam of the Divine promise. . . . And particularly is it the deeply-rooted custom of this Shrine that we should bring no Buddhist rosary or offering, or any special petition in our hearts and this is called "Inner Purity." Washing in sea water and keeping the body free from all defilement is called "Outer Purity." And when both these Purities are attained there is then no barrier between our mind and that of the Deity. And if we feel to become thus one with the Divine, what more do we need and what is there to pray for? When I heard that this was the true way of worshiping at the Shrine, I could not refrain from shedding tears of gratitude.[8]

Becoming one with kami, what more does one need? In and through these forms of worship of the kami, people are helped to regain their original purity and brightness and to live life in reverence for the kami. Fellowship with the kami helps one discover the inexhaustible sacred life that has its source in them, for renewal and transformation, enabling one to contribute to the continuing evolution of the kami-based world.

The need for transformation extends to the family and the community as well, and so the path provides family rituals as well as communal festivals. The family rituals serve especially to bond the family together with the ancestors, as people renew their sense of gratitude to the ancestors for giving life, protection, and blessing; and they resolve to realize their hopes and ideals by passing love and care to their descendants. Many of the rituals of worshiping the ancestors are Buddhist rituals, but reverence and gratitude to the ancestors and the continued transformation of the family through their blessings is certainly also a central Shinto concern. Festivals also have a transformative effect on the community, for these are sacred times when the whole community purifies itself and renews its life and harmony by joyful communion with the kami.

So the path of transformation begins with purification of the physical world and of the inner heart, and it leads to renewal of life in communion with the kami, the source of all goodness and blessing.

ULTIMATE REALITY AND THE PATH IN JAPANESE BUDDHISM

The perspective of Buddhism, discussed in Part I, plays an important role in Japanese thinking about ultimate reality. The ideas of the Dharma Body of the Buddha and emptiness (*shunyata*) are central in Japanese Buddhist thought. Japanese Zen thinkers reinforced the Mahayana nondualistic interpretation of reality: samsara is nirvana. In a series of writings Dogen, for example, argued forcefully that there is a universal Buddha-nature. Whereas Mahayana scriptures had said that all beings have Buddha-nature, Dogen wrote that all beings *are* Buddha-nature. Thus Buddha-nature is not some unchanging entity beyond the world but it is precisely inseparable from the transiency common to all beings. In fact, Dogen wrote, impermanence and even birth-and-death—the conditioned character common to all beings—are Buddha-nature. In this way Dogen pushed the Mahayana teaching that samsara is nirvana to a radical level of understanding.

One tendency in Mahayana Buddhism, to elevate a particular Buddha toward ultimate status, may be seen in some of the Japanese sects. For Pure Land Buddhists of Shinran's school, Amida is the supreme Buddha for this age, the only saving power available; and his Pure Land paradise is almost identified with nirvana itself. For Shinran, Amida is not just one Buddha among others, limited to his period of enlightenment ten kalpas ago. Rather, he is the eternal Buddha, the formless Dharma Body that took form to manifest his essential nature, making his eternal compassion and wisdom available for the salvation of living beings.

Tantric Buddhism in Japan, that is, Kukai's Shingon school, elevated Mahavairocana, the Sun Buddha (Dai Nichi, Great Sun) to the status of the all-encompassing Buddha reality whose body is the whole universe. Shingon thinks of Mahavairocana as the eternal Dharma Body of the Buddha. But whereas the Dharma Body was traditionally thought of as formless and totally beyond conceptualization, Mahavairocana's attributes are represented in the Buddhas and gods of the universe. Mahavairocana transcends the universe, yet this material

At Sanjusangendo Temple in Kyoto, a thousand and one statues of the thousand-armed Bodhisattva Kannon (Avalokiteshvara) provide an overwhelming sense of sacred reality.

universe is his body. Kukai wrote, "The Buddha Dharma is nowhere remote. It is in our mind; it is close to us. Suchness is nowhere external. If not within our body, where can it be found?"[9] So the Dharma Body is the ultimate pantheistic-monotheistic reality with personality, wisdom, and compassion, who is found in the world and in our mind.

For the Nichiren Buddhists of Japan, it is the Lotus Sutra that embodies all the power and perfection of Buddhahood. Shakyamuni Buddha is the eternal reality, of whom all other Buddhas are emanations. But the absolute truth of Shakyamuni Buddha and the whole universe is embodied in the Daimoku, the sacred title of the Lotus Sutra that is chanted in the formula "Namu myoho rengekyo" (Praise to the wondrous truth of the Lotus Sutra).

The Japanese Buddhist Perspective on Human Existence

Though Japanese culture is permeated with the Shinto sense for the world and human nature, Japanese people have also been deeply influenced by the perspective of Buddhism, discussed in Part I, on topics of the universal Buddha-nature, impermanence, no-self, conditioned arising, and karma. This perspective operates for many people in a complementarity (or in a certain tension) with the Shinto perspective.

Whereas Shinto teaches that nature and humans are originally bright and pure, Japanese Buddhists stressed, for example, the notion of "original enlightenment" (*hongaku*), the innate enlightenment or Buddha-nature that all people, and even plants and animals, possess. This means that there is a Buddha quality about life and nature—a quality that was aesthetically explored in poetry, painting, and other arts. But, as Shinto holds that pollution and impurity obscure the original nature, Japanese Buddhists teach that original enlightenment is obscured by ignorance and desire. As Kukai said, "All sentient beings are innate bodhisattvas; but they have been bound by defilements of greed, hatred, and delusion."[10]

Some schools of Japanese Buddhism, as we saw, have taken over the notion of the "three ages of the Dharma" from China, the idea that we are now living in the third, totally degenerate age of this world cycle. Consequently, life in the world is depicted as corrupt and degenerate, and the purgatories and hells awaiting after death are described or painted in pictures with gory details. Other schools resist such a gloomy picture of human existence. But all agree on the basic Buddhist perspective that it is ignorance and clinging that cause suffering and continued samsaric existence.

Japanese writers have provided striking portrayals in literature of this human problem. For example, building on a traditional theme, a short story by a modern author, Akutagawa Ryunosuke,[11] tells how one day the celestial Buddha, sauntering by the lotus pond of paradise, happened to look down through the crystal water and saw hell far below. Among the sinners squirming on the bottom of hell he spotted Kandata, a great murderer and robber. The Buddha remembered that, among his innumerable crimes, Kandata had one good deed to his credit: one day he had spared a spider's life rather than step on it. Thinking he might deliver him from hell, the Buddha took some silvery thread from a spider of paradise and let it down to the bottom of hell. Below, Kandata chanced to see the thread and, wearied though he was from all the torments, began to climb with all his might to get out of hell. He was having a fair amount of success and began to think he might even climb to paradise, even though hell is myriads of miles removed. Finally he stopped to rest, but now he noticed to his horror that countless other sinners were climbing eagerly after him, like a procession of ants. How could this slender spider thread support these hundreds and thousands of sinners without breaking? He cried to them that this thread was his and they should get off. At that moment the thread, which had shown no signs of breaking, snapped above Kandata and he fell headlong back into the Pool of Blood at the bottom of hell.

Selfish struggle and desire are common human tendencies, but they do not lead to liberation.

Buddhist Paths of Transformation in Japan

Many, if not most, Japanese follow in some degree the Mahayana Buddhist paths of transformation, either exclusively or together with the Shinto path. Buddhists in Japan have taken over the full path from India and China, and they have given it characteristic Japanese accents. We find these accents in the path as taught, for example, in Shingon, Pure Land, Nichiren, and Zen, and carried over into some New Religions of today.

Resonating to the concrete, this-worldly emphasis of Japanese culture, one strand of the Buddhist path in Japan has long focused on the possibility of achieving Buddhahood in this very body, this very existence. Kukai, founder of Shingon, provided particular emphasis on this goal, as he taught the esoteric (Tantric) form of Buddhism, but these basic perspectives came to permeate other schools of Japanese Buddhism as well. The whole universe is really the body of the great cosmic Buddha, Mahavairocana or Dainichi (Great Sun), Kukai taught. Since our real nature is the great Buddha, it is possible by meditation and ritual action to realize one's Buddhahood. The body, speech, and

mind of Mahavairocana—the Three Mysteries—permeate the whole cosmos. But these three mysteries are innate to all living beings, and therefore it is possible through meditation and ritual to integrate the microcosmic activities of our body, speech, and mind into the Body, Speech, and Mind of Mahavairocana. This is done in meditation by symbolic ritual acts of body, such as sitting in meditation and use of hand gestures (mudras); by recitation of mantras, symbols of Mahavairocana's cosmic speech; and by rituals of the mind involving thinking, imagining, and visualizing, focusing especially on symbolic paintings of the sacred cosmos (mandalas). Kukai wrote:

> If there is a Shingon student who reflects well upon the meaning of the Three Mysteries, makes mudras, recites mantras, and allows his mind to abide in the state of samadhi [meditative trance], then, through grace, his three mysteries will be united with the Three Mysteries [of Mahavairocana]; thus, the great perfection of his religious discipline will be realized. . . . If there is a man who whole-heartedly disciplines himself day and night according to the prescribed methods of discipline, he will obtain in his corporeal existence the Five Supernatural Powers. And if he keeps training himself, he will, without abandoning his body, advance to the stage of the Buddha. The details are as explained in the sutras. For this reason it is said, "When the grace of the Three Mysteries is retained, [our inborn three mysteries will] quickly be manifested." The expression "the grace . . . is retained" indicates great compassion on the part of the Tathagata and faith on the part of sentient beings. The compassion of the Buddha pouring forth on the heart of sentient beings, like the rays of the sun on water, is called *ka* [adding], and the heart of sentient beings which keeps hold of the compassion of the Buddha, as water retains the rays of the sun, is called *ji* [retaining]. If the devotee understands this principle thoroughly and devotes himself to the practice of samadhi [meditation], his three mysteries will be united with the Three Mysteries, and therefore in his present existence, he will quickly manifest his inherent three mysteries.[12]

Kukai's words reflect the characteristic Japanese Buddhist double emphasis on the grace or power of the Buddha and on meditation and discipline on the part of the meditator. These two emphases are reflected, in somewhat different configurations, in the Pure Land and Zen paths of transformation.

The one strand of the path takes over the Chinese Pure Land tradition of depending on the power of Amida Buddha. Honen, considered the real founder of the Pure Land movement in Japan, felt deeply that humankind had entered into the third stage of the Dharma, the "latter end of the Dharma," the period of hopeless degeneracy. In this situation it is no longer possible to follow the path of meditation and discipline and reach enlightenment, so the only hope is to rely on the power of Amida Buddha, on the basis of Amida's original vows to save all those who have faith in him and call on his name. The power of Amida is made available through his name, so it is by repeating the Nembutsu, that is, the phrase "Namu Amida Butsu" (Praise to Amida Buddha), that the mind becomes fixed on Amida and, at death, one is reborn in the Pure Land paradise. Honen taught:

> The method of final salvation that I have propounded is neither a sort of meditation, such as has been practiced by many scholars in China and Japan, nor is it a repetition of the Buddha's name by those who have studied and understood the deep meaning of it. It is nothing but the mere repetition of the "Namu Amida Butsu," without a doubt of His mercy, whereby one may be born into the Land of Perfect Bliss.[13]

Shinran, a disciple of Honen, articulated this emphasis on help from Amida into a full theology of salvation by grace and faith. If we have feelings of merit, Shinran felt, these can stand in the way of total dependence on Amida's saving grace. Likewise, if we feel we first need strong faith and goodness before Amida helps us, we will despair. Rather, Shinran taught, even before we are moved to recite Amida's name, we are already embraced by Amida's saving light from which we will not be forsaken. Faith is really a gift from Amida, transforming our minds and giving hope and confidence of salvation. It matters not whether one is saint or sinner—Amida's original vow saves all. Honen had taught that since Amida can save even an evil person, surely he can easily save a good person. To make his point effectively, Shinran turned this saying around: "If even a good man can be reborn in the Pure Land, how much more so a wicked man!"[14] Self-confidence and reliance on "self-power" (jiriki) are grand illusions, for in this degenerate age good deeds are impos-

sible for mortal beings. In place of such pride and illusion, Shinran urged complete reliance on the "other power" (tariki) of Amida, for it is through the Buddha's act of compassion and his gift that faith arises in our hearts, and that is none other than attaining the Buddha-nature:

> One who lives in faith is equal
> To Tathagata, the Buddha.
> Great Faith is the Buddha Nature.
> This at once is Tathagata.[15]

At the moment that faith arises in the mind, according to Shinran, one has total assurance of salvation, for she has entered into the company of the assured, to remain in this state of nonretrogression until she is born into the Pure Land paradise. So the moment of faith brings salvation now, determining once and for all the destiny of the individual and thus assuring salvation. Thus the life of faith is marked by joy, gratitude, and thankfulness.

In contrast to the "other power" emphasis of Pure Land, Zen (Chan) Buddhism in Japan has self-consciously cultivated an approach to transformation that relies on one's own powers and abilities to see the Buddha-nature within. The Japanese Zen master Dogen said, "Any person at any time can attain enlightenment by following the path of the Buddha. . . . In following the Law of the Buddha, there is no difference in the kinds of people. Every being in the realm of man is endowed with the capacity to follow the Law of the Buddha."[16] There is no need to rely on "other power," or to look to future rebirth in the faraway Pure Land paradise. The Buddha is our own mind; the Pure Land is here this very instant.

Like Chan in China, Japanese Zen teaches a path of transformation that is without goal or purpose. There is no goal to be attained, no purpose to strive for. Goal, purpose, future reward, striving for—all such concepts suggest that the Buddha-nature is something other than the immediate here-and-now existence. All such concepts of the mind need to be discarded, for they only stand in the way of direct seeing. Just sit quietly and do nothing, Dogen counseled, emptying the mind and seeing directly into your own nature. This is to realize the pure mind of Buddhahood and to experience awakening—satori. There is no difference between the practice of meditation and enlightenment itself; doing zazen is itself experiencing enlightenment.

Work is considered a part of the path of meditation for Zen Buddhist monks, here at Eiheiji Temple in Fukui Prefecture.

Dogen's school of Zen, the Soto school, teaches the path toward a "gradual enlightenment," a deepening experience of awakening arising from daily zazen. The Rinzai school has traditionally practiced the path with a view toward "sudden enlightenment," an intense experience of awakening that comes suddenly after much practice and floods the consciousness. To help disciples toward the experience, Rinzai masters make use of the koan (Chinese gong-an), a question or riddle often taken from the sayings of the early Chinese Chan masters, as we saw in our discussion of Chinese Chan Buddhism. For example, a favorite koan tells how Zhao-zhou, when asked about the Buddha-nature of a dog, replied simply: "Wu" (nothingness). One koan often used in Japan stems from Japanese master Hakuin: "Listen to the Sound of the Single Hand." Hakuin explained: "What is the Sound of the Single Hand? When you clap together both hands a sharp sound is heard; when you raise the one hand there is neither sound nor smell."[17] The disciple meditates on the koan, striving to understand it and explain it in daily interviews with the master. Since the koan cannot be answered by ordinary rational, logical thinking, gradually the conceptual operation of the mind breaks down, and the disciple may experience the "great doubt" and the "great death," which culminates in the "great enlightenment," in Master Hakuin's words.

If you take up one koan and investigate it unceasingly your mind will die and your will will be destroyed. It is as though a vast, empty abyss lay before you, with no place to set your hands and feet. You face death and your bosom feels as though it were afire. Then suddenly you are one with the koan, and both body and mind are cast off. This is known as the time when the hands are released over the abyss. Then when suddenly you return to life, there is the great joy of one who drinks the water and knows for himself whether it is hot or cold. This is known as rebirth in the Pure Land. This is known as seeing into one's own nature.[18]

Whether through gradual enlightenment or sudden enlightenment, the Zen path leads to the transformation of life that results from seeing the "suchness" of reality, the Buddha quality that is inherent in every moment of existence.

So we see that, with the Mahayana emphasis on realizing Buddhahood, Japanese Buddhists shaped paths that emphasize either "other power" or one's own discipline and meditation—with many different shadings of these possibilities. We should remember that many Japanese have retained a sense of the basic identity of kami and Buddhas and that the Confucian path of transformation has also remained influential for many Japanese. So it is typical in Japan not to remain strictly within the confines of the Shinto path or the Buddhist path but to integrate elements of Shinto, Buddhism, and Confucianism in a "way" (*michi*) of self-cultivation. Examples of such syntheses abound, such as the way of the warrior (bushido) or the way of the mountain priests. Even though most of the "New Religions" tend to fall into either the Shinto or the Buddhist tradition, the way as practiced in many of them combines elements from Shinto, Buddhism, Confucianism, and folk traditions. Finally, we might mention that for some Japanese even the practice of the traditional arts, such as poetry, noh drama, the tea ceremony, and flower arranging, is filled with disciplines and rituals and considered a way of self-transformation.

DISCUSSION QUESTIONS

1. What is the nature of the kami? What does it mean to say this is a "kami-saturated" cosmos?
2. What does it mean to say humans are "children of the kami"? Why is there evil and suffering in the world, in the Shinto view?
3. What is the importance of "purification" in the Shinto path of transformation? What is meant by a "pure and bright heart"?
4. What does the Buddhist idea of the Three Ages of the Dharma imply about the nature of human existence?
5. Explain Kukai's view of the use of the Three Mysteries in the path of transformation.
6. What is the double emphasis in the Japanese Buddhist path of transformation, as exemplified in Pure Land and Zen?
7. What are meant by "gradual enlightenment" and "sudden enlightenment"? What is a koan and how is it used?

Worship and the Good Life in Japan

WORSHIP AND RITUAL

How can we find new power for life? How can we find meaning in the humdrum of daily existence? Answers to questions like these are given through worship and sacred times in Japan as elsewhere. Japanese religion is practical more than theoretical. Colorful ceremonies, exuberant sacred dances, quiet meditation sessions, pilgrimages to sacred mountains—more than articulating doctrines and beliefs, Japanese traditionally have performed their religion.

The worship and ritual of Confucianism and Daoism are intertwined in varying degrees in Japanese religious life. But most characteristic of Japan are the specifically Shinto practices of worshiping the kami and the Buddhist worship of Buddhas and rituals of meditation. For many Japanese these are not exclusive practices. For example, traditional families often have both a kamidana (altar for the kami) and a butsudan (altar for the Buddha) in their home, with appropriate daily rituals performed at both.

Rituals of Worshiping In Daily Life

Worshiping the Kami

Since all life, growth, and goodness come from communion with the kami, the Japanese have from ancient times cultivated the art of worshiping the kami, based on the patterns given in the mythology. When, for example, Amaterasu the sun kami withdrew into a cave, all the myriads of kami celebrated a matsuri (festival) to please her and entice her to come out of the cave. Shinto worship and festivals today are patterned after that event. The main ingredients of worshiping the kami are purification, an attitude of respect and gratitude, presenting offerings, and saying prayers—accompanied, of course, with a dedication of one's life in harmony with the will of the kami.

Where does one worship? Wherever the presence of kami is felt it is appropriate to worship them. Primarily this will be at home, at the shrines, on neighborhood streets during community festivals, and, of course, in beautiful places of nature.

Actually, since all life is lived in communion with the kami, even ordinary daily life is thought of as matsuri, service to the kami. But it is important to maintain harmony and unity with the kami by specific rituals of worship growing out of a sincere heart, in a sacred time and a setting of purity.

Devout Japanese often begin the day by worshiping the kami at the kamidana (kami-altar) in the central room of the home, a high shelf with a miniature shrine containing talismans of the kami, with a rope stretched over the shrine. The ritual of worship is very simple. The worshiper washes the hands and rinses the mouth and then places fresh offerings before the kami, consisting of clean rice, water, and salt. On special occasions, rice cakes, sea fish, fowl, seaweed, vegetables, or fruit might also be offered. Facing the shrine, a slight bow is made, followed by two deep bows. A brief prayer may be offered audibly or silently. Then the worship is ended with two deep bows, clapping the hands together twice, another deep bow and a slight bow. Later the special food offerings may be served at mealtime when a special act of reverence would again be made.

On many special occasions individuals or families go to a shrine to worship the kami, and the general attitude of worship is the same as at home. Proceeding on foot, the worshipers pass through the first *torii* (shrine gate) with a sense of entering sacred space. At the ablution pavilion they purify their mouth and hands with water from a wooden dipper. Standing in front of the worship hall, they jangle a bell, toss a coin into the offering box, and then perform the bows, hand claps, and prayers. On occasions of special significance, such as starting a new business venture or entering college, they may go inside the worship hall with a priest for a more formal ritual before the kami, with offerings and a prayer. Before leaving the shrine they may obtain a printed oracle that tells what fortune or misfortune lies ahead, and after reading these they usually twist them around a twig of a tree or some other convenient object, as a petition to the kami for fulfillment (or warding off, if a misfortune is predicted). They leave the shrine with an inexpressible feeling of peace and renewal.

Some of the most joyous and renewing times come when the whole community shares in a Shinto festival. It is said that many people in Japan today are secular, and perhaps not a large percentage would call themselves Shinto believers. But when a community festival comes along, many of these people join in. Communal worship at a shrine typically includes four major movements: purification, presentation of offerings, intoning of prayers, and communal participation.

In preparation for a festival the priests do many acts of purification, cleaning the shrine and abstaining from forbidden acts. The people also purify themselves with water upon entering the shrine. The festival typically begins with the priests appearing in their special garments, and one of them performs a formal purification, waving a purification wand with sweeping arm movements and sprinkling salt.

As all bow deeply, the chief priest opens the doors of the inner sanctuary (where the symbol of the kami is kept)

to the accompaniment of music and a special "oo-ing" sound. Then the special food offerings, having been ceremonially prepared and purified and arranged on trays with exquisite aesthetic taste, are passed from one priest to another until they are placed before the kami. The food items typically consist of rice, rice wine, salt, vegetables, seafood, and fruit. There may also be other special offerings of silk, money, or other items from the Association of Shinto Shrines or, in the case of some shrines, from the Imperial Household.

With the offerings in place, the priest recites the ancient prayers (Norito) in a dignified, high, chanting voice. The prayers thank the kami for benefits over the past year, asking for continued health and prosperity. After the prayers, the offerings are removed, later to be consumed by the priests and their families, and the chief priest closes the doors to the inner sanctuary, accompanied by the "oo-ing" sound.

At this point the fourth movement of the matsuri begins, the communal participation. Laypeople may come forward to make offerings and receive a sip of the wine offered previously to the kami. Often there will be a dance (kagura) performed by the young shrine maidens, both solemn and colorful, according to the tradition of the local shrine. Another special dance is the ancient Chinese court dance called bugaku. In addition, there will usually be a variety of other entertainment presented at the festival, such as horse races, archery, folk dancing, Japanese wrestling (sumo), pageants, and processions—all designed to entertain the kami and the human participants as well. A special part of local shrine festivals is the procession of the palanquin with the kami-symbol through the streets of the community. These processions can be solemn, but nowadays one may see sturdy young men carry the palanquin on their shoulders, zigzagging down the street shouting "washo, washo," under the watchful eyes of the shrine priests. Usually the people go to visit the kami; during the procession the kami comes to visit the people and bless the community with divine presence.

Buddhist Elements of Worship in Japan
Traditional homes also have a *butsudan* in the central room, a lacquered cabinet containing images of Buddhas and small containers for offerings. Offerings are made to

The Gion Festival held during July in Kyoto is one of the most famous festivals in Japan.

the Buddhas and prayers and sutras recited in daily devotions. The butsudan also typically contains the wooden tablets representing the spirits of the family ancestors, so worshiping at the butsudan is at the same time venerating the ancestors, praying to them to ensure their continued blessing for the family.

Worship at Buddhist temples has a somewhat different character from that at Shinto shrines. Whereas shrines are usually simple and natural, without statues, in Buddhist temples there are usually elaborate altars and statues of Buddhas and bodhisattvas, the inner darkness of the ornate temple rooms illuminated with candles that reflect

light off the gilded statues and decorations. Many villages and neighborhoods have parish Buddhist temples, where not only Buddhas but also the ashes of ancestors of parish families are enshrined. Often these parish temples have cemeteries where families erect memorial stones dedicated to the ancestors. As at the butsudan in the home, so also at the temple people make offerings and speak prayers and sutras before the altars. Priests associated with these temples perform worship services, commemorative rituals, memorial rites, and the like, for their own needs and for the welfare of the laypeople. The temple cultic life is especially active, of course, during the major annual and seasonal festivals.

The ultimate purpose of Buddhist worship is to attain enlightenment and Buddhahood, but, as we have seen, the path toward the ultimate transformation is broad and can find expression in many types of ritual and worship. One prays before the Buddhas and ancestors to achieve ends such as the protection of the nation, success in life, healing of the sick, or repose for the dead. Several of the Buddhas and bodhisattvas are widely worshiped for such benefits. Very popular is Kannon (the bodhisattva Avalokiteshvara), the "goddess of mercy," who provides help in almost any kind of need, such as conceiving a child, easy childbirth, safe travel, and much more. In times of sickness people pray and recite scripture before a statue of Yakushi, the healing Buddha; and to request repose and merit for the dead, people pray before statues of Jizo, patron saint of the spirits of the dead, especially of dead children. Whereas such acts of worship are directed toward immediate needs, we should remember that the power for these benefits comes from the wisdom and compassion of those beings who have achieved Buddhahood and who are believed, through various means, to lead their devotees toward that goal.

Many of these activities of worship can be carried out by laypeople with little or no priestly help. Sometimes a group of laypeople will form their own association for the purpose of worshiping a particular Buddha, holding regular meetings in their homes during which they have simple services and social gatherings.

Japanese following the popular Pure Land and Nichiren traditions exemplify typical patterns of group worship, whether at home or temple, with or without priests participating. The Pure Land worship service includes the usual elements of Buddhist worship, but a special focus is on reciting the Nembutsu, "Namu Amida Butsu," over and over again, for this is the formula by which the worshipers receive the merit and compassion of Amida Buddha. Worship might include chanting verses from Shinran's writings, reading Shinran's biography, listening to sermons, and discussing the teachings.

Buddhists following the Nichiren tradition, one of the most lively and populous of the various traditions in modern Japan, follow Nichiren's special design for worship, focusing on the gohonzon as the object of worship and using the daimoku chant. The gohonzon, as designed by Nichiren, is a kind of mandala without pictorial images; it is a scroll inscribed with names of leading Buddhas and bodhisattvas of the Lotus Sutra, with the sacred words of the daimoku chant at the center. This is the chief object of worship both in homes and in temples. The daimoku is the formula, "Namu myoho rengekyo" (Praise to the wonderful truth of the Lotus Sutra), which Nichiren considered to contain the universal Buddha nature. Nichiren worship thus consists of reciting the daimoku before a gohonzon, to the accompaniment of drums, with worshipers often fingering the particular Nichiren rosary of 108 beads. The worship is dramatic and intense and is felt to produce many spiritual benefits as well as benefits for everyday life. Modern Nichiren groups in Japan often include informal small group discussion sessions that provide opportunity for individuals to share their personal problems and receive Buddhist insight in dealing with them.

In contrast to the Pure Land and Nichiren forms, the characteristic Zen Buddhist rituals are carried on primarily by Zen monks and nuns, although certain laypeople may also participate on occasion. Whereas priests of Zen temples may perform the usual types of Buddhist worship, also for the benefit of the laypeople, the distinctive Zen ritual discipline is meditation. The typical daily ritual in a Chan (Zen) monastery is discussed earlier concerning traditional China. Here let us look more closely at the actual practice of zazen, sitting in meditation. The simplicity of the meditation hall and rituals of sutra-chanting, bowing, and offering incense before a statue of the Buddha help set the atmosphere for the period of quiet sitting. Practitioners in the Soto tradition sit facing the wall; in the Rinzai tradition, the meditators face into the room, looking down to the floor in front. The basic ritual discipline is the art of sitting itself. Here is Master Dogen's famous description of how to sit:

> At the site of your regular sitting, spread out thick matting and place a cushion above it. Sit either in the full-lotus or half-lotus position. In the full-lotus position, you first place your right foot on your left thigh and your left foot on your right thigh. In the half-lotus, you simply press your left foot against your right thigh. You should have your robes and belt loosely bound and arranged in order. Then place your right hand on your left leg and your left palm [facing upwards] on your right palm, thumb-tips touching. Thus sit upright in correct bodily posture, neither inclining to the left nor to the right, neither leaning forward or backward. Be sure your eyes are on a plane with your shoulders and your nose in line with your navel. Place your tongue against the front roof of your mouth, with teeth and lips both shut. Your eyes should always remain open, and you should breathe gently through your nose. Once you have adjusted your posture, take a deep breath, inhale and exhale, rock your body right and left and settle into a steady immobile sitting position. Think of not-thinking. How do you think of not-thinking? Non-thinking. This in itself is the essential art of zazen.[1]

During the meditation session, which may last thirty to forty minutes, one monk may walk slowly among the

Zen monks sitting in mediation at Eiheiji Temple, with one monk receiving "encouragement" from a fellow monk.

seated meditators carrying the long flat *keishaku* stick; when someone feels drowsy or unalert, she may bow toward the monk who will then strike her sharply on her shoulders, an act of compassion to assist in meditation. In the Soto tradition, the meditator simply practices zazen and empties the mind, without effort, without purpose. In the Rinzai tradition, the meditator may work on such koans as "The sound of one hand clapping," "What was your face before you were born?" or simply "Mu!" (nothingness), allowing that koan to break through ordinary dualistic notions of self and object. Regular interviews with the master for testing and growing insight also form part of the meditation discipline and ritual.

Sacred Times in Japan

There are a great number of festivals in Japan, depending on the region and specific community, and these festivals may be predominantly Shinto or Buddhist, often containing elements from both traditions together with many local popular traditions. Probably the most highly ranked festivals are those at the Grand Shrines of Ise where Amaterasu is enshrined: the Spring Festival, the Autumn Festival, and especially the Niiname-sai (November 23–24) at which the emperor offers the first fruits of the grain harvest. The Niiname-sai is modeled on the ancient ceremony in which a newly enthroned emperor first offers the new food to Amaterasu and the other kami. Other important local Shinto festivals are widely attended by tourists, such as the Aoi Matsuri in Kyoto on May 15, involving a procession through the streets with ox-drawn carts, horses with golden saddles, and everything decorated with wisteria.

Among the universally celebrated festivals are some that no longer have specific religious significance such as the Doll Festival (for girls) on March 3, Boys' Day on May 5 (now Children's Day, a national holiday), and the Star Festival on July 7. Of important religious significance are the Great Purification celebrated at local shrines on June 30 and also the spring and fall festivals for the tutelary kami. There is also the festival of the Buddha's birthday, celebrated in Japan on April 8, when temples perform a special ritual of pouring sweet tea over a statue of the infant Buddha, in memory of the story of Shakyamuni's birth when flower petals and sweet tea rained from the sky. More solemn than this festive springtime celebration is the observance marking the Buddha's attainment of enlightenment, generally held on December 8. At this time Zen monasteries hold specially intensive training sessions over a seven-day period, culminating in all-night sitting until the dawn of December 8.

The Obon Festival (Ullambana), celebrated in the middle of the seventh lunar month (today most Japanese observe it in the middle of July), is Buddhist-inspired and related completely to the ancestors, like the similar festival in China discussed earlier. The spirits of the ancestors are welcomed in the home at the butsudan with special offerings, and the families visit the ancestral graves and clean the area and place new flowers. Although the festival has to do with the dead, it tends to be joyful, with the spirits warmly welcomed on the night of the thirteenth day of the month, entertained with colorful dances and singing, and then, after two days, sent off by fires to the graveyards. In some places lanterns are floated on a nearby river. Obon festivals often conclude with people dancing around a temporary tower holding singers and drummers. During the festival Buddhist priests hold memorial services in temples and homes. Services remembering the dead and visits to the family graves also take place during the spring and autumn equinoxes (Higan-e); rituals include repenting of past sins and praying for enlightenment in the next life.

The New Year Festival, now almost universally observed at the beginning of January (the old lunar calendar has it in February), is the most vigorously celebrated festival of the year and the most important family event. Toward the end of December there is much bustle as workers leave the cities to journey back to the country to be with their families. Business and industry shut down for a number of days, and the perpetual smog over industrial cities even lifts a bit. Shrines perform a great purification to purify people of defilements from the previous year. Each family cleans and symbolically purifies the house, putting a pine branch on the outside gate and hanging a straw rope over the entrance. Special New Year foods are prepared, especially dried fish and *o-mochi*, a sticky rice cake. Offerings are made to the ancestors, the family eats, drinks, and relaxes together, and with midnight the cry goes up, "Akemashite omedeto gozaimasu!" (Happy New Year!). At Buddhist temples at midnight the temple gongs are struck 108 times, signifying the 108 kinds of blind passions that should be purged out in the coming year.

On New Year's Day people make their first visit of the New Year to the local shrine, wearing traditional kimono, to begin the New Year with luck and happiness. Buddhist temples are also visited, but the bulk of the seventy million people who make the New Year visit go to Shinto shrines. Many buy new shrine symbols and paper to place in their household shrines, since the old ones have been used up in absorbing all the bad luck and illness in the past year. For the next few days there is general relaxing and visiting of family and friends. Gradually the festivities end, people journey back to the cities, and around January 15 in a bonfire celebration the New Year decorations are burned. So the people have purified the home and the community, renewed family bonds and contacts with the ancestors, visited the kami and Buddhas anew, and now they start off the new year with fresh vitality.

Besides these rituals and festivals there are still other opportunities for personal spiritual growth. People can go individually to the shrine and apologize to the kami for wrongdoing, or, for stronger penance, perform the ritual of the "hundredfold repentance"—walking between two stone markers one hundred times reciting repentance. Going on pilgrimages to special temples, shrines, sacred mountains, and the like, is another well-used ritual of spiritual transformation. Since the Heian era (794–1185) there have been people who engaged in special training and practices on sacred mountains, combining Buddhist practices with local Shinto traditions, and these mountain priests (yamabushi) would serve as guides to pilgrims going on retreats to these mountains. Today there still are some Shinto organizations that continue the traditions of these earlier mountain ascetics, and there are in addition many formal and informal mountain pilgrimage groups. A popular Buddhist pilgrimage takes the devotee to eighty-eight special temples on the island of Shikoku, worshiping the main Buddhas enshrined in these temples. The main emphasis on the Shikoku pilgrimage is "walking with St. Kukai," the holy man born in Shikoku who founded Shingon Buddhism in Japan and is widely believed to be alive yet today, walking with the pilgrims and helping those who need assistance. The pilgrimage is made by individuals, family groups, groups of friends, and even more formally organized pilgrimage groups.

Rituals of the Passages of Life

At the great moments of life passages or crises, many Japanese look especially to the assistance of guardian kami, whose protective arms enfold all their children. Unlike Western ideas of change and decay, the Shinto view is of life as a clear and pure river with endless change, freshness, and renewal. And so the main passages of life are dedicated to the kami for purification and renewal.

The kami are frequently invoked to assist couples who want to have a baby. In earlier times there were many avoidances associated with childbirth, an impure situation especially because of the blood involved. After a month the child is considered free from impurities and is taken to the shrine of the tutelary kami, to be dedicated to the kami who is affirmed as the source of life and protection. There are special events the family celebrates with the young child, on the first birthday, for example, or the first par-

The bride and groom worshiping the kami at a modern Shinto wedding ceremony.

ticipation in the Doll Festival or Boys' Day. A special festival on November 15 is "Seven-Five-Three Festival"—for girls of seven and three and boys of five—when the children dress up in their best and visit the shrine.

The passage from childhood to adulthood is marked in a number of ways, for example, when a young man first participates in the local festival by helping to carry the portable shrine. For many Japanese youth, the "examination hell," which finally leads to entrance to a good university, is a critical passage in life, and there are visits to the kami for help in learning. Today Japan has a national holiday on January 15 called "Adult Day," on which all twenty-year-olds are formally recognized as adults and show their gratitude by visiting a local shrine. This very modern tradition is a good example of how Shinto has adapted its institutions to modern-day life.

Marriage is an important affair, joining not only two lives but also two families. Even in modern Westernized Japan, many families prefer to arrange marriages for their children, using a family friend as a "go-between," with, of course, considerable input from the young people about the prospective mate. Weddings traditionally occurred in the home, and the crucial ceremony was the ritual exchange of *o-sake* (rice wine) between the bride and groom. In modern times it has become customary to have the wedding ceremony at a shrine with very formal Japanese (or Western) dress. The couple sit before a priest in the presence of family and close friends. The priest waves the purification wand and offers prayers that they may be free of ill fortune and blessed by good things. And all present receive some o-sake as a sharing with the protective kami who have been invoked. If and when the new couple is able to build their own house, they will have a Shinto priest perform a purification ritual at the site, and there will also be a framework-raising ceremony to thank the kami and invoke their continued protection.

Whereas Japanese turn to the kami during the changes in the flow of life, when death approaches their thoughts turn to Buddhist teachings, and most observe Buddhist funeral practices. In a sense, Shinto has to do with life, fertility, and growth; Buddhism in Japan has to do especially with death and the ancestral existence after death. So the funeral service is conducted by Buddhist priests, reciting Buddhist scriptures at the wake, in the funeral service, and at the cremation. A Buddhist posthumous name is given to the deceased and written on a memorial tablet, which is set up in front of the butsudan in the home. The family is in mourning for forty-nine days, after which the dead person is considered to be transformed into an ancestral spirit. After this memorial masses are held on the anniversary days of the death, often ending with the thirty-third anniversary, when the deceased joins the more general generations of ancestors.

Art in Japanese Religion

A deep aesthetic sense permeates Japanese culture, and this sense has roots both in Shinto and in Buddhist-Confucianist traditions from China. Many of the arts are closely related to Buddhism, especially Zen, but the indigenous Japanese outlook on life first established the integration of art and religion that is so characteristic of Japanese culture.

The Shinto attitude is that the elements of nature are the pure and beautiful children of the kami, and humans are to cooperate with the kami to promote this goodness and beauty. The land itself is pure, sacred, and beautiful as created by the kami, and therefore the presence of the kami is revealed not only by words but especially by aesthetic awareness of the beauty of nature. Leaders of craft guilds in ancient times acted as priests, invoking the kami of the tree and the metal before cutting wood or forging metal to create cultural objects. Still today carpenters may intone prayers to the kami when raising the head beam of a building. Further, the idea that human cultural creations are made in service to the kami inspires artists to create the most aesthetically pleasing houses, shrines, clothing, food, and the rest. The Shinto perspective has contributed an emphasis on the natural and the simple in art forms, a reflection of the true pure heart.

The Shinto tradition has not done much with iconography—rarely have there been statues or images to represent the kami, for example. Rather, the arts to which Shinto has contributed are those related to ritual, such as dance, music, drama, poetry, clothing, food, and so forth.

In Shinto worship, the kami are summoned to this world and this shrine, entertained here, and then sent away again—and the arts flourished in this setting, as entertainment for the kami and the people as well. The shrine dance-drama, kagura, has its origins in the mythology of the kami, when one of the heavenly kami performed an ecstatic dance, entertaining the kami so as to entice Amaterasu out of the rock-cave into which she had withdrawn. In ancient times, Shinto shamanesses drew on that heavenly model as they performed kagura, to the accompaniment of music, for entertaining the kami in worship festivals. Today, kagura has many different forms throughout Japan, performed by young women of the shrine, called miko, as a central part of shrine festivals.

Japanese poetry likewise grew up in a strong Shinto world, with poems in the classical uta or waka form (with 5- and 7-syllable lines) found already in the mythological texts and in the eighth-century poetic collection, the *Manyoshu*. These poems express the free interchange between kami and humans, reflecting the seamless, natural early Shinto world of meaning.

Buddhist art in Japan is influenced both by developments in China and by the pre-Buddhist Japanese sensitivity for the natural and the simple as appropriate for sacred power. Much use is made of art in Buddhist practice in Japan, serving to enhance rituals, create a sense of sacred time and space, make present the Buddha power, or assist in realizing the Buddha-nature. Chinese Buddhist art was carried over into Japan—iconography, including sculptures and paintings of Buddhas and bodhisattvas, paintings of mandalas, temple architecture, literature, music, drama, and the like. But in appropriating this art the Japanese also transformed it in keeping with the Japanese aesthetic tradition, as is evident in the simple, natural, and open architecture of some monastery halls, slender and graceful sculptures of Buddhas and bodhisattvas, simple gardens of rocks and sand, and Buddhist poetry inspired by nature.

Kukai, the founder of Shingon Buddhism in Japan and himself an excellent calligrapher, laid a strong foundation for the use of art in Japanese Buddhism by emphasizing the universal Buddha-nature in all of nature. Using the art of poetry, Kukai wrote:

> The three Mysteries [body, speech and mind of Mahavairocana] pervade the entire universe,
> Adorning gloriously the mandala of infinite space.
> Being painted by brushes of mountains, by ink of oceans,

> Heaven and earth are the bindings of a sutra revealing the Truth.
> Reflected in a dot are all things in the universe;
> Contained in the data of senses and mind is the sacred book.[2]

Kukai influenced the arts especially by promoting the Tantric idea that through ritual and art forms one experiences the universal Buddha-nature. Since, as he taught, all the world is the Dharma Body, identical with the cosmic Sun Buddha Mahavairocana, through aesthetic forms like hand gestures, chanted formulas, paintings, and the like, it is possible to experience that Buddha-nature. One must take care, Kukai cautioned, not to take the finger pointing to the moon for the moon itself. The highest truths cannot be expressed in words or forms. Yet through ritual use of speech and forms, especially paintings of mandalas, in meditative practice, one can act out the cosmic drama of Mahavairocana's self-activity, "entering self into Self [Mahavairocana] so that the Self enters into the self."[3] The aesthetic forms thus aid in awakening to the Buddha nature.

Zen Buddhist art in Japan, deeply influenced by Chinese aesthetic developments in the Song era, uses restraint, empty space, and natural materials to heighten the Mahayana awareness that "form is emptiness, emptiness is form." A painting such as Sesshu's (1420–1506) misty landscapes often leaves much empty space and merely suggests the lines of the form. Zen temples may have rock gardens, such as the one at Ryoanji Temple in Kyoto, created from scattered rocks on a base of raked sand; here emptiness and form seem to interact with each other, creating an atmosphere of stillness and tranquility resonating with the "suchness" that underlies all reality.

Buddhist art in Japan, like Shinto art, has always reflected a concern for the natural and the simple, bringing to fruition the notion that life is art lived beautifully and purely. Under Buddhist influence, many of the traditional Japanese arts are thought of as "ways," complete with spiritual training and discipline—for example, the way of the sword, the way of poetry, the way of painting, the way of noh drama, the way of flowers, and the way of tea. Basic to these arts is the Mahayana Buddhist sense of the nonduality of samsara and nirvana—that is, the experience of the Buddha-nature can be expressed aesthetically in the commonness of daily life, whether that is the sparse brushstrokes of a landscape paint-

A *rock garden at a sub-temple in Daitokuji Temple in Kyoto.*

ing, a few common words put together in a short poem, or a social gathering for a cup of tea.

For example, the poems of Japanese Buddhist poets attain a deep sense of the immediacy of the nirvanic experience in the midst of natural life. A waka poem from Saigyo (1118–1190) expresses the sense of impermanence:

> In deep reverie
> On how time buffets all,
> I hear blows fall

On a temple bell . . . drawing out more
Of its sounds and my sadness.[4]

In even terser form, haiku (seventeen-syllable) poems present a snapshot of reality that can only be understood intuitively by the mind, as in Basho's (1644–1694) celebrated haiku:

furu ike ya	An ancient pond, ah!
kawazu tobikomu	A frog leaps in—
mizu no oto	Water's sound.

Such a poem presents the suchness of reality in its undivided immediacy, devoid of our mental and emotional interpretations; it returns one, for a moment at least, to the "original mind" of enlightenment.

Japanese culture produced a rich set of theater arts, evolving from the kagura dance-drama and various kinds of popular plays and drama, further influenced by Buddhist ideals. Lively, colorful kabuki plays and bunraku (puppet theater) are well known theater arts still today flourishing and popular among the Japanese. An important form of theater that developed early in medieval times is noh drama, a sophisticated art of traditional drama and music brought to its height by master Zeami (1363–1443). Noh is closely connected to the classical literary tradition as well as the ritual tradition of music and dance. But it also came under the strong influence of Zen Buddhism, in the creation of its aesthetic ideals. The goal, according to Zeami, is for the actor to use his spiritual strength (developed through long, intense discipline) to take the audience beyond the outer appearance, to reveal the inner essence and depth of reality. The term yugen ("sublime beauty") is used to speak of this form of beauty through which we experience the profound, ineffable, inner qualities of existence. The long, piercing flute sound that opens the play transports us beyond the normal world; the chanting of the chorus and the music of flute and drums; the elaborate costume and masks of the actors; and the slow, exquisite dance movements of the actors all reveal a spiritual quality of great profundity. To the actors (and the well informed audience), the way of noh is a spiritual path as well as an artistic pursuit.

Besides the artistic ideals, the plots of noh dramas typically express religious meaning, with the appearance of kami, bodhisattvas, demons, priests, and various spirits;

and themes of karma, reincarnation, spirit possession, worshiping the Buddha, and attainment of salvation. The typical plot would have a troubled ghost first appear, drawn to a particular place because of attachments and passions still remaining from life. The ghost then is induced to tell her or his story, often reenacting those crucial parts that have to do with the continuing passions and attachments. Through all of this, a deliverance occurs and the ghost (and perhaps the audience) is granted release and salvation.

The way of tea (chanoyu or chado) is perhaps the epitome of a "secular" Japanese art that was interpreted by some great masters of the art as a way of enlightenment. The way of tea is a way of life focused on the tea ceremony, encompassing many of the traditional arts like gardening, architecture, flower arranging, and calligraphy. It involves stringent training and discipline, and it moves toward self-transformation and awakening. But the materials of the art are precisely common everyday experiences: rustic utensils (highly valued, of course, for their rustic beauty) for preparing tea, a simple hut, a tranquil garden, a sprig of flowers, some food and a cup of tea shared between friends.

Wabi is an essential aesthetic quality sought after in the practice of the tea ceremony art. It is the aesthetic experience of poverty and insufficiency, of the bare bone of reality, of the pith or essence that underlies the abundance. Wabi, one great tea master said, is seeing the moon dimly shining through a veil of clouds. It is the appreciation of the cold and withered branch in winter. The great master Sen Rikyu (1521–1591), considered the main founder of the tea ceremony art, taught the meaning of wabi by means of this poem:

> To those who await
> only the cherry blossoms—
> how I would like to show
> the first patches of green grass
> through the snow of the mountain village.

The art of chanoyu involves a whole way of life, with years of discipline and practice required to master all the arts and cultural knowledge and to develop the aesthetic sensitivity required of a tea master—and of a guest. Training typically includes Zen discipline as well as training in all the cultural arts of Japan. The tea ceremony gathering itself is a very slow, deliberate affair—a formal tea ceremony with a full meal and two servings of tea lasts four hours. The host and the handful of invited guests are co-actors in a kind of plotless drama as they share food, drink tea, and enjoy the unique experience of this particular moment. The ritual art of the tea ceremony slows down this common everyday experience, as it were, savoring the aesthetic quality of each movement, sound, sight, and taste. Every action, every sense, every aesthetic form is attuned to the real. The tea ceremony is "a one-time meeting once in a lifetime"—that is, it focuses all of life's experience in the timelessness of the present moment, touching that depth of reality that, to Buddhists, is none other than the Buddha-nature. Sen Rikyu is said to have expressed the spiritual meaning of the tea ceremony art in this way:

> The essential meaning of *wabi* [Rikyu's style of tea ceremony] is to manifest the Buddha-world of complete purity free from defilements. In this garden path and in this thatched hut every speck of dust is cleared out. When host and guest together commune direct from the heart, no ordinary measures of proportion or ceremonial rules are followed. A fire is made, water is boiled, and tea is drunk—nothing more! For here we experience the disclosure of the Buddha-mind.[5]

To the twenty million people today, in Japan and elsewhere, who involve themselves to some extent in chanoyu, this art has many meanings. In a primary way, it represents to them an important and authentic piece of traditional Japanese culture. But it is perhaps unique among the arts in that what appears to be a purely secular social gathering can be in fact a disciplined way to experience qualities of enlightenment.

SOCIETY AND THE GOOD LIFE

How should we live? To be Japanese means to live as part of the Japanese people. The sense of community in Japan has been strong from ancient times, and the good life means living in accordance with the role one has within the family, the community, and the nation.

Structure of Japanese Society: Sacred Community

An outstanding feature of Japanese society is the strong group solidarity, as in China. The sense of individualism is minimized; it is the social nexus that provides identity and meaning. Perhaps because of insular isolation, Japanese society is more homogeneous than Chinese society. Emigrants from outside were assimilated already in the prehistorical period, and since that time there have been only a few divisions in Japanese society along ethnic or cultural lines. So the concentric circles of group solidarity move out without disruption from family to clan to village/town to the whole people as one large family.

The importance of the family in Japan is much like that in China, and indeed the influence of Confucianism imported from China played a big part in structuring the family values of Japan. But even before Confucian influence, ancient Japanese society was already based in clans (*uji*) that bound familial groups together around tutelary kami, clan shrines, and a clan leader. The clans in ancient Japan each had their own family kami (*uji-gami*), which they worshiped through the head of the clan acting as the priest of the kami. This tradition of tutelary kami has continued in a modified form up to the present, at least in areas where families have maintained connections with their family shrines or with local tutelary shrines. Children, for example, are taken to the family shrine a month after birth to be dedicated to the tutelary kami. The family is certainly the keystone of Japanese society and religion; in fact, most participation in society and in religious practices is based in the family.

The traditional family often includes at least three generations, the oldest son of a family continuing the primary line and the other sons setting up branch families. The importance of the family for one's personal identity is illustrated by the common practice of referring to family members by their particular position or roles in the family. A sociological study of a village in Japan provides this typical conversation of a mother speaking to her small daughter:

"Ma-chan, has West-Grandmother gone across to the store yet?"
"No, she went out to see Eldest-Sister-Uphill first."

"Well, go tell her that Grandfather-Within wants her to bring him something from the store."[6]

Whereas everyone has a personal name, in this short conversation only the little girl's name (in diminutive form) is used, the others being designated by their place within the extended family.

The cohesion of the family is closely linked to the ancestors. A traditional family will place ancestral tablets on a butsudan (Buddhist altar) in the home and make offerings and prayers to the ancestors in household rituals. They believe that the ancestors make special visits to the family homes during the New Year celebrations and during the festival of the dead in late summer. In this way the ancestors provide blessing and protection within the ongoing family unit.

The family naturally broadens out through participation in the local community, which traditionally was the village but in modern Japan is often a city or an urban district. In the rural areas a number of farming families form a village community for economic and religious cooperation, making practical decisions for the welfare of the community and sponsoring the village shrines and festivals. Neighborhood groups in the cities sponsor local shrines and festivals in which many of the people participate.

The notion of the Japanese people as a sacred nation (*kokutai*) has been a long and powerful tradition, reaching back to the ancient mythology of the descent of people

Children dressed in their finest, visiting a shrine for the Seven-Five-Three children's festival.

from the kami and continuing in varying forms up to the disestablishment of Shinto after World War II. Throughout much of Japanese history religion has been closely bound up with the nation, focusing on the emperor as the head of the people, descended from Amaterasu, the sun kami. Often this was expressed in terms of a "father-child" relation between emperor and people, with the people expected to dedicate themselves wholeheartedly to the welfare of the emperor and the whole nation. It is true that this ideology of loyalty to the emperor and the nation was abused as a tool of totalitarianism in the hands of military expansionists in the World War II tragedy. But at the end of the war Emperor Hirohito issued an Imperial Rescript to renounce the emperor's "divinity" and reinterpret the relationship:

> The ties between us and our people have always stood upon mutual trust and affection. They do not depend upon mere legends and myths. They are not predicated on the false assumption that the Emperor is divine and that the Japanese people are superior to other races and fated to rule the world.[7]

And under the Allied occupation, the disestablishment of Shinto and the separation of government and religion in Japan were carried out.

But still today the nation has a semireligious character for many Japanese. Many have deep respect and reverence for the emperor as the symbol of the unity of the whole people. They recognize that the state no longer supports religious activities but feel it is important nevertheless, for example, that the special shrine of Amaterasu at Ise is maintained, that the emperor performs the special thanksgiving rites at harvest time for the welfare of the whole nation, and that those who died for the nation be remembered through special rituals at Yasukuni Shrine (the national shrine for war dead). Most Japanese took much interest in the recent funeral rites for Emperor Hirohito, and the rituals associated with the enthronement of the new emperor, Akihito. National observances like these are somewhat controversial today, given the official separation of state and religion. But the important point is that the Japanese people are more than just a people who happen to live in a certain place; the people still in some sense make up a sacred community that gives its people a special sense of belonging.

There are, of course, other kinds of community identity in Japan. In the early Tokugawa period, following Neo-Confucian ideas, the samurai (warriors) cultivated loyalty to superiors into a path of self-transformation called bushido (way of the warrior). Bushido involved an elaborate code of ethical honor and spiritual conduct, focusing on unlimited loyalty to one's lord (daimyo), bravery and self-sacrifice to the point of death, and a rigorous spiritual discipline often based in Zen meditation. That same kind of group loyalty focused on a master or leader can be seen in schools of the traditional arts, where the head of the lineage (the *iemoto*) is the focus of intense group tradition and loyalty. Some sociologists have pointed out that a similar type of group loyalty operates in many modern Japanese corporations.

Other groups are more specifically religious. There are Buddhist lay societies, for example. Community identity is especially important for members of the New Religions, the recently formed religious movements that have incorporated many of the traditional religious forms but offer to the believers a more personal and intimate sense of belonging to a large family of like-minded believers. These New Religions usually have a powerfully charismatic founder or leader, and the new believers can enter into a "parent-child" relationship with that leader. Typically there are many group activities, including regular meetings, pilgrimages, and even sports events, to recreate the sense of belonging that perhaps has been lost with the decline of the traditional communities in Japan. These New Religions have grown tremendously in Japan since World War II and for many Japanese appear to provide a most important sense of community identity and belonging.

Religious Leadership in Japan

From ancient times there has not been a sharp line separating kami and humans, and Japanese have always looked on great ancestors and powerful leaders as personifications of kami. In certain periods the emperor was considered "manifest kami" as direct descendant of Amaterasu and as father of the Japanese national family. Through the centuries the role of the emperor waxed and waned, but in general he (or she, in some early cases) always had the double role of being the chief of state and the chief priest of Shinto, since politics and religion were closely bound together. Even though Shinto is disestablished from state support today, the emperor still performs certain rituals such as the harvest thanksgiving ceremony, acting in his capacity as the spiritual head of the traditional Japanese religion.

In early times the head of each clan had special responsibilities to act as priest in worshiping the kami, sometimes communicating with the kami through a priestess or shamaness. Gradually special families of Shinto priests developed, regulated by the government, and today the priests of most of the shrines are educated and certified under the auspices of the Association of Shinto Shrines. There is no longer a hereditary priesthood. During the wartime shortage of priests, wives of some priests performed the priestly duties in place of their husbands, and today some 1,300 of the nearly 20,000 Shinto priests are women.

Of course, as in other Buddhist lands, Buddhist monks and nuns are also holy persons who provide important religious leadership for the Japanese people. A special characteristic of Japanese Buddhism is the tradition, starting with Shinran of the Pure Land school, of married Buddhist priests. Shinran broke with the Buddhist tradition of celibacy for monks because of his conviction that in this degenerate age such practices bring no merit and are not helpful. Following Shinran's example, the tradition of a "household Buddhism" developed in all Japanese Buddhist schools, with married Buddhist priests in charge of local temples.

Among the holy persons in Japan is also the shaman or medium who lives among the people and serves as healer and exorcist apart from the organized religions. One important tradition in northern Japan was the blind shamaness who received special training and was able to communicate with the dead. Founders of some of the New Religions have also shown shamanistic traits, believed to be possessed by sacred power and thus qualified to give revelation and guidance. It is not unusual that the leader of a New Religion is considered to be a "living kami" (*ikigami*).

Though in Japan women have generally had roles subordinate to men, there are certainly many examples of powerful, leading women, both divine and human. There is, first of all, Amaterasu, the sun kami, the divine ancestor of the imperial family, the Ruler of the Plain of High Heaven. It seems that in prehistoric times the Japanese

had women rulers, and an important early emperor was Empress Jingu. There was the tradition of the princess-priestess, rooted in ancient shamanism in Japan. A woman relative—niece, sister, or wife—of the clan chieftain would be consecrated and would live apart to maintain absolute purity. She would go into trances, possessed by the kami of the clan, giving advice to the chieftain. This system was institutionalized by the emperor, with the Ise princess-priestess performing this function with relation to the great kami Amaterasu. But after Chinese culture and Confucian ideas entered in the eighth century women seldom attained leadership roles.

In the feudal era, court women were educated and strong, at the center of court intrigues. One of Japan's greatest literary works, the *Genji Monogatari*, was written by a woman, Lady Murasaki, providing a look at court life and with that a glimpse into women's lives in the centers of power in the Heian era. Throughout the centuries there have been shamanesses (*miko*), especially in rural areas, playing heroic roles, healing the sick, helping those in need, and telling fortunes.

It is significant that many of the New Religions, such as Tenrikyo, Omoto, and Tensho-kotai-jingu-kyo, have been founded by women. These women often gained their transformatory experiences later in life, having gone through the whole life cycle of a woman. Some of these women are considered by their followers to be *ikigami*, "living kami." Despite the traditional split in Japan between women's roles in the domestic arena and men's roles in the public business world, women today are highly educated and are making an impact in the public realm. There are some women functioning as Shinto priests, and women practice Zen meditation and serve as masters in some cases.

The Good Life in the Japanese View

How should we live? What is the good life for us and our community? Like people of all cultures, Japanese also are interested in these questions. It is typical of the Japanese to be directed more toward actually living the good life rather than discussing what it is. It goes without saying that the Buddhist and the Confucian ethical views, discussed earlier, are very important for most Japanese. But the Japanese understanding of Buddhist and Confucian ethics has been tempered and shaped by the traditional Shinto outlook on life.

Unlike many religions, Shinto has never had any standardized written law code to guide behavior, nor are ideas of morality and ethics discussed in the sacred texts. Once, in Tokugawa times, a Confucian scholar argued that the lack of such codes showed the ancient Japanese were morally deficient: "As proof of this there is the fact that no native Japanese words exist for the concepts of humanity, righteousness, decorum, music, filial piety, and fraternal affection." A leading scholar of the Shinto restoration movement, Hirata Atsutane (1776–1843), responded indignantly:

> Humanity, righteousness, filial piety, and the rest are all principles governing the proper conduct of man. If they are always automatically observed and never violated, it is unnecessary to teach them. . . . The ancient Japanese all constantly and correctly practiced what the Chinese called humanity, righteousness, the five cardinal virtues and the rest, without having any need to name them or to teach them.[8]

It is Shinto belief that a moral sense is a natural property of human beings. In proper harmony with the kami, people will naturally do what is good and right in their personal lives and in family and community.

Not only does Shinto not have any written moral code, but it also does not have a strict sense of what is right and what is wrong or what is good and what is evil. Nothing is unconditionally evil, even illicit sexual relations or killing. Good and evil are relative notions, to be understood in the context of family, clan, community, nature, and the rest. The meaning and value of a particular action depend on the motivations, purpose, circumstances, time, and place. In the myths and legends about the kami and the early ruling families, there is much killing, sex, stealing, and the like. But "evil" arises when a kami becomes angry and rough and obstructs the processes of life, and "good" occurs when the kami is quieted down and brings benefits. Similarly, something is good when fortunate things happen and bad when unlucky things happen, apart from considerations based on some standard of morality.

This is not to say that Shinto is immoral or amoral. Traditions of proper behavior have been passed on in families and communities, and there is wide consensus on the general outlines of the good life. It is recognized, according to Shinto scholar Sokyo Ono, that "that which disturbs the social order, causes misfortune, and obstructs worship of the kami and the peaceful development of this world of kami is evil." There is also consensus on what is good: "Generally speaking, however, man's heart must be sincere; his conduct must be courteous and proper; an evil heart, selfish desire, strife, and hatred must be removed; conciliation must be practiced; and feelings of goodwill, cooperation and affection must be realized."[9]

The emphasis here is on the inner motivation, the need for a sincere and pure heart. Thus the important moral quality of an act depends on intentionality, on the sincerity or honesty (*makoto*) of the heart. That sincerity is common to kami and to humans, and if one is in harmony with the kami and acts in sincerity, she will be doing the best, being "true" to the whole situation.

From this perspective we can see that the Shinto view of right behavior is not only situational and intentional; it is also naturalistic. Since our nature, and the nature of all the world, is pure and good as given from the kami, the good life is also the most fully natural life. There is no fundamental breech between humans and the natural world. This means that all natural needs, instincts, desires, and passions are also good and can be indulged in with a sincere and honest heart—sexuality, acquiring wealth, drinking and eating, playing, and the rest. It further means that the good life brings people into close harmony with nature itself, for together the world and humans are siblings, children of the kami. So the good life means an ecological balance, with respect and love for nature as well as human society. One aspect of this ethical harmony with nature is the value Japanese have always placed on art; part of human responsibility is to assist the kami in making human life and nature as beautiful as possible.

Buddhist Ethical Contributions in Japan

The Buddhist ethical system has also been very influential in Japan, of course. The most characteristically Japanese developments in Buddhism—Pure Land, Nichiren, and Zen—have each contributed to the shaping of the Japanese view of the good life. Shinran's writings place much stress on the gratitude that should permeate the life of one who knows she is saved by Amida's power. "When I consider well the Vow upon which Amida Buddha thought for five aeons, (I reflect) it was for me Shinran alone. O how grateful I am for the Original Vow which aspired to save one who possesses such evil karma."[10] The sense of deep obligation to the compassion of the Buddha is to find expression not only in reciting the Nembutsu but also in showing sympathy for others and in refraining from speaking ill of others. Later interpreters of Pure Land ethics tended somewhat toward a passive quietism, based on the view that human life is inevitably under the sway of passion even for those who have faith in Amida. Rennyo (1414–1499), for example, constructed a theory of two levels of moral truth: the believer should obey the conventional morality, at the same time knowing that he is free from such obligations because his destiny is determined solely through faith in Amida.

Nichiren Buddhism, at least in some of its sects, has tended to emphasize the positive value of the world and ordinary human activities, arising from the Mahayana equation of nirvana and samsara. The Nichiren perspective often includes a wholehearted affirmation of the positive benefits offered by the modern world, with its science and technology, its opportunities for a happy, prosperous life. Some of the new Nichiren movements of today, such as Soka Gakkai, explicitly direct concern toward human fulfillment and worldly benefits that accrue to the person following the Nichiren path.

Zen Buddhism, in a somewhat different way, also affirms a this-worldly ethical outlook, building on the Mahayana idea that the ultimate truth transcends all dualities, including those of right and wrong or good and evil. Of course, Zen masters do not promote immorality, but they remind Buddhists that all moral values are relative. Right conduct does not result from following rules but from the spontaneous expression of inner awakening. A popular figure in the Japanese Zen tradition is Ikkyu Sojun (1394–1481), an eccentric Zen master who gained a reputation for tavern and brothel hopping, claiming they were far better places for attaining enlightenment than the corrupt establishment temples. But despite his flaunting of accepted standards of morality, Ikkyu pursued the rigors of the meditative life in preference to the pomp and rewards that could have been his through the established Zen in-

stitutions. The ideal Zen life transcends standards of right and wrong—but it results in a life of selflessness and compassion.

Principles of the Good Life: Filial Piety and Loyalty

We have emphasized the personal, subjective aspect of the good life. But we cannot forget that the main context for this life is the community—the community that includes the kami and the Buddhas, the family together with the ancestors, and the larger community and nation. In traditional Japan, questions about how one should live are inseparable from the welfare of family and nation. This does not mean that the individual is sacrificed to the group—although that mentality did have some backing during the nationalistic World War II period. The central paradigm, as in China, is the family, writ large as the national family, and the twin ethical principles are filial piety and loyalty. These principles the Japanese learned from China and Confucianism, but they are simply ways of expressing deeply held ancient Japanese values. Hirata Atsutane, a Shinto thinker deeply influenced by Neo-Confucian values, summed up this context in these words:

> Inasmuch as we originally came out of the creative spirit of the kami, [we] are endowed with the way of the kami. It implies therefore that we have the innate capacity to venerate the kami, the sovereign, and our parents, to show benevolence to our wives and children, and to carry out other obligations. . . . To live according to these [kami-given virtues] without distorting them is nothing but to follow the way of the kami.[11]

Hirata uses the same word, *venerate*, to speak of proper actions toward kami, parents, and emperor—and this is appropriate, since in the traditional Japanese view humans are children of the kami, children of their parents and ancestors, and children of the emperor. Here we see the concentric circles of the good life, with duties to family and nation simply extensions of worship of the kami. The good life is really a way of showing gratitude to the kami by contributing to the continuing evolution and welfare of the kami-based family and nation.

Duties within the family have tended to be defined in Confucian terms, with the virtue of filial piety as the core.

This is broadened to put emphasis on each person's responsibility upward toward seniors or superiors. There is, of course, a family hierarchy, and the specific grade of privilege and responsibility of each member is clearly understood—whether that be where to sit for meals, in what order to bathe, what subtleties of speech formality to use, or the degree of authority over the family budget. A major obligation, as a member of the family, is to live up to the standards of the family and do nothing to discredit it. Such "loss of face" for the family would be a serious affront to one's parents and ancestors.

The traditional Japanese idea of the good life maintains the centrality of the family, at the same time incorporating the nation itself as the larger context. Here the Confucian key term is loyalty. Since early times the political rule of Japan has been closely united with religion, and loyalty to the rulers, especially the emperor, has been highly valued. This sense of loyalty to one's superior was highly cultivated in bushido, the way of the samurai.

One of the reasons Japanese society has never needed strong law enforcement is the deep sense of reciprocal social obligation and duty that forms the heart of the social system. A key term is *giri*, the social obligation to help those who have helped one and to promote the welfare of the group of which one is part. Each person has obligations to live up to the standards of his or her family, rank, class, or group and to do nothing to discredit them. To fulfil these obligations, no matter what the cost, is the highest moral worth. To fail in this is *giri-shirazu*, "not knowing *giri*"— one of the worst insults imaginable. This system of reciprocal obligations works in many contexts. One important arena is the workplace, where a person is a part of a large family, the business company. Here loyalty to the company and to superiors in the company takes on important moral force. As in the family and in the nation, there are reciprocating relationships in the company structure, with duties going both ways among superiors and employees.

Concern for the Betterment of Human Society

The strong Japanese sense of group loyalty translates into a feeling of responsibility for the welfare of society. The most dramatic evidence of that is the way the person in charge assumes complete responsibility when misfortune or disaster befalls the people—whether the person is a government official or a company head. In present-day Japan the ethic of productive work for the welfare of the group (the company) and the whole nation is likewise strong. Each company employee has responsibility for the good of the whole.

According to Shinto thinkers, there is in the Shinto outlook a vision that lends itself to social change and progress. As children of the kami, people show their gratitude to the kami by working toward the fuller goodness of this evolving kami-world. As one modern Shinto author says,

> It is further believed that the *kami* who created this land are those who bless and sustain life in this world and that human participation in and advancement of this life constitute at once a realization of the will of these deities and the fulfillment of the meaning and purpose of individual existence. . . .
>
> Some people, not yet understanding Shinto, criticize it as a religion that has a primary interest in this-worldly benefits. From a Shinto perspective, however, an interest in tangible benefits that will promote life in this world is regarded as a perfectly natural consequence of its esteem for the *kami* that bestow and enhance life.[12]

From this Shinto point of view, Japanese people can participate wholeheartedly in promoting the betterment and further evolving of life in the world, realizing it as the unfolding of kami-life that is infinite and inexhaustible.

In a land that has had its share of bloody violence down through the centuries, many Japanese today draw on the harmony promoted in Shinto and the pacificism of Buddhism to present to the world a voice for peace and reconciliation. Like all religions, the Japanese religions also have in the past been used to lend support to violence and war. But many religious leaders today, freed from political ideology, continue to support the unique heritage of Japan while seeking the betterment and harmony of the whole world. The Association of Shinto Shrines has stated these three principles:

1. To express gratitude for divine favor and the benefits of ancestors, and with a bright, pure, sincere mind to devote ourselves to the shrine rites and festivals.
2. To serve society and others and, in the realization of ourselves as divine messengers, to endeavor to improve and consolidate the world.
3. To identify our minds with the Emperor's mind and, in loving and being friendly with one another, to

pray for the country's prosperity and for peaceful co-existence and co-prosperity for the people of the world.[13]

Some Buddhist groups in Japan have been engaged actively in promoting interreligious cooperation and in efforts to end the risk of nuclear war in the world. Interestingly, one of the groups leading the peace movement is Rissho Koseikai, a new religious movement in the Nichiren tradition. Nichiren groups have traditionally been known for their nationalism and exclusive claims to truth, but Rissho Koseikai has launched an international movement for attaining world peace through interreligious cooperation. With Japan's unique status as the only country to have suffered from nuclear bombing, these Japanese voices for peace carry a compelling message to the rest of humankind.

DISCUSSION QUESTIONS

1. What are the four main movements of matsuri (Shinto shrine festivals)?
2. What is the main worship for Pure Land Buddhists? For Nichiren Buddhists?
3. Describe zazen.
4. Outline the interaction of Shinto and Buddhism in the rituals of life and death in Japan.
5. What is the religious significance of the artistic ways in Japan, such as poetry, noh drama, the tea ceremony (chanoyu), and others?
6. In what senses is the Shinto vision of the good life situational, intentional, and naturalistic?
7. Discuss the importance of group loyalty in Japan, as well as the sense of *giri*, in terms of Shinto and Confucianist ideals.

KEY TERMS IN JAPANESE RELIGION

Amaterasu   Sun kami, ruler of the Plain of High Heaven, ancestress of the Japanese emperors

Bushido   "Way of the warrior," the Japanese code of self-discipline for warriors, based on Zen, Shinto, and Neo-Confucian ideals

butsudan   in Japan, Buddhist altar in the home

chado   *See* **chanoyu**

chanoyu   the art of the Japanese tea ceremony; also called *chado*, "the way of tea"

Daimoku   formula used in Nichiren Buddhist worship: *Namu myoho rengekyo*, "Praise to the wonderful law of the Lotus Sutra"

Dogen   important thinker (1200–1253) and founder of Soto Zen in Japan

Eisai   founder (1141–1215) of Rinzai Zen in Japan

giri   important Japanese sense of social obligation and duty

Hidden Christians   Christians in Japan who continued their religion secretly after Christianity was outlawed in the mid-seventeenth century

Honen   founder (1133–1212) of Pure Land Buddhism as a separate sect in Japan

Ise Shrine   shrine of Amaterasu, the Japanese Sun Kami.

Izanagi and Izanami   the pair of kami who created the world, according to Japanese mythology

Jizo   popular Buddhist divinity in Japan known as the savior of the dead and helper of dead children

kami   spirits or divinities in Shinto, including mythological beings, powerful and awesome aspects of nature, and important humans

kamidana   Kami altar in the home in Japan

Kannon   Bodhisattva Avalokiteshvara, popular goddess of mercy in Japan. Guan Yin in China

koan   Zen saying or riddle used in meditation

Kojiki   records of Ancient Matters, earliest writing in Japan, a compilation of stories about the age of the kami and the beginnings of Japan

Kukai   great Japanese Buddhist thinker (773–835) and founder of Shingon

matsuri   Shinto shrine festival

Meiji Restoration   restoration of imperial rule in Japan in 1868

Motoori Norinaga   leading scholar (1730–1801) of the National Learning movement that advocated the restoration of Shinto as Japan's central religion

nembutsu   formula of calling on Amida Buddha: *Namu Amida Butsu*, "Praise to Amida Buddha"

New Religions   new religious movements in Japan, often drawing on and combining aspects of Buddhism, Shinto, and folk religion

Nichiren   Japanese Buddhist sect based single-mindedly on the Lotus Sutra, founded by the monk Nichiren (1222–1282)

Nihon Shoki   chronicles of Japan, compiled shortly after the Kojiki and containing stories about the kami and early emperors

Ninigi   grandson of Amaterasu, sent to earth to begin kami rule on earth, ancestor of first legendary Japanese emperor

noh   classical Japanese theater, closely linked to the religious traditions, especially Zen

Norito   ancient Shinto ritual prayers

Obon (Ullambana)   festival of the seventh month in Japan welcoming the ancestors

pollution   in the Shinto view, anything that hinders life and fertility by causing separation from the kami

Pure Land   popular school of Buddhism, founded in Japan especially by Honen and Shinran, focusing on the worship of Amida Buddha

purification   rituals, important in Shinto, to remove pollution and reinstate harmony and communion with the karmi

Saicho   founder (767–822) of Tendai Buddhism in Japan

samurai   the Japanese class of warriors influenced by Zen and Neo-Confucianism

School of National Learning   Shinto restoration movement during the Tokugawa period

Shingon   esoteric (Tantric) Buddhism in Japan

Shinran   disciple (1173–1262) of Honen and founder of the True Pure Land Buddhist sect in Japan

Shinto   Chinese term (**shen-dao**) used to designate the Japanese "way of the kami"

Shotoku   prince regent (573–621) who advocated Buddhism as one of the pillars of Japan

shrine (jinja)   sacred place because of the presence of a kami; usually has appropriate buildings where a symbol of the kami is housed and where worshipers can consult priests

Soka Gakkai   largest New Religion in Japan, based on Nichiren Buddhism

Susanoo   storm kami in Japanese mythology, unruly brother of Amaterasu

Tendai   important school of Buddhism in Japan (Tian-tai in China)

Tenrikyo   the oldest of the existing New Religions in Japan, founded in 1838

torii   characteristic gateway to the Shinto shrine

way of art   in Japan, practice of an art (such as poetry, noh drama, or the tea ceremony) as a way of self-cultivation

zazen   Zen central practice of sitting in meditation

Zen   important school of meditation Buddhism in Japan (Chan in China)

NOTES

Chapter 1
Introduction: Basic Dimensions of Religion

[1] Ruldolph Otto, *The Idea of The Holy*, trans. John Harvey (London: Oxford University Press, 1958).

[2] Joachim Wach, *Sociology of Religion* (Chicago: University of Chicago Press, 1944), pp. 17–34.

[3] Mircea Eliade, *The Sacred and the Profane: The Nature of Religion*, trans. Willard R. Trask (New York: Harcourt, Brace & World, 1959).

[4] The terms *kenosis* and *plerosis* are used by Theodor H. Gaster, *Thespis: Ritual, Myth, and Drama in the Ancient Near East* (New York: Doubleday, 1961), pp. 23–49.

[5] The structure of the rites of passage was first analyzed by Arnold van Gennep, *The Rites of Passage*, trans. Monika Vizedom and Gabrielle Caffee (Chicago: University of Chicago Press, 1960).

[6] Eliade, *The Sacred and the Profane*, pp. 20–65.

PART ONE
RELIGIONS ARISING FROM INDIA

Chapter 2
Hinduism: Sacred Story and Historical Context

[1] Wendy Doniger O'Flaherty, trans., *The Rig Veda: An Anthology* (New York: Penguin Books, 1981), pp. 211–212.

[2] Ibid., p. 149.

[3] Wing-tsit Chan et al., comps., *The Great Asian Religions: An Anthology* (New York: Macmillan, 1969), p. 13.

[4] O'Flaherty, *Rig Veda*, p. 134.

[5] Ibid., p. 25.

[6] Chan et al., *Great Asian Religions*, p. 24.

[7] Robert Ernest Hume, trans., *The Thirteen Principal Upanishads Translated from the Sanskrit*, 2nd ed. (New York: Oxford University Press, 1931), p. 76.

[8] Barbara Stoler Miller, trans., *The Bhagavad-Gita: Krishna's Counsel in Times of War* (New York: Columbia University Press, 1986), p. 39.

[9] Ibid., p. 87.

[10] John M. Koller, *The Indian Way* (New York: Macmillan, 1982), p. 257.

Chapter 3
Hindu Worlds of Meaning

[1] Wendy Doniger O'Flaherty, trans., *The Rig Veda: An Anthology* (New York: Penguin Books, 1981), pp. 25–26.

[2] Robert Ernest Hume, trans., *The Thirteen Principal Upanishads Translated from the Sanskrit*, 2nd ed. (New York: Oxford University Press, 1931), pp. 119–120.

[3] Ibid., pp. 117–119.

[4] Ibid., p. 147.

[5] Ibid., p. 210.

[6] Troy Wilson Organ, *Hinduism: Its Historical Development* (Woodbury, NY: Barron's Educational Series, 1974), p. 256.

[7] Barbara Stoler Miller, trans., *The Bhagavad-Gita: Krishna's Counsel in Time of War* (New York: Columbia University Press, 1986), pp. 99–105.

[8] Ramanuja on Bhagavad Gita 6.47, in R. C. Zaehner, *Hinduism* (London: Oxford University Press, 1962), p. 99.

[9] A. K. Ramanujan, trans., *Speaking of Shiva* (Baltimore: Penguin Books, Inc., 1973), p. 84.

[10] Swami Nikhilananda, trans., *The Gospel of Sri Ramakrishna* (New York: Ramakrishna-Vivekananda Center, 1952), pp. 134–135.

[11] Hume, *Thirteen Principal Upanishads*, p. 81.

[12] Ibid., p. 248.

[13] Ibid., p. 140.

[14] Ibid., pp. 413–414.

[15] Ibid., p. 143.

[16] Wing-tsit Chan et al., comps., *The Great Asian Religions: An Anthology* (New York: Macmillan, 1969), p. 45.

[17] Hume, *Thirteen Principal Upanishads*, pp. 83–84.

[18] Ibid., p. 142.

[19] Ibid., p. 353.

[20] Ibid., p. 141.

[21] Ibid., p. 393.

[22] Miller, *Bhagavad-Gita*, pp. 52, 43.

[23] Ibid., p. 87.

[24] Ibid., p. 79.

[25] David R. Kinsley, *The Sword and the Flute* (Berkeley: University of California Press, 1977), pp. 52–53.

[26] O'Flaherty, *Shiva: The Erotic Ascetic* (Oxford: Oxford University Press, 1981), p. 149.

27 Manikka Vasager, quoted in R. C. Zaehner, *Hinduism*, pp. 133–134.

28 Translated in Leonard Nathan and Clinton Seely, *Grace and Mercy in Her Wild Hair: Selected Poems to the Mother Goddess* (Boulder: Great Eastern, 1982), pp. 62, 25.

29 Nikhilananda, *The Gospel of Sri Ramakrishna*, pp. 261–262.

Chapter 4
Hindu Worship and the Good Life

1 Robert C. Lester, "Hinduism: Veda and Sacred Texts," in *The Holy Book in Comparative Perspective*, edited by Frederick M. Denny and Rodney L. Taylor (Columbia: University of South Carolina Press, 1985), p. 128.

2 McKim Marriot, "The Feast of Love," in *Krishna: Myths, Rites, and Attitudes*, edited by Milton Singer (Chicago: University of Chicago Press, 1968), p. 212.

3 Mariasusai Dhavamony, *Classical Hinduism* (Roma: Universita Gregoriana Editrice, 1982), pp. 181–183.

4 Charles White, "Mother Guru: Jnanananda of Madras, India," *Unspoken Worlds: Women's Religious Lives*, ed. Nancy Auer Falk and Rita M. Gross (Belmont, CA: Wadsworth Publishing Company, 1989), pp. 20, 15–24.

5 Patrima Bowes, *The Hindu Religious Tradition: A Philosophical Approach* (London: Routledge and Kegan Paul, 1977), p. 296.

6 Law-code of Manu, 3:55; 9:3–4, 11, 26, in Wm. Theodore de Bary et al., comps., *Sources of Indian Tradition* (New York: Columbia University Press, 1959), p. 233.

7 Law-code of Manu, 6:2, in de Bary et al., *Sources*, p. 234.

8 Law-code of Manu, 6:33, 42, in de Bary et al., *Sources*, p. 234.

9 Law-code of Manu, 6:45–81, in R. C. Zaehner, *Hinduism* (London: Oxford University Press, 1966), p. 113.

10 Pratap Chandra Roy, trans., *The Mahabharata*, vol. IX (Calcutta: Oriental Publishing, 1927–1932), p. 110.

11 Written in *The Harijan* for December 8, 1946; in Troy Wilson Organ, *Hinduism: Its Historical Development* (Woodbury, NY: Barron's Educational Series, 1974), p. 368.

12 S. Radhakrishnan, *Eastern Religions and Western Thought* (Oxford: Clarendon Press, 1939), p. 327.

Chapter 5
Buddhism: Sacred Story and Historical Context

1 From the Suvarnaprabhasa, a Mahayana text, in Edward Conze, trans., *Buddhist Scriptures* (Baltimore: Penguin Books, 1959), pp. 24–26.

2 From the Buddhacarita, a Sanskrit poem said to have been composed by Ashvaghosha between the first and second centuries C.E., Wm. Theodore de Bary, ed., *The Buddhist Tradition in India, China, and Japan* (New York: Vintage Books, 1972), p. 58. We follow the main outlines of the Buddhacarita in telling the Buddha's story.

3 Ibid., p. 59.

4 Ibid., pp. 61–62.

5 Ibid., p. 66.

6 Henry Clarke Warren, *Buddhism in Translation: Passages Selected from the Buddhist Sacred Books* (Cambridge: Harvard University Press, 1947), pp. 60–61.

7 de Bary, *Buddhist Tradition*, p. 68.

8 Warren, *Buddhism*, p. 76.

9 Stephan Beyer, *The Buddhist Experience: Sources and Interpretations* (Belmont, CA: Dickenson Publishing, 1974), p. 197.

10 From the Samyutta Nikaya; in Walpola Rahula, trans., *What the Buddha Taught*, rev. ed. (New York: Grove Press, 1974), p. 93.

11 From the Mahaparinibbana Sutta, in de Bary, *Buddhist Tradition*, p. 29.

12 From Digha Nikaya, in ibid.

Chapter 6
Buddhist Worlds of Meaning

1 Wm. Theodore de Bary, ed., *The Buddhist Tradition in India, China and Japan* (New York: Vintage Books, 1972), p. 29.

2 Majjhima Nikaya, in David J. Kalupahana, "Pratityasamutpada," *Encyclopedia of Religion*, vol. 11, edited by Mircea Eliade (New York: Macmillan, 1987), p. 486.

3 Edward Conze et al., eds., *Buddhist Texts Through the Ages* (New York: Harper and Row, 1964), p. 95.

4 Conze, *Buddhism: Its Essence and Development* (New York: Harper and Row, 1959), p. 40.

5 From the Samyutta Nikaya, in Wapola Rahula, *What the Buddha Taught* (New York: Grove Press, 1974), p. 27.

6 Digha Nikaya, *Sources of Indian Tradition*, compiled by Wm. Theodore de Bary et al. (New York: Columbia University Press, 1958), pp. 130–131.

7 Conze, trans., *Buddhist Scriptures* (Baltimore: Penguin Books, 1959), pp. 222–224.

8 From Samyutta Nikaya, in Rahula, *What the Buddha Taught*, p. 93.

9 From Majjhima Nikaya, in John M. Koller, *The Indian Way* (New York: Macmillan, 1982), p. 158.

10 Rahula, *What the Buddha Taught*, p. 73.

11 From Bodhicaryavatarapanjika, in Wing-tsit Chan et al. comps., *The Great Asian Religions: An Anthology* (New York: Macmillan, 1969), p. 74.

12 Conze, ed., *Buddhist Texts Through the Ages*, p. 130.

13 Siksasamuccaya Vajradhvaja Sutra, in Conze, *Buddhist Texts*, p. 131.

Chapter 7
Buddhist Worship and the Good Life

1 In Melford E. Spiro, *Buddhism and Society: A Great Tradition and Its Burmese Vicissitudes* (New York: Harper and Row, 1972), p. 210.

2 Ibid., p. 212.

3 Stephen Beyer, *The Buddhist Experience: Sources and Interpretations* (Belmont, CA: Dickenson Publishing, 1974), p. 241.

4 Spiro, *Buddhism*, pp. 283–284.

5 Suttanipata, I, 8; in Walpola Rahula, *What the Buddha Taught* (New York: Grove Press, 1959), pp. 97–98.

6 Siksasamuccaya, pp. 278–283, in Wm. Theodore de Bary et al., *Sources of Indian Tradition* (New York: Columbia University Press, 1958), pp. 163–165.

7 Dhammapada, vss. 3, 50, 223, in Rahula, *What the Buddha Taught*, pp. 125–132.

8 Majjhima Nikaya, 2:147ff., in de Bary et al., *Sources of Indian Tradition*, pp. 144–145.

9 Sutta Nipata, v. 136, in ibid., p. 143.

10 Digha Nikaya, 3:180ff, in ibid., pp. 125–127.

11 Rahula, *What the Buddha Taught*, pp. 81–84.

12 Ibid., pp. 84–85.

13 First Pillar Edict, in de Bary et al., *Sources of Indian Tradition*, p. 148.

14 Twelfth Rock Edict, in ibid., p. 151.

Chapter 8
The Path of the Jains

1 Padmanabh S. Jaini, *The Jaina Path of Purification* (Berkeley: University of California Press, 1979), p. 1.

2 Ibid., pp. 11–12.

3 Ibid., p. 26.

4 Ibid., p. 38.

5 Ibid., pp. 45–46.

6 Wm. Theodore de Bary et al., comps., *Sources of Indian Tradition* (New York: Columbia University Press, 1958), pp. 79–81.

7 Ibid., pp. 59–60.

8 Jyotiprasad Jain, *Religion and Culture of the Jains* (New Delhi: Bharatiya Jnanpith Publication, 1975), p. 114.

9 Vilas Adinath Sangave, *Jaina Community: A Social Survey*, rev. ed. (Bombay: Popular Prakashan Private, Ltd., 1980), pp. 245–247.

10 Jaini, *Jaina Path*, p. 247, n. 8.

11 Jain, *Religion*, p. 176.

Chapter 9
The Way of the Disciples: The Sikhs

1 W. Owen Cole, *The Guru in Sikhism* (London: Darton, Longman and Todd, 1982), pp. 15–16.

2 Ibid., p. 15.

3 Trilochan Singh et al., trans., *Selections from the Sacred Writings of the Sikhs* (London: George Allen and Unwin, 1960), p. 28.

4 W. H. McLeod, *Guru Nanak and the Sikh Religion* (New York: Oxford University Press, 1968), p. 216.

5 Ibid., p. 165.

6 Ibid., p. 196.

7 Trilochan Singh et al., *Selections from the Sacred Writings of the Sikhs*, pp. 103–105.

8 *Sikh Religion* (Detroit: Sikh Missionary Center, 1990), p. 258.

9 Ibid., p. 265.

10 Trilochan Singh, *Selections*, p. 91.

11 Ibid., p. 203.

12 Ibid., p. 102.

13 McLeod, *Guru Nanak*, p. 205.

14 Taran Singh, quoted in Cole, *The Guru*, p. 89.

15 Gopal Singh, *The Sikhs: Their History, Religion, Culture, Ceremonies, and Literature* (Madras: M. Seshachalam, 1970), p. 64.

16 Trilochan Singh, *Selections*, p. 56.

17 Ibid., p. 60.

18 Pritam Singh Gill, *Heritage of Sikh Culture: Society, Morality, Art* (Jullundur: New Academic Publishing Co., 1975), p. 229.

19 Ibid., p. 159.

20 Avtar Singh, *Ethics of the Sikhs* (Patiala: Punjabi University, 1970), p. 29.

21 Ibid., p. 85.

22 Ibid., p. 112.

23 Trilochan Singh, *Selections*, p. 93.

24 *Sikh Religion*, p. 286.

25 McLeod, *Textual Sources for the Study of Sikhism* (Totowa, NJ: Barnes and Noble Books, 1984), p. 57.

26 Quoted in Cole, *The Guru*, pp. 93–94.

PART TWO
RELIGIONS OF CHINA AND JAPAN

Chapter 10
China: Sacred Story and Historical Context

1 Howard Smith, *Chinese Religions: From 1000 B.C. to the Present Day* (New York: Holt, Rinehart and Winston, 1971), p. 16.
2 Ibid., pp. 22–23.
3 Ibid., pp. 27–28.
4 Wing-tsit Chan, *A Source Book in Chinese Philosophy* (Princeton, NJ: Princeton University Press, 1969), p. 38.
5 Ibid., p. 36.
6 Chan et al., comps., *The Great Asian Religions: An Anthology* (London: Macmillan, 1969), p. 109.
7 Chan, *Source Book*, p. 78.
8 Ibid., p. 152.
9 Ibid., p. 148.
10 Ibid., p. 197.

Chapter 11
Transformations in Chinese Religious History

1 Holmes Welch, *Taoism: The Parting of the Way* (Boston: Beacon Press, 1966), p. 159.
2 Michael Saso, *The Teachings of Taoist Master Chuang* (New Haven: Yale University Press, 1978), p. 46.
3 Wm. Theodore de Bary et al., comps., *Sources of Chinese Tradition*, vol. 1 (New York: Columbia University Press, 1960), pp. 469–470.

Chapter 12
Chinese Worlds of Meaning

1 Translated in Milton M. Chiu, *The Tao of Chinese Religion* (New York: University Press of America, 1984), pp. 58, 108, 112–113.
2 D. Howard Smith, *Chinese Religions: From 1000 B.C. to the Present Day* (New York: Holt, Rinehart and Winston, 1968), p. 19.
3 Wing-tsit Chan, *A Source Book in Chinese Philosophy* (Princeton, NJ: Princeton University Press, 1969), p. 35.
4 Wing-tsit Chan et al., comps., *The Great Asian Religions: An Anthology* (London: Macmillan, 1969), p. 135.
5 Translated by James Legge, in Daniel L. Overmyer, *Religions of China* (San Francisco: Harper and Row, 1986), pp. 71–72.
6 Translated in Chiu, *The Tao*, p. 138.
7 Chan, *Source Book*, p. 139.

8 Burton Watson, trans., *The Complete Works of Chuang Tzu* (New York: Columbia University Press, 1968), p. 302.
9 Chan, *Source Book*, p. 203.
10 Wm. Theodore de Bary, et al., comps., *Sources of Chinese Tradition*, vol. I (New York: Columbia University Press, 1960), p. 58.
11 Chan, *Source Book*, pp. 156–157.
12 Ibid., p. 194.
13 Michael R. Saso, *Taoism and the Rite of Cosmic Renewal* (Pullman: Washington State University Press, 1972), p. 51.
14 Chan, *Source Book*, p. 638.
15 Joseph Needham, *Science and Civilisation in China*, vol. II, *History of Scientific Thought* (London: Cambridge University Press, 1956), p. 492.
16 Quoted in Richard H. Robinson and Willard L. Johnson, *The Buddhist Religion: A Historical Introduction*, 3rd ed. (Belmont, CA: Wadsworth Publishing, 1982), p. 178.
17 From *San-wu Li-ji*, in N. J. Gerardot, *Myth and Meaning in Early Taoism: The Theme of Chaos* (Berkeley: University of California Press, 1983), p. 193.
18 Derk Bodde, "Myths of Ancient China," in *Mythologies of the Ancient World*, edited by Samuel Noah Kramer (New York: Doubleday, 1961), p. 383.
19 Girardot, *Myth and Meaning*, p. 54.
20 Chan, *Source Book*, p. 160.
21 Guan-zi, ch. 40, in Chiu, *The Tao*, pp. 147–148.
22 Ibid., p. 173.
23 From Liu An (d. 122 B.C.E.), ibid., p. 176.
24 In Chan, *Source Book*, p. 280, and de Bary et al, *Sources of Chinese Tradition*, pp. 163–164.
25 de Bary et al., *Sources of Chinese Tradition*, p. 91.
26 W. A. C. H. Dobson, *Mencius: A New Translation Arranged and Annotated for the General Reader* (Toronto: University of Toronto Press, 1963), pp. 141–142.
27 de Bary et al., *Sources of Chinese Tradition*, p. 104.
28 From Yang Xiung (53 B.C.E.–18 C.E.), in Chan, *Source Book*, p. 289.
29 de Bary et al., *Sources of Chinese Tradition*, vol. I, pp. 88–89.
30 Burton Watson, trans., *The Complete Works of Chuang Tzu* (New York: Columbia University Press, 1968), pp. 99–100.
31 Chan et al., *Great Asian Religions*, p. 209.
32 Translated by Herbert A. Giles, quoted in Laurence G. Thompson, *The Chinese Way in Religion* (Belmont, CA: Dickenson Publishing Company, 1973), pp. 187, 195.
33 de Bary et al., *Sources of Chinese Tradition*, p. 22.
34 Chan, *Source Book*, pp. 86–87.

[35] Ibid., p. 87.
[36] de Bary et al., *Sources of Chinese Tradition*, p. 109.
[37] Ibid., p. 33.
[38] Chan et al., *Great Asian Religions*, p. 110.
[39] Ibid.
[40] Chan, *Source Book*, p. 148.
[41] Ibid., p. 147.
[42] de Bary et al., *Sources of Chinese Tradition*, p. 74.
[43] Ibid., pp. 71–72.
[44] Chang Chung-yuan, trans., *Original Teachings of Ch'an Buddhism: Selected from The Transmission of the Lamp* (New York: Vintage Books, 1971), pp. 116–117.
[45] Chan, *Source Book*, pp. 446–448.

Chapter 13
Worship and the Good Life in China

[1] See Wm. Theodore de Bary et al., comps., *Sources of Chinese Tradition*, vol. I (New York: Columbia University Press, 1960), p. 109.
[2] Francis L. K. Hsu, *Under the Ancestors' Shadow: Kinship, Personality and Social Mobility in China* (Stanford: Stanford University Press, 1971), pp. 184–192.
[3] John K. Shryock, *The Origin and Development of the State Cult of Confucius* (New York: Paragon Book Reprint Corp., 1966; originally printed 1932), pp. 175–176.
[4] Translated in Laurence G. Thompson, *Chinese Religion: An Introduction*, 3rd ed. (Belmont, CA: Wadsworth, Inc., 1979), p. 83.
[5] Michael R. Saso, *Taoism and the Rite of Cosmic Renewal* (Pullman: Washington State University Press, 1972), pp. 70–72.
[6] Michael Saso, "Orthodoxy and Heterodoxy in Taoist Ritual," in *Religion and Ritual in Chinese Society*, edited by Arthur P. Wolf (Stanford: Stanford University Press, 1974), pp. 329–331.
[7] David K. Jordan, *Gods, Ghosts and Ancestors: Folk Religion in a Taiwanese Village* (Berkeley: University of California Press, 1972), pp. 56–59.
[8] Holmes Welch, *The Practice of Chinese Buddhism, 1900–1950* (Cambridge: Harvard University Press, 1967), pp. 269–301; quotation from p. 274.
[9] Ibid., pp. 53–77.
[10] Margery Wolf, *Women and the Family in Rural Taiwan* (Stanford: Stanford University Press, 1972), pp. 135–136.
[11] Bruce Watson, trans., *Basic Writings of Hsun Tzu* (New York: Columbia University Press, 1967), pp. 117–118.
[12] Osvald Siren, *The Chinese on the Art of Painting: Translations and Comments* (New York: Schocken Books, 1963), pp. 54–56.
[13] de Bary et al., *Sources of Chinese Tradition*, p. 118.
[14] Wing-tsit Chan, *A Source Book in Chinese Philosophy* (Princeton, NJ: Princeton University Press, 1963), p. 226.
[15] de Bary et al., *Sources of Chinese Tradition*, p. 31.
[16] Thompson, *Chinese Religion*, p. 40.
[17] James Legge, trans., *The Sacred Books of China: Part III, The Li Ki, I-K* (Delhi: Motilal Banarsidass, 1966; orig. published by the Clarendon Press, 1885), pp. 450–451.
[18] Chan, *Source Book*, p. 77.
[19] Marcel Granet, *The Religion of the Chinese People*, translated by Maurice Freedman (New York: Harper & Row, 1977), pp. 88–89.
[20] Classic of Filiality, in Thompson, *Chinese Religion*, p. 42.
[21] Li Ji, in Legge, *Sacred Books*, pp. 71–72.
[22] Wing-tsit Chan et al., comps., *The Great Asian Religions: An Anthology* (London: Macmillan, 1969), pp. 107–108.
[23] Doctrine of the Mean, ch. 14, in Chan, *Source Book*, p. 101.
[24] Ibid., p. 22.
[25] Holmes Welch, *Taoism: The Parting of the Way* (Boston: Beacon Press, 1966), p. 125.
[26] D. Howard Smith, *Chinese Religions: From 1000 B.C. to the Present Day* (New York: Holt, Rinehart and Winston, 1968), p. 73.
[27] de Bary et al., *Sources of Chinese Tradition*, p. 81.
[28] Chan, *Source Book*, p. 166.
[29] Saso, *Taoism*, pp. 48–51.
[30] de Bary et al., *Sources of Chinese Tradition*, pp. 175–176.
[31] Chan, *Source Book*, pp. 497–498.
[32] Ibid., pp. 731–734.

Chapter 14
Japan: Sacred Story and Historical Context

[1] Nihongi, Bk. 6, 25th yr., translated in Wing-tsit Chan et al., comps., *The Great Asian Religions: An Anthology* (New York: Macmillan, 1969), p. 240.
[2] Nihongi, Bk, 19, 13th yr., in ibid., p. 249.
[3] Ibid., p. 250.
[4] Nihongi, Bk. 22, 12th yr., in ibid., p. 252.
[5] Ibid., p. 279.

Chapter 15
Japanese Worlds of Meaning

[1] Ichiro Hori et al., eds., *Japanese Religion: A Survey by the Agency for Cultural Affairs*, translated by Yoshiya Abe and David Reid (Tokyo: Kodansha International Ltd., 1972), pp. 37–38.
[2] Nihon Shoki, Bk. 5, 7th year, in Wing-tsit Chan et al., *Great Asian Religions: An Anthology* (London: Macmillan, 1969), p. 240.

3 Chan et al., *Great Asian Religions*, p. 239.

4 From the Engi Shiki, ibid., p. 265.

5 Ibid., pp. 297–298.

6 Chan et al., *Great Asian Religions*, pp. 265–266.

7 Tsunetsugu Muraoka, *Studies in Shinto Thought*, translated by Delmer Brown and James Araki (Tokyo: Ministry of Education, 1964), p. 37.

8 A. L. Sadler, *The Ise Daijingu Sankeiki or Diary of a Pilgrim to Ise* (Tokyo: Zaidan Hojin Meiji Seitoku Kinen Gakkai, 1940), pp. 34, 48; quoted in H. Byron Earhart, *Religion in the Japanese Experience: Sources and Interpretations* (Belmont, CA: Dickenson Publishing, 1974), p. 25.

9 Yoshito S. Hakeda, trans., *Kukai: Major Works* (New York: Columbia University Press, 1972), p. 93.

10 Hakeda, *Kukai*, p. 218.

11 Akutagawa Ryunosuke, "The Spider's Thread," in *Rashomon and Other Stories*, translated by Glenn W. Shaw (Tokyo: Hara Publishing Co., 1964), pp. 164–174.

12 Hakeda, *Kukai*, pp. 230–232.

13 Ryusaku Tsunoda et al., comps., *Sources of Japanese Tradition*, vol. I (New York: Columbia University Press, 1964), p. 202.

14 Ibid., p. 211.

15 Alfred Bloom, *Shinran's Gospel of Pure Grace* (Tucson: University of Arizona Press, 1965), p. 40.

16 Chan et al., *Great Asian Religions*, p. 287.

17 Philip B. Yampolsky, trans., *The Zen Master Hakuin: Selected Writings* (New York: Columbia University Press, 1971), pp. 163–164.

18 Ibid., pp. 135–136.

Chapter 16
Worship and the Good Life in Japan

1 Norman Waddell and Masao Abe, trans., "Dogen's Fukanzazengi and Shobogenzo zazengi," *The Eastern Buddhist*, NS VI, no. 2 (1973), pp. 122–123.

2 Yoshito S. Hakeda, trans., *Kukai: Major Works* (New York: Columbia University Press, 1972), p. 91.

3 Ibid., p. 98.

4 William R. LaFleur, trans., *Mirror for the Moon: A Selection of Poems by Saigyo (1118–1190)* (New York: New Directions Publishing, 1978), p. 33.

5 From the *Namboroku*, in *Chado koten zenshu*, Vol. IV, edited by Sen Soshitsu (Kyoto: Tanko Shinsha, 1956–1962), p. 264.

6 Richard K. Beardsley, John Hall, and Robert E. Ward, *Village Japan* (Chicago: University of Chicago Press, 1969), p. 220.

7 Floyd Hiatt Ross, *Shinto: The Way of Japan* (Boston: Beacon Press, 1965), p. 155.

8 Ryusaku Tsunoda et al., comp., *Sources of Japanese Tradition*, vol. II (New York: Columbia University Press, 1964), pp. 42–43.

9 Sokyo Ono, *The Kami Way* (Tokyo: International Institute for the Study of Religions, 1959), pp. 106–107.

10 Alfred Bloom, *Shinran's Gospel of Pure Grace* (Tucson: University of Arizona Press, 1965), p. 73.

11 Wing-tsit Chan et al., comps., *The Great Asian Religions: An Anthology* (London: Macmillan, 1969), p. 300.

12 Kenji Ueda, "Shinto," in *Japanese Religion: A Survey by the Agency for Cultural Affairs*, edited by Ichiro Hori et al. (Tokyo: Kodansha International Ltd., 1972), pp. 38–41.

13 Ono, *Kami Way*, p. 82.

BIBLIOGRAPHY

This selection of suggested readings is intended to help students to move toward a deeper understanding of the religions. For more extensive bibliographies and more specialized scholarly works, the student is advised to consult the bibliographies in *The Encyclopedia of Religion* (see asterisk in first section) and in the other works listed here.

Introduction:
Basic Dimensions of Religion

Carmody, Denise Lardner. *Women and World Religions*. 2nd ed. Englewood Cliffs: Prentice Hall, 1989.

Christ, Carol P., and Judith Plaskow, eds. *Womanspirit Rising: A Feminist Reader in Religion*. San Francisco: Harper & Row, 1979.

De Vries, Jan. *The Study of Religion: A Historical Approach*. Translated by Kees W. Bolle. New York: Harcourt, Brace & World, 1967.

Denny, Frederick M., and Rodney L. Taylor, eds. *The Holy Book in Comparative Perspective*. Columbia: University of South Carolina Press, 1985.

*Eliade, Mircea, ed. *The Encyclopedia of Religion*. 15 vols. New York: Macmillan, 1987. An excellent resource for all religions and religious subjects, with up-to-date information and bibliographies, written by a large international team of scholars.

Eliade, Mircea. *Patterns in Comparative Religion*. Translated by Rosemary Shee. Cleveland: World Publishing, 1963.

———. *The Sacred and the Profane: The Nature of Religion*. Translated by Willard R. Trask. New York: Harcourt, Brace & World, 1959.

Falk, Nancy Auer and Rita M. Gross, eds. *Unspoken Worlds: Women's Religious Lives*. Belmont, CA: Wadsworth Publishing Company, 1989.

Graham, William A. *Beyond the Written Word: Oral Aspects of Scripture in the History of Religion*. New York: Cambridge University Press, 1987.

Hall, T. William, Richard B. Pilgrim, and Ronald R. Cavanagh. *Religion: An Introduction*. San Francisco: Harper & Row, 1985.

Livingston, James C. *Anatomy of the Sacred: An Introduction to Religion*. New York: Macmillan Publishing Company, 1989.

Sharma, Arvind, and Katherine Young, eds., *Women in World Religions*. Buffalo: State University of New York Press, 1986.

Slater, Peter. *The Dynamics of Religion: Meaning and Change in Religious Traditions*. San Francisco: Harper & Row, 1978.

Streng, Frederick J. *Understanding Religious Life*. 3rd ed. Belmont, CA: Wadsworth Publishing Company, 1985.

Wach, Joachim. *The Comparative Study of Religions*. Edited by Joseph M. Kitagawa. New York: Columbia University Press, 1958.

Wilson, John F. *Religion: A Preface*. 2nd ed. Englewood Cliffs, NJ: Prentice-Hall, 1989.

PART ONE
RELIGIONS ARISING FROM INDIA

General

Basham, A. L. *The Wonder That Was India: A Survey of the Culture of the Indian Sub-Continent Before the Coming of the Muslims*. New York: Grove Press, 1959.

de Bary, Wm. Theodore, Stephen N. Hay, Royal Weiler, and Andrew Yarrow, comps. *Sources of Indian Tradition*. New York: Columbia University Press, 1958.

Koller, John M. *The Indian Way*. New York: Macmillan, 1982.

Nakamura Hajime. *Ways of Thinking of Eastern Peoples: India-China-Tibet-Japan*. Edited by Philip P. Wiener. Honolulu: East-West Center Press, 1964.

Hinduism

Bharati, Agehananda. *The Tantric Tradition*. New York: Doubleday, 1970.

Bowes, Pratima. *The Hindu Religious Tradition: A Philosophical Approach*. London: Routledge & Kegan Paul, 1976.

Brockington, J. L. *The Sacred Thread: Hinduism in Its Continuity and Diversity*. New York: Columbia University Press, 1981.

Dimmitt, Cornelia, and J. A. B. van Buitenen, trans. *Classical Hindu Mythology: A Reader in the Sanskrit Puranas*. Philadelphia: Temple University Press, 1978.

Dumont, Louis. *Homo Hierarchicus: The Caste System and Its Implications*. London: Paladin, 1972.

Eck, Diana L. *Banaras: City of Light*. Princeton, NJ: Princeton University Press, 1982.

———. *Darshan: Seeing the Divine Image in India*. 2nd ed. Chambersburg, PA: Anima Publications, 1985.

Eliade, Mircea. *Yoga: Immortality and Freedom*. Translated by Willard R. Trask. Princeton, NJ: Princeton University Press, 1970.

Embree, Ainslie T., ed. *The Hindu Religious Tradition: Readings in Oriental Thought*. New York: Random House, 1966.

Hawley, John S. *At Play With Krishna: Pilgrimage Dramas from Brindavan*. Princeton, NJ: Princeton University Press, 1985.

Hawley, John Stratton, and Donna Marie Wulff, eds. *The Divine Consort: Radha and the Goddesses of India*. Boston: Beacon Press, 1986.

Hopkins, Thomas. *The Hindu Religious Tradition*. Belmont, CA: Dickenson Publishing Company, 1971.

Kinsley, David R. *Hindu Goddesses: Visions of the Divine Feminine in the Hindu Religious Tradition*. Berkeley: University of California Press, 1985.

———. *Hinduism: A Cultural Perspective*. Englewood Cliffs, NJ: Prentice-Hall, 1982.

———. *The Sword and the Flute: Kali and Krishna, Dark Visions of the Terrible and the Sublime in Hindu Mythology*. Berkeley: University of California Press, 1977.

Kramrisch, Stella. *The Hindu Temple*. 2 vols. Delhi: Motilal Banarsidass, 1976.

Miller, Barbara Stoler, trans. *The Bhagavad-Gita: Krishna's Counsel in Time of War*. New York: Columbia University Press, 1986.

Nathan, Leonard, and Clinton Seely, trans. *Grace and Mercy in Her Wild Hair: Selected Poems to the Mother Goddess*. Boulder: Great Eastern, 1982.

Nikhilananda, Swami, trans. *The Gospel of Sri Ramakrishna: Originally Recorded in Bengali by M. [Mahendranath Gupta], a Disciple of the Master*. New York: Ramakrishna-Vivekananda Center, 1952.

O'Flaherty, Wendy Doniger. *The Origins of Evil in Hindu Mythology*. Berkeley: University of California Press, 1976.

———, trans. *The Rig Veda: An Anthology*. New York: Penguin Books, 1981.

———. *Shiva: The Erotic Ascetic*. Oxford: Oxford University Press, 1981.

Organ, Troy Wilson. *Hinduism: Its Historical Development*. Woodbury, NY: Barron's Educational Series, 1974.

Ramanujan, A. K., trans. *Speaking of Shiva*. Baltimore: Penguin Books, Inc., 1973.

Singer, Milton, ed. *Krishna: Myths, Rites, and Attitudes*. Chicago: University of Chicago Press, 1968.

Waghorne, Joanne Punzo and Norman Cutler, eds., in association with Vasudha Narayanan. *Gods of Flesh/Gods of Stone: The Embodiment of Divinity in India*. Chambersburg, PA: Anima Publications, 1987.

Zaehner, R. C. *Hinduism*. London: Oxford University Press, 1962.

Zimmer, Heinrich. *Myths and Symbols in Indian Art and Civilization*. New York: Harper & Row, 1962.

Buddhism

Beyer, Stephen, trans. *The Buddhist Experience: Sources and Interpretations*. Belmont, CA: Dickenson Publishing Company, 1974.

Chen, Kenneth K. S. *Buddhism: the Light of Asia*. Woodbury, NY: Barron's Educational Series, 1968.

Conze, Edward. *Buddhism: Its Essence and Development*. New York: Harper & Row, 1959.

———, ed. *Buddhist Texts Through the Ages*. New York: Harper and Row, 1964.

Corless, Roger J. *The Vision of Buddhism: The Space Under the Tree*. New York: Paragon House, 1989.

de Bary, Wm. Theodore, ed. *The Buddhist Tradition in India, China and Japan*. New York: Vintage Books, 1972.

Dumoulin, Heinrich, and John C. Maraldo. *Buddhism in the Modern World*. New York: Macmillan, 1976.

Harvey, Peter. *An Introduction to Buddhism: Teachings, History and Practices*. Cambridge: Cambridge University Press, 1990.

Kalupahana, David J. *Nagarjuna: The Philosophy of the Middle Way*. New York: State University of New York Press, 1986.

Kitagawa, Joseph M., and Mark D. Cummings. *Buddhism and Asian History*. New York: Macmillan Publishing Company, 1989.

LaFleur, William R. *Buddhism: A Cultural Perspective*. Englewood Cliffs: Prentice Hall, 1988.

Lester, Robert C. *Theravada Buddhism in Southeast Asia*. Ann Arbor: University of Michigan Press, 1973.

Paul, Diana Y. *Women in Buddhism: Images of the Feminine in the Mahayana Tradition*. Berkeley: University of California Press, 1979.

Prebish, Charles S. *American Buddhism*. Belmont, CA: Wadsworth Publishing Company, 1979.

_____, ed. *Buddhism: A Modern Perspective*. University Park: Pennsylvania State University Press, 1975.

Rahula, Walpola. *What the Buddha Taught*. Rev. ed. New York: Grove Press, 1974.

Robinson, Richard H., and Willard L. Johnson. *The Buddhist Religion: A Historical Introduction*. 3rd ed. Belmont, CA: Wadsworth Publishing Company, 1982.

Spiro, Melford E. *Buddhism and Society: A Great Tradition and Its Burmese Vicissitudes*. New York: Harper & Row, 1972.

Swearer, Donald K. *Buddhism and Society in Southeast Asia*. Chambersburg, PA: Anima Publishing, 1981.

Takakusu, Junjiro. *The Essentials of Buddhist Philosophy*. 3rd ed. Edited by Wing-tsit Chan and Charles A. Moore. Honolulu: University of Hawaii Press, 1956.

Tambiah, Stanley J. *The Buddhist Saints of the Forest and the Cult of Amulets*. New York: Cambridge University Press, 1984.

Tucci, Giuseppe, *The Religions of Tibet*. Translated by Geoffrey Samuel. Berkeley: University of California Press, 1980.

Williams, Paul. *Mahayana Buddhism: The Doctrinal Foundations*. London: Routledge, 1989.

[See also below under Religions of China and Religions of Japan.]

Jainism

Jain, Jyotiprasad. *Religion and Culture of the Jains*. New Delhi: Bharatiya Jnanpith Publications, 1975.

Jaini, Padmanabh. *The Jaina Path of Purification*. Berkeley: University of California Press, 1979.

Sangave, Vilas Adinath. *Jaina Community: A Social Survey*. 2nd, rev. ed. Bombay: Popular Prakashan, 1980.

Sikhism

Cole, W. Owen. *The Guru in Sikhism*. London: Darton, Longman and Todd, 1982.

_____ and Piara Singh Sambi. *The Sikhs: Their Religious Beliefs and Practices*. London: Routledge and Kegan Paul, 1978.

McLeod, W. H. *The Evolution of the Sikh Community*. Oxford: Clarendon Press, 1976.

_____. *Guru Nanak and the Sikh Religion*. New York: Oxford University Press, 1968.

Sikh Religion. Detroit: Sikh Missionary Society, 1990.

Singh, Avtar. *Ethics of the Sikhs*. Patiala: Punjabi University, 1970.

Singh, Khushwant. *The Sikhs Today: Their Religion, History, Culture, Customs, and Way of Life*. Rev. ed. New Delhi: Orient Longmans, 1964.

PART TWO
RELIGIONS OF CHINA AND JAPAN

General

DeVos, George A., and Takao Sofue, eds. *Religion and the Family in East Asia*. Berkeley: University of California Press, 1984.

Religions of China

Bodde, Derk. *Festivals in Classical China*. Princeton, NJ: Princeton University Press, 1975.

Chan, Wing-tsit. *A Source Book in Chinese Philosophy*. Princeton, NJ: Princeton University Press, 1969.

Chappell, David W., ed. *Buddhist and Taoist Practice in Medieval Chinese Society*. Honolulu: University of Hawaii Press, 1987.

Ch'en, Kenneth K. S. *The Chinese Transformation of Buddhism*. Princeton, NJ: Princeton University Press, 1973.

Chiu, Milton M. *The Tao of Chinese Religion*. New York: University Press of America, 1984.

Chung-Yuan, Chang, trans. *Original Teachings of Ch'an Buddhism: Selected from The Transmission of the Lamp*. New York: Vintage Press, 1971.

de Bary, Wm. Theodore, Wing-tsit Chan, and Burton Watson, comps. *Sources of Chinese Tradition*. 2 vols. New York: Columbia University Press, 1960.

Dumoulin, Heinrich. *Zen Buddhism: A History*. Vol. I (India and China). New York: Macmillan Publishing Company, 1988.

Eber, Irene, ed. *Confucianism: The Dynamics of Tradition*. New York: Macmillan, 1986.

Girardot, N. J. *Myth and Meaning in Early Taoism: The Theme of Chaos*. Berkeley: University of California Press, 1983.

Hsu, Francis L. K. *Under the Ancestors' Shadow: Kinship, Personality and Social Mobility in China*. Stanford: Stanford University Press, 1971.

Jochim, Christian. *Chinese Religions: A Cultural Perspective*. Englewood Cliffs, NJ: Prentice-Hall, 1986.

Jordon, David K. *Gods, Ghosts, and Ancestors: Folk Religion in a Taiwanese Village*. Berkeley: University of California Press, 1972.

_____ and Daniel K. Overmyer. *The Flying Phoenix: Aspects of Chinese Sectarianism in Taiwan*. Princeton, NJ: Princeton University Press, 1986.

Lagerwey, John. *Taoist Ritual in Chinese Society and History*. New York: Macmillan, 1987.

Maspero, Henri. *Taoism and Chinese Religion*. Translated by Frank A. Kierman. Amherst: University of Massachusetts Press, 1981.

Moore, Charles A., ed. *The Chinese Mind*. Honolulu: University of Hawaii Press, 1967.

Overmyer, Daniel L. *Folk Buddhist Religion: Dissenting Sects in Late Traditional China*. Cambridge: Harvard University Press, 1976.

_____. *Religions of China: The World As a Living System*. San Francisco: Harper & Row, 1986.

Saso, Michael. *Taoism and the Rite of Cosmic Renewal*. Pullman: Washington State University Press, 1972.

_____. *The Teachings of Taoist Master Chuang*. New Haven: Yale University Press, 1978.

Schwartz, Benjamin I. *The World of Thought in Ancient China*. Cambridge: Belknap Press of Harvard University Press, 1985.

Smith, D. Howard. *Chinese Religions: From 1000 B.C. to the Present Day*. New York: Holt, Rinehart & Winston, 1971.

_____. *Confucius*. New York: Scribner's, 1973.

Taylor, Rodney L. *The Religious Dimensions of Confucianism*. Albany: State University of New York, 1990.

_____. *The Way of Heaven: An Introduction to the Confucian Religious Life*. Leiden: E. J. Brill, 1986.

Thompson, Laurence G. *Chinese Religion: an Introduction*. 4th ed. Belmont, CA: Wadsworth Publishing Company, 1989.

_____. *The Chinese Way in Religion*. Belmont, CA: Dickenson Publishing Company, 1973.

Weinstein, Stanley. *Buddhism Under the T'ang*. Cambridge: Cambridge University Press, 1987.

Welch, Holmes. *The Practice of Chinese Buddhism, 1900–1950*. Cambridge: Harvard University Press, 1967.

Welch, Holmes, and Anna Seidel. *Facets of Taoism: Essays in Chinese Religion*. New Haven: Yale University Press, 1979.

_____. *Taoism: The Parting of the Way*. Boston: Beacon Press, 1966.

Wolf, Arthur P., ed. *Religion and Ritual in Chinese Society*. Stanford: Stanford University Press, 1974.

Wolf, Margery. *Women and the Family in Rural Taiwan*. Stanford: Stanford University Press, 1970.

Wright, Arthur F. *Buddhism in Chinese History*. Stanford: Stanford University Press, 1959.

Yang, C. K. *Religion in Chinese Society*. Berkeley: University of California Press, 1961.

Religions of Japan

Beardsley, Richard K., John Hall, and Robert E. Ward. *Village Japan*. Chicago: University of Chicago Press, 1969.

Bellah, Robert N. *Tokugawa Religion*. Boston: Beacon Press, 1970.

Blacker, Carmen. *The Catalpa Bow: A Study of Shamanistic Practices in Japan*. London: George Allen & Unwin, 1975.

Bloom, Alfred. *Shinran's Gospel of Pure Grace*. Tucson: University of Arizona Press, 1965.

Collcutt, Martin. *Five Mountains: The Rinzai Monastic Institution in Medieval Japan*. Cambridge: Harvard University Press, 1981.

Dobbins, James C. *Jodo Shinshu: Shin Buddhism in Medieval Japan*. Bloomington: Indiana University Press, 1989.

Dumoulin, Heinrich. *Zen Buddhism: A History*. Vol. II (Japan). New York: Macmillan Publishing Company, 1988.

Earhart, H. Byron. *Japanese Religion: Unity and Diversity*. 3rd ed. Belmont, CA: Wadsworth Publishing Company, 1982.

_____. *Religion in the Japanese Experience: Sources and Interpretations*. Belmont, CA: Dickenson Publishing Company, 1974.

Ellwood, Robert S., and Richard Pilgrim. *Japanese Religion: A Cultural Perspective*. Englewood Cliffs, NJ: Prentice-Hall, 1985.

Hakeda, Yoshito S., trans. *Kukai: Major Works*. New York: Columbia University Press, 1972.

Hardacre, Helen. *Kurozumikyo and the New Religions of Japan*. Princeton, NJ: Princeton University Press, 1986.

_____. *Shinto and the State, 1868–1988*. Princeton: Princeton University Press, 1989.

Hoover, Thomas. *Zen Culture*. New York: Vintage Books, 1978.

Hori, Ichiro. *Folk Religion in Japan: Continuity and Change*. Edited by Joseph M. Kitagawa and Allan L. Miller. Chicago: University of Chicago Press, 1968.

Hori, Ichiro, Ikado Fujio, Wakimoto Tsuneya, and Yanagawa Keiichi, eds. *Japanese Religion: A Survey by the Agency for Cultural Affairs*. Translated by Yoshiya Abe and David Reid. Tokyo: Kodansha International, 1972.

Kageyama, Haruki. *The Arts of Shinto*. New York: Weatherhill Press, 1973.

Kasulis, T. P. *Zen Action/Zen Person*. Honolulu: University of Hawaii Press, 1981.

Kato, Genichi. *A Historical Study of the Religious Development of Shinto*. New York: Greenwood Press, 1988.

Kim, Hee-jin. *Dogen Kigen—Mystical Realist*. Tucson: University of Arizona Press, 1975.

Kitagawa, Joseph M. *On Understanding Japanese Religion*. Princeton, NJ: Princeton University Press, 1987.

———. *Religion in Japanese History*. New York: Columbia University Press, 1966.

Kraft, Kenneth, ed. *Zen: Tradition and Transition*. New York: Grove Press, 1988.

LaFleur, William R. *The Karma of Words: Buddhism and the Literary Arts in Medieval Japan*. Berkeley: University of California Press, 1983.

McFarland, H. Neill. *The Rush Hour of the Gods: A Study of New Religious Movements in Japan*. New York: Macmillan, 1967.

Matsunaga, Daigan, and Alicia Matsunaga. *Foundation of Japanese Buddhism*. 2 vols. Los Angeles: Buddhist Books International, 1974.

Muraoka, Tsunetsugu. *Studies in Shinto Thought*. Translated by Delmer Brown and James Araki. Tokyo: Ministry of Education, 1964.

Ono, Sokyo. *Shinto: The Kami Way*. Rutland, VT: Charles E. Tuttle, 1967.

Reader, Ian. *Religion in Contemporary Japan*. Honolulu: University of Hawaii Press, 1991.

Ross, Floyd Hiatt. *Shinto: The Way of Japan*. Boston: Beacon Press, 1965.

Suzuki, Daisetz T. *Zen and Japanese Culture*. Princeton, NJ: Princeton University Press, 1970.

Suzuki, Shunryu. *Zen Mind, Beginner's Mind*. Tokyo: John Weatherhill, 1970.

Tsunoda, Ryusaku, Wm. Theodore de Bary, and Donald Keene, comps. *Sources of Japanese Tradition*. New York: Columbia University Press, 1964.

Varley, H. Paul. *Japanese Culture*. 3rd ed. Honolulu: University of Hawaii Press, 1984.

Yampolsky, Philip B., trans. *The Zen Master Hakuin: Selected Writings*. New York: Columbia University Press, 1971.

Index

Acknowledgments

TEXT

Verses reprinted with permission of Columbia University Press from *The Bhagavad-Gita: Khrishna's Counsel in Time of War*, translated by Barbara Stoller Miller. Copyright © 1986 Columbia University Press, New York. Used by permission.

Excerpts reprinted with permission of Wing-Tsit Chan, Joseph M. Kitagawa, and P. T. Raju from *Great Asian Religions: An Anthology*, by Chan *et al.* Copyright © 1969.

Excerpts reprinted with permission of Oxford University Press from *The Thirteen Principal Upanishads*, translated from the Sanskrit by Robert Ernest Hume. Copyright © 1931 Oxford University Press.

Excerpts reprinted from deBary *et al. Sources of Indian Tradition*. Copyright © 1959 Columbia University Press. Used by permission.

Excerpts reprinted with permission of Unwin Hyman Limited from *The Sacred Writings of the Sikhs*, translated by Kushwant Singh. Copyright © 1960 Unwin Hyman Limited.

Excerpts from *Chinese Religions: From 1000 B.C. to the Present Day*, by D. Howard Smith. Copyright © 1968 D. Howard Smith. Reprinted by permission of Henry Holt and Company, Inc.

A Source Book in Chinese Philosophy, translated by Wing-Tsit Chan. Copyright © 1963 Princeton University Press. Scattered excerpts reprinted with permission of Princeton University Press.

Excerpts from deBary *et al. Sources of Chinese Tradition*. Copyright © 1960 Columbia University Press. Used by permission.

Excerpts reprinted with permission of Washington State University Press from *Taoism and the Rite of Cosmic Renewal*, by Michael Saso. Copyright © 1972 Washington State University Press.

ILLUSTRATIONS

Chapter 1

Bruno Barby/Magnum Photos: p. 1; Courtesy of the India Tourist Office: p. 3; Courtesy of the Japan National Tourist Office: p. 6; Bruno Barby/Magnum Photos: p. 12; The Metropolitan Museum of Art, Harris Brisbane Dick Fund, 1929: p. 16; Courtesy of the United Nations: p. 18.

Part I

Religious News Service: p. 23.

Chapter 2

Marc Ribaud/Magnum Photos: p. 26; Religious News Service: p. 27; The Asia Society, NY; Mr. & Mrs. John D. Rockefeller III: p. 37; Marc Ribaud/Magnum Photos: p. 41; Mary Evans Picture Library/Photo Researchers, Inc.: p. 44; Amy Stromsten/Photo Researchers, Inc.: p. 45.

Chapter 3

Marilyn Silverstone/Magnum Photos: p. 47; The Bettmann Archive: p. 50; The Asia Society, NY; Mr. & Mrs. John D. Rockefeller III: p. 52; Bruno Barby/Magnum Photos: p. 55; Marilyn Silverstone/Magnum Photos: p. 58; The Asia Society, NY; Mr. & Mrs. John D. Rockefeller III: p. 61.

309

Chapter 4

The Asia Society, NY; Mr. & Mrs. John D. Rockefeller III: p. 64; The New York Public Library Picture Collection: p. 65; Courtesy of the India Tourist Office: p. 66; Bernard Pierre Wolff/Photo Researchers, Inc. p. 68; The Asia Society, NY; Mr. & Mrs. John D. Rockefeller III: p. 70; Courtesy of the India Tourist Office: p. 77.

Chapter 5

Courtesy of the Japan National Tourist Office: p. 81; Religious News Service: p. 84, 87, 94, 96, 97.

Chapter 6

The Asia Society, NY; Mr. & Mrs. John D. Rockefeller III: p. 99; Religious News Service: p. 100; The Asia Society, NY; Mr. & Mrs. John D. Rockefeller III: p. 102; Courtesy of the Japan National Tourist Office: p. 108; The Asia Society, NY; Mr. & Mrs. John D. Rockefeller III: p. 111.

Chapter 7

Renee Lynn/Photo Researchers, Inc.: p. 113; Courtesy of the India Tourist Office: p. 114; Renee Lynn/Photo Researchers, Inc.: p. 119; Courtesy of the Japan National Tourist Office: p. 122; The Bettmann Archive: p. 126.

Chapter 8

Magnum Photos/Alex Webb: p. 130; Woodfin Camp & Associates: p. 132; Magnum Photos/Alex Webb: p. 134; Raghu Rai/Magnum Photos: p. 137; Magnum Photos/Alex Webb: p. 138.

Chapter 9

Raghu Rai/Magnum Photos: p. 142; Marilyn Silverstone/Magnum Photos: p. 144; Raghu Rai/Magnum Photos: p. 147; Raghu Rai/Magnum Photos: p. 150.

Part II

Courtesy of the Japan National Tourist Office: p. 155.

Chapter 10

The Bettmann Archive: p 157; The Metropolitan Museum of Art, Rogers Fund, 1943: p. 159; The Bettmann Archive: p. 163; The Bettmann Archive: p. 166; Photo Researchers, Inc.: p. 170.

Chapter 11

Paolo Koch/Photo Researchers, Inc.: p. 173; Courtesy of the Cleveland Museum of Art, John L. Severance Fund: p. 175; The Bettmann Archive: p. 179; Robert E. Murowchick/Photo Researchers, Inc.: p. 182; Paolo Koch/Photo Researchers, Inc.: p. 182.

Chapter 12

Audrey Topping/Photo Researchers, Inc.: p. 189; Bruno Barby/Magnum Photos: p. 195; Audrey Topping/Photo Researcher, Inc.: p. 201; Rene Burri/Magnum Photos: p. 205; Paolo Koch/Photo Researchers, Inc.: p. 209.

Chapter 13

Catherine Ursillo/Photo Researchers, Inc.: p. 211; Audrey Topping/Photo Researchers, Inc.: p. 213; Catherine Ursillo/Photo Researchers, Inc.: p. 220; The Bettmann Archive: p. 224; Fredrico Arborio Mellas/Photo Researchers, Inc.: p. 230; Paolo Koch/Photo Researchers, Inc.: p. 233.

Chapter 14

Courtesy of the Japan National Tourist Office: pp. 237, 241, 250, 252; The Asia Society, NY; Mr. & Mrs. John D. Rockefeller III: p. 239.

Chapter 15

Courtesy of the Japan National Tourist Office: pp. 254, 256, 260, 262, 265.

Chapter 16

Courtesy of the Japan National Tourist Office: pp. 267, 269, 270, 272, 275, 277.